JUDICIAL DIALOGUE AND HUMAN RIGHTS

This book offers a comprehensive analysis of the extent, method, purpose and effects of domestic and international courts' judicial dialogue on human rights. The analysis covers national courts' judicial dialogue from different regions of the world, including Eastern Europe, Latin America, Canada, Nigeria and Malaysia. The text is complemented by studies on specific subject matters, such as LGTBI people's and asylum seekers' rights that further contribute to a better understanding of factors that stimulate or hold back judicial dialogue, as well as by first-hand insights of domestic and European Court of Human Rights judges into their courts' involvement in judicial dialogue. The volume contains contributions from leading scholars and judges, whose combined perspectives provide an interesting and timely study.

AMREI MÜLLER is currently a post-doctoral fellow at the Centre of Excellence 'PluriCourts' for the Study of the Legitimate Roles of the Judiciary in the Global Order, at the University of Oslo.

HEGE ELISABETH KJOS is Assistant Professor at the Amsterdam Center for International Law, University of Amsterdam.

STUDIES ON INTERNATIONAL COURTS AND TRIBUNALS

General Editors

Andreas Føllesdal, University of Oslo
Geir Ulfstein, University of Oslo

Studies on International Courts and Tribunals contains theoretical and interdisciplinary scholarship on legal aspects as well as the legitimacy and effectiveness of international courts and tribunals.

OTHER BOOKS IN THE SERIES

Mads Andenas *and Eirik Bjorge (eds.) A Farewell to Fragmentation: Reassertion and Convergence in International Law*

Cecilia M. Bailliet and Nobuo Hayashi (eds.) *The Legitimacy of International Criminal Tribunals*

JUDICIAL DIALOGUE AND HUMAN RIGHTS

Edited by

AMREI MÜLLER

(in collaboration with Hege Elisabeth Kjos)

CAMBRIDGE
UNIVERSITY PRESS

CAMBRIDGE
UNIVERSITY PRESS

University Printing House, Cambridge CB2 8BS, United Kingdom
One Liberty Plaza, 20th Floor, New York, NY 10006, USA
477 Williamstown Road, Port Melbourne, VIC 3207, Australia
4843/24, 2nd Floor, Ansari Road, Daryaganj, Delhi – 110002, India
79 Anson Road, #06-04/06, Singapore 079906

Cambridge University Press is part of the University of Cambridge.

It furthers the University's mission by disseminating knowledge in the pursuit of education, learning, and research at the highest international levels of excellence.

www.cambridge.org
Information on this title: www.cambridge.org/9781107173583
10.1017/9781316780237

First published 2017

A catalogue record for this publication is available from the British Library.

Library of Congress Cataloging-in-Publication data
Names: Müller, Amrei, editor. | Kjos, Hege Elisabeth, editor.
Title: Judicial dialogue and human rights / edited by Amrei Müller ; (in collaboration with Hege Elisabeth Kjos).
Description: New York: Cambridge University Press, 2017. | Includes bibliographical references and index.
Identifiers: LCCN 2016047833 | ISBN 9781107173583 (hardback)
Subjects: LCSH: International human rights courts. | Human rights. | Communication in law. | Judicial process.
Classification: LCC K3240.5 .J83 2017 | DDC 342.08/5–dc23
LC record available at https://lccn.loc.gov/2016047833

ISBN 978-1-107-17358-3 Hardback

CONTENTS

CONTRIBUTORS

AZIZAT O. AMOLOYE-ADEBAYO holds a PhD in *Sharī'ah* and international human rights law from the University of Nottingham. She currently lectures in the Islamic Law department, Faculty of Law, University of Ilorin, Ilorin, Nigeria. She is a barrister and solicitor of the Supreme Court of Nigeria and an associate of the Chartered Institute of Arbitrators, Nigeria and United Kingdom.

THE RIGHT HONOURABLE LORD CARNWATH OF NOTTING HILL is Justice of the United Kingdom Supreme Court.

DANIELE GALLO (PhD, Sapienza University) is a senior lecturer at Luiss University (Rome, Italy) and holds the qualification of associate professor of international law and EU law.

GIANLUCA GENTILI (PhD) is a lecturer in law at the University of Sussex, School of Law. His research and teaching focus on Canadian, US and UK public law, in a comparative perspective.

LUIS LÓPEZ GUERRA holds a licenciado en derecho from Universidad Complutense (School of Law), a master's in political science from Michigan State University and a doctorate in law from Universidad Complutense. He is a professor of constitutional law, Universidad de Extremadura (1979–1995) and Universidad Carlos III de Madrid (1996–today). He has been a Judge at the Spanish Constitutional Court (1986–1995), Secretary of State of Justice (2004–2007) and is currently (since 2008) a Judge at the European Court of Human Rights.

NAOMI HART is a PhD candidate in law at St John's College, University of Cambridge. She is also currently in training to become a barrister of England and Wales.

HEGE ELISABETH KJOS is assistant professor at the Amsterdam Center for International Law, University of Amsterdam. She holds a doctorate, a JD, a Cand. Mag. degree and a Bachelor's degree following studies in the United States, the Netherlands, France and Norway. Her courses and research at the University of Amsterdam focus on international law and international dispute settlement in general, and specialise in international investment law and arbitration.

ELAINE MAK is an endowed professor of empirical study of public law, in particular of rule-of-law institutions, at Erasmus University Rotterdam, Erasmus School of Law. Her research interests include legal theory, (comparative) constitutional law and socio-legal analysis, focusing on the functioning of public institutions in liberal-democratic systems. She has published a monograph on *Judicial Decision-Making in a Globalised World* (Hart Publishing, 2013).

CLARA MARSAN-RAVENTÓS is a public law lecturer at Universitat Oberta de Catalunya, associate professor at Universitat Pompeu Fabra and visiting professor at Universitat de Girona. She holds a PhD from the European University Institute and has devoted her research to constitutional theory and practice from comparative and multilevel perspectives.

MICHAEL FREITAS MOHALLEM is a lecturer in human rights law and head of the Center for Justice and Society at Fundação Getulio Vargas (FGV) Law School, Rio de Janeiro (Brazil). He is a PhD candidate at the University College London (UCL, School of Law). He holds an LLM degree in public law and human rights from UCL, a postgraduate degree in political science from the University of Brasília and an LLB from the Catholic University of São Paulo (Brazil).

ERIK MØSE is a Judge at the European Court of Human Rights. He has been a judge in the Supreme Court of Norway and was previously President of the International Criminal Tribunal for Rwanda.

AMREI MÜLLER is a post-doctoral fellow at the department of public and international law of the University of Oslo (*PluriCourts*). She has obtained her PhD degree from the University of Nottingham, School of Law, United Kingdom. Her research interests lie in the area of public international law and human rights, in particular economic, social and cultural rights, the law of the European Convention on Human Rights and international humanitarian law.

ANGELIKA NUßBERGER has been a Judge at the European Court of Human Rights since January 2011 and the President of the 5th Section since November 2015. She is also a professor of public international law and comparative constitutional law at Cologne University since 2002.

LUCA PASQUET holds a PhD in international law from the Graduate Institute of International and Development Studies, Geneva and a law degree from the University of Torino. His research interests are the relation between human rights and other branches of international law (in particular the law of immunities), legal pluralism and legal theory.

ANDREAS PAULUS (Dr. juris) is Justice at the Federal Constitutional Court (Germany), professor of international and public law at the University of Göttingen and co-director of the Institute of International and European Law of the Georg-August-University Göttingen.

RAFFAELE SABATO is a doctor of law (Naples, Italy), a doctor of political sciences (Macerata, Italy) and holds a master's degree of comparative jurisprudence (University of Texas at Austin, USA). He is a Justice at the Supreme Court of Cassation (Rome, Italy); a member of the board of directors, coordinator for the international department, School for the Judiciary (Rome, Italy); a member, and past chair, Consultative Council of European Judges, Council of Europe (Strasbourg, France); and a fellow and member of the Council, European Law Institute (Vienna, Austria).

IZABELA SKOMERSKA-MUCHOWSKA (PhD) is assistant professor at the Jaen Monet Chair of European Constitutional Law at the faculty of law and administration of the University of Łodź. Her research interests lie in the area of European institutional law and public international law.

LAURA VAN DEN EYNDE is a research fellow (F.R.S.-F.N.R.S.) at the Université libre de Bruxelles (Belgium). She holds a master of laws from ULB, a European master's degree in human rights and democratisation (EUIC – Venice) and a master of the science of the law from Stanford University.

MATTEO M. WINKLER (PhD, Bocconi University; LLM, Yale Law School) is assistant professor at HEC Paris, which he joined in 2014 after a long experience as a litigator in Italy. He has published extensively in the fields of transnational litigation, international commercial law, international commercial arbitration and human rights, in particular lesbian, gay, bisexual and transgender (LGBT) rights. In 2014 he was a visiting professor at Humboldt University in Berlin.

TABLE OF CASES

International

International Court of Justice

Jurisdictional Immunities of the State (Germany v. Italy: Greece intervening), ICJ Reports (2012) 99.

Application of the International Convention on the Elimination of All Forms of Racial Discrimination (Georgia v. Russian Federation) ICJ Reports (2011), 70.

Certain Property (Liechtenstein v. Germany) ICJ Reports (2005), 6.

LaGrand Case (Germany v. United States of America) ICJ Reports (2001), 466.

Case Concerning Avena and Other Mexican Nationals (Mexico v. United States of America) ICJ Reports (2004) 12.

International Criminal Tribunal for the Former Yugoslavia Cases

Prosecutor v. Limaj, Bala and Musliu, Judgment (Trial Chamber II), Case No. IT-03-66-T, 30 November 2005.

Prosecutor v. Tadić, Decision on the Defence Motion for Interlocutory Appeal on Jurisdiction (Trial Chamber), Case No. IT-94-1-AR72, 2 October 1995.

UN Committee against Torture

Chahin v. Sweden, Communication No. 310/2007, 8 July 2011, UN Doc. CAT/C/46/D/310/2007.

EA v. Switzerland, Communication No. 28/1995, 10 November 1997, UN Doc. CAT/C/19/D/28/1995.

Mutombo v. Switzerland, Communication No. 13/1993, 27 April 1994, UN Doc. CAT/C/12/D/013/1993.

UN Human Rights Committee

Regional

Court of Justice of the European Union

European Court of Human Rights

Bordikov v. Russia (Appl. No. 921/03), Judgment (Chamber), 8 October 2009, not reported.

Bosphorus Hava Yollari Turizm v. Ireland (Appl. No. 45036/98), Judgment (Grand Chamber), 30 June 2005, ECHR 2005-VI.

Bosphorus v. Ireland (Appl. No. 45036/98), Judgment (Grand Chamber), 30 June 2005, ECHR 2005-VI.

Buldashev v. Russia (Appl. No. 46793/06), Judgment (Chamber), 18 October 2011, not reported.

Catan and Others v. Moldova and Russia (Appl. Nos. 43370/04, 8252/05 and 18454/06), Judgment (Grand Chamber), 19 October 2012, ECHR 2012-V.

Center of Legal Resources on behalf of V. Câmpeanu v. Romania (Appl. No. 47848/08), Judgment (Grand Chamber), 17 July 2014, selected for publication 2014.

Chahal v. the United Kingdom (Appl. No. 22414/93), Judgment (Grand Chamber), 15 November 1996, Reports 1996-V.

Christine Goodwin v. the United Kingdom (Appl. No. 28957/95), Judgment (Grand Chamber), 11 July 2002, ECHR 2002-VI.

Coban v. Spain (Appl. No. 17060/02), Judgment (Chamber), 25 September 2006, not reported.

Communist Party and Others v. Russia (Appl. No. 29400/05), Judgment (Chamber), 19 June 2012, not reported.

Craxi v. Italy (No.2) (Appl. No. 25337/94), Judgment (Chamber), 17 July 2003, not reported.

D.H. v. Czech Republic (Appl. No. 57325/00), Judgment (Grand Chamber), 13 November 2007, ECHR 113.

Dahlab v. Switzerland (Appl. No. 42393/98), Decision (Chamber), 15 February 2001, ECHR 2001-V.

Davydov and Others v. Russia (Appl. No. 75947/11), communicated on 18 March 2014.

De Souza Ribeiro v. France (Appl. No. 22689/07), Judgment (Grand Chamber), 13 December 2012, ECHR 2012-VI.

Demir and Baykara v. Turkey (Appl. No. 34503/97), Judgment (Grand Chamber), 12 November 2008, ECHR 2008-V.

Denisov v. Russia (Appl. No. 33408/03), Decision (Chamber), 6 May 2004, not reported.

Dirdizov v. Russia (Appl. No. 41461/10), Judgment (Chamber), 27 November 2012, not reported.

Dmitriy Ryabov v. Russia (Appl. No. 33774/08), Judgment (Chamber), 1 August 2013, not reported.

Göbel v. Germany (Appl. No. 35023/04), Judgment (Chamber), 8 December 2011, not reported.

Görgülü v. Germany (Appl. No. 74969/01), Judgment (Chamber), 26 February 2004, not reported.

Gracia Cancio v. Germany (Appl. No. 19488/09), Decision (Chamber), 29 May 2012, not reported.

Gross v. Switzerland (Appl. No. 67810/10), Judgment (Chamber), 30 September 2014, selected for publication 2014.

Guja v. Moldova (Appl. No.14277/04), Judgment (Grand Chamber), 12 February 2008, ECHR 2008 II.

Guzzardi v. Italy (Appl. No. 7367/76), Judgment (Plenary), 6 November 1980, Series A, No. 39.

H.W. v. Germany (Appl. No. 17167/11), Judgment (Chamber), 19 September 2013, not reported.

Hämäläinen v. Finland (Appl. No. 37359/09), Judgment (Grand Chamber), 16 July 2014, selected for publication 2014.

Heinisch v. Germany (Appl. No. 28274/08), Judgment (Chamber), 21 July 2011, ECHR 2011-V.

Hermann v. Germany (Appl. No. 9300/07), Judgment (Grand Chamber), 26 June 2012, not reported.

Hirsi Jamaa v. Italy (Appl. No. 27765/09), Judgment (Grand Chamber) 23 February 2012, ECHR 2012-II.

Hirst v. the United Kingdom (No.2) (Appl. No. 74025/01), Judgment (Grand Chamber), 6 October 2005, ECHR 2005-XI.

Hirst v. the United Kingdom (No.2) (Appl. No. 74025/01), Judgment (Chamber), 30 March 2004, not reported.

HLR v. France (Appl. No. 24573/94), Judgment (Grand Chamber), 29 April 1997, Reports 1997-III.

Hoffer and Annen v. Germany (Appl. Nos. 397/07 and 2322/07), Judgment (Chamber), 13 January 2011, ECHR 2011.

Hromadka and Hromadkova v. Russia (Appl. No. 22909/10), Judgment (Chamber), 11 December 2014, not reported.

Hümmer v. Germany (Appl. No. 26171/07), Judgment (Chamber), 9 July 2012, not reported.

Idalov v. Russia (Appl. No. 5826/03), Judgment (Grand Chamber), 22 May 2012, not reported.

Igual Coll v. Spain (Appl. No. 37496/04), Judgment (Chamber), 10 March 2009, not reported.

Imbrioscia v. Switzerland (Appl. No. 13972/88) Judgment (Chamber) 24 November 1993, Series A, No. 275.

Incal v. Turkey (Appl. No. 22678/93), Judgment (Grand Chamber), 9 June 1998, ECHR 1998-IV.

Ireland v. the United Kingdom (Appl. No. 5310/71), Judgment (Plenary), 18 January 1978, Series A, No. 25.

Isayeva and Others v. Russia (Appl. Nos. 57947/00, 57948/00 and 57949/00), Judgment (Chamber), 24 Febuary 2005, not reported.

Iskandarov v. Russia (Appl. No. 17185/05), Judgment (Chamber), 23 September 2010, not reported.

James and Others v. the United Kingdom (Appl. No. 8793/79), Judgment (Plenary), 21 February 1986, Series A, No. 98.

John Murray v. the United Kingdom (Appl. No. 18731/91), Judgment (Grand Chamber), 8 February 1996, Reports 1996-I.

K.A. v. Finland (Appl. No. 27751/95), Judgment (Chamber), 14 January 2003, not reported.

Kamaliyevy v. Russia (Appl. No. 52812/07), Judgment (Chamber), 3 June 2010, not reported.

Karner v. Austria (Appl. No. 40016/98), Judgment (Chamber), 24 July 2003, ECHR 2003-IX.

Kasparov and Others v. Russia (Appl. No. 21613/07), Judgment (Chamber), 3 October 2013, not reported.

Kaya v. Turkey (Appl. No. 22729/93), Judgment (Chamber), 19 February 1998, not reported.

Keegan v. Ireland (Appl. No. 16969/90), Judgment (Chamber), 26 May 1994, Series A, No. 290.

Khamidov v. Russia (Appl. No. 72118/01), Judgment (Chamber), 15 November 2007, not reported.

Khashiyev and Akayeva v. Russia (Appl. Nos. 57942/00 and 57945/00), Judgment (Chamber), 24 February 2005, not reported.

Khaydarov v. Russia (Appl. No. 21055/09), Judgment (Chamber), 20 May 2010, not reported.

Khlyustov v. Russia (Appl. No. 28975/05), Judgment (Chamber), 11 July 2013, not reported.

Khodorkovskiy v. Russia (Appl. No. 5829/04), Judgment (Chamber), 31 May 2011, not reported.

Khodzhayev v. Russia (Appl. No.52466/08), Judgment (Chamber), 12 May 2010, not reported.

Khudoyorov v. Russia (Appl. No. 6847/02), Judgment (Chamber), 8 November 2005, ECHR 2005-X.

Kiyutin v. Russia (Appl. No. 2700/10), Judgment (Chamber), 10 March 2011, ECHR 2011-II.

X. and Others v. Austria (Appl. No. 19010/07), Judgment (Grand Chamber), 19 February 2013, ECHR 2013-II.
X. v. Latvia (Appl. No. 27853/09), Judgment (Grand Chamber), 26 November 2013, ECHR 2013-VI.
Yuriy Rudakov v. Russia (Appl. No. 48982/08), Judgment (Chamber), 15 January 2015, not reported.
Z. and Others v. the United Kingdom (Appl. No. 29392/95) Judgment (Grand Chamber), 10 May 2001, ECHR 2001-V.
Zaunegger v. Germany (Appl. No. 22028/04), Judgment (Chamber), 3 December 2009, not reported.
Zimin v. Russia (Appl. No. 48613/06), Judgment (Chamber), 6 February 2014, not reported.
Związek Nauczycielstwa Polskiego v. Poland (Appl. No. 42049/98), Judgment (Chamber), 21 September 2004, ECHR 2004-IX.

Inter-American Court of Human Rights

Bámaca Velásquez v. Guatemala, Judgment, 25 November 2000, Series C, No. 91.
Enforceability of the Right to Reply or Correction, Advisory Opinion, 29 August 1986, Opinion OC-7/86.
Escher v. Brazil, Judgment, 9 July 2009, Series C, No. 200.
Godínez-Cruz v. Honduras, Judgment (Reparations and Costs), 21 July 1989), Series C, No. 8.
Maritza Urrutia v. Guatemala, Judgment, 27 November 2003, Series C, No. 103.
Tibi v. Ecuador, Judgment, 7 September 2004, Series C, No. 114.

National

Argentina

Supreme Court of Justice, *Maza, Ángel E. s/* amparo medida cautelar, nº M. 1514. XLIII, October 6, 2009.
Supreme Court of Justice, *S., V. c/ M., D.A.* s/medidas precautorias, nº S. 622 XXXIII, 3 April 2001.
Supreme Court of Justice, *Ekmekdjian v. Sofovich y otros*, Recurso Extraordinario, nº E. 64. XXIII, 315 Fallos 1492, 7 July 1992.
Supreme Court of Justice, *Petric, Domagoj, Antonio c/ diario Página 12*, nº P.534.XXXI, 16 April 1998.

Australia

Administrative Appeals Tribunal, *W97/164 v. Minister for Immigration and Multicultural Affairs* [1998] AATA 618.

Federal Court of Australia, *A v. Minister for Immigration and Multicultural Affairs* [1999] FCA 116.

Federal Court of Australia, *Arquita v. Minister for Immigration and Multicultural Affairs* [2000] 106 FCR 465.

Federal Court of Australia, *Betkoshabeh v. Minister for Immigration and Multicultural Affairs* [1998] 157 ALR 95.

Federal Court of Australia, *Minister for Immigration and Citizenship v. MZYYL* [2012] FCAFC 147.

High Court of Australia, *Kartinyeri v. Commonwealth* [1998] 195 CLR 337.

High Court of Australia, *Minister for Immigration and Ethnic Affairs v. Guo* [1997] 191 CLR 559.

High Court of Australia, *Minister for Immigration and Multicultural Affairs v. Singh* [2002] 209 CLR 533.

Austria

Constitutional Court of Austria, Judgments of 10 December 2013, G 16/2013, G 44/2013.

Constitutional Court of Austria, Judgment of 27 February 1989, B 821/88.

Bolivia

Constitutional Tribunal of Bolivia, Acción de Inconstitucionalidad, *Verónica Laura Guiteras Aramayo*, Sentencia Constitucional Plurinacional, 1250/2012, Sala Plena, Expediente 00130-2012-01-AIC, 20 September 2012.

Constitutional Tribunal of Bolivia, Acciones de Inconstitucionalidad, *Morales, Melgar, Feraudy y Quiroga*, Sentencia Constitucional Plurinacional, 0300/2012 (TIPNIS), Sala Plena, Expedientes 00157-2012-01-AIA, 00188-2012-01-AIA (acumulado), 18 June 2012.

Constitutional-Tribunal-of Bolivia, Recurso Directo de Inconstitucionalidad, *Luis Eduardo Siles Pérez*, Sentencia Constitucional nº 0045/2006, Sala Plena, Expediente 2005-12440-25-RDI, 2 June 2006.

Constitutional Tribunal of Bolivia, Sentencia Constitucional 0221/2011-R, Revisión nº 0221, Expediente: 2009-19965-40-AL, 11 March 2011.

Constitutional Tribunal of Bolivia, Sentencia Constitucional 1321/2011-R, Revisión nº 1321, Expediente: 2010-21993-44-AL, 26 September 2011.
Constitutional Tribunal of Bolivia, Sentencia Constitucional 2334/2010-R, Revisión nº 2334, Expediente: 2008-17607-36-RHC, 19 November 2010.

Brazil

Supreme Federal Court, Arguição de Descumprimento de Preceito Fundamental (ADPF) nº132, proposta por Estado do Rio de Janeiro, 5 May 2011.
Supreme Federal Court, *Ellwanger v. Superior Tribunal de Justiça*, Habeas Corpus nº 82424/RS, Tribunal Pleno, DJ 19-03-2004, 17 September 2003.
Supreme Federal Court, *Silvan Guedes v. Superior Tribunal Militar*, Habeas Corpus nº 79285-RJ, 31 August 1999.
Supreme Federal Court, Ação Direta de Inconstitucionalidade (ADI) nº 4277-DF proposta por Procuradoria-Geral da República, 5 May 2011.
Supreme Federal Court, Arguição de descumprimento de preceito fundamental (ADPF) nº 153- DF proposta pelo Conselho Federal da Ordem Dos Advogados do Brasil – OAB, 29 April 2010.

Canada

Federal Court of Appeal, *Bazargan v. Canada (Minister of Citizenship and Immigration)* (1996) 205 NR 282.
Federal Court of Appeal, *Gonzalez v. Canada (Minister of Employment and Immigration)* 1994 FC 646.
Federal Court of Appeal, *Li v. Canada (Minister of Citizenship and Immigration)* 2005 FCA 1.
Federal Court of Appeal, *Nagamany v. Canada (Minister of Citizenship and Immigration)* 2005 FC 1554.
Federal Court of Appeal, *Ramirez v. Canada (Minister of Employment and Immigration)* (1992) 89 DLR (4th) 173.
Immigration and Refugee Board (Refugee Protection Division), *Re IVH* [2004] RPDD No. 57.
Privy Council, *Bank of Toronto v. Lambe* [1887] 12 AC 575.
Privy Council, *Edward v. Canada (AG)* [1930] 124 AC 136.
Supreme Court of British Columbia, *The Crookes v. Wikimedia Foundation* 2008 BCSC 1424.

Supreme Court of Canada, *Alberta v. Hutterian Brethren of Wilson Colony* [2009] 2 SCR 567.
Supreme Court of Canada, *Andrews v. Law Society of British Columbia* [1989] 1 SCR 143.
Supreme Court of Canada, *BC v. Imperial Tobacco Canada Ltd* [2005] 2 SCR 473
Supreme Court of Canada, *Canadian Western Bank v Alberta* [2007] 2 SCR 3.
Supreme Court of Canada, *Charkaoui v. Canada (Citizenship and Immigration)* [2007] 1 SCR 350.
Supreme Court of Canada, *Charkaoui v. Minister of Citizenship and Immigration* [2007] 1 SCR 350.
Supreme Court of Canada, *Committee for the Commonwealth of Canada v. Canada* [1991] 1 SCR 139.
Supreme Court of Canada, *Consolidated Fastfrate Inc v. Western Canada Council of Teamsters* [2009] 3 SCR 407.
Supreme Court of Canada, *General Motors of Canada Ltd v. City National Leasing* [1989] 1SCR 641.
Supreme Court of Canada, *Gosselin (Tutor of) v. Quebec (Attorney General)* [2005] 1 SCR 238.
Supreme Court of Canada, *Hunter v. Southam* [1984] 2 SCR 145.
Supreme Court of Canada, *Kindler v. Canada (Minister of Justice)* [1991] 2 SCR 779.
Supreme Court of Canada, *Lavigne v. Ontario Public Service Employees Union* [1991] 2 SCR 211.
Supreme Court of Canada, *Miron v. Trudel* [1995] 2 SCR 418.
Supreme Court of Canada, *Ontario Hydro v. Ontario (Labour Relations Board)* [1993] 3 SCR 327.
Supreme Court of Canada, *Pushpanathan v. Canada* [1998] 1 SCR 982.
Supreme Court of Canada, *R v. Advance Cutting & Coring Ltd* [2001] 3 SCR 209.
Supreme Court of Canada, *R v. Butler* [1992] 1 SCR 452.
Supreme Court of Canada, *R v. Elshaw* [1991] 3 SCR 24, 57.
Supreme Court of Canada, *R v. Kalanj* [1989] 1 SCR 1594.
Supreme Court of Canada, *R v. Kang-Brown* [2008] 1 SCR 456.
Supreme Court of Canada, *R v. Morgentaler* [1988] 1 SCR 30.
Supreme Court of Canada, *R v. Oakes* [1986] 1 SCR 103.
Supreme Court of Canada, *R v. Rahey* [1987] 1 SCR 588.
Supreme Court of Canada, *R v. Ruzic* [2001] 1 SCR 687.
Supreme Court of Canada, *R v. Seaboyer* [1991] 2 SCR 577.
Supreme Court of Canada, *R v. Simmons* [1988] 2 SCR 495.

Supreme Court of Canada, *R v. Smith* [1987] 1 SCR 1045.
Supreme Court of Canada, *R. v. Borden* [1994] 3 SCR 145.
Supreme Court of Canada, *R. v. Keegstra* [1990] 1 SCR 697.
Supreme Court of Canada, *Reference re Ng Extradition (Canada)* [1991] 2 SCR 858.
Supreme Court of Canada, *Reference re Secession of Quebec* [1998] 2 SCR 217.
Supreme Court of Canada, *Saumur v. City of Quebec* [1953] 2 SCR 299.
Supreme Court of Canada, *Sauvé v. Canada (Chief Electoral Officer)* [2002] 3 SCR 519.
Supreme Court of Canada, *Solski (Tutor of) v. Quebec (Attorney General)* [2005] 1 SCR 201.
Supreme Court of Canada, *United Food & Commercial Workers Local 1518 v. Kmart CanLtd* [1999] 2 SCR 1083.
Supreme Court of Canada, *United States v. Burns* [2001] 1 SCR 283.
Supreme Court of Canada, *Vriend v. Alberta* [1998] 1 SCR 493.
Supreme Court of Canada, *Wayne Crookes, et al. v. Jon Newton* [2011] 3 SCR 269.
Supreme Court of Canada, *Winnipeg Child and Family Services (Northwest Area) v. G (DF)* [1997] 3 SCR 925.

Chile

Constitutional Court of Chile, Requerimiento de Inaplicabilidad por Inconstitucionalidad, *Sepúlveda Álvarez*, Sentencia Rol 1683-10-INA n° 1683-10, 4 January 2011.
Constitutional Court of Chile, Requerimiento de Inaplicabilidad por Inconstitucionalidad, *Andrade y Vignau*, Sentencia Rol n° 2153-2011 INA, 11 September 2012.
Constitutional Court of Chile, *Wetzel, Antonio, y otros v. Soto Silva*, Sentencia Rol n° 1881-10-INA, 3 November 2011.

Colombia

Constitutional Court of Colombia, Demanda de Inconstitucionalidad, *Carlos Andrés Echeverry Restrepo y otros*, Sentencia C-577/11, Sala Plena, 26 July 2011.
Constitutional Court of Colombia, Demanda de Inconstitucionalidad, *Daniel Bonilla Maldonado y otros*, Sentencia C-417/09, Sala Plena, 26 June 2009.

Constitutional Court of Colombia, *Lais v. Bar Discoteca Pandemo*, Sentencia T-629/10, Sala Tercera de Revisión de la Corte Constitucional, 13 August 2010.

Constitutional Court of Colombia, Revisión Constitucional de la Ley 765 de 2002, Sentencia C- 318/03, Sala Plena, 24 April 2003.

Constitutional Court of Colombia, Revisión Constitucional, Sentencia C-225/95, 18 May 1995.

Constitutional Court of Colombia, Demanda de Inconstitucionalidad, *Carlos Humberto García Guzmán y Jorge Eliecer Peña Pinilla*, Sentencia C-575/09, Sala Plena, 26 August 2009.

Constitutional Court of Colombia, Revisión de Constitucionalidad de la Ley 1354 de 2009, Sentencia C-141/10, Sala Plena, 26 February 2010.

Constitutional Court of Colombia, *Oscar Carupia Domicó y otros v. Ministerios de Transporte y otros*, Sentencia T-129/2011, Sala Quinta de Revisión de la Corte Constitucional, 3 March 2011.

Czech Republic

Constitutional Court of the Czech Republic, Judgment of 15 April 2003, I. ÚS 752/02.

Constitutional Court of the Czech Republic, Judgment of 24 June 2003, Pl. ÚS 44/02.

Constitutional Court of the Czech Republic, Judgment of 25 April 2005, Pl. ÚS 11/04.

Constitutional Court of the Czech Republic, Judgment of 25 June 2002, Pl. ÚS 36/01.

Finland

Supreme Administrative Court, KHO:2010:84, 30 December 2010.

France

Constitutional Council, Decision 99–419 DC, 9 November 1999.

Constitutional Council, *Mme. Corinne C. et Sophie H. v. France*, Decision 2010–92 QPC, 28 January 2011.

Court of Cassation, *Vilela v. Mme Weil*, 1998 JCP II–10093, 17 December 1997.

Refugee Appeals Board, *MA*, Case 508193, 22 November 2005.

Refugee Appeals Board, *MK*, Case 494377, 21 April 2005.

Germany

Federal Constitutional Court (BVerfG), Judgment of 21 July 2010, 1 BvR 420/09.

Federal Constitutional Court (BVerfG), Judgment of 22 October 1986, 2 BvR 197/83.

Federal Constitutional Court (BVerfG), Judgment of 23 March 2006, 1 BvR 204/03.

Federal Constitutional Court (BVerfG), Judgment of 24 April 2013, 1 BvR 1215/07.

Federal Constitutional Court (BVerfG), Judgment of 24 July 1986, 1 BvR 331/85.

Federal Constitutional Court (BVerfG), Judgment of 26 February 2008, 1 BvR 1602/07, 1 BvR 1606/07 and 1 BvR 1626/07.

Federal Constitutional Court (BVerfG), Judgment of 26 January 1982, 1 BvR 1925/80.

Federal Constitutional Court (BVerfG), Judgment of 27 November 1990, 1 BvR 402/87.

Federal Constitutional Court (BVerfG), Judgment of 29 January 2003, 1 BvL 20/99 and 1 BvR 933/01.

Federal Constitutional Court (BVerfG), Judgment of 29 May 1974, 2 BvL 52/71.

Federal Constitutional Court (BVerfG), Judgment of 3 April 1990, 1 BvR 680/86.

Federal Constitutional Court (BVerfG), Judgment of 4 May 2011, 2 BvR 2365/09, 2 BvR 740/10, 2 BvR 2333/08, 2 BvR 1152/10 and 2 BvR 571/10.

Federal Constitutional Court (BVerfG), Judgment of 4 October 1993, 1 BvR 640/93.

Federal Constitutional Court (BVerfG), Judgment of 5 November 2013, 2 BvR 1579/11.

Federal Constitutional Court (BVerfG), Judgment of 7 July 2009, 1 BvR 1164/07.

Federal Constitutional Court (BVerfG), Judgment of 8 May 2013, 1 BvL 1/08.

Federal Constitutional Court (BVerfG), Judgment of 9 March 1992, 1 BvR 74/92.

Federal Constitutional Court, Judgment of 30 June 2009, 2 BvE 2/08, 2 BvE 5/08, 2 BvR 1010/08, 2 BvR 1022/08, 2 BvR 1259/08 and 2 BvR 182/09.

Federal Constitutional Court, Order for a Preliminary Ruling of 14 January 2014, 2 BvR 2728/13, 2 BvR 2729/13, 2 BvR 2730/13, 2 BvR 2731/13 and 2 BvE 13/13.

Hungary

Israel

Italy

Court of Cassation, Judgment of 17 January 2006, No. 788/2006.
Court of Cassation, Judgment of 18 July 2012, No. 12357/2012.
Court of Cassation, Judgment of 20 May 2011, No. 11163/2011.
Court of Cassation, Judgment of 21 October 2008, No. 1072/2008.
Court of Cassation, Judgment of 29 May 2008, No. 14201/2008.
Court of Cassation, Judgment of 4 May 2000, No. 11/2000.
Court of Cassation, Judgment of 9 February 2015, No. 2400/2015.
Court of Cassation, Order of 4 September 2008, No. 400/2008.
Tribunal of Reggio Emilia, Judgment of 13 February 2012, No. 1401/2011.

Lithuania

Constitutional Court of Lithuania, Judgment of 25 May 2004, No. 24/04.
Constitutional Court of Lithuania, Judgment of 5 September 2012, No. 8/2012.

New Zealand

Court of Appeal, *S v. Refugee Status Appeals Authority* [1998] 2 NZLR 291.
Court of Appeal, *X v. Refugee Status Appeals Authority; Attorney-General (Minister of Immigration) v. Y* [2009] NZLR 73.
Immigration and Protection Tribunal, *AB (Iraq)* [2011] NZIPT 800014.
Immigration and Protection Tribunal, *AC (Syria)* [2011] NZIPT 800035.
Immigration and Protection Tribunal, *AZ (Iran)* [2012] NZIPT 800237.
Immigration and Protection Tribunal, *BG (Fiji)* [2012] NZIPT 800091.
Immigration and Protection Tribunal, *BS (Fiji)* [2012] NZIPT 800041.
Supreme Court of New Zealand, *Attorney General v. Tamil X* [2011] 1 NZLR 721.

Nigeria

Court of Appeal of Nigeria, *Nwosu v. Nwosu* (2012) 8 NWLR (Pt. 1301) 1 CA.
Supreme Court of Nigeria, *Cross-River v. AG. Federation* (2012) 16 NWLR (Pt. 1327) 425.
Supreme Court of Nigeria, *C.O.P. Western Region v. Igwe & Ors* (1961) 2 NSCC 1.
Supreme Court of Nigeria, *Kalu v. State* (1998) 12 SCNJ 1.

Paraguay

Appellate Court, Primera Sala, Itapúa, nº 38-08-01, 3 March 2008.
Supreme Court of Justice, *Radio Ñanduti S.A. v. Artículos 305 y 329 de la Ley N° 834/1996 (Código Electoral)*, Acuerdo y Sentencia nº 1287, Sala Constitucional de la Corte Suprema, 3 December 2007.

Peru

Constitutional Court of Peru, Demanda de Inconstitucionalidad, 002-2009-PI/TC.

Poland

Appellate Court of Katowice, Judgment of 8 February 2013, I ACa 971/12.
Appellate Court of Rzeszów, Judgment of 27 June 2013, I ACa 181/13.
Appellate Court of Warsaw, Judgment of 17 October 2012, I ACa 367/12.
Appellate Court of Warsaw, Judgment of 21 November 2012, II AKa 335/12.
Constitutional Court of Poland, Judgment of 1 April 2009, SK 77/06.
Constitutional Court of Poland, Judgment of 10 December 2014, K 52/13.
Constitutional Court of Poland, Judgment of 10 May 2000, K. 21/99.
Constitutional Court of Poland, Judgment of 11 May 2005, K 18/04.
Constitutional Court of Poland, Judgment of 14 December 2005, SK 61/03.
Constitutional Court of Poland, Judgment of 15 July 2009, K 63/07.
Constitutional Court of Poland, Judgment of 15 May 2014, III SK 28/13.
Constitutional Court of Poland, Judgment of 16 November 2011, SK 45/09.
Constitutional Court of Poland, Judgment of 18 November 2010, K 29/09.
Constitutional Court of Poland, Judgment of 18 October 2004, P 8/04.
Constitutional Court of Poland, Judgment of 19 December 2006, P 37/05.
Constitutional Court of Poland, Judgment of 19 July 2011, K 11/10.
Constitutional Court of Poland, Judgment of 2 June 2007, K 41/05.
Constitutional Court of Poland, Judgment of 20 October 2009, SK 15/08.
Constitutional Court of Poland, Judgment of 21 April 2004, K 33/03.
Constitutional Court of Poland, Judgment of 22 June 2010, SK 25/08.
Constitutional Court of Poland, Judgment of 23 February 2010, P 20/09.

Constitutional Court of Poland, Judgment of 24 June 1997, K 27/91.
Constitutional Court of Poland, Judgment of 24 November 2010, K 32/09.
Constitutional Court of Poland, Judgment of 27 April 2005, P 1/05
Constitutional Court of Poland, Judgment of 28 June 2008, K 51//07.
Constitutional Court of Poland, Judgment of 30 July 2014, K 23/11.
Constitutional Court of Poland, Judgment of 30 September 2008, K 44/07.
Constitutional Court of Poland, Judgment of 6 July 2011, P 12/09.
Constitutional Court of Poland, Judgment of 7 January 1992, K 8/91.
Constitutional Court of Poland, Judgment of 7 May 2002, SK 20/00.
Constitutional Court of Poland, Judgment of 9 July 2009, SK 48/05.
Regional Administrative Court of Warsaw, Judgment of 29 October 2014, II SA/Wa 437/14.
Regional Administrative Court of Wrocław, Decision of 15 May 2015, IV SAB/Wr 101/13.
Regional Court in Częstochowa, Decision of 20 December 2013, IV U 1470/12.
Supreme Administrative Court, Decision of 30 May 2014, I ONP 1/14.
Supreme Administrative Court, Judgment of 16 May 2014, II FSK 1395/12.
Supreme Administrative Court, Judgment of 26 August 1999, V SA 708/99.
Supreme Administrative Court, Judgment of July 2015, II GSK 1365/14.
Supreme Court of Poland, Decision of 11 January 1995, III ARN 75/94.
Supreme Court of Poland, Decision of 25 August 1987, II PRZ 8/87.
Supreme Court of Poland, Decision of 29 October 2010, IV CSK 465/09.
Supreme Court of Poland, Decision of 9 December 2014, III SPP 231/14.
Supreme Court of Poland, Judgment of 10 November 1980, I CR 283/81.
Supreme Court of Poland, Judgment of 12 December 1992, CZP III 48/92.
Supreme Court of Poland, Judgment of 13 April 2007, I CSK 31/07.
Supreme Court of Poland, Judgment of 23 November 2012, I CSK 292/12.
Supreme Court of Poland, Judgment of 23 October 2012, SK 11/12.
Supreme Court of Poland, Judgment of 29 November 2005, II PK/100/05.
Supreme Court of Poland, Judgment of 3 June 2007, I UK 40/07.
Supreme Court of Poland, Judgment of 6 December 2013, I CSK 146/13.
Supreme Court of Poland, Resolution of 12 July 2001, III CZP 22/01.
Supreme Court of Poland, Resolution of 17 December 2009, III PZP 2/09.

Russia

Constitutional Court of the Russian Federation, Judgment of 10 October 2013, No. 20-P.

Constitutional Court of the Russian Federation, Judgment of 22 April 2013, No. 8-P.

Constitutional Court of the Russian Federation, Judgment of 27 June 2000, No. 11-P.

Constitutional Court of the Russian Federation, Judgment of 5 February 2007, No. 2-P.

Constitutional Court of the Russian Federation, Judgment of 6 December 2013, No 27-P.

Constitutional Court of the Russian Federation, Judgment of 8 April 2014, No. 10-P.

Constitutional Court of the Russian Federation, Ruling of 15 January 2009, No. 187-O-O.

Constitutional Court of the Russian Federation, Ruling of 19 January 2010, No. 151-O-O.

Constitutional Court of the Russian Federation, Ruling of 19 November 2009, No. 1344-O-R.

Constitutional Court of the Russian Federation, Ruling of 24 October 2013, No. 1718-O.

Supreme Court of the Russian Federation, Resolution of the Plenum of 10 October 2003, No. 5.

Supreme Court of the Russian Federation, Resolution of the Plenum of 19 December 2013, No. 41.

Supreme Court of the Russian Federation, Resolution of the Plenum of 27 June 2013, No. 21.

Supreme Court of the Russian Federation, Resolution of the Plenum of 29 October 2009, No. 22.

Supreme Court of the Russian Federation, Ruling of 15 August 2012, No. 1-APG12-11.

Supreme Court of the Russian Federation, Ruling of 9 November 2012, No. 14-KF-12–560.

Slovakia

Constitutional Court of Slovakia, Judgment of 11 February 2004, Pl. ÚS. 15/03.

Spain

Constitutional Court of Spain, Judgment of 11 December 1995, STC 176/ 1995.

Constitutional Court of Spain, Judgment of 28 June 2010, STC 31/2010.
Supreme Court of Spain, Judgment of 11 October 2012, STS 757/2012.
Supreme Court of Spain, Judgment of 25 January 2012 STS 406/2012.
Supreme Court of Spain, Judgment of 29 May 2013, STS 474/2013.

Sweden

Migration Court of Appeal, Decision of 23 February 2007, UM 23-06.

The Netherlands

The Council of State, Case 200608939/1 LJN BB0917, 20 July 2007.

Ukraine

Constitutional Court of Ukraine, Judgment of 29 December 1999, No. 11- rp/99.
District Administrative Court of Kiev, *Person v. Darnitsa District of Kiev Center for Social Assistance*, Judgment of 26 June 2008, No. 4/337.

United Kingdom

Asylum and Immigration Tribunal, *IH (s 72; 'Particularly Serious Crime') Eritrea v. Secretary of State for the Home Department* [2009] UKAIT 12.
Asylum and Immigration Tribunal, *KH (Article 15(c) Qualification Directive) Iraq v. Secretary of State for the Home Department, CG* [2008] UKAIT 23.
Asylum and Immigration Tribunal, *SZ and JM (Christian – FS confirmed) Iran v. Secretary of State for the Home Department, CG* [2008] UKAIT 82.
England and Wales Court of Appeal, *Ahmed v. Inner London Education Authority* [1978] QB 36.
England and Wales Court of Appeal, *Al-Skeini & Ors, R (on the application of) v. Secretary of State for Defence* [2005] EWCA Civ 1609.
England and Wales Court of Appeal, *El-Ali v. Secretary of State for the Home Department* [2002] EWCA Civ 1103.
England and Wales Court of Appeal, *JS (Sri Lanka) v. Secretary of State for the Home Department* [2010] 2 WLR 17.
England and Wales Court of Appeal, *QD & AH (Iraq) v. Secretary of State for the Home Department* [2009] EWCA Civ 620.

United Kingdom Supreme Court, *Manchester City Council v. Pinnock (No.2)* [2011] UKSC 6.

United Kingdom Supreme Court, *R (on the application of ClientEarth) v. The Secretary of State for the Environment, Food and Rural Affairs* [2013] UKSC 25.

United Kingdom Supreme Court, *R (on the application of ClientEarth) v. The Secretary of State for the Environment, Food and Rural Affairs* [2015] UKSC 28.

United Kingdom Supreme Court, *R (on the application of Nicklinson) (Appelants) v. Ministry of Justice* [2014] UKSC 38.

United Kingdom Supreme Court, *R v. Horncastle and Others* [2009] UKSC 14.

Upper Tribunal (Asylum and Immigration Chamber), *AK (Article 15(c)) Afghanistan v. Secretary of State for the Home Department, CG* [2012] UKUT 163.

Upper Tribunal (Asylum and Immigration Chamber), *AMM and Others (Conflict; Humanitarian Crisis; Returnees; FGM) Somalia v. Secretary of State for the Home Department, CG* [2011] UKUT 445.

Uruguay

Supreme Court of Justice, Casación nº 418, 17 December 1997.

Supreme Court of Justice, Excepción de Inconstitucionalidad arts. 1, 3 y 4 de la Ley Nº 15.848, Sentencia nº 365/2009, 19 October 2009.

Supreme Court of Justice, *Marabotto [r], Cairoli, Torello, Alonso de Marco y Mariño*, Acción de Reclamación de Identidad Sexual nº 139, 5 May 1997.

USA

Supreme Court of California, *DVD Copy Control Association Inc. v. A.T. McLaughlin*, 21 January 2004, No. CV 786804.

Supreme Court of Illinois, *Society v. Kohrig*, 1 October 1986, 62719–24, 498 N.E. 2d 1158.

Supreme Court of Iowa, *State v. Hartog*, 17 May 1989, 88–383, 440 N.W. 2d 852.

Supreme Court of Washington, *State v. Eckblad*, 14 October 2004, 74109-3, 152, Wn.2d 515, 98 3d 1184.

US Supreme Court, *Katz v. United States*, 18 December 1967, 389 US 347.

US Supreme Court, *Lawrence v. Texas*, 26 June 2003, 539 US 558.
US Supreme Court, *Obergefell et al. v. Hodges, Director, Ohio Department of Health et al.*, 26 June 2015, 576 US ___.
US Supreme Court, *Rasul v. Bush*, 28 June 2004, 542 US 466.
US Supreme Court, *Roe v. Wade*, 22 January 1973, 410 US 113.
US Supreme Court, *Romer v Evans*, 20 May 1996, 517 US 620.
US Supreme Court, *R.A.V. v. City of St.Paul, Minnesota*, 22 June 1992, 505 US 377.
US Supreme Court, *Schenck v. U.S.*, 3 March 1919, 249 US 47.
US Supreme Court, *Terminiello v. Chicago*, 16 May 1949, 337 US 1.
US Supreme Court, *Texas v. Johnson*, 21 June 1989, 491 US 397.
US Supreme Court, *United States v. Eichman*, 11 June 1990, 496 US 310.
US Supreme Court, *Virginia v. Black et al.*, 7 April 2003, 538 US 343.

Venezuela

Supreme Tribunal of Justice, *Asociación Civil Espacio Público v. Contraloría General de la República Bolivariana de Venezuela*, Acción de Amparo Constitucional nº 09-1003, Sala Constitucional, 15 July 2010.
Supreme Tribunal of Justice, *Bloque de Prensa Venezolano (BPV) y Andrés De Armas Silva y Eduardo Alemán Pérez*, Sentencia nº 00-1445, Sala Constitucional, 27 July 2004.

TABLE OF CONVENTIONS AND STATUTES

African Charter on Human and Peoples' Rights, 1520 UNTS 217, entered into force 21 October 1986.

American Convention on Human Rights, 1144 UNTS 123, entered into force 18 July 1978.

Arab Charter on Human Rights, created 15 September 1994, revised and adopted 23 May 2004 by the League of Arab States, entered into force 15 March 2008.

Cairo Declaration on Human Rights in Islam, adopted on 5 August 1990 by the Organization of the Islamic Conference, Annex to Res. No. 49/19-P.

Charter of Fundamental Rights of the European Union, Official Journal C 326, 26 October 2012.

Charter of the Organization of American States, 119 UNTS 1609, entered into force 13 December 1951.

Consolidated Version of the Treaty on the Functioning of European Union, Official Journal 326 (26 October 2012).

Consolidated Version of the Treaty on European Union, Official Journal 326 (26 October 2012).

Constitution of the United Nations Educational, Scientific and Cultural Organization, 4 UNTS 275, entered into force 4 November 1946.

Convention Against Torture and Other Cruel, Inhuman or Degrading Treatment or Punishment, 1465 UNTS 85, entered into force 26 June 1987.

Convention for the Protection of Human Rights and Fundamental Freedoms, 213 UNTS 222; 312 ETS 5, entered into force 3 September 1953.

Convention on Jurisdictional Immunities of States and their Property (2 December 2004), UN Doc. A/RES/59/38, not yet in force.

Convention on the Prevention and Punishment of the Crime of Genocide, 78 UNTS 227, entered into force 12 January 1951.

Convention on the Rights of the Child, 1577 UNTS 3, entered into force 2 September 1990.

Convention relating to the Status of Refugees, 189 UNTS 137, entered into force 22 April 1954.

Geneva Convention for the Amelioration of the Condition of the Wounded and Sick in Armed Forces in the Field, 75 UNTS 35, entered into force 21 October 1950.

Hague Convention of 25 October 1980 on the Civil Aspects of International Child Abduction, 1343 UNTS 89, entered into force 1 December 1983.

Indigenous and Tribal Peoples Convention, International Labour Organization (ILO), C169, entered into force 5 September 1991.

Inter-American Convention on Forced Disappearance of Persons, Organization of American States, OAS Treaty Series A-60; 33 ILM 1429 (1994), entered into force 28 March 1996.

Inter-American Convention to Prevent and Punish Torture, OAS Treaty Series No. 67, 9 entered into force 28 February 1987.

International Convention on the Elimination of All Forms of Racial Discrimination, 660 UNTS 195, entered into force 4 January 1969.

International Covenant on Civil and Political Rights, 993 UNTS 3, entered into force 3 January 1976.

International Covenant on Economic, Social and Cultural Rights, 993 UNTS 171, entered into force 3 January 1976.

Protocol Additional to the Geneva Conventions of 12 August 1949, and relating to the Protection of Victims of International Armed Conflicts, 1125 UNTS 3, entered into force 7 December 1979.

Protocol Relating to the Status of Refugees 606 UNTS 267, entered into force 4 October 1967.

Protocol to the Convention for the Protection of Human Rights and Fundamental Freedoms, 213 UNTS 262, entered into force 18 May 1954.

Treaty of Lisbon amending the Treaty on European Union and the Treaty establishing the European Community, Official Journal C 306 (17 December 2007), entered into force 1 December 2009.

Vienna Convention on the Law of Treaties, 1155 UNTS 331, entered into force 27 January 1980.

ACKNOWLEDGEMENTS

This volume is the result of the research project 'International Law through the National Prism: The Impact of Judicial Dialogue' funded by the European Science Foundation (ESF) as a European Collaborative Research Project in the Social Sciences (ECRP). As part of this project, a conference hosted by the University of Oslo in 2013 (re-)examined and discussed whether, how, when and why courts engage in judicial dialogues on human rights, and what the purpose and effects are of this practice. Thoroughly revised and updated as contributions to this book, the papers presented at the conference formed the basis for these contributions. They were also brought in line with a common framework for the analysis of domestic and international courts' judicial dialogue that allows drawing comparative conclusions which are presented in the final chapter of the volume. The volume takes a particular interest in the potential of judicial dialogue for advancing the rule of human rights law at the international and domestic level in light of 'present-day conditions' (to use the language of the European Court of Human Rights).

Financial support was provided from a number of sources. The original conference and the editorial work occurred under the auspices of the Norwegian Research Council / European Science Foundation (ECRP) project 'Judicial Dialogues on the Rule of Law: Interaction between National Courts and the European Court of Human Rights'; the European Research Council (ERC) Advanced Grant 69841 *MultiRights* – on the Legitimacy of Multi-Level Human Rights Judiciary; and was partly supported by the Norwegian Research Council through its Centres of Excellence Funding Scheme, project number 223274 *PluriCourts* – on the Legitimacy of the International Judiciary. The editor is thankful for this generous support.

The book could not have been published without the support of many people. The editor is particularly grateful to the authors who readily revised their contributions throughout the editing process so that this volume could become a coherent whole. Thanks also to Geir Ulfstein, Andreas

Føllesdal and André Nollkaemper for their insights and ideas shared on various aspects of judicial dialogue, and their encouragement to pursue this publication.

Warm thanks are extended to Lisa Findley and Claire Poppelwell-Scevak for their dedicated language editing and proofreading, as well as to Eirik Torsvoll, Chrysa Alexandraki, Maria Antonieta Alfaro Calvo and Lars Jørgen Røed for their invaluable work, *inter alia*, on the footnotes and bibliography. With its supportive colleagues and friends, the Centre of Excellence *PluriCourts* in Oslo provided an excellent working environment for the completion of this volume. Thank you to all of you.

The findings presented in the chapters of this book are current as of August 2015.

ABBREVIATIONS

ACHR	American Convention on Human Rights
CCJE	Consultative Council of European Judges
CIS	Commonwealth of Independent States
CJEU	Court of Justice of the European Union
CoE	Council of Europe
CoM	Committee of Ministers, Council of Europe
CPT	European Committee for the Prevention of Torture
ECHR	European Convention of Human Rights
ECRI	European Commission against Racism and Intolerance
ECtHR	European Court of Human Rights
EU	European Union
IACHR	Inter-American Commission on Human Rights
IACtHR	Inter-American Court of Human Rights
ICCPR	International Covenant on Civil and Political Rights
ICERD	International Convention on the Elimination of All Forms of Racial Discrimination
ICESCR	International Covenant on Economic, Social and Cultural Rights
ICJ	International Court of Justice
ICTR	International Criminal Tribunal for Rwanda
ICTY	International Criminal Tribunal for the former Yugoslavia
JCPC	Judicial Committee of the Privy Council
LGTBI	Lesbian, Gay, Bisexual, Transgender, Intersex
NATO	North Atlantic Treaty Organisation
NGO	Non-Governmental Organisation
NZIPT	New Zealand Immigration and Protection Tribunal
OIC	Organisation of Islamic Cooperation
PACE	Parliamentary Assembly of the Council of Europe
PCIJ	Permanent Court of International Justice
PIL	Public International Law
SADC	South African Development Community
SCA	*Sharīʿah* Court of Appeal
SCC	Supreme Court of Canada

SECA	Supreme and Exchequer Courts Act
TEU	Treaty on European Union
TFEU	Treaty on Functioning of European Union
UNCAT	United Nations Convention against Torture
UNESCO	United Nations Educational, Scientific and Cultural Organisation
UNHCR	United Nations High Commissioner for Refugees
VCLT	Vienna Convention on the Law of Treaties
WTO	World Trade Organisation

1

Introduction

AMREI MÜLLER AND HEGE ELISABETH KJOS

1.1 Background

Domestic and international courts across the world play an important role in giving effect to international human rights law. What sort of judicial dialogue do they engage in when protecting human rights? That is the topic of this volume. Such dialogues are particularly important for securing human rights in a world affected by rapid changes. Human rights provisions are often open-ended and require an 'evolutive' interpretation.[1] Hence, judges applying human rights instruments or parallel domestic provisions are given the challenging task of ensuring 'practical and effective' protection in the light of 'present-day conditions'.[2] 'Present-day conditions' can often be characterised by new or newly recognised threats to people's ability to enjoy their human rights. A prominent example is the so-called war on terror. In the aftermath of 9/11, many countries rushed to adopt comparable counterterrorism measures, some of which have been found to violate international human rights law and/or domestic constitutional law.[3] Other current human rights issues affecting numerous countries concern the right to privacy vis-à-vis activities of intelligence services

[1] T. Makkonen, 'Between Anti-Essentialism and Anti-Everything – Is There Anything?', J. Petman and J. Klabbers (eds.), *Nordic Cosmopolitanism: Essays in International Law for Martti Koskenniemi* (Leiden: Brill, 2003) 251–61, at 257; D. Harris *et al.* (eds.), *Law of the European Convention on Human Rights*, 3rd ed. (Oxford University Press, 2014) at 8–10; M. Sepúlveda, *The Nature of the Obligations under the International Covenant on Economic, Social and Cultural Rights* (Antwerpen: Intersentia, 2003) at 81.

[2] E.g. *Tyrer v. the United Kingdom* (Appl. No. 5856/72), Judgment (Chamber), 25 April 1978, Series A, Vol. 26, para. 31, a statement that the ECtHR repeated many times in other judgments and which has become an established doctrine of the ECtHR's jurisprudence. See also Harris *et al.*, Law of the European Convention, *supra* note 1, at 8–10.

[3] E.g. D. Moeckli, *Human Rights and Non-Discrimination in the 'War on Terror'* (Oxford University Press, 2008); R.A. Wilson (ed.), *Human Rights in the War on Terror* (Cambridge University Press, 2005).

and of big internet providers and companies,[4] the protection of migrants'[5] and LGTBI people's rights,[6] as well as measures taken to address the global financial and economic crisis, some of which conflict with socio-economic rights.[7]

The interpretation and application of domestic and international human rights law concerning these and other areas often involve controversial debates, which can encompass political, historical, cultural, religious and economic interests. The controversies may involve collisions between domestic laws and international human rights law; and they can also reflect broader disagreement about the appropriate scope of protection of a particular right within a country, between states and/or within regional and international fora. When rendering judgments in human rights cases, domestic and international judges are constantly asked to find the right balance between the protection of individual rights and public interests, between the rights of different people, and between respect for international (universal) human rights law and principles on the one hand and respect for legitimate diversity in the interpretation and application of human rights on the other.

This book analyses whether, how and with what effect domestic and international courts engage in dialogue when addressing these and other challenges in securing human rights. Judicial dialogue occurs when national and international judges construing and giving effect to a particular norm look at how their colleagues in other states or international courts have construed the same or a similar norm. This practice of looking beyond 'borders' has been coined in various terms: 'transnational', 'global' or 'international' judicial dialogue,[8]

[4] E.g. L. Paquette, 'The Whistleblower as Underdog: What Protection Can Human Rights Offer in Massive Secret Surveillance?', *The Int'l J. of Human Rights* 17:7–8 (2013) 796–809; and A. Mihr, 'Public Privacy: Human Rights in Cyberspace', *SIM Working Paper, The Netherlands Institute of Human Rights*, Utrecht University (2013).

[5] R. Rubio-Marin (ed.), *Human Rights and Immigration* (Oxford University Press, 2014).

[6] E.g. M. O'Flaherty and J. Fisher, 'Sexual Orientation, Gender Identity and International Human Rights Law: Contextualising the Yogyakarta Principles', *Human Rights Law Review* 8:2 (2008) 207–48; and S. Goldberg, *Sexuality and Equality Law* (Franham: Ashgate, 2013).

[7] E.g. A. Nolan (ed.), *Economic, Social and Cultural Rights after the Global Financial Crisis* (Cambridge University Press, 2014); D. Bilchitz, 'Socio-economic Rights, Economic Crisis, and Legal Doctrine', *Int'l J. of Constitutional L.* 12:3 (2014) 710–39; A. Kentikelenis *et al.*, 'Greece's Health Crisis: From Austerity to Denialism', *The Lancet* 383 (2014) 748–53.

[8] See e.g. R. Krotoszynski, '"I'd Like the World to Sing (in Perfect Harmony)": International Judicial Dialogue and the Muses – Reflections in the Perils and the Promise of International Judicial Dialogue', *Michigan L. Rev.* 104:6 (2006) 1321–59; D. Law and W.C. Chang, 'The Limits of Global Judicial Dialogue', *Washington L. Rev.* 86 (2011) 523–77; M. Waters, 'Mediating Norms and Identity: The Role of Transnational Judicial Dialogue in Creating

'conversation'[9] or 'engagement';[10] 'transjudicial dialogue'[11] or 'communication';[12] 'inter-judicial coordination';[13] 'transjudicialism',[14] 'judicial comparativism';[15] 'comparative international law';[16] and 'transnational interaction'[17] of courts.[18] The interaction between courts is facilitated by increased cross-border communication in most regions of the world, which has also become possible through technological advances combined with publication and reporting of (translated) court decisions.[19]

and Enforcing International Law', *Georgetown L. J.* 93 (2005) 487–574; G.S. Goodwin-Gill and H. Lambert (eds.), *The Limits of Transnational Law – Refugee Law, Policy Harmonization and Judicial Dialogue in the European Union* (Cambridge University Press, 2010); M. Kirby, 'Transnational Judicial Dialogue, Internationalisation of Law and Australian Judges', *Melbourne J. of Int'l L.* 9:1 (2008) 171–90; G. Martinico and O. Pollicino, *The Interaction between Europe's Legal Systems: Judicial Dialogue and the Creation of Supranational Laws* (Cheltenham: Edward Elgar, 2012); and A. Strauss, 'Beyond National Law: The Neglected Role of International Law of Personal Jurisdiction in Domestic Courts', *Harvard Int'l L. J.* 36:2 (1995) 373–425, introducing the phrase 'international judicial dialogue' in 1995, at 378.

9 See e.g. C. McCrudden, 'A Common Law of Human Rights?: Transnational Judicial Conversations on Constitutional Rights', *Oxford J. of Legal Studies* 20:4 (2000) 499–532; and M. Kirby, 'Domestic Court and International Human Rights Law – The Ongoing Judicial Conversation', *Utrecht L. Rev.* 6:1 (2010) 168–81.

10 V. Jackson, *Constitutional Engagement in a Transnational Era* (Oxford University Press, 2010) at 71.

11 M. R. Ferrarese, 'When National Actors Become Transnational: Transjudicial Dialogue between Democracy and Constitutionalism', *Global Jurist* 9:1 (2009) 1–31.

12 A. M. Slaughter, 'A Typology of Transjudicial Communication', *University of Richmond L. Rev.* 29:1 (1994–1995) 99–139.

13 E. Benvenisiti and G. Downs, 'Towards Global Checks and Balances', *Constitutional Political Economy* 20:3–4 (2009) 366–87, at 382.

14 R. Bahdi, 'Globalisation of Judgment: Transjudicialism and the Five Faces of International Law in Domestic Courts', *George Washington Int'l L. Rev.* 34 (2002) 555–88.

15 E. Örücü (ed.), *Judicial Comparativism in Human Rights Cases* (London: British Institute for International and Comparative Law, 2003); M. Bobek, *Comparative Reasoning in European Supreme Courts* (Oxford University Press, 2013). See also G. Canivet, M. Andenæs and D. Fairgrieve (eds.), *Comparative Law Before the Courts* (London: British Institute for International and Comparative Law, 2004); and B. Markesinis and J. Fedtke, *Engaging with Foreign Law* (Oxford: Hart, 2009).

16 A. Roberts, 'Comparative International Law? The Role of National Courts in Creating and Enforcing International Law', *Int'l and Comparative L. Quarterly* 60:1 (2011) 57–93.

17 See A. Hol, 'Highest Courts and Transnational Interaction – Introductory and Concluding Remarks', *Utrecht L. Rev.* 8:2 (2012) 1–7. This editorial relates to a number of articles discussing this phenomenon.

18 For the terminology used in this book, see *infra* section 1.2.1.

19 Roberts, 'Comparative International Law?', *supra* note 16, at 58; Jackson, Constitutional Engagement, *supra* note 10, at 5–6. Note in particular International Law in Domestic Courts (ILDC), published by Oxford University Press as part of the Oxford Reports on

Dialogue can help courts in the interpretation and application of domestic constitutional law and/or international human rights law, to solve a concrete dispute and to find common solutions to current human rights problems. To return to the example of counterterrorism measures, a study of how other courts have balanced the various interests involved can enhance a judge's understanding of what solution works best. In this way, international and domestic courts can arrive at shared solutions to bring these measures in line with international human rights law and/or parallel domestic norms. References to interpretations that carry transnational support can be particularly valuable as a means to strengthening judicial credibility in cases that are politically charged or otherwise controversial. From this perspective, judicial dialogue in the area of human rights can also be seen as a tool for the incremental development of *international* human rights law and principles.[20] A 'conversation' between domestic and international judges, including when it involves an acknowledgement of differentiated solutions, could help to resolve conflicting interpretations at the national, regional and international levels or promote the acceptance of legitimate national or regional differences. Yet disparities in the participation of different national and international courts in a judicial dialogue[21] may undermine the development of a *truly international* understanding of human rights law and principles.[22]

This brings us to another, larger role that national and international courts play in today's world, and that could be enhanced through dialogue through human rights:[23] ensuring the 'rule of law'.[24] While there

International Law (ORIL) and Cambridge Law Reports (CLR), published by Cambridge University Press.

[20] In this context see the observation by Esin Örücü that 'comparativism must be at the heart of human rights cases, if human rights are to be regarded as embodying principles that are "universal" rather than purely domestic or even "European"'. See E. Örücü, 'Whither Comparativism in Human Rights Cases?', E. Örücü (ed.), *supra* note 15, 229–43, at 230; see also C. Koch, 'Judicial Dialogue for Legal Multiculturalism', *Michigan J. of Int'l L.* 25:4 (2003–04) 879–903.

[21] See text accompanying *infra* notes 28–35.

[22] For example, if dialogue takes place primarily between courts of 'Western' liberal democracies, it is unlikely that socio-economic rights will gain a prominent place in this dialogue.

[23] The phrase 'judicial dialogue *through* international human rights law' is meant to take account of the fact that most of the time domestic courts do not apply international human rights law directly, but interpret domestic law in light of international human rights law. This results in a more indirect dialogue *through* international human rights law, not a direct dialogue *on* international human rights law. See also *infra* section 1.2.1 for a more detailed explanation of what we mean by 'judicial dialogue'.

[24] A. Nollkaemper, *National Courts and the International Rule of Law* (Oxford University Press, 2011); UN GA, Declaration of the High-level Meeting of the General Assembly on

is no exact definition of this term, a common explanation contains the following three core elements: a government of laws, the supremacy of the law and equality before the law.[25] In the latter part of the twentieth century, the rule of law ceased to be an exclusively national concept, and contours of an 'international rule of law' emerged. Widely supported interpretations of the 'rule of law' that encompass both its national and international dimensions require that laws and the exercise of public power are consistent with international human rights norms.[26] It has been suggested, therefore, that when domestic judges give effect to international human rights law,[27] they guard the rule of (human rights) law both at home and globally. Contributions to this edited volume discuss how judicial dialogue can facilitate the task shared by domestic and international courts of ensuring and developing the international rule of (human rights) law.

Much research has already been conducted into various aspects of the phenomenon of judicial dialogue in the area of human rights and other fields of law. Empirical data has been collected on whether and how various domestic, regional and international courts use international and foreign legal material. Yet, concerning domestic courts, the focus has mainly been on Western European states,[28] the United States

the Rule of Law at the National and International Levels, 30 November 2012, UN Doc. A/RES/67/1, para.32.

25 See S. Chesterman, 'Rule of Law', *Max Planck Encyclopedia of Public International Law* (Oxford University Press, 2007) accessed online (opil.ouplaw.com/home/epil).

26 See e.g. UN Secretary-General, 'Report of the Secretary-General on the Rule of Law and Transitional Justice in Conflict and Post-conflict States', 23 August 2004, UN Doc. S/2004/61623, para.6; The World Justice Project, 'What is the Rule of Law?', available at world-justiceproject.org/what-rule-law; Nollkaemper, National Courts, *supra* note 24, at 4–5; B. Tamanaha, *On the Rule of Law: History, Politics, Theory* (Cambridge University Press, 2010) at 112; B. Zangl, 'Is there an Emerging International Rule of Law?', *European Review* 13 (2005) 73–91. Others suggest a narrower definition, see e.g. J. Waldron, 'Are Sovereigns Entitled to the Benefits of the International Rule of Law?', *European J. of Int'l L.* 22:2 (2011) 315–43.

27 This can happen either through the direct application of international human rights treaties at the domestic level, or through the interpretation of domestic law in light of and conformity with international human rights law.

28 See e.g. the focus of the edited volumes by Canivet, Andenæs and Fairgrieve, Comparative Law, *supra* note 15; Örücü, Judicial Comparativism, *supra* note 15; Bobek, Comparative Reasoning, *supra* note 15; and Markesinis and Fedtke, Engaging with Foreign Law, *supra* note 15; M. Gelter and M. Siems, 'Networks, Dialogue or One-Way Traffic? An Empirical Analysis of Cross-Citations Between Ten of Europe's Highest Courts', *Utrecht L. Rev.* 8:2 (2012) 88–99; and H. Keller and A. Stone-Sweet (eds.), *A Europe of Rights: The Impact of the ECHR on National Legal Systems* (Oxford University Press, 2008), covering also several Central and Eastern European states.

Supreme Court,[29] as well as Commonwealth countries,[30] among them Australia,[31] Canada[32] and South Africa.[33] While there are several studies covering single countries[34] or countries from a particular region,[35] the practice of courts in many Asian, Latin American, African, Arab and

[29] G. Neuman, 'The Uses of International Law in Constitutional Interpretation', *American J. of Int'l L.* 98 (2004) 82–91; S. Calabresi and S. D. Zimdahl, 'The Supreme Court and Foreign Sources of Law: Two Hundred Years of Practice and the Juvenile Death Penalty Decision', *William and Mary L. Rev.* 47:3 (2005) 743-909; C. L'Heurreux-Dube, 'The Importance of Dialogue: Globalisation and the International Impact of the *Rehnquist* Court', *Tulsa L. J.* 34:1 (1998) 15–40; and critical: R. Brok, *Coercing Virtue: The Worldwide Rule of Judges* (Cambridge, MA: Aei Press, 2003); R. Alford, 'Misusing International Sources to Interpret the Constitution', *American J. of Int'l L.* 98 (2004) 57–69; R. Posner, 'No Thanks, We Already Have Our Own Laws', *Legal Affairs* July/August 2004, available at www.legalaffairs.org/issues/July-August-2004/feature_posner_julaug04.msp; and M. Ramsey, 'International Materials and Domestic Rights: Reflections on Atkins and Lawrence', *American J. of Int'l L.* 98:1 (2004) 69–82; Jackson, Constitutional Engagement, *supra* note 10.

[30] B. Flanagan and S. Ahern, 'Judicial Decision-Making and Transnational Law: A Survey of Common Law Supreme Court Judges', *Int'l and Comparative L. Quarterly* 60:1 (2011) 1–28 (covering the UK House of Lords, the Caribbean Court of Justice, the High Court of Australia, the Constitutional Court of South Africa, and the Supreme Courts of Canada, India, Ireland, Israel, New Zealand and the United States).

[31] Kirby, Transnational Judicial Dialogue, *supra* note 8. M. Weisbrud, 'Using International Law to Interpret National Constitutions – Conceptual Problems: Reflections on Justice Kirby's Advocacy of International Law in Domestic Constitutional Interpretation', *American University Int'l L. Rev.* 21:3 (2006) 365–79.

[32] K. Roach, 'Constitutional, Remedial and International Dialogues About Rights: The Canadian Experience', *Texas J. of Int'l Law* 40:3 (2004–05) 537–77; G. van Ert, *Using International Law in Canadian Courts* (Toronto: Irwin Law, 2008); and older: P. McCormick, 'The Supreme Court of Canada and American Citations 1945–1994: A Statistical Overview', *Supreme Court L. Rev.* 8 (1997) 527–33.

[33] A. Lollini, 'The South African Constitutional Court Experience: Reasoning Patterns Based on Foreign Law', *Utrecht L. Rev.* 8 (2012) 55–88; D. Carey-Miller, 'The Great Trek to Human Rights: The Role of Comparative Law in the Development of Human Rights in Post-reform South Africa', E. Örücü (ed.), *supra* note 15, 201–26; and M. Martinek, 'Comparative Jurisprudence – What Good Does It Do – History, Tasks, Methods, Achievements and Perspectives of an Indispensable Discipline of Legal Research and Education', *J. of South African L.* 1 (2013) 39–57.

[34] E.g. Law and Chang, Limits of Global Judicial Dialogue, *supra* note 8, studying the practice of the Taiwanese Constitutional Court; A. Ejima, 'Enigmatic Attitude of the Supreme Court of Japan towards Foreign Precedents – Refusal at the Front Door and Admission at the Back Door', available at www.juridicas.unam.mx/wccl/ponencias/12/200.pdf; W.C. Chang, 'The Convergence of Constitutions and International Human Rights: Taiwan and South Korea Comparisons', *North Carolina J. of Int'l L. and Commercial Regulation* 36:3 (2011) 593–625; and E. Örücü, 'The Turkish Experience with Judicial Comparativism in Human Rights Cases', E. Örücü (ed.), *supra* note 15, 131–55, studying Turkish court's involvement in judicial dialogue.

[35] M. Adjami, 'African Courts, International Law, and Comparative Case Law: Chimera or Emerging Human Rights Jurisprudence?', *Michigan J. of Int'l L.* 24:1 (2002) 103–69;

Eastern European countries remains under-researched, or any existing research is overlooked by ('Western') scholars and judges. With respect to international courts, research on their use of 'external'[36] legal material often only covers some aspects of such dialogue[37] or focuses on a specific court like the International Court of Justice (ICJ), the Court of Justice of the European Union (CJEU) or Investment Arbitration Tribunals.[38] Thus, to fully understand the phenomenon of national and international courts' dialogue in the area of human rights, including its potential to strengthen the rule of (international human rights) law, the existing data from some courts and regions must first be complemented by empirical material from other courts and regions. Concerning national courts' engagement in dialogue, this book provides some of this material by examining Eastern Europe (with a focus on Poland), Latin America and Nigeria and Malaysia. Concerning international human rights courts, this book contributes to our understanding of one prominent court's engagement in dialogue: it sheds light on the ECtHR's dialogue with domestic courts in the Council of Europe's (CoE) member states, non-member states and international courts and quasi-judicial bodies.

The limited and uneven availability of empirical data has not prevented theoretical literature on the phenomenon of judicial dialogue in general, and in particular the area of human rights. Different positions have been taken regarding the practice and its possible purpose and effects. Anne-Marie Slaughter, for example, suggests that the dialogue unites judges

and M. Killander (ed.), *International Law and Human Rights Litigation in Africa* (Cape Town: Pretoria University Law Press, 2010), covering Benin, Botswana, Cote d'Ivoire, Ghana, Kenya, Namibia, Nigeria, Senegal, Tanzania, Uganda and Zambia.

[36] That is, domestic law and 'external' international law as well as decisions of domestic courts and decisions of other international courts.

[37] E.g. in relation to the sources of law, see A. Nollkaemper, G. Bos and W. Schabas, 'Decisions of National Courts as Sources of International Law: An Analysis of the Practice of the ICTY', G. Boas and W. Schabas (eds.), *International Criminal Law Developments in the Case Law of the ICTY* (Leiden: Brill, 2003) 277–96; or in relation to international law, see e.g. M. Forovicz, *The Reception of International Law in the European Court of Human Rights* (Oxford University Press, 2010).

[38] See respectively A. Nollkaemper, 'The Role of Domestic Courts in the Case Law of the International Court of Justice', *Chinese J. of Int'l L.* 5:2 (2006) 301–22; B. Simma, 'Mainstreaming Human Rights: The Contribution of the International Court of Justice', *J. of Int'l Dispute Settlement* 3:1 (2012) 7–29; F.G. Jacobs, 'Judicial Dialogue and the Cross-Fertilization of Legal Systems: The European Court of Justice', *Texas Int'l L. J.* 38:3 (2003) 547–57; and V. Vadi, 'Towards Arbitral Path Coherence and Judicial Borrowing: Persuasive

around the world in a 'common global judicial enterprise'[39] or a 'global community of courts'.[40] Slaughter describes judges as 'remarkably self-consciousness about what they are doing',[41] engaging in 'open'[42] debates with courts in other countries on both procedural and substantive questions of law, most notably in the area of human rights.[43] She argues that these 'interactions both contribute to a nascent global jurisprudence' and 'improve the quality of particular national decisions'.[44] Even though she recognises that the global community of courts 'does not yet include all courts from all countries, or even all international courts and tribunals',[45] she is confident that judicial dialogue will ultimately strengthen the international rule of law, in particular the rule of international human rights law.[46]

Others are more cautious. They observe that the participation of courts in judicial dialogues is vastly inconsistent.[47] Among the reasons offered are that judges may be prevented by domestic law, procedure, established practice or ideological reasons from referring to external legal material; some judges may regard it as improper, even if they are not impeded by these factors.[48] Other courts may engage in selective dialogue, for example

Precedent in Investment Arbitration', *Transnational Dispute Management* 5:3 (2008), available at www.transnational-dispute-management.com/article.asp?key=1240.

39 A.-M. Slaughter, *A New World Order* (Princeton University Press, 2004) at 99.

40 A.-M. Slaughter, 'A Global Community of Courts', *Harvard Int'l L. J.* 44:1 (2003) 191–221; see also L. Helfer and A.-M. Slaughter, 'Toward a Theory of Effective Supranational Adjudication', *Yale L. J.* 107:2 (1997) 273–391, at 372–73 (referring to conferences and networks).

41 Slaughter, A Global Community, *supra* note 40, at 195.

42 *Ibid.*

43 Slaughter, A Typology, *supra* note 12, at 99–100.

44 Slaughter, A Global Community, *supra* note 40, at 195.

45 *Ibid.*, at 194.

46 This view is supported by e.g. Bahdi, Globalisation of Judgment, *supra* note 14; Helfer and Slaughter, Supranational Adjudication, *supra* note 40; L'Heureux-Dube, The Importance of Dialogue, *supra* note 29, at 21; and Waters, Mediating Norms and Identity, *supra* note 8.

47 See e.g. Law and Chang, Limits of Global Judicial Dialogue, *supra* note 8, at 530–35. See also Jackson, Constitutional Engagement, *supra* note 10, at 8–9 (referring to three different postures courts can take: resistance, convergence and engagement).

48 This is the opinion of some justices of the US Supreme Court, see sources cited in *supra* note 29; and A. Harding, 'Comparative Case Law in Human Rights Cases in the Commonwealth: The Emerging Common Law of Human Rights', E. Örücü (ed.) *supra* note 15, 183–201 (discussing Malaysia); J. Tsen-Ta Lee, 'Interpreting Bills of Rights: The Value of a Comparative Approach', *Int'l J. of Constitutional L.* 5:1 (2007) 122–52, at 125–27 (on Singapore courts); Law and Chang, Limits of Global Judicial Dialogue, *supra* note 8, at 531–32; and M. Killander and H. Adjolohoun, 'International Law and Domestic Human Rights Litigation in Africa: An Introduction', M. Killander (ed.), *supra* note 15, 3–25, at 18–19.

by only referring to judgments of courts that they deem prestigious.[49] Brian Flanagan and Sinéad Ahern, for instance, observe that 'critical opportunism and the aspiration to membership of an emerging international "guild" appear to be equally important strands in judicial attitudes towards foreign law'.[50] This means that frequently the 'transnational winds blow only in one direction',[51] resulting in a skewed and uneven contribution of domestic and international courts to a 'universal' understanding of judicial practice in various areas of international law, including human rights law. The function of court-to-court dialogue in securing and developing the rule of truly *international* human rights law, to which *all* courts can contribute, can be questioned under these circumstances.[52]

Questions about the appropriateness and legitimacy of judicial dialogue are also raised. Concerning dialogue between domestic courts, Ronald Krotoszynski, for instance, asks whether a judge can reliably 'borrow' from a decision of a foreign court when he or she 'lacks even the most rudimentary understanding of the institution that issued the opinion and the legal, social and cultural constraints that provided the context for this decision'.[53] For example, domestic jurisdictions have different conceptions of 'positive' and 'negative' human rights obligations, and there are variations as to the scope and function of judicial review.[54] Misinterpretation may even occur when the external decision references international human rights provisions that are also binding on the 'receiving' court. Countries differ in the way they incorporate or transpose human rights law in their domestic legal order, and the degree of bindingness may impact on the interpretation of the relevant norm and also the outcome of the case.

Critics have also voiced concerns about the lack of clarity with respect to the legal principles in accordance with which judicial dialogue is

[49] See Alford, Misusing International Sources, *supra* note 29, at 64–69; A. Smith, 'Making Itself at Home: Understanding Foreign Law in Domestic Jurisprudence: The Indian Case', *Berkeley J. of Int'l L.* 24:1 (2006) 218–73, at 265–66; Y. Ghai, 'Sentinels of Liberty or Sheep in Wolf's Clothing? Judicial Politics and the Hong Kong Bill of Rights', *Modern L. Rev.* 60:4 (1997) 459–81, at 479.

[50] Flanagan and Ahern, Judicial Decision-Making, *supra* note 30.

[51] J. Hermida, 'A New Model of Application of International Law in National Courts: The Transjudicial Vision', *Waikato L. Rev.* 11 (2003) 37–58, at 54.

[52] See e.g. Law and Chang, Limits of Global Judicial Dialogue, *supra* note 8, at 527.

[53] Krotoszynski, I'd Like the World to Sing, *supra* note 8, at 1325 and 1340. This danger is also highlighted by Alford, Misusing International Sources, *supra* note 29, at 64–69; and McCrudden, A Common Law *supra* note 9, at 526.

[54] Krotoszynski, *ibid.*, at 1342. This is a common problem of comparative law; see e.g. G. Frankenberg, 'Comparing Constitutions: Ideas, Ideals and Ideology – Towards a Layered Narrative', *Int'l J. of Constitutional L.* 4:3 (2006) 439–59, at 441.

conducted. They have noted the absence of a rigorous theory, and argue that proponents of the practice have failed to ground it in any of the standard approaches to constitutional interpretation[55] or the interpretation of international law.[56] This ambiguity can give judges too much discretion[57] in deciding whether and when to follow decisions of which foreign domestic or international courts. A practice of selectiveness or 'cherry-picking' can undermine the credibility of courts as independent guardians of the rule of law. The related fear has been voiced that judicial dialogue may lead to circumvention of the checks and balances at the domestic level and ultimately of democratic accountability, in particular when courts use (certain) foreign decisions to justify their reasoning in cases that involve issues lacking consensus within their jurisdiction.[58]

This brief overview of existing research on judicial dialogue shows that questions of both a practical and theoretical nature remain on the practice, including its potential to strengthen an international rule of human rights law to which international and national courts from all regions of the world should contribute. Many of these questions formed the background for the project 'International Law through the National Prism: the

55 See the criticism by R. Alford, 'In Search of a Theory for Constitutional Comparativism', *University of California L. Rev.* 52:3 (2005) 639–715.

56 E.g. under article 31(3)(b) Vienna Convention on the Law of Treaties ((VCLT) (23 May 1968) 1155 UNTS 311, entered into force 27 January 1980), allowing taking account 'of any subsequent practice in the application of the treaty which establishes the agreement of the parties regarding its interpretation' in the interpretation of an international treaty; or article 38(1)(d) Statute of the International Court of Justice ((ICJ Statute) (26 June 1945) 3 Bevans 1179; 59 Stat 1055, entered into force 24 October 1945), allowing to take account of relevant judicial decisions in the interpretation of international law.

57 See e.g. J. Larson, 'Importing Constitutional Norms from a "Wider Civilization": Lawrence and the Rehnquist Court's Use of Foreign and International Law in Domestic Constitutional Interpretation', *Ohio State L. J.* 65:5 (2004) 1283–1329, at 1303–26. This is also discussed by McCrudden, A Common Law *supra* note 9, at 517, who, however, suggests that there are some criteria that regulate the rules of referencing foreign legal material. Vicki Jackson also examines this challenge in regard to the use of foreign and international legal material by the US Supreme Court. She argues that the challenge can well be overcome by integrating the use of foreign and international law in the constitutional interpretation of the common law tradition that involves consideration of multiple interpretative sources; see V. Jackson, 'Constitutional Comparisons: Convergence, Resistance, Engagement', *Harvard L. Rev.* 119:1 (2005) 109–28, at 122–23.

58 Krotoszynski, I'd Like the World to Sing, *supra* note 9, at 1333; the question about (democratic) legitimacy of judicial dialogue has also been asked by McCrudden, A Common Law *supra* note 9, at 530; and Jackson, Constitutional Comparisons, *supra* note 57, at 120–22, dispersing this fear for the context of the use of foreign and international law by the US Supreme Court.

Impact of Judicial Dialogue', funded by the European Science Foundation (ESF) as a European Collaborative Research project in the Social Sciences (ECRP).[59] As part of this project, a conference hosted by the University of Oslo in 2013 was organised to (re-)examine and discuss whether, how, when and why courts engage in judicial dialogue through international human rights law, and what the purpose and effects are of this practice. The conference focused on judicial dialogues on/through international human rights law, and took a particular interest in their potential for advancing the rule of (human rights) law at the international and domestic level in light of 'present-day conditions'. Viewpoints were sought both from scholars and domestic supreme/constitutional court judges and judges at the European Court of Human Rights (ECtHR). This edited volume is a result of these 'dialogues on dialogues'.

In individual contributions, authors give evidence of recent dialogues involving international human rights law in different regions of the world. Building on existing scholarship and following a common analytical framework, they explore and offer new insights on the extent, method, purpose and effects of judicial dialogue in the area of human rights law, pointing also to legal, practical and normative reasons why some courts may not engage in this practice. Moreover, answers are sought to some of the pressing theoretical and normative questions about the ultimate purpose and effects of judicial dialogue.

A valuable and unique contribution is offered by the main characters involved in judicial dialogue: the judges themselves. In response to questionnaires distributed to them by the editors in advance of the conference,[60] they reflect on their role in the process. The judges' contributions are included in the form of comprehensive summaries of their discussions during the conference. They provide refreshing insights into the actual practice of judicial dialogue through international human rights law that complement the observations made in the other contributions.

The conference furthermore examined the extent, method, purpose and effects of one regional human rights court's engagement in judicial dialogue in detail: the ECtHR. This is continued and elaborated upon in the present book. The analysis includes how the ECtHR's interaction with domestic courts in the member states of the CoE can encourage domestic

[59] Amsterdam Center for International Law, 'International Law through the National Prism: the Impact of Judicial Dialogue', available at http://acil.uva.nl/research/research-projects/current-projects/current-projects/current-projects/content/folder/international-law-through-the-national-prism.html.

[60] The questionnaires can be found in the annexes to this book.

courts to take on an active role in the application and interpretation of the European Convention on Human Rights (ECHR),[61] and in the development of European/international human rights law. Furthermore, the book investigates the role non-governmental organisations (NGOs) play in encouraging the ECtHR's engagement in dialogue, in particular through their submission of *amicus curiae* briefs to the Court. The in-depth case study of this one regional court promises to move the discussion on regional human rights courts' judicial dialogue forward, and result in a more detailed understanding of the underlying reasons for regional courts' dialogue. Conclusions from the case study on the ECtHR may also inspire the judicial dialogue of regional courts and UN human rights treaty bodies that have not been discussed at the conference and as part of this book. In particular, insight into how the ECtHR uses its engagement with domestic courts to disperse criticism that is raised against international or regional judicial mechanism and supervision of states' human rights obligations,[62] can also be of relevance for the dialogue of other international and regional courts with domestic courts.

The following sections provide the framework of the book. It outlines our understanding of the concept of judicial dialogue, and it elaborates on the questions about the extent, method, purpose and effect of judicial dialogue which the contributors set out to answer.

1.2 Framework

1.2.1 The Concept of Judicial Dialogue

In order to facilitate the 'dialogue on dialogue', we adopt a wide definition of judicial dialogue. Judicial dialogue is understood as the use of external judicial decisions by courts as an element of influence (even if very limited) in interpretation and application of the law. External judicial decisions include judicial decisions of foreign national and international courts, as well as of quasi-judicial UN human rights treaty bodies. Judicial dialogue can be direct or indirect[63] and may be stimulated in various ways,

[61] Convention for the Protection of Human Rights and Fundamental Freedoms (4 November 1950) 213 UNTS 222; 312 ETS 5, entered into force 3 September 1953.

[62] In the CoE's system for the protection of human rights, this criticism comes in particular from the United Kingdom. For an overview of the situation, see J. Henley, 'Why is the European Court of Human Rights Hated by the UK Right?', *The Guardian*, 22 December 2013, available at www.theguardian.com/law/2013/dec/22/britain-european-court-human-rights.

[63] Direct dialogue implies that courts are explicit about how they have used external legal material, whereas indirect dialogue implies that (members of) the court engages with external legal material, but that any influence is not directly traceable. See also the distinction drawn by Cian Murphy between 'explicit' and 'implicit' dialogue; C. Murphy, 'Human

for example, by domestic and international judges reading (about) external judicial decisions through their own research or that of counsel or *amici*, as well as through interactions between judges, lawyers and scholars outside the courtroom, including at conferences, specifically organised meetings and in telephone conversations.[64] Our focus is on possible (legal) effects of external judicial decisions on judgments of domestic and international courts concerning human rights. When looking at individual cases, these may range from the resistance to use it, to engagement with such material, to direct embracement and convergence.[65] We also consider the broader effects that the (lack of) influence of external judicial decisions may have on either fostering or restraining the (international) rule of (human rights) law.

In our definition, judicial dialogue does not need to be equal or reciprocal.[66] Not all practice analysed in this book will thus be 'dialogue' between courts in the true sense of the word that involves an ongoing and reciprocal 'conversation' between different courts on questions of law during which the courts oppose or support each other. In other words, the book also covers judicial interaction where a court makes a mere reference to a foreign or international judicial decision or it is otherwise clear that such a decision was considered (if only to be rejected). For that reason, the broader term 'engagement', as suggested by Vicki Jackson, may better capture the practice studied in this book.[67]

In terms of direction, dialogue can be horizontal, taking the form of interaction between two or more domestic courts in different states or between different international courts. In horizontal dialogue, the participating courts are either all domestic or regional/international.[68] Dialogue can also be vertical – that is, it can take place between international/

Rights Law and the Challenges of Explicit Judicial Dialogue', *Jean Monnet Working Paper*, NYU School of Law 12:10 (2012) 1–32, at 11–13.

64 For an overview of the different forms in which judicial dialogue can take place, see Slaughter, A Typology, *supra* note 12.

65 For a typology of different effects that judicial dialogue can have on court decisions, see Jackson, Constitutional Comparisons, *supra* note 57.

66 In this context, we note that the use of the term 'dialogue' has raised some debate, since it implies an inclusive process of mutual engagement with different positions. This is frequently missing in the phenomenon of judicial interaction that is analysed in this book and existing literature on the topic. See e.g. the observations by Law and Chang, Limits of Global Judicial Dialogue, *supra* note 8, at 528–34; and by L. Pasquet in Chapter 17 of this volume. However, due to the fact that the European Collaborative Research Project of which this edited volume is a result, uses the term 'judicial dialogue', we retain this term.

67 Jackson, Constitutional Engagement, *supra* note 10.

68 Slaughter, A Typology, *supra* note 12, at 103.

regional courts on the one hand, and domestic courts on the other;[69] or it can be 'mixed vertical-horizontal'. The latter occurs when an international court serves as a channel for horizontal communication between national courts, or when an international court or tribunal distils common legal principles from domestic legal orders and distributes them to domestic courts and other international courts or tribunals.[70]

With the exception of dialogue between a domestic court and an international court involving a judgment of the latter by which the domestic court is legally bound, the book focuses on 'voluntary' use of foreign and international judicial decisions, that is, sources that may be considered 'persuasive authority' rather than legally binding.[71] In most cases analysed in this book, the decision as to whether to engage in judicial dialogue remains a choice of the court in question,[72] even if more and more courts might feel pressured into taking account of foreign and international legal material in a world in which globalisation does not stop at the doorsteps of courthouses. In this sense, judicial dialogue can be distinguished from 'reception', which was common between colonies and their colonial power, involving the colonies' strict adherence to the law and court decisions of colonial powers.[73] However, reception has also been used to describe the gradual incorporation and transformation of ratified international treaties into domestic law, for example through the influence of a regional human rights court.[74] In this understanding, 'reception' also includes some elements of dialogue between domestic and international courts on treaties that are binding on the respective state. This form of dialogue on binding human rights treaties is also part of our analysis.[75]

With this definition as its basis, the contributions to this book explore different aspects concerning the extent, method, purpose and effect of horizontal, vertical and mixed vertical-horizontal judicial dialogue of domestic courts and the ECtHR. While these four categories were chosen

[69] *Ibid.*, at 106–11.

[70] *Ibid.*, at 111–12.

[71] Jackson, Constitutional Engagement, *supra* note 10, at 10 and chapter 6.

[72] The ECtHR's reliance on domestic courts' and other international courts' decisions is to some extent an exception in this context. The ECtHR regularly holds that it interprets and applies the law of the ECHR in light of the 'practice of European States reflecting their common values' and that it will take account of 'elements of international law other than the Convention [and] the interpretation of such elements by competent organs'. See e.g. *Demir and Baykara v. Turkey* (Appl. No. 34503/97), Judgment (Grand Chamber), 12 November 2008, ECHR 2008-V, 427, para. 85.

[73] L'Heureux-Dube, The Importance of Dialogue, *supra* note 29, at 21.

[74] See e.g. Keller and Stone Sweet, A Europe of Rights, *supra* note 29.

[75] See Chapter 11 in this volume.

to give some common structure to the chapters, it is noted that there is an overlap between these different aspects, and authors were given some freedom to put more or less weight on the various aspects. The categories are also relied upon in the concluding chapter, which compares, synthesises and builds on the findings made in the other contributions.

1.2.2 Extent

The authors first examine the *extent* of judicial dialogues on human rights that are taking place between different domestic courts in different countries and regions, as well as the extent of the ECtHR's judicial dialogue. Questions were posed by the editors about possible variances in the scope, reach and frequency of judicial dialogue by reference to the following factors:

Time: Are we right to assume that the process of judicial dialogue has accelerated in recent years in different regions around the world?[76]

Space: Can we say that judicial dialogue is a global phenomenon, or are there countries whose courts participate less or not at all in any form of judicial dialogue?[77]

Type of judicial system: Can we detect differences between common law and civil law countries in their involvement in judicial dialogues?[78] And what is the influence of a country's framework for accepting international law (monism versus dualism) or for reconciling conflicts between domestic and international norms?

Subject matter: Is judicial dialogue particularly prone to occur in the field of human rights, especially in regard to issues where the law is developing, for example in regard to LGTBI rights, migrants' rights, data protection, environmental rights, the protection of whistle-blowers or freedom of religion?

What material: The decisions of which foreign and/or international courts are used most frequently, and how often is such material taken on or rejected?[79] Are there variations in regard to what foreign and international

[76] The presumption that the use of foreign legal material by domestic courts is a recent phenomenon is questioned by some. See e.g. Law and Chang, Limits of Global Judicial Dialogue, *supra* note 8, at 526, citing various sources supporting their argument.

[77] Contributions that focus on the analysis of judicial dialogue in a particular region also ask whether the extent to which courts engage in dialogue varies across the countries within a region.

[78] Some existing research suggests that common law countries are more open to use foreign or international material, see e.g. Killander and Adjolohoun, International Law and Domestic Rights, *supra* note 48, at 5–16.

[79] In this context, see the observations by McCrudden, A Common Law *supra* note 9, at 512.

legal material courts actually use – that is, are apex court decisions used more frequently than decisions of lower courts?

Following this more empirical or descriptive examination that is meant to fill knowledge gaps in these areas, the contributions seek to explain possible variations with regard to the extent of judicial dialogues. While there are more, the editors suggested considering in particular the following factors that could serve as explanations.

Are there provisions in domestic law that encourage or obstruct domestic courts' engagement in judicial dialogues?[80] Moreover, to what extent can variations be explained by the status of decisions of foreign domestic and international courts' decisions within domestic law?[81] What role do the characteristics of domestic or regional structures play in encouraging or discouraging dialogue, for example the existence of regional human rights courts like the ECtHR or the Inter-American Commission on Human Rights, the Inter-American Court of Human Rights and the African Court on Human and Peoples' Rights? Can the extent to which a particular court engages in dialogue be explained by the degree of openness of individual judges to look beyond their own jurisdiction, and/or by the extent to which they have been educated in comparative law?[82] What role do language skills play?[83] Can regular or irregular, informal or formal meetings of judges help to explain the extent to which judicial dialogue is taking place in a particular country or region?[84] What role do the demands for external validation of more controversial judgments play that may be voiced by society, the parties to a dispute or other branches of government?[85] Or is the process and extent of judicial dialogue rather driven by parallel non-judicial transnational processes? If there is a country or region in which judges and courts engage in none or very limited dialogue,

80 Some constitutions include provisions that directly authorise courts to refer to foreign and international material, see the observations by Kirby, Domestic Courts, *supra* note 9, at 171.

81 For a debate of the Australian context, see *ibid.*, at 174–76.

82 There is evidence that education in comparative law is a key precondition for judges' engagement in judicial dialogue. See, McCrudden, A Common Law, *supra* note 9, at 526–27, holding that judges are unlikely use foreign material if they fear that their lack of judicial competence in the technical legal aspects of another country will lead to mistakes being made.

83 See Örücü, Whither Comparativism, *supra* note 20, at 230; and Gelter and Siems, Networks, Dialogue, *supra* note 28, at 28, suggesting that courts from the same legal tradition and language group are more likely to cite each other.

84 There are suggestions that face-to-face meetings of judges play little role in encouraging engagement in judicial dialogue. See e.g. Law and Chang, Limits of Global Judicial Dialogue, *supra* note 8, at 565–66.

85 See also related questions about the purpose of judicial dialogue *infra* section 1.2.4.

what are the reasons for this? And why are the decisions of some foreign or international courts cited more often than others?

1.2.3 Method

Contributions analyse the *method* that domestic and international courts use when engaging in judicial dialogue. How do judges become aware of the external judgments that they may cite or use in some way? Do they (or their clerks) conduct their own research on the Internet and/or through more traditional methods, for example by using libraries? Do they benefit from face-to-face meetings with judges from foreign domestic courts or international courts? Do they rely on personal contacts when they wish to find out about a particular decision in another country or of an international court? What role do the parties to a dispute play in drawing the judges' attention to foreign and international legal material? Are academics from countries whose decisions are particularly frequently used by a particular court invited to provide information about jurisprudential developments from the courts of their countries?[86] And what role do *amicus curiae* briefs or NGO reports play in raising judges' awareness of foreign and international legal material?[87]

1.2.4 Purpose

Here, the authors focus on analysing the *purpose* of judicial dialogue: What motivates judges to partake in or to refrain from engaging in judicial dialogue, and what do they believe this practice aims at?

Do judges only seek to solve the legal issue in the case at hand, or do they aim to increase the quality of their court's decision by using external decisions? Do they rely on such decisions to progressively develop the legal protection of individual rights in domestic law or to fill gaps in domestic law or jurisprudence, which can stimulate self-reflection?[88] In other words, by pointing to solutions taken abroad or at the international level, do judges seek to raise awareness of insufficiencies at home? Or is the purpose

[86] This practice can be observed in some courts, see Law and Chang, Limits of Global Judicial Dialogue, *supra* note 8, at 566.

[87] See Jackson, Constitutional Engagement, *supra* note 10, at 1 (referring to pressures and influences from third parties, including NGOs).

[88] In this context, see the observations by McCrudden, A Common Law *supra* note 9, at 523–24; Bahdi, Globalisation of Judgment, *supra* note 14, at 575; and Slaughter, A Typology, *supra* note 12, at 117–18.

of dialogue to avoid the progressive interpretation of domestic law[89] or international human rights law? Stated differently, is dialogue used as a tool to deliberately highlight and justify the differences between the 'internal' and the 'external' scope of protection of human rights? Do judges wish to honour and 'distribute' foreign or international decisions that they regard as highly persuasive? Especially in cases where domestic courts apply international human rights law, do they seek to lend weight to their decisions by referring to similar applications of international human rights law by other courts?[90] Can it be confirmed that some domestic and international judges feel that they are part of a 'global community of courts'[91] whose purpose is to secure the implementation and progressive development of international human rights law through judicial dialogue? Furthermore, is it their aim to promote (and develop) the international rule of (human rights) law?[92] And, concerning domestic courts' vertical dialogue, do they want to express their (dis)agreement with the interpretation of a certain international human rights provision by an international court?

Some contributions also consider wider political or social purposes that may explain courts' (non-)engagement in judicial dialogues. To the extent that these purposes play a role, who is the audience judges wish to influence or convince through their reliance on or rejection of solutions reached elsewhere?[93] Is it the immediate parties to the case, fellow judges, the legislative and executive branches, a particular group within a society, society as a whole? Or is there (also) a foreign or global audience? Do judges wish to sway or take a stand as concerns certain domestic political processes, or non-judicial transnational processes? For instance, by referring to the jurisprudence of a certain country or group of countries, do judges wish to support/discourage political associations with these countries?[94] Do they engage in dialogues with the purpose of avoiding negative assessments of the domestic situation by the international community,[95] for example through the finding of violations of human rights by a regional human rights court? Concerning the ECtHR, does it seek to build

[89] See the examples discussed by Bahdi, Globalisation of Judgment, *supra* note 14, at 575.

[90] *Ibid.*, at 584; and Slaughter, A Typology, *supra* note 12, at 119.

[91] Slaughter, A Global Community, *supra* note 40.

[92] Bahdi, Globalisation of Judgment, *supra* note 14, at 560–68.

[93] McCrudden, A Common Law, *supra* note 9, at 519–29.

[94] *Ibid.*, at 521–23; see also Law and Chang, Limits of Global Judicial Dialogue, *supra* note 8, at 570, on possible 'political' motives of Taiwanese judges to cite foreign cases despite limited abilities to participate in face-to-face dialogue with foreign judges due to Taiwan's diplomatic isolation.

[95] This is suggested by, e.g. Bahdi, Globalisation of Judgment, *supra* note 14, at 590–97.

strategic alliances with domestic courts for the effective implementation of the ECHR through dialogue;[96] or does it aim to avoid criticism of its judgments from executive and legislative branches of government through dialogue with domestic courts?

Furthermore, chapters towards the end of the book pose broader, theoretical and normative questions about the desired purpose and aims of judicial dialogue. When participating in dialogue on human rights, do judges seek to promote the inherent dignity and equal worth of all individuals around the world? In other words, do they follow a 'universalist' or cosmopolitan impulse?[97] Should they do so? Or is judicial dialogue in reality a (random) interaction of different entities, all seeking to promote and achieve their particularised purposes and aims?

1.2.5 Effects

Closely related to the questions about purposes, contributions to this book also analyse the legal and other *effects* of judicial dialogue, both at the domestic and regional/international level.

Concerning legal effects at the national level, contributions take an interest in how decisions that refer to foreign and international jurisprudence differ from those that are solely based on national material and domestic dialogue. Are the former decisions of a 'better' legal quality than the latter (e.g. do courts give better reasons for their decisions)? Do external judicial decisions have an impact on the interpretation of domestic or international law similar to that of legal precedent, or do they have some other, weaker influence, serving rather as a 'source of inspiration'? Or perhaps citations merely have a 'decorative' effect/purpose?[98] Does use of foreign or international material result in a progressive or, rather, a regressive interpretation of domestic (human rights/constitutional) law?

Furthermore, some contributions engage with the political and social effects of judicial dialogue at the national level. Does the engagement in judicial dialogue result in greater credibility of domestic judgments that

[96] Slaughter suggests that this could be one of the functions of judicial dialogue by international courts; see Slaughter, A Typology, *supra* note 12, at 114 and 121.

[97] Bahdi, Globalisation of Judgment, *supra* note 14, at 568–75.

[98] In this context, Krotoszynski has drawn the distinction between 'strong form' and 'weak form' of international judicial dialogue. Krotoszynski, I'd Like the World to Sing, *supra* note 8, at 1324–25. Vicki Jackson distinguishes between 'convergence', 'resistance' and 'engagement', see Jackson, Constitutional Comparisons, *supra* note 57. See also related questions on the purpose of judicial dialogue *infra* section 1.2.4.

is demanded and/or recognised by society, the legislative/executive powers or other actors? Or does it have the opposite effect: Do references by a domestic court to external judicial decisions diminish the credibility of that court in the eyes of society, the executive/legislative or other actors? Can such practice lead to legislative revision of domestic law? Likewise, does the practice of judicial dialogue by domestic courts reflect a 'transnationalisation' of judicial power that is establishing itself besides 'transnational' executive power which has traditionally ruled the domain of international lawmaking and application?[99]

Concerning the legal effects of judicial dialogues at the regional and international level, contributions address the effects the practice may have on the interpretation and development of international human rights law. Does dialogue contribute to progressively develop human rights standards, or does it rather result in a practice of avoiding or restricting the application of international human rights law?[100] In other words, is judicial dialogue used as a vehicle to advance or restrict the international rule of (human rights) law?

Several contributions also pose questions about possible effects of judicial dialogues on the legitimacy of European-level decision-making on human rights. For example, does the ECtHR's use of domestic court decisions result in, or at least contribute to, silencing critics who at times question the (democratic) legitimacy of this regional court? Does it strengthen the ECtHR's role as a subsidiary actor (in relation to domestic courts) in securing the rights of the ECHR? Moreover, does the ECtHR's engagement with domestic and international court decisions help to create common European human rights law and principles that are accepted widely by the member states of the CoE?

Some authors also query the broader, global effects of judicial dialogue: Does the practice promote the unity and consistency of international human rights law? Can we even speak about judicial dialogue 'producing'/'promoting' universal (cosmopolitan) norms? Or are (legitimate) polyphone voices of less 'authoritative' courts silenced through judicial dialogues, and thus existing power imbalances are reinforced? Or perhaps judicial dialogues promote the (legitimate) local differentiation of

99 As suggested by E. Benvenisti and G. Downs, 'The Democratising Effects of Transjudicial Coordination', *Utrecht L. Rev.* 8:2 (2012) 158–71; see also Kirby, Domestic Courts, *supra* note 9, at 177.

100 In this context, contributions will critically examine Slaughter's claim that one of the effects of judicial communication is that it will spread and enhance the protection of universal human rights. See Slaughter, A Typology, *supra* note 12, at 134.

human rights standards, for instance when domestic courts deliberately use foreign and international judicial decisions to explain differences and reinforce national solutions?[101] In addition, is it even desirable or realistic to rely on courts, several of which may engage in selective or superficial dialogues, to serve as fora for the promotion of cosmopolitan/universal norms?[102]

1.3 Methods Used to Study Judicial Dialogue

The authors use different methods to study the extent, purpose and effects of judicial dialogue. Among them is the more traditional doctrinal legal analysis of relevant international and domestic law and jurisprudence. Other contributions use quantitative approaches such as the counting and coding of citations of external judicial decisions used by the courts that are the object of the respective analyses. Some chapters also use more qualitative approaches, relying, for instance, on interviews with judges. The perspectives provided by the domestic and ECtHR judges in response to the editors' questionnaires can also be seen to fall in this category. Authors moreover rely on the work of philosophers and political theorists to approach normative questions about the (legitimate) purposes and effects of judicial dialogues in a globalised world.

1.4 Outline

Structured through the common framework, the book covers various aspects of the extent, method, purpose and effect of different national courts' and of the ECtHR's engagement in judicial dialogue in the area of human rights. The two last chapters offer a normative and theoretical appraisal of the practice of dialogue. Short contributions by domestic and ECtHR judges complement and expand on the analysis in the chapters. The chapters and short judges' contributions are briefly introduced in the following.

Chapters 2–5 of Part I systematically analyse the extent, method, purpose and effects of different domestic courts' dialogue. They cover the dialogue by Polish and other Eastern European courts, South American courts, the Canadian Supreme Court and *Sharīʿah* courts in Nigeria and

[101] See Jackson, Constitutional Engagement, *supra* note 10, at 38 ('Exceptionalists' impulses may support the use of foreign legal experiences to differentiate the polity, but not as a positive normative example.')

[102] Örücü, Whither Comparativism, *supra* note 20, at 231.

Malaysia. These chapters fill gaps in the knowledge about domestic courts' dialogue in some regions of the world that have not been studied extensively before. The impact that regional human rights courts like the ECtHR and the Inter-American Court of Human Rights have on fostering domestic courts' interaction in the area of human rights is also assessed, as is the relevance of the broader legal, political and social environment. Chapters 6 and 7 concentrate on domestic and regional courts' judicial dialogue on particular issues: the protection of migrants that may not qualify as refugees under the UN Refugee Convention,[103] and same-sex families. These two thematic chapters are included to increase our understanding of certain factors that stimulate or hold back the practice of judicial dialogue by domestic courts. Both subject matters are politically charged. This is one factor that influences the practice of judicial dialogue in these areas, and, among other things, results in a situation where not only domestic courts are involved in dialogue but also national parliaments and civil society organisations.

The chapters on different national courts' judicial dialogue are followed by short reports on practice (Chapters 8–10) of three national judges. Justice Andreas Paulus at the German Federal Constitutional Court (*Bundesverfassungsgericht*), Lord Carnwath of Notting Hill, Justice of the United Kingdom Supreme Court, and Raffaele Sabato, Justice at the Italian Court of Cassation (*Corte Suprema di Cassazione*), give some first-hand insight into their respective courts' engagement in dialogue. They discuss the varying intensity of their courts' interaction with different foreign national, regional or international courts; how they find out about relevant foreign and international case law; and what effect foreign and international material has on their courts' deliberations and decision-making. They also examine some prominent cases in which their respective court engaged in extensive dialogue.

Chapters 11 and 12 in Part II analyse the ECtHR's judicial dialogue in depth. The ECtHR's extensive case law and the diversity of state parties that submitted to its jurisdiction provide a particularly fertile ground to trace and assess the extent, method, purpose and effects of a regional court's dialogue. These chapters explore how the ECtHR's dialogue contributes to ensuring the rule of (European) human rights law within member states of the CoE, and how this dialogue influences the development of European and international human rights law. In this context, a particular

[103] Convention Relating to the Status of Refugees (28 July 1951) 189 UNTS 137, entered into force 22 April 1954.

emphasis is placed on the ECtHR's dialogue with domestic courts that have considered the case before it reached the ECtHR (Chapter 11). The question is posed whether this dialogue contributes to a strengthening of the Convention system as a 'cooperative system' where domestic courts and the ECtHR effectively cooperate to 'secure ... the rights and freedoms ... of the Convention'.[104] Chapter 12 promises new insights as to whether *amicus curiae* briefs could make up for one of the deficits in the ECtHR's dialogue: its uneven use of comparative material (cherry-picking). NGOs submitting *amicus curiae* briefs might bring forward relevant material to the ECtHR from countries or international or regional courts that so far do not feature frequently in the ECtHR's judgments. Overall, the analysis in Chapter 12 of the briefs' content and their influence on the ECtHR's judgments helps to explain one of the methods through which ECtHR judges become aware of foreign and international decisions.

Complementing and expanding on the analysis in these chapters, Part II includes short reports on practice (Chapters 13 to 15) from three judges at the ECtHR. Judge López Guerra shares his first-hand experiences of the Court's interaction with domestic courts of the respondent state. He identifies and discusses four different ways in which the ECtHR enters into dialogue with these courts: confirmative, corrective and proposed dialogue, as well as dialogue with discrepancy. Judge Erik Møse offers his insights on the ECtHR's dialogue with domestic courts not involved in the case at hand and with other bodies and organs of the CoE. Among other things, he gives his tentative assessment of the extent and effects of this dialogue on the ECtHR's jurisprudence, and highlights the importance of the Court's own Research Division for bringing relevant foreign and international material to the attention of the ECtHR judges. Judge Angelika Nußberger discusses the ECtHR's dialogue with other international and regional courts, and with quasi-judicial bodies, such as the UN human rights treaty bodies. She sets out the different ways in which the Court engages with material from these courts and bodies, and discusses the effects of this dialogue on the Court's interpretation and application of different Convention rights, sharing her views on considerations that may determine whether and how the Court decides to use the material in question.

Chapters 16 and 17 in Part III offer normative and theoretical appraisals of the practice of judicial dialogue by national and international courts. Chapter 16 discusses the purposes and (desired) effects of domestic apex courts' dialogue on human rights through the lens of cosmopolitan theory.

[104] Article 1 ECHR.

It asks whether this dialogue can lead to the creation of cosmopolitan norms that not only enhance the protection of individual rights but also contribute towards enhancing the capacity of democracies to represent their people, a capacity that has been diminished through globalisation processes. Chapter 17 critically analyses the alleged purposes and effects of judicial dialogue by questioning the assumptions held by most legal scholars who study the phenomenon of judicial dialogue and who are influenced by (Western) liberal thinking. The great expectations that many share about judicial dialogue as an effective tool to unite a fragmented world driven by like-minded judges who share common values are based on (Western) liberal thinking. Chapter 17 critically asks whether 'dialogue' should not rather be construed as a form of unsystematic interaction of courts that occurs regardless of a particular court's willingness to engage with its counterparts, the effects of which can be contingent or even random, including on the protection of human rights.

The concluding remarks in Chapter 18 draw together and reflect on the findings made in the separate parts of the book. In putting in place the 'pieces of the puzzle', the analysis is aided by the common framework used in the chapters and the judges' contributions. The overall findings indicate that by and large, domestic, regional and international courts' dialogue on human rights strengthens the rule of (human rights) law at the national and international levels. The incremental addition of courts that are not yet included to this dialogue, as well as the expansion of dialogue on all human rights, including economic, social and cultural rights, could further enhance this effect.

PART I

Judicial Dialogue in Domestic Courts

2

Judicial Dialogue on International Human Rights Law in Poland and Eastern Europe

IZABELA SKOMERSKA-MUCHOWSKA

2.1 Introduction

In the early 1990s, Eastern European courts, including Polish courts, became members of the European and global 'community' of judges. Active participation in the community requires not only compliance with its rules, but also co-creation of its normative framework through active interpretation and application of relevant rules. This chapter presents the results of research into the extent, method, purpose and effects of Polish courts' engagement in judicial dialogue in the area of human rights. Where relevant for clarifying certain developments, the practice of Polish courts will be compared to and contrasted with dialogue of courts in other Eastern European countries, especially the Czech Republic, Hungary, Lithuania, Russia and Ukraine.

The term 'Eastern Europe' is used to describe 'the portion of the European landmass that lies east of Germany and the Alps and west of the Ural Mountains. It includes the former Eastern bloc countries of Poland, the Czech Republic and Slovakia (formerly as Czechoslovakia), Hungary, Romania, and Bulgaria, as well as the Baltic republics of Estonia, Latvia, and Lithuania, and the former Soviet republics of Belarus and Ukraine, along with Russia west of the Urals.'[1] The reason for singling out the Eastern European judiciary as a subject of research in this chapter is not only the geographical closeness of the studied jurisdictions but also their shared experiences in recent history. As a social phenomenon, law is determined by history, geography and culture, so a regional approach to studying judicial dialogue is justified. Especially the experience of the period of socialist government can be recognised as a point of common departure for the judiciaries of the states under examination

[1] Oxford Dictionaries, 'Eastern Europe', available at www.oxforddictionaries.com/definition/english/Eastern-Europe.

in their way into the 'global community of courts' through engagement in judicial dialogue, as described by Anne-Marie Slaughter.[2]

Socialist constitutions, including the Constitution of the Republic of Poland of 1952, did include provisions on fundamental rights and freedoms.[3] However, according to the socialist fundamental rights doctrine, collective interest of the state prevailed over individual rights.[4] As a result, human rights provisions in socialist constitutions were not recognised as rights that individuals could invoke before the courts. Moreover, the 1952 Polish Constitution did not explicitly recognise international law, including human rights instruments, as part of the internal Polish legal order.[5] Some distinguished Polish scholars advocated the idea that ratified international treaties should be acknowledged to form part of domestic law and be applied *ex proprio vigore*.[6] Courts, however, were reluctant to apply international law at the time, mainly for political reasons.[7] Exceptions were made in areas where domestic statutes clearly referred to a particular international treaty.[8]

2 See the introduction to this volume (Chapter 1), Section 1.1, and A.-M. Slaughter, 'A Global Community of Courts', *Harvard Int'l L. J.* 191:4 (2003) 191–219.

3 Chapter VIII of the Constitution of the People's Republic of Poland (*Konstytucja Polskiej Rzeczpospolitej Ludowej*) of 22 July 1952, Official Journal (*Dziennik Ustaw*) of 23 July 1952, No. 33, 232.

4 Article 6 of the Constitution of the Union of Soviet Socialist Republics of 7 October 1977 stated that 'enjoyment of the rights and freedoms of citizens must not be to the detriment of the interests of society or the state'.

5 For more details, see S. Pomorski, 'International Law in the Polish Municipal Legal Order: A Historical Overview and the Current Constitutional Status', R. Clark, F. Feldbrugge and S. Pomorski (eds.) *International and National Law in Russia and Eastern Europe, Essays in Honor of George Ginsburgs* (The Hague: M. Nijhoff Publishers, 2001) 295–317, at 295–300. As to other Eastern European states see *inter alia*: G. M. Danilenko, 'Implementation of International Law in CIS States: Theory and Practice', *European J. of Int'l L.* 10:1 (1999) 51–69; M. Frei and M. MacLaren, 'A "Common European Home"? The Rule of Law and Contemporary Russia', *German L. J.* 5:10 (2004) 1295–1315; S. Y. Marochkin, 'International Law in the Courts of the Russian Federation: Practice of Application', *Chinese J. of Int'l L.* 6:2 (2007) 329–44.

6 For more details, see L. Garlicki, M. Marsternak-Kubiak and K. Wójtowicz, 'Poland', D. Sloss (ed.) *The Role of Domestic Courts in Treaty Enforcement: A Comparative Study* (Cambridge University Press, 2009) 370–409, at 371–73; K. Skubiszewski, 'Traktaty a prawo krajowe', *Państwo i Prawo* 8–9 (1977) 255–65, at 257–59; and K. Skubiszewski, 'Prawa jednostki, umowy międzynarodowe i porządek prawny PRL', *Państwo i Prawo* 7 (1981) 9–23, at 9–12.

7 As it has been rightly noticed by Czaplinski, 'the courts under communist rule, for manifestly political reasons, did not accept the possibility of direct application and effectiveness of international law within the Polish legal order. Individuals could not claim any rights granted under human rights treaties'. See W. Czaplinski, 'International Law and the Polish Constitution', M. Wyrzykowski (ed.) *Constitutional Essays* (Warsaw: Instytut Spraw Publicznych, 1999) 289–306, at 291.

8 In the decision of 1987, the Polish Supreme Court stated: 'Under the Polish Constitution there is no ground to recognise that ratification of a treaty results in its transformation

But already by the 1980s, forerunners of future transformations emerged in Poland. Polish courts tried to use international law as a source to enhance the protection of human rights and fundamental freedoms.[9] The Polish Constitutional Court was established in 1985.[10] However, it was only in the 1990s, when the true transformation process gained pace, that the direct effect of ratified treaties was recognised by Polish courts.[11] This transformation process from a socialist to a democratic system in Poland and other Eastern European states was influenced and dynamised to a large extent by European rule of law standards and the common framework for the protection of human rights.[12] The main reason for this was the recognition that 'a democratic system after the collapse of a communist system require[d] a new legal axiology; restoration of the adequate relations between the state and the individual, a dramatic breakthrough in legal thinking, [and]

into domestic law.' Decision of 25 August 1987, II PRZ 8/87 (translation after Garlicki, Marsternak-Kubiak and Wójtowicz, 'Poland', *supra* note 6, at 373).

9 See especially: Polish Supreme Court, Judgment of 10 November 1980, Ref. No. I CR 283/81 on the registration of the trade union *Solidarność* and the judgment of Military Court in Olsztyn of 8 June 1982, in which the Court recognised article 61 of martial law contrary to article 15 of the ICCPR (*lex retro non agit* principle). See A. Wyrozumska, *Umowy międzynarodowe. Teoria i praktyka* (Warszawa: Wydawnictwo Prawo i Praktyka Gospodarcza, 2006), at 545. However, courts were still rather reluctant to apply international agreements. See K. Skubiszewski, 'Umowy międzynarodowe w porządku prawnym PRL', *Państwo i Prawo* 6 (1989) 135–45, at 143.

10 Act of 29 April 1985 on the Constitutional Tribunal. For more information about the role of constitutional courts in the process of systemic transformation, see W. Sadurski, *Postcommunist Constitutional Courts in Search of Political Legitimacy* (1999), available at www.law.wustl.edu/harris/conferences/constitutionalconf/Constitutional_Courts_Legitimacy.pdf; L. Sólyom, 'The Role of Constitutional Courts in the Transition to Democracy: With Special Reference to Hungary', *International Sociology* 18:1 (2003) 133–61; J. Kurczewski and B. Sullivan, 'The Bill of Rights and the Emerging Democracies, Law and Contemporary Problems', *Law and Contemporary Problems* 65:2 (2002) 251–94; and R. Müllerson, M. Fitzmaurice and M. Andenas (eds.), *Constitutional Reforms and International Law in Central and Eastern Europe* (The Hague: Brill, 1997).

11 In the judgment of 12 June 1992, the Supreme Court stated that '[t]he relationship of international treaty norms to municipal law will be explicitly defined in the new Constitution of the Republic of Poland. Before this happens, it can be recognised, as in jurisprudence of the interwar period, that the issuance of a statute expressing consent to ratification of an international agreement transforms a treaty into municipal law of statutory rank.' (translation by author). The same argument was made by the Supreme Court in a judgment of 12 December 1992, Ref. No. CZP III 48/92. The Supreme Court stated that when ratifying international treaties, the parliament grants its consent in the form of statute. Therefore, ratified international agreements should be applied by all courts as statutes.

12 See E. Łętowska, 'Human Rights as a Pillar of Transformation: A Polish Perspective', R. Arnold (ed.), *The Universalism of Human Rights, Ius Gentium: Comparative Perspective on Law and Justice* (Berlin: Springer, 2013) 341–55, at 344.

a localisation of fundamental constitutional rights in the centre of legal system'.[13] In line with this acknowledgement, in the beginning of the 1990s, there was a strong political motivation in Eastern Europe to follow international standards of human rights protection, to enshrine these standards in national constitutions and states' practice, and to join the Council of Europe (CoE)[14] and the European Union (EU).[15] In 1992, the Polish Supreme Court declared that both the European Convention of Human Rights (ECHR) and the International Covenant on Civil and Political Rights (ICCPR) are sources of universally binding law in Poland.

In the years when Poland transitioned from a socialist to a democratic state, human rights and rule of law standards were 're-imported' from international law into Polish law and the legal orders of other Eastern European states.[16] History has shown that judicial activity cannot be reduced to the mechanical application of the law in the form of judicial syllogism, and in recent years the role of judges has become increasingly relevant, in particular when it comes to the effective protection of human rights.

With this historical background of Eastern Europe in mind, this chapter aims to shed more light on Polish courts' engagement in judicial dialogue in the area of human rights. The chapter first analyses the extent of Polish courts' engagement in judicial dialogue (Section 2.2) by giving an overview of the frequency with which Polish courts engage with judgments of the European Court of Human Rights (ECtHR), the Court of Justice of the European Union (CJEU) and with foreign domestic courts. Section 2.3 gives some insights into the methods that Polish judges use to find out about relevant international and foreign domestic courts' decisions. The different purposes and actual effects of the Polish courts' engagement in dialogue are discussed in Section 2.4. Concluding remarks are offered in Section 2.5. Throughout, the analysis focuses on Polish courts' dialogue

[13] M. Safjan, 'Transitional Justice: The Polish Example, the Case of Lustration', *European J. of Legal Studies* 1:2 (2007) 1–20, at 2.

[14] Poland acceded to the CoE in 1991 and ratified the ECHR in 1993. Other states under consideration joined the CoE in the 1990s as well: the Czech Republic in 1993 (from 1991 to 1992 member as part of Czechoslovakia), Hungary in 1990, Lithuania in1993, Ukraine in 1995 and the Russian Federation in 1996. These states also ratified ECHR: the Czech Republic in 1992, Hungary in 1992, Lithuania in 1995, Ukraine in 1997, and the Russian Federation in 1998.

[15] See A. Peters, 'Supremacy Lost: International Law Meets Domestic Constitutional Law', *Vienna Online J. on Int'l Constitutional L.* 3:3 (2009) 170–98, at 174.

[16] *Ibid.*, at 175.

on human rights, leaving aside dialogue on other areas of law. Where relevant, the practice of Polish courts is compared and contrasted with the practice of domestic courts in other Eastern European countries to highlight broader trends affecting the region.

2.2 The Extent of Polish Courts' Engagement in Judicial Dialogue on Human Rights

This section starts by explaining the legal context in which judicial dialogue takes place by highlighting how international human rights treaties are incorporated into Polish law (subsection 2.2.1). This can have a significant influence on the extent of Polish courts' dialogue with international and foreign domestic courts in the area of human rights. The discussion then moves to examine with which regional and foreign domestic courts Polish courts enter into dialogue most frequently, looking at their dialogue with the ECtHR, with the CJEU and with foreign domestic courts separately (subsections 2.2.2–2.2.4). Throughout, attempts are made to explain the varying extent of Polish courts' dialogue with these courts. In subsection 2.2.5, some general trends in the extent of Polish courts' engagement in judicial dialogue are summarised.

2.2.1 The Legal Context of Judicial Dialogue: The Position of International Law in the Polish Legal Order

The prerequisite for dialogue on international law is the validity of that law in the domestic legal order. The Constitution of the Republic of Poland of 1997 has explicitly incorporated international law into the Polish legal order.[17] Article 9 of the Polish Constitution sets out the general rule on the position of international law in Polish law: 'The Republic of Poland shall respect international law binding upon it.' This provision is understood as a universal one, referring not only to treaties but also to other sources of international law (customary law, general principles of law

[17] See W. Czapliński, 'Relationship between International Law and Polish Municipal Law in the Light of the 1997 Constitution and of the Jurisprudence', *Revue Belge du Driot International* 1 (1998) 259–71. On the practice of application of international law in Poland, see: A. Preisner, 'Prawo międzynarodowe w orzecznictwie sądów polskich', M. Kruk-Jarosz (ed.) *Prawo międzynarodowe i wspólnotowe w orzecznictwie sądów polskich* (Warszawa: Wydawnictwo Sejmowe, 1997); and A. Wyrozumska, 'Zapewnianie skuteczności prawu międzynarodowemu w prawie krajowym w projekcie konstytucji', *Państwo i Prawo* 11 (1997) 16–34.

and legally binding decisions of international organisations).[18] The Polish Constitutional Court has described article 9 of the Constitution not only as 'a grandiose declaration addressed to the international community, but also an obligation of state authorities, including the government, parliament and the courts, to observe the international law, which is binding for the Republic of Poland.'[19] The provision is also the basis of state organs' obligation to interpret and apply national law in conformity with international law,[20] an obligation that also addresses Polish courts.

Other provisions of the Constitution refer directly to the position of treaties ratified by Poland. In line with articles 87 and 91 of the Polish Constitution, ratified international agreements are directly applicable sources of universally biding law and have precedence over statutes.[21] Sources other than ratified international agreements (such as customary law, general principles of international law and non-ratified international treaties to which Poland is a party) are applied by Polish courts

[18] Garlicki, Masternak-Kubiak and Wójtowicz, Poland, *supra* note 6, at 376.

[19] See Polish Constitutional Court, Judgment of 27 April 2005, Ref. No. P 1/05 available in English at http://trybunal.gov.pl/fileadmin/content/omowienia/P_1_05_full_GB.pdf.

[20] See *inter alia*, Polish Supreme Court, Judgment of 29 November 2005, Ref. No. II PK 100/05 in which the Court stated that article 9 of the Polish Constitution obliges Polish courts to favour an interpretation that is sympathetic to international law. This means courts should interpret internal Polish law in conformity with the content of international law. Concerning EU law see: Polish Constitutional Court, Judgments of 21 April 2004, Ref. No. K 33/03 and of 11 May 2005, Ref. No. K 18/04. See also the Polish Supreme Administrative Court, Judgment of 26 August 1999, Ref. No. V SA 708/99.

[21] Article 87 states that ratified international agreements are sources of universally binding law of the Republic of Poland. According to article 91, after publication in the Journal of Laws of the Republic of Poland (*Dziennik Ustaw*), a ratified international agreement constitutes part of the domestic legal order and is applied directly, unless its application depends on the enactment of a statute. An international agreement ratified with prior consent of the parliament through a statute has precedence over other statutes if such an agreement cannot be reconciled with the provisions of such other statutes. The same provision provides that if the Republic of Poland ratifies an agreement that establishes an international organisation, the laws adopted by this organisation are applied directly and have precedence over domestic law in the event of a conflict of laws, if the ratified agreement so provides. (English translation of the Constitution of the Republic of Poland available at www.sejm.gov.pl/prawo/konst/angielski/kon1.htm). Article 91 of the Constitution contains a so-called formal condition of direct application, i.e. ratification and publication, as well as substantive condition which requires 'the completeness of the treaty provision that enables its operation without any additional implementation' (see Polish Supreme Court, Judgment of 21 November 2003, Ref. No. I CK 323/02). For more details about the relationship between international law and Polish law, see A. Wyrozumska, 'Poland', D. Shelton (ed.), *International Law and Domestic Legal Orders, Incorporation, Transformation and Persuasion* (Oxford University Press, 2011) 468–516; and Garlicki, Marsternak-Kubiak and Wójtowicz, Poland, *supra* note 6, at 373 and 381.

on the basis of the aforementioned general clause contained in article 9 of the Constitution.[22] Both judiciary and doctrine accepted that 'article 9 expresses the principle of … the Polish legal order in respect to the norms of international law and establishes a presumption of automatic, even if only indirect, incorporation of those norms into that order.'[23]

Ratified international agreements prevail over statutory law, but not over the Constitution, which, according to its article 8, is the 'supreme law of the Republic of Poland'. However, as the Constitutional Court stated in a judgment of 11 May 2005, this provision 'is accompanied by the requirement to respect and to be favourably inclined towards appropriately drafted regulations of international law binding upon the Republic of Poland.' This means that also the Polish Constitution is regularly interpreted and applied in light of and in conformity with Poland's obligations under international law, including international human rights treaties.[24]

Other Eastern European constitutions are equally open to international law. Like the Polish Constitution, the Constitutions of the

[22] P. Sarnecki, 'Commentary to Article 9', L. Garlicki (ed.), *Konstytucja Rzeczypospolitej Polskiej, Komentarz* t. V (Warszawa: Wydawnictwo Sejmowe, 1999) 1–37, at 2 and 5; K. Działocha, 'Commentary to Article 87', L. Garlicki (ed.), *Konstytucja Rzeczypospolitej Polskiej, Komentarz* (Warszawa: Wydawnictwo Sejmowe, 1999) 1–14, at 5; A. Wasilkowski, 'Przestrzeganie prawa międzynarodowego (art. 9 Konstytucji RP)', K. Wójtowicz (ed.), *Otwarcie Konstytucji RP na prawo międzynarodowe i procesy integracyjne* (Warszawa: Wydawnictwo Sejmowe, 2006) 9–29, at 15; A. Wyrozumska, 'Prawo międzynarodowe oraz prawo Unii Europejskiej a konstytucyjny system źródeł prawa', K. Wójtowicz (ed.), *Otwarcie Konstytucji RP na prawo międzynarodowe i procesy integracyjne* (Warszawa: Wydawnictwo Sejmowe, 2006) 31–108, at 36–37 and 39; and M. Masternak-Kubiak, *Przestrzeganie prawa Międzynarodowego w świetle Konstytucji Rzeczpospolitej Polskiej* (Warszawa: Zakamycze, 2003) at 259.

[23] See R. Szafarz, 'Międzynarodowy porządek prawny i jego odbicie w polskim prawie konstytucyjnym', M. Kruk (ed.), *Prawo międzynarodowe i wspólnotowe w wewnętrznym porządku prawnym* (Warszawa: Wydawnictwo Sejmowe, 1997) 19–42, at 19.

[24] Polish Constitutional Court, Judgment of 11 May 2005, Ref. No. K 18/04. The Constitutional Court further explained that 'the Constitution enjoys precedence of binding force and precedence of application within the territory of the Republic of Poland. The precedence over statutes of the application of international agreements which were ratified on the basis of a statutory authorisation or consent granted … in no way signifies an analogous precedence of these agreements over the Constitution.' (English translation available at http://trybunal.gov.pl/fileadmin/content/omowienia/K_18_04_GB.pdf). A few years later the Constitutional Court ruled that 'the principle of favourable predisposition and respect of EU Treaties and international law obligations which bind the Republic of Poland expressed in article 9 of the Constitution … cannot undermine article 8 of the Constitution, which stipulates the primacy of the Constitution in the Polish legal order' (Polish Constitutional Court, Judgment of 24 November 2010, K 32/09, English translation available at http://trybunal.gov.pl/fileadmin/content/omowienia/K_32_09_EN.pdf).

Czech Republic,[25] Hungary,[26] Lithuania,[27] the Russian Federation[28] and Ukraine[29] explicitly state that international law forms an integral part of the respective legal orders. The Hungarian and Czech Constitutional Courts have confirmed that international human rights treaties have the same rank as constitutional norms.[30] In Lithuania, Russia and Ukraine, the strong position of international law in the domestic legal order has also been confirmed by statutes or the decisions of the respective Supreme and Constitutional Courts.[31]

[25] Article 1 of the Constitution of the Czech Republic of 16 December 1992. For more information, see questionnaire on the Czech Republic prepared as part of the project 10-ECRP-028: P. Mikeš, 'International Law through the National Prism: The Impact of Judicial Dialogue' available at http://wpia.uni.lodz.pl/struktura/zespol-ds-funduszy-ue/realizowane-projekty/international-law-through-the-national-prism/about-the-project.

[26] Article Q of the Fundamental Law of Hungary of 18 April 2011. For more information, see questionnaire on Hungary prepared as part of the project 10-ECRP-028: N. Chronowski, E. Csatlós and T. Hoffmann, 'International Law through the National Prism: the Impact of Judicial Dialogue' available at http://wpia.uni.lodz.pl/struktura/zespol-ds-funduszy-ue/realizowane-projekty/international-law-through-the-national-prism/about-the-project and N. Chronowski, T. Drinóczi and I. Ernszt, 'Hungary', in D. Shelton (ed.) *International Law and Domestic Legal Systems. Incorporation, Transformation and Persuasion* (Oxford University Press: 2011) 256–87 available at http://eltelawjournal.hu/wp-content/uploads/2014/03/ELJ_Separatum_csatlos_chronowski.pdf

[27] Articles 138 and 135 of the Constitution of the Republic of Lithuania of 25 October 1992. For more information, see questionnaire on Lithuania prepared as part of the project 10-ECRP-028: V. Vaičaitis, 'International Law through the National Prism: the Impact of Judicial Dialogue' available at http://wpia.uni.lodz.pl/struktura/zespol-ds-funduszy-ue/realizowane-projekty/international-law-through-the-national-prism/about-the-project.

[28] Article 15(4) of the Constitution of the Russian Federation of 12 December 1993. For more information, see questionnaire on the Russian Federation prepared as part of the project 10-ECRP-028: E. Ivanov, 'International Law through the National Prism: the Impact of Judicial Dialogue' available at http://wpia.uni.lodz.pl/struktura/zespol-ds-funduszy-ue/realizowane-projekty/international-law-through-the-national-prism/about-the-project.

[29] Article 9 of the Constitution of Ukraine.

[30] Decisions of the Constitutional Court of Hungary No. 45/2012 (XII. 29.) AB and No. 1/2013. (I. 7.). See also the detailed discussion by N. Chronowski and E. Csatlós, 'Judicial Dialogue or National Monologue? The International Law and Hungarian Courts', *ELTE Law Journal* 1 (2013) 7–29, at 16–18; and the respective decisions of the Constitutional Court of the Czech Republic, Judgment of 25 June 2002, Pl. ÚS 36/01; and Judgments of 15 April 2003, I. ÚS 752/02 and of 24 June 2003, Pl. ÚS 44/02.

[31] Concerning Lithuania, see Act of the Supreme Council of the Republic of Lithuania on the Re-establishment of the State of Lithuania adopted in 1990, available at www3.lrs.lt/seimu_istorija/w3_viewer.ViewTheme-p_int_tv_id=281&p_kalb_id=2&p_org=0.htm. Concerning Ukraine see the Declaration of State Sovereignty of Ukraine, passed by the *Verkhovna Rada* of the Ukrainian Soviet Socialist Republic, Kyiv, 16 July 1990, available

2.2.2 *Polish Courts' References to the Case Law of the ECtHR*

We now move to have a closer look at the extent to which the Polish courts refer to ECtHR jurisprudence and are thus entering into a dialogue with the ECtHR. Shortly after Poland's accession to the ECHR, the Polish Supreme Court declared that the 'case law of the European Court of Human Rights in Strasbourg should be applied as an essential source of interpretation of the provisions of Polish domestic law'. The Court referred for the first time to the 'right to a court' guaranteed under article 6(1) ECHR in the context of the requirement to pay court fees for lodging a claim or appeal.[32]

According to the general constitutional provisions discussed, the ECHR, as a ratified international agreement, is directly applicable and has precedence over statute. In contrast to some other constitutions of Eastern Europe, the Polish Constitution does not give international human rights treaties a special position in the Polish legal order. Nonetheless, it is clear from the *travaux préparatoires* of the 1997 Polish Constitution that the Chapter II of this Constitution "The Freedoms, Rights and Obligations of Persons and Citizens" has been inspired by international human rights standards, especially by the ECHR and the ICPPR.[33]

In addition, the Polish Constitutional Court has recognised the evolving standard of ECHR rights protection as established by the ECtHR as a substantive part of the constitutional standard of human rights protection in Poland.[34] Consequently, constitutional provisions on human rights and freedoms should be interpreted in the light of the ECHR and ECtHR

at http://static.rada.gov.ua/site/postanova_eng/Declaration_of_State_Sovereignty_of_Ukraine_rev1.htm, and articles 9 and 55 of the Ukrainian Constitution. Concerning Russia, see Articles 15(4), 79, 90 and 113 of the Russian Constitution; Federal Law 'On the Ratification of the Convention on Protection of Human Rights and Basic Freedoms and Protocols thereto', No 54-FZ of 30 March 1998; Ruling of the Plenum of the Supreme Court of the Russian Federation of 10 October 2003, No 5; and Ruling of the Plenum of the Supreme Court of the Russian Federation of 27 June 2013, No 21. For more details on the situation in Russia, see also Marochkin, 'International Law in the Courts', *supra* note 5.

32 Polish Supreme Court, Decision of 11 January 1995, Ref. No. III ARN 75/94.

33 See M. Jabłoński, 'Identyfikacja wolności i praw jednostki w pracach nad treścią Konstytucji RP z dnia 2 kwietnia 1997 roku', M. Jabłoński (ed.), *Realizacja i ochrona konstytucyjnych praw jednostki w polskim porządku prawnym* (Wrocław: Uniwersytet Wrocławski, 2014) 15–28, at 17.

34 In the Judgment of 28 June 2008, Ref. No. K 51//07, the Polish Constitutional Court explicitly stated that it is necessary to refer to human rights treaties and practice of their application to establish the standard of constitutional protection.

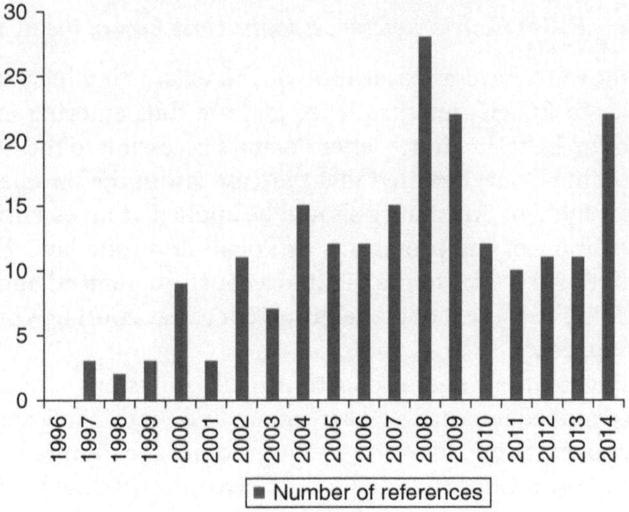

Figure 2.1 References to ECtHR Jurisprudence in the Polish Constitutional Court (1996–2014)

jurisprudence.[35] This includes the interpretation and application of the Polish Constitution.

Due to the strong position of the ECHR and the ECtHR's jurisprudence in Polish law, the Constitutional Court of Poland refers to the case law of the ECtHR in its application of human rights rather often. This is clear in particular from the fact that Polish courts refer to the ICCPR and output of the UN Human Rights Committee much less frequently.[36] In the period between 1996 and 2014, the Constitutional Court resolved more than 2,600 cases concerning human rights Protection. In 208 of these decisions, the Constitutional Court referred to ECtHR jurisprudence.[37] Figure 2.1 gives an indication of the number of references in the Polish Constitutional Court.

The number of references is determined by the subject matter of the case and by the grounds of action brought before the court. Case law of the ECtHR is thus invoked mainly in 'problematic' cases, some of which

35 Polish Constitutional Court, Judgment of 23 February 2010, Ref. No. P 20/09.

36 See *inter alia* Polish Constitutional Court, Judgments of 1 April 2009, Ref. No. SK 77/06; and of 18 November 2010, Ref. No. P 29/09.

37 Research based on the database of the Polish Constitutional Court, available at www.otk.trybunal.gov.pl/orzeczenia/.

are discussed in detail in Section 2.4. These 'problematic' cases most often concern alleged violations of article 6 (right to fair trial) as well as alleged violations of article 1 Protocol I to the ECHR (the right to property). Most of the Polish cases before the ECtHR have concerned these two provisions. If there is no doubt about the scope and content of the right in question, there is no need for the Polish Constitutional Court to refer to ECtHR jurisprudence.

Concerning the grounds of action influencing the number of references of the Polish Constitutional Court to the ECHR and ECtHR jurisprudence, it has to be noted that the ECHR may be invoked directly before the Polish Constitutional Court only in the so-called procedure of abstract norm control of constitutionality of national provisions.[38] As a result, it is in these cases in which most references to the ECHR are found. In these cases, international human rights treaties (including the ECHR) are applied directly to control whether laws and other acts conform to the Polish Constitution and international human rights treaties. However, the ECHR is also used as an interpretative tool by the Constitutional Court in the individual complaint procedure.[39] In this procedure, the Polish Constitution is applied in light of international human rights law.

As it was already mentioned, both the ECHR and the ICCPR, as ratified international treaties, have been recognised by the Supreme Court of Poland as part of Polish legal order.[40] The Supreme Court also frequently refers to the ECtHR jurisprudence. Between 2010 and 2015 it did so in almost 300 cases.[41] In the same period, the Supreme Administrative Court made more than 700 references to the ECtHR.[42] The high number of references made by these courts is determined by the number of cases decided in the period

[38] See the procedure provided for in article 188(1)-(3) of the Polish Constitution concerning review of conformity of statutes with the Constitution and ratified international treaties.

[39] In the Judgment of 20 October 2009, SK 15/08 the Constitutional Court stated: 'Article 79 of the Constitution may only concern pleas of exception of infringement of constitutional rights and freedoms or obligations of plaintiff provided for in the Constitution of Poland and not rights provided for in international treaties' (translation by author). The Constitutional Court constantly stresses that international agreements on human rights protection may not be applied directly in this procedure (see Judgments of 7 May 2002, Ref. No. SK 20/00; of 14 December 2005, Ref. No. SK 61/03; and of 22 June 2010, Ref. No. SK 25/08). However, they are frequently applied indirectly for interpretative purposes. See judgments discussed in Section 2.3.

[40] See Polish Supreme Court, Resolution of 12 July 2001, Ref. No. III CZP 22/01.

[41] Research based on the database of the Polish Supreme Court, available at www.sn.pl/orzecznictwo/SitePages/Baza_orzeczen.aspx.

[42] Research based on the database of the Polish Supreme Administrative Court, available at www.orzeczenia.nsa.gov.pl/.

under consideration, which is considerably higher than the number of cases of the Constitutional Court.[43] Since the ECHR is directly applicable in the Polish legal order, parties quite often invoke the Convention before the courts. Although the number of references to ECtHR jurisprudence in the three highest Polish courts has constantly increased over the years, lower courts are still rather reluctant in applying ECHR and ECtHR jurisprudence when they decide cases in the field of human rights.[44]

In most cases in which the Polish Constitutional Court, the Supreme Court and the Supreme Administrative Court cite the ECHR/ECtHR jurisprudence, the ECHR was invoked by the parties to the proceedings, and the courts rely on the arguments brought forward by the parties. Otherwise, the selection of ECtHR judgments that are cited is highly dependent on accessibility to the judges of their Polish translation. The courts mainly refer to ECtHR judgments discussed in Polish legal literature,[45] judgments that are available in the Electronic System of Legal Information (LEX) or judgments that can be found on the website of the Ministry of Justice that publishes in Polish ECtHR judgments to which Poland was a party[46] (however, this last source is used rarely). The problem of accessibility of ECtHR judgments in the respective national languages of judges also limits the number of references to these judgments in other Eastern European states.

43 According to available data in the period of 2010–2015, the Supreme Administrative Court issued more than 100,000 judicial decisions. The Constitutional Court issued 4,240 judicial decisions.

44 D. R. Swenson, K. Stasiak and A. Szarek, *Poland and the European Court of Human Rights. Selected Issues and Recommendations* (Lublin: The Rule of Law Institute Foundation, 2011) at 16–19.

45 The most popular source is the commentary to ECHR and ECtHR jurisprudence by M. A. Nowicki, *Europejski Trybunał Praw Człowieka – orzecznictwo* (Kraków: Zakamycze, 2002). This commentary has been referred to in 36 cases of the Polish Supreme Court and in many decisions of lower courts (see e.g. Judgment of the Appellate Court of Warsaw of 21 November 2012, Ref. No. II AKa 335/12; and the decision of the Supreme Court of 9 December 2014, Ref. No. III SPP 231/14). However, courts also use other academic sources. For example, in the Judgment of 13 April 2007, Ref. No. I CSK 31/07, the Supreme Court referred to the ECtHR Judgment *A. Cordoba v. Italy* which was discussed in the journal *Przegląd Sejmowy* (Parliamentary Review): *Przegląd Sejmowy* 61:2 (2004), at 200. The argumentation of the Constitutional Court in a judgment of 22 July 2011, Ref. No. P 12/09 which in part concerned questions of the ECHR, is almost fully based on a monograph by I.C. Kamiński, *Ograniczenia swobody wypowiedzi dopuszczalne w Europejskiej Konwencji Praw Człowieka. Analiza krytyczna* (Warszawa: Wolters Kluwer, 2010).

46 See the relevant website, available at www.bip.ms.gov.pl/pl/prawa-czlowieka/europejski-trybunal-praw-czlowieka/orzecznictwo-europejskiego-trybunalu-praw-czlowieka/orzeczenia-w-sprawach-dotyczacych-polski/.

2.2.3 *Polish Courts' References to the Jurisprudence of the CJEU*

Although Polish courts refer to CJEU jurisprudence in the application of both EU law and national law implementing EU law very often, this is not common practice in the field of human rights protection. In the Polish Constitutional Court, in the 1996–2015 period, only thirty-one references were made to the CJEU practice concerning human rights. It must be noted that the Constitutional Court recognised the EU Charter of Fundamental Rights (EU Fundamental Rights Charter)[47] as part of the standard of human rights protection in cases covered by EU law. For example, in case No. SK 45/09 of 16 November 2011, in which the Polish Constitutional Court recognised its own jurisdiction to review the constitutionality of EU regulations, it also broadly referred to the jurisprudence of the CJEU, concerning questions about the exact content and scope of the right to fair trial.[48]

The reasons for the otherwise limited extent of dialogue on human rights between the CJEU and the Polish Constitutional Court lie in the limited overlap of jurisdiction between the two courts in the area of human rights. In principle, the preliminary ruling procedure constitutes a mechanism of direct judicial dialogue between the CJEU and domestic courts in EU member states, among which are Polish courts.[49] Because of the limited scope of application of fundamental rights enshrined in article 6 of the Treaty on European Union (TEU)[50] and the Fundamental Rights Charter, the preliminary ruling procedure is not used very often in the field of human rights.[51] However, when applying the EU Fundamental

[47] Charter of Fundamental Rights of the European Union, Official Journal C 326, 26 October 2012.

[48] Judgment of the Constitutional Court of 16 November 2011, Ref. No. SK 45/09, para. 6.4.

[49] The preliminary ruling procedure is set out in article 267 of the TFEU (Consolidated Version of the Treaty on the Functioning of European Union, Official Journal 326 (26 October 2012).

[50] Consolidated Version of Treaty on European Union, Official Journal 326 (26 October 2012).

[51] According to article 51 of the EU Fundamental Rights Charter, 'the provisions of the Charter are addressed to the institutions, bodies, offices and agencies of the Union with due regard for the principle of subsidiarity and to the Member States only when they are implementing Union law. They therefore respect the rights, observe the principles and promote the application thereof in accordance with their respective powers and respecting the limits of the powers of the Union as conferred on it in the Treaties. At the same time, the Charter does not extend the field of application of Union law beyond the powers of the Union or establish any new power or task for the Union, or modify powers and tasks as defined in the Treaties.'

Rights Charter, Polish courts refer to the case law of the CJEU,[52] and if necessary, ask the CJEU about the interpretation of EU law in the light of the Charter.[53]

In addition, possibilities for (indirect) dialogue on the ECHR between the CJEU and Polish courts through article 6(3) TEU are limited. To explain this, it is necessary to determine the position of the ECHR in the legal system of the EU and the obligations of national courts in this area. This question emerged in a case before the Polish Supreme Administrative Court.[54] Referring to relevant judgments the CJEU,[55] the Supreme Administrative Court stated that according to article 6(3) TEU, fundamental rights as guaranteed by the ECHR and as they result from the constitutional traditions common to EU member states, are to constitute general principles of EU law. However, this provision does not govern the relationship between the ECHR and the legal systems of the member states, nor does it determine the consequences to be drawn by a national court in case of conflict between the rights guaranteed by the ECHR and a provision of national law. As a result, the reference in article 6(3) TEU to the ECHR does not require the national court, in case of conflict between a provision of national law and the ECHR, to apply the provisions of the Convention directly and thus to dis-apply the provision of national law incompatible with the Convention. This decision of the Supreme Administrative Court confirmed that the dialogue with the CJEU is limited to cases covered by EU law.

These limits to the possibilities of dialogue between Polish courts and the CJEU in the area of human rights are not always clear to lower Polish courts. In these cases, the CJEU can correct the approach of national courts through the preliminary ruling procedure. An example is the case C-28/14 *Pańczyk*.[56] In this case, the CJEU dismissed the preliminary reference issued by a regional court in Częstochowa[57] concerning the interpretation

[52] See *inter alia* Judgment of the Supreme Administrative Court of 3 July 2015, Ref. No. II GSK 1365/14; and the Judgment of the Regional Administrative Court in Warsaw of 29 October 2014, Ref. No. II SA/Wa 437/14.

[53] See decision of the Polish Supreme Court of 15 May 2014, Ref. No. III SK 28/13.

[54] Polish Administrative Court's Decision of 30 May 2014, Ref. No. I ONP 1/14.

[55] E.g. Case C-571/10, *Servet Kamberaj v. Istituto per l'Edilizia sociale della Provincia autonoma di Bolzano (IPES) and Others* [2012] ECR I-233; ECLI:EU:C:2012:233.

[56] Case C-28/14, *Ryszard Pańczyk v. Dyrektor Zakładu Emerytalno-Rentowego Ministerstwa Spraw Wewnętrznych i Administracji w Warszawie* [2014], ECR I-0000; ECLI:EU:C:2014:2003.

[57] Decision of the Regional Court in Częstochowa of 20 December 2013, Ref. No. IV U 1470/12.

of article 2 of the TEU and several provisions of the EU Fundamental Rights Charter. It did so because the referring court had not demonstrated that EU law applied to the facts of the case, that is, that there had been a link between national law and EU law. The case therefore lay outside the scope of application of the EU Fundamental Rights Charter and the jurisdiction of the CJEU.

2.2.4 Polish Courts' Engagement with Jurisprudence of Foreign Domestic Courts

The discussion now moves to an analysis of the extent of Polish courts' engagement with the case law of foreign domestic courts. First of all, it has to be noted that the number of references to foreign national courts in Polish courts differs considerably from references to jurisprudence of the ECtHR and the CJEU. Except from cases that involve private international law and mutual recognition, as well as other cases in which the consideration of foreign law is compulsory,[58] decisions of foreign courts are not binding for Polish courts. As a consequence, Polish courts use decisions of foreign domestic courts mainly as sources of inspiration in the process of interpretation and application of Polish law.[59] References to foreign courts' judgments are made mainly by the Polish Constitutional Court.[60] Figure 2.2[61] indicates the foreign domestic court cases the Polish Constitutional Court refers to in cases involving human rights questions in the period between 1996 and 2014.

The most frequent references in the field of human rights protection are made by the Polish Constitutional Court to the Federal Constitutional Court of Germany (47), the French courts, especially the Constitutional Council but also the Council of State (8), US courts (10) and the Austrian Constitutional Court (8). The choice of which court to refer to seems to be determined by several factors, including availability of jurisprudence in the language of the judges, and also of Polish reports and literature discussing case law in the foreign domestic court in question. In regard to

[58] See M. Bobek, *Comparative Reasoning in European Supreme Courts* (Oxford University Press, 2013) at 21–23.

[59] See *ibid.*, at 28.

[60] For a broad analysis of the practice of the Polish Constitutional Court, see J. Krzemińska, 'Courts as Comparatists: References to Foreign Law in the Case-law of the Polish Constitutional Court', *Jean Monnet Working Paper* 05/12, available at www.jeanmonnetprogram.org.

[61] Research based on the database of the Polish Constitutional Court, available at www.otk.trybunal.gov.pl/orzeczenia/.

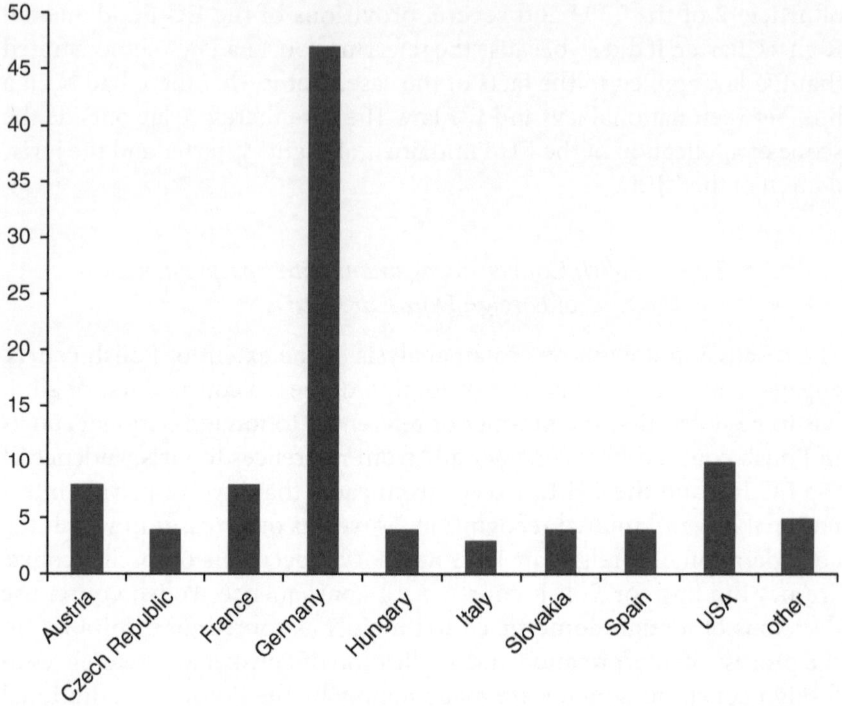

Figure 2.2 Polish Constitutional Court – References to Jurisprudence of Foreign Domestic Courts

the Federal Constitutional Court, it is useful to remember that because of proximity and common history, for many years German was the most popular 'Western' language in Poland, and comparative research in many fields has been conducted in regard to Poland and Germany. In addition, many areas of Polish law, especially criminal law, are based on German law. The same arguments may be used to explain references to French case law.

There are also references to foreign jurisprudence in the practice of the Supreme Court[62] and the Supreme Administrative Court.[63] In lower courts, references to foreign courts' decisions seem rather incidental, mainly because the lower courts have limited access to foreign judgments. Judges from both the Polish Constitutional Court and Supreme Court

[62] See *inter alia* Polish Supreme Court, Decision of 29 October 2010, Ref. No. IV CSK 465/09.

[63] See *inter alia* Polish Supreme Administrative Court, Judgment of 16 May 2014, Ref. No. II FSK 1395/12.

cooperate with their counterparts in other countries through various fora, which gives them the opportunity to exchange information with judges from abroad concerning similar legal questions they are faced with.[64]

2.2.5 General Observations on the Extent of Polish Courts' References to International and Foreign Jurisprudence

The level of detail in the analysis of international and foreign domestic jurisprudence in Polish courts' judgments varies from simple mention of a particular concept or statement of other courts to more detailed analysis of their case law. A non-specific reference, used in majority of cases before Polish courts, is made by simple invocation of the case law of an international or foreign court (without reference to particular cases) like 'according to the case law of the European Court of Human Rights' or a 'similar interpretation can be found in the case law of the courts of country ... '.[65] This kind of reference is used mainly in order to confirm a view already adopted by the citing court, and it is hard to determine to what extent the foreign or international case influenced the final decision of the Polish courts. Such references are common not only in Polish courts but are also prevalent in the practice of courts of other Eastern European states.[66] When making such references in their decisions, Polish and other Eastern European courts do not describe, contextualise or evaluate the decision referred to in more detail. In other words, the classic comparative reference to foreign jurisprudence seems to be limited to the statement that there is an external authority following a similar approach.[67]

[64] For more on this cooperation, see Section 2.3.

[65] See *inter alia* Polish Supreme Court, Judgment of 6 December 2013, Ref. No. I CSK 146/13; and the Judgment of 23 November 2012, Ref. No. I CSK 292/12; Polish Appellate Court in Rzeszów, Judgment of 27 June 2013, Ref. No. I ACa 181/13; Polish Appellate Court in Katowice, Judgment of 8 February 2013 I ACa 971/12; and Polish Appellate Court in Warsaw, Judgment of 17 October 2012, I ACa 367/12.

[66] In regard to Ukraine, see P. Nesterenko, 'Some Issues Concerning Application of the Practice of the European Court of Human Rights in Ukraine', *European Integration Studies* 6 (2012) 41–46, at 43. The author indicates that the judicial practice in Ukraine shows that many national judges are not ready to effectively apply the ECHR and engage with ECtHR jurisprudence. In many cases, Ukrainian judges have no clear understanding of the legal status of the ECHR and ECtHR jurisprudence in Ukrainian law, and thus do not understand the implications that the content of ECtHR judgments should have for the interpretation and application of Ukrainian law. Therefore, it is fairly common for domestic courts to use an abstract reference to the ECtHR's jurisprudence, without indicating a specific ECtHR judgment or decision.

[67] M. Wendel, 'Comparative Reasoning and the Making of a Common Constitutional Law – The Europe-Decisions of National Constitutional Courts in a Transnational Perspective', *Jean Monnet Working Paper* 25:13, available at www.jeanmonnetprogram.org, at 24.

When making more specific references to a foreign or international judgment, Polish courts explicitly mention a specific judgment, and they include excerpts of such rulings or engage in an in-depth analysis of foreign or international case law. Such references are mainly found in the jurisprudence of the Polish Constitutional Court, in particular in cases that concern questions on limitations of fundamental rights. When balancing conflicting rights, the Constitutional Court looks for inspiration abroad to find out about the common democratic European standard.[68] Even if to a lesser extent than the Constitutional Court, in some cases involving human rights questions, the Polish Supreme Court also looks very carefully at international and foreign practice. In many cases, especially in cases of lower courts, a single passage or concept from the foreign or international judgment is quoted, without the citing Polish court giving any explanation concerning the similarity of circumstances of the quoted case with the current case.[69] Generally, lower Polish courts (both administrative courts and courts of general jurisdiction) focus on the interpretation and application of domestic law and standards. In many cases, their references can therefore be described as 'decorative', that is, they do not have real influence on the final decision.[70] This may be caused by the limited accessibility of international and foreign case law in Polish, as discussed in Section 2.2.2. Sometimes, the choice of judgments to which Polish courts refer seems to be random, especially in cases in which Polish courts do not explain why they referred to a particular judgment. However, this is a typical problem of the comparative approach which is sometimes described as subjectivist or arbitrary.[71] As discussed further in Section 2.4, engagement in dialogue of Polish courts may also have a specific purpose, and can thus be an instrumental and result-oriented mechanism. This also explains why Polish courts will not always disclose the reasons for why they refer to a particular international or foreign judgment in their own decision.

[68] See J. Krzemińska, Courts as Comparatists, *supra* note 59, at 34.

[69] See e.g. many cases concerning questions on access to justice and legal assistance in different administrative courts quoted. In many of these cases, the administrative courts quote a passage from the ECtHR case *Związek Nauczycielstwa Polskiego v. Poland* (Appl. No 42049/98) Judgment (Chamber), 21 September 2004, ECHR 2004-IX, 102: 'the right of access to a court is not, however, absolute. It may be subject to legitimate restrictions, for example, statutory time-limits or prescription periods, security for costs orders, regulations concerning minors and persons of unsound mind, etc.' See: Regional Administrative Court of Wrocław, Decision of 15 May 2015, Ref. No. IV SAB/Wr 101/13; and Judgment of the Supreme Court of 3 June 2007, Ref. No. I UK 40/07.

[70] See Bobek, Comparative Reasoning, *supra* note 58, at 227–28.

[71] *Ibid.*, at 240–44, and literature referred to by Bobek.

As noted by Michal Bobek, it is even possible that in some cases courts quote a foreign or international authority that they did not read. Unfortunately, sometimes this is the case in Polish courts as well. Bobek indicates that the reason for this is the fact that judges frequently act under time pressure. This constrains the study of foreign and international jurisprudence, and can lead judges to rely on references to foreign and international case law that they made in earlier judgments or that they find in academic literature.

The last point to make about the extent to which Polish and other Eastern European courts engage in judicial dialogue is that not all of this dialogue might be visible in the judgments that these courts issue. Due to shared constitutional values, courts may follow each other's argumentation without making direct references. An example can be taken from the Ukrainian Constitutional Court, which has developed the doctrine of recognising a 'common European standard of the rule of law'. This doctrine played an important role, for example, in the decision of the Constitutional Court of Ukraine of 29 December 1999[72] on the death penalty. In this judgment, the Constitutional Court avoided a direct reference to the legal position of the ECtHR on the non-conformity of the death penalty as a type of punishment with article 3 of the ECHR. However, it is obvious from the content of the judgment that it was influenced by the ECtHR judgment *Soering v. the United Kingdom*.[73]

2.3 The Method of Polish Courts' Engagement in Judicial Dialogue

Our analysis now moves to the method of Polish courts' engagement in judicial dialogue, particularly how Polish courts find out about the domestic and international decisions that they refer to.

Regrettably, Polish judges rarely indicate in their judgments in which they refer to foreign and international material how they found out about this material. As indicated earlier, the most important source for Polish judges to find out about relevant international and foreign cases is the Electronic System of Legal Information (LEX), which contains this material in Polish.[74] Academic literature also plays an important role. These

[72] Constitutional Court of Ukraine, Judgment of 29 December 1999, No. 11- rp/99.

[73] *Soering v. the United Kingdom* (Appl. No. 14038/88), Judgment (Plenary), 7 July 1989, Series A, Vol. 161.

[74] See the earlier discussion – text accompanying *supra* notes 45 and 46.

sources are particularly important when it comes to finding relevant ECtHR and CJEU jurisprudence. In regard to foreign judicial decisions cited by Polish courts, the main sources for Polish courts to find out about them seems to be scientific literature and arguments presented by parties to the proceeding.

The participation of judges of the Polish Constitutional Court, the Supreme Court and the Supreme Administrative Court in various European and international networks also helps these courts to get to know relevant international and foreign decisions. For example, the Constitutional Court of Poland is a member of international judicial associations such as the World Conference on Constitutional Justice[75] and the Conference of European Constitutional Courts.[76] Both associations organise regular meetings for constitutional court judges from different countries. The Polish Constitutional Court also organises international conferences and seminars itself, and is visited by judges from European and non-European states.[77] Similarly, the Supreme Court is a member of the Network of the Presidents of the Supreme Judicial Courts of the European Union[78] and specialised judicial organisations such as European Forum of Commercial Judges.[79] The Polish Supreme Administrative Court is a member of the International Association of Supreme Administrative Jurisdictions[80] and of the Association of Councils of State and Supreme

[75] The World Conference on Constitutional Justice unites 71 Constitutional Courts, Councils, and Supreme Courts in Africa, the Americas, Asia and Europe. It promotes constitutional justice – understood as constitutional review including human rights case law – as a key element for democracy, the protection of human rights and the rule of law: www.venice.coe.int/WCCJ/WCCJ_E.asp.

[76] Among other things, the Conference of European Constitutional Courts organises regular conferences for judges of European constitutional courts: www.confeuconstco.org/en/common/home.html.

[77] See e.g. the report on a conference held by the Constitutional Court in 2015: 'Informacja o istotnych problemach wynikających z działalności i orzecznictwa Trybunału Konstytucyjnego' ('Information on Important Problems Arising from the Activity and Jurisprudence of the Constitutional Court'), (Warszawa, Wydawnictwo Trybunału Konstytucyjnego, 2015), at 70–71, available at www.trybunal.gov.pl/publikacje/informacje-o-problemach-wynikajacych-z-dzialalnosci-i-orzecznictwa-tk/od-2003/.

[78] See 'Informacja o działalności Sądu Najwyższego w roku 2014' (Information on the activity of the Supreme Court in 2014), available at www.sn.pl/osadzienajwyzszym/SitePages/Sprawozdania_z_dzialalnosci.aspx; and at www.network-presidents.eu/

[79] *Ibid.*

[80] The purpose of the International Association of Supreme Administrative Jurisdictions (IASAJ), created in 1983, is to promote exchanges of ideas and experiences between jurisdictions empowered to adjudicate, in the last instance, disputes arising from the action of public administrations. It seeks to encourage cooperation on questions of law pending

Administrative Jurisdictions of the European Union (ACA-Europe).[81] Judges of the Supreme Administrative Court also take part in international working groups of administrative courts.[82]

2.4 Purpose and Effects of Polish Courts' Engagement in Judicial Dialogue on Human Rights

The discussion now moves to why Polish and other Eastern European courts refer to international and foreign case law and what effect these references have. Almost any reference to an external authority, be it to a foreign national or international judgment, constitutes an intentional act of Polish courts designed to attain a specific purpose. As in many other countries, the Polish practice of judicial dialogue usually occurs in complex or novel cases where domestic authority is conflicting, lacking or in need of an update.[83] While recognising that it is sometimes difficult to clearly define one specific purpose of a Polish court's engagement in judicial dialogue, and without any claim to exhaustiveness, the following prominent purposes and effects of Polish courts' references to foreign and international law are analysed in more detail below: legitimising the transition process (subsection 2.4.1); ensuring that domestic law is interpreted in a manner that is consistent with international and European human rights law (subsection 2.4.2); solving 'difficult' cases (subsection 2.4.3); widening the competences of a particular domestic court (subsection 2.4.4); and highlighting specificities of the Polish legal system and justifying the retaining of these specificities (subsection 2.4.5). Specific cases from Polish courts and other Eastern European courts are discussed to illustrate these purposes and effects of dialogue on human rights.

2.4.1 Dialogue with the Purpose to Legitimise the Transition Process

Reference to international or foreign courts' decisions not only demonstrates that the court has looked at international or foreign practice in

before these courts or related to their organisation and functioning. It is a network of more than 100 supreme administrative jurisdictions of the world: www.aihja.org/

[81] ACA-Europe is composed of the Court of Justice of the European Union and the Councils of State or the supreme administrative jurisdictions of each of the members of the European Union. For more information on the activities of ACA-Europe see: www.aca-europe.eu

[82] For example in the Czech-Polish working group of administrative judges and the German-Polish working group of administrative judges. For more information, see the website of the Supreme Administrative Court, at www.nsa.gov.pl.

[83] See Bobek, Comparative Reasoning, *supra* note 58, at 280.

determining the content and scope of a particular right, but in many cases it is proof (at least in the mind of the judge) that the decision is in conformity with common European and international standards of protection. In this regard, the evolution of the Polish practice is significant. In the 1990s, references to international and foreign judicial decisions were used mainly as a legitimising tool in the transition process. The courts' main aim was to demonstrate that the Republic of Poland was a democratic state based on the rule of law, and that Poland regarded international human rights standards binding upon it. The courts referred both to the case law of the ECtHR and to foreign judicial decisions to find 'democratic standards' or 'typical solutions' to the legal question before it.

To some extent, this purpose of judicial dialogue was determined by the legal framework at the time. Before the adoption of the Constitution in 1997, there was no explicit legal basis for the application of international law in the Polish legal order. In the jurisprudence of the Polish Constitutional Court, the basis for the protection of human rights in conformity with international standards as interpreted by international courts, especially of ECtHR, was the rule of law clause included in article 1 of the so-called Small Polish Constitution of 1992.[84] However, the political motivation for engagement in judicial dialogue on human rights that is characteristic for young democracies also is visible in Polish courts' practice, in particular in the 1990s. Already in a judgment of 11 January 1995, the Polish Supreme Court argued that the case law of ECtHR must be taken into account by Polish courts as an important source of interpretation of national law. It held that

> it is obviously *against the interest of the State* if judicial and administrative decisions are negatively evaluated by the Court [ECtHR] and give rise to critical statements on Poland in professional literature and even in newspapers. It is therefore necessary to make every effort to maintain conformity

[84] Constitutional Act of 17 October 1992 on mutual relations between legislative and executive powers of the Republic of Poland and on self-government (Ustawa Konstytucyjna z 17 października 1992 o wzajemnych stosunkach między władzą ustawodawczą i wykonawczą Rzeczpospolitej Polskiej oraz o samorządzie terytorialnym, Dz. U. nr 84, poz. 426). In the Judgment of 24 June 1997, K 27/91 in regard to right to privacy, the Constitutional Court stated that 'the fact that international treaties on human rights recognise the right to privacy and that in international jurisprudence the right is strictly connected with general principle of the rule of law, is decisive for the recognition of the right to privacy as a constitutional right. It is therefore justified to assume that due legal protection of the right to privacy forms a necessary element of a democratic state based on the rule of law and is covered by general clause of Article 1 of the Constitution' (translation by the author). See also Judgment of the Constitutional Court of 7 January 1992, Ref. No. K 8/91.

> of Polish administrative and judicial practice with recommendations of the Council of Europe and European case law in the field of protection of human rights.[85]

In the twenty-first century, the rhetoric of Polish courts evolved in the direction of identifying 'European standards' through their engagement with foreign and international material, understood not only in terms of international obligations but as a common value protected at the European and national level as a part of the rule of law. Poland's membership in the EU was a significant factor in this development, contributing to linking the international with the European and the national provisions on the protection of fundamental rights. This is supported by the fact that the Polish Constitution does not distinguish between international and EU law, a distinction that is absent also in the jurisprudence of the Constitutional Court.[86] Poland's integration into the European Union made its judges more open not only towards norms of international law, but also towards the subsequent practice of interpretation and application of these norms by regional courts. Polish courts' references to international and foreign judicial decisions became more specific and detailed over time, and the impact of judicial dialogue on Polish judgments became more visible. The number of judgments of the Polish Constitutional Court that included an in-depth analysis of international and foreign case law increased over time.

2.4.2 Ensuring Interpretation of National Law Consistent with International Human Rights Standards

A prominent purpose and effect that Polish courts allegedly wish to attain with their engagement in judicial dialogue is very much related to the purpose just discussed: the purpose of ensuring that domestic law is interpreted and applied effectively in line with European and international human rights law.

There is no doubt that human rights granted in the ECHR reflect a common standard agreed between the state parties to the Convention. As is clear from the ECtHR's concept of the Convention as a 'living instrument', the content of ECHR rights evolves over time.[87] This fact makes judicial

[85] Decision of the Supreme Court of 11 of January 1995, Ref. No. III ARN 75/04 (emphasis added).

[86] See especially Judgment of the Constitutional Court of 19 December 2006, Ref. No. P 37/05 and of 16 November 2011, Ref. No. SK 45/09.

[87] In 1968, in its judgment *Wemhoff v. Germany* (Appl. No 2122/64), Judgment (Chamber), 27 June 1968, Series A, Vol. 7, the ECtHR had already rejected the restrictive interpretation

dialogue an important tool for the development of the evolving European consensus on the scope of human rights.[88]

Consistent interpretation is a well-established method used by national courts to avoid conflicts between domestic constitutional law and international and regional human rights law. Polish courts use judicial dialogue, especially with the ECtHR, to achieve this purpose. As mentioned before, shortly after Poland's accession to the ECHR, the Polish Supreme Court recognised the necessity to take the jurisprudence of the ECtHR into account; and to interpret and apply Polish law in light of this jurisprudence was confirmed also by the Polish Constitutional Court.[89] One prominent example of dialogue that resulted in bringing Polish law in line with the ECHR is a case concerning the reorganisation of intelligence services.[90] In this case, the Constitutional Court held that although it was unnecessary to refer to article 6 of the ECHR since the right of fair trial was enshrined in article 45 of the Polish Constitution, it was necessary to refer to human rights treaties and the judicial practice of the ECtHR and other international human rights bodies to establish the (evolving) standard of constitutional protection.

Similar arguments can be found in the statements of other Eastern European courts, which suggests that the purpose of dialogue to bring

of the Convention and stated that '[g]iven that [the Convention] is a law-making treaty, it is … necessary to seek the interpretation that is most appropriate in order to realise the aim and achieve the object of the treaty, not that which would restrict to the greatest possible degree the obligations undertaken by the Parties'. The Court first mentioned the 'living instrument' doctrine explicitly in *Tyrer v. the United Kingdom* (Appl. No. 5856/72 Judgment (Chamber), 25 April 1978, Series A, Vol. 26. See also the discussion of the 'living instrument' doctrine in the academic literature: M. Cartabia, 'Europe and Rights: Taking Dialogue Seriously', *European Constitutional L. Rev.* 5:1 (2009) 5–31; G. Letsas, 'The ECHR as a Living Instrument: Its Meaning and Legitimacy', A. Føllesdal *et al.* (eds.), *Constituting Europe: The European Court of Human Rights in a National, European and Global Context* (Cambridge University Press, 2013), 106–41.

[88] As a former judge of the ECtHR Anatoly Kovler stated, the process of development of the Convention as living instrument 'is not possible without on the one hand a more active response to the Court's judgments at national level, particularly from the courts, and on the other hand a more detailed study of innovative legal practice in the member States (on this last point allow me to remark that in recent years the Court has taken increasing account of the case law of the national courts in its decisions and judgments). It is therefore a two-way process'. *Dialogue between Judges*, European Court of Human Rights, 2008, available at www.echr.coe.int/Documents/Dialogue_2008_ENG.pdf, at 8. See also A. Garapon, 'The Limits to the Evolutive Interpretation of the Convention', *Dialogue between Judges: What are the Limits to the Evolutive Interpretation of the Convention?*, European Court of Human Rights, 2011, at 28–37.

[89] Judgment of the Polish Constitutional Court of 18 October 2004, Ref. No. P 8/04.

[90] Judgment of the Polish Constitutional Court of 27 June 2008, Ref No. K. 51/07, para III. 4.2.

domestic law into line with international human rights standards is shared by these courts. An example is ruling No. 21 of 2013 of the Russian Supreme Court. The Supreme Court stated that '[t]he legal positions of the European Court [ECtHR] are taken into consideration when the Russian legislation is applied. In particular, the content of the rights and freedoms provided by the laws of the Russian Federation must be defined in view of the content of similar rights and freedoms displayed by the European Court when applying the Convention and the Protocols thereto'.[91]

When judicial dialogue is relied on to achieve consistent interpretation of domestic and international human rights law in Polish courts, the foreign or international courts' judgments do not usually form part of the legal reasoning in the determination of the content and scope of the applicable norm. Rather, Polish courts use international and foreign material to support or supplement their primarily Polish law-based argument.[92] In this regard, the judgment of the Polish Constitutional Court on the retirement age of men and women is a good example. The Constitutional Court clearly stated that the case was concerned exclusively with establishing whether national provisions that set a different retirement age for men and women were in conformity with article 32 (non-discrimination) and article 33 (equality of men and women) of the Polish Constitution. It nonetheless dedicated two separate parts in the judgment to a discussion of relevant EU and international standards of protection, including the case law of both the CJEU and the ECtHR. In addition, the Constitutional Court noted explicitly, albeit in an *obiter dictum*, that the relevant provisions of domestic law were consistent with these European and international standards.[93]

By contrast, in other Eastern European countries, the case law of the ECtHR has been used as a persuasive authority to alter the scope of human rights protection granted under domestic law. An example is the case that is known as the *Maslov* case, handed down by the Russian Constitutional Court in 2000.[94] Interpretation of domestic law in conformity with the

91 Ruling of the Plenary of the Supreme Court of the Russian Federation No. 21 of 27 June 2013, para. 2.

92 M. Wendel, Comparative Reasoning, *supra* note 67, at 9; J. Krzemińska, Courts as Comparatists, *supra* note 60, at 49–50.

93 See point III.3 under the heading 'EU law provisions concerning equal retirement age of men and women' and III. 4 under the heading 'International law provisions concerning equal retirement age of men and women' of the Judgment of 15 July 2009 Ref. No. K 63/07.

94 Russian Constitutional Court, Judgment of 27 June 2000, No. 11-P.

jurisprudence of the ECtHR[95] resulted in the alteration of the scope of rights of defendants in the Russian Code of Criminal Procedure. The Russian Constitutional Court stressed the obligation of law enforcement agencies to enable detained persons to access a defence counsel in the first hours of police questioning, even though neither the Russian Code on Criminal Procedure nor the Russian Constitution contained such an obligation at the time.[96]

Polish courts in dialogue with the CJEU may also bring domestic law into line with the European standard of human rights protection, especially in cases concerning measures implementing EU law in the Polish legal system.[97] However, the practice of the Polish Constitutional Court is inconsistent in that regard. On the one hand, in a case concerning ritual slaughter strictly connected to the implementation of EU Regulation (EC) No 1099/2009,[98] the Constitutional Court did not refer to relevant jurisprudence of the CJEU.[99] On the other hand, the Constitutional Court sometimes refers to CJEU case law in cases not covered by EU law. It does so with the purpose of highlighting the existence of a 'European standard' of protection to interpret domestic law in conformity with this standard. The notion of a 'European standard' followed by the Polish Constitutional Court is based on jurisprudence of the ECtHR, the CJEU and national European (constitutional) courts.[100]

Reliance on a common 'European standard' through (indirect) dialogue with the CJEU with the aim to bring national law in line with this standard can be observed not only in the domestic courts of the EU member states but also in courts of third states. Although courts in non-member states of the EU are not bound by EU law, the case law of

[95] ECtHR judgments cited by the Russian Constitutional Court were *Quaranta v. Switzerland* (Appl. No. 12744/87) Judgment (Chamber) 24 May 1991, Series A, Vol. 205; and *Imbrioscia v. Switzerland* (Appl. No. 13972/88), Judgment (Chamber), 24 November 1993, Series A, Vol. 275.

[96] For a detailed analysis of case law of the Constitutional Court of the Russian Federation, see National Report, Russian Federation, XVI Congress of the Conference of European Constitutional Courts, 'Cooperation of Constitutional Courts in Europe – Current Situation and Perspectives', Vienna, May 2014, available at www.vfgh.gv.at/cms/vfgh-kongress/downloads/landesberichte/LB-Russie-EN.pdf.

[97] Polish Constitutional Court, Judgment of 2 June 2007, Ref. No. K 41/05; and Judgment of 30 July 2014, Ref. No. K 23/11. The reason for this might be, however, that Polish law was in conformity with the EU regulation.

[98] Council Regulation 1099/2009/EEC of 24 September 2009 on the protection of animals at the time of killing, OJ L 303, 18 November 2009, 1–30.

[99] Polish Constitutional Court, Judgment of 10 December 2014, Ref. No. K 52/13.

[100] Polish Constitutional Court, Judgment of 23 October 2012, Ref. No. SK 11/12.

the CJEU may be used by these courts as a source of inspiration in the process of strengthening the rule of law and principles of human rights protection in their countries. An example can be given from Ukraine. In cases related to state liability towards the individual, Ukrainian administrative courts have adopted and developed the concept of legal certainty through their reliance on CJEU jurisprudence. The concept of legal certainty was previously unknown to the Ukrainian legal system. To determine the scope of the principle, Ukrainian courts referred to case law of the CJEU.[101]

2.4.3 *Polish Courts' Dialogue with the Purpose to Solve 'Difficult' Cases*

Another purpose of Polish courts' engagement in dialogue with foreign domestic and international courts is to strengthen their argumentation in cases involving difficult questions about which there is no consensus in Polish society. In these cases, Polish courts regularly try to formulate a convincing legal answer to difficult social questions that is in conformity with standards of international human rights protection through a proper balancing of conflicting interests.

An example revealing this purpose of dialogue is the judgment of the Polish Constitutional Court on the constitutionality of a domestic law that provided for the possibility of shooting down a passenger aircraft (the *Aerial Law* case).[102] Shooting down was permitted by the law if the aircraft constituted a threat to the state's security, and where an organ of the air defence command had found that the aircraft in question was used for unlawful acts, in particular as a means for carrying out a terrorist attack. The objective of the proposed regulation was to facilitate an efficient

[101] See R. Petrov and P. Kalinichenko, 'The Europeanization of Third Country Judiciaries though the Application of the EU Aquis: The Cases of Russia and Ukraine', *Int'l and Comparative L. Quarterly* 60:2 (2011) 325–53, at 348–50. Authors refer in particular to the case of *Person v. Darnitsa District of Kiev Center for Social Assistance*, Judgment of the District Administrative Court of Kiev of 26 June 2008, No. 4/337, concerning the rights to benefits of those who took part in the operation during the Chernobyl catastrophe. The court provided that the principle of state liability to offer compensation to those involved in the Chernobyl disaster flows from the Case 41/74, *Van Duyn v. Home Office* [1974] ECR 1337; 1 CMLR 1, Ch. 358. In particular, the court stated that if the state formally acknowledged its commitment to offer compensation to those affected by the Chernobyl disaster, it could not refer to its own failure to fulfil its commitments in order to avoid liability, which would also violate the legitimate expectations of Ukrainian nationals (principle of legal certainty).

[102] Polish Constitutional Court, Judgment of 30 September 2008, Ref. No. K 44/07.

response to any potential aerial terrorist attack, and to allow the air forces of NATO member states to operate in Polish airspace.

In its judgment, the Polish Constitutional Court rejected the arguments that fundamental human rights have to be reinterpreted in order to maintain public security at a time when the threat of terrorist attacks is high, and declared the Polish law in question unconstitutional. To strengthen this conclusion, the Polish Constitutional Court referred to the case law of the UK House of Lords,[103] the German Federal Constitutional Court,[104] the Israeli Supreme Court[105] and the US Supreme Court.[106] The Polish Constitutional Court only explicitly relied on the German Federal Constitutional Court's judgment in one part of its judgment: to underline the highly controversial nature of the authorisation to shoot down a passenger aircraft if this constituted the only means to prevent a direct threat to the life of persons not on the aircraft. However, the Polish Constitutional Court also adopted some of the German Constitutional Court's arguments (without explicit reference) to determine the standard of protection, involving the question of defining the appropriate limitations to the rights to life. The Court noted that there are two specific requirements that need to be complied with if the right to life is limited. First, the necessity of a limitation to the right to life must be interpreted particularly restrictively. As developed in the jurisprudence of the ECtHR on article 2 ECHR, the appropriate standard is that of 'absolute necessity'. Secondly, the Polish Constitutional Court observed that due to the fundamental nature of the right to life in the Polish constitutional axiology, only the presence of other fundamental interests could justify solutions that interfere with the right to life of a certain group of people (i.e. the passengers of the aircraft being shot down). Limitation of the right to legal protection of life is conditional upon the existence of a situation in which the right cannot be reconciled with analogous rights of other persons. According to the Polish Constitutional Court, this prerequisite may generally be defined as the requirement of 'a symmetry of values': the sacrificed value and the saved value need to be of equal importance.

[103] House of Lords, *A (FC) and others (FC) v. Secretary of State for the Home Department* [2005] UKHL 71; and *A (FC) and others (FC) v. Secretary of State for the Home Department* [2004] UKHL 65.

[104] German Constitutional Court, Judgment of 16 February 2006, 1 BvR 357/05.

[105] Israeli Supreme Court, *Public Committee Against Torture on Israel v. The State of Israel et al.*, Case HCJ 5100/94; *The Center for the Defence of the Individual v. The Commander of IDF Forces in the West Bank*, Case HCJ 3278/02; and *Marab v. The Commander of IDF Forces in the West 14 Bank*, Case HCJ 3239/02.

[106] US Supreme Court, *Rasul v. Bush*, 28 June 2004, 542 US 466.

In the *Aerial Law* case, the Polish Constitutional Court used international and foreign case law in the process of balancing competing interests: the need to uphold public security by fighting terrorism on the one hand and the need to protect human rights on the other. References performed two functions here: they were a source of inspiration for the Polish Constitutional Court's arguments, but also helped to legitimise the decision of the Court by reference to similar solutions that had been accepted in other jurisdictions concerning this difficult and controversial question. The Court referred to the 'European standards' as established by the ECtHR, and as implemented in other countries. It thus relied on a combination of international and foreign decisions to determine the existence of common standards, and used these standards as an external authority reinforcing its conclusion.[107]

Another example of the determination of a common standard through judicial dialogue, and the use of these standards to decide cases that involve difficult questions of balancing of interests, are the Hungarian cases concerning the prohibition to publicly display totalitarian symbols.[108] The first in a sequence of cases involving various national constitutional courts and the ECtHR came up before the Hungarian Constitutional Court. It concerned the prohibition under the Hungarian Criminal Code to use and wear totalitarian symbols, including the 'five-point red star'. The relevant provision of the Criminal Code was challenged before the Hungarian Constitutional Court in 2000 by Mr Vajnai who had been sanctioned for wearing a five-point red star in public. However, the Hungarian Constitutional Court did not find that the prohibition was unconstitutional. Subsequently, Mr Vajnai challenged this decision before the ECtHR.[109] In its judgment *Vajnai v. Hungary*, the ECtHR concluded that the applicant's criminal conviction for simply having worn a red star had to be considered unnecessary, as it did not respond to a 'pressing social need'. Furthermore, the sanction against the applicant, although relatively light, came under criminal law, entailing serious consequences for the applicant. The sanction had therefore not been proportionate to the legitimate aim pursued. Accordingly, there had been a violation of article 10 ECHR.

[107] See J. Krzemińska, Courts as Comparatists, *supra* note 60, at 56.

[108] See the Hungarian Constitutional Court's Decision of 9 May 2000, Ref. No. 14/2000 (V. 12) AB. English translation available at www.alkotmanybirosag.hu/letoltesek/en_0014_2000.pdf.

[109] *Vajnai v. Hungary* (Appl. No. 33629/06), Judgment (Chamber), 8 July 2008, ECHR 2008-IV, 173.

After the ECtHR had issued its judgment in the *Vajnai* case, a similar case concerning the public use of totalitarian symbols came up before the Polish Constitutional Court. The Constitutional Court referred to the jurisprudence of the Hungarian Constitutional Court as well as the ECtHR's *Vajnai* judgment. In addition, it considered the case law of the German Federal Constitutional Court, which appeared to be the main persuasive source for the finding of the Polish Constitutional Court when it balanced the competing interests involved: the individual right to freedom of expression with the need to maintain public safety.[110]

Back in Hungary, Mr Vajnai had again been accused for wearing the red star in public. The Hungarian Supreme Court submitted a legal question to the Hungarian Constitutional Court. The Constitutional Court reversed its earlier judgment, finding that the domestic provision in question (§ 269/B of the Hungarian Criminal Code) was unconstitutional. In coming to this conclusion and establishing the proper level of protection, the Hungarian Constitutional Court not only relied on the ECtHR's *Vajnai* judgment but also referred to domestic law of Slovakia, Germany, Italy, Lithuania, Latvia, Romania, Poland and Ukraine, as well as to the decisions of foreign constitutional courts on the subject, including to the decision of the Polish Constitutional Court mentioned earlier.[111] It relied on this foreign and international material to hold that the broad and general prohibition in the challenged provision of the Hungarian Criminal Code was disproportionate and thus imbalanced, and therefore incompatible with Hungarian Constitution. From the argumentation of the Constitutional Court of Hungary, it seems that although the ECtHR's *Vajnai* judgment had been the main reason for it to change its interpretation of the Hungarian Constitution on the matter, foreign judicial decisions offered important additional arguments made in similar social and political contexts underlying the legal problems at hands.

In other, less controversial cases, Polish and other Eastern European courts also rely on dialogue to determine appropriate limitations to rights.

[110] See the Polish Constitutional Court, Judgment of 19 July 2011, Ref. No. K 11/10, point III. 3 with the heading 'The standards and jurisprudence of other states and of the European Court of Human Rights.'

[111] Judgments of the German Federal Constitutional Court, of 3 April 1990, 1 BvR 680/86; of 23 March 2006, 1 BvR 204/03; of 1 June 2006, 1 BvR 150/03; and of 18 May 2009, 2 BvR 2202/08; and the Italian Constitutional Court, Judgment 74/1958 of 20 December 1958 were referred to in the judgment of 19 July 2011, *ibid*. The Hungarian Constitutional Court mentioned that the Polish Constitutional Court had considered the ECtHR judgment when it had annulled the respective provision in the Polish Criminal Code based on the finding of a violation of the principle of *nullum crimen sine lege*.

An example is a case that came before the Polish Constitutional Court in 2009,[112] challenging the constitutionality of the obligation to fasten seat belts in cars under the Polish Road Traffic Act. The applicant had been stopped by the police and had been fined for not fastening his seat belt. The applicant refused to pay the fine on the ground that the obligation in question was contrary to the right of privacy and violated his dignity. The Polish Constitutional Court referred to several cases of the ECtHR[113] as well as of foreign national courts[114] to strengthen its argumentation concerning the acceptable scope of limitations to the protection of the right to privacy. Similarly, the Constitutional Court of Czech Republic had to decide about the scope of the right to judicial review in a judgment of 26 April 2005 involving the question of the right to access classified information. In its judgment,[115] the Court broadly referred to the decisions of the Slovak[116] and Polish[117] Constitutional Courts, laws of the Netherlands and Lithuania, and the jurisprudence of the ECtHR.[118] It used these references in its arguments that the right to an effective remedy was broader under the Czech Constitution than the protection granted by the ECHR.

2.4.4 *Polish Courts' Dialogue with the Purpose of Widening the Competences of a Particular Domestic Court*

Sometimes references to the practice of foreign domestic and international courts may be used by Polish courts to justify the expansive interpretation of domestic law, a practice that can amount to judicial lawmaking. This

[112] Polish Constitutional Court, Judgment of 9 July 2009, Ref. No. SK 48/05.

[113] Among them *X v. Belgium* (Appl. No. 8707/79), Decision (Commission, Plenary), 13 December 1979, Series D.R., Vol. 18, 257; *Schmautzer v. Austria* (Appl. No. 15523/89), Judgment (Chamber), 10 May 1993, Series A, Vol. 328-A; *Viel v. France* (Appl. No. 41781/98), Decision (Chamber), 14 December 1999, not reported.

[114] For example, the Federal Constitutional Court of Germany: Judgment of 26 January 1982, 1 BvR 1925/80; Judgment of 24 July 1986, 1 BvR 331/85; and Judgment of 9 March 1992, 1 BvR 74/92; Austrian Constitutional Court: Judgment of 27 February 1989 in the case of *Schmautzer*, B 821/88; Judgments of the US Supreme Courts: Illinois, of 1 October 1986, *Society v. Kohrig*, No. 62719–24, 498 N.E. 2d 1158; Iowa, of 17 May 1989, *State v. Hartog*, No. 88–383, 440 N.W. 2d 852; and Washington, of 14 October 2004, *State v. Eckblad*, No. 74109-3, 152 Wn.2d 515, 98 3d 1184.

[115] Czech Constitutional Court, Judgment of 25 April 2005, Pl. ÚS 11/04.

[116] The Czech Constitutional Court referred to the Judgment of the Slovak Constitutional Court of 11 February 2004, Pl. ÚS. 15/03.

[117] The Czech Constitutional Court referred to the Judgment of the Polish Constitutional Court of 10 May 2000, Ref. No. K. 21/99.

[118] Among them were *Incal v. Turkey* (Appl. No. 22678/93), Judgment (Grand Chamber), 9 June 1998, ECHR 1998-IV; *Sramek v. Austria* (Appl. No. 8790/79), Judgment (Plenary), 22

is particularly prominent among the judges of the Polish Constitutional Court. An example is the judgment of the Polish Constitutional Court in which it arguably widened its own competences by developing the concept of 'interpretative rulings'.[119] The jurisdiction of the Constitutional Court in Poland is limited to the judicial control of laws (normative acts) for their conformity with the Polish Constitution. It does not cover the constitutional review of the application of these laws by lower courts and administrative authorities. However, the Polish Constitutional Court declared itself competent to give rulings also on the constitutionality of a specific interpretation of a legal provision established by lower courts in cases where the underlying legal provision is a constitutional provision ('interpretative rulings'). When developing its argument that this power came with its competence to control the constitutionality of Polish law (effectiveness), the Polish Constitutional Court adopted a comparative perspective and relied on the practice of other foreign domestic courts. In a subsequent resolution, the Polish Supreme Court questioned this practice and stated:

> When issuing interpretative rulings, the Constitutional Court refers to the standards and traditions developed by constitutional courts of other states. These are not reasons which could justify the practice of handing down interpretative judgments. Polish law neither provides for nor allows rulings based on constitutional practice of other European courts, which, after all, do not work and have not decided on the basis of the same legislation. The fact that constitutional courts in Europe have similar, or even more nuanced decision making formulas, does not justify duplication of those formulas that have no basis in the Polish constitutional or statutory order. The practice of constitutional courts of other states should not be uncritically transposed, reproduced, or copied.[120]

The resolution of the Supreme Court made the Polish Constitutional Court's interpretative judgments unenforceable. The Supreme Court stated that interpretative judgments in which the Constitutional Court does not establish that a particular provision of domestic law is unconstitutional, but indicates wrong interpretation in the process of its application, may not constitute ground for reopening the case. The Constitutional Court

October 1984, Series A, Vol. 84; *Pellegrin v. France* (Appl. No. 28541/95), Judgment (Grand Chamber), 8 December 1999, ECHR 1999-VIII, 251.

[119] See *inter alia* Polish Constitutional Court, Judgment of 10 February 2003, Ref. No. P11/02, para III.5.

[120] Polish Supreme Court, Resolution of 17 December 2009, Ref. No. III PZP 2/09, translation after J. Krzemińska, Courts as Comparatists, *supra* note 60, at 30.

was thus unsuccessful in its attempt to widen its competences through its engagement in judicial dialogue.

2.4.5 *References to International and Foreign Judgments with the Purpose to Justify a Particular Domestic Solution*

Sometimes Polish courts' purpose in referencing case law of a foreign jurisdiction or an international court is not to prove the existence of a common standard of protection or to solve a 'difficult' case, but to point out and justify a particular domestic solution that differs from the solutions proposed by the cited foreign and international material. Three examples of judgments from the Polish Constitutional Court, the Russian Constitutional Court and the Constitutional Court of Lithuania shall be given to illustrate this point.

The first example is the judgment of the Polish Constitutional Court concerning the insult of the President of the Republic of Poland.[121] In this case, the Constitutional Court had to answer the question of the conformity of penal provisions on public insult of the President of Republic of Poland (article 135(2) of the Polish Penal Code) with both article 54 (right to freedom of expression) of the Polish Constitution and article 10 of the ECHR. The Polish Constitutional Court analysed the jurisprudence of the ECtHR with the clear intention to prove the conformity of article 135 (2) of the Polish Penal Code with article 10 of ECHR. To achieve this, the Court based its main argument on (an artificial) distinction between an 'insult' and a 'defamation'. It found that most ECtHR judgments concerned the question of defamation, whereas the case before the Polish Constitutional Court concerned a question of insult. In consequence, it held that ECtHR jurisprudence was of low relevance for the solution of the case before the

121 Polish Constitutional Court, Judgment of 6 July 2011, Ref. No. P 12/09. The proceedings before the Constitutional Court were initiated by a question posed by the Regional Court in Gdansk concerning the conformity of article 135 (2) of the Penal Code with article 54(1) in conjunction with article 31(3) of the Constitution of the Republic of Poland and article 10 of the ECHR. The question arose in the context of a complaint about the decision of the Regional Prosecutor's Office in Warsaw to discontinue the investigation of the alleged insult of the President of the Republic of Poland Lech Kaczyński by the former President of Poland, Lech Wałęsa. The latter had called the former a 'fool' during a TV programme. The Public Prosecutor decided to discontinue the proceedings against Lech Wałęsa because the statement should be interpreted in the context in which it was made, as an inherent part of the substance of the articulated criticism. The Prosecutor found that the choice of words might seem controversial; however, they could not be the basis for the declaration of an offence of insulting the President. The Prosecutor's decision was challenged by the Representative of the President of the Republic of Poland Lech Kaczyński.

Polish Constitutional Court, including the ECtHR's judgment issued in a very similar case of defamation of the King of Spain, *Otegi Mondragon v. Spain*.[122] It stated that

> numerous interesting views were presented by the ECtHR with regard to the infringement of Article 10 of the Convention in cases related to actions aimed against the head of state. However, in the context of the present case, the significance of that jurisprudence is limited, due to the fact that, to a large extent, it concerns defamation, and not an insult to the head of state.[123]

The Polish Constitutional Court further observed that only the ECtHR's judgment *Pakdemirli v. Turkey* of 2005[124] – in which the President of Turkey was referred to *inter alia* as 'a liar', 'a slanderer', 'a political invalid', 'a narrow-minded person' and 'a person who corrupts clean consciences' – may be regarded as an example of an *insult* of the head of state. However, after the Polish Constitutional Court had heard the opinion of an expert on the question, it nonetheless concluded that the judgment *Pakdemirli v. Turkey* was irrelevant for the case before it. The reason for this was that *Pakdemirli v. Turkey* concerned the question of civil law compensatory sanctions (financial compensation) for undermining good reputation. The case before the Polish Constitutional Court, by contrast, concerned a criminal sanction.

The Court concluded its analysis of ECtHR jurisprudence with a statement that revealed the purpose of its dialogue with the ECtHR in this case: to uphold the particular Polish law on the criminalisation of the insult of the president of the Poland. It observed that one should not

> overlook the fact that the ECtHR, by its nature, resolves whether a ruling issued by a domestic court with regard to specific circumstances of a given case (the result of the application of a provision in a particular situation) complies with a standard of the Convention, and does not adjudicate on the conformity of a provision of the national law to the Convention. Therefore, views formulated by the ECtHR directly refer only to the circumstances of a particular case and the ruling related thereto which has been issued by a domestic court.[125]

122 *Otegi Mondragon v. Spain*, (Appl. No 11662/85), Judgment (Chamber), 15 March 2011, ECHR 2011-I, 385. The Polish Public Prosecutor General had relied on this judgment in its submissions to the Polish Constitutional Court.

123 Judgment of 6 July 2011, *supra* note 121, para.3.4. English version available at www.trybunal.gov.pl.

124 *Pakdemirli v. Turkey*, (Appl. No. 5839/97), Judgment (Chamber), 22 February 2005, not reported.

125 Judgment of 6 July 2011, *supra* note 121, para.3.4.

This statement of a full bench of the Polish Constitutional Court seems to question the idea of judicial dialogue between the ECtHR and national courts as the main tool of creation of common European standard of protection discussed earlier. However, as judge Stanisław Biernat pointed out in the separate opinion, the statement should not be absolutised,[126] but rather understood to point to the limitations of Polish courts' dialogue with the ECtHR. In this context it is necessary to remember that constitutional courts, including the Polish one, are first of all guardians of the constitutional identity of their states. In a judgment adopted by the Polish Constitutional Court of 13 October 2009,[127] the Court reiterated the supremacy of the Polish Constitution in the Polish legal order based on article 8 of the Polish Constitution, and thus clarified some of the limitations of the dialogue in which it is ready to enter with the ECtHR. The Constitutional Court observed that although the normative content of rights granted by the ECHR is determined in the jurisprudence of the ECtHR, which should be taken into account when the fundamental rights in the Polish Constitution are interpreted, the Polish Constitutional Court nonetheless enters into a dialogue with the ECtHR within the limits of its own jurisdiction. In the jurisdiction of the Polish Constitutional Court, the Polish Constitution is the supreme law.[128] The statement of the Polish Constitutional Court above can be understood as a reservation to taking on the jurisprudence of the ECtHR: this jurisprudence will only be given effect if it does not undermine a higher standard of protection granted by the Polish Constitution and in the established jurisprudence of the Polish Constitutional Court.

[126] As judge Stanislaw Biernat pointed out in the dissenting opinion, '[o]ne may only partially agree with that statement. In its more recent jurisprudence, the ECHR requires the states, being the High Contracting Parties to the Convention, to take action in order to adjust the domestic law and the practice of the application thereof to the requirements of the Convention. This is the notion of "positive obligations of the state".... I do not think that the said kind of obligation could apply to Poland in the context of Article 135(2) of the Penal Code, taking into account the present practice of applying the provision. My point is that the above-cited statement about the case-specific character of the ECHR rulings, voiced by the Constitutional Tribunal (full bench) in this particular context, would not be absolutised.' (author's translation).

[127] Polish Constitutional Court, Judgment of 13 October 2013, Ref. No. P 4/08, para 3.2

[128] In its Judgment of 11 May 2005, Ref. No. K 18/04, the Polish Constitutional Court noticed that norms of the Constitution within the field of individual rights protection of rights and freedoms indicate a minimum and unsurpassable threshold which may not be lowered or questioned as a result of the principle of interpreting domestic law in a manner 'sympathetic to European law'. The latter principle is also formulated in the Constitutional Court's jurisprudence.

The second example of an Eastern European court engaging in judicial dialogue with the aim to protect a particular domestic solution can be taken from the Russian Federation: the *Markin* case decided by the Russian Constitutional Court. Mr Markin, Russian citizen and military serviceman, applied for paternal leave to take care of his three children. His request was denied on the grounds that Russian law only grants this benefit to female military personnel. In 2009, the Constitutional Court of the Russian Federation considered the case for the first time and did not find violations of the Russian Constitution. It held that the difference in treatment between male and female military personnel was justified in order to ensure the effective functioning of the Russian military, because of the 'limited participation of women in military service' and the 'special social role of women associated with motherhood.'[129] In its judgment, the Russian Constitutional Court also engaged with ECtHR jurisprudence, but concluded that this jurisprudence justified upholding the Russian law in question, which was inspired by article 38(1) of the Russian Constitution that mandated the state to protect 'maternity and childhood, and the family'.[130] This suggests that the main argument of the Russian Constitutional Court rested on the need to protect constitutional values as a part of identity of the Russian state.

Mr Markin brought his case before ECtHR, and in October 2010 the Court issued its judgment,[131] which was challenged by Russia before the Grand Chamber.[132] The ECtHR found a violation of the ECHR, criticised

[129] Russian Constitutional Court, Ruling of 15 January 2009, No. 187-O-O. The Constitutional Court stated that: 'Owing to the specific demands of military service, non-performance of military duties by military personnel en masse must be excluded as it might cause detriment to the public interests protected by law. Therefore, the fact that servicemen under contract are not entitled to parental leave cannot be regarded as a breach of their constitutional rights or freedoms, including their right to take care of, and bring up, children.... Moreover, this limitation is justified by the voluntary nature of the military service contract. By granting, on an exceptional basis, the right to parental leave to servicewomen only, the legislature took into account, firstly, the limited participation of women in military service and, secondly, the special social role of women associated with motherhood. [Those considerations] are compatible with Article 38 § 1 of the Constitution of the Russian Federation. Therefore, the legislature's decision cannot be regarded as breaching the principles of equality of human rights and freedoms or equality of rights of men and women, as guaranteed by Article 19 §§ 2 and 3 of the Constitution of the Russian Federation.' Translation after the ECtHR *Konstantin Markin v. Russia* (Appl. No. 30078/06), Judgment (Grand Chamber), 22 March 2012, ECHR 2012-III, 77 (extracts), para 34.

[130] Article 38(1) of the Russian Constitution.

[131] *Konstantin Markin v. Russia* (Appl. No. 30078/06), Judgment (Chamber), 7 October 2010, not reported.

[132] *Konstantin Markin v. Russia* (GC), *supra* note 129.

the Russian Constitutional Court's reasoning as 'unconvincing' and pointed to 'gender prejudices' in the decision.[133] The decision was subsequently criticised by the Russian authorities, including the President of the Constitutional Court, Valeri Zorkin, who claimed that the ECtHR had not shown sufficient respect for Russia's sovereignty and its legislature, which was better placed to solve questions related to national security and determining the scope of individual rights in this context.[134] He further declared that the interpretation of the Russian Constitution by the Russian Constitutional Court could not automatically be overridden by an interpretation of the ECHR offered by the ECtHR.[135]

In 2013, Mr Markin asked for the reopening of his case before a regional court in St. Petersburg, in consequence of the ECtHR's ruling. The regional court referred the case to the Russian Constitutional Court as it was faced with the legal question of how to reconcile contradicting judgments of the Russian Constitutional Court and the ECtHR. In its decision, the Russian Constitutional Court made sure that it left a backdoor open that would allow it to protect specific domestic solutions in the future, in particular solutions that were based on its own interpretation of the Russian Constitution. The Russian Constitutional Court ruled that generally, the district court was under an obligation to reopen the proceedings after the ECtHR had found a violation of the ECHR by Russia. However, the Court also noted that if a lower court is able to comply with the judgment of the ECtHR only by disregarding an interpretation of the Constitution and a finding of the constitutionality of an ordinary law by the Russian Constitutional Court that was binding on lower courts, the lower court in question is obliged to refer the case to the Russian Constitutional Court. The Constitutional Court will then reassess its interpretation of the Russian Constitution and/or its finding on the constitutionality of a domestic provision in light of the ECtHR judgment. The Russian Constitutional Court did not indicate how it would solve such cases in detail. Nevertheless, the judgment indicates that the Russian Constitutional Court also recognises that its dialogue with the ECtHR has certain limitations that are to be found in the fundamental values protected by the Russian Constitution. In the case at hand, the decision on Mr Markin's right to parental leave

[133] See *Konstantin Markin v. Russia* (Chamber), *supra* note 131, paras. 57–59.

[134] See W. E. Pomeranz, '*Uneasy Partners*: *Russia* and the *European Court* of *Human Rights*', *Human Rights Brief* 19:3 (2012) 17–21, at 19.

[135] See G. Vaypan, 'Acquiescence Affirmed, Its Limits Left Undefined: The *Markin* Judgment and the Pragmatism of the Russian Constitutional Court vis-a-vis the European Court of Human Rights', *Russian L. J.* 2:3 (2014) 130–40, at 134–35.

became redundant because his children attained an age that no longer entitled him to parental leave.

The last example of an Eastern European court using dialogue to assert and justify a particular domestic constitutional standard that differs from the solution offered under international human rights law comes from Lithuania: the *Paksas* case of the Constitutional Court of Lithuania of 25 May 2012.[136] In this case, the Lithuanian Constitutional Court emphasised the need to protect the 'very constitutional identity' of Lithuania when it justified its rejection of ECtHR jurisprudence. The case in question concerned the effects of the ECtHR judgment *Paksas v. Lithuania*,[137] which criticised an earlier decision of the Constitutional Court of Lithuania of 2004 concerning the Lithuanian constitutional order.[138] In its 2004 judgment, the Lithuanian Constitutional Court had held that a person who had been removed from the office of the president for a gross violation of the Lithuanian Constitution or a breach of oath could never be elected president of the republic or a member of the *Seimas* (lower chamber of Lithuanian Parliament) again, nor could he or she hold an office for which it was necessary to take an oath in accordance with the Lithuanian Constitution. The ECtHR, reviewing this decision, found a violation of the right to vote and stand in parliamentary elections under article 3 of the First Protocol to the ECHR.[139] In its subsequent decision of 2012, the Lithuanian Constitutional Court questioned the ECtHR's arguments and set out the limits of the legal consequences of the ECtHR judgments in the Lithuanian legal order based on two arguments. First, the Constitutional Court of Lithuania pointed to the subsidiary nature of the ECHR system. It noted that

> the European Court of Human Rights plays a subsidiary role in the implementation of the Convention and Protocols thereto; it does not replace the competence and jurisdiction of national courts, nor is it an appeal or cassation instance with regard to judgments of the latter. Even though the jurisprudence of the European Court of Human Rights, as a source for construction of law, is important also for construction and application of Lithuanian law, the jurisdiction of the said Court does not replace the powers of the Constitutional Court to officially construe the Constitution.[140]

[136] Constitutional Court of Lithuania, Judgment of 22 May 2012, Case No. 8/2012/05/09/2012.

[137] *Paksas v. Lithuania* (Appl. No. 34932/04), Judgment (Grand Chamber), 6 January 2011, ECHR 2011-I, 1.

[138] Constitutional Court of Lithuania, Judgment of 25 May 2004, Ref. No. 24/04.

[139] Protocol to the Convention for the Protection of Human Rights and Fundamental Freedoms (20 March 1952), 213 UNTS 262, CETS 009, entered into force 18 May 1954.

[140] Constitutional Court of Lithuania, *supra* note 136, para III.2. English translation available at www.lrkt.lt/en/court-acts/search/170/ta1055/content.

The Lithuanian Constitutional Court's second argument related to the need to protect the constitutional identity of the state. It observed that there was a close relationship between the impeachment procedure, breach of oath and electoral rights under the Lithuanian Constitution. It stressed that a change of any of these three elements would influence the balance of the Lithuanian constitutional system and the constitutional values behind this system. The Constitutional Court of Lithuania declared the Lithuanian Constitution as the supreme law of the land. It further stated that ECtHR judgments may not serve as a constitutional basis for the reinterpretation of the official constitutional doctrine if such reinterpretation, in the absence of corresponding amendments to the Lithuanian Constitution, affects the essence of the constitutional provision in question. Such reinterpretation based on ECtHR judgments could also not be accepted if it unduly interfered with the values entrenched in the Lithuanian Constitution and undermined the level of protection of fundamental rights offered by it.

Similar to the Polish and Russian Constitutional Courts, the Lithuanian Constitutional Court thus engaged in dialogue with the ECtHR to ensure that it retained its room of manoeuvring in cases where the judgments of the ECtHR might conflict with the Lithuanian Constitution and its interpretation by the Lithuanian Constitutional Court. It proves that constitutional courts of Eastern Europe, similar to constitutional courts in Western Europe,[141] protect their role as guardians of national constitutions. These courts are eager to retain the last word when it comes to the protection of fundamental constitutional values.

2.5 Concluding Remarks

Judges in Eastern Europe, especially the judges of supreme and constitutional courts, increasingly rely on foreign sources of law and thus participate in a transnational judicial discourse. This is particularly visible in the area of human rights and constitutional law that was analysed in this chapter. Courts in Eastern Europe today actively engage with jurisprudence of international courts and foreign domestic courts, and often, such engagement leads them to arrive at their own, well-reasoned conclusions on a human rights question.

Polish and other Eastern European courts' most common reason for referencing an 'external' judicial decision is to strengthen their argumentation

[141] See Federal Constitutional Court of Germany, Judgment of 14 October 2004, 2 BvR 1481/04; and UK Supreme Court, *Manchester City Council v. Pinnock (No.2)* [2011] UKSC 6.

and to thus increase the authority of their own judgments. Sometimes this can lead to the impression that the use of foreign and international decisions is rather 'decorative', as references to them do not have any noticeable influence on the respective courts' legal argumentation. Polish and other Eastern European courts do not normally begin their explanations of the reasons for their decisions with references to 'external' practice (in order to analyse the content of norms). Rather, they first present their views construed independently from 'external' practice, and only at a later stage add arguments that are supported by decisions of foreign or international courts. The practice of courts in 'hard cases' shows that it is particularly in these cases that courts support their findings on questions of substantive law with references to practice of foreign courts in jurisdictions that face similar legal problems. This is especially true for the Polish Constitutional Court, which has to decide on more cases that involve difficult social, ethical or political cases than common courts do.

Finally, it should be recalled that courts in Poland and other Eastern European states have yet relatively little experience with engaging in judicial dialogue. The membership of Eastern European states in the EU and/or the CoE, involving acceptance of the jurisdiction of the CJEU and/or the ECtHR, provides an impetus for national courts to follow the developments in the jurisprudence of the CJEU and the ECtHR. Overall, faced with the challenge of their countries' participation in these international organisations, Polish and other Eastern European judges display an eagerness to engage in judicial dialogue. This chapter traced a significant increase of references to the standards of the ECHR as developed by the ECtHR, in particular in human rights cases in Eastern European courts. These references range from courts simply observing the fact that the Convention exists, to quotations of ECtHR judgments, to extensive and critical engagements with the ECHR and ECtHR jurisprudence.

3

Horizontal Judicial Dialogue on Human Rights

The Practice of Constitutional Courts in South America

MICHAEL FREITAS MOHALLEM

3.1 Introduction

The reference by courts to foreign judgments is not an exclusive phenomenon of any region, country or legal tradition.[1] This chapter adds to the existing literature on this practice by focusing on a region that has attracted little attention so far. It analyses South American domestic constitutional and supreme courts' engagement in horizontal judicial dialogue in cases involving human rights through an assessment of the constitutional jurisprudence of Argentina, Bolivia, Brazil, Chile, Colombia, Ecuador, Paraguay, Peru, Uruguay and Venezuela. It assesses the extent to which national courts rely on foreign material; the method by which they do so; the purpose of this engagement in judicial dialogue in the area of human rights; and the effects that foreign and international judgments have on the development of national law in this region. In accordance with the definition of this book, the term 'judicial dialogue' refers to the use of external legal material as an element of influence in legal interpretation and application; and 'horizontal' dialogue connotes that the interaction takes place between different domestic legal orders.[2] Next to external judicial decisions, the chapter also considers other legal material, such as foreign statutes and constitutions.

[1] Considering common law jurisdictions, see e.g. B. Flanagan and S. Ahern, 'Judicial Decision-Making and Transnational Law: a Survey of Common Law Supreme Court Judges', *Int'l and Comp. L. Quarterly* 60:1 (2011) 1–28. For the Canadian view, see B. Roy, 'An Empirical Survey of Foreign Jurisprudence and International Instruments in Charter Litigation', *University of Toronto Fac. L. Rev.* 62:99 (2004) 99–148; for the UK and the Netherlands, see E. Mak, 'Why Do Dutch and UK Judges Cite Foreign Law?' *Cambridge L. J.* 70:2 (2011) 420–50; E. A. Posner and C. R. Sunstein, 'The Law of Other States', *Stanford L. Rev.* 59:1 (2006) 131–79. For different jurisdictions, see E. Örücü (ed.), *Judicial Comparativism in Human Rights Cases* (London: British Institute of International and Comparative Law, 2003).

[2] 'Rejection of decisions of other courts by a judge or judges' should be included in this understanding of 'dialogue'. See, e.g. P. Webb, 'Immunities and Human Rights: Dissecting

In recent years, the concept of (mutual) judicial 'dialogue' has become prevalent, as countries have moved away from the process of mere (unilateral) 'reception' of foreign law. 'Reception' implies bilateral relationships between states in which courts in one country are exclusively on the receiving end when it comes to the use of and engagement with foreign jurisprudence. This has often been the case of former colonies.[3] By contrast, 'judicial dialogue' describes the mutual consideration of the other's jurisprudence and legal material.[4] Argentina is a good example of a country that, while 'breaking away from the Spanish tradition', simultaneously engaged in another relation of 'reception' with the United States.[5] The adherence to a new source of foreign legal influence was based on the 'conviction that the US Constitution had instilled the germ of political and economic progress in the United States, and it was assumed that the same germ would penetrate Argentina'.[6]

Notwithstanding this example, the process in South America of communication and exchange between courts is better defined as 'judicial dialogue' – as opposed to 'reception' – since it occurs in multiple directions, beyond the confines of a particular court's legal material, and because it is characterised by the voluntary embracing of external reasoning patterns. The phenomenon of judicial dialogue can be understood as a modern expansion of comparative horizons[7] that produces original outcomes when compared to the centuries-old method of foreign law reception.[8] This is also the approach of South American courts as they look across borders for solutions adopted in cases concerning the interpretation and

the Dialogue in National Courts', O. K. Fauchald and A. Nollkaemper (eds.), *The Practice of International and National Courts and the (De-)Fragmentation of International Law* (Oxford: Hart Publishing, 2012) 245–67, at 245. See also the Introduction to this book, subsection 1.2.1.

[3] C. L'Heureux-Dube, 'The Importance of Dialogue: Globalization and the International Impact of the Rehnquist Court' *Tulsa L. J.* 34:15 (1998) 15–40, at 21 and 17.

[4] *Ibid.*

[5] C. F. Rosenkrantz, 'Against Borrowings and Other Nonauthoritative Uses of Foreign Law' *Int'l J. Constitutional L.* 1:269 (2003) 269–95, at 272.

[6] *Ibid.*, at 271.

[7] Koh refers to the 'emergence and expansion of an extensive body of transnational law which is essentially public in character'. Human rights law plays an important role in this body of transnational law. H.H. Koh, 'Transnational Legal Processes Illuminated', M. Likosky (ed.), *Transnational Legal Processes: Globalisation and Power Disparities* (London: Butterworths, 2002) 327–32, at 331.

[8] The examination of foreign law and jurisprudence was common in the colonial period, particularly between the empires and their colonies. Furthermore, it is an established practice between states party to the Commonwealth of Nations (or British Commonwealth) and common among states that have informally elected the post–World War II jurisprudence of the United States as reference; see A.M. Slaughter, *A New World Order* (Princeton

application of the same treaties and similar domestic provisions. This practice is facilitated by an increased access to foreign judicial decisions, *inter alia* through publications in English. Yet, the comparative horizons also grow from the direct judicial cooperation set up by courts and judges in the region, which can be seen in conferences, bilateral meetings, thematic debates and institutional agreements.[9] These are no longer (solely) ceremonial events, but can be described as processes of institutionalisation of judicial dialogue, which not only broadens South American judges' legal perspectives but also contributes to an increased affinity and solidarity among judges who share similar professional challenges.[10]

The argument is made that the extent of this horizontal dialogue in the region is related to the strong position of international human rights treaties in the constitutional law of many Latin American states, as well as the construction of permanent spaces for the exchange of legal ideas (in the form of regional institutions) in the region. Furthermore, the practice in South America is facilitated by cultural, linguistic and legal similarities, and by ongoing regional political integration processes. These favour not only the borrowing of legal provisions but also the constant communication among the courts.

This chapter is structured as follows. Section 3.2 presents the context in which the research results are evaluated and the line of argument developed, with an emphasis on the constitutional evolution of the region. It highlights the relationship between increased judicial dialogue and a recent trend in South American countries to incorporate international human rights law into domestic law at the level of national constitutions. Section 3.3 analyses the extent of horizontal judicial dialogue in South America. It uses a quantitative methodology to explore the frequency with which foreign material is referred to in domestic human rights cases, the

University Press, 2005) at 71. Giuseppe De Vergottini, by the same token, acknowledges that 'in fact there [have] always been cases in which one court used as [a] paradigm the decision of another court, which serves as a model for the lending court'. Nevertheless the 'phenomenon of transferring ideas and political programmes' as well as the 'migration of constitutional ideas' have become more frequent and faster in the second half of the last century. G. De Vergottini, *Oltre il Dialogo tra le Corti. Giudici, Diritto Straniero, Comparazione* (Bologna: Il Mulino, 2010) at 18.

9 Slaughter notes the occurrence and institutionalisation of meetings between constitutional courts since the 1980s, and draws attention to personal meetings between judges as instruments of 'cross-fertilisation', capable of broadening the legal perspectives of participating judges and contributing to the development of solidarity networks. Slaughter, A New World Order, *supra* note 8, at 99.

10 *Ibid.*, at 91.

evolution of such practice in the years between 1990 and 2012, and the occurrence of foreign citations in the majority and/or minority opinions of the different courts; and it assesses whether the adjudication of specific rights attracts more foreign citations than others. Section 3.4 explores the methods by which judges and courts engage in dialogue in the region; and Section 3.5 assesses the purposes and motivations of South American courts and judges practicing judicial dialogue. Finally, Section 3.6 discusses some of the effects of referencing foreign material in domestic jurisprudence, notably in cases where answers in existing domestic law and jurisprudence are unavailable; where a South American court intends to 'update' the understanding of domestic law; where citations of external material guide the implementation of human rights treaties by domestic courts; and where the prominence of the foreign and international material makes it difficult for a South American court to ignore it.

First, however, an explanation on scope and methodology. This chapter assesses constitutional or supreme court cases from Argentina, Brazil, Bolivia, Chile, Colombia, Ecuador, Paraguay, Peru, Uruguay and Venezuela. This group of cases is more comprehensive than a random representative sample, but it does not include all cases in which foreign material was considered in domestic constitutional cases. The focus is on the use of references to foreign material (domestic foreign legal decisions or statutes) in cases that involve human rights law. This includes references to decisions by foreign domestic courts that interpret and apply international human rights treaties. Excluded from the analysis is, however, South American courts' engagement in vertical judicial dialogue with international or regional human rights courts and/or quasi-judicial bodies, or mere reference to the text of international or regional human rights treaties. Figure 3.1 illustrates this scope: the chapter is concerned with the analysis of South American apex courts' decisions in the circle on the left.

The analysed cases were obtained from the database of each supreme or constitutional court's website through keyword searches. The main search conducted in the case law of each jurisdiction was made after finding the term 'human rights' in the text of the decisions. Where the search produced an excessive number of results, further filters were added, such as 'Inter-American' and 'treaties'. Further cases were found with the keywords 'hierarchy', 'international jurisprudence', 'foreign jurisprudence', 'foreign law', 'international tribunals', 'constitutional tribunals', 'foreign tribunals' and 'judicial cooperation'. The possibilities to further filter the searches varied among each jurisdiction. Where the supreme or constitutional tribunal

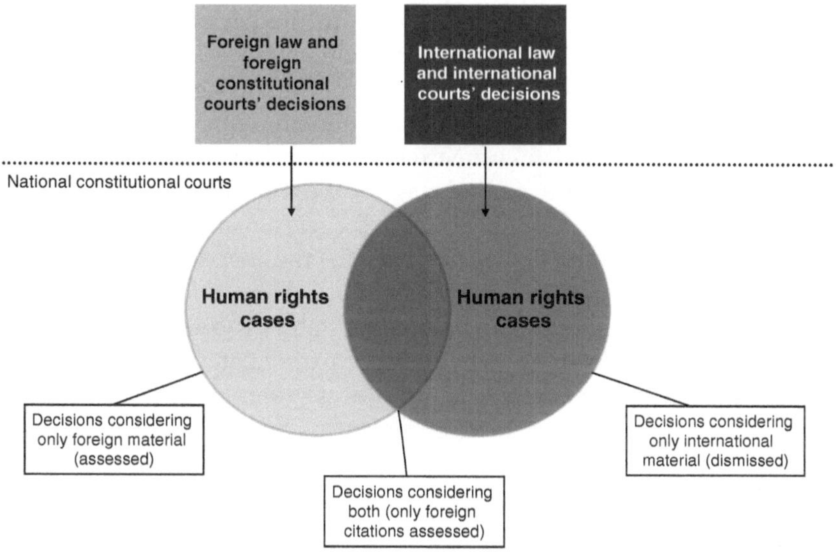

Figure 3.1 Cases Considered

was divided into thematic chambers, the cases from the 'constitutional chamber'[11] were given particular attention. Similarly, where a court's website provided for searches in accordance with the internal classification of the respective court's cases, the option 'constitutional matters' was chosen.[12] In other cases, the search was done on the available database of the court.[13] Where available, the decisions adopted in the period between 1990 and 2012 were analysed; otherwise the analysis started from the date after 1990 when the cases became available.[14]

[11] This was the case of Venezuela. Concerning this country, the searches were only done for cases of the *Sala Constitucional* within the *Tribunal Supremo de Justicia* and aimed for *texto completo* (complete text). See the Annex to this chapter.

[12] Chilean cases were selected from the *Corte Suprema de Justicia* database but restricted to *matéria constitucional* (constitutional issues). For Paraguay, the cases were searched on the *Corte Suprema de Justicia's* website and equally restricted to *matéria constitucional*. For Uruguay, the cases were restricted to *derecho constitucional* (constitutional law) within the database of the *Corte Suprema*.

[13] The cases of Argentina, Bolivia, Brazil, Colombia, Ecuador and Peru were selected through searches on the entire database of each supreme or constitutional court.

[14] Not all constitutional courts make their cases available from 1990. Although all jurisdictions were considered until the end of 2012, the starting dates were the following: Argentina (1990), Bolivia (1994), Brazil (1990), Chile (1990), Colombia (1992), Ecuador (2008), Paraguay (1995), Peru (1996), Uruguay (1990), Venezuela (2000). See the Annex to this chapter for further details.

The total number of cases resulting from the keyword searches was 1,173 for all 10 states.[15] Each case was individually assessed, and those captured by the keyword filters that were not human rights cases (i.e. not dealing with or considering international human rights law or equivalent domestic constitutional law) were excluded from the next stage, resulting in a total of 562 cases. The second stage of the analysis was the coding of the cases. Among many coded variables, the relevant ones for this chapter are the following: (a) the year of decision; (b) the country of origin of the cited material (exclusively the citation of foreign law or foreign decisions, not including factual references to foreign states or foreign policies); (c) the legal right considered; (d) whether the foreign material was 'verifiable' or only 'superficially' considered;[16] and (e) whether the foreign material was used in the majority, separate or dissenting opinion. Of the total relevant cases, 236 (42 per cent) contained a reference to foreign material.

Section 3.3 examines the extent of the dialogue by analysing the collected data (based on the crossing of the aforementioned codes) both qualitatively and quantitatively. The quantitative assessment of constitutional cases elucidates the significance of horizontal judicial dialogue in the South American region, since it gives an overall picture of the practice in relation to the total number of human rights cases. In addition, the quantitative method offers a view of the evolution of the practice over time, making it possible to find associations with particular legal moments such as specific constitutional reforms. The qualitative approach in the second part of Section 3.3 is used to identify whether the majority or the minority of the court used foreign material, and also to assess whether the frequent reliance on foreign material may be associated with specific human rights.

Sections 3.4 and 3.5 analyse the methods employed by judges and courts to find out about relevant foreign law and jurisprudence, and discuss the purposes of dialogue. Section 3.6 adopts a qualitative method to discuss the effects of judicial dialogue on domestic judicial decisions and national law in South America in depth. The individual assessment of each case indicates four different legal effects deriving from the practice of citing

[15] Argentina (86), Bolivia (154), Brazil (107), Chile (87), Colombia (99), Ecuador (144), Paraguay (104), Peru (74), Uruguay (173), Venezuela (145). See Annex for further details.

[16] By 'verifiable' I mean the cases in which the citation or quotation transcribes a section of the foreign law or jurisprudence and/or identifies the source, such as the case number or the law's name and relevant article. The 'superficial' classification refers to the foreign material mentioned generically as part of a group of states with a similar approach to the matter. For instance, when a decision refers to a group of constitutions that have similar norms in relation to a specific matter, or when it refers to a group of states whose courts adopt a certain interpretation, with no mention of the relevant articles or case names.

and engaging with foreign legal material. The classification in Section 3.6 does not follow a strict procedure in which each of the 562 cases was allocated to one of the four categories. Instead, the four categories reflect general trends of the legal effects that foreign jurisprudence can have on the respective domestic legal systems.

3.2 Judicial Dialogue and Constitutional Evolution in South America

Judicial dialogue in South America has been influenced by the recent trend in the region to incorporate international human rights law into domestic law at the constitutional level. As Vicki Jackson reminds us, 'The idea of a constitution is itself one that may seem to invite resistance or indifference to foreign or international law'.[17] Constitutions are documents associated with individual national histories, charged with identifiers and political goals, and the 'expressive components' of constitutions, beyond any rhetorical purpose, may serve as differentiators.[18] As the argument goes, 'if part of their very purpose is … to express how one national group differs from all others', the resistance to external references may be a natural consequence.[19] However, not all constitutions develop insulated from foreign influence. On the contrary, there are constitutions that are explicitly developed with the influence of other constitutional documents and/or international human rights law. Once established, these constitutions may be more receptive to the jurisprudence construed in the 'exporter' state or by international human rights courts or quasi-judicial bodies.[20] Inversely, older and traditional constitutional schools may be more likely to adopt interpretive theories such as originalism, and may consequently show more resistance to foreign influence.[21]

The influence of the Spanish, Portuguese (in the case of Brazil) and US constitutions was particularly important in the development of constitutionalism in South America in the early years following independence in the nineteenth century. In some cases, this influence remains relevant

[17] V. Jackson, *Constitutional Engagement in a Transnational Era* (Oxford University Press, 2013) at 20.

[18] *Ibid.*, at 19.

[19] *Ibid.*

[20] Rosenkratz, Against Borrowings, *supra* note 5, at 278.

[21] Jackson, Constitutional Engagement, *supra* note 17, at 20. Some scholars sustain the view that comparativism may even diminish human rights standards in countries with a tradition of human rights compliance. See e.g. R. P. Alford, 'Misusing International Sources to Interpret the Constitution', *Am. J. Int'l of L.* 98:1 (2004) 57–69, at 67.

today. Moreover, recent transformations, either through constitutional amendments or through the adoption of entirely new constitutions, force constitutional interpreters to expand their horizons. These recent transformations led to the incorporation of international and regional human rights treaties ranked at the level of the domestic constitution in each of the ten legal systems examined in this chapter. These incorporations represent a dramatic transformation of the way in which international and foreign law is perceived in these legal systems.[22]

Direct incorporation of international human rights law requires contextual interpretation of the relevant international and regional conventions, notably the American Convention on Human Rights (ACHR).[23] To achieve this, South American judges openly use legal comparison as a method of legal interpretation.[24] In other words, national judges seem to react to the process of internationalisation of domestic law through their engagement in judicial dialogue. They need to decide issues that are no longer exclusively part of domestic law, taking on an international function of human rights adjudication, which they assimilate with their domestic legal competences. South American courts are thus taking part in the creation of principles, rules and legal concepts 'rooted in shared national norms and emerging international norms, that have similar or identical meaning in every national system'.[25]

The incorporation of regional and international human rights treaties in South American domestic legal systems is paralleled by the increase in the number of these treaties after the end of the Cold War. This has also contributed to the expansion of horizontal judicial dialogue in the field of human rights in the region, particularly so considering that often, human rights treaties are intended to be enforceable as domestic law,[26] leaving a complementary or subsidiary role for regional and international fora.[27]

22 The engagement in judicial dialogue has been associated with judges embracing a 'more internationalist attitude' and their readiness to 'assimilate the national and the international interest, and seek to converse with an international audience'. Y. Shany, 'National Courts as International Actors: Jurisdictional Implications' *Rivista di Diritto Pubblico Italiano, Comunitario e Comparato* 15:1 (2009) 1–31, at 30.

23 American Convention on Human Rights (20 November 1969) 1144 UNTS 123, entered into force 18 July 1978.

24 See E. V. Foruria, 'Métodos y Principios de Interpretación Constitucional. Un Catálogo de Problemas', *Revista de Derecho Constitucional Europeo* 13:1 (2010) 379–414, at 379–85.

25 H. H. Koh, 'The Globalization of Freedom', *Yale J. Int'l L.* 26:305 (2001) 305–12, at 306.

26 E.g. article 2(2) ICCPR; article 2(1) ICESCR; article 2 ACHR.

27 This complementary/subsidiary role of regional human rights courts in relation to domestic courts also flows from the exhaustion of domestic remedies rule found in e.g. article 35(1) ECHR and article 46(1)(a) ACHR.

For example, at the regional level, the ACHR entitles individuals, groups or non-governmental entities to lodge petitions with the Inter-American Commission on Human Rights (IACHR). Only a small part of the complaints is transferred to the Inter-American Court of Human Rights (IACtHR).[28] In this context, national courts are crucial to securing rights set out in regional and international human rights treaties. When domestic courts are willing and able to take on this task of enforcing international treaties, the range of their legal references will inevitably increase. This will favour the search for developed or paradigmatic jurisprudence from foreign states where such international-domesticated law has already been interpreted in more detail over a longer period.

To summarise, constitutional design may open national legal systems to the world and thus stimulate the use of foreign material in the domestic interpretation of internalised international material. In South American countries, this is particularly prevalent, as international human rights law has been incorporated into domestic law at the constitutional level, so that its interpretation and application have become part of South American supreme or constitutional courts' mandates. This stimulates judges to search for foreign references of domestic interpretation of international human rights law. In addition, the limited capacity of the IACtHR to absorb individual complaints invites supreme and constitutional courts in the region to act in a more internationalised fashion. As shown in the following analysis, Latin American courts frequently seek to embed their decisions in the human rights law in the region, and they do so through comparison with and references to foreign jurisprudence. The extent, method, purpose and effects of this judicial dialogue are analysed in more detail in the following sections.

[28] In 2010 the IACHR evaluated 1676 petitions. Out of those cases, 275 were declared admissible. In the same year, 16 cases were submitted to the ICtAHR (IACHR, Annual Report of the Inter-American Commission on Human Rights 2010 (2011), OEA/Ser.L/V/II. Doc. 5, rev. 1). The annual average was even smaller in previous years, as 'the Court [IACtHR] received not a single case between 1979 and 1986, the first seven years of its operation, it received seven cases between 1986 and 1993, and thirty-two cases between 1994 and 2001. In the three-year period between 2001 and 2004, the Court received twenty-nine cases, a doubling of the rate immediately prior to the 2000 amendment to the Commission's Rules of Procedure.' See: T. J. Melish, 'The Inter-American Court of Human Rights: Beyond Progressivity', M. Langford (ed.), *Social Rights Jurisprudence: Emerging Trends in International and Comparative Law* (Cambridge University Press, 2008) 372–409, at 185, fn 43; and D. Sloss, *The Role of Domestic Courts in Treaty Enforcement: a Comparative Study* (Cambridge University Press, 2009) at 2.

3.3 The Extent of Judicial Dialogue in South American Courts

Employing the comparative method allows us to discern whether various South American states' engagement with foreign sources follows specific national standards or whether it is possible to talk about regional characteristics of judicial dialogue. This section discusses the number of cases in which foreign material is referred to in apex court decisions in the region, as well as the variation of such practice over time. Judicial dialogue will also be measured in relation to who employs such materials (the majority or minority of the respective courts). Following that, an analysis of individual cases with a great number of foreign references will be conducted. This analysis aims to detect whether any preference for the comparative method exists in regard to some specific topic(s) and/or specific human right(s).

The evaluation of the adoption of foreign sources in judicial decisions of South American courts during the last two decades reinforces the claim that courts worldwide have increasingly adopted legal considerations that are external to their respective jurisdictions. In the case of the countries at hand, the data also suggest a causal relationship between the aforementioned constitutional reforms or judicial interpretations that give international human rights treaties the status of constitutional law and the increase in national courts' engagement in judicial dialogue in the region.

3.3.1 The Frequency of Judicial Dialogue

The frequency with which South American courts resort to foreign law and jurisprudence in human rights cases shows a reasonable degree of similarity (see Figure 3.2, marking 10 year average trends). Most courts relied on foreign material in 30–50 per cent of the cases. Bolivia (59 per cent) and Venezuela (15 per cent) are the exceptions to both ends of the spectrum.

In spite of the textual openness of the Venezuelan Constitution towards international law, notably human rights treaties,[29] during the last decade, the country and its courts have been undergoing a process that is inverse to those of most other states and their courts in the region. In fact, in the face of external political pressure, the Venezuelan government and judiciary have become increasingly critical of international decisions, including those regarding human rights. Venezuela has systematically criticised

[29] Treaties, pacts and conventions relating to human rights that have been ratified by Venezuela have a constitutional rank, and thus prevail over internal legislation. See: Constitución de la República de Venezuela, 20 December 1999, article 23.

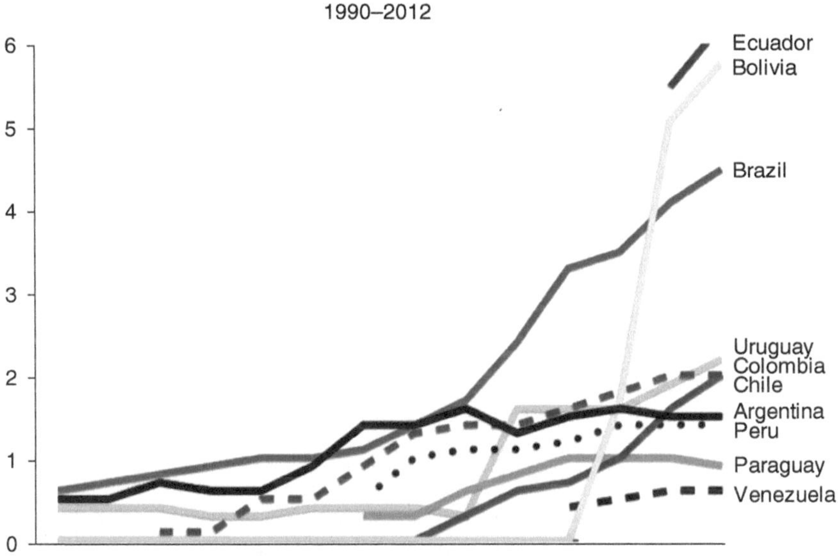

Figure 3.2 Average Number of Cases Referring to Foreign Law/Jurisprudence per State (10 years average, from 1990 to 2012)

the decisions of the IACtHR, and ultimately withdrew from the jurisdiction of the Court and subsequently from the ACHR in 2012.[30] In this context, domestic courts' references to external material in legal decisions would probably provoke further criticism from the Venezuelan executive and legislative branches, and make these decisions vulnerable to political review.

As for Bolivia, its Constitutional Tribunal saw a high increase in the number of cases in 2009, the same year that the country adopted a new constitution formally establishing the 'constitutional bloc'. The 'constitutional bloc' includes human rights treaties ratified by Bolivia and directly incorporated into domestic law at the same level as the Bolivian Constitution.[31] Consequently, many litigants sought to explore and assert the pre-eminence of human rights treaties in relation to domestic law before Bolivian courts, including the Bolivian Constitutional Tribunal.[32] These cases included a backlog of claims filed before 2009,

[30] See: 'Venezuela Denounces American Convention on Human Rights as IACHR Faces Reform', available at www.ijrcenter.org/2012/09/19/venezuela-denounces-american-convention-on-human-rights-as-iachr-faces-reform/.

[31] Bolivia, Constitucíon Política del Estado de Bolivia, 9 February 2009, article 410 (II).

[32] R. B. Guzmán, 'Los Derechos Fundamentales. La Constitución y los Tratados en el Ordenamiento Jurídico de Bolivia', *Ius et Praxis* 9:1 (2003) 193–200.

which now had to be assessed under the new regime. In this context, the high number of cases and the proportionally higher number of foreign references may be a temporary phenomenon at this stage of adjustment, and not necessarily representative of a regular national practice. In addition, a further element may contribute to the high number of results from Bolivia. In cases that deal with similar issues, parts of the actual texts of the Constitutional Tribunal's decisions are identical. It is not clear whether this is a common practice or the result of the accumulation of cases in the mentioned period.[33] Nonetheless, entire sections of decisions are identical – but not cited as precedents – and some of these repeated extracts contained foreign references. This inflates the number of cases with such references.

3.3.2 *The Evolution of Judicial Dialogue*

South America serves as an example of a more general trend that the reliance on foreign and international law and jurisprudence is increasing worldwide.[34] A closer look at the collected data shows that there is a direct correlation between giving domestic pre-eminence to international human rights law as constitutional law and the increasing use of foreign material.

Figure 3.2 shows this trend in relation to each state on an average ten-year period.[35] It reveals how the use of foreign sources in human rights constitutional adjudication evolved from the moment the data is available until the end of 2012. The frequency – on average – of foreign citations has not only increased consistently with time; the graph also suggests that there is an increase in the number of cases referring to foreign material in the period following constitutional reforms in the various countries. In other words, the abrupt change in the trend of using

33 Many constitutional courts, even when accumulating competences of appellant courts for constitutional violations in ordinary cases and abstract considerations of constitutional infringement by legal acts, have mechanisms to select representative cases and thus avoid repetitive litigation at this level. This was not the case for Bolivia, at least during this initial period under the new Constitution.

34 Posner and Sunstein, The Law of Other States, *supra* note 1, at 135 ('Consultation of the foreign law seems to be the rule, not the exception').

35 Trend lines are imprecise as to the exact number of cases in each year. Instead, it allows a general view of evolving averages in each jurisdiction. Thus, the initial marks of the graph in Figure 3.2 show that the average number of cases referring to foreign material in Brazil, Argentina and Uruguay from 1990 until 2000 was less than one per country per year. The last marks, on the opposite side, indicate the average between 2002 and 2012.

foreign sources in Bolivia is clearly a response to the new constitutional openness towards international human rights law. Between 1994 and 2009, none of the ten cases in which human rights issues were discussed by the Bolivian court contained a reference to foreign sources. From 2010 until the end of 2012, there were 89 cases referencing international human rights law sources, and 59 per cent of them also considered foreign material.

A similar transformation can also be observed in respect to Uruguay in the period following the Supreme Court's first decision of 1997, which established that international norms of superior rank must trump domestic legislation. Despite the non-existence of a clear constitutional norm stipulating the hierarchy of international human rights law in domestic law and adjudication, the Court implemented the doctrine of superiority by referring to neighbouring Argentina, which since 1994 had explicitly constitutionalised the superior rank of international human rights law in its domestic legal system.[36]

Colombia is another example of this correlation. In 1995, the Supreme Court of Colombia implemented the aforementioned theory of the 'constitutional bloc'. The Court stated that 'the only reasonable meaning to be conferred to the notion of priority of international human rights and international humanitarian law [by the Colombian Constitution[37]] … is that they form, together with the remaining articles of the Constitution, a "bloc of constitutionality", which imposes authority over the [domestic] law'.[38] The subsequent jurisprudence of Colombia reinforced, polished and even exported this doctrine.[39] The period following the adoption of the 'constitutional bloc' also saw the expansion of vertical judicial dialogue on human rights.

Finally, Brazil shows a constant progression in the number of cases considering foreign materials. This trend was reinforced by the 2004

36 Suprema Corte de Justicia (Uruguay), Casación nº 418, 17 December 1997.

37 Article 93 of the Colombian Constitution establishes that 'rights and duties mentioned in this Charter will be interpreted in accordance with international treaties on human rights ratified by Colombia', and article 214 (2) states that human rights and fundamental liberties cannot be suspended except when regulated by law.

38 Corte Constitucional (Colombia), *Revisión constitucional*, Sentencia C-225/95, 18 May 1995, para. 12.

39 The Bolivian tribunals adopted the controversial concept of the 'constitutional bloc' years before it was formally inserted into the constitutional text of 2009, openly inspired by the Colombian jurisprudence. See e.g. Tribunal Constitucional de Bolivia (Bolivia), Recurso Directo de Inconstitucionalidad, *Luis Eduardo Siles Pérez*, Sentencia Constitucional nº 0045/2006, Sala Plena, Expediente 2005-12440-25-RDI, 2 June 2006.

constitutional reform, which explicitly granted constitutional status to all ratified human rights treaties.[40]

3.3.3 *Judicial Dialogue in Majority Judgments and Minority Opinions*

As Figure 3.3 shows, the use of foreign material in South American domestic courts is more frequent in the votes of the majority of the respective courts than in minority opinions. Once again, Bolivia is an exception to this rule. The dissenting opinions in the Bolivian Tribunal relied repetitively on the Colombian Constitutional Court's interpretation of the application of the *pro homine* principle. These dissenting opinions held that the Bolivian Tribunal should 'apply the more comprehensive norm or interpretation when it comes to recognising rights' protected by the Constitution and by international law, and 'adopt the most restrictive interpretation when it comes to setting restrictions' to fundamental rights.[41] Despite the inflation of references to foreign material arising from the issue of identical reasoning in different cases discussed above (this also applies to dissenting opinions), the dissenting opinions' insistence on foreign decisions may be seen as part of a strategy of the Bolivian Tribunal's minority to change a predominant view or doctrine over time.

Although the frequency of dissenting opinions may depend on the respective court's culture and structure of the elaboration of votes, the presence of foreign and international material in a great number of both majority and dissenting opinions signals that judicial dialogue is not contested as a method of interpretation. The case of Argentina is emblematic, as this is one of the most internationalised courts in the region, with strong reliance on international human rights law and international courts' jurisprudence. Indeed, in 23 per cent of the Argentine cases where foreign material is used, it is found in both the majority and the dissenting opinions. Foreign material is no longer a 'wild card' in the argumentation and justification of a decision. Instead, both competing views may find support

[40] Constitution of Brazil (1988), article 5(3): 'International human rights treaties and conventions which are approved in each House of the National Congress, in two rounds of voting, by three fifths of the votes of the respective members shall be equivalent to constitutional amendments'.

[41] Among many see: Tribunal Constitucional de Bolivia (Bolivia), Sentencia Constitucional 2334/2010-R, Revisión nº 2334, Expediente: 2008-17607-36-RHC, 19 November 2010; Sentencia Constitucional 0221/2011-R, Revisión nº 0221, Expediente:2009-19965-40-AL, 11 March 2011; and Sentencia Constitucional 1321/2011-R, Revisión nº 1321, Expediente: 2010-21993-44-AL, 26 September 2011.

in the foreign arena. The discussion of different views based on foreign references is also common in majority and dissenting opinions of Chilean courts. For instance, the Constitutional Tribunal of Chile was asked to assess article 365 of the Chilean Criminal Code,[42] which criminalises consensual male homosexual relationships when involving a minor. It had to evaluate whether this provision violates the dignity and right to privacy of the involved persons, and whether it is discriminatory against male homosexuals. The Tribunal was divided. The majority found no violation of the Chilean Constitution and upheld the prohibition. The point to be emphasised in this decision is that both the majority and the minority of the Tribunal carefully considered the jurisprudence and legislation of many foreign states. The majority referred to the application of the international principle of the best interests of the child as recognised by Colombian Constitutional Court jurisprudence.[43] In relation to the right to privacy, it referred to the Brazilian Supreme Court's view that 'the inviolability of intimacy is not an absolute right to be used as a guarantee for the practice of sexual crimes'.[44] Further, it discussed the European Human Rights Court (ECtHR) case *X and Y v. the Netherlands*,[45] citing the ECtHR's conclusion that the respondent state was in violation of the European Convention on Human Rights (ECHR)[46] because the Dutch Criminal Code did not provide practical and effective protection to the claimant.[47]

The minority's opinion summarised legislation and decisions from national and international tribunals in a section of the judgment entitled 'The International Standards'. It stated that 'the examination of comparative law and international instruments on the matter allows us to conclude that today the criminalisation of consented sodomy has been declared unconstitutional in many states, as have the rules establishing the age of consent in relation to sexual relations among persons of the same sex.'[48] The minority opinion arrived at its conclusion of unconstitutionality after considering cases of the South African Constitutional Court, the Austrian

[42] Chile, Codigo Penal (Penal Code), 12 November 1874, article 365.

[43] Corte Constitucional (Colombia), *Revisión constitucional de la Ley 765 de 2002*, Sentencia C-318/03, Sala Plena, 24 April 2003.

[44] Supremo Tribunal Federal (Barzil), *Silvan Guedes v. Superior Tribunal Militar*, Habeas Corpus nº 79285-RJ, 31 August 1999.

[45] *X and Y v. The Netherlands* (Appl. No. 8978/80), Judgment (Chamber), 23 March 1985, Series A, Vol.91.

[46] Convention on the Protection of Human Rights and Fundamental Freedoms (4 November 1950) 213 UNTS 222; 312 ETS 5, entered into force 18 May 1954.

[47] Tribunal Constitucional (Chile), nº 1683-10, 11 January 2011, s. 30 and 39.

[48] *Ibid.*, s. 5.

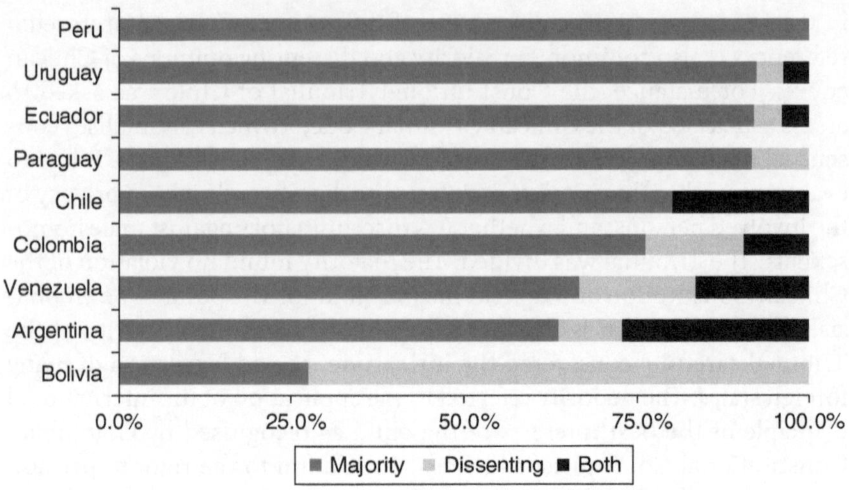

Figure 3.3 Majority vs. Dissenting Opinions Considering Foreign Material in Constitutional Court Decisions

Constitutional Tribunal, the US Supreme Court, the Indian High Court and the ECtHR.[49] As to legislative practices, it mentioned a 'tendency not to consider sexual identity as criteria for defining punishment regarding specific sexual practices' as seen in the laws of Argentina, Brazil, Ecuador, Honduras, Mexico, Paraguay, Peru and Uruguay.[50]

3.3.4 *The Correlation between Specific Rights and the Extent of Judicial Dialogue*

When assessed individually, the cases with the largest number of cited foreign references suggest that some rights may stimulate the respective court's engagement in judicial dialogue more than others do. This section takes a closer look at a few cases from each analysed jurisdiction with the greatest number of references to foreign material. In half of the jurisdictions, cases involving freedom of expression and the related 'right to reply' that is specific to the region were among those with the most foreign references. Unlike in other international and regional human rights treaties, the right to reply is treated as a distinct right in article 14 of the ACHR and aims to protect the honour and reputation of individuals 'injured by

[49] *Ibid.*
[50] *Ibid.*

inaccurate or offensive statements or ideas disseminated to the public in general by a legally regulated medium of communication'.[51]

Concerning Argentina, the three cases with the highest number of foreign material concerned the right to freedom of expression. Two of them discuss the right to reply, and cite 38 and 16 different jurisdictions, respectively.[52] The third case deals with the right to access state-held information, citing material from 20 different foreign jurisdictions.[53] Venezuela, which has a low record of judicial dialogue, also has two freedom-of-expression cases that cite six and seven foreign jurisdictions, respectively.[54] Likewise, Paraguay, Chile and Bolivia's freedom-of-expression cases are among those that attracted the highest number of cited foreign material.[55]

The second issue that attracts a large number of foreign references is that of crimes against humanity, sometimes treated specifically under the crime of forced disappearance.[56] Finally, a third topic that appears to stimulate foreign comparison in Latin American courts is cases involving the rights of homosexuals. Cases discussing equal treatment for homosexuals generated a wide comparative assessment in two Chilean cases, each of them referring to 22 different jurisdictions,[57] in Colombia one case with

[51] See also the IACtHR, Enforceability of the Right to Reply or Correction, Advisory Opinion, OC-7/86 of 29 August 1986.

[52] Corte Suprema de Justicia de la Nación (Argentina), *Ekmekdjian v. Sofovich y otros*, Recurso Extraordinario, nº E. 64. XXIII, 315 Fallos 1492, 7 July 1992; and *Petric, Domagoj, Antonio c/ diario Página 12*, nº P.534.XXXI, 16 April 1998.

[53] Corte Suprema de Justicia de la Nación (Argentina), *S., V. c/ M., D.A.* s/medidas precautorias, nº S. 622 XXXIII, 3 April 2001.

[54] Tribunal Supremo de Justicia (Venezuela), *Recurso de Nulidad de Bloque de Prensa Venezolano (BPV) y Andrés De Armas Silva y Eduardo Alemán Pérez*, Sentencia nº 00-1445, Sala Constitucional, 27 July 2004; and *Asociación Civil Espacio Público v. Contraloría General de la República Bolivariana de Venezuela*, Acción de amparo constitucional nº 09-1003, Sala Constitucional, 15 July 2010.

[55] Corte Suprema de Justicia (Paraguay), *Radio Ñanduti S.A. v. Artículos 305 Y 329 de la ley N° 834/1996, Código Electoral*, Acuerdo y Sentencia nº 1287, Sala Constitucional de la Corte Suprema, 3 December 2007; and Tribunal Constitucional (Chile), *Requerimiento de Inaplicabilidad Por Inconstitucionalidad de Andrade y Vignau*, Sentencia Rol nº 2153-2011 INA, 11 September 2012; and Tribunal Constitucional de Bolivia (Bolivia), *Acción de Inconstitucionalidad de Verónica Laura Guiteras Aramayo*, Sentencia Constitucional Plurinacional, 1250/2012, Sala Plena, Expediente 00130-2012-01-AIC, 20 September 2012.

[56] Forced disappearance is a politically relevant topic in the region, as this type of crime was committed by most of the military regimes in the region. Thus, some of the cases would refer to or apply the specific Inter-American Convention on this issue (Inter-American Convention on the Forced Disappearance of Persons (9 June 1994), A-60, entered into force 28 March 1996).

[57] Tribunal Constitucional (Chile), *Requerimiento de Inaplicabilidad por Inconstitucionalidad de Sepúlveda Álvarez*, Sentencia Rol 1683-10-INA nº 1683-10, 4 January 2011; and *Wetzel, Antonio, y otros v. Soto Silva*, Sentencia Rol n° 1881-10-INA, 3 November 2011.

references to 25 jurisdictions[58] and in Uruguay two cases with references to two and four jurisdictions, respectively.[59]

The frequency with which a court engages in some horizontal judicial dialogue is disproportionate to the number of actual references to external material. The human rights issue at hand seems to determine whether the number of actual references will be high. For example, 39 per cent of all cases analysed in this chapter concerned due process rights and guarantees. However, when the number of foreign citations in those cases is considered, it becomes clear that there are only very few such references in each case and their effect on the actual decisions of South American courts is limited. This is even clearer if due process rights cases are compared with the cases involving freedom of expression/right of reply, the rights of homosexuals and crimes against humanity, which make up only 5, 2.5 and 1.5 per cent, respectively, of all cases analysed in this chapter. Nonetheless, these cases were among those that stimulated the highest number of references to foreign material in individual decisions.

How can this be explained? For instance, when dealing with issues that could not have been predicted by those who wrote the original constitutional text or other legal document, the use of foreign reference may prove worthwhile.[60] Indeed, academics have argued that judicial dialogue is particularly useful when domestic law seems to provide no clear answer, or when the scope of a right in international human rights law is unclear.[61] This may explain the search for foreign references in cases involving rights of homosexuals. Most countries' jurisprudence on these rights is recent,[62] and not even the IACtHR has thus far provided sufficient

[58] Corte Constitucional (Colombia), *Demanda de inconstitucionalidad de Carlos Andrés Echeverry Restrepo y otros*, Sentencia C-577/11, Sala Plena, 26 July 2011.

[59] Suprema Corte de Justicia (Uruguay), *Marabotto [r], Cairoli, Torello, Alonso de Marco y Mariño*, Acción de reclamación de identidad sexual nº 139, 5 May 1997.

[60] It has been suggested that an originalist view in constitutional interpretation is less appealing than an internationalist position which 'focuses on the usefulness of an integrated legal interpretation' in cases dealing with modern legal challenges, such as terrorism. C. Marian, 'Learning from Others: The Scalia-Breyer Debate and the Benefits of Foreign Sources of Law to U.S. Constitutional Interpretation of Counter-Terrorism Initiatives', *Vienna Online J. on Int'l Const. L.* 4:1 (2010) 5–19, at 5 and 8.

[61] T. H. Bingham, *Widening Horizons: The Influence of Comparative Law and International Law on Domestic Law* (Cambridge University Press, 2010) at 8 ('there are perhaps two situations in which foreign authority may exert a significant if not a decisive influence. One is where domestic authority points towards an answer that seems inappropriate or unjust. The other is where domestic authority appears to yield no clear answer'.). See also the discussion below, sections 5 and 6.

[62] See also the analysis in Chapter 7 of this volume.

guidance on the matter. By contrast, due process rights, although present in the International Covenant on Civil and Political Rights (ICCPR)[63] and the ACHR, are explicitly embedded in domestic law. Comparison in these cases may not be as helpful, since the regulation of due process rights within domestic law is well developed. Thus, the less developed a human right is within domestic law, and the more open questions there are on the balancing of different interests, the more likely it is that domestic courts will enter into a judicial dialogue.

The more frequent search for foreign and international material in areas such as freedom of expression and crimes against humanity could also be explained by the recent importance that these issues have obtained in the region. Both topics have been the subject of many cases before the IACHR and the IACtHR, and at least the former has received attention from domestic courts for many years.

It is also clear that the aforementioned recent constitutional transformations in the region that made international human rights law a direct part of national law lie behind the increased reliance on foreign jurisprudence in these areas by South American courts. The accumulated jurisprudence of the Inter-American System might not be sufficient to provide all the necessary references for domestic courts to effectively solve a case before them involving the rights of homosexuals or freedom of expression. This provokes Latin American courts to assess human rights cases in light of not only their own domestic law and the law of the ACHR, but also in the interpretation and application of the relevant rights by other national courts. A reasonable move, notably when the contextual similarities exist, is to rely on the interpretation given by distinct domestic constitutional courts that are bound by the same international treaties.

3.3.5 The Most Cited Jurisdictions

This subsection analyses the origin of the foreign cases and legislation cited by South American judges and courts. The purpose is to identify which jurisdictions have the most influence on South American law and jurisprudence. Each foreign jurisdiction has been counted only once per case in which it is mentioned, regardless of the number of cases or the references to the same foreign legislation, cited in a single case.

[63] International Covenant on Civil and Political Rights (16 December 1966) 999 UNTS 171, entered into force 14 June 1998.

Spain is the most cited country overall. Jurisprudence and legislation from Spain were mentioned in 79 cases (10 per cent between 1990 and 2012) spread throughout the ten assessed jurisdictions in South America. The second most cited jurisdiction is Colombia (9.1 per cent), followed by the USA (8.1 per cent), Germany (7.6 per cent) and Argentina (7.1 per cent).[64] Colombia is particularly influential among its closest neighbours. It is the most cited jurisdiction in Ecuador, Bolivia and Venezuela. In addition, Argentinian jurisprudence and legislation are frequently referred to by its neighbours, particularly Paraguay and Uruguay.

If we consider the two most influential regions of the world in the formation of South American domestic jurisprudence: inter-Latin American citations and references to decisions of European domestic courts make up 86 per cent of all citations by South American courts. But when Spain – which is understandably influential as the former colonial empire for all assessed countries except Brazil – is removed from this account, inter-Latin American references become the most dominant. This is despite the relative younger constitutional legal tradition in the region, and the limited experience South American courts have with the interpretation and application of national and international human rights law, when compared to 'global favourites' such as the United States, the United Kingdom, Germany, France and Italy.[65]

3.4 The Method of Transnational Judicial Dialogue in South America

This section turns to the question of the judicial dialogue method in South America. It inquires how courts and judges in the region find out about relevant foreign and international jurisprudence. As argued earlier, the internalisation of the main international and regional human rights instruments by South American states as constitutional law stimulates courts and judges in the region to look for the application of the same treaty by a peer court. Furthermore, judgments in the region have a 'generally discursive' style, and they use non-legislative sources of law such as domestic and international academic work as well as national and foreign jurisprudence, as they constitute a legitimate 'form of comparative

[64] See full table with all jurisdictions mentioned in the cases assessed in the Annex of this chapter.

[65] The frequency of inter-Latin-American dialogue reflects not only the common legal and historical elements discussed earlier but also the method by which judicial dialogue is implemented in the region as discussed in Section 3.4.

legal reasoning'.[66] This tradition favours a practice whereby judges look for relevant comparative material. In this process, South American courts familiarise themselves more and more with relevant foreign cases while deciding their own cases. As will be elaborated later in the chapter,[67] in some situations the cited case might be so relevant and well known that the courts feel almost compelled to discuss it. In most cases, however, it is likely that the citations are a product of judges (or their law clerks) searching for related and relevant foreign cases on the basis of which they engage in comparative reflections.

The method of finding relevant foreign cases can also take informal forms. Ran Hirschl has recently exposed an example of such an informal process of selecting foreign jurisprudence: once a law clerk working for a UK Supreme Court Justice contacted him in Canada, seeking information about how a similar issue in Israel had been discussed.[68] Such informal conversations likely also take place between South American judges who are linked up through various networks.

These established networks constitute another medium or 'method' through which Latin American courts and judges find out about relevant foreign material. As discussed elsewhere in this book, judicial dialogue is associated with aspects of modernity, such as the facilitation of communication and access to information, including translated material.[69] In the following, it is shown that in South America, the real-time, face-to-face interaction between judges through consolidated networks plays an important role in strengthening the relationships between judges and substantially increases their propensity to rely on decisions issued by their peers.

South America has seen an intense process of institutional integration, which brings along conferences and other meetings of judges where views

[66] H. P. Glenn, 'Comparative Legal Reasoning and the Courts: A View from the Americas', G. Canivet, M. Andenas and D. Fairgrieve (eds.), *Comparative Law Before the Courts* (London: British Institute of International and Comparative Law, 2004) 217–28, at 222.

[67] See *infra* section 5.4.

[68] R. Hirschl, 'Politicising Law, Judicialising Politics: A Realist Approach to Comparative Constitutionalism', *FLJS Annual Lecture in Law and Society*, Annual Lecture held in association with the Centre for Socio-Legal Studies, University of Oxford, Thursday, 20 May 2010, Magdalen College, Oxford, podcast available at www.fljs.org/content/politicizing-law-judicializing-politics-realist-approach-comparative-constitutionalism-0. Cf. *R (E) v Governing Body of JFS and the Admissions Appeal Panel of JFS and others*, [2009] UKSC 15 & 1 (United Kingdom, Supreme Court), referring to the decision HCJ 1967/08 (Israel, Supreme Court). See also the observations by Lord Carnwath in this volume (8.1).

[69] See e.g. Chapter 1 in this volume.

on common legal issues are exchanged. At the global level, the World Conference on Constitutional Justice was established. Among its statutory objectives is the promotion of the 'exchange of experiences and case law within the regional and linguistic groups, between them and with individual members'.[70] The World Conference is a relatively recent enterprise (it was founded in 2009), and its creation was sponsored by the Venice Commission of the Council of Europe.[71] Its second meeting was held in Rio de Janeiro in 2011. One of the purposes of this meeting was to enable interaction among judges in order 'to draw inspiration … from their peers in other countries'.[72] According to the Venice Commission's Annual Report of 2011, conversations among judges 'may provide the moral support necessary [for judges] to remain faithful to the[ir] Constitution even in difficult situations'. The report also notes that by referring to each other's case law, judges 'can give an added legitimacy to a judgement'.[73]

At the regional level, there is the already well-established Permanent Forum of Supreme Courts of Mercosur, which has held its ninth meeting since it was established in 2004.[74] The Forum's purposes include the promotion of cooperation among member states' courts and tribunals, the support for exchange programs with courts in non-member states, regional groups or supranational organisations and the sharing of legal decisions that apply or relate to Mercosur's laws.[75] In addition, there are two other organisations whose membership is based on linguistic and geographic criteria and that promote contacts between Latin American

[70] The World Conference on Constitutional Justice congregates 62 constitutional courts and equivalent bodies, such as Constitutional Councils, Supreme Courts exercising constitutional jurisdiction and Constitutional Chambers. The current membership composition has Brazil, Chile and Peru as the South American participant courts.

[71] See the preamble of the Statute of the World Conference on Constitutional Justice, 23 May 2011, available at www.venice.coe.int/WebForms/pages/?p=02_WCCJ.

[72] The Second Conference's theme was 'Separation of Powers and Independence of Constitutional Courts and Equivalent Bodies' (16–18 January 2011). Eighty-eight constitutional and supreme courts and 10 regional groups were participating. The information, presented papers and programme are available at www.venice.coe.int/WCCJ/WCCJ_Rio_E.asp.

[73] European Commission for Democracy through Law – The Venice Commission of the Council of Europe, Annual Report of Activities 2011, at 19, available at www.venice.coe.int/WebForms/documents/?pdf=CDL-RA(2011)001-e.

[74] The Permanent Forum of Supreme Courts of Mercosur was created by the *Carta de Brasília*, Declaration of November 2004, available at www.cortesmercosul.jus.br.

[75] The initiative of sharing jurisprudence has resulted in the adoption of the 'Cooperation Agreement for the Exchange of Information and Publications through the Mercosur Jurisprudence Database' (2007). According to the agreement, state parties provide domestic jurisprudence related to the Mercosur treaties and respective national laws to be made available at www.cortesmercosul.jus.br/forum/jurisprudencia/pesquisarJurisprudencia .asp.

judges. The first is the Ibero-American Conference on Constitutional Justice, which includes all constitutional courts (or equivalent courts responsible for interpreting the constitution) of Portuguese- and Spanish-speaking states.[76] This association also has among its objectives to promote a 'close, continuous and fluid relationship', the 'exchange of information' and 'networks for knowledge management and exchange of experiences' between the organs of constitutional justice in Ibero-American countries.[77] The second is the Conference of Portuguese Language Constitutional Jurisdictions (CPLCJ), inaugurated in 2008. This organisation of judicial and jurisprudential cooperation seeks to promote 'human rights, democracy and judicial independence' and to stimulate 'the exchange of judicial review experiences' between its members.[78]

One could argue that the choice of participating in such organisations is already a sign of approval of and adherence to the practice of judicial dialogue. Despite the increased possibilities of engagement with foreign and international material via the Internet, the frequency and variety of encounters through these networks undoubtedly expose judges to contextual material and allow the building of personal affinities with other judges and jurisdictions. For instance, there is no question that a lecture on 'The Constitutional Gender Doctrine' by the Chief Justice of the Constitutional Court of Costa Rica given at the 2011 meeting of the Ibero-American Conference on Constitutional Justice[79] offered information, views and opportunities for debate that go beyond what internet-based research on comparative material can offer. The same can be said for a discussion on 'Public Hearings in Abstract Judicial Review in Chile' presented by a Chilean Supreme Court justice at the Second World Conference on Constitutional Justice.[80]

[76] The Ibero-American Conference has 22 member courts (including the 10 South American states included in this research) and was officially created in 2005. It held the ninth meeting in May 2012. More information is available at www.cijc.org/acercaCIJC/es-ES/Paginas/default.aspx.

[77] *Ibid.*

[78] Charter of the Conference of Portuguese Language Constitutional Jurisdictions (2011), article 2, available at www.venice.coe.int/CJCA/CJCA_Statute_E.pdf. The Conference is composed by the constitutional tribunals of Angola and Portugal, Supreme Courts of Brazil, Cape Verde, Guinea-Bissau and S. Tome and Principe, Mozambique's Constitutional Council and the Court of Appeal of Timor-Leste.

[79] See the programme of the 2011 meeting of the Ibero-American Conference on Constitutional Justice, La Antigua, Guatemala, available at www.cijc.org/actividades/SeminarioAntiguaGuatemala/Paginas/programa.aspx.

[80] Justice Marisol Peña Torres, paper presented at the II World Conference on Constitutional Justice (2011), available at <http://www.venice.coe.int/WCCJ/Rio/Papers/CHI_Penna%20Torres_ESP.pdf> accessed 02/03/2013.

Furthermore, the institutionalisation of meetings and conferences produces ancillary services that are now available to judges and courts of the region, directly responding to their needs. The CPLCJ, for instance, implemented an integrated website that allows searching for thematic jurisprudence of all member states.[81] Moreover, some domestic courts in the region have decided to translate their most important decisions into English, as is the case with the Colombian Constitutional Court.[82] Likewise, the Brazilian Supreme Court translates its main jurisprudence into English and Spanish, and periodically distributes an electronic newsletter (*MercoJur*) which contains information concerning jurisprudence and legal issues of Mercosur countries.[83]

The consequences of face-to-face encounters and the providing of means to conduct comparative research are seen in South American courts' increasing reliance on foreign materials, and in the consequential by-product of raised awareness of constitutional developments and crises in the region. According to Giuseppe De Vergottini, the encounters can be described as 'initiatives that rationalise the relationship between courts and, through discussion and study, contribute to strengthening the common cultural context that tends to homogenise constitutional justice systems, at least in certain geographic areas'.[84] Accordingly, it is possible to speak about a real jurisdictional dialogue between Latin American courts.[85]

Importantly, it is a non-hierarchical authority that characterises and sustains these networks insofar as the meaning of a standard or interpretation by a foreign body is not imposed, but is reconstructed 'in light of the receiving order'.[86] Marcelo Neves defines this process as a constitutional conversation (which he names 'transconstitutionalism') in which the 'legal orders inter-relate on the reflexive level of their normative structures'. In this conversation, each order is 'self-binding and possesses primacy' over any other.[87]

The trend observed in the South American region seems to be there to stay. For instance, on the 2015 agenda of the Brazilian Constitutional

81 See the CPLCJ's jurisprudence website at www2.stf.jus.br/cjcplp/cjcplp_jurisprudencia .html.
82 See the court's website at http://english.corteconstitucional.gov.co.
83 See 'STF International' at www.stf.jus.br/internacional.
84 De Vergottini, Oltre il Dialogo Tra le Corti, *supra* note 8, at 100.
85 *Ibid.*
86 M. Neves, *Transconstitucionalismo* (São Paulo: Martins Fontes, 2009), at 118.
87 *Ibid.*

Court were no fewer than ten international face-to-face meetings.[88] And there are no signs of resistance or opposing movements 'that would push courts back to a state of intellectual self-sufficiency'.[89] It appears that the South American judiciary, traditionally closed in its endogenous decision-making processes, has finally been absorbed by globalisation.

3.5 The Purpose of Judicial Dialogue for South American Courts

This section asks why South American judges cite foreign decisions. Tom Bingham has suggested that the use of comparative jurisprudence may 'illustrate the way in which courts across the world, grappling with the same problem arising under an international convention, seek, collaboratively, to feel their way towards a consensual international solution'.[90] To Esin Örücü, the reason behind the engagement with foreign jurisprudence may be a different one. She proposes that comparison at this level is brought forward to 'show that while a problem is universal, there are in fact different solutions'.[91] It is not always easy to identify judges' motivations for referring to a foreign decision. In the face of an expanding practice by national courts to look beyond the confines of national law, this section will analyse the motivations of South American judges for engaging with foreign law and jurisprudence.

Four key reasons are proposed here for South American judges' use of foreign material. The first is the search for interpretive material that assists in construing or transforming domestic law. The second is the desire to ascend to an international circuit of judges and courts by sharing similar legal views on a range of subjects. A third purpose of dialogue in the region might be a more practical one: the need of South American courts to protect their independence from political pressure. And the fourth purpose is related to the fulfilment of the expanded constitutional mandate of the courts of the region that requires them to actively interpret and apply regional and international human rights treaties.

88 The international meetings of the Brazilian Supreme Court include the Global Law Summit in London, the BRICs Supreme Courts Forum in China, four ordinary sessions of the Venice Commission and other meetings. See www2.stf.jus.br/portalStfInternacional/cms/verConteudo.php?sigla=portalStfAgenda_pt_br&idConteudo=283782.

89 B. S. Markesinis and J. Fedtke, *Engaging with Foreign Law* (Oxford: Hart Publishing, 2009), at 374.

90 Bingham, Widening Horizons, *supra* note 61, at 44.

91 E. Örücü, 'Whither Comparativism in Human Rights Cases?', E. Örücü, (ed.), *Judicial Comparativism in Human Rights Cases* (London: British Institute for International and Comparative Law, 2003) 229–42, at 235.

In relation to the first purpose of South American courts' engagement with foreign jurisprudence as an interpretative aid, it has to be noted that legal decisions cannot solely be made based on a survey of foreign courts' decisions, no matter how many cultural, political or legal similarities there are between the 'importing' and the 'exporting' state.[92] The rule of law requires that judges indicate the set of legal rules on which they base their judicial decisions. Moreover, judges are aware that their decisions are authoritative not because of the decisions' consistency with foreign courts' jurisprudence, but because they are issued in accordance with the laws and the constitution of their state. Thus, judges formally refer to domestic and constitutional law as the binding instruments for their decisions, and further justify the interpretation of these instruments on the basis of foreign material.[93] Particularly in human rights cases, constitutional norms and (constitutionalised) human rights treaties have porous language, the meaning of which may change in line with jurisprudential developments. If the law and tradition in a particular state do not require that the concretisation of domestic human rights be based solely on domestic material, foreign law and jurisprudence can be used as interpretive sources. This happens frequently in Latin America. Moreover, in a progressively internationalised and integrated world of which South American courts have become a part, judges are aware of the authority that can be added to their own decisions by way of references to foreign legal decisions. They therefore search for an international consensus, if there is one, or at least for decisions within a global marketplace of legal ideas that resonate with a domestic audience, that may legitimise their decisions further. This is especially so in cases where national law points to a solution that seems 'unjust or inappropriate', or when there is no apparent answer to the problem in national law.[94] In fact, the consideration of a source as a persuasive

[92] Alford, Misusing International Sources, *supra* note 21, at 61 ('Constitutional decision making is not a scatter diagram in which all data points, domestic and global, are used to plot a constitutional line of best fit').

[93] See section 5 *infra* for a discussion on the effects of the use of foreign material. Judges are conscious of those effects, and commonly employ foreign jurisprudence when intending to have them.

[94] See Bingham, Widening Horizons, *supra* note 61, at 8. See also Bohmer's impressions that 'when the status quo of national political systems perpetuates the democratic deficit, the incorporation of foreign legislation can produce the necessary impulse to force collective deliberation in the enforcement stage of norms that we agree to assume, albeit imperfectly, as our own.… During crucial moments of its history, Argentina looked to foreign law in order to force the dialogue that its institutions could not produce on their own. After the massive violation of rights in the 1970s and the permanent impossibility of building

resource or as a 'value to be noted' influences 'primarily at the level of deliberation and justification'.[95]

The second purpose behind South American judges' increasing reliance on foreign material is their wish to be part of an international community of judges, or simply put, their wish to relate their own legal views to the views of a larger group of international and foreign judges and courts. Of interest in this respect is a recent survey that showed that aspiration to membership of an emerging international judicial 'guild' appears to be an important reason for judges to engage in judicial dialogue.[96] It can also be assumed that judges hope to add legitimacy and persuasiveness to their own decisions by relating them to the legal views of a more international group of judges and courts, in particular where this practice is widely accepted by their audience. Furthermore, the consolidation of judicial networks has the potential to create supportive and inspirational links between progressive judges who are more willing to go beyond interpretations of domestic law based exclusively on the plain text of the respective national provision, when an effective protection of human rights requires them to do so.

Concerning the third alleged purpose of South American judges' engagement in transnational judicial dialogue – the protection against undue political pressure or coercion that might compromise domestic courts' independence – one can note that although there have not been known regional cases in which judges of constitutional courts have received support from foreign courts, their established networks create an additional layer of support if they are under pressure from the domestic executive or legislative branches.[97] In South America, the ties between courts are built and strengthened independently of the executive branch, through engagement in judicial dialogue, exchange programmes and regular visits.[98] They can be crucial in politically difficult times, and thus

democracy for more than a hundred years, Argentina looked once more into other legislations and judicial decisions, searching for the texts that our incapacity could not produce'. M. Bohmer, 'Use of Foreign Law as a Strategy to Build Constitutional and Democratic Authority', *Revista Jurídica de la Universidad de Puerto Rico* 77:411 (2008) 411–32, at 430.

95 M. Moran, 'Shifting Boundaries: The Authority of International Law', J. Nijman and A. Nollkaemper (eds.), *New Perspectives on the Divide Between National and International Law* (Oxford University Press, 2007) 163–91, at 166.

96 Flanagan and Ahern, Judicial Decision-Making, *supra* note 1, at 60.

97 For instance, Slaughter mentions the support of international networks in a case regarding pressure and threats by the Zimbabwean government on the Supreme Court Chief Justice. Slaughter, New World Order, *supra* note 8, at 99.

98 Since 2009 the state parties to the Mercosur have adopted a programme for regular visits and exchanges of magistrates and civil servants of the judicial branches. For instance, two

judicial dialogue can have a greater systemic purpose aimed at ensuring self-preservation of independent domestic courts in the region.

Finally, the fourth purpose of domestic courts' use of foreign jurisprudence is related to the implementation of constitutional reforms in the region. As discussed, recent constitutional changes have enlarged the constitutional mandate of apex courts by bringing international human rights treaties to the level of constitutional law, allowing for their direct application by domestic judges. The rapid increase in the required legal competences and the enlargement of the legal grounds on which domestic courts in the region may now decide their cases, have pushed Latin American courts to actively look for more foreign references as a way to fulfil these broadened constitutional mandates.

3.6 The Effects of Judicial Dialogue by South American Courts

This section considers possible effects of foreign material in domestic jurisprudence and discusses whether the use of this material is in fact achieving the purposes identified in the previous section. The assessment of the cases is divided according to the four most common contexts in which foreign law is relied upon, and in which the reliance on such material can have different effects. The first context is where answers are not available domestically. In these situations, the effect of judicial dialogue is that the gap in domestic law and jurisprudence is closed (subsection 3.6.1). The second context is where judges seek to 'update' or synchronise their understanding of relevant law with the rest of the world. When engaging in dialogue in this context, the effect of this dialogue is precisely a synchronisation or 'update' (subsection 3.6.2). Third, citations are made to guide the implementation of human rights treaties that have recently become binding on the state. Dialogue of South American courts often has this effect (subsection 3.6.3). The fourth context in which foreign cases are cited frequently are those in which these foreign cases can arguably not be neglected due to their importance. As the examples that follow show, in these cases the effects of dialogue can vary (subsection 3.6.4).

Before discussing these contexts in more detail, some aspects of human rights jurisprudence should be considered as it can help to understand

Ecuadorian Justices spent 10 days in the Brazilian Supreme Court in 2009 and two Bolivian first instance judges spent 30 days in Brazil. Programme available at www.stf.jus.br/repositorio/cms/portalStfInternacional/portalStfDestaque_es_es/anexo/liv_cortes_supremas_Joaquim_Nabuco1_semestre_2011_web2.pdf.

South American courts' wide adoption of foreign material in human rights cases compared to the rather limited use of private or general foreign or international law and jurisprudence by the same courts.

First, domestic jurisprudence on human rights generally develops with a significant contribution from the jurisprudence of international judicial and quasi-judicial human rights bodies. This is particularly so in South America, where international human rights treaties are firmly incorporated into domestic law. Thus, it is reasonable for a constitutional court to assume that courts in a foreign state, which is a party to the same or similar human rights treaties and hence subject to the jurisdiction of the same or similar human rights courts or treaty bodies, may have helpful jurisprudence. They may also assume that the respective legislatures of these foreign countries and/or the review of regional human rights courts or UN human rights treaty bodies have ensured the compatibility of domestic law with regional and international human rights treaties in these countries. Therefore, domestic constitutional law and jurisprudence can be assumed to be in line with relevant treaties that the South American courts apply as well; consequently, an engagement with such external material seems reasonable and likely.

A second particularity of human rights law that might explain the effects of South American courts' engagement in dialogue in this area is the fact that the language of human rights is generally highly abstract. This may stimulate the search for examples on the concrete application of those same rights by foreign constitutional courts.[99] Although it has to be acknowledged that some domestic interpretation of international treaties is done through the lens of domestic values, courts regularly combine the application of domestic constitutional law with the use of foreign domestic and international jurisprudence interpreting a specific right or treaty. This is particularly the case when a bill of rights in a national constitution mimics international human rights instruments, as is the case in many modern constitutions.[100] When interpreting and applying similarly worded

[99] Even the binding character of domestic precedents in human rights on future domestic cases is not clear, as many are recently settled and sometimes weak if compared to other areas of law. See C. McCrudden, 'Common Law of Human Rights? Transnational Judicial Conversations on Constitutional Rights', *Oxford J. of Legal Studies* 20:4 (2000) 499–532, at 512.

[100] See J. Levit, 'The Constitutionalization of Human Rights in Argentina: Problem or Promise?', *Colum. J. Transnat'l L.* 37:281 (1999), 281–355, at 297: 'Some constitutional provisions in this group [constitutions that incorporate the "spirit" of human rights treaties] ostensibly mimic international treaties but carve elastic exceptions that envelop the substantive right'; and T. Buergenthal, 'Modern Constitutions and Human Rights Treaties', *Colum. J. Transnat'l L.*, 36:216 (1998) 211–23, at 217: 'Various Latin American countries,

provisions, most judges see no reason why they should not look into how this interpretation and application is developing elsewhere.

The last particularity that might help to explain the effects of judicial dialogue in human rights cases in South America is the fact that, unlike in many other states – mostly those where judicial precedent is equivalent to parliamentary law – South American judges, academics and lawyers do not raise significant objections to the consideration of foreign material in judicial decisions.[101] No matter how much influence a foreign case may have on a national court's decision, domestically it will be seen as a legitimate interpretive aid, even in constitutional interpretation. However, foreign material is never used as a formally binding source of law. Hence, the usual dichotomy between 'binding' and 'persuasive' authority, so common in the debate involving the use of foreign sources in common law states, is not entirely transferable to the jurisdictions assessed in this work, and perhaps not to any civil law jurisdiction.[102]

With these three particularities of human rights law and the interpretative weight given to foreign jurisprudence in South American court decisions in mind, we now move to discuss the four main contexts in which

no doubt influenced by article 10(2) of the Spanish Constitution of 1978, have accorded constitutional rank to human rights treaties'.

[101] In Brazil the use of foreign jurisprudence by courts raises no relevant opposition, G. V. Cardoso, 'The Comparative Law in the Constitutional Adjudication', *Revista de Direito Getulio Vargas* 6:2 (2010) 469–92, at 487. Similarly, in Argentina 'there has not been enough critical reflection', Rosenkratz, Against Borrowings, *supra* note 5, at 277. There are, nevertheless, isolated reactions against the use of foreign jurisprudence as binding precedent. For instance, the Paraguayan Appeal Tribunal of Itapúa stated that the use of foreign material 'has brought contradictory interpretations among legal interpreters seeking to apply the doctrine and jurisprudence based on foreign law'. The Tribunal then concluded that the national Civil Procedural Code 'is not subordinated' to the requirements of Argentine Law and that 'the opinion of national scholars or the comparative law are not formal sources of Paraguayan law, however laudable or authoritative they may be, except when domestic law refer to them expressly (article 7, 3rd para. Civil Code)'. Tribunal de Apelación (Paraguay), Primera Sala, Itapúa, nº 38-08-01 (2008) (translation by author).

[102] The difference is emphasised by a number of scholars: '[I]t is one thing to find in international [and foreign] materials an illuminating argument or insight and adopt as one's own. It is quite another to cite [them] as authority, as though they deserved deference independent of their persuasive force'; see M. Wells, 'International Norms in Constitutional Law', *Georgia J. of Int'l & Comp. L.* 32 (2004) 429–36, at 433. Also on the binding-persuading dichotomy, see C. McCrudden, 'Human Rights and Judicial Use of Comparative Law', E. Örücü, (ed.), *Judicial Comparativism in Human Rights Case* (London: British Institute for International and Comparative Law, 2003) 1–23; and J. Waldron, 'Foreign Law and the Modern Ius Gentium', *Harvard L. Rev.* 119:1 (2005) 125–47, at 129.

Latin American courts engage in horizontal judicial dialogue, and the effect this has on the development of law and jurisprudence in the region.

3.6.1 No Clear Answer in Domestic Law

The reliance on foreign jurisprudence is more common in cases where the constitution, domestic law or jurisprudence seem to provide no clear answer. One of the most prominent effects of the use of foreign material by South American courts is, consequently, the closing of gaps in domestic law. For instance, in an emblematic case, the Supreme Court of Uruguay overturned the decision of the Appellate Family Tribunal that had denied the request of the complainant to change gender identity after a sex change operation. The Supreme Court reasoned that 'there is no legal definition of what is sex' and the attempts to define it consider the morphologic-genital aspect of an individual from birth. However, sex change surgeries 'change the originally morphologic sex of the individual to its own psychological' identity, requiring a rectification of the public registration.[103] To reach this conclusion, the Court considered the ACHR and foreign legislation of Italy and Germany, which allow the change of name through a judicial procedure. The Uruguayan Supreme Court recognised that the 'issue under consideration has not received specific normative regulation' in Uruguay. It nevertheless held that the 'law is a normative plexus and therefore no individual rights may be hindered on the pretext of lack of explicit rules'.[104]

In a different case, the Colombian Constitutional Court was asked to assess a claim challenging the constitutionality of a bill proposing a national referendum[105] to decide whether the Colombian president would be entitled to run for a third consecutive term.[106] The decision found the proposal incompatible with the 'original axis' of the Colombian Constitution, and held that not even Congress had the power to alter this 'original axis'. It referred to different presidential regimes (such as in Brazil, Uruguay, Mexico and the United States) to emphasise the necessity of alternating government and the risk of interfering with the separation of

[103] Suprema Corte (Uruguay), Acción de reclamación de identidad sexual, nº 139 (5 May 1997).

[104] *Ibid.*

[105] Corte Constitucional (Colombia), *Revisión de constitucionalidad de la Ley 1354 de 2009*, Sentencia C-141/10, Sala Plena, 26 February 2010, s.6.3.2

[106] The Colombian Constitution allows a maximum of two presidential mandates consecutively. Constitution of Colombia (1991), article 197.

powers should the bill pass. Although the Colombian Court enjoys strong public support in the country, the danger of isolation of the Court in cases such as this, in which the law was already approved by the Colombian parliament and had the support of the executive, stimulated the search for supporting ideas and arguments in foreign law and jurisprudence. One may argue that the Colombian Court's reliance on the very fundamental structure of the Colombian Constitution would suffice to justify the decision. Nevertheless, the emphasis on the foreign models may have added the necessary strength to this delicate political decision.

The *Ellwanger* case decided by the Brazilian Supreme Court also illustrates the search for answers that are not clearly available domestically. The Court decided that the publication and dissemination of anti-Semitic ideas would amount to the crime of racism.[107] In the absence of any explicit domestic norms in this regard, foreign legislation criminalising the denial of crimes against humanity, and specifically of the Holocaust, directly influenced the Court's conclusions. The Brazilian Supreme Court referred *inter alia* to relevant legislation and jurisprudence of France,[108] Spain,[109] Portugal,[110] the United Kingdom[111], Germany[112] and the United States.[113]

3.6.2 Lost in Time: Synchronising Rights Evolution through Judicial Dialogue

Another effect that South American courts' engagement in judicial dialogue can produce is that of updating domestic legislation in light of developments in foreign and international human rights law. The Supreme Court of Argentina's decision of 2009 about the constitutionality of a specific penalty listed in the Constitution itself is a good example of this

[107] Supremo Tribunal Federal (Brazil), *Ellwanger v. Superior Tribunal de Justiça*, Habeas Corpus nº 82424/RS, Tribunal Pleno, DJ 19-03-2004, 17 September 2003. For a complete discussion of the case, see J. Z. Benvindo, *On the Limits of Constitutional Adjudication: Deconstructing Balancing and Judicial Activism* (Berlin: Springer, 2010).

[108] France, Act No 90615 (1990).

[109] Constitucional Court of Spain, Judgment of 11 December 1995, STC 176/1995.

[110] Portugal, Penal Code 1982, article 240

[111] UK House of Lords, *Mandla v. Dowell-Lee* [1983] 2 AC 548.

[112] Judgments of the Federal Constitutional Court (Germany): of 15 January 1958, 1 BvR 400/51; of 11 January 1994, 1 BvR 434/87; of 10 October 1995, 1 BvR 1476/91, 1 BvR 1980/91, 1 BvR 102/92 and 1 BvR 221/92; and of 29 November 1990, 1 BvR 402/87.

[113] US Supreme Court, *Terminiello v. Chicago*, 16 May 1949, 337 US 1; *R.A.V. v. City of St.Paul, Minnesota*, 22 June 1992, 505 US 377; and *Texas v. Johnson*, 21 June 1989, 491 US 397.

effect of judicial dialogue.[114] Although substantially reformed in 1994, the Argentine Constitution is one of the oldest in the world, dating from 1853.[115] In one of it its original sections, it still provides the penalty of 'disqualification in perpetuity from holding public offices' for various activities, including for serious criminal offences against the state entailing personal enrichment.[116]

In 2009, the Supreme Court of Argentina was faced with a case in which the governor of a province had been sentenced to 'perpetual disqualification' because of poor performance of his duties, dereliction of duty and common crimes. He appealed to the Supreme Court, challenging the constitutionality of the constitutional norm itself.[117] In its decision, the Court interpreted the rule by looking at the US and British laws on impeachment that inspired the provision at hand. It also compared the provision in the Argentine Constitution to the adaptation of impeachment rules in the French and Colombian constitutions that were made over time, as well as to the evolution of its interpretation in the United States. For the Supreme Court of Argentina, imposing the sanction of disqualification may have made sense two centuries ago.[118] Considering the evolution of legal thinking outside Argentina as well as the 1994 Argentine constitutional reform, it concluded that 'sanctions such as civil death have completely disappeared from contemporary law and would not be compatible with the international law incorporated into the Constitution'.[119]

[114] Although the possibility of judicial review of constitutional amendments is accepted in many jurisdictions, this case inverted the reasoning by declaring an original clause 'obsolete' and not applicable. On the discussion of judicial review of constitutional amendments see G. J. Jacobsohn, 'Unconstitutional Constitution – A Comparative Perspective', *Int'l J. Const. L.* 4:3 (2006) 460–87, at 460; A. Barak, 'Unconstitutional Constitutional Amendments', *Isr. L. Rev.* 44:321 (2011) 321–41; and Y. Roznai and S. Yolcu, 'An Unconstitutional Constitutional Amendment 'The Turkish Perspective: A Comment on the Turkish Constitutional Court's Headscarf Decision', *Int'l J. of Constitutional L.* 10:1 (2012) 175–207.

[115] Argentine scholars and official documents refer to the constitutional text of 1994 as a reform text (the seventh) of the 1853 constitution rather than as a new constitution. Nevertheless, the current text, available on the federal government's website (www.argentina.gov.ar) is signed by the Constitutional Assembly of 1994, which (despite the adoption of some identical norms in relation to the previous constitution) could be considered a formal criterion making the reform text a new constitution.

[116] Constitución de la Nación Argentina, 22 August 22 1994, section 36.

[117] Corte Suprema de Justicia de la Nación (Argentina), *Maza, Ángel E. s/ amparo medida cautelar*, nº M. 1514. XLIII, 6 October 2009, para. 6.

[118] *Ibid.*, para. 4.

[119] *Ibid.*, paras. 6, 8.

The role of foreign material in this case was essential to show how the norm, which originated from abroad, had evolved away from the meaning that the lower Argentine courts had adopted. Thus, based on the understanding that the constitutional provision was no longer synchronised with the global evolution of similar laws, and that it contradicted the provisions of international treaties on human rights that also form part of the Argentine Constitution, the Supreme Court held that the provision and related laws were to be considered 'obsolete clauses'.[120]

A decision of the Colombian Constitutional Court regarding the discriminatory treatment of a sex worker is another example of a case where a court relied on foreign material to develop the interpretation of the national constitution.[121] The Court's comparative legal analysis on the regulation of prostitution showed that generally, the activity was not criminalised. It also observed a trend to recognise prostitution as a profession in foreign law and jurisprudence.[122] In light of the foreign material, the Colombian Constitutional Court held that the association between the claimant and the establishment where she conducted her regular activities as a sex worker constituted a work contract. Thus, the Court found that she was protected against illegal dismissal during her pregnancy.[123]

A final example is a case in which the Supreme Court of Brazil unanimously recognised a 'homoaffective union' as a family entity.[124] The decision was the result of two cases challenging the constitutionality of the Civil Code's definition of a 'family entity' as a 'stable union between man and woman, configured through continuous and abiding public life, with the purpose of constituting a family'.[125] The claimants argued it violated their constitutional rights to equality, legal protection, freedom and human dignity. Rather than striking down the questioned norm, the Court gave the

[120] *Ibid.*, para. 8.

[121] Corte Constitucional (Colombia), *Lais v. Bar Discoteca Pandemo*, Sentencia T-629/10, Sala Tercera de Revisión de la Corte Constitucional, 13 August 2010.

[122] *Ibid.*, s. 2.4.1.

[123] The use of foreign material as evidence for global trends is particularly frequent in decisions arguing in favour of new interpretations of certain rights. See, for instance, Corte Constitucional (Colombia), *Demanda de inconstitucionalidad de Daniel Bonilla Maldonado y otros*, Sentencia C-417/09, Sala Plena, 26 June 2009, s.2.b.e. These cases considered the 'tendency' of changing laws criminalising slander and libel against public agents within the Inter-American System.

[124] Supremo Tribunal Federal (Brazil), *Arguição de Descumprimento de Preceito Fundamental (ADPF) nº132, proposta por Estado do Rio de Janeiro*, 5 May 2011, at 148. The case was decided in conjunction with *Ação Direta de Inconstitucionalidade (ADI) nº 4277-DF proposta por Procuradoria-Geral da República*, 5 May 2011, also before the Tribunal Federal, both challenging the same issue.

[125] Código Civil (Civil Code) nº 10.406, 10 January 2002, article 1723.

norm a broad interpretation,[126] excluding any meaning from the Brazilian Civil Code that impedes the recognition of unions between two people of the same sex as family.[127] It also held that such recognition would have the same legal consequences as 'heteroaffective' unions.[128]

In constitutional decisions involving disputed issues such as these, it is common to have multiple sources of interpretation, including national and international jurisprudence and scholarship. As an illustration, this decision on the Brazilian Constitutional Court consists of 274 pages in which more than 40 statutes, 55 national decisions, 12 foreign statutes and constitutions, 11 foreign courts' decisions and 96 pieces of national and international academic scholarship were cited. Evidently, in long and complex decisions with different opinions and lines of reasoning, the key elements forming the *ratio decidendi* of the court may not always be clear.[129] However, foreign jurisprudence and statutes are certainly relevant for South American courts in these types of cases. As in the Brazil case, such external material serves less as a normative reference (of how the specific domestic law should be interpreted) and more as an indication that even basic definitions such as 'marriage' are changing elsewhere,[130] a fact that cannot be ignored in the Brazilian Supreme Court's jurisdiction.

3.6.3 Foreign Material as a Guide for Compliance with Human Rights Treaties

It has been argued that 'foreign case law puts flesh onto otherwise bare [international] treaty provisions … by providing evidence of

[126] The Court frequently adopts such doctrine, borrowed from the German Constitutional Court, which is a type of judicial review with no reduction of text, called 'interpretation in accordance with the Constitution'.

[127] Supremo Tribunal Federal (Brazil), Arguição de Descumprimento de Preceito Fundamental (ADPF) nº132, proposta por Estado do Rio de Janeiro, 5 May 2011, at 5.

[128] *Ibid.*

[129] This feature of the decision-making process of the Brazilian Supreme Court was criticised for its apparent lack of collective reasoning: 'If we try to take the Court's arguments seriously, however, we face another difficulty: the 'Tribunal's arguments almost never exist, except through a metaphor'. C. H. Mendes, 'Onze ilhas [Eleven islands]', *Folha de São Paulo*, 1 February 2010, available at www1.folha.uol.com.br/fsp/opiniao/fz0102201008.htm.

[130] Posner and Sunstein have argued that the persuasiveness of this practice is explained by the 'condorcet jury theorem'. The theorem suggests that 'if many courts have decided on a particular course of action, and if each of them is likely to make choices that are better than random, there is excellent reason to believe that the course of action is right'. However, in some cases, judges seem to believe that one or a few foreign references in a principled decision suffice to have a high degree of persuasiveness. Posner and Sunstein, The Law of Other States, *supra* note 1, at 138.

"international opinion" on the proper interpretation of these provisions'.[131] This specific use of foreign material is indeed common in South America, driven in particular by the direct incorporation of international human rights treaties into domestic law. In this context, it is not uncommon for decisions of foreign domestic courts applying similar international treaties to be cited. Hence, judicial dialogue with foreign domestic courts is, in some circumstances, used by South American courts as an auxiliary tool to verify whether the domestic interpretation given to a certain human right is adequate in the light of these other peer courts' interpretation. However, the citations do not always refer to foreign material interpreting international treaties by the exporting court, as the exporting court may solely be interpreting a constitutional right also present in the international instrument under consideration by the receiving court. In both cases, from the perspective of the citing court, international human rights law seems to be a conduit for dialogue, despite having international *or* domestic law on the other (exporting) side of the dialogue.

An interesting example of jurisprudence with this effect comes from the Supreme Court of Chile when it assessed whether the definition of marriage in the Chilean Civil Code violates the Chilean Constitution, the ICCPR or the ACHR.[132] The Chilean Civil Code defines marriage as a 'solemn contract by which a man and a woman come together'.[133] The majority of the Court, in distinct concurrent opinions, found no violation of article 23(2) ICCPR and article 17(2) ACHR. These articles expressly recognise 'the right of men and women' to marry and have a family. The majority found support of such interpretation in the decision of the French *Conseil Constitutionnel* interpreting article 34 of the French Constitution as well as decisions of the German Constitutional Court which hold marriage to be a union between a man and a woman.[134]

The same rationale can be observed in the Bolivian Constitutional Court's decision assessing whether the approval of two national statutes – without prior consultation of the affected indigenous people – had violated the 'duty to consult' established by article 6 of the Indigenous

[131] M. A. Waters, 'Creeping Monism: The Judicial Trend toward Interpretive Incorporation of Human Rights Treaties', *Columbia L. Rev.* 107:3 (2007) 628–706, at 691.

[132] Tribunal Constitucional (Chile), nº 1881-10, 4 January 2011.

[133] *Ibid.*

[134] Le Conseil Constitutionnel (France), *Mme. Corinne C. et Sophie H. v. France*, Decision 2010–92, QPC, 28 January 2011, interpreting article 34 of the French Constitution as well as a Judgment of 17 July 2002, 1 BvF 1/01 and 1 BvF 2/01 of the German Constitutional Court.

and Tribal Peoples Convention (ILO Convention 169).[135] Two members of the Bolivian Parliament filed the case, arguing that the requirement of consultation before the implementation of public policies under domestic law was incompatible with the ILO Convention 169 and the Bolivian Constitution. This was due to the obligation on the state to have consulted the indigenous people prior to the enactment of 'any legislative or administrative measures susceptible of affecting them', not only after the adoption of these legislative or administrative measures.[136] The Court dismissed the case and concluded that the consultation process established by the domestic laws was compatible with both the Bolivian Constitution and ILO Convention 169. The decision relied on the interpretation given to the 'duty to consult' in international and foreign jurisprudence. In particular, the Bolivian Court relied on rulings of Colombian[137] and Peruvian[138] courts to form its interpretation of international law on the consultation of indigenous populations.[139]

In another case, the Colombian Constitutional Court was asked to decide whether the freedom to burn the national flag should be protected as an exercise of the right to freedom of expression. The claimants argued that the right to freedom of expression should be construed not only in light of the Colombian constitutional guarantee to 'express and disseminate thoughts and opinions'[140] but also in light of international human

[135] Convention concerning Indigenous and Tribal Peoples in Independent Countries (ILO No. 169) (27 June 1989), entered into force 5 September 1991, article 6(1)(a). In applying the provisions of this Convention, governments shall 'consult the peoples concerned, through appropriate procedures and in particular through their representative institutions, whenever consideration is being given to legislative or administrative measures which may affect them directly'.

[136] Bolivia, Ley n. 180, 24 October 2011 and Ley n. 222, 10 February 2012. Tribunal Constitucional de Bolivia (Bolivia), Acciónes de Inconstitucionalidad, *Morales, Melgar, Feraudy y Quiroga*, Sentencia Constitucional Plurinacional 0300/2012 (TIPNIS), Sala Plena, Expedientes 00157-2012-01-AIA, 00188-2012-01-AIA (acumulado), 18 June 2012, s. I(1).

[137] Corte Constitucional (Colombia), *Oscar Carupia Domicó y otros v. Ministerios de Transporte y otros*, Sentencia T-129/2011, Sala Quinta de Revisión de la Corte Constitucional, 3 March 2011.

[138] Tribunal Constitucional del Peru (Peru), Demanda de inconstitucionalidade 002-2009-PI/TC.

[139] The rulings were clear on the necessity of consultations prior to the intervention, but not necessarily prior to the enactment of a statute. The Bolivian Court held that the latter parameter was to be followed also by Bolivia. In its decision, the Bolivian Constitutional Court emphasised that the jurisprudence issued by constitutional courts of other countries are not binding on Bolivian jurisdiction, but that they can provide an understanding of the circumstances in which the duty to consult under ILO Convention 169 has been implemented elsewhere (*ibid*., s. III.4).

[140] Constitution of Colombia (1991), article 20.

rights treaties ratified by Colombia and that form part of the Colombian 'constitutional bloc'.[141] The Court considered whether article 461 of the Colombian Criminal Code, which can impose a fine on those who 'insult ... the flag, national anthem or emblem of Colombia',[142] violates article 19 UDHR, article 19 ICCPR and article 13 ACHR. It found that these international provisions, 'together with the Constitution, indicate the reach of this right [to freedom of expression] and the extent of the protected acts'.[143] The reasoning emphasised the strong relationship between the protection of the right to freedom of expression and the development of democratic societies. This required that any attempt to limit this right must be subject to 'very strict examination to avoid situations in which states unnecessarily abridge the free expression of personal opinions'.[144] When considering whether the specific provision of the Criminal Code could be considered as one of the legitimate limitations to the exercise of the right to freedom of expression, the Court thoroughly set out the reasoning and findings from related US cases. Consequently, it held that acts of apparent aggression to a national symbol might represent legitimate forms of political expression, particularly of those opposing the current regime.[145]

3.6.4 Unavoidable Dialogue: Similarity, Relevance and Context

The use of judicial dialogue is almost unavoidable when the relevant foreign jurisprudence has attained global importance to the point that it cannot be ignored by domestic courts; in particular, this is seen in South American courts due to their respective constitutional mandates to enforce international human rights law. This 'unavoidable' dialogue can have varying effects: it can bring either the interpretation and application or relevant law into line with an emerging regional or international

[141] Corte Constitucional (Colombia), *Demanda de inconstitucionalidad de Carlos Humberto García Guzmán y Jorge Eliecer Peña Pinilla*, Sentencia C-575/09, Sala Plena, 26 August 2009, s. 4.

[142] Colombia, Código Penal (Penal Code), Ley nº 599/2000, 24 July 2000, article 461.

[143] *supra* note 141, s. 4.

[144] *Ibid.*

[145] *Ibid.* ('In sum, it is not hard to imagine many circumstances in which symbols are instruments of social protest, when they are used as a means of communication to express personal positions on issues regarding community life ... [F]reedom of expression protects the public expression of individual opinion even if it does not coincide with the majority view, or even when repulsive or disagreeable to common and widely accepted social standards'). (Translation by author). The foreign cases considered 'highly pertinent' were from the US Supreme Court, *Texas v. Johnson*, 21 June 1989, 491 US 397 and *United States v. Eichman*, 11 June 1990, 496 US 310.

consensus on a certain matter, or it can prompt courts to point out domestic particularities that justify a domestic court coming to a country-specific solution.

Examples are the respective responses of the Uruguayan and Brazilian Constitutional Courts to amnesty laws. The Uruguayan case challenged the Uruguayan 'expiration law',[146] an amnesty law that precluded the prosecutions of crimes committed before 1 March 1985 by military and police officials during the performance of their duties, or when the said crime had been perpetrated with a political motive. A relative of a woman killed in 1974 while in military detention initiated the case. The relative requested a genuine investigation of the circumstances into her death. The judge of the Uruguayan criminal court of first instance requested the executive branch to clarify whether the facts under investigation were covered by the 'expiration law'. The government at the time replied positively to the question.[147] The public prosecutor, however, argued for the unconstitutionality of articles 1, 3 and 4 of the 'expiration law' on the basis that it violates the Uruguayan Constitution and the international human rights treaties to which Uruguay was a party.[148] The key constitutional arguments brought forth by the prosecutor were first that the amnesty law had been adopted in violation of the sovereignty of the Uruguayan electorate, since it had been passed by a parliament under the threat of the armed forces at the time. Second, the prosecutor argued that the amnesty law violated the constitutional right to equality by creating a privileged category of individuals 'exempt from criminal jurisdiction'. Third, the prosecutor stated that the expiration law violated the constitutional principle of the separation of powers because it transferred the power to decide whether the judiciary may exercise its jurisdictional prerogatives to the executive.[149] Last, the expiration law was challenged because of its incompatibility with the right to a fair trial and to judicial protection (articles 8(1) and 25 ACHR).

The Uruguayan Constitutional Court declared the impugned section of the expiration law unconstitutional and inapplicable. It accepted the public prosecutor's arguments of the violation of people's sovereignty, of the separation of powers and of the violation of the mentioned articles of the ACHR. All three elements equally formed the Court's *ratio decidendi*. In reaching this conclusion, the Court first declared the ACHR an

146 Uruguay, Ley de Caducidad ('expiration law'), Ley N° 15.848, 22 December 1986.

147 Suprema Corte de Justicia (Uruguay), *Excepción de Inconstitucionalidad arts. 1, 3 Y 4 de la Ley N° 15.848*, Sentencia n° 365/2009, 19 October 2009.

148 *Ibid.*

149 *Ibid.*

'integral' part of the Uruguayan Constitution and referred to the similar constitutional design of Argentina. Subsequently, it considered the Argentine jurisprudence regarding Argentina's own amnesty law.[150] Instead of simply citing the relevant Argentine cases, the Uruguayan Court referred to one of the Argentine decisions as an 'authentic leading case'.[151] Subsequently, the Court justified the crucial influence of the cited foreign cases on its own decision with the factual resemblance, importance and context of the foreign case:

> Amnesty laws enacted for the benefit of military officers and police who committed crimes of this nature have been declared illegal by both international courts and judiciaries of countries who went through similar processes as that experienced by Uruguay at the same time. Because of the similarity with the issue analysed here and the importance they have had, these decisions could not be ignored when assessing the constitutionality [of the 'expiration law']; and they have been taken into account by this Court before issuing this ruling.[152]

Judicial dialogue in this context is not a mere representation of similar cases. Although the historical resemblance seems to be one of the elements driving the court to consider the Argentine experience on the matter, the Uruguayan court borrowed more than just one argument and adopted *inter alia* the doctrinal construction of the 'constitutional bloc' on the basis of judicial dialogue.[153] Dialogue in this case thus had the clear effect of bringing Uruguayan law into line with regional and international developments, enhancing the protection of individuals in Uruguay.

A similar 'unavoidability' of reliance on foreign law and jurisprudence can be seen in the Brazilian Supreme Court's decision regarding the revision of the Brazilian amnesty law.[154] The effect of this dialogue was, however, different from the effect on Uruguayan law. Although the Brazilian Supreme Court held that it did not have jurisdiction to review the amnesty law, it assessed the political processes that followed the enactment of amnesty laws in some of its neighbouring countries. It did so in order to justify the outcome of its

150 *Ibid.*, s. III.8.

151 *Ibid.*

152 *Ibid.*

153 The Uruguayan parliament has not passed any constitutional amendment explicitly conferring to human rights treaties the status of constitutional law, but the Uruguayan Supreme Court adopted the interpretation influenced by the Argentine reference.

154 Supremo Tribunal Federal (Brazil), *Arguição de descumprimento de preceito fundamental (ADPF) nº 153-DF, Conselho Federal da Ordem Dos Advogados do Brasil – OAB*, ILDC 1495 (BR 2010), 29 April 2010.

own decision as it differed from parallel decisions of apex courts in these neighbouring countries. The winning vote of the Brazilian justice rapporteur described at length the parliamentary processes that had led to the later repeal of amnesty laws in Chile, Argentina and Uruguay.[155] As noted by the Supreme Court, Brazil differed from these countries by the absence of parallel parliamentary and wider political processes.[156] For this reason, it held that the question of reviewing the effects of the Brazilian amnesty law should be initiated by the legislature reviewing the law, not the courts.

Apparently, the Brazilian Supreme Court deemed it important, and even necessary, to thoroughly justify why it arrived at a decision that differed from notable courts in neighbouring states in similar cases. What could have been seen as weakening their reasoning – that is, discussing how other courts in the region came to opposite outcomes – was instead used in support of its ruling as it allowed it to point out contextual differences with the Brazilian amnesty law. Yet, the case also shows that simply ignoring how a major regional issue of amnesties was decided by other courts in the region is no longer a viable option for South American courts.[157]

3.7 Conclusion

This chapter discussed the practice of citing foreign law and jurisprudence in cases involving human rights in South American apex courts. With the use of quantitative and qualitative methods, 562 cases from 10 different countries were analysed to assess the extent, method, purpose and effects of this horizontal judicial dialogue in the region.

It was argued that the increase in the number of international human rights treaties and their direct incorporation into the national legal systems in South America stimulates their courts' engagement in judicial dialogue. Newly domestically enforceable international human rights treaties require contextual knowledge for their application, which can *inter alia* be found in foreign jurisdictions that are bound by the same treaties and that have a similar legal tradition.

[155] The decision mistakenly included the plebiscites initiatives in Uruguay as a decision taken by parliamentarians (*ibid*, s. 49).

[156] *Ibid*., s. 46–49.

[157] In other regions, 'unavoidable' dialogue may refer to the use of citations from a very influential jurisdiction to the extent that it is so 'common that [it] is almost necessary to explain when it is not appropriate', such as the use of German law references by Austrian judges. See M. Gelter and M. Siems, 'Citations to Foreign Courts – Illegitimate and Superfluous, or Unavoidable? Evidence from Europe', *Am. J. Comparative L.* 62:1 (2014) 35–86, at 64.

The chapter also discussed the extent of the practice of horizontal judicial dialogue by South American courts. References to foreign law and jurisprudence in the region are widely present in court decisions. With the exception of Bolivia (59 per cent) and Venezuela (15 per cent), the cases of all other countries contained references to foreign materials in 30–50 per cent of the decisions. The evaluation of the use of foreign sources by South American courts in the last two decades reinforces the claim that courts have become increasingly open to adopting legal reasoning that is external to their respective jurisdictions. The data also suggests a causal relationship between constitutional reforms or judicial interpretation of domestic constitutional law that gives international human rights treaties the status of constitutional law, and the expansion of judicial dialogue between 1990 and 2012.

The methods by which Latin American courts and judges engage in horizontal judicial dialogue includes constitutional judges' attendance at conferences where the development of relevant national or international law and jurisprudence is discussed; their increasing access to translated foreign material; the specialised work of law clerks who are instructed to look for relevant foreign jurisprudence; and visiting programmes for judges.

As concerns the purposes of considering foreign material when deciding domestic human rights law cases, four motivations were identified. First, South American courts rely on such material to assist them in the interpretation of domestic law and, where legitimate, to adapt national law in a way that ensures the effective protection of human rights. In this context, foreign material is only used as an interpretative aid. In other words, Latin American courts ensure that they do not subject the practice to the criticism of bypassing the enforcement of national law or any formal limitation set by domestic law. A second purpose of South American courts' engagement in horizontal judicial dialogue in the area of human rights appears to be the desire of these courts to become part of an international community of courts that share similar views on similar legal questions. Domestic judges search for international consensus when dealing with universal themes such as human rights. If there is none, the legitimacy of decisions might be enhanced through references to relevant decisions from the global marketplace of legal ideas. The reliance on external material may also have a third, more practical purpose: the protection of the court's independence from political pressure. Fourth, transnational judicial dialogue can be used as a tool in the implementation of Latin American apex courts' expanded legal competences following the direct incorporation and constitutionalisation of international human rights treaties.

With respect to the effects of horizontal judicial dialogue on South American law and jurisprudence, it was argued that references to foreign material are made in order to close gaps in domestic law. The reliance on foreign law and jurisprudence also seems to have the effect of 'updating' or synchronising the understanding of domestic constitutional law, thus transforming the meaning and protective scope of a certain right. Court engagement with foreign jurisprudence may also have the effect of guiding the correct domestic implementation of international or regional human rights treaties that are binding on both the citing and cited court. Finally, in a few cases, the citation of foreign jurisprudence seems to have the main purpose and effect of preventing criticism that the court failed to look to solutions adopted elsewhere. This is most obvious when courts refer to foreign judicial decisions dealing with similar fact patterns, such as amnesty laws. This also suggests that the practice of citing foreign law and jurisprudence is well established in the South American region.

Annex: Data Summary

Overview of Cases Considered

	Time Frame	Cases Filtered	Relevant Cases (human rights)	Cases with Dialogue	% Dialogue in Relevant Cases	Different Cited Jurisdictions
South America	–	1173	562	236	42.0%	65
Argentina	1990–2012	86	51	22	43.1%	43
Bolivia	1994–2012	154	98	58	59.2%	15
Brazil	1990–2012	107	54	32	59.3%	33
Chile	1990–2012	87	43	20	46.5%	23
Colombia	1992–2012	99	64	21	32.8%	49
Ecuador	2008–2012	144	66	25	37.9%	10
Paraguay	1995–2012	104	31	12	38.7%	7
Peru	1996–2012	74	48	14	29.2%	13
Uruguay	1990–2012	173	66	26	39.4%	12
Venezuela	2000–2012	145	41	6	14.6%	12

Effect of Citations

	South America		Argentina (1990–2012)		Bolivia (1994–2012)		Brazil (1990–2012)		Chile (1990–2012)	
number of cases	562	–	51	–	98	–	54	–	43	–
foreign citations	236	42.0%	22	43.1%	58	59.2%	33	61.1%	20	46.5%
verifiable citations	151	64.0%	10	45.5%	43	74.1%	25	75.8%	12	60.0%
superficial citations	47	19.9%	5	22.7%	11	19.0%	0	0.0%	5	25.0%
both superficial and verifiable	37	15.7%	7	31.8%	4	6.9%	8	24.2%	3	15.0%
cited by majority	163	69.1%	15	68.2%	16	27.6%	26	78.8%	16	80.0%
cited by minority	51	21.6%	2	9.1%	42	72.4%	1	3.0%	0	0.0%
both minority and majority	20	8.5%	5	22.7%	0	0.0%	6	18.2%	4	20.0%

Most Cited Jurisdictions (individual cases mentioning law or jurisprudence from a foreign jurisdiction)

South America		Argentina		Bolivia		Brazil		Chile		Colombia	
Spain	79	USA	16	Colombia	37	Spain	20	Spain	17	Spain	13
Colombia	72	Germany	10	Peru	20	Germany	19	Germany	10	Germany	10
USA	64	Spain	7	Costa Rica	19	Portugal	18	USA	8	USA	9
Germany	60	France	7	Ecuador	18	USA	17	Colombia	6	Italy	8
Argentina	56	Italy	5	Argentina	16	France	17	Argentina	5	France	7
Italy	49	Peru	5	Spain	6	Italy	13	Italy	5	Argentina	5
Peru	47	Brazil	5	USA	1	UK	11	Peru	4	Portugal	5
France	38	Venezuela	4	Germany	1	Argentina	10	France	3	UK	4
Costa Rica	26	Uruguay	4	Venezuela	1	Peru	7	Ecuador	3	Mexico	3
Portugal	26	Chile	4	Paraguay	1	Netherlands	7	Mexico	3	Brazil	3
Ecuador	25	Colombia	3	Guatemala	1	Mexico	5	Brazil	3	Uruguay	3
Mexico	18	UK	3	Honduras	1	Paraguay	5	Venezuela	2	Austria	3
UK	18	Paraguay	3	Nicaragua	1	Russia	5	Paraguay	2	Switzerland	3
Brazil	15	Canada	3	Panama	1	Colombia	3	S. Africa	2	Ireland	3
Venezuela	14	Guatemala	3	El Salvador	1	Venezuela	3	Costa Rica	1	Costa Rica	2
Paraguay	12	Costa Rica	2	Italy	0	Uruguay	3	Uruguay	1	Ecuador	2
Uruguay	11	Portugal	2	France	0	Canada	3	Canada	1	Canada	2
Canada	10	Mexico	2	Portugal	0	Belgium	3	Netherlands	1	Chile	2
Chile	10	Belgium	2	Mexico	0	Chile	2	Belgium	1	Netherlands	2
Netherlands	10	Austria	2	UK	0	Austria	2	Austria	1	Belgium	2
Belgium	9	Switzerland	2	Brazil	0	S. Africa	2	Honduras	1	S. Africa	2
Austria	8	Denmark	2	Uruguay	0	Denmark	2	Bolivia	1	Finland	2
Russia	7	Nicaragua	2	Canada	0	Nicaragua	2	India	1	Hungary	2
S. Africa	7	Panama	2	Chile	0	Bulgaria	2	Portugal	0	Luxemb.	2
Guatemala	6	El Salvador	2	Netherlands	0	Greece	2	UK	0	N. Zealand	2

Colombia (1992–2012)		Ecuador (2008–2012)		Paraguay (1995–2012)		Peru (1996–2012)		Uruguay (1990–2012)		Venezuela (2000–2012)	
64	–	66	–	31	–	48	–	66	–	41	–
21	32.8%	25	37.9%	12	38.7%	14	29.2%	26	39.4%	6	14.6%
11	52.4%	17	68.0%	8	66.7%	10	71.4%	13	50.0%	4	66.7%
4	19.0%	5	20.0%	2	16.7%	2	14.3%	12	46.2%	1	16.7%
6	28.6%	3	12.0%	2	16.7%	2	14.3%	1	3.8%	1	16.7%
16	76.2%	23	92.0%	12	100.0%	14	100.0%	24	92.3%	4	66.7%
3	14.3%	1	4.0%	0	0.0%	0	0.0%	1	3.8%	1	16.7%
2	9.5%	1	4.0%	0	0.0%	0	0.0%	1	3.8%	1	16.7%

Ecuador		Paraguay		Peru		Uruguay		Venezuela	
Colombia	18	Argentina	8	Spain	7	Italy	15	Colombia	3
Peru	6	USA	4	Germany	6	Argentina	9	Peru	3
Spain	3	Spain	3	Colombia	2	USA	5	USA	2
Argentina	2	Germany	2	USA	1	Spain	3	Brazil	2
USA	1	Italy	1	Argentina	1	France	3	Costa Rica	1
Germany	1	France	1	Italy	1	Mexico	2	Mexico	1
Italy	1	Mexico	1	Costa Rica	1	Germany	1	Paraguay	1
Venezuela	1	Colombia	0	Portugal	1	Peru	1	Canada	1
Chile	1	Peru	0	Ecuador	1	Brazil	1	Chile	1
S. Africa	1	Costa Rica	0	Mexico	1	Venezuela	1	Honduras	1
France	0	Portugal	0	Brazil	1	Belgium	1	Panama	1
Costa Rica	0	Ecuador	0	Venezuela	1	Guatemala	1	Bolivia	1
Portugal	0	UK	0	Hungary	1	Colombia	0	Spain	0
Ecuador	–	Brazil	0	Peru	–	Costa Rica	0	Germany	0
Mexico	0	Venezuela	0	France	0	Portugal	0	Argentina	0
UK	0	Paraguay	–	UK	0	Ecuador	0	Italy	0
Brazil	0	Uruguay	0	Paraguay	0	UK	0	France	0
Paraguay	0	Canada	0	Uruguay	0	Paraguay	0	Portugal	0
Uruguay	0	Chile	0	Canada	0	Uruguay	–	Ecuador	0
Canada	0	Netherlands	0	Chile	0	Canada	0	UK	0
Netherlands	0	Belgium	0	Netherlands	0	Chile	0	Venezuela	–
Belgium	0	Austria	0	Belgium	0	Netherlands	0	Uruguay	0
Austria	0	Russia	0	Austria	0	Austria	0	Netherlands	0
Russia	0	S. Africa	0	Russia	0	Russia	0	Belgium	0
Guatemala	0	Guatemala	0	S. Africa	0	S. Africa	0	Austria	0

(*continued*)

South America		Argentina		Bolivia		Brazil		Chile		Colombia	
Switzerland	6	R. Domin.	2	Belgium	0	Bhutan	2	Chile	–	Croatia	2
Denmark	5	Ecuador	1	Austria	0	Yemen	2	Russia	0	Peru	1
Honduras	5	Russia	1	Russia	0	Japan	2	Guatemala	0	Venezuela	1
Nicaragua	5	Honduras	1	S. Africa	0	Mauritania	2	Switzerland	0	Russia	1
Panama	5	Bolivia	1	Switzerland	0	S. Arabia	2	Denmark	0	Guatemala	1
Bolivia	4	Bulgaria	1	Denmark	0	Switzerland	1	Nicaragua	0	Denmark	1
Bulgaria	4	Greece	1	Bolivia	–	Australia	1	Panama	0	Honduras	1
El Salvador	4	Finland	1	Bulgaria	0	Turkey	1	Bulgaria	0	Panama	1
Greece	4	Luxemb.	1	Greece	0	Costa Rica	0	El Salvador	0	Bolivia	1
Finland	3	N. Zealand	1	Finland	0	Ecuador	0	Greece	0	Bulgaria	1
Hungary	3	Malta	1	Hungary	0	Brazil	–	Finland	0	El Salvador	1
Ireland	3	Poland	1	Ireland	0	Guatemala	0	Hungary	0	Greece	1
Luxemb.	3	Cyprus	1	Luxemb.	0	Honduras	0	Ireland	0	Australia	1
N. Zealand	3	Ethiopia	1	N. Zealand	0	Panama	0	Luxemb.	0	India	1
Australia	2	Morocco	1	Australia	0	Bolivia	0	N. Zealand	0	Malta	1
Croatia	2	Norway	1	Croatia	0	El Salvador	0	Australia	0	Poland	1
India	2	Syria	1	India	0	Finland	0	Croatia	0	Andorra	1
Malta	2	Taiwan	1	Malta	0	Hungary	0	Malta	0	Armenia	1
Poland	2	Argentina	–	Poland	0	Ireland	0	Poland	0	Azerbaijan	1
R. Domin.	2	Netherlands	0	R. Domin.	0	Luxemb.	0	R. Domin.	0	Cuba	1
Bhutan	2	S. Africa	0	Bhutan	0	N. Zealand	0	Bhutan	0	CzechRep	1
Yemen	2	Hungary	0	Yemen	0	Croatia	0	Yemen	0	Israel	1
Japan	2	Ireland	0	Japan	0	India	0	Japan	0	Slovenia	1
Mauritania	2	Australia	0	Mauritania	0	Malta	0	Mauritania	0	Sweden	1
S. Arabia	2	Croatia	0	S. Arabia	0	Poland	0	S. Arabia	0	Colombia	–
Andorra	1	India	0	Andorra	0	R. Domin.	0	Andorra	0	Paraguay	0
Armenia	1	Bhutan	0	Armenia	0	Andorra	0	Armenia	0	Nicaragua	0
Azerbaijan	1	Yemen	0	Azerbaijan	0	Armenia	0	Azerbaijan	0	R. Domin.	0
Cyprus	1	Japan	0	Cyprus	0	Azerbaijan	0	Cyprus	0	Bhutan	0
Cuba	1	Mauritania	0	Cuba	0	Cyprus	0	Cuba	0	Yemen	0
CzechRep	1	S. Arabia	0	CzechRep	0	Cuba	0	CzechRep	0	Japan	0
Ethiopia	1	Andorra	0	Ethiopia	0	CzechRep	0	Ethiopia	0	Mauritania	0
Israel	1	Armenia	0	Israel	0	Ethiopia	0	Israel	0	S. Arabia	0
Morocco	1	Azerbaijan	0	Morocco	0	Israel	0	Morocco	0	Cyprus	0
Norway	1	Cuba	0	Norway	0	Morocco	0	Norway	0	Ethiopia	0
Syria	1	CzechRep	0	Syria	0	Norway	0	Syria	0	Morocco	0
Slovenia	1	Israel	0	Slovenia	0	Syria	0	Slovenia	0	Norway	0
Sweden	1	Slovenia	0	Sweden	0	Slovenia	0	Sweden	0	Syria	0
Taiwan	1	Sweden	0	Taiwan	0	Sweden	0	Taiwan	0	Taiwan	0
Turkey	1	Turkey	0	Turkey	0	Taiwan	0	Turkey	0	Turkey	0
Total	791		121		125		196		82		126
Latin America	338	Latin America	46	Latin America	117	Latin America	40	Latin America	32	Latin America	28
% citations of Latin American material	43%	% citations of Latin American material	38%	% citations of Latin American material	94%	% citations of Latin American material	20%	% citations of Latin American material	39%	% citations of Latin American material	22%

Ecuador		Paraguay		Peru		Uruguay		Venezuela	
Switzerland	0	Switzerland	0	Guatemala	0	Switzerland	0	Russia	0
Denmark	0	Denmark	0	Switzerland	0	Denmark	0	S. Africa	0
Honduras	0	Honduras	0	Denmark	0	Honduras	0	Guatemala	0
Nicaragua	0	Nicaragua	0	Honduras	0	Nicaragua	0	Switzerland	0
Panama	0	Panama	0	Nicaragua	0	Panama	0	Denmark	0
Bolivia	0	Bolivia	0	Panama	0	Bolivia	0	Nicaragua	0
Bulgaria	0	Bulgaria	0	Bolivia	0	Bulgaria	0	Bulgaria	0
El Salvador	0	El Salvador	0	Bulgaria	0	El Salvador	0	El Salvador	0
Greece	0	Greece	0	El Salvador	0	Greece	0	Greece	0
Finland	0	Finland	0	Greece	0	Finland	0	Finland	0
Hungary	0	Hungary	0	Finland	0	Hungary	0	Hungary	0
Ireland	0	Ireland	0	Ireland	0	Ireland	0	Ireland	0
Luxemb.	0	Luxemb.	0	Luxemb.	0	Luxemb.	0	Luxemb.	0
N. Zealand	0	N. Zealand	0	N. Zealand	0	N. Zealand	0	N. Zealand	0
Australia	0	Australia	0	Australia	0	Australia	0	Australia	0
Croatia	0	Croatia	0	Croatia	0	Croatia	0	Croatia	0
India	0	India	0	India	0	India	0	India	0
Malta	0	Malta	0	Malta	0	Malta	0	Malta	0
Poland	0	Poland	0	Poland	0	Poland	0	Poland	0
R. Domin.	0	R. Domin.	0	R. Domin.	0	R. Domin.	0	R. Domin.	0
Bhutan	0	Bhutan	0	Bhutan	0	Bhutan	0	Bhutan	0
Yemen	0	Yemen	0	Yemen	0	Yemen	0	Yemen	0
Japan	0	Japan	0	Japan	0	Japan	0	Japan	0
Mauritania	0	Mauritania	0	Mauritania	0	Mauritania	0	Mauritania	0
S. Arabia	0	S. Arabia	0	S. Arabia	0	S. Arabia	0	S. Arabia	0
Andorra	0	Andorra	0	Andorra	0	Andorra	0	Andorra	0
Armenia	0	Armenia	0	Armenia	0	Armenia	0	Armenia	0
Azerbaijan	0	Azerbaijan	0	Azerbaijan	0	Azerbaijan	0	Azerbaijan	0
Cyprus	0	Cyprus	0	Cyprus	0	Cyprus	0	Cyprus	0
Cuba	0	Cuba	0	Cuba	0	Cuba	0	Cuba	0
CzechRep	0	CzechRep	0	CzechRep	0	CzechRep	0	CzechRep	0
Ethiopia	0	Ethiopia	0	Ethiopia	0	Ethiopia	0	Ethiopia	0
Israel	0	Israel	0	Israel	0	Israel	0	Israel	0
Morocco	0	Morocco	0	Morocco	0	Morocco	0	Morocco	0
Norway	0	Norway	0	Norway	0	Norway	0	Norway	0
Syria	0	Syria	0	Syria	0	Syria	0	Syria	0
Slovenia	0	Slovenia	0	Slovenia	0	Slovenia	0	Slovenia	0
Sweden	0	Sweden	0	Sweden	0	Sweden	0	Sweden	0
Taiwan	0	Taiwan	0	Taiwan	0	Taiwan	0	Taiwan	0
Turkey	0	Turkey	0	Turkey	0	Turkey	0	Turkey	0
	35		20		25		43		18
Latin America	28	Latin America	9	Latin America	8	Latin America	15	Latin America	15
% citations of Latin American material	80%	% citations of Latin American material	45%	% citations of Latin American material	32%	% citations of Latin American material	35%	% citations of Latin American material	83%

4

The Supreme Court of Canada's Transnational Judicial Communication on Human Rights (1982–2014)

An Empirical Assessment

GIANLUCA GENTILI AND ELAINE MAK

4.1 Introduction

Since the adoption of the 1982 Canadian Charter of Rights and Freedoms[1] (Charter), the Supreme Court of Canada (SCC or Court) has come to be regarded as one of the most progressive constitutional judiciaries worldwide. The Court today appears to be at the forefront of judicial globalisation[2] when it comes to its transnational connections with other courts.[3] In a system that originally mirrored the British tradition of legislative supremacy, the Charter, enacted in 1982 as a constitutional declaration of rights, has markedly changed the Court's role and approach to judicial interpretation. It has vested the Court with powers of constitutional review with a view to protect constitutionally entrenched rights.[4] A significant outcome of the Charter's enactment, in part also due to the influence of the US Bill of Rights and several international human rights documents,

1 Charter of Rights and Freedoms, Part I of the Constitution Act, 1982 being Schedule B to the Canada Act 1982 (UK), 1982, c 11.

2 B. Markesinis and J. Fedtke, *Engaging with Foreign Law* (Oxford University Press, 2009); V. C. Jackson, *Constitutional Engagement in a Transnational Era* (Oxford University Press, 2010).

3 In S. Muller and S. Richards (eds.), *Highest Courts and Globalisation* (The Hague: Hague Academic Press, 2010), the term 'judicial internationalisation' is used to capture the increased exchange of legal ideas and experiences between judges in different legal systems, a trend also referred to as 'transjudicialism, … judicial cosmopolitanism, judicial globalisation, the migration of legal ideas, legal transplants'; see also Introduction to this volume, subsection 4.2.1. The practice is also referred to as judicial *engagement* with foreign law in Jackson, Constitutional Engagement, *supra* note 2, at 71 *et seq* or 'judicial dialogue' in S. Harding, 'Comparative Reasoning and Judicial Review', *Yale J. of Int'l L.* 28:2 (2003) 409–64, at 424–39.

4 In a legal system based on this principle, no constraints are imposed upon what Parliament can do, because it is thought that Parliament represents the best place to draw the appropriate balance between individual freedoms and a broader public interest.

was to increase the openness to foreign legal sources of the Court called to interpret it. As will be shown in this chapter, this openness is discernible in the SCC's case law, which regularly contains citations of judgments handed down by courts in foreign jurisdictions.[5]

However, it remains unclear to what extent this trend of judicial globalisation has actually affected court practices in Canada. Normative frameworks for judicial decision-making, including the Canadian one, generally allow judges considerable discretion regarding the legal sources which they are allowed to consider.[6] Therefore, foreign legal materials may play a role in both the heuristic phase of judicial deliberations and in legitimising a decision through the Canadian courts' reasoning. The question thus arises: In which circumstances and with what effect do judges use foreign legal sources, particularly the case law of foreign courts? Answering this question may prove important in light of the limitations and risks allegedly associated with the transnational exchange of ideas and experiences between courts, such as criticism of the choice of the cited jurisdictions (a contentious practice usually referred to as cherry-picking), the supposed increase in judicial activism or the alleged harm to the principle of sovereignty.

This chapter investigates the engagement of the SCC in transnational judicial communication practices while exercising its adjudicatory functions in cases dealing with human rights.[7] It systematically analyses the extent, method, purpose and effects of this engagement. In what manner does the SCC make use of references to foreign case law in human rights cases, with regard to both the selection of foreign decisions and their use in the reasoning part of judgments? Which purposes does the SCC further by engaging with foreign case law and to what extent are these purposes specific to human rights cases? What are the possible effects of the SCC's developed practice of comparative engagement on its case law and on the development of this case law over the years? Throughout, we are particularly interested in the Charter's impact on the SCC's engagement in transnational judicial dialogue, as well as in the role that judges and their particular mind-set play in fostering or limiting such dialogue.

In order to answer these questions, we analyse the Court's engagement with foreign case law both from a quantitative and a qualitative

[5] See Section 4.3.

[6] B. Markesinis and J. Fedtke, *Judicial Recourse to Foreign Law* (Abingdon: Routledge-Cavendish, 2006) 7–46.

[7] We will use the term 'communication' rather than the less neutral term 'dialogue' to refer to the interaction between highest courts. See in this regard G. de Vergottini, *Oltre il dialogo tra le Corti. Giudici, diritto straniero, comparazione* (Bologna: Il Mulino, 2010). See also Chapter 17 by L. Pasquet in this book.

perspective. Concerning the quantitative aspects, we systematically counted citations of foreign case law in the SCC's judgments. Concerning the qualitative perspective, the research relied on interviews with past and current Justices of the Supreme Court of Canada to better understand, complement and evaluate the results of the quantitative research. In light of the complexity of Canada's legal history and constitutional system and the limited scope of this chapter, a few methodological choices had to be made. First, in regard to the quantitative analysis, our examination focuses on what has been defined as 'horizontal communication' between national courts, to the exclusion of vertical and mixed vertical-horizontal interactions.[8] Therefore, with the exception of jurisprudence of the European Court of Human Rights (ECtHR), the Court of Justice of the European Union (CJEU) and the Inter-American Court of Human Rights (IACtHR), citations of judgments of international adjudicatory bodies, such as the International Court of Justice or the International Criminal Court, were excluded from consideration. The reasons for including the SCC's citation of ECtHR and CJEU jurisprudence is that since 1986[9] and increasingly in the past 20 years, judgments of the ECtHR and the CJEU have represented a fundamental point of reference for the SCC in the effort to enhance protection of fundamental rights domestically. This is despite the fact that Canada is subject to neither of the European Courts' jurisdictions, and decisions of these two Courts have thus only persuasive, rather than binding, authority in Canada.[10] The same considerations apply with regard to the IACtHR, since Canada became a member of the Organization of American States (OAS) in 1990, but it has never ratified the American Convention on Human Rights.[11] Second, for the same reason (i.e. the focus on investigating trans-judicial horizontal communication), citations of sources of law other than case law (such as international treaties, foreign statutes or codes) were excluded.

[8] See A.-M. Slaughter, 'A Typology of Transjudicial Communication', *University of Richmond L. Rev.* 29 (1994) 99–137; and the Introduction to this volume, subsection 1.2.1.

[9] In *R v. Oakes* [1986] 1 SCR 103, the SCC cited a decision of the European Commission of Human Rights for the first time, a body operating until 1998 as a 'filter' to the ECtHR. See Table 4.2.

[10] On the difference between persuasive and binding authority, see H. P. Glenn, 'Persuasive Authority', *McGill L. J.* 32:2 (1987) 261–98, at 263, emphasising that persuasive authority is an 'authority which attracts adherence as opposed to obliging it'.

[11] Canada signed the Charter of the Organization of American States ((30 April 1948), 119 UNTS 1609, entered into force 13 December 1951) on 13 November 1989 and ratified it on 8 January 1990. OAS established the IACtHR in 1979 to enforce and interpret

As mentioned, one of the main purposes of the study is also to assess the Charter's impact on the SCC's attitude towards engagement with foreign jurisprudence. A third methodological choice therefore was to cover the years from 1982 – when the Charter came into effect – to 2014.[12] Despite alternative views of other authors,[13] the decision to focus on this window of time reflects our view that so-called formative periods of domestic jurisprudence are relevant to a comprehensive assessment of citations of foreign case law and trans-judicial communication, and should be included in the analysis. Doing so helps to determine the effects of the new document on the constitutional system as a whole and on the Court's functions and role, and eliminates the arbitrariness involved in defining the temporal limits of the 'formative periods'.

The qualitative part of the study aims to complement the quantitative analysis, in particular concerning questions about the purpose of the SCC's engagement in judicial dialogue in the area of human rights, as well as in the search for explanations of the practice's actual extent and effect on Canadian fundamental rights jurisprudence. The qualitative analysis is based on interviews conducted in April 2010 with two of the then-sitting Justices and two former Justices of the SCC (see Annex 1 for information on the interview design).[14] Until now, it was unclear to what extent the personal approaches of judges – their perceptions or opinion regarding their own role – influenced the extent, purpose and effects of

the provisions of the American Convention on Human Rights (22 November 1969) 1144 UNTS 123, entered into force 18 July 1978.

12 Embracing therefore the work of four Chief Justices: Bora Laskin (CJ from 1973 to 1984), Brian Dickson (1984–90), Antonio Lamer (1990–2000) and Beverley McLachlin (2000–present).

13 See, for example, B. Roy, 'An Empirical Survey of Foreign Jurisprudence and International Instruments in Charter Litigation', *University of Toronto Faculty L. Rev.* 62:2 (2004) 99–148, at 103. The author regards as potentially anomalous the uncommonly high number of references to foreign jurisprudence that is likely to occur during the 'formative period' of domestic jurisprudence and decides to exclude this period from his study.

14 The interviews were conducted by Elaine Mak. Letters requesting an interview were sent to all nine of the Justices of the Court at the beginning of 2010. In light of the Justices' busy schedules, they agreed that meetings with two of them would be possible. The personal contacts of the researcher were used to establish contact with two former Justices of the Court. Three interviews were conducted in personal meetings with the Justices. One interview was conducted by telephone. The achievement of a representative selection is a common problem regarding elite interviews. See U. Jaremba and E. Mak, 'Interviewing Judges in the Transnational Context', *Law and Method* 5:3 (2014) 1–15. To make sure that the views of judges with 'open' and with 'closed' attitudes to the transnational context were both sufficiently represented in the research, additional information was obtained through the analysis of publications and speeches of judges.

the citation of foreign case law. Our interviews with a number of Justices made it possible to identify a series of different approaches which may co-exist within a single court and allowed us to assess the influence of these approaches on the extent, purpose and effect of dialogue as well as on the decision-making process of the Court as a whole.[15] Additional information concerning the views and approaches of the Canadian Justices was gathered through the study of published interviews, public speeches, and academic articles authored by former and current members of the Court. Information is moreover gathered from the analysis of case law that was mentioned in the interviews with the Justices. Through a combination of these sources of information, a picture can be sketched of the Canadian Justices' approaches to the use of foreign judgments in human rights cases.

To set the scene, this chapter first presents the constitutional context to the practice of the SCC (Section 4.2). We then analyse, from a quantitative and qualitative points of view, the extent (Section 4.3), the method (Section 4.4), the purpose and the effects (Section 4.5) of the SCC's engagement in transnational judicial dialogue in the area of human rights. Finally, conclusions are drawn from this analysis, summarising our findings on the extent, method, purpose and effects of the SCC's citations of foreign jurisprudence in human rights cases, and providing some tentative conclusions on the possible future of these citations (Section 4.6).

4.2 The Context: Human Rights Cases before the Supreme Court of Canada

The use of foreign law can be enabled or constrained by the constitutional system in which a national court operates. A court's jurisdiction, organisation and working methods may also influence its ability to consider foreign case law. These different aspects will be described in the following paragraphs, focusing on the history of the SCC and on the development of human rights adjudication in the Canadian legal system.[16]

[15] See further E. Mak, *Judicial Decision-Making in a Globalised World: A Comparative Analysis of the Changing Practices of Western Highest Courts* (Oxford: Hart Publishing, 2013), at 6–8 and 62–66.

[16] Studies concerning the decision-making by the Supreme Court of Canada have also been conducted by I. Bushnell, *The Captive Court: A Study of the Supreme Court of Canada* (Montreal: McGill-Queen's University Press, 1992); R. Martin, *The Most Dangerous Branch: How the Supreme Court of Canada Has Undermined Our Law and Our Democracy* (Montreal/Kingston: McGill-Queen's University Press, 2005); D. Muttart, *The Empirical*

4.2.1 *The Supreme Court of Canada*

Canada's political formation arose in 1867 following the unification of several political systems north of the United States into a Federation. The Dominion of Canada was created out of three separate entities by the British North America Act of 1867 (BNAA or Act), which served also as Canada's constitution until 1982. The Act also established a guideline for admitting other colonies and territories in the future.[17] Domestic popular and political pressure for the development of a national High Court for Canada led to the adoption, in 1875, of the Supreme and Exchequer Courts Act (SECA), an ordinary Act of Parliament, and to the creation of the SCC.[18] The SECA established the Court's jurisdiction over all provincial and federal legal questions, on both common and statutory law. The SCC, however, did not immediately become the court of last resort for Canada. Its decisions remained subject to appeal to the Judicial Committee of the Privy Council in London until 1949, when that right was terminated. This occurred gradually: criminal appeals to the Privy Council were terminated in 1933 (with a few exceptions) after the adoption of the Statute of Westminster in 1931, while civil appeals ended in 1949 after a reform of the Supreme Court Act.[19] Until then, the Privy Council had a significant influence on the evolution of the Canadian constitution, establishing the principles used to guide interpretation of the BNAA. In this process, the Privy Council favoured a strict literal interpretation, and promoted provincial powers over those of the federal government.[20]

While no major changes occurred between 1949 and 1975, in 1975, an amendment to the Supreme Court Act abolished most appeals as

Gap in Jurisprudence: A Comprehensive Study of the Supreme Court of Canada, 2nd ed. (University of Toronto Press, 2007); and D. R. Songer, *The Transformation of the Supreme Court of Canada: An Empirical Examination* (University of Toronto Press, 2008).

[17] The original three provinces were New Brunswick, Nova Scotia and the United Province of Canada, comprising present-day Ontario and Quebec. Between 1867 and 1949, six more Provinces joined (British Columbia, Prince Edward Island and Newfoundland) or were created from federal territories (Manitoba, Saskatchewan and Alberta). Now Canada has ten provinces and three federal territories (Yukon, Northwestern Territories and Nunavut).

[18] Supreme and Exchequer Courts Act, RS, 1900, c 154, later known as the Supreme Court Act.

[19] G. P. Browne, *The Judicial Committee and the British North America Act* (University of Toronto Press, 1967). Interestingly, one of the interviewed Justices pointed out that following Canada's claim of independence from the British colonial power in the 1920s, judgments of the British highest courts were not considered binding on Canadian courts anymore.

[20] W. Kaplan, *Canadian Maverick. The Life and Times of Ivan C. Rand* (University of Toronto Press, 2009) at 98 *et seq.*

of right, introducing a leave-to-appeal mechanism that gave the Court control over its own docket.[21] Since the Court could now select the cases it would review, its docket decreased rapidly, enabling the Court to focus on cases with national relevance. Furthermore, unlike its US counterpart, the Court has the possibility of delivering advisory opinions – so-called reference cases – on constitutional or other issues referred to it by federal or provincial governments.[22] All decisions of the Supreme Court of Canada are published in English and in French in the Canada Supreme Court Reports. This publication encompasses the written and oral judgment of the Court as well as the reason for the judgment.[23]

Originally composed of six members, the Court's membership grew over the years to reach the current total of nine. According to the Supreme Court Act, the Court is composed of one Chief Justice and eight Puisne (Associate) Justices exercising jurisdiction over appeals from provincial courts in civil and criminal matters.[24] These are appointed by the Governor in Council, that is, the Governor General of Canada acting on the advice of the Federal Cabinet.[25] The Court's composition takes into account regional representation.[26] Cases in the Supreme Court of Canada are resolved by a minimum of five Justices,[27] but in most cases the judicial panel is composed of seven or nine Justices. Each judge is assisted by three law clerks, who provide research assistance.

[21] Cases can be resolved by the Supreme Court of Canada if leave to appeal is granted by a panel of three justices on the court. The leave is granted only if a question of public importance is at stake or if a relevant legal issue warrants consideration of the Court: Supreme Court Act 1985 (Canada), ss 40(1) and 43(3). Between 2003 and 2013, the number of applications for leave to appeal which were granted fluctuated between 11 per cent and 18 per cent of the applications submitted to the Court. Further statistics from 2003 to 2013 can be retrieved from the SCC's website at www.scc-csc.gc.ca/case-dossier/stat/index-eng.aspx

[22] Supreme Court Act, RSC, 1985, c S-26, s 53.

[23] The judgments are also available online at scc-csc.lexum.com/scc-csc/en/nav.do

[24] Supreme Court Act, RSC, 1985, c S-26, s 4(1).

[25] *Ibid.*, s 4(2). In order to be eligible to become a Supreme Court Justice, candidates must be superior court judges or barristers with at least ten years' standing at the Bar of a province or a territory. Justices can sit in the Supreme Court until the age of 75 (Supreme Court Act, 1985, s 9(2)).

[26] Regional representation results from a combination of legislation and conventions. The Supreme Court Act requires three Justices to come from Quebec (Supreme Court Act, RSC, 1985, c S-26, s 6). Of the Court's remaining seats, conventionally, three are allocated to Ontario, two to the Western Provinces and one to Atlantic Canada.

[27] Supreme Court Act, RCS, 1985, s 25. In exceptional circumstances, the quorum can consist of four Justices: see *ibid.*, ss 28(2) and 29.

4.2.2 *The Canadian Charter of Rights and Freedoms*

The Charter is a constitutional declaration of fundamental rights drawing inspiration from various international human rights covenants[28] and from the 1791 Bill of Rights to the US Constitution. Due to their similarity – both in terms of wording of the provisions and of the legal culture they promote – these two declarations of rights can be described as 'genetically related'.[29] However, the Canadian Charter goes beyond its more than 200-year-old US predecessor in its reflection of an expansive conception of rights – a hallmark of modern constitutionalism. This was the direct result of the influence of international human rights treaties and conventions on the Charter's drafters, and consequently, on its content.[30]

The Charter has supremacy over all federal and provincial enactments. The power to strike down legislation inconsistent with the Charter is expressly codified in section 52(1) of the Constitution Act, 1982, which entrenches the Canadian version of the US Supremacy Clause. It provides that the constitution, including the Charter, is the supreme law of Canada, and mandates that laws that are inconsistent with it are of no force or effect 'to the extent of the inconsistency'.[31] This makes the Charter a stronger Bill of Rights than its predecessor, the interpretative Bill of Rights enacted in 1960 in Canada[32] and those still in force in New Zealand and the United Kingdom.[33] At the same time, the Charter differs from the US

[28] Especially the European Convention on Human Rights (*infra* note 36), as indicated by Kent Roach: see K. Roach, 'Constitutional, Remedial and International Dialogues about Rights: The Canadian Experience', *Texas Int'l L. J.* 40 (2005) 537–76, at 541–46.

[29] See L. Henkin, 'A New Birth of Constitutionalism: Genetic Influences and Genetic Defects', *Cardozo L. Rev.* 14 (1993) 533–47, at 536–38; and L. Weinrib, 'Review: Of Diligence and Dice, Reconstituting Canada's Constitution', *University of Toronto L. J.* 42:2 (1992) 207–27, at 220.

[30] See J. Claydon, 'International Human Rights Law and the Interpretation of the Canadian Charter of Rights and Freedoms', *Supreme Court L. Rev.* 4:1 (1982) 287–302, at 295–302, noting the influence of the European Convention on Human Rights, the UN Universal Declaration of Human Rights and other international human rights instruments on the Charter.

[31] Constitution Act, 1982 being Schedule B to the Canada Act, 1982 (UK), 1982, c 11, s 52(1).

[32] In 1960 a Canadian Bill of Rights was enacted as an ordinary statute by the Canadian Parliament. The Bill, still in effect today, is an interpretive Bill of Rights listing a series of fundamental freedoms and providing that all other laws be 'so construed and applied so as not to abrogate, abridge or infringe' any of the rights or freedoms declared in the Bill itself. Canadian Bill of Rights, 'An Act for the Recognition and Protection of Human Rights and Fundamental Freedoms', SC 1960, c 44.

[33] For a comparison of the Bills of Rights adopted in Canada, the United Kingdom and New Zealand, which, in different forms, accommodate judicial protection of fundamental rights

Bill of Rights in that it includes a general 'salvage' or 'limitations' clause in its section 1. This clause allows the government to justify reasonable limits on rights,[34] an innovation subsequently adopted in New Zealand and South Africa.[35] Unlike under the constitutions of other common law jurisdictions – like India or Ireland, for example – or under the European Convention on Human Rights (ECHR),[36] the Canadian limitations clause is open-ended and does not prescribe the reasons that can justify limitations of rights.[37] The Charter thereby implicitly acknowledges that no right can be treated as absolute in the Canadian legal system.[38] This way courts are permitted to uphold statutes found to interfere with Charter rights, provided that legislation meets the procedural ('prescribed by law') and substantive ('demonstrably justified in a free and democratic society') requirements of section 1.[39] Section 24(1) gives the Court the power to

with claims of parliamentary sovereignty, see S. Gardbaum, *The New Commonwealth Model of Constitutionalism: Theory and Practice* (Cambridge University Press, 2013).

[34] s 1 Charter states: 'The *Canadian Charter of Rights and Freedoms* guarantees the rights and freedoms set out in it subject only to such reasonable limits prescribed by law as can be demonstrably justified in a free and democratic society'.

[35] See s 5 ('Justified Limitations') of the New Zealand Bill of Rights Act 1990 and s 36 ('Limitation of Rights') of the 1996 Constitution of South Africa.

[36] Convention for the Protection of Human Rights and Fundamental Freedoms (4 November 1950) 213 UNTS 222; 312 ETS 5, entered into force 3 September 1953.

[37] This clause derives from some earlier twentieth-century human rights instruments. See Jackson, Constitutional Engagement, *supra* note 2 at 86, fn 88–91.

[38] Section 1 applies to all individual rights entrenched in the Charter. Although this was a much-debated issue back in the mid-1980s, the SCC eventually indicated that the general limitations clause of section 1 does, in fact, find application also to s. 12 of the Charter which prohibits 'cruel and unusual punishment' (and therefore torture); see *R v. Smith*, [1987] 1 S.C.R. 1045. Canadian constitutional law scholar Peter Hogg, however, believes that section 1 can never apply to section 12 of the Charter. He indicated that section 12 'may be an absolute right. Perhaps it is the only one': P. W. Hogg, *Constitutional Law of Canada. 2003 Student Edition* (Scarborough: Thomson Canada Limited, 2003), at 822.

[39] In *R v. Oakes*, 1 SCR 103 (1986), a case dealing with the constitutionality of a reverse onus provision of the Narcotic Control Act, RSC 1970, the SCC developed the test for the application of the balancing mechanism set out in Section 1. According to the two-stage *Oakes* test, courts first need to establish whether there has been an interference with a Charter right. If an interference is found, and the government action has been authorised by law, the Court then moves to the second step to decide whether the right was legitimately denied under Section 1 and the interference - and corresponding law - can be 'demonstrably justified in a free and democratic society', and therefore 'salvaged' from a declaration of unconstitutionality. This second step has three important components, requiring a court to assess whether: (1) 'the measures adopted … [are] reasonably connected to the objective' (rationality); (2) 'the means … impair "as little as possible" the right or freedom in question' (minimal impairment); (3) there is 'proportionality between the effects of the measure responsible for limiting the Charter right and the objective which has been identified as of "sufficient importance"' (proportionality as such): *R v. Oakes*, 139.

devise remedies for individuals whose Charter rights have been violated.[40] A joint reading of sections 52(1) and 24(1) of the Charter vests the power of judicial review in the Canadian courts. The power of courts to declare statutes unconstitutional is, however, not without limits: a further defining feature of the Charter is its section 33, which allows provincial and federal legislatures to enact laws for a renewable five-year period, notwithstanding the fundamental freedoms and legal rights protected by the Charter, as interpreted by the courts.[41] Section 33 has indeed been employed to re-enact legislation in response to a declaration of unconstitutionality. Finally, section 32(2) of the Charter originally provided that the right to equality protected by section 15 would become effective three years after enactment of the Charter.

4.3 The Extent of the SCC's Engagement in Judicial Dialogue

With the new functions that the Constitution Act 1982 vested with the Court, the vast majority of judicial review cases now fell under the Charter's purview, and civil liberties cases rapidly increased in number, bringing Canada closer to the United States in the level of rights-based litigation.[42] The majority of citations of comparative material are in cases involving questions of individual rights rather than questions of allocation of powers among the levels of government.[43] This section

[40] s 24(1) Charter provides that '[a]nyone whose rights or freedoms, as guaranteed by this Charter, have been infringed or denied may apply to a court of competent jurisdiction to obtain such remedy as the court considers appropriate and just in the circumstances.'

[41] *Ibid.*, s 33: '(1) Parliament or the legislature of a Province may expressly declare in an Act of Parliament or of the legislature, as the case may be, that the act or a provision thereof shall operate notwithstanding a provision included in section 2 or sections 7 to 15 of this Charter ... (3) A declaration made under subsection (1) shall cease to have effect five years after it comes into force or on such earlier date as may be specified in the declaration.'

[42] Table 4.1 shows that the SCC's total case load increased significantly in the first 10 years under the Charter, with constitutional cases accounting for around 40 per cent of the Court's total judgments. However, the case load rapidly decreased in the second half of the 2000s, bringing the SCC even closer to the US Supreme Court in terms of cases adjudicated per year. The US Supreme Court handed down full opinions in 78 cases in 2013, 27 of which concerned constitutional questions. See 'The Supreme Court 2013 Term: The Statistics', *Harvard L. Rev.* 128:1 (2014), 401–15.

[43] However, use of foreign case law is certainly not reserved only to fundamental rights cases. A small number of significant institutional cases - addressing the boundaries between federal and provincial powers - is dealt with each year by the Court. See, for example, *General Motors of Canada Ltd v. City National Leasing* [1989] 1 SCR 641; *Ontario Hydro v. Ontario (Labour Relations Board)* [1993] 3 SCR 327; *Reference re Secession of Quebec* [1998] 2 SCR 217; *BC v. Imperial Tobacco Canada Ltd* [2005] 2 SCR 473; *Canadian Western Bank*

first provides a general overview of the SCC's references to foreign case law (subsection 4.3.1). Next, the analysis focuses on trends in the SCC's citations of foreign case law (subsection 4.3.2). Thirdly, it is examined in which parts of the judgments foreign jurisprudence is relied on (subsection 4.3.3). Finally, the reasons behind the frequency of citations of foreign law and its development over time are analysed, discussing *inter alia* the example of the SCC's case law on the interpretation of the limitation clause (subsection 4.3.4).

4.3.1 General Overview

We first consider the number of decisions and citations of foreign case law in the SCC's judgments in human rights cases between 1982 and 2014. Next, the influence of judges' attitudes towards the use of foreign case law in adjudication is analysed on the basis of the information obtained through interviews. Finally, particularities of the Canadian system are addressed, which might also influence the frequency with which foreign case law is cited.

4.3.1.1 Number of Citations

Table 4.1 shows that the number of cases granted leave to the SCC increased between the end of the 1980s and the first half of the 1990s,[44] reaching its peak in 1990 and remaining high at least until 1997. Arguably, therefore, 1990–97 was the period when most of the new Charter cases reached the Court.

A comparison of columns B and D and columns E and F of Table 4.1 illustrates that the SCC's tendency to refer to foreign case law is present not only in constitutional cases,[45] but also in other areas of law, a fact highlighting the SCC's generally favourable attitude towards citation of foreign case law.

Human rights cases predominately cite US, Australian, ECtHR and New Zealand judgments. The steady increase in human rights cases reaching

v. Alberta [2007] 2 SCR 3; and *Consolidated Fastfrate Inc v. Western Canada Council of Teamsters* [2009] 3 SCR 407.

[44] This is roughly the time when s 15, which took effect in 1985, received its first serious judicial interpretation by the SCC, in *Andrews v. Law Society of British Columbia* [1989] 1 SCR 143.

[45] The expression 'constitutional cases' is used here broadly, to include not only cases involving the interpretation and application of constitutional provisions but also those dealing with institutional and/or human rights issues.

Table 4.1 *Number of Decisions and Citations of Foreign Case Law (CFCL) (1982–2014)*

Year	- A - Total decisions per year	- B - Cases with CFCL (constitutional & others)	- C - Constitutional cases	- D - Constitutional cases with CFCL (% of total decisions)	- E - Total CFCL per year	- F - Total CFCL in constitutional cases per year
1982	119	39 (32.8%)	15	4 (3.4%)	113	10
1983	90	17 (18.9%)	12	2 (2.2%)	36	4
1984	64	15 (23.4%)	13	3 (4.7%)	112	13
1985	84	31 (36.9%)	28	9 (10.7%)	182	48
1986	76	32 (42.1%)	19	9 (11.8%)	200	97
1987	94	28 (29.8%)	34	12 (12.8%)	178	89
1988	106	31 (29.2%)	32	12 (11.3%)	155	66
1989	133	49 (36.8%)	61	26 (19.5%)	209	122
1990	144	60 (41.7%)	80	33 (22.9%)	327	196
1991	108	29 (26.8%)	38	15 (13.9%)	180	103
1992	109	39 (35.7%)	49	20 (18.3%)	235	57
1993	138	40 (28.9%)	53	21 (15.2%)	204	88
1994	111	33 (29.7%)	41	17 (15.3%)	169	81
1995	108	37 (34.2%)	39	21 (22.7%)	201	122
1996	121	39 (32.2%)	54	23 (19.0%)	136	78
1997	110	43 (39.1%)	33	18 (16.4%)	195	83
1998	90	27 (30.0%)	33	15 (16.7%)	80	37
1999	80	26 (32.5%)	36	13 (16.3%)	163	82
2000	69	21 (30.4%)	20	7 (10.1%)	111	26
2001	94	32 (34.0%)	34	15 (16.0%)	161	90
2002	86	38 (44.2%)	38	21 (24.4%)	184	55
2003	74	21 (28.4%)	27	8 (10.8%)	67	21
2004	83	18 (21.7%)	28	7 (8.4%)	53	26
2005	87	19 (21.8%)	30	8 (9.2%)	59	19
2006	59	20 (33.8%)	18	3 (5.1%)	64	3
2007	55	28 (50.9%)	20	12 (21.8%)	157	77
2008	72	25 (34.7%)	19	7 (9.7%)	110	52
2009	62	19 (30.6%)	18	7 (11.3%)	114	86
2010	67	17 (25.4%)	27	9 (13.4%)	84	66
2011	67	16 (23.9%)	20	5 (7.5%)	100	37
2012	75	24 (32.0%)	19	10 (13.3%)	55	18
2013	74	30 (40.5%)	16	8 (10.8%)	106	20
2014	78	19 (24.4%)	31	13 (16.7%)	153	109

the SCC, combined with the lack of domestic jurisprudence interpreting the Charter, account for the extensive use of US judgments displayed in Table 4.2. Frequent citations of British judgments are not surprising, given the historical ties that exist between the Canadian court system and the UK and Commonwealth systems. The Charter's enactment, however, at least with regard to constitutional cases, soon brought the 'English captivity'[46] to an end, as it resulted in a rapid decline in institutional cases and a corresponding decrease in the number of UK judgments cited by the SCC. Conversely, the increase in human rights cases reaching the SCC made US judgments valuable resources, and these are extensively resorted to, reaching a peak in the early 1990s. It is our view that this rise was determined mainly by two reasons: first, claims of civil rights' violations previously filed under the BNAA's provisions concerning the allocation of legislative competences between the Federation and the provinces started to be filed under Charter provisions;[47] second, the Charter's enactment changed citizens' attitudes towards the protection of fundamental rights. The Parliament was no longer the only appropriate place to protect and advance fundamental rights, and courts became a preferred locus for raising rights claims.

Arguably, language also plays an important role in the choice of the foreign jurisdictions considered. This was confirmed by the interviewed Justices.[48] As it can be inferred from Table 4.2, in the 32 years of the SCC's activity surveyed in this chapter, more than 98 per cent of the SCC's decisions in constitutional cases made reference to six main jurisdictions and one supranational court. These were either former members of the British Commonwealth, or they were speaking the same languages, English and French (both official languages in Canada): the United States, the United Kingdom, Australia, the ECtHR (whose decisions are generally issued in both English and French), New Zealand, France and South Africa, listed in order of frequency of citations. Citations of US and UK judgments alone account for more than 86 per cent of the total foreign citations in constitutional cases.

[46] B. Laskin, 'The Supreme Court of Canada: A Final Court of and for Canadians', *Canadian Bar Rev.* 29:10 (1951) 1038–79, at 1045–46.

[47] For example, in *Saumur v. City of Quebec* (1953) 2 SCR 299, the SCC upheld a Jehovah's Witness's challenge to a Quebec law against distribution of literature on the streets without prior police permission. Although the case addressed religious freedom issues, the SCC based its judgment on the federal division of power, ruling that the power to regulate religious practices fell under the purview of the national government rather than of the provinces.

[48] See subsection 4.3.2 *infra*.

Table 4.2 *Citations of Foreign Case Law in Constitutional Cases per Country (1982–2014)*

YEAR	UK	US	AU	ECtHR	NZ	Other Jurisdictions
1982	5	5	–	–	–	–
1983	4	–	–	–	–	–
1984	6	6	1	–	–	–
1985	12	31	–	–	–	Bahamas: 2; Cyprus: 1; Pakistan: 2
1986	12	70	–	4	2	–
1987	18	69	–	1	1	–
1988	22	33	4	7	2	Germany: 1
1989	32	74	5	9	–	Belgium: 1; EU: 1
1990	23	157	2	9	1	India: 2
1991	5	92	2	2	1	Ireland: 1
1992	20	25	1	2	–	–
1993	31	50	2	2	2	–
1994	32	40	11	1	1	Germany: 2; Hong Kong: 1; Israel: 1; South Africa: 1
1995	39	77	3	2	–	–
1996	24	50	1	–	3	–
1997	12	63	6	–	2	–
1998	18	14	2	2		France: 1
1999	34	33	5	–	5	EU: 1; India: 1; South Africa: 1
2000	11	15	-	–	–	–
2001	23	51	10	6		–
2002	22	24	4	4	–	Israel: 1; South Africa: 1
2003	10	11	–	–	–	–
2004	2	23	–	1	–	–
2005	5	8	–	–	–	EU: 2; France 4
2006	–	3	–	–	–	–
2007	14	40	5	4	2	France: 4; Israel: 4; South Africa: 1
2008	19	24	6	–	2	Hong Kong: 1
2009	26	30	7	3	4	South Africa: 3
2010	19	28	4	8	4	Netherlands: 1; South Africa: 1
2011	4	13	6	2	1	France: 7; Germany: 4
2012	7	9	–	–	2	–
2013	3	17	–	–	–	–

(*continued*)

Table 4.2 *(continued)*

YEAR	UK	US	AU	ECtHR	NZ	Other Jurisdictions
2014	29	33	6	3	4	EU: 6; Inter-American Court of Human Rights: 4; Belgium: 5; France: 3; Germany: 2; Ireland: 2; Hong Kong: 1; Singapore: 1; South Africa: 1;
Total	**545**	**1216**	**93**	**72**	**39**	France: **19**; EU: **10**; Germany: **9**; South Africa: **9**; Belgium: **6**; Israel: **6**; Inter-American Court of Human Rights: **4**; Hong Kong: **3**; India: **3**; Ireland: **3**; Bahamas: **2**; Pakistan: **2**; Cyprus: **1**; Singapore: **1**; The Netherlands: **1**.

4.3.1.2 Attitudes of Individual Justices

Individual Justices are considered to have left their mark on the development of the use of comparative law in the Supreme Court of Canada. Former Justice Gérard La Forest, who was a member of the Supreme Court from 1985 until 1997, was cited in an interview as an example of a Justice who had been very interested in foreign law. One of the interviewees felt that the influence of comparative law on the Supreme Court's decision-making diminished after Justice La Forest left the Court.[49] Still, the interest in comparative law within the Court is visible in various publications and public speeches of current and former Justices, including Justice L'Heureux-Dubé,[50] Justice LeBel[51] and Justice Binnie.[52]

[49] The interest of this Justice in comparative law transpires from his publications. See G.V. La Forest, 'The Use of International and Foreign Material in the Supreme Court of Canada' *Canadian Council on International Law. Proceedings* 17 (1988) 230–41; G.V. La Forest, 'The Expanding Role of the Supreme Court of Canada in International Law Issues' *Canadian Yearbook of Int'l L.* 34 (1996) 89–102.

[50] C. L'Heureux-Dubé, 'The Importance of Dialogue: Globalization and the International Impact of the Rehnquist Court', *Tulsa L. J.* 34 (1998–1999) 15–40.

[51] Justice L. LeBel and G. Chao, 'The Rise of International Law in Canadian Constitutional Litigation: Fugue or Fusion? Recent Developments and Challenges in Internalizing International Law', *Supreme Court L. Rev.* 16 (2002) 23–60; Justice L. LeBel and A. Gonsalves, 'Comments on the Integration of International Law into the Canadian Legal System', Federal Judicial Center of the American Society of International Law (ed.), *International Law and Litigation for US Judges* (30 October 2006) retrieved from www.fjc.gov/public/pdf.nsf/lookup/Intl0616.pdf/$file/Intl0616.pdf

[52] Justice I. Binnie, 'Judging the Judges: May They Boldly Go Where Justice Rand Went Before', *Canadian J. of L. and Jurisprudence* 26 (2013) 2–21.

Despite the described willingness of the members of the Canadian Supreme Court to engage with foreign law, one interviewed Justice observed that the members' interest in international consensus, and in foreign law as such, has faded over the years. Only in exceptional cases, for example a case in which the question of the definition of 'torture' arose,[53] this interest can still be discerned.

The Canadian Justices mentioned the controversy in the US Supreme Court,[54] and pointed out that no similar debate exists within the SCC concerning the legitimacy of considering foreign law. In particular, no theory of originalism, as was advocated by Justice Scalia in the United States,[55] is present in the Supreme Court of Canada. Conversely, the progressive hermeneutical approach embraced by the SCC (the 'living tree' metaphor) arguably plays a central role in explaining the Court's use of foreign case law.[56] As pointed out by Vicki Jackson, 'while living constitutionalism need not embrace the consideration of transnational sources, it is more open to them than, for example, highly intentionalist or originalist modes of interpretation'.[57]

The Justices thought that the search for guidance in comparative law is possibly accepted more easily in Canada because it is a less-populated country than the United States is and because it was recently a colony. The smaller size of the country's population might encourage judges to look beyond national borders sooner than judges in countries with bigger populations would do, because of a generally more 'open' outlook towards the transnational context in countries that experience influences from 'bigger' neighbouring countries in the political, economic, social and legal domains.[58] Moreover, a former member of the Canadian Supreme Court

[53] See subsection 4.4.2 *infra*.

[54] See in particular N. Dorsen, 'The Relevance of Foreign Legal Materials in US Constitutional Cases: A Conversation between Justice Antonin Scalia and Justice Stephen Breyer', *Int'l J. of Constitutional L.* 3:4 (2005) 519–41.

[55] A. Scalia, *A Matter of Interpretation: Federal Courts and the Law* (Princeton University Press, 1998).

[56] The 'living tree' metaphor and corresponding doctrine of constitutional interpretation trace back to Lord Sankey's opinion for the Privy Council in the *Persons Case* recognising the right of women to sit in the Canadian Senate: 'The British North America Act planted in Canada a living tree capable of growth and expansion within its natural limits ... Their Lordships do not conceive it to be the duty of this Board ... to cut down the provisions of the Act by a narrow and technical construction, but rather to give it a large and liberal interpretation' (*Edward v. Canada (AG)*, AC 124 (1930) 136).

[57] Jackson, Constitutional Engagement, *supra* note 2, at 97

[58] The correctness of this assumption seems to be confirmed by M. Gelter and M. M. Siems, 'Language, Legal Origins, and Culture before the Courts: Cross-Citations between Supreme Courts in Europe', *Supreme Court Economic Rev.* 21:1 (2013) 215–69.

considered that the Canadian heritage of two legal systems (the British and the French) stimulates judges to keep multiculturalism and multi-legalism alive. Finally, an 'evolutionary' aspect in the Supreme Court's decision-making, including the citation of cases from other Commonwealth jurisdictions, is considered natural in light of the Court's role in further developing the common law.[59]

4.3.1.3 Particularities of the Canadian Legal System

Several other reasons, more specifically related to Canada, have been put forth by legal scholars to explain the SCC's use of foreign judgments. From an institutional standpoint, Canada is a bilingual and bijural country. It is thought that familiarity with more than one language and legal tradition - originating from Quebec's French linguistic heritage and civil law tradition - makes Canadian lawyers and judges more accustomed to understanding multiple legal systems. This increases the likelihood that Canadian lawyers and judges access and understand foreign legal materials and are more prone to include them in their submissions and *amici curiae* briefs (lawyers) and their decisions (judges).[60] Finally, considering the experiences of Hungary and South Africa, extensive revision or enactment of a new constitutional document and corresponding lack of a line of domestic precedents interpreting the new provisions or document may have promoted recourse to foreign case law by the SCC.[61]

While the openness to foreign jurisprudence has remained unchanged over the years, citation rates of foreign jurisprudence declined between the end of the 1990s and the end of the 2000s (see Table 4.1, column D), indicating that once the SCC had developed a sufficient domestic jurisprudence, it relied less on foreign sources and more on its own domestic body of established case law. More generally, today the attitude of the

[59] See subsection 4.5.1 *infra*.

[60] However, as Table 4.2 shows, the citation process is dominated by decisions from common law countries, that is, from only one of Canada's languages and legal cultures. On this point, see also P. McCormick, 'Waiting for Globalization: An Empirical Study of the McLachlin Court's Foreign Judicial Citations', *Ottawa L. Rev.* 41:2 (2010) 209–44.

[61] Charter claims were qualitatively different from earlier arguments relying on the BNAA in that they were based on direct constitutional protection of civil liberties. This made pre-Charter precedent of little help to judges seeking guidance on civil liberties issues. On this, then-Justice McLachlin noted: '[T]he difficulty is that the Canadian Charter ... is a new experience. We have not had anything like it before. Our judges cannot rely on their own experience to breathe life into the Charter; instead they must find that life elsewhere'; B. McLachlin, 'The Charter of Rights and Freedoms: A Judicial Perspective', *University of British Columbia L. Rev.* 23 (1989) 579–90, at 580. The tendency to resort to foreign case law is likely to decline when a significant line of domestic jurisprudence becomes available.

SCC towards citation of foreign case law is still in flux. Confronted with the major demands that the Charter's enactment brought on the Court, the SCC resorted to the example provided by foreign judgments to develop domestic jurisprudence.

4.3.2 Trends in the SCC's Citations of Foreign Case Law

This section will use both quantitative and qualitative information to identify trends in the SCC's citations of foreign case law, including which jurisdictions are most frequently cited by the SCC, the possible existence of a common legal and cultural heritage with these jurisdictions and the type of use – whether positive or aversive – that the SCC makes of the cited foreign jurisprudence.

In Canada, the use of foreign jurisprudence seems to have received stimulus from a variety of factors. First and foremost, there is the Commonwealth practice of considering the common law as a single, unified legal system with a high degree of permeability between jurisprudences.[62] When addressing judicial review issues under the Constitution of one Commonwealth member, the Privy Council would refer to cases involving other members' Constitutions, making comparison a familiar exercise in constitutional adjudication and practice.[63] Canadian legal actors therefore became accustomed to reading cases from the United Kingdom, Australia and New Zealand, all English-speaking countries sharing the same Commonwealth history and similar social and economic conditions. While Canada is no longer a member of this system, extra-systemic materials are today resorted to due to perceived membership of a single cultural space which justifies jurisprudential cross-references. The numerous references to UK, Australian and New Zealand judgments illustrated by Table 4.2 can therefore be explained through the 'genealogic interpretation'[64] theory: a common law court may find it useful to resort to judgments of a foreign court of a country belonging (presently or in the past) to the same cultural or legal space to solve controversial cases,

[62] The theory was that there was a single, monolithic body of common law, see W. R. Lederman, *Continuing Canadian Constitutional Dilemmas* (Toronto: Butterworths, 1981) at 68; also described as 'a comprehensive body of doctrine … uniform throughout the British Empire' by P. W. Hogg, *Constitutional Law of Canada. 2007 Edition* (Scarborough: Thomson Canada Limited, 2007) at 32.

[63] Jackson, Constitutional Engagement, *supra* note 2, at 96

[64] S. Choudhry, 'Globalization in Search of Justification: Toward a Theory of Comparative Constitutional Interpretation', *Indiana L. J.* 74:3 (1999) 819–92, at 838 *et seq.*

whenever suitable legislative or jurisprudential aids are missing within its own legal system.[65]

Concerning US cases specifically, it is important to note that since the early days of the Canadian Confederation, the Canadian judiciary was aware of and referred to cases decided by US state and federal courts. The first years after 1867 were also characterised by discussions about the similarities and differences of the two constitutional systems and by Canadian courts' references to US constitutional cases.[66] The Privy Council, however, soon established a formalist approach to statutory interpretation and indicated that US decisions bore no relevance in the adjudication of cases arising from Canada.[67] As a result, the Constitution Act of 1867 came to be interpreted almost exclusively on the basis of domestic (i.e., Canadian and Commonwealth-based) legal materials. This approach discouraged any investigation into or exploration of foreign case outcomes, which remained the practice even after the SCC became Canada's highest appellate court in 1949.

This scenario was drastically altered by the adoption of the Charter, whose drafters incorporated the US experience with civil rights jurisprudence but also modified the original draft of the Charter to enhance its compatibility with a distinctively Canadian conception of rights and as a result of concerns arising from the US experience.[68] Once enacted,

[65] De Vergottini, Oltre il Dialogo, *supra* note 7, at 108.

[66] The use of US case law by Canadian courts has been studied extensively: Lex, 'The Authority of American Decisions in Canadian and English Courts', *Canada L. J.* 35 17–18 (1899) 518–20; J.M. MacIntyre, 'The Use of American Cases in Canadian Courts', *University of British Columbia L. Rev.* 2:3 (1964–1966) 478–90: the articles suggest that, after an initial period of acceptance, a bias emerged against American authorities; S.I. Bushnell, 'Comment: The Use of American Cases', *University of New Brunswick L. J.* 35:1 (1986) 157–81. Bushnell found that the use of American cases declined in the 1920s to re-emerge only in the 1970s. C.P. Manfredi, 'The Use of United States Decisions by the Supreme Court of Canada under the Charter of Rights and Freedoms', *Canadian J. of Political Science* 23:3 (1990) 499–518. Manfredi notes that between 1949 and 1968, American cases constituted less than 2 per cent of all citations; conversely, between 1969 and 1978, a significant increase in US citations occurred. American jurisprudence therefore influenced Canadian legal doctrine even before 1982. This shows that the enhancement of fundamental rights in Canada was connected to references to US cases even before the Charter's enactment. See also P.W. Hogg, 'Canada: From Privy Council to Supreme Court', J. Goldsworthy (ed.), *Interpreting Constitutions. A Comparative Study* (Oxford University Press, 2007) 55–105.

[67] Early Privy Council case law rejected the view that US authority would be controlling in the interpretation of the Canadian constitution: *Bank of Toronto v. Lambe* [1887] UKPC 29 (Privy Council) (appeal taken from Canada).

[68] The October 1980 draft of s 1 referred to 'reasonable limits … in a free and democratic society with a parliamentary system of government'. The Charter's drafters eventually removed reference to 'a parliamentary system of government' from s 1 in order not to imply the

the Charter's language similarities with the US Bill of Rights made US jurisprudence immediately relevant.[69] Indeed, on the one hand, the sections dealing with group rights addressed distinctive aspects of Canadian society, and the override provision of Section 33 reflected concerns of judicial activism and the willingness to safeguard – at least to some extent – the British tradition of parliamentary sovereignty. On the other hand, both the US and Canadian declarations entrench a series of negative rights (substantive and procedural) protecting individuals from unconstitutional state action, leaving outside of their purview positive or social rights. These negative rights are included in section 2 and sections 7 to 15 of the Charter and are expressed in broad terms analogous to the First, Fourth, Fifth, Sixth, Eighth and Fourteenth Amendments to the US Constitution, subject only to the limitation of section 1. The Charter, therefore, brought the US and the Canadian legal systems closer, the latter acquiring a rights-based foundation which had characterised the former for several decades. It came naturally to the SCC to resort to US case law that interpreted constitutional provisions cognate to those entrenched in the Charter[70] Furthermore,

irrelevance of US jurisprudence in Charter adjudication: P.W. Hogg, *Constitutional Law of Canada, 1985 Edition* (Toronto: Carswell, 1985) at 679, fn 149. On the other hand, provincial concerns about the interpretation given to the expression 'due process' by US courts led to its replacement with 'principles of fundamental justice' in s 7 of the *Charter*: R. Romanow, J. White and H. Leeson, *Canada Notwithstanding: The Making of the Constitution, 1976–1982* (Toronto: Carswell, 1984), at 245–46. More generally, on the influence of the US *Bill of Rights* on the drafting of the Charter, see Y. Dotan, 'The Spillover Effect of Bills of Rights: A Comparative Assessment of the Impact of Bills of Rights in Canada and Israel', *American J. of Comparative L.* 53:2 (2005) 293–341.

69 For early comparisons between the Charter and the US Constitution, see D. Stone and F.K. Walpole, 'The Canadian Constitution Act and the Constitution of the United States: A Comparative Analysis' *Canadian-American L. J.* 2:1 (1983) 1–36; W.S. Tarnopolsky, 'The New Canadian Charter of Rights and Freedoms as Compared and Contrasted with the American Bill of Rights', *Human Rights Quarterly* 5:3 (1983) 227–74; P. Bender, 'The Canadian Charter of Rights and Freedoms and the United States Bill of Rights: A Comparison' *McGill L. J.* 28:4 (1983) 811–66; and F.L. Morton, 'The Politics of Rights: What Canadians Should Know About the American Bill of Rights', *Windsor Rev. of Legal and Social Issues* 1:1 (1989) 61–96.

70 CJ Dickson expressed willingness to examine US case law: 'the American courts have the benefit of two hundred years of experience in constitutional interpretation. This wealth of experience may offer guidance to the judiciary in this country', *R v. Simmons* [1988] 2 SCR 495, 516. The same spirit is evident in Justice L'Heureux-Dubé's concurring opinion in *R v. Elshaw* [1991] 3 SCR 24, 57: 'to reject the American experience out of hand and to refuse to engage in its examination, at least as a comparative exercise, would surely be … a [great] mistake'. See also C. L'Heureux-Dubé, 'Two Supreme Courts: A Study in Contrast', M. McKenna (ed.), *The Canadian and American Constitutions in Comparative Perspectives* (Calgary University Press, 1993) 149–66, at 163.

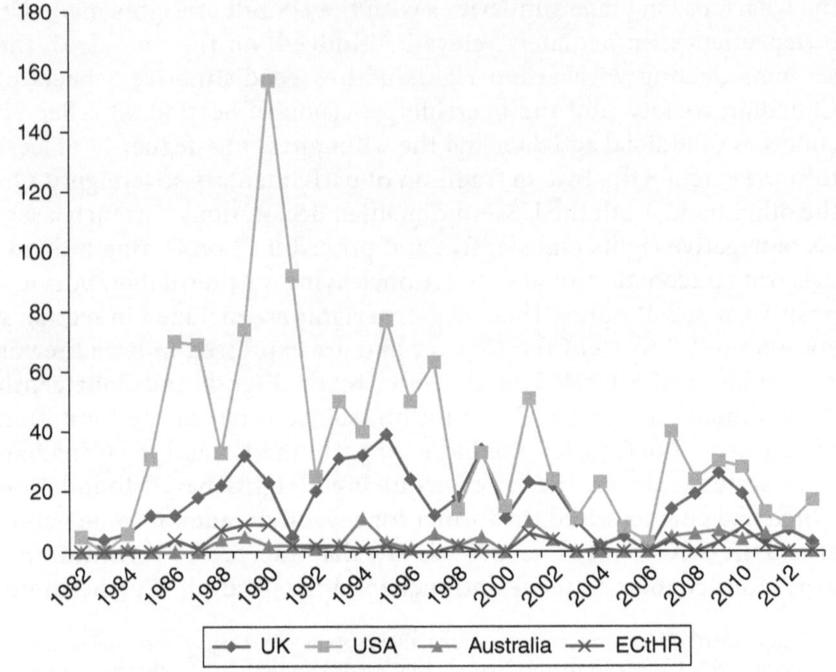

Figure 4.1 Citations of Foreign Judgments per Country in Constitutional Cases (four most-often cited jurisdictions) (1982–2014)

even when the language of the Charter differed from the one of the US Bill of Rights, US cases represented a useful source of ideas and comparisons, in order to foresee possible, long-term outcomes of certain interpretations.

US judgments, therefore, soon became a valuable resource, and one that was resorted to with increasing frequency. As shown in Figure 4.1, citations to US judgments soon exceed by far citations to cases decided in other jurisdictions. They reached a peak in the early 1990s, roughly the time when the first cases based on s 15 - the Charter's equality provision which took effect in 1985 - reached the Supreme Court. Since then, the trend of citations to US cases has been slowly decreasing, but it is undeniable that the United States still represents the most cited foreign jurisdiction for the Supreme Court of Canada.

From a qualitative standpoint, our research shows that while the SCC's use of American judgments in constitutional cases is focused on US cases decided in the latter half of the twentieth century, this US jurisprudence relied on is not necessarily the most recent.[71] Furthermore, the fact that the SCC has cited US rulings coming not only from the US Supreme Court but from across all levels of American courts (including lower US federal and state court judgments) suggests a rather sophisticated understanding of US jurisprudence by Canadian judges.

The Court has proven to be very conscious of the risks involved in citing foreign case law. In *Lavigne v. Ontario Public Service Employees Union*, Justice Wilson wrote:

> This Court has consistently stated that even though it may undoubtedly benefit from the experience of American and other courts in adjudicating constitutional issues, it is by no means bound by that experience or the jurisprudence it generated. The uniqueness of the Canadian Charter of Rights and Freedoms flows not only from the distinctive structure of the Charter as compared to the American Bill of Rights but also from the special features of the Canadian cultural, historical, social and political traditions.[72]

With regard to references to international case law, it can be recalled that international human rights treaties played an important role in the Charter's drafting. It should not come as a surprise, therefore, that in interpreting the Charter, the SCC is open to citation of foreign materials coming from the ECtHR or from other jurisdictions.[73]

Finally, as concerns language, sources used by the Canadian judges are most often in English or in French. The quantitative results presented in subsection 4.3.1 of this chapter highlighted that the vast majority of citations are to cases coming from English-speaking jurisdictions. Most judges in the Supreme Court of Canada would have trouble in consulting, for example, Romano-German legal sources. However, one interviewed

[71] The majority of Canadian citations concern US Supreme Court decisions taken during the Warren and Burger Courts (1953 to 1986). See C. L'Heureux-Dubé, The Importance of Dialogue, *supra* note 50, at 29: 'An informal analysis of Canadian Supreme Court decisions since 1986 revealed that the Rehnquist court was cited in fewer than one-half as many cases as the Warren Court, and in just under one-third the number of Burger Court cases.'

[72] *Lavigne v. Ontario Public Service Employees Union* [1991] 2 SCR 211.

[73] On the Charter's relationship to other international and human rights documents, see A.F. Bayefsky, 'International Human Rights Law in Canadian Courts', I. Cotler and F.P. Eliadis (eds.), *International Human Rights Law: Theory and Practice* (Montreal: Canadian Human Rights Foundation, 1992) 115–51, at 115 and 125–29. The timing of the adoption of the Charter may have reinforced Canadian openness to foreign influences, particularly since the Charter was drafted, negotiated and adopted shortly after Canada's 1976 ratifications of the International Covenant on Civil and Political Rights (ICCPR) and the International Covenant on Economic, Social and Cultural Rights (ICESCR): Jackson, Constitutional Engagement, *supra* note 2, at 239.

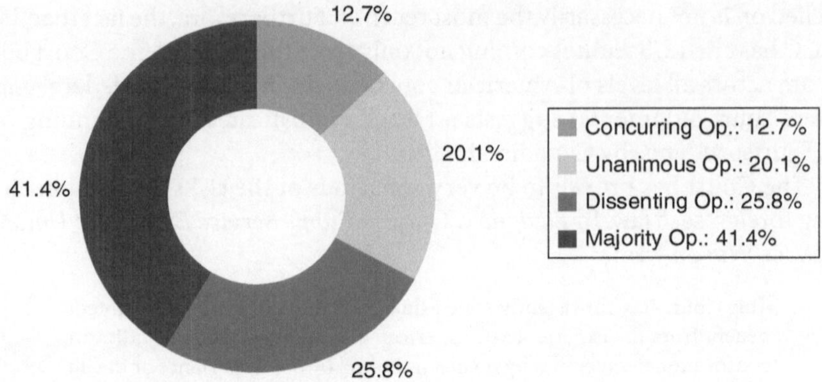

Figure 4.2 Location of Citations to Foreign Judgments in Constitutional Cases (1982–2014)

judge mentioned that he sometimes looked at decisions of the German Constitutional Court that have been translated into English.

4.3.3 Use of Comparative Material in Deliberations and Judgments

Finally, the comparative material is used by the Justices of the SCC in all parts of their judgments. The Justices usually strive to reach a unanimous judgment, but each Justice has the possibility to issue a concurring or dissenting opinion. Such opinions can provide judges with an opportunity to discuss elements of foreign law which they consider relevant for a specific judgment. However, one of the interviewed Justices observed that he would rather not make use of the possibility to write a separate opinion for the sole reason of bringing up a point of foreign law. This judge considered that it is more important to reach a majority decision in the case at hand. The quantitative analysis corroborates these reflections. While SCC decisions are notable for their high rate of unanimity (around 65 per cent of the total),[74] as Figure 4.2 shows, the highest numbers of citations of foreign judgments are found in majority and dissenting opinions. This is a sign that the number of foreign judgments cited increases with the level of disagreement on a specific issue and the number of opinions filed. Judges seem to feel compelled to cite a higher number of judgments

[74] This attitude did not change after the Charter's enactment, despite the increase in more controversial cases. See Songer, Transformation, *supra* note 16, at 210.

not only to overcome opposition from colleagues but also to make their decisions more acceptable to the public and to other institutional actors with enforcement powers. Also, on average, judges appear to resort more often to foreign case law when overturning government action than when upholding it.[75]

4.3.4 *Frequency of Citations of Foreign Case Law and Development over Time*

In addition to the general factors presented in the foregoing, a more specific, textual factor has played a fundamental role in promoting comparison with other jurisdictions and in furthering the SCC's recourse to foreign case law: we are referring here to the general 'salvage' or 'limitations' clause included in section 1 of the Charter. As previously indicated, as an explicit balancing and limiting provision, section 1 mandates courts to take into account public interests in a 'free and democratic society' in the process of reviewing governmental activity that allegedly infringes such rights.

Determining what limitations are justified in a 'free and democratic society', however, requires some degree of comparison, since the words 'free and democratic' imply a contrast with societies that are not 'free and democratic' and, conversely, commonality with others sharing those features of a 'free and democratic society'. It is clear, therefore, that such a provision represents 'a directive to engage in comparative exercise and research the position in other jurisdictions' and not to 'blindly [accept] the Canadian experience as the last word on how a free and democratic society ought to conduct itself'.[76] Indeed, in some scholars' view, section 1 represents something analogous to the express authorisation to cite foreign judgments codified in the Constitutions of South Africa and Malawi,[77] and

[75] See e.g. *R v. Morgentaler* [1988] 1 SCR 30 (19 foreign judgments); *Committee for the Commonwealth of Canada v. Canada* [1991] 1 SCR 139 (20 foreign judgments); *R v. Seaboyer* [1991] 2 SCR 577 (18 foreign judgments); *Miron v. Trudel* [1995] 2 SCR 418 (14 foreign judgments); *R v. Ruzic* [2001] 1 SCR 687 (23 foreign judgments); and *R v. Kang-Brown* [2008] 1 SCR 456 (13 foreign judgments).

[76] L'Heureux-Dubé, Two Supreme Courts, *supra* note 70, at 164; see also La Forest, The Use of International and Foreign Material, *supra* note 49, at 236.

[77] s 11(2)(c) of the Constitution of the Republic of Malawi, 1994; s 39(1) of the Constitution of South Africa, 1996. See B.-O. Bryde, 'The Constitutional Judge and the International Constitutionalism Dialogue', Markesinis and Fedtke, Judicial Recourse, *supra* note 6, 295–308, at 306; C. Saunders, 'Judicial Engagement with Comparative Law', T. Ginsburg and R. Dixon (eds.), *Comparative Constitutional Law* (Cheltenham: Edward Elgar Publishing, 2012) 571–98, at 574; Jackson, Constitutional Engagement, *supra* note 2, at 73.

provides Canadian judges with a framework where 'comparative analysis is regarded as internal to the activity of constitutional adjudication'.[78]

More generally, however, the Court's use of foreign material in Charter cases has been described by Justice Binnie as 'a question of evolution':

> In the early years, the Dickson court did make broad, sweeping pronouncements because they were laying the groundwork.... As you work through all these different situations ... you get down to much shorter strokes and much more difficult calls.... Now, we are much more into a phase of tying up loose ends and adding precision to the general principles that were enunciated.... I think the legal landscape has changed and the court has evolved with the landscape.[79]

This also confirms our introductory observations about the 'formative period' of domestic jurisprudence.[80] The interviewed Justices confirmed that the Court was initially more interested in comparative law, right after the Charter entered into force. As mentioned in subsection 4.3.2, the Charter refers to the values of a 'free and democratic society'[81] and contains similarities with catalogues of fundamental rights in national constitutions elsewhere and with the ECHR. These similarities provide a basis for legal comparison. Furthermore, Justice Dickson, who was the first to write judgments on the basis of the Charter, thought it important to take into account general international consensus when adjudicating Charter cases.[82] Amongst the interviewed Justices, several observed that the study of comparative law is part of the intellectual perspective of the SCC. These judges pointed out that Canada is a fairly new country and has inherited both British and French influences. A judge further added that one cannot help but notice what other courts do, in particular very visible ones such as the ECtHR and the Supreme Court of Israel.

4.4 The Method of the SCC's Engagement in Judicial Dialogue

The Court's working methods of how it finds out about relevant foreign and international material are discussed next. In this context, it should

[78] L. Weinrib, 'Constitutional Conceptions and Constitutional Comparativism', V. Jackson and M. Tushnet (eds.), *Defining the Field of Comparative Constitutional Law* (Westport: Praeger, 2002) 3–34, at 3–4.

[79] K. Makin, 'Justice Ian Binnie's Exit Interview', Toronto, *Globe and Mail*, 23 September 2011. See also subsection 4.3.2 *supra*.

[80] See Section 4.1 *supra*.

[81] Charter, s 1.

[82] See also R.J. Sharpe and K. Roach, *Brian Dickson: A Judge's Journey* (University of Toronto Press, 2003).

be noted at the outset that in recent years, the research on and discussion about foreign case law in the SCC has been institutionalised to some degree. Methods used by single judges are also analysed based on information obtained from the interviews with judges.

We first address the Court's internal research on foreign law (subsection 4.4.1). Second, we look at the role of external actors involved in the decision-making of the Court that may draw the Court's attention to relevant international and foreign comparative material (subsection 4.4.2).

4.4.1 Research of Foreign Law by the Judges

Research on relevant foreign and international jurisprudence is carried out by the Justices themselves or by their judicial assistants. The Justices' personal interests in and affinities to comparative law and specific foreign legal systems seem to play an important role in how this research is conducted. As an example, a former Justice of the Supreme Court reported to have done specific research in a case concerning Canada's bilingualism in connection with the Canadian Constitution and the right to education.[83] This Justice felt that the development of the Internet has had significant influence on the research of foreign law, as online databases facilitate easy access to foreign case law and other useful resources.[84] Moreover, the emergence of transnational judicial networks and the increase of bilateral exchanges between highest courts provide judges with opportunities to learn about foreign law and to exchange ideas with their counterparts in foreign jurisdictions.[85]

Comparative legal research is also conducted by judicial assistants. A former Justice of the SCC indicated that he often asked his law clerks to do research on foreign judgments, including the case law of the ECtHR. A current Justice estimated asking law clerks to do research in approximately one-third of the cases brought before the Court. Another Justice estimated doing this in about half of the cases. The frequency of citations to foreign case law appears to be lower than these estimations. Table 4.1, giving details about the citations to foreign case law between 1982 and 2014, shows that a citation rate of 50 per cent occurred only in 2007 and

[83] See for example *Solski (Tutor of) v. Quebec (Attorney General)* [2005] 1 SCR 201; and Gosselin (*Tutor of) v. Quebec (Attorney General)* [2005] 1 SCR 238.

[84] M. Bastarache, 'The Globalisation of the Law and the Work of the Supreme Court of Canada', Muller and Richards (eds.), Highest Courts, *supra* note 3, at 54.

[85] See M. Claes and M. de Visser, 'Are You Networked Yet? On Dialogues in European Judicial Networks', *Utrecht L. Rev.* 8:2 (2012) 100–14.

that in 11 of the examined years the citation rate was below 30 per cent.[86] Therefore, either not all comparative legal research seems to have yielded helpful arguments to be discussed in the Court's decisions, or not all of the comparative research conducted by the judges and their assistants is discussed in the reasoning of the Court's judgments.

4.4.2 *The Role of Counsel,* Amici Curiae *and Interveners*

Information about comparative law can also be introduced in the court proceedings by external actors. The interviewed judges made observations about the role of the parties and their counsel, *amici curiae* and interveners[87] in the proceedings before the highest courts and about the information on foreign law obtained through these actors.

It should be kept in mind that in all cases before the Supreme Court of Canada, the parties have the right to raise constitutional questions.[88] This way, one of the parties can present the case in a manner that invites comparative research into similar legal questions adjudicated by courts in other jurisdictions. This might be a useful approach if the available foreign case law supports the outcome desired by this party. In a published interview, the recently retired Justice Ian Binnie confirmed the importance of the persuasive powers of lawyers and individual judges in directing the focus of the case: 'It is the art of the advocate to frame the question in a way that suits his or her interest. … The effective judge is the judge who frames the question in a way the other judges accept as a legitimate characterization of what we have to decide'.[89] Still, the legal question to be answered by the Court is framed by the Chief Justice,[90] who therefore has the final say on the angle taken by the Court for deciding the case, including the relevance of comparative material.

Several Justices observed that counsel for a party sometimes also introduces foreign sources in the procedure. A former Justice specified that lawyers bring forward both primary sources (foreign case law) and secondary

[86] See Table 4.1. See also Roy, Empirical Survey, *supra* note 13, at 123–24.

[87] Like in the legal system of the United Kingdom, in the Canadian legal system *amici curiae* are experts who do not have a direct interest in the outcome of the case. Interveners, such as non-governmental organisations, are third parties who have a direct interest in the outcome of the case and who have been allowed to submit their arguments to the Court. See the more detailed discussion later in the chapter.

[88] Rules of the Supreme Court of Canada, 2002, r 60.

[89] Makin, Justice Ian Binnie, *supra* note 79.

[90] Rules of the Supreme Court of Canada, 2002, rr 60–61.

sources (analyses and academic literature on foreign law and foreign case law). However, another Justice pointed out that counsel usually does not conduct this type of comparative research. The focus of the lawyers is regularly on the legal questions under Canadian law raised by the parties' case. The research of foreign law is often considered time-consuming or costly compared to the possible benefits that could arise from this research.

Furthermore, one Justice was of the opinion that sometimes foreign legal sources are misused. According to this Justice, this occurs, for example, when counsel does not check the relevance of a foreign reference for the case at hand. Misuse also occurs when counsel resorts to foreign law merely as a rhetorical device. Another Justice stressed the significance of the input of counsel but pointed out that this input is sometimes of insufficient quality. This member of the Court recalled a controversy in which he had asked counsel for the appellant what the risk of 'torture' meant in that specific case. Counsel stated that it was relying on the definition of torture given in the UN Convention against Torture.[91] However, according to the Justice, counsel could not reproduce this definition during the hearing of the appeal and did not know how to classify a number of examples based on incidences at Guantanamo. This example seems to corroborate the observation made by Justice Binnie that Members of the Supreme Court 'suffer from the absence of a specialised Supreme Court bar'.[92]

The Justices also mentioned that interveners, such as non-governmental organisations, sometimes bring foreign case law to the attention of the SCC. Their input is appreciated by the Court, as interveners often are represented by specialised counsel.[93] *Amici curiae*, who do not have an interest in the direct outcome of the case, can be requested by the SCC to provide information and arguments which could contribute to the Court's deliberations.[94]

4.5 The Purpose and Effects of the SCC's Engagement in Judicial Dialogue

Why does the SCC cite foreign case law in its judgments? What effects does this practice have? Without any claim of comprehensiveness, these

[91] Convention against Torture and Other Cruel, Inhuman or Degrading Treatment or Punishment (10 December 1984) 1465 UNTS 85, entered into force 26 June 1987.

[92] Makin, Justice Ian Binnie, *supra* note 79.

[93] *Ibid.*

[94] Rules of the Supreme Court of Canada, 2002, r 92.

two questions are addressed in this section, considering first the main purposes pursuant through citations of foreign case law (subsection 4.5.1) and then the effects of the SCC's citation practice (subsection 4.5.2).

4.5.1 Purposes of the SCC's Engagement in Dialogue

At the outset, in the interviews the Justices confirmed that they do not look at foreign judgments for solutions, but for ideas. They considered that the transplanting of solutions from one legal system into another is often not possible because of contextual differences.[95] This statement is consistent with the view that engagement with foreign law is first and foremost an exercise in enhancing self-understanding, which leads to identification of the distinguishing elements of Canadian society. In other words, 'engagement' with foreign material is a stance 'primarily concerned with the self-reflective elements of constitutional adjudication',[96] rather than a finalistic exercise in comparative reasoning within judicial decision-making.

An example of this purpose can be found in the judgment of the SCC in the case of *United States v. Burns*. In this case, which was also mentioned by the interviewed Justices, the SCC looked at international opinion and other states' experiences.[97] This case concerned the requested extradition of two Canadians to the United States, where these persons could be sentenced to death. The SCC decided that it was unconstitutional under the Charter to extradite the persons in question if no assurances were given that the death sentence would not be imposed or carried out.[98] This decision, overturning earlier judgments of the Canadian Supreme Court,[99] was reached partly on the basis of a reflection on international experience that resonated with the attitudes of Canadian society at large:

> International experience, particularly in the past decade, has shown the death penalty to raise many complex problems of both a philosophical and pragmatic nature. While there remains the fundamental issue of whether the state can ever be justified in taking the life of a human being within its power, the present debate goes beyond arguments over the effectiveness of deterrence and the appropriateness of vengeance and retribution. It strikes at the very ability of the criminal justice system to obtain a uniformly correct result even where death hangs in the balance.

95 See also subsection 4.3.2 *supra*.

96 Jackson, Constitutional Engagement, *supra* note 2, at 71.

97 *United States v. Burns* [2001] 1 SCR 283.

98 *Ibid.*, [143–44].

99 *Kindler v. Canada (Minister of Justice)* [1991] 2 SCR 779; and *Reference re Ng Extradition (Canada)* [1991] 2 SCR 858.

> International experience thus confirms the validity of concerns expressed in the Canadian Parliament about capital punishment. It also shows that a rule requiring that assurances be obtained prior to extradition in death penalty cases not only accords with Canada's principled advocacy on the international level, but is also consistent with the practice of other countries with whom Canada generally invites comparison, apart from the retentionist jurisdictions in the United States.[100]

With regard to this judgment, which contained further references to foreign case law and to foreign factual developments, Justice Binnie observed: 'I do not suggest that the outcome in the *Burns* case depended on this review of foreign sources but it assisted us in clarifying our own approach.'[101]

Secondly, one of the interviewed Members of the Court also observed that the Supreme Court of Canada has a strong responsibility towards the Canadian legal community to show that the Court has informed itself about relevant foreign sources, even though their citation is not mandatory. This would show the Court's awareness of these sources and help to make sure that as much relevant material as possible has been collected and considered by the Court. In particular, the Justice thought that the Courts of Appeal in the Canadian provinces appreciate the citation of foreign sources by the Supreme Court. After all, the Courts of Appeal do not have the same resources as the Supreme Court regarding the research of foreign legal sources.

These observations are corroborated by the view expressed by Justice Binnie in a lecture delivered in London in 2010, and are also possibly linked to a different and additional purpose. Indeed, he indicated that one of the reasons why Canadian judges cite foreign sources is 'to encourage re-examination of earlier Canadian precedents'.[102] He mentioned the example of cases concerning the extradition of individuals to countries where they would face the death penalty. Justice Binnie felt that the review of foreign sources in these cases 'assured the legal community and the broader public in Canada that all potential sources of enlightenment had been taken into account'.[103]

This observation is consistent with the information obtained from the interviewed Justices with regard to a possible additional purpose for the

[100] *United States v. Burns* [2001] 1 SCR 283 [127–28].

[101] Justice I. Binnie, 'Foreign Sources: Searching for Enlightenment or a Fig Leaf?' (speech given in London, July 2010).

[102] *Ibid.*

[103] *Ibid.* See also subsection 4.3.1 *supra*.

SCC's practice of citing foreign case law: the Justices clarified that research concerning foreign law is sometimes conducted to improve the process of decision-making and the Court's reasoning in specific cases. Indeed, if the use of comparative law and recourse to foreign judgments are not done with finalistic intents aiming to support a certain (sometimes preferred) outcome, the utility of the practice is, conversely, undeniable. When domestic jurisprudence on the interpretation of a newly enacted legal document is insufficiently developed, judges resort to foreign solutions in order to foresee possible consequences for the various interpretations of the constitutional provisions theoretically available.[104] This 'dialogical interpretation' helps the Court to become more aware of the direction that its own jurisprudence is taking.[105] Moreover, foreign case law can 'alert [the Court] to some of the theories about which [it] might want to think.'[106]

Finally, according to the interviewed Canadian justices, comparative legal analysis increasingly forms part of the judicial deliberations. A former Justice thought that the consultation of foreign legal sources is likely to continue in the future as a result of the increased role played by uniform legal instruments, such as international treaties or transnational regulation. If these instruments are used more often, it is likely that more trans-border mechanisms of judicial decision-making will develop as well. In this regard, the process of legal integration in Europe, in particular the influence of the ECHR and the case law of the ECtHR in contracting states, can remain an example for the SCC.

4.5.2 *Effects of the SCC's Engagement in Dialogue*

Our research indicates that the Court is receptive to foreign solutions only when they are compatible with the principles informing Canadian society and its legal system. This finding confirms Justice Wilson's statement that 'our courts have found the experience in other "free and democratic" societies useful in determining whether means adopted in this country are the best alternative.'[107] In this regard, the SCC has cited foreign judgments and made use of the experience of other 'free and democratic' countries at both

[104] S. I. Smithey, 'A Tool, Not A Master. The Use of Foreign Case Law in Canada and South Africa', *Comparative Political Studies* 34:10 (2001) 1188–1211.

[105] Choudhry, Globalization, *supra* note 64, at 836; and C. Saunders, 'Judicial Dialogue in Common Law Countries', Pierre Bon *et al* (Comité d'Organisation), *Renouveau du droit constitutionnel. Mélanges en l'honneur de Louis Favoreau* (Paris: Dalloz, 2007) 413–28, at 423.

[106] M. Tushnet, 'The Possibilities of Comparative Constitutional Law', *Yale L. J.* 108:6 (1999) 1225–1309.

[107] *Lavigne v. Ontario Public Service Employees Union* [1991] 2 SCR 211, 298 (Can).

stages of the interpretive process required by the Charter, as identified by the SCC: that is, not only in defining the substance of the specific right at issue but also in assessing the constitutionality of limitations.[108]

However, looking beyond one's own borders does not necessarily imply automatic acceptance and adoption of foreign solutions, and the Court certainly does not cite comparative sources only to support a desired outcome.[109] This is probably and most strikingly reflected in the Canadian attitude towards citation of US judgments. Firstly, with regard to US case law, the SCC seems to consider discussion of the legal treatment of specific issues in the United States almost as a necessary step in constitutional interpretation, in order to then draw conclusions with regard to the treatment of that same issue in the Canadian legal system.[110] Secondly, despite the SCC's high number of citation of US judgments, our research reveals that in the majority of cases results reached by US courts have not been followed.[111] Indeed, while there have been a few instances of endorsement of US interpretations of the Bill of Right's provisions,[112] the different

[108] See *supra* note 38. This dynamic is clear, for example, in *Charkaoui v. Canada (Citizenship and Immigration)* [2007] 1 SCR 350.

[109] Critics of the use of foreign case law in constitutional adjudication argue that when judges start to quote foreign decisions, they will soon be unable to use these resources in a principled manner and will not resist 'cherry-picking': citing only foreign decisions supporting their preferred result. See, for example, Judge John Roberts Confirmation Hearings available at www.gpo.gov.

[110] Relevant US case law is often presented to the Court in the briefs submitted by the parties. The immediate aim of this practice is to provide the SCC with readily available material that could be useful for a comparison between the solution found to a legal question in the United States and in Canada (therefore saving the Court the effort to embark in time- and resource-consuming research).

[111] With regard to the outcome of the cases, between 1982 and 2014, out of 291 constitutional cases with citations to US case law, US solutions have been followed in only 13.8 per cent of these cases, while being distinguished in 29 per cent of them. The remainder of cases (57.2 per cent) presents merely neutral and informative references to US case law (which is, therefore, neither followed nor distinguished).

[112] For example, in *Hunter v. Southam* [1984] 2 SCR 145, when interpreting the Charter guarantee of freedom from unreasonable search or seizure (s 8), the SCC adopted the warrant requirement set forth in *Katz v. United States* 389 US 347 (1967). It did so despite the fact that the Charter does not make reference to such a requirement. In cases involving obscenity, the SCC has relied extensively on US case law to develop a similar test for assessing the constitutionality of obscenity statutes: see *The Queen v. Butler* [1992] 1 SCR 452. In *United Food & Commercial Workers Local 1518 v. Kmart Can Ltd* [1999] 2 SCR 1083, in determining whether different standards apply in reviewing the constitutionality of leafleting and picketing bans, the SCC adopted the distinction between these two activities established in US First Amendment jurisprudence. In *Vriend v. Alberta* [1998] 1 SCR 493, the SCC, in dealing with employment discrimination based on sexual orientation, cited with approval the US Supreme Court's decision in *Romer v. Evans*, 517 US 620 (1996).

structure of the Charter, especially with regard to its general limitation clause (section 1), has become a catalyst for the development of a distinctively Canadian jurisprudence.[113] Therefore, and as a result also of the approach set out in the *Lavigne* judgment,[114] consideration of US judgments by the SCC is mainly 'aversive' or 'negative'.[115]

A more positive approach, conversely, is adopted by the SCC with regard to the case law of European supranational courts and especially towards decisions of the European Court of Human Rights. Indeed, since the mid-1980s, the SCC has extensively referred to decisions of the ECtHR when deciding landmark cases in the area of fundamental rights.[116] Furthermore, in the majority of cases, these references led to a positive endorsement of the approach taken by the ECtHR in the interpretation of the rights protected in the European Convention on Human Rights, which find corresponding protection in the Charter.

An example is provided by references to ECtHR decisions that were included in Justice Cory's dissenting opinion in *Kindler v. Canada (Minister of Justice)* and in the *United States v. Burns* judgment,[117] two cases addressing the legality of the practice to extradite individuals to countries where they may face the death penalty, with the latter decision overruling the former and establishing that under these circumstances, extradition

[113] In *R v. Keegstra* [1990] 3 SCR 697, 740, Chief Justice Dickson stated for the majority: '... applying the *Charter* to the legislation challenged in this appeal reveals important differences between Canadian and American constitutional perspectives.... Section 1 has no equivalent in the United States, a fact previously alluded to by this Court in selectively utilizing American constitutional jurisprudence'.

[114] As discussed earlier; see text accompanying *supra* note 72.

[115] C.L. Ostberg, M.E. Wetstein and C.R. Ducat, 'Attitudes, Precedents, and Cultural Change: Explaining the Citation of Foreign Precedents by the Supreme Court of Canada', *Canadian J. of Political Science* 34:2 (2001) 377–99.

[116] See, for example, the citations to ECtHR cases included in the decision *R v. Rahey* [1987] 1 SCR 588 and in the dissenting opinion of Justice Lamer in *R v. Kalanj* [1989] 1 SCR, two cases dealing with the right to a trial within a reasonable period of time. Other citations of ECtHR cases have been made in the SCC's decisions dealing with the right to freedom of expression (see the opinion of Chief Justice Dickson in *R. v. Keegstra* [1990] 1 SCR 697 and by Justice Gonthier in *R v. Butler* [1992] 1 SCR. 452), the right to life (see the opinion by then Justice McLachlin in *Winnipeg Child and Family Services (Northwest Area) v. G (DF)* [1997] 3 SCR 925), the right to liberty (in connection with a detention under a certificate; see *Charkaoui v. Canada (Citizenship and Immigration)* [2007] 1 SCR 350), freedom of religion (*Alberta v. Hutterian Brethren of Wilson Colony*, [2009] 2 SCR 567), freedom of association (see the dissenting opinion by Justice Bastarche in *R v. Advance Cutting & Coring Ltd* [2001] 3 SCR 209) and the right to vote (see the dissenting opinion by Justice Gonthier in *Sauvé v. Canada (Chief Electoral Officer)* [2002] 3 SCR 519).

[117] *Kindler v. Canada (Minister of Justice)* [1991] 2 SCR 779; and *United States v. Burns* [2001] 1 SCR 283.

amounts to a breach of the principle of fundamental justice under section 7 of the Charter.[118] In *Burns*, the SCC referred extensively, and with approval, to *Soering v. the United Kingdom*,[119] ultimately reaching the same conclusions that the European Court of Human Rights had reached twelve years earlier.

More recently, the SCC has also referred to judgements of the Inter-American Court of Human Rights. In *Kazemi Estate v. Islamic Republic of Iran*, one of the most contentious cases decided by the SCC in 2014, the Court had been called upon to decide whether Canadians had a right to sue foreign governments for damages resulting from acts of torture to a next of kin. In this context, both the majority and dissenting opinions relied on the views of the IACtHR to describe the effects of impunity on victims of torture.[120]

More generally, however, it is important to note that external sources – whether cited positively or aversively – have never been dispositive of the outcome of a case before the Court. The SCC, through a principled approach towards citation of foreign jurisprudence, seems to provide evidence that concerns about 'cherry-picking' should be, at least to some extent, reconsidered, in light of the numerous aversive citations. More precisely, the SCC shows that comparative reasoning - usually associated with a finalistic approach, aiming to emphasise analogies more than differences - can also be used aversively, in order to reassert differences with other jurisdictions and define the identity of a domestic system ('self-reflection purpose').[121] In this sense, we can understand the view of the interviewed

[118] Section 7 of the Charter provides that 'everyone has the right to life, liberty and security of the person and the right not to be deprived thereof except in accordance with the principles of fundamental justice'.

[119] *Soering v. the United Kingdom* (Appl. No. 14038/88), Judgment (Plenary), 7 July 1989, Series A, Vol. 161. In this case, the ECtHR established that extradition of an individual to the United States to face charges of capital murder violated article 3 of the ECHR (right to be protected from inhuman and degrading treatment).

[120] *Kazemi Estate v. Islamic Republic of Iran* [2014] 3 SCR 176. The majority opinion delivered by Justice LeBel referred to IACtHR, *Tibi v. Ecuador*, Judgment, 7 September 2004, Series C, No. 114 and to IACtHR, *Bámaca Velásquez v. Guatemala*, Judgment, 25 November 2000, Series C No. 91, while Justice Abella, in her dissenting opinion cited *Godínez-Cruz v. Honduras*, 21 July 1989 (Reparations and Costs), Series C, No. 8. In *R. v. Quesnelle*, [2014] 2 SCR 390, a 2014 case addressing the intersection between right to privacy and right to defence, the Court cited the IACtHR's decision in *Escher v. Brazil*, Judgment, 9 July 2009, Series C, No. 200.

[121] A concept defined by Pierre Legrand as 'prioritization of difference': P. Legrand, 'The Same and the Different' P. Legrand and R. Munday (eds.), *Comparative Legal Studies: Traditions and Transitions* (Cambridge University Press, 2003) 240–311, at 240 *et seq*. and 292 *et seq*.; De Vergottini, Oltre il Dialogo, *supra* note 7, at 35.

Justices, who think that most Justices of the Supreme Court consider that comparative law does not have any real influence on the domestic legal system.[122]

4.6 Concluding Remarks

This chapter has analysed the extent, method, purpose and effects of transnational judicial communication in the Supreme Court of Canada with regard to human rights cases. Rather than summarising the analysis, we conclude with some final observations which build on the outcomes of our quantitative and qualitative analysis of the SCC's case law and the views and approaches of judges on the Court concerning citations of foreign law.

An important outcome of the research is that, along with reasons connected to processes of legal adjudication, citation of foreign case law may also involve some additional purposes and strategic reasons that aim to have effects beyond the Canadian legal system. The SCC has become aware of the role that its jurisprudence can play in the international arena, and has recognised the importance of being regarded as a progressive and outward-looking judicial body in the area of fundamental rights protection. By citing civil liberties cases from other countries extensively, Canadian judges have become part of a global debate on human rights in democratic societies. According to former Justice Bastarache, foreign legal sources are cited by the SCC in human rights cases 'to demonstrate established or emerging patterns informing human rights jurisprudence throughout the world'.[123] Openness towards citation of foreign judgments has also been perceived as an invitation to other courts to interact and has in fact encouraged other jurisdictions to cite Canadian judgments in the exercise of their own adjudicatory functions.[124] This has also had an effect on constitution-drafting efforts worldwide, leading some scholars to observe that 'the Canadian Charter of Rights and Freedoms has, in recent

[122] One of the exceptions, according to several of the interviewed justices, is considered to be former Justice C L'Heureux-Dubé, who served on the Court from 1987 until 2002. See L'Heureux-Dubé, The Importance of Dialogue, *supra* note 50.

[123] Bastarache, The Globalization of the Law, *supra* note 84, at 44

[124] 'Canadian law serves as a source of inspiration for many countries around the world', A. Barak, 'Foreword: A Judge on Judging: The Role of a Supreme Court in a Democracy', *Harvard L. Rev.* 116:16 (2002) 19–162, at 114. Recent studies detailed the influence of the SCC's decisions on high courts of other jurisdictions: T. Groppi, 'A User-friendly Court. The Influence of Supreme Court of Canada Decisions Since 1982 on Court Decisions in Other Liberal Democracies', *Supreme Court L. Rev.* 36 (2007) 337–64.

years, become a leading alternative' to the US Bill of Rights as a model for constitution-making.[125]

One may wonder, given these broader purposes and effects, whether the SCC's citations of foreign judgments in recent years are still genuine or have rather begun to reflect ulterior political motives. After all, 'judges from Canada may experience satisfaction from being regarded as committed to a cooperative transnational project of judging and human rights'.[126] Regarding this aspect, our research shows a recent trend in citation of foreign case law. While citations occur less frequently as Canada develops significant lines of domestic precedents, the SCC – particularly in dealing with previously unaddressed issues – has continued to reference foreign case law. Despite a decline in the number of foreign citations and the inevitable political influences on judges, our research suggests the SCC still genuinely perceives itself as operating within a new 'worldwide rights culture',[127] implicitly embracing legal cosmopolitanism and a 'sincere outward-looking interest in the views of other societies'.[128]

Acknowledgments

This article is the result of the joint reflections of the two authors. Still, the quantitative analysis is based on research conducted by Gianluca Gentili, who wrote most of Sections 4.2 and 4.3; the qualitative research was conducted by Elaine Mak, who wrote most of Section 4.4; while sections 4.1 and 4.5 were developed and written jointly. Gianluca Gentili wishes to acknowledge the helpful comments of Tania Groppi, Marie-Claire Ponthoreau, Cheryl Saunders, Jean-François Gaudreault-DesBiens and Richard Kay on his quantitative research outputs. Part of the quantitative research outputs presented in this chapter was included in the author's earlier contribution to T. Groppi and M.-C. Ponthoreau (eds.), *The Use of Foreign Precedents*

[125] Choudhry, Globalization, *supra* note 64, at 822; Anne-Marie Slaughter suggests that Canada and South Africa are 'looking around the world and canvassing the opinions of their fellow constitutional courts, and each is disproportionally influential as a result', A.-M. Slaughter, 'A Brave New Judicial World', M. Ignatieff (ed.), *American Exceptionalism and Human Rights* (Princeton University Press, 2005) 277–303, at 289. See also D.S. Law and M. Versteeg, 'The Declining Influence of the United States Constitution' *New York University L. Rev.* 87:3 (2012) 762–858.

[126] Jackson, Constitutional Engagement, *supra* note 2, at 240.

[127] Remarks of Chief Justice McLachlin on 'The Use of Foreign Law' delivered at the 104th ASIL's Annual Meeting held from 24–27 April 2010 in Washington, DC, USA. Materials available at: www.fora.tv,

[128] G.V. La Forest, 'The Use of American Precedents in Canadian Courts', *Maine L. Rev.* 46:2 (1994) 211–20.

by Constitutional Judges (Oxford: Hart Publishing, 2013). The author is responsible for any remaining errors. Elaine Mak's research was supported by a post-doctoral VENI grant from the Netherlands Organisation for Scientific Research (NWO). She wishes to thank the Justices who participated in the interviews as well as Sam Muller, John Bell and Ryan Gauthier for their help and suggestions. The qualitative research outcomes regarding Canada have been integrated in a comparative analysis in E. Mak, *Judicial Decision-Making in a Globalised World: A Comparative Analysis of the Changing Practices of Western Highest Courts* (Oxford: Hart Publishing, 2013). Any mistakes remain the authors' own.

Annex: Interview Design

In order to obtain as much useful information as possible, a semi-structured interview technique was chosen. A list of themes was formulated in advance. These themes were brought up during the interviews, while flexibility in the formulation and the sequence of questions was allowed.[129]

Letter

> Dear *[title and name of the judge]*,
>
> I am writing to ask you whether you would be available for an interview in the course of my post-doctoral research on highest courts and globalisation. Your name and contact details were given to me by *[name of contact person]*.
>
> My research concerns the changing role of highest courts in western legal systems under the influence of globalisation. In particular, I look at the extent to which legal ideas and experiences from other jurisdictions play an influencing role on the decisions of the highest national courts. My research is linked to the HiiL project in the Netherlands concerning the study of judicial networks (www.hiil.org). For this research, I am studying a number of jurisdictions, including the ones mentioned above. With regard to *[jurisdiction of the judge]*, the research focuses on *[examined court(s)]*. I have already begun my analysis of the functioning of this institution/these institutions on the basis of relevant legislation, case law and literature. In order to complete the picture, I would be much helped by getting first-hand information from (former) judges.

[129] Concerning this research methodology, see J.A. Maxwell, *Qualitative Research Design: An Interactive Approach*, 2nd ed. (Thousand Oaks: Sage, 2005).

In particular, I would like to find out how judges see their role within a globalised legal community both in relation to their national public and in relation to national government and Parliament. Also, I would like to get a better understanding of the institutional dynamics which influence the functioning of the highest courts. Specific questions in this respect concern the use of foreign sources (such as international treaty law and foreign case law) in judicial decision-making, and the institutional position of the highest courts in the balance of powers at the domestic level.

Given your experience as a judge in *[name of the court]*, I would be very grateful to have a conversation with you regarding the matters described above. Could you please let me know if you would be willing to meet with me? If so, would you have time for a meeting between *[available timeframe for the interview]*?

For your information, I would like to point out that the interview would not be tape-recorded and all uses of information in future publications would be unattributed. If you would like, I would be happy to submit to you any version of the unattributed information before submission for publication.

I look forward to hearing from you.

With kind regards,
Elaine Mak

Interview Questions

General: the role and impact of the highest court

1. What do you think is the role of the highest court on which you are serving in the national legal system? What do you think should be its role?
2. What impact does the court have on the national level? What impact does the court have on the international level? What impact do you think the court should have?
3. Do you perceive that the role or impact of the court has changed over time? If so, in what way has the court's role or impact changed? What reasons do you think have incited these changes?

Institutional arrangements

4. How do you perceive the institutional framework for the court's functioning? (that is: relation to other courts, relation to the political powers, NGO's, citizens, etc.)
5. To what extent do you think the institutional arrangements for the court have an influence on the court's role in theory and in practice?

The use of comparative law

6. Do you take elements of international and comparative law into account in your decision-making? If so, do you take these elements into account:
   - as an argument which justifies your decision?
   - as an additional justification of your decision, not being an authoritative source of itself?
7. Do you think/know that decisions of your Court are used as a source by judges in other legal systems? If so, can you give examples? Do you think this is important? Do you take this into account when deciding cases?
8. If you make use of comparative law sources, how do you obtain information?
   - Do you receive input from your support staff?
   - Do you discuss with colleagues or with judges in other courts or in other countries?
   - Do you take a passive or an active approach, that is:

by reading about international law and foreign case law?
by actively looking for clues in order to solve pending cases? If so, which types of cases?
by participating in international judicial networks and/or international conferences? If so, which ones?

The judge as a person

9. Could you give some details regarding your background? This information can include:
   - training and experience as a judge in the national system;
   - experience as a judge in a European or an international court;
   - experience in a specific field of law: private law; criminal law; administrative law; constitutional law;
   - other professional experiences: government; academia; etc.
10. Do you think your professional background has an influence on your decision-making, in particular as regards the way in which you make use of international and comparative law sources? Could you give examples which illustrate this influence?

The role of the court in the future

11. What do you think the future of your court will look like? Will it get a more important or a less important role under the effects of globalisation?

5

Ideological Barriers to Judicial Dialogue

A Study of the Laws Establishing *Sharī'ah* Courts in Malaysia and Nigeria

AZIZAT O. AMOLOYE-ADEBAYO

5.1 Introduction

This chapter analyses a major constraint to judicial dialogue, particularly the explicit citing of foreign national and international jurisprudence in judicial decisions,[1] which affect *Sharī'ah* courts in Malaysia and Nigeria. The analysis is limited to these *Sharī'ah* courts, and does not include the dialogue of other courts within these jurisdictions.[2] Moreover, the chapter focuses on *Sharī'ah* courts' (non-)dialogue on issues concerning Islamic

[1] That is to say, of the variety of comparative legal analysis. Various kinds of judicial dialogue have been identified in relevant sources ranging from formal citing/consultation of foreign jurisprudence in judicial decisions to informal meetings and quasi-official gatherings of judicial officials. (See the broad definition of the term 'judicial dialogue' adopted under subsection 1.2.1 in Chapter 1 in this volume). This chapter focuses on whether or not *Sharī'ah* courts in Malaysia and Nigeria can make explicit reference to or seek guidance from foreign national and international decisions in the discharge of their judicial duties (explicit dialogue). It does not consider the notion of implicit dialogue by Malaysian and Nigerian *Sharī'ah* courts with foreign national and international jurisprudence, as no judge of the *Sharī'ah* court in either jurisdiction was interviewed.

[2] As a matter of practice, other domestic court types (particularly the apex courts) in both Malaysia and Nigeria engage in dialogue (particularly of the typology of comparative legal analysis or the citing of foreign and international jurisprudence) with other national and supranational courts, especially in, but not limited to, matters involving the violation of human rights standards. As this is further afield from the focus of the present analysis, for more discussion on this point, the reader is referred to the following judicial authorities where foreign jurisprudence is cited, and to relevant academic texts. On Malaysia, see e.g. *Pet Far Eastern v. Tay Young Haut* (1999) 5 MLJ 558; S.B. Lyke, '*Brown* Abroad: An Empirical Analysis of Foreign Judicial Citation and the Metaphor of Cosmopolitan Conversation', *Vanderbilt J. of Transnational L.* 45:83 (2012) 83–144, at 97 and 135. In Nigeria, with a legal history connected to its British colonial past, it is commonplace for the judges of the Nigerian apex court (the Supreme Court) to cite or be guided by foreign jurisprudence in their decisions. See, for example, *C.O.P. Western Region v. Igwe &*

personal laws such as family law and inheritance, as the jurisdiction of the Malaysian and Nigerian *Sharīʿah* courts is limited to these subject matters.[3]

According to the laws establishing Malaysian and Nigerian *Sharīʿah* courts, these courts cannot engage in dialogue, neither with one another (and in the same sense, not with *Sharīʿah* courts in other Muslim countries where a different Islamic school of law operates) nor with foreign national non-*Sharīʿah* or international human rights courts. This chapter explains why there is no explicit dialogue between these courts, and why such dialogue is not possible.[4] The chapter also engages with the question of whether the situation should be changed, thus encouraging *Sharīʿah* courts to enter into dialogue with *Sharīʿah* courts in other Muslim jurisdictions and/or foreign national and international human rights courts. If so, how could this be achieved, and what purpose could such dialogue have? With the exception of a discussion of the possible purpose of *Sharīʿah* courts' engagement in judicial dialogue, this chapter does not address the questions of the extent, method, purpose and effects of dialogue as set out in the Introduction of this volume. This is due to the fact that little or no dialogue exists to date involving *Sharīʿah* courts.

This chapter's substantive analysis spans three sections (5.2, 5.3 and 5.4). Sections 5.1 and 5.5 are the introduction and the conclusion, respectively. The first substantive section (5.2) discusses and questions

Ors (1961) 2 NSCC 1, where the court, in determining 'whether knowledge that a police officer is executing his duty is a necessary ingredient to the offence of assault' on that police officer, cited the English cases of *R v. Forbes and Webb* [1865] 10 COX 362 and *R v. Lisle* [1936] 2 KB 434 amongst others; *Kalu v. State* [1998] 12 SCNJ 1, where the Supreme Court, in determining the legality or otherwise of the death penalty in Nigeria, cited various decisions from other municipal jurisdictions and international instruments, e.g. the Constitutional Court of South Africa, *De Reuck v. Director of Public Prosecution* [2003] 50 WRN 58 CCSA; *Satchwell v. President of the Republic of South Africa* [2003] 49 WRN 139 CCSA. See also numerous references to other foreign courts' decisions in the Nigerian Supreme Court's judgments *AG. Cross-River v. AG. Federation* (2012) 16 NWLR (Pt. 1327) 425 and *Nwosu v. Nwosu* (2012) 8 NWLR (Pt. 1301) 1 CA. On both Malaysia and Nigeria, see generally A. M. Smith, 'Making Itself at Home-Understanding Foreign Law in Domestic Jurisprudence: The Indian Case', *Berkeley J. of Int'l L.* 24:1 (2006) 218–72, at 218–19 and fn 1.

[3] For a more detailed explanation of the Malaysian and Nigerian *Sharīʿah* courts' jurisdiction, see subsection 3.1.

[4] Concerning Malaysian and Nigerian *Sharīʿah* courts' dialogue with international courts, unlike other chapters in this edited volume, the analysis in this chapter excludes an examination of their dialogue with UN human rights treaty bodies. This is to avoid repetition of analysis and arguments, as discussion on why there is no dialogue between *Sharīʿah* courts and international courts as set out in this chapter can also be entirely adopted for the idea of dialogue between *Sharīʿah* courts and UN human rights treaty bodies.

some of the underlying assumptions of the dominant notion of judicial dialogue as it relates to the practice of the courts discussed in the chapter. Following from this interrogation, Section 5.3 presents a legal analysis of why *Sharī'ah* courts in Malaysia and Nigeria[5] exist at the margins, if they participate at all, in the process of transnational judicial dialogue. Section 5.4 suggests some provisions in the laws examined for each domestic context on the *Sharī'ah* court that may be constructively construed in ways that can make transnational dialogue with other *Sharī'ah* courts, as well as with foreign national and international human rights courts, possible in spite of ideological variations. It also engages with the question of whether such dialogue is desirable and what its purpose could be.

5.2 The Notion of Judicial Dialogue

Increasingly, courts now communicate with each other across varied contexts as autonomous players in a global judicial enterprise, claims Anne-Marie Slaughter.[6] Slaughter describes a typology of this communication or dialogue, from official and unofficial direct meetings of judges to the consultation of foreign jurisprudence in domestic adjudication, whether or not explicitly acknowledged.[7] This notion has received some attention and agreement by other scholars as well.[8] Even if it is acknowledged as

[5] Malaysia and Nigeria were chosen as examples of jurisdictions where *Sharī'ah* courts form part of the national judicial structure under a federal system of government. Additionally, as discussed later in the chapter, there are four major schools of Islamic law. The *Sharī'ah* courts in Malaysia adjudicate on the basis of a school that is different from the officially recognised school applied by the *Sharī'ah* courts in Nigeria. This is also a factor in the choice of the jurisdictions.

[6] A.-M. Slaughter, 'A Typology of Transjudicial Communication', *University of Richmond L. Rev.* 29:1 (1994–95) 99–137; A.-M. Slaughter, 'A Global Community of Courts', *Harvard J. of Int'l L.* 44:1 (2003) 191–219, at 191–93. This perspective continues to permeate this author's latter works on the subject such as 'Judicial Globalization' *Virginia J. of Int'l L.* 40:4 (2000) 1103–24, at 1103.

[7] *Ibid.*, (1994–95), at 103–14. See also the all-encompassing description offered in subsection 1.2.1 in the Introduction.

[8] For instance, R. Bahdi, 'Globalization of Judgment: Transjudicialism and the Five Faces of International Law in Domestic Courts', *The George Washington Int'l L. Rev.* 34 (2002–03) 554–603, at 555, asserts at the beginning of this work: 'Globalization has infiltrated judicial decision making'. Also, M. Kirby, 'Commentaries: Transnational Judicial Dialogue, Internationalisation of Law and Australian Judges', *Melbourne J. of Int'l Law* 9:1 (2008) 171–89, at 179, postulates that 'the transnational judicial conversation is likely to continue and to expand'. See also J.S. Martinez, 'Towards an International Judicial System', *Stanford L. Rev.* 56:2 (2003) 429–529, at 429; R.B. Ahdieh, 'Between Dialogue and Decree: International Review of National Courts', *New York University L. Rev.*79 (2004) 2029–2163, at 2029; M.A. Waters, 'Mediating Norms and Identity: The Role of Transnational

an empirically verifiable matter that national, regional and international courts continually and routinely engage in one form of dialogue or the other, a worrisome point is that this notion of judicial dialogue does not always pay sufficient attention to a practical consideration of why such dialogue was possible in the first place. The question can be asked whether courts that participate in these dialogues do so as a natural and inevitable consequence of globalising trends, because of the progressing integration of international human rights law and domestic constitutional law that is affecting many countries, and because of the easy availability of and access to foreign judgments, or whether there are some ideological considerations involved that induce such dialogue. No matter what answer scholars give to this question, in this author's opinion, the prevalent notion of judicial dialogue tends to postulate judges, particularly those within domestic contexts, as adjudicators who may use relevant foreign jurisprudence at their discretion to aid the discharge of their duties, especially, but not limited to, when there seems to be a gap on a matter in national law.

The main plank of this chapter's objection to this notion of judicial dialogue and its understanding of the role of domestic judges is this conception of judges as relatively 'autonomous' entities. It is as though judges involved in judicial dialogue are seen as connected to the process of transnational communication largely at their own free will; committed to developing 'a common judicial ideology' or 'a common law on human rights',[9] and who may to some extent disconnect ideologically from the immediate location of adjudication.[10] Illustrating this perception of judicial dialogue further, Tara Leigh Grove, commenting on the apparent reluctance of the US Supreme Court to participate in the transnational dialogue process, posits that

> The U.S. Supreme Court seems to regard the U.S. Constitution as a document that should not be informed by outside jurisprudence. Courts that

Judicial Dialogue in Creating and Enforcing International Law', *Georgetown L. J.* 93:2 (2005) 487–574, at 529; M.A. Waters 'Creeping Monism: The Judicial Trend Toward Interpretative Incorporation of Human Rights Treaties', *Columbia L. Rev.* 107:3 (2007) 628–705, at 628; M.A. Waters, 'Normativity in the "New" Schools: Assessing the Legitimacy of International Legal Norms Created by Domestic Courts', *Yale J. Int'l L.* 32:2 (2007) 455–84, at 455; D.J. Bederman, 'Diversity and Permeability in Transnational Governance', *Emory L. J.* 57:1 (2007) 201–33, at 201; and N.I. Turner, 'Transnational Networks and International Criminal Justice', *Michigan L. Rev.* 105:5 (2007) 985–1032, at 985.

9 C. McCurdden, 'A Common Law of Human Rights? Transnational Judicial Conversations on Constitutional Rights', *Oxford J. of Legal Studies* 20:4 (2000) 499–532, at 499.

10 Consider an anecdotal account by one judge of a situation where his reference in a judgment to a principle of international law not recognised by the domestic law of the court

> have joined the international judicial dialogue, by contrast, seem to perceive their constitutions as documents that "speak to", and listen to, the entire international community.[11]

By contrast, here it should be observed that even where judges are minded to engage in such judicial activism or creativity, or where they are aware of foreign or international jurisprudence that may have resolved a comparable issue presented before them in an admirable way, dialogue may be impossible for the reason that the extent of and limits to their activism is clearly defined through national law. Judges are not necessarily as autonomous as sometimes conveyed by prevalent understandings of judicial dialogue, but are in actual fact dependent on the extent to which the instruments of their appointment and enabling laws actually allow and accommodate engagement with foreign and international jurisprudence. As Paul Stefan has rightly argued concerning judicial behaviour and domestic judges' engagement in transnational judicial dialogue:

> What drives judicial behavior ... is a traditional understanding of the judicial function, in particular respect for the instructions given by competent authorities and caution in the face of unclear instructions. Judicial mandates arise out of specific commitments by these authorities, rather than a general command to do what is best for the public as a whole. These commitments necessarily are incomplete and thus require courts to develop a gap-filling strategy. Modern contract theory posits that courts should and do fulfil their mandates by attempting to ascertain the instructors' preferences and not their own ... This approach, which counsels judges to act as agents, not trustees, dictates the outcomes of international judicial encounters.[12]

Therefore, in particular if a court has been established on the basis of certain ideological considerations, this may constitute a barrier to dialogue with courts elsewhere that function on the basis of some other ideologies, religious or otherwise. This is the case especially with courts based on some religious tenets, such as the *Sharīʿah* courts considered in this chapter. What follows is an examination of this perspective.

in question occasioned some strong criticisms even from other judicial colleagues, in M. Kirby, 'Domestic Courts and International Human Rights Law: The Ongoing Judicial Conversation', *Utrecht L. Rev.* 6:1 (2010) 168–81, at 173–74.

11 T. L. Grove, 'The International Judicial Dialogue: When Domestic Constitutional Courts Join the Conversation', *Faculty Publications* (2001) Paper 1226, at 2072–73, available at scholarship.law.wm.edu/facpubs/1226.

12 P.B. Stephan, 'Courts on Courts: Contracting for Engagement and Indifference in International Judicial Encounters', *Virginia L. Rev.* 1:100 (2014) 17–109, at 20.

5.3 Ideological Barriers to Dialogue: Islamic Legal Thought and the Process of Judicial Dialogue

Dialogue between *Sharīʿah* courts and other courts may be limited or impossible due to ideological barriers of a religious nature in the process of adjudication. This may be observed across two levels. Firstly, the tradition of Islamic legal thought has historically 'recognized and accommodated a certain level of acceptable diversity of practice and belief'.[13] Four schools of law (*Madhāhib* in Arabic, or *Madhhab* in its singular form) comprising *Hanafī*, *Mālikī*, *Shāfi'ī* and *Hanbalī* schools jointly form the majority *Sunnī* schools of law in Islamic jurisprudence. From around the tenth century, these four schools for the majority of Muslims 'define both an arena of legitimate disagreement and the outer limits of acceptable diversity'[14] in respect of doctrinal interpretation and application of *Sharīʿah*. The consequence is the recognition in municipal law of one or the other of these schools as the official scheme of adjudication in various Muslim jurisdictions. For example, as discussed later in the chapter, the *Shāfi'ī Madhhab* is the official school in Malaysia, while in Nigeria it is the *Mālikī* school of law. It is important to note that although these four *Sunnī* schools presently comprise the mainstream regimes for the application of *Sharīʿah* across the majority of Muslim jurisdictions, there is also the *Shi'ī* minority school which has some measure of Muslim followership in Pakistan and is the official school in Iran. It is also pertinent to state that, at present, the majority of Muslims do not consider the views of the jurists of the *Shi'ī* school to be within the limits of acceptable diversity.

This demonstrates that even among Muslims themselves there is an 'intra communal plurality' and they may not necessarily 'have identical interpretations of their foundational texts.'[15] Zulfikar Hirji describes this as the process whereby Muslims debate Islam from within, which results in some varied and, at times, irreconcilable constructions of the 'self' and the 'internal other' by an individual Muslim.[16] This is the first type of ideological barrier envisaged in this chapter, a barrier at the official

[13] M.E. Cammack, 'Islam and Nationalism in Indonesia: Forging an Indonesian Madhhab', P. Bearman *et al.* (eds.), *The Islamic School of Law: Evolution, Devolution, and Progress* (Harvard University Press, 2005), at 175.

[14] *Ibid.*, at 175–76.

[15] Z. Hirji, 'Debating Islam from Within: Muslim Constructions of the Internal Other', Z. Hirji (ed.) *Diversity and Plurality in Islam: Historical and Contemporary Discourses amongst Muslims* (London: IB Tauris, 2010), at 7.

[16] *Ibid.*, at 4–7.

level of adjudication – that is, a barrier based on different hermeneutical constructions of identical religious texts by religious courts which may have similar objectives but operate in different contexts.

One could ask whether an international instrument could serve as a conduit to dialogue between different *Sharī'ah* courts that follow one of the four different *Sunnī* schools of Islamic jurisprudence – like the Malaysian and Nigerian *Sharī'ah* courts – to overcome this barrier. In many other jurisdictions horizontal dialogue between domestic courts is facilitated by the fact that domestic courts apply common international human rights treaties and/or interpret relevant domestic law in light of these common international human rights treaties.[17] In the context of Islamic jurisdictions, the Cairo Declaration on Human Rights in Islam (Cairo Declaration)[18] could potentially serve as such a conduit to dialogue between *Sharī'ah* courts that follow different *Sunnī* schools of Islamic jurisprudence. Both Malaysia and Nigeria are members of the Organisation of Islamic Cooperation (OIC),[19] and are thereby also parties to the Cairo Declaration. Together with the Arab Charter on Human Rights (Arab Charter),[20] the Cairo Declaration is an instrument regarded as compatible with Islam, reflecting that Islam 'is a relevant factor in the human rights discourse in the Muslim world'.[21] However, the Cairo Declaration's preamble establishes that the provisions of the document are meant to only 'serve as a general guidance for Member States in the field of human rights'.[22] In addition, the Declaration goes on to provide in articles 24 and 25 respectively that '[all] the rights and freedoms stipulated in this Declaration are subject to the Islamic Shari'ah' and '[t]he Islamic Shari'ah is the only source of reference for the explanation of any of the articles of this Declaration.' This means that even if different

[17] See e.g. the analysis in Chapters 2, 3 and 4 of this volume.

[18] Cairo Declaration on Human Rights in Islam, adopted in 1990 by the Organization of the Islamic Conference (now Organization of Islamic Cooperation), Annex to RES.NO. 49/19-P.

[19] Established in 1969 as 'Organization of the Islamic Conference' and now 'Organization of Islamic Cooperation' with the stated purpose of acting as a collective voice for the Muslim World. The organisation is presently comprised of 57 member states across four continents. See www.oic-oci.org/page_detail.asp?p_id=40.

[20] The Arab Charter on Human Rights was adopted on 15 September 1994 by the League of Arab States. A revised version was adopted in 2004 and entered into force 15 March 2008. Neither Malaysia nor Nigeria is a member of the Arab League. More discussion on the relevance of mentioning this Charter in this work is given below in this section.

[21] M. A. Baderin, 'Islam and the Realization of Human Rights in the Muslim World: A Reflection on Two Essential Approaches and Two Divergent Perspectives', *Muslim World J. of Human Rights* 4:1 (2007): contribution 5, at 2.

[22] See para. 6 of the Cairo Declaration.

Sharīʿah courts would apply the Declaration,[23] they would do so in light of their own school of Islamic jurisprudence, preventing any dialogue with *Sharīʿah* courts following another school. Other international and regional human rights treaties ratified by Malaysia and Nigeria cannot induce horizontal dialogue between different *Sharīʿah* courts for ideological reasons.

This brings us to the second type of barrier that prevents *Sharīʿah* courts' dialogue with foreign national and international courts. This barrier has to do with how Islamic legal thought views and interacts with other external thoughts. In other words, any of the *Sharīʿah* courts in the contexts examined in this chapter may not be able to engage in dialogue with a non-*Sharīʿah* court whether or not that other court is a foreign national or a supranational court. The reason, as shall be seen in the discussions that follow, is that *Sharīʿah* courts must at all times base their considerations on Islamic law. Therefore, there is a fundamental ideological barrier to dialogue with any other foreign national or international court whose decisions are not guided by the same ideology.

For example, *Sharīʿah* courts could interact with international human rights courts and their jurisprudence, or domestic courts applying international human rights treaties and/or relevant domestic law in light of these treaties. The mentioned Arab Charter and Cairo Declaration, and their enforcement mechanisms, could be possible institutions to interact with. A revised Arab Charter on Human Rights[24] entered into force in 2008 two months after it received seven ratifications in accordance with its article 45.[25] The Arab Charter contains no provision for the establishment of a court. However, article 45 (1) provides for the establishment of an Arab Human Rights Committee to supervise the implementation of its provisions; this committee became a reality in 2009.[26] Since neither Nigeria nor Malaysia has ratified the Arab Charter and the output of the Arab Human Rights Committee is limited, there are limited possibilities for Nigerian and Malaysian courts to interact with this Committee. While both Malaysia and Nigeria are amongst the membership of the OIC[27] and are therefore parties to the Cairo Declaration, the OIC at present has

[23] This is unlikely for reasons given the discussion that follows in this section and in subsection 5.3.1.1.

[24] The original version from 1994 was revised after it had received criticism from international observers that it was inconsistent with international standards. See M. Rishmawi, 'The Arab Charter on Human Rights and the League of Arab States: An Update', *Human Rights Law Review* 10:1 (2010) 169–78, at 170.

[25] *Ibid.*, at 169.

[26] *Ibid.*, at 172.

[27] See *supra* note 20.

no judicial organ generally or specifically on human rights matters with whom Malaysian or Nigerian *Sharīʿah* courts could interact.

As the discussion so far has shown, the human rights monitoring and enforcement machinery of the Muslim world is still evolving. The situation is the same for the African and Asian regional human rights machineries.[28] For example, the African Court of Human and Peoples' Rights[29] has, to date, finalised around 19 of the applications so far submitted to it for consideration.[30] Out of all these decisions, none touched on the question of Islamic personal law, which is the main jurisdictional area of the Malaysian and Nigerian *Sharīʿah* courts as shall later be explained in more detail.[31] Therefore, so far there is no decision of the African Court of Human Rights that *Sharīʿah* courts could potentially cite.

On account of the preceding discussions, the analysis in this chapter on the possibility of dialogue between *Sharīʿah* courts and a non-*Sharīʿah* court focuses on a more developed supranational human rights court, the European Court of Human Rights (ECtHR). This is because this court's extensive human rights jurisprudence[32] has also touched on different aspects of family law, specifically but not limited to questions of inheritance rights which might be a potential subject for dialogue with the *Sharīʿah* courts discussed in this chapter. Another and perhaps more interesting reason for the choice of the ECtHR in this typology of dialogue is that unlike the Cairo Declaration and the Arab Charter that make the Islamic ideology a factor in the protection and guarantee of the recognised rights, the European Convention on Human Rights (ECHR),[33] which establishes the ECtHR,[34] makes no overt concession to any religious ideology.[35] This chapter posits that in construing a particular human rights issue, it is highly improbable that a *Sharīʿah* court will enter into a dialogue with ECtHR by engaging with the ECtHR's jurisprudence in its own decision.

[28] See for a more detailed discussion: A. O. Amoloye-Adebayo, *The Right to Inheritance under Sharīʿah and International Human Rights Law*, PhD Thesis, University of Nottingham, 2012, chapter 3.

[29] Which interprets the provisions of human rights instruments in the African region such as the Africa Charter on Human and Peoples' Rights (26 June 1981) OAU Doc. CAB/LEG/67/3 rev.5; 1520 UNTS 217, entered into force 21 October 1986.

[30] The details of which are available at the Court's website at www.african-court.org/en/index.php/2012-03-04-06-06-00/finalised-cases-closed.

[31] See relevant discussion in the sections that follow.

[32] Available at www.echr.coe.int/Pages/home.aspx?p=home.

[33] Convention for the Protection of Human Rights and Fundamental Freedoms (4 November 1950), 213 UNTS 222, entered into force 3 September 1953.

[34] Article 19 of the ECHR.

[35] See the preambular provisions as well as the entire text of the ECHR.

The two identified categories of possible ideological/religious barriers are examined in more detail below in the order of formulation.

5.3.1 Sharī'ah *Courts Operating in Different Muslim Jurisdictions*

Two courts that administer *Sharī'ah* in two different jurisdictions (Malaysia and Nigeria) are examined in this section vis-à-vis the recognised official school of law for the interpretation and application of *Sharī'ah*.

5.3.1.1 The Malaysian Syariah (or *Sharī'ah*) Court

The 1957 Constitution of Malaysia, as amended (hereinafter Constitution), in article 3 (1), while acknowledging that other religions may freely be practiced, recognises Islam as the religion of the federation.[36] Sub-article 5 of the same article confers on the Malaysian Parliament the power to 'by law make provisions for regulating Islamic religious affairs'. The Ninth Schedule to the Constitution houses the legislative lists. The provisions of list I (4a) under the 'federal list' grant the federal legislature the power to constitute and organise all Malaysian courts except the '*Syariah* Courts'. Such powers are vested, according to the provisions enshrined in list II (1) under the 'state list', in the state legislatures. The state legislatures are responsible not only for the constitution and organisation of the *Syariah* courts but also for their procedure. The same provision goes on to state that the *Syariah* courts 'shall have jurisdiction only over person [sic] professing the religion of Islam and in respect only of any of the matters included in this paragraph'.[37] In order to analyse the state initiative as regards the carrying into effect the constitutional provisions on the *Syariah* courts, the Malaysian Administration of Islamic Law (Federal Territories) Act, 1993 (AIL) is examined. This law is applicable only in the territories of Kuala Lumpur and Labuan in Malaysia, being federal territories.[38]

[36] For an in-depth historical and descriptive analysis of the extent and scope of the application of *Sharī'ah* in Malaysia, see F. S. Shuaib, 'The Islamic Legal System in Malaysia', *Pacific Rim Law and Policy J.* 21:1 (2012) 85–113.

[37] These matters are stated in the preceding part of the paragraph as 'Islamic law and personal and family law of persons professing the religion of Islam, including the Islamic law relating to succession, testate and intestate, betrothal, marriage, divorce, dower, maintenance, adoption, legitimacy guardianship, gifts, partitions and non-charitable trusts; *Wakafs* and the definition and regulation of charitable and religious endowments, institutions, trusts, charities and charitable institutions operating wholly within the State; Zakat, Fitrah and Baitulmal or similar Islamic religious revenue, mosques or any Islamic public places of worship'.

[38] See section 1(1) of the AIL.

It is to be noted that, according to the provisions of article 1(2) of the Malaysian Constitution discussed earlier, there are 13 federating units in Malaysia. Therefore, there are 14 *Syariah* courts in Malaysia, one for the federal territories and one each for all the federating units.[39] A perusal of the preliminary provisions contained in the AIL[40] shows that the federal territories of Kuala Lumpur and Labuan (the loci of the application of the AIL) were formerly parts of the Malaysian state of Selangor. Both territories appear to have been subject to an earlier law on the matter, which is the Administration of Muslim Law Enactment, 1952 of the State of Selangor. It appears reasonable to suppose, therefore, that the provisions of the AIL which are applicable in the federal territories of Malaysia should be representative enough of the provisions of other states' laws on the Constitution and the applicable laws of the *Syariah* courts in that context.

The provisions of the AIL[41] recognise three tiers of the *Syariah* Courts in Malaysia. These are the *Syariah* subordinate courts, the *Syariah* High Court and the *Syariah* Appeal Court. A detailed analysis of the composition, jurisdiction and practice and procedure before these courts will take this chapter far afield from its focus of concern.[42] What is important is that by the provisions of sections 32–34 of the AIL, there shall be appointed a 'Mufti' (a person qualified to give a legal opinion/ruling called *fatwa* in Islamic law) and a deputy Mufti. The Mufti is recognised as the adviser to the administrative authority (the Yang di-Pertuan Agong) in respect of all matters in Islamic law. In these matters, the Mufti is 'the chief authority in the Federal Territories after the Yang di-Pertuan Agong, except where otherwise provided in this Act'.[43] Section 34 empowers the Mufti to, at will or upon request by the administrative head or in response to a letter by any person, make *fatwa* on any 'unsettled' or 'controversial' question of Islamic law for publication in the gazette. Such published *fatwa* 'shall be binding on every Muslim resident' in the region and 'shall be recognized by all Courts in the Federal territories as authoritative of all matters laid down therein'.[44]

A salient point for this chapter is the provision in respect of authorities to be followed by the Mufti in the making of *fatwas*. The prescription of section 39 (1) AIL is that 'the Mufti shall ordinarily follow the accepted views (*qaul muktamad*) of the *Mazhab Syafie*'. It is useful to recall that

[39] See Shuaib, The Islamic Legal System, *supra* note 36, at 97.

[40] Section 2 of the AIL.

[41] *Ibid.*, sections 40–57.

[42] However, see parts IV and V of the AIL for the details regarding the above matters.

[43] See section 33 of the AIL.

[44] *Ibid.*, section 34 (3) and (4).

Mazhab Syafie or the *Shāfi'ī* school of law is one of the four mainstream schools of interpretation and application of Islamic law discussed at the beginning of this section.

5.3.1.2 The Nigerian *Sharī'ah* Court of Appeal

By the provisions of section 2 (1) and (2) of the 1999 Constitution of Nigeria[45] (1999 CFRN), Nigeria is a federation comprising 36 states and a Federal Capital Territory. Further, section 6 (1)–(6) of the 1999 CFRN titled 'Judicial Powers' vests the judicial authority of the federation and the states in the 'superior courts of record.' Accordingly, it is stated that 'the courts to which this section relates, established by this Constitution for the Federation and for the states … shall be the only superior courts of record in Nigeria' and 'each court shall have all the powers of a superior court of record.'[46] Section 5 (a) to (i) specifies the courts being referred to, and, in particular, paragraphs (f) and (g) respectively contain 'the *Sharī'ah* Court of Appeal of the Federal Capital Territory, Abuja and a *Sharī'ah* Court of Appeal of a State.' The provisions of section 6 (6) (a) and (b) require that the judicial powers vested in the identified courts 'extend, notwithstanding anything to the contrary in this Constitution, to all inherent powers and sanctions of a court of law' and shall also 'extend to all matters between persons, or between government or authority and to any person in Nigeria, and to all actions and proceedings relating thereto, for the determination of any question as to the civil rights and obligations of that person.'

In furtherance of the above requirements for this type of court in Nigeria, section 275 (1) 1999 CFRN establishes a *Sharī'ah* Court of Appeal 'for any State that requires it.' The jurisdiction of the *Sharī'ah* Court of Appeal (SCA) is contained in section 277 (1) and (2) (a)–(e) where it is provided that the court shall

> in addition to such other jurisdictions as may be conferred upon it by the law of the state, exercise such appellate and supervisory jurisdiction in civil proceedings involving –
>
> a. any question of Islamic personal law regarding marriage concluded in accordance with that law, including a question relating to the validity or dissolution of such marriage or a question that depends on such a marriage and relating to family relationship or the guardianship of an infant;

[45] The Constitution of the Federal Republic of Nigeria (Promulgation) Act, 1999, Cap C23 Laws of the Federation of Nigeria, 2010 (1999 CFRN).

[46] See section 6 (3) 1999 CFRN.

b. where all the parties to the proceedings are Muslims, any question of Islamic personal law regarding marriage, including the validity or dissolution of that marriage, or regarding family relationship, a foundling or the guardianship of an infant;
c. any question of Islamic Personal Law regarding a *wakf*,[47] gift, will or succession where the endower, donor, testator or deceased person is a Muslim;
d. any question of Islamic Personal Law regarding an infant, prodigal or person of unsound mind who is a Muslim or the maintenance or the guardianship of a Muslim who is physically or mentally infirm; or
e. where all the parties to the proceedings, being Muslims, have requested the court that hears the case in the first instance to determine that case in accordance with Islamic personal law, any other question.

In the exercise of any jurisdiction constitutionally conferred on the SCA, the court is duly constituted with at least three Kadis (or Judges).[48] It is important to state at this juncture that all the provisions discussed earlier are *in pari materia* with the establishment, jurisdiction and composition of the SCA of the Federal Capital Territory, Abuja.[49] The power to make rules to govern the practice of the SCA of a state as well as its procedural requirements, according to section 279, is conferred on the Grand Kadi (or Chief Judge) of the court. Such power is, however, subject to the provisions of 'any law made by the House of Assembly of the State.'[50]

At this point, it is important to further examine how this power is exercised in the context of a state in Nigeria. As stated earlier, Nigeria is a federation comprised of 36 states. Thus, as far as the establishment of a state SCA is concerned, the implication of the constitutional provisions examined earlier is that it is theoretically possible to have up to a maximum of 37 SCAs in the whole of Nigeria. In reality, however, 19 SCAs operate in 18 Northern Nigerian states[51] and the Federal Capital Territory, Abuja. For the purposes of this chapter, the laws of one Nigerian state, Kwara, are

[47] This translates to mean 'endowment'.

[48] See section 278 of the 1999 CFRN.

[49] *Ibid.*, sections 260–64.

[50] *Ibid.*, section 279.

[51] There are six geopolitical zones in Nigeria comprising the North-Central, North-East, North-West, South-East, South-South and South-West zones. For more information, see Federal Ministry of Women Affairs, Nigeria, '*Nigeria's Report on the Implementation of the Beijing Platform for Action and Commonwealth Plan of Action*', April 2004, available at www.genderandtrade.org/shared_asp_files/uploadedfiles/911B9951-F8D0-41C5-8B26-0E717C6CD34B_Nigeria.pdf.

examined in respect of the applicable law, practice and procedure of the SCA in a Nigerian state. This is to avoid replication of arguments, since it appears that the state laws are *in pari materia* regarding this court type in Nigeria. Additionally, Kwara is one of the states in the North-Central geopolitical zone[52] of Nigeria. Its demography is such that the state is an ideal choice for illustration because it appears representative in significant terms of some of the major Nigerian tribes.[53] The law that establishes a SCA for the state of Kwara is the *Sharīʿah* Court of Appeal Law.[54] The relevant part of this law in the context of this chapter is the provision contained in section 13(1). It requires that in the exercise of the jurisdiction conferred on it, the SCA shall 'administer, observe and enforce the observance of, the principles and provisions of – (a) Islamic law of the Maliki school'. Again, the stated school is one of the four schools of Islamic law discussed earlier.

The examination of the court type and applicable laws within the two jurisdictions discussed earlier is to demonstrate, in the first place, that the *Sharīʿah* courts are not bound by any other law except the national constitution in each case and Islamic law based on the officially recognised scheme of interpretation. A careful perusal of the provisions of the constitutions of both Malaysia and Nigeria does not disclose any duty on the *Sharīʿah* court in each case to do more than apply Islamic law in the manner analysed previously. For example, the duty appears not to extend to interpreting Islamic law provisions in the light of the human rights obligations of the country concerned under either regional or international human rights instruments.[55] Secondly, the earlier examination also indicates how statutorily recognised official schemes for the application of Islamic law may differ across national contexts. It demonstrates that judges of these courts are not statutorily expected to consider, let alone cite, the opinions of the jurists of the other schools (or refer to the decisions of comparable courts that apply them) in the discharge of their duties. That is to say, even where a judge in the contexts examined is desirous of dialogue with another court whose basis is a scheme of interpretation other than the officially recognised school of law of that judge, the statutory provisions examined earlier constitute a barrier based on religious ideology. However, such dialogue

[52] *Ibid.*

[53] It is such that it roughly comprises the Northern mix (a term popularly understood in its widest terms to include such cultural affiliations as the Hausas, Fulanis, the Nupes and the Baribas) as well as the South-West mix (generally comprising the various Yoruba tribes).

[54] Cap. S4, 2006 Laws of Kwara State of Nigeria.

[55] See *supra* note 2.

may be possible between *Sharīʿah* courts in different Muslim jurisdictions when they both have the same officially recognised school of law.

5.3.2 *The* Sharīʿah *Courts and the ECtHR*

As a result of my deep interest in the concept of human rights as well as the rationale given at the beginning of this section, the ECtHR, being a court with an extensive human rights jurisprudence, is selected for an analysis of the possibility of a dialogue between this Court and a *Sharīʿah* court in Malaysia or Nigeria. An area covered by the jurisdiction of the *Sharīʿah* court in both Malaysia and Nigeria[56] that may give rise to some human rights issues and, therefore, theoretically make the jurisprudence of the ECtHR relevant is the question of inheritance rights. Although there are several judicial pronouncements by the ECtHR on the subject of inheritance rights, for the most part, they deal with the effect of 'illegitimacy' (i.e. concerning children born out of wedlock) on these rights.[57] The ideology of the ECtHR on this issue, upon due observation, is that whether or not a child was born in or out of wedlock is immaterial for the recognition of her/his right to inherit from the putative father. For example, in *Marckx v. Belgium*[58] the ECtHR held that drawing a distinction between a 'legitimate' and an 'illegitimate' family for the purpose of protecting the right to family life, as enshrined in article 8 of the ECHR, could no longer be justified.

By contrast, the question of legitimacy is a primordial consideration under the Islamic inheritance system. Under *Sharīʿah*, an 'illegitimate' child enjoys the right to inherit only from the birth mother but never from the putative father.[59] On the issue of inheritance rights, therefore, there are ideological differences between the perspectives of the ECtHR and any *Sharīʿah*

56 See relevant discussion *supra* in this section.

57 For example, see the decisions of this court in *Marckx v Belgium* (Appl. No. 6833/74), Judgment (Plenary), 13 June 1979, Series A, Vol. 31; *Mazurek v. France*, (Appl. No. 34406/97) Judgment (Chamber), 1 February 2000, ECHR 2000-II, 1; *X, Y and Z v. the United Kingdom (1)*, (Appl. No. 21830/93), Judgment (Grand Chamber), 22 April 1997, ECHR 1997-II, 130; and *Fabris v. France*, (Appl. No. 16574108), Judgment (Grand Chamber), 7 February 2013, ECHR 2013-I, 381.

58 *Marckx v. Belgium, supra* note 57, paras. 14–15.

59 For a discussion of this Islamic perspective and its rationale, see H. Khan, *The Islamic Law of Inheritance: A Comparative Study of Recent Reforms in Muslim Countries*, 2nd ed. (Oxford University Press, 2007); J.J. Nasir, *The Islamic Law of Personal Status* (London: Graham & Trotman, 1990); and N.J. Coulson, *Succession in the Muslim Family* (Cambridge University Press, 1971).

court, whether Malaysian or Nigerian. Thus, it is highly unlikely that the *Sharī'ah* court will look to the jurisprudence of the ECtHR for direction when there is the need to supplement national law on the matter, assuming in the first instance that making such reference is statutorily recognised.

5.4 Overcoming Barriers: Exploring Possible Approaches to Encourage Judicial Dialogue between *Sharī'ah* Courts and Other National and International Courts and the Possible Purpose of Such Dialogues

5.4.1 *Dialogue between* Sharī'ah *Courts in Different Domestic Jurisdictions*

The easy diffusion of knowledge and ideas is an effect of globalisation which continues to dictate that no nation can exist as an island immune to the occurrences in other nations and societies. Not only may one regard this position as true in matters of law[60] and its interpretation and application generally, it is also true of the agglomeration of individuals into societies such as the Muslim world.[61] On account of this, it is important to encourage and establish the cross-fertilisation of ideas in the form of overt consultation/citation of foreign jurisprudence by *Sharī'ah* courts in any Muslim jurisdiction regardless of the officially recognised school. While the long-term sustainability of this process may necessitate an eventual amendment of enabling laws in each case, I am of the opinion that it is still possible for a lot to be achieved with the present state of the enabling laws on the *Sharī'ah* courts considered in this chapter.

Thus, on the possibility of dialogue between *Sharī'ah* courts in different contexts and with different officially recognised schools of law, it appears that some judicial creativity may be encouraged, in theoretical terms at least. I have argued for this elsewhere, on the issue of the construction and enforcement of inheritance rights of women and children in Muslim jurisdictions.[62] In the Nigerian context, as earlier discussed, section 13

[60] W. Twining, 'Diffusion of Law: A Global Perspective', *J. of Legal Pluralism and Unofficial L.* 36:49 (2004) 1–45, at 4–5. See also a further illumination of the theme in a sequel to this by W. Twinning, 'Social Science and Diffusion of Law', *J. of L. and Society* 32:2 (2006) 203–40, at 204–07; and also 'Implications of "Globalisation" For Law As A Discipline', Presented at the Commonwealth Scholarship Commission Legal Network Launch Conference, 13–14 June 2009, at 1–3. On file with the author.

[61] A. Shari'ati, *On the Sociology of Islam*, translated from Persian by H. Algar (Berkeley: Mizan Press, 1979), at 122.

[62] See Amoloye-Adebayo *supra* note 28, chapters 6 and 7.

(1) (a) of the *Sharīʿah* Court of Appeal Law stipulates that the scheme of interpretation of Islamic law is the *Mālikī* school. This same section further provides in its paragraph (d) that in the process of adjudication, the court will also have regard to 'natural justice, equity and good conscience according to Islamic law'. In my view, this paragraph may be interpreted as empowering the court to give consideration to the view of other schools of law of the *Hanbalī*, *Shāfiʾī*, *Hanafī* and *Shiʾī* schools where they appear to be better attuned to modern challenges and social reality. It is not clear, however, if the practitioners will be favourably disposed to this suggestion, especially as regards the view of the *Shiʾī* school in the application of Islamic law generally.[63] In fact, a consultation of the existing jurisprudence of the *Sharīʿah* courts does not disclose that such consideration has taken place in an explicit form.

One might present the same argument as made earlier for the Malaysian context, given that section 39(2)of the AIL also empowers the Mufti to follow the views of the other three schools other than the recognised scheme in cases where following the official scheme 'will lead to a situation which is repugnant to public interest.' In fact, subsection 3 of the same section goes further to state that where the Mufti is of the opinion that none of the views of the four schools is apposite on ground of public interest, the matter may be resolved by the Mufti by an exercise of personal judgment. However, the Mufti is not a judge who can engage in the process of judicial dialogue. This means that unlike the Nigerian situation, Malaysian *Syariah* courts are not granted the powers of independent reflection but must merely apply duly made and published *fatwas* of the Mufti. A way out may be for the judges of these courts to 'unofficially' engage in dialogue with relevant jurisprudence of the other schools and to thereafter initiate the process of a fresh *fatwa* under section 34(1) AIL.[64]

5.4.2 *Dialogue between* Sharīʿah *Courts and Non-*Sharīʿah *Courts*

As alluded to in the beginning of the preceding section, legal restrictions in the form of enabling laws as well as differences in ideology may be creatively manipulated to achieve constructive dialogue between courts of varying religious or legal ideologies. Concerning the possible dialogue between *Sharīʿah* courts and other national courts or transnational courts

[63] My conclusion from a conversation I had with the chief librarian of the Kwara State SCA in the process leading up to the writing of my thesis in 2011 at the University of Nottingham.

[64] See the earlier discussion of the requirements of this *supra* in section 3.

such as the ECtHR, I am of the view that the purpose of judicial dialogue is not necessarily to highlight similarities in perspectives, ideologies or expected outcomes in the process of adjudication. In some cases, the purpose could also be to explore differences of perspectives and outcomes that may lead to an in-depth and holistic analysis of a legal problem. As Jacobs has correctly argued, it may be that

> it is precisely the differences in "outcomes" [sic] between the two systems which throw the most light on the nature of each system. Perhaps the most interesting question to explore is why the outcomes are different. In that perspective, differences may even be more significant than similarities.[65]

The idea here is that in spite of what is dictated by the particular legal context within which a judge operates vis-à-vis the process of judicial dialogue, there can be much room for judicial activism depending on the judge in question. The preceding quote is instructive of the fact that the purpose of judicial dialogue may be viewed not only in terms of the generation of norms which aspire to universality but also to comprehend how different contexts dictate divergent applications of a widely understood concept. Viewed in such a manner, it is here argued that *Sharīʿah* courts can overtly cite foreign jurisprudence rooted in some other ideologies where relevant to an instant consideration. Doing so will, in the my opinion, foster a better understanding of why in a particular case the Islamic prescription is different from that other held by the consulted foreign ideology. This could also help to feed well-reasoned decisions of a diverse voice into the international human rights discourse that so far have not been heard and engaged with in this discourse.

To use the earlier example of the un-severable connection between the inheritance rights and the 'il/legitimate' status of an inheriting heir in relation to a putative father, the outcome of the process of comparative legal analysis by a *Sharīʿah* court vis-à-vis a relevant decision of the ECtHR may lead non-adherents of Islam to appreciate how, in the Islamic law perspective, disinheriting an 'illegitimate' child is not discriminatory.[66] The jurisprudence of the ECtHR on article 14 ECHR[67] and the United Nations

[65] F. G. Jacobs, 'Judicial Dialogue and the Cross-Fertilization of Legal Systems: The European Court of Justice', 38 *Texas Int'l L. J.* 38:3 (2003) 547–56, at 556.

[66] For a discussion of the Islamic point of view, see the cited texts in *supra* note 59.

[67] See, for example, the following cases: *Sejdic and Finci v. Bosnia Herzegovina* (Appl. No. 27996/06 and 34836/06), Judgment (Grand Chamber), 22 December 2009, ECHR 2009-VI, 273 and *Orsus and Others v. Croatia* (Appl. No.15766/03), Judgment (Grand Chamber), 16 March 2010, ECHR 2010-II, 247.

Human Rights Committee[68] is clear on the fact that 'not every differentiation of treatment will constitute discrimination, if the criteria for such differentiation are reasonable and objective and if the aim is to achieve a purpose which is legitimate under the Covenant (the International Covenant on Civil and Political Rights (ICCPR)).'[69] Through references to and engagement with the relevant ECtHR jurisprudence as well as statements of the UN Human Rights Committee, *Sharī'ah* courts could highlight the 'reasonable and objective criteria' for the differentiation in treatment of 'legitimate' and 'illegitimate' children 'to achieve a purpose that is legitimate under the Covenant' with references to the Islamic law which these courts are charged with applying. The basic sources of this Islamic law are no less than a thousand years old,[70] and the schemes of interpretation and application of the provision of these sources consist of centuries-old juristic elaborations of classical jurists, recorded in volumes of Islamic law books.[71] While it is unlikely that this will lead the ECtHR or the UN Human Rights Committee[72] to change their interpretation of the ECHR and ICCPR on this matter, the process of judicial dialogue may aid a modern understanding of why some age-long concepts in Islamic law continue to retain their social relevance for Muslims in contemporary times.

One can, however, pose the question of how such dialogue can be made possible without running afoul of statutory limits of Malaysian and Nigerian *Sharī'ah* courts that were discussed earlier in the chapter. To answer this question, one can recall one of the basic principles of *Sharī'ah* as a belief system. It appears that this belief system sanctions constructive dialogue with other ideologies in the *Qur'ānic* provision contained in Q16:125: 'and reason with them in ways that are best and most gracious'. This could be relied on by judges of *Sharī'ah* courts who may wish to refer to and/or cite foreign or international jurisprudence while they interpret

[68] This is the international treaty body under the auspices of the United Nations responsible for monitoring State Parties' compliance with International Covenant on Civil and Political Rights (16 December 1966), 993 UNTS 3, entered into force 3 January 1976.

[69] HRC, General Comment No. 18, UN Doc. 10/11/89 (1989), para. 13. See also the decisions of the HRC on this point in *Haraldson and Sveinsson v. Iceland*, Communication No. 1306/2004, 24 October 2007, UN Doc. CCPR/C/91/D/1306/2004, paras. 10.2 and 13; *Jongenburger-Veerman v. the Netherlands*, Communication No. 1238/2004, 1 November 2005, UN Doc. CCPR/C/85/D/1238/2004, para. 7.2; *Love et al. v. Australia*, Communication No. 983/2001, 25 March 2003, U.N. Doc. CCPR/C/77/D/983/2001, paras. 8.2-3.

[70] See more detailed discussions in Amoloye-Adebayo, *supra* note 28, chapter 2.

[71] *Ibid.*

[72] HRC, General Comment No. 17, UN Doc. A/44/40 (1989), para.5, urging states to end discrimination against 'illegitimate' children.

and apply Islamic law of their respective school. Moreover, it is posited that the statutory limits will not be breached if the purpose of the dialogue is to aid the interpretation of a relevant issue, but not as a basis of the *Sharīʿah* court's decision. Aiding interpretation of Islamic law applied by *Sharīʿah* courts is certainly one of the purposes of the process of judicial dialogue.[73]

5.5 Conclusion

This chapter has demonstrated that whether or not a court (in this case the *Sharīʿah* court) is able to participate in the process of judicial dialogue, especially comparative legal analysis of foreign jurisprudence, is largely dependent upon the context of the court in question and the extent to which such practice is accommodated in domestic law. As officials of the state, judges must adjudicate within the ambits of the clearly defined limits contained in the legal instruments establishing the powers and jurisdiction of the court in question. Notwithstanding this recognition, however, it is my conception that courts will also be acting within their powers if they creatively interpret relevant provisions that make dialogue with foreign courts possible on comparable issues regardless of ideological/religious considerations.

On the issue of dialogue between *Sharīʿah* courts operating in different Muslim jurisdictions with divergent officially recognised schools of law, it has been suggested that a more elaborate construction of enabling laws may make dialogue possible. As regards dialogue between *Sharīʿah* courts and other foreign national or international courts that operate on the basis of some other ideologies, it has been suggested that *Sharīʿah* courts can overtly cite foreign jurisprudence rooted in some other ideologies where relevant to an instant consideration. The purpose of this dialogue, in my opinion, will most often be to foster a better understanding of why in a particular case, the Islamic prescription is different from that held by the consulted foreign ideology. In this way, *Sharīʿah* courts could also enrich the international human rights discourse with detailed and well-reasoned decisions.

[73] According to a proposition in E. Egede, 'Bringing Human Rights Home: An Examination of the Domestication of Human Rights Treaties in Nigeria' *J. of African L.* 51:2 (2007) 249–84, at 284, one way for judicial officers to domesticate international human rights treaties that have not been legislatively incorporated into domestic law is through judicial activism, whereby the provisions of such treaties are employed as an aid to interpret and apply domestic legislation.

6

Complementary Protection and Domestic Courts

The Extent, Method, Purpose and Effects of Judicial Dialogue

NAOMI HART

6.1 Introduction

International refugee law, one of the earliest supranational legal regimes for protecting human rights, can boast numerous achievements in the relief of human suffering. One deficit, however, is that its protective ambit has not historically extended to individuals who are highly vulnerable but do not meet the strict test for refugee status set out in the 1951 Convention relating to the Status of Refugees and the 1967 Protocol relating to the Status of Refugees (collectively, Refugee Convention).[1] Over the last decade, a doctrine of complementary protection has emerged in some industrialised states, extending those states' protective legal obligations to individuals in 'refugee-like' situations. Although both traditional refugee protection (bestowed upon so-called Convention refugees) and complementary protection rely on an applicant proving that he or she faces a risk of persecution or other serious harm in their country of origin, a key distinguishing feature is that beneficiaries of complementary protection are not required to prove that the threat they face is related to one of the five grounds enumerated in the Refugee Convention.[2] In addition, although the harm they face must be serious, they need not prove that it reaches the high threshold

[1] Convention relating to the Status of Refugees (28 July 1951) 189 UNTS 137, entered into force 22 April 1954; Protocol relating to the Status of Refugees (31 January 1967) 606 UNTS 267, entered into force 4 October 1967 (collectively, Refugee Convention).

[2] The five grounds are race, religion, nationality, membership of a particular social group or political opinion: Refugee Convention, *ibid.*, article 1A. For example, in introducing the Australian Migration Amendment (Complementary Protection) Bill 2011, Julie Owens MP conjectured that the new protection regime could cover those at risk of female genital mutilation and honour killings, and victims of rape from countries where rape victims are executed along with their attackers, all of whom may fall outside of the Refugee

of 'persecution'.[3] The United Nations High Commissioner for Refugees (UNHCR) has described complementary protection as protecting individuals deemed equivalent to refugees 'in the broader sense, to denote persons outside their countries who are in need of international protection because of a serious threat to their life, liberty or security of person in their country of origin as a result of persecution or armed conflict, or serious public disorder'.[4]

This chapter considers one dimension of the interpretation and application of the concept of complementary protection in the countries in which it has been enacted: the extensive dialogue between domestic judges in these various jurisdictions. The paucity of international sources which could offer interpretive guidance relating to complementary protection, as well as the absence of an international judicial or quasi-judicial body with an explicit mandate to enforce obligations in this field, make this area particularly interesting for studying the extent, method, purpose and effects of judicial dialogue. This absence arguably amplifies the incentives for domestic decision-makers, including judges, to collaborate with and derive lessons from their counterparts in other national jurisdictions. Alongside horizontal dialogue between domestic courts, some vertical dialogue has occurred, whereby national judges have drawn on decisions of international and regional courts and quasi-judicial bodies for guidance on certain facets of complementary protection. This chapter focuses on horizontal dialogue. Unlike other areas of human rights which have, to a large extent, been forged through diplomatic conferences and international treaties, the pioneers in the field of complementary protection obligations have been national governments which have voluntarily assumed new obligations without them first becoming mandatory under an international regime.[5]

Convention: House of Representatives, Second Reading Speech: Migration Amendment (Complementary Protection) Bill 2011 (Parliament of Australia, 19 September 2011) at 4498, 4503 (Julie Owens MP).

[3] For example, the Australian Migration Act states that, in order to acquire refugee status, a person must show a risk of persecution amounting to 'serious harm' that involves 'systematic and discriminatory conduct': Migration Act 1958 (Cth) (Australia), Act No. 62, 1958, dated 8 October 1958, as last amended 6 July 2015, s 91R. In contrast, under the complementary protection provisions, it is only necessary to show 'significant harm': see s 36(2A) of the same Act. The latter is considered a lower threshold: Migration Review Tribunal (MRT) and Refugee Review Tribunal (RRT) (Australia), 'Complementary Protection Training Manual' (January 2012) at 10, www.law.unsw.edu.au/sites/law.unsw.edu.au/files/images/rrt_manual_jm_6.1.12_final_sent_0.pdf.

[4] UNHCR, Note on International Protection, 9 June 2000, UN Doc. A/AC.96/830, para. 32.

[5] Member states of the European Union (EU) are obligated to implement in their national laws European secondary legislation, including Directive 2011/95/EU of the European

Few states have enacted complementary protection legislation, and those that have are almost exclusively western and industrialised. This chapter limits itself to the practices of courts in Australia, Canada, New Zealand and the member states of the European Union (EU). These states have framed their obligations in similar terms and their respective courts have engaged in prolific dialogue. Notably, these are not the only states to have enacted complementary protection laws: the United States and Mexico have also done so.[6] Judges in these latter countries have not, however, participated in dialogue on complementary protection with national courts elsewhere. Section 6.3 offers some explanation for why judicial dialogue has been concentrated in this way.

This chapter, in line with the themes of the edited collection in which it is included, explores the extent, method, purpose and effects of judicial dialogue. Section 6.2 outlines the complementary protection laws of Canada, New Zealand, EU member states and Australia. Section 6.3 examines the extent of judicial dialogue. It explains this chapter's focus on horizontal, rather than vertical, dialogue between courts, and sketches the patterns to which this horizontal dialogue conforms, speculating as to why some states have been excluded from the conversation. Section 6.4 addresses the method of judicial dialogue in relation to complementary protection, emphasising extra-curial opportunities for judges to engage with their colleagues in other states. Section 6.5 explores the purpose and effects of this practice of exchange between courts. It argues that such dialogue is motivated by an aspiration to harmonise standards of complementary

Parliament and of the Council of 13 December 2011 on standards for the qualification of third-country nationals or stateless persons as beneficiaries of international protection, for a uniform status for refugees or for persons eligible for subsidiary protection, and for the content of the protection granted (recast), OJ 2011 No. L 337/9, 20 December 2011 (EU Qualification Directive). In this sense, these states have not adopted these obligations wholly without supranational compulsion. However, there is still evidence of voluntariness. Most European states had implemented complementary protection laws of some sort before the EU Qualification Directive was enacted. In any event, the EU, as a regional bloc, assumed complementary protection obligations without them being imposed internationally.

6 A risk of torture in an applicant's home country has been grounds for barring deportation in a small number of cases in Hong Kong: see K. Loper, 'Human Rights, *Non-refoulement* and the Protection of Refugees in Hong Kong', *Int'l J. of Refugee L.* 22:3 (2010) 404–39. While the promising case law surrounding *non-refoulement* may assist refugees and other asylum seekers, Hong Kong does not formally offer asylum. Hong Kong's system, based solely on compliance with its obligations under the Convention Against Torture and Other Cruel, Inhuman or Degrading Treatment or Punishment (CAT (10 December 1984) 1465 UNTS 85, entered into force 26 June 1987), does not include a robust complementary protection regime akin to those in other jurisdictions in this chapter. For this reason, Hong Kong is excluded from further discussion in this chapter.

protection across different national jurisdictions. The effects springing from this purpose have been mixed: on some questions, the level of protection afforded to forced migrants has been enhanced, while on others the protection has been diluted. Section 6.6 provides case studies which illustrate the extent, method, purpose and effects of judicial dialogue in relation to certain aspects of complementary protection.

6.2. Complementary Protection Regimes

This section examines the complementary protection legislation of Canada, New Zealand, the EU and Australia, the latter having introduced complementary protection legislation most recently. There are terminological differences between the domestic laws, with some of the legislative instruments using terms such as 'subsidiary protection' or 'humanitarian protection' in place of complementary protection. For the sake of simplicity, this chapter uses the term 'complementary protection' to denote protection outside the Refugee Convention, and the term 'international protection' to encompass both traditional refugee protection and complementary protection.

In the past, most of the aforementioned states had laws which endowed their governments with discretion to grant protection visas on humanitarian or compassionate grounds. Now, however, the conferral of complementary protection is framed as a legal duty.[7] These countries label and define their obligations differently, though in all jurisdictions the laws cover both an individual's eligibility for protection, and their status (that is, the treatment to which they are entitled) after being granted protection.[8]

6.2.1 Canada

Canada's Immigration and Refugee Protection Act (2001) refers to an individual entitled to complementary protection as a 'person in need of protection'. Persons in need of protection are those whose removal to their country of origin would 'subject them personally ... to a danger, believed on substantial grounds to exist, of torture ... or ... to a risk to their life or to

[7] J. McAdam, 'From Humanitarian Discretion to Complementary Protection: Reflections on the Emergence of Human Rights-based Refugee Protection in Australia', *Australian Int'l L. J.* 18 (2011) 60–76; J. McAdam, *Complementary Protection in International Refugee Law* (Oxford University Press, 2007) at 2–3 and 42.

[8] McAdam, Complementary Protection, *ibid.*, at 1–2.

a risk of cruel and unusual treatment or punishment'.[9] Persons in need of protection are granted the same status as Convention refugees.[10]

6.2.2 New Zealand

New Zealand's Immigration Act (2009) uses the term 'protected person' to denote a person in relation to whom there are 'substantial grounds for believing that he or she would be in danger of being subjected to torture ... or ... arbitrary deprivation of life or cruel treatment' if deported from New Zealand.[11] These provisions are linked explicitly to violations of the rights set out in the Convention Against Torture (CAT) and the International Covenant on Civil and Political Rights (ICCPR), respectively.[12] Similarly to those recognised as Convention refugees, protected persons cannot be deported from New Zealand except under certain statutorily limited circumstances.[13]

6.2.3 EU Member States

Member states of the EU are obliged to incorporate into their domestic laws the protections conferred by Directive 2011/95/EU (2011) (EU Qualification Directive).[14] This Directive – a recast version of a 2004 directive which was the first supranational instrument to codify complementary protection obligations – uses the term 'subsidiary protection', stating that a person entitled to subsidiary protection is

> a third country national or a stateless person who does not qualify as a refugee but in respect of whom substantial grounds have been shown for

[9] Immigration and Refugee Protection Act (Canada), SC 2001, c 27, dated 1 November 2001, as last amended 1 July 2015, s 97(1).

[10] *Ibid.*, s 95(1)(b).

[11] Immigration Act 2009 (New Zealand), Public Act No. 51, 2009, dated 16 November 2009, as last amended 6 November 2015, ss 130(1), 131(1).

[12] CAT, *supra* note 6; International Covenant on Civil and Political Rights (ICCPR) (16 December 1966) 999 UNTS 171, entered into force 23 March 1976.

[13] Immigration Act 2009, *supra* note 11, ss 129(2), 130(4), 131(4), 164(3), 164(4). These sections stipulate that protected persons can be deported on the grounds of national security or public safety, or if they are convicted of a 'particularly serious crime' – exceptions also set down in articles 32(1) and 33(2) of the Refugee Convention.

[14] EU Qualification Directive, *supra* note 5. The EU Qualification Directive recasts and amends Directive 2004/83/EC of the Council of 29 April 2004 on minimum standards for the qualification and status of third-country nationals or stateless persons as refugees or as persons who otherwise need international protection and the content of the protection granted, OJ 2004 No. L 304/12, 30 September 2004. This chapter analyses the more recent instrument.

> believing that the person concerned, if returned to his or her country of origin, or in the case of a stateless person, to his or her country of former habitual residence, would face a real risk of suffering serious harm as defined in Article 15.[15]

Article 15 of the Directive defines 'serious harm' as 'the death penalty or execution; ... torture or inhuman or degrading treatment or punishment ... or ... [a] serious and individual threat to a civilian's life or person by reason of indiscriminate violence in situations of international or internal armed conflict'.[16] Complementary protection offers its beneficiaries a less favourable status than that bestowed on Convention refugees. For example, a Convention refugee must be granted a renewable residence permit which is valid for at least three years, while beneficiaries of complementary protection are entitled to a residence permit that is valid for only one year (or, if renewed, two years).[17]

Like all directives of EU institutions, the EU Qualification Directive is binding upon member states, although national authorities may choose the form and methods of implementing it in national law.[18]

6.2.4 Australia

In 2011, the Australian government amended the Migration Act (1958) to introduce a complementary protection regime. Since the amendments came into effect in 2012, the Migration Act now grants protection to non-citizens

> in respect of whom the Minister is satisfied Australia has protection obligations because the Minister has substantial grounds for believing that, as a necessary and foreseeable consequence of the non-citizen being removed from Australia to a receiving country, there is a real risk that the non-citizen will suffer significant harm.[19]

The Act defines 'significant harm' as arbitrary deprivation of life, the carrying out of the death penalty, the infliction of cruel or inhuman treatment or punishment, and degrading treatment or punishment.[20]

[15] EU Qualification Directive, *supra* note 5, article 2(f).

[16] *Ibid*., article 15.

[17] *Ibid*., article 24. Other differences which previously existed between the two statuses were removed by the recast version of the Directive in 2011.

[18] Consolidated Version of the Treaty on the Functioning of European Union (TFEU), Official Journal C 326/01 (26 October 2012), article 288.

[19] Migration Act 1958, *supra* note 3, s 36(2)(aa).

[20] *Ibid*., s 36(2A).

Individuals in this category receive protection visas identical to those given to Convention refugees.[21]

6.3 The Extent of Judicial Dialogue in Relation to Complementary Protection

The decisions of national courts dealing with matters of complementary protection contain extensive evidence of dialogue with judges in other countries. This section explores the extent of this dialogue. The first part analyses why horizontal dialogue has been so influential in the field of complementary protection. It argues that vertical judicial dialogue, while of some assistance to national courts, is limited because of textual and structural disparities between domestic complementary protection laws and existing regional and international human rights regimes. The second part explains the broad contours of this practice of horizontal dialogue, and considers why certain national jurisdictions have been absent from the exchange.

6.3.1 The Prevalence of Horizontal Judicial Dialogue

The focus of this chapter is on dialogue that occurs horizontally between national courts in different countries. Although national courts have also engaged in some vertical dialogue with regional and international bodies, this section points out that none of these bodies provide holistic interpretive guidance on questions of complementary protection, giving national courts an incentive to engage instead in dialogue on the horizontal plane.

There is no international human rights treaty which explicitly contains a right to complementary protection or governs the conditions under which such a status must be conferred.[22] This fact makes it less likely

[21] *Ibid.*, s 36(2).

[22] This distinguishes complementary protection from other fields of international human rights law where treaties set out clear obligations based on international or regional agreement. For example, civil and political rights are enshrined in the ICCPR, *supra* note 12. Discrimination based on race is governed by the International Convention on the Elimination of All Forms of Racial Discrimination (21 December 1965) 660 UNTS 195, entered into force 4 January 1969. The use of torture and other forms of ill-treatment is governed by CAT, *supra* note 6; within Europe, by the European Convention for the Prevention of Torture and Inhuman or Degrading Treatment or Punishment (26 November 1987) ETS 126, entered into force 1 February 1989; and, within the Inter-American system, by the Inter-American Convention to Prevent and Punish Torture (9 December 1985) OAS Treaty Series No. 67, entered into force 28 February 1987.

that domestic courts will engage in vertical dialogue with regional or international human rights courts or quasi-judicial bodies when interpreting and applying complementary protection laws. This distinguishes complementary protection from other areas of human rights law. In other fields, even in dualist national legal systems in which treaties are not automatically incorporated into municipal law, courts frequently look to international conventions as a source of guidance on how to interpret legislative provisions.[23] For example, in the field of traditional refugee law, both the Refugee Convention[24] and its *travaux préparatoires*[25] have been used as guides for interpreting domestic statutes. The fact that complementary protection norms are not codified in an international treaty removes one possible source of international interpretive guidance for domestic courts, rendering these courts more likely to look horizontally to their counterparts in other domestic jurisdictions.

The EU Qualification Directive provides an exception to this observation. This Directive is a supranational instrument regulating complementary protection. Courts within EU member states frequently draw directly on the text of the operative paragraphs of the Qualification Directive, as well as its preambular paragraphs and preparatory documents, in order to evince the object and purpose of the instrument. But as with other areas of international human rights law which are governed by treaty, although the EU Qualification Directive itself is a pre-eminent authority, its terms have contested meanings which must be interpreted and applied by courts and tribunals. This provides the courts of European states with additional reasons to engage in horizontal judicial dialogue regarding complementary protection obligations, as explored below.

Aside from the absence of an international convention governing complementary protection, there is also no international court or

[23] To take but one jurisdiction as an example, the High Court of Australia has found that where domestic laws are ambiguous, it will 'adopt that meaning which conforms to the principles of universal and fundamental rights rather than an interpretation which would involve a departure from such rights': *Kartinyeri v. Commonwealth* (1998) 195 CLR 337, at 418.

[24] By way of example, the authoritative value of the Refugee Convention has been acknowledged by the Supreme Court of the United Kingdom in *Al-Sirri (FC) v. Secretary of State for the Home Department; DD (Afghanistan) (FC) v. Secretary of State for the Home Department* [2012] UKSC 54, para. 75.

[25] See for example *El-Ali v. Secretary of State for the Home Department* [2002] EWCA Civ 1103 (Court of Appeal of England and Wales), paras. 18–21. Under the Vienna Convention on the Law of Treaties, the *travaux* of an international treaty are a source that may be consulted as a supplementary means of interpreting the terms of that treaty: Vienna Convention on the Law of Treaties (23 May 1969) 1155 UNTS 331, entered into force 27 January 1980, article 32.

quasi-judicial body dedicated to overseeing complementary protection norms. Again, this absence differentiates complementary protection from other branches of human rights law.[26] For example, a national court wishing to interpret legislation banning racial discrimination may look to the documents and quasi-judicial decisions of the United Nations Committee on the Elimination of Racial Discrimination, and on children's rights it may look to the United Nations Committee on the Rights of the Child. There is no body whose mandate involves enforcing all aspects of complementary protection obligations, as these obligations (with the exception of those contained in the EU Qualification Directive) have their provenance in national governments' legislative initiatives, rather than in international treaties. As a result, horizontal dialogue between national courts is especially influential,[27] and for that reason national judges have been pioneers in forging complementary protection standards.[28]

It would be misleading to suggest that national courts engage in no vertical dialogue with regional and international courts and tribunals. Indeed, there are a number of international and regional authorities to which national courts may look to interpret certain aspects of their complementary protection regimes. The essential point, however, is that each of these supranational authorities has limitations in how it contributes to the oversight of complementary protection. Three existing options for international oversight are explored here.

First, UNHCR, as a key custodian of international protection generally, plays some role in overseeing the implementation of complementary protection laws. UNHCR's mandate formally covers only those seeking protection under the Refugee Convention,[29] and yet in the past UNHCR has assumed *de facto* authority over other forced migrants, such as internally displaced persons.[30] In the same vein, UNHCR has engaged in questions

[26] See H. Lambert, 'Transnational Law, Judges and Refugees in the European Union', G.S. Goodwin-Gill and H. Lambert (eds.), *The Limits of Transnational Law: Refugee Law, Policy Harmonization and Judicial Dialogue in the European Union* (Cambridge University Press, 2010) 1–16, at 4.

[27] For a similar argument in relation to Convention refugee protection, see G.S. Goodwin-Gill, 'The Search for the One, True Meaning…', G.S. Goodwin-Gill and H. Lambert (eds.), *The Limits of Transnational Law: Refugee Law, Policy Harmonization and Judicial Dialogue in the European Union* (Cambridge University Press, 2010) 204–40, at 207.

[28] J.C. Hathaway, 'A Forum for the Transnational Development of Refugee Law: The IARLJ's Advanced Refugee Law Workshop', *Int'l J. Refugee L.* 15:3 (2003) 418–21, at 418–19.

[29] Statute of the Office of the UNHCR, UN GA Resolution 428(V), 14 December 1950, UN Doc. A/RES/428(V), article 6.

[30] J.C. Hathaway, 'Who Should Watch over Refugee Law?', *Forced Migration Rev.* 14 (July 2002) 23–26, at 23; V. Türk, 'UNHCR's Supervisory Responsibility', *Revue Québécoise de Droit*

of complementary protection, including by publishing a commentary on the predecessor to the EU Qualification Directive.[31] Even if UNHCR continues in this pattern, its rigour as an oversight mechanism will remain limited. Despite the persuasive value of its published opinions,[32] UNHCR's inadequacies as a monitoring body for refugee law are well documented.[33] Article 35 of the Refugee Convention imposes on states an obligation to 'cooperate' with UNHCR, but this provision is largely aspirational and defies enforcement.[34] Unlike reporting obligations imposed by other United Nations (UN) human rights treaties, states bear no duty to report periodically on their implementation of and compliance with the Refugee Convention (or other international protection obligations), and UNHCR is not empowered to publish reports on the extent to which individual states have discharged their obligations. In contrast to other UN treaty bodies[35] and regional human rights courts and commissions,[36] which have exerted immense influence in refining legal norms, there is

International 14:1 (2001) 135–58, at 147–48; R. Mandal, 'Protection Mechanisms outside of the 1951 Convention ("Complementary Protection")', *Legal and Protection Policy Research Series for the Division of International Protection*, PPLA/2005/02 (UNHCR, June 2005), at 3. Note that internally displaced persons do not formally qualify as refugees because they are not outside their country of origin.

31 UNHCR, Annotated Comments on the EC Council Directive 2004/83/EC of 29 April 2004 on minimum standards for the qualification and status of third country nationals or stateless persons as refugees or as persons who otherwise need international protection and the content of the protection granted (OJ L 304/12 of 30.9.2004) (January 2005), www.unhcr.org/43661eee2.pdf.

32 S. Takahashi, 'Recourse to Human Rights Treaty Bodies for Monitoring of the Refugee Convention', *Netherlands Quarterly of Human Rights* 20:1 (2002) 53–74, at 57. For example, the House of Lords has stated that 'the UNHCR plays a critical role in the application of the Refugee Convention', stating that 'it is not surprising therefore that the UNHCR Handbook [on Procedures and Criteria for Determining Refugee Status under the 1951 Convention and the 1967 Protocol relating to the Status of Refugees], although not binding on states, has high persuasive authority, and is much relied on by domestic courts and tribunals': *R v. Secretary of State for the Home Department, ex parte Adan* [2000] UKHL 67, [2001] 2 WLR 143, at 520.

33 See, for example, Türk, Supervisory Responsibility, *supra* note 30, at 147–48; Takahashi, Human Rights Treaty Bodies, *supra* note 32, at 56; H. Lambert, 'Transnational Judicial Dialogue, Harmonization and the Common European Asylum System', *Int'l & Comp. L. Q.* 58:3 (2009) 519–43, at 521; S.W. Allard, 'Casualties of Disharmony: The Exclusion of Asylum Seekers under the Auspices of the Common European Asylum System', *Emory Int'l L. Rev.* 24:1 (2010) 295–330, at 302.

34 Takahashi, Human Rights Treaty Bodies, *ibid.*, at 54.

35 Examples include the Committee Against Torture, Committee on the Rights of the Child, Human Rights Committee and Committee on the Elimination of Racial Discrimination.

36 Examples include the European Court of Human Rights (ECtHR), the Inter-American Court of Human Rights and the African Commission on Human and Peoples' Rights.

no mechanism by which individuals can submit complaints to UNHCR for impartial adjudication. UNHCR can publish opinions and guidelines on issues of international protection, but these lack binding force.[37] Indeed, numerous commentators have claimed that UNHCR has essentially become an operational agency devoted almost exclusively to the delivery of humanitarian services, performing only minimal functions relating to clarifying or developing legal standards.[38]

The second possible supranational oversight mechanism is the Court of Justice of the European Union (CJEU), a body which provides opportunities for vertical dialogue by domestic courts within EU member states. States may refer questions to the CJEU where there is uncertainty surrounding obligations under EU law.[39] For example, in *Elgafaji v. Staatssecretaris van Justitie*, the Dutch Council of State requested the CJEU's opinion on the interpretation of article 15(c) of the EU Qualification Directive, particularly regarding the threshold of armed conflict required to animate this provision.[40] CJEU decisions may offer clarity on the questions posed, useful for both the requesting court and courts in other EU jurisdictions. The CJEU is not, however, a perfect oversight mechanism. First, some authors express concern about a lack of expertise in international protection among CJEU judges.[41] Second, decisions of the CJEU are binding only on the EU member states (or other parties) to which they are addressed.[42] Third, the CJEU can rule on a complaint of a private individual against a national government only if requested by a court of that state[43] – a system that means that CJEU rulings on complementary protection are few in number.[44] Given the scarcity

[37] James Hathaway observes that the sole human rights treaty which predates the Refugee Convention, the Convention on the Prevention and Punishment of the Crime of Genocide (9 December 1948) 78 UNTS 227, entered into force 12 January 1951, is similarly bereft of any enforcement or oversight mechanism. He posits that, at the point in the history of international human rights law at which these instruments were concluded, the notion of state conduct being internationally monitored and evaluated did not yet command international support: Hathaway, Who Should Watch over Refugee Law, *supra* note 30, at 24.

[38] See for example Hathaway, *ibid.*, at 24; Takahashi, Human Rights Treaty Bodies, *supra* note 32, at 54.

[39] Article 267 TFEU.

[40] Case C-465/07, *Elgafaji v. Staatssecretaris van Justitie* [2009] ECR I-921, ECLI:EU:C:2009:94.

[41] See, for example, Lambert, Transnational Law, *supra* note 26, at 8–9.

[42] TFEU, *supra* note 18, article 288.

[43] *Ibid.*, article 267. The situation is different for actions brought against a member state by European Union institutions or other member states: in these cases, no preliminary reference by a domestic court is required: see TFEU, articles 258–59. To date, no inter-state actions have been instituted in relation to complementary protection obligations.

[44] J. McAdam, 'Regionalizing International Refugee Law in the European Union: Democratic Revision or Revisionist Democracy', *Vict. U. Well. L. Rev.* 38:2 (2007) 255–80, at 266. Even

of decisions, the CJEU is unable to develop a sophisticated jurisprudence over several opinions. Interpretation of the EU Qualification Directive – as well as interpretation of the small number of CJEU rulings – falls to a large extent to domestic courts, the decisions of which in turn become sources of interpretive guidance for other national courts. For example, in interpreting the CJEU's ruling in *Elgafaji*, Finland's Supreme Administrative Court alluded to jurisprudence from the United Kingdom, Sweden and Germany.[45]

Fourth, national courts may look to existing tribunals for the enforcement of human rights, such as the United Nations Human Rights Committee (UNHRC), the United Nations Committee against Torture (UNCAT) and the European Court of Human Rights (ECtHR). These bodies have numerous strengths: for example, individuals may bring complaints before them; they typically issue dozens of decisions every year and so refine their jurisprudence through successive cases; and, for at least some of the bodies (such as the ECtHR and the Inter-American Court of Human Rights), their decisions are binding on national governments. Such human rights courts and quasi-judicial bodies have played a critical role in guaranteeing certain fundamental rights of asylum seekers and forced migrants, including freedom from arbitrary detention,[46]

since McAdam's research in 2007, the CJEU has issued preliminary rulings on only a handful of issues relating to complementary protection. These include: *Elgafaji*, *supra* note 40 (on the meaning of 'internal armed conflict' and 'indiscriminate violence'); Case C-277/11, *MM v. Minister for Justice, Equality and Law Reform and Attorney General of Ireland* [2012] ECR ECR I-0000, ECLI:EU:C:2012:744 (on due process during hearing of complementary protection claims); Case C-285/12, *Diakité v. Commissaire Général aux Réfugiés et aux Apatrides* [2014] ECR I-0000, ECLI:EU:C:2014:39 (on whether the term 'internal armed conflict' has a meaning independent of the meaning under international humanitarian law); Case C-604/12, *HN v. Minister for Justice, Equality and Law Reform and Attorney General of Ireland* [2014] ECR I-0000, ECLI:EU:C:2014:302 (on procedural rules concerning whether a court must consider an application for refugee status before determining eligibility for complementary protection); Case C-542/13, *M'Bodj v. État Belge* [2014] ECR I-0000, ECLI:EU:C:2014:2452 (on whether returning a person to a state where they will be unable to receive treatment for a serious illness amounts to inhuman or degrading treatment).

45 KHO:2010:84, 30 December 2010 (Finland, Supreme Administrative Court), at 5, 14 (unofficial English translation available at www.refworld.org/docid/4ea028162.html). See also N. Hart, 'Complementary Protection and Transjudicial Dialogue: Global Best Practice or Race to the Bottom?', *Int'l J. of Refugee L.* 28:2 (2016) 171-209, at 200-07 (exploration of a number of CJEU cases, variously favourable and unfavourable to applicants for complementary protection).

46 *MSS v. Belgium and Greece* (Appl. No. 30696/09), Judgment (Grand Chamber), 21 January 2011, ECHR 2011-I, 255; UNHRC, *A v. Australia*, Communication No. 560/1993, 30 April 1997, UN Doc. CCPR/C/59/D/560/1993; UNHRC, General Comment No. 20,

freedom from expulsion to face torture,[47] and the right to family unity and privacy.[48] In complementary protection cases, domestic courts have exhibited a willingness to engage vertically with these courts and treaty bodies in interpreting those aspects of national complementary protection laws with a clear link to international and regional human rights provisions. For example, the New Zealand Immigration and Protection Tribunal (NZIPT) has considered the jurisprudence of the UNHRC in interpreting its country's complementary protection laws and, specifically, whether 'socio-economic deprivation' can amount to torture.[49] Similarly, the Upper Tribunal of the United Kingdom gave extensive consideration to jurisprudence of the ECtHR in addressing the weight to be given to evidence of the situation in an applicant's country of origin.[50]

Despite the contribution of these bodies, there are textual and structural disparities between national complementary protection legislation and other areas of human rights law adjudicated by existing supranational courts, commissions and treaty bodies. As a result, these bodies lack jurisdiction to consider key features of complementary protection regimes that may arise before national courts. For example, the CAT stipulates that torture can only be committed 'by or at the instigation of or with the consent or acquiescence of a public official or other person acting in an

3 October 1992, UN Doc. HRI/GEN/1/Rev.1 at 30, para. 9; UNCAT, *Chahin v. Sweden*, Communication No. 310/2007, 8 July 2011, UN Doc. CAT/C/46/D/310/2007.

47 Landmark cases of the ECtHR include *Chahal v. the United Kingdom* (Appl. No. 22414/93), Judgment (Grand Chamber), 15 November 1996, Reports 1996-V; *Othman (Abu Qatada) v. the United Kingdom* (Appl. No. 8139/09), Judgment (Chamber), 19 May 2012, ECHR 2012-I, 259. For more recent applications of the principles relevant to expulsions of refugees and the risk of torture or inhuman or degrading treatment or punishment, see *Tatar v. Switzerland* (Appl. No. 65692/12), Judgment (Chamber), 14 April 2015, not reported; *Mamazhonov v. Russia* (Appl. No. 17239/13), Judgment (Chamber), 23 October 2014, not reported. See also UNHRC, General Comment No. 31, 26 May 2004, UN Doc. CCPR/C/21/Rev.1/Add. 13, para. 12.

48 On family unity, see *Berrehab v. Netherlands* (Appl. No. 10730/84), Judgment (Chamber), 21 June 1998, Series A, Vol. 138; *Bajsultanov v. Austria* (Appl. No. 54131/10), Judgment (Chamber), 12 June 2012, not reported; H. Lambert, 'The European Court of Human Rights and the Right of Refugees and Other Persons in Need of Protection to Family Reunion', *Int'l J. Refugee L.* 11:3 (1999) 427–50, at 436. On the right to private life, see *Bensaid v. the United Kingdom* (Appl. No. 44599/98), Judgment (Chamber), 6 February 2001, ECHR 2001-I, 303.

49 *BG (Fiji)* [2012] NZIPT 800091 (New Zealand, Immigration and Protection Tribunal (NZIPT)), paras. 174–79.

50 *AMM and Others (Conflict; Humanitarian Crisis; Returnees; FGM) Somalia v. Secretary of State for the Home Department, CG* [2011] UKUT 445 (United Kingdom, Upper Tribunal, Asylum and Immigration Chamber). Most notably the Tribunal (especially at paras. 55–133) referred to *Sufi and Elmi v. United Kingdom* (Appl. Nos. 8319/07 and 11449/07), Judgment (Chamber), 28 June 2011, not reported.

official capacity' and imposes the same requirement on 'other acts of cruel, inhuman or degrading treatment or punishment'.[51] In contrast, Canada's Immigration and Refugee Protection Act does not require that 'cruel and unusual treatment or punishment' be inflicted by or with the acquiescence of a state official.[52] Similarly, the definition of torture in Australia's Migration Act does not require that the impugned conduct occurs at the hands of public agents,[53] rendering total reliance on decisions of UNCAT problematic.[54] Due to such differences, domestic judges cannot always look for interpretive guidance by engaging in vertical dialogue. Instead, they may look horizontally to courts in other countries for their interpretations of similar provisions.[55] Section 6.6 discusses some aspects of complementary protection which have been the subject of extensive horizontal dialogue, in part because the legislative terms in question do not have equivalents in international and regional treaties interpreted by supranational bodies.

6.3.2 *The Contours of Horizontal Judicial Dialogue*

This part explores the most common channels of exchange between national courts; that is, the question of which courts consult which other courts most

[51] CAT, *supra* note 6, articles 1 and 16. It should be noted that this restriction on the definition of torture and inhuman and degrading treatment and punishment does not arise in all supranational jurisdictions. For example, the ECtHR has found that the *non-refoulement* principle applies where the risk of ill-treatment arises from private actors against which public officials are unable or unwilling to provide protection: see for example *HLR v. France* (Appl. No. 24573/94), Judgment (Grand Chamber), 29 April 1997, Reports 1997-III, paras. 39–40.

[52] Immigration and Refugee Protection Act 2001, *supra* note 9, s 97(1)(b); and J. Reekie, 'Part III: Canada', International Association of Refugee Law Judges (IARLJ), 'Convention Refugee Status and Subsidiary Protection Working Party: First Report' (7th World Conference, Mexico City, November 2006) 36–52, at 39–40.

[53] Migration Act 1958, *supra* note 3, s 36(2A)(c); J. McAdam, 'Australian Complementary Protection: A Step-by-Step Approach', *Sydney L. Rev.* 33:4 (2011) 687–734, at 697.

[54] *Minister for Immigration and Citizenship v. MZYYL* [2012] FCAFC 147 (Australia, Full Court of the Federal Court), paras. 18–19. As an additional point, the Australian Migration Act grants complementary protection where a person is at risk of 'significant harm', which is lower than the threshold for *non-refoulement* of 'irreparable harm' imposed by the UNHRC (see UNHRC, General Comment No. 31, *supra* note 47, para. 12).

[55] For example, a Canadian or Australian judge faced with a claim of harm by private actors may look to decisions of French courts (*Commission des Recours des Réfugiés*) which have recognised that all of the following may constitute torture or other forms of mistreatment, despite not being carried out by state officials: threats by employers (*MK*, Case 494377, 21 April 2005); threats by criminal gangs against which the applicant may be called to testify (*Mlle Z*, Case 493983, 8 February 2005); and domestic violence which the state had failed to

prolifically. Specifically, this section considers, first, the nationality and, second, the seniority of the courts engaged in dialogue.

First, there is variety as to the nationality of courts which participate in dialogue. Although European courts frequently rely on other jurisdictions in which the EU Qualification Directive applies and Commonwealth countries have a tendency to draw on each other's authorities,[56] there is extensive cross-referencing that defies these trends.[57]

Despite this variety, some patterns as to the nationalities of courts involved in dialogue emerge. There are also some contextual reasons for why certain jurisdictions are more likely to engage in, and be drawn on as a source for, transnational judicial dialogue. To date, domestic courts in states which were admitted to the EU in the mid- to late 2000s have decided very few cases and so are rarely looked to as a source of guidance.[58] Countries which publish their decisions in languages which are widely spoken around the world – especially English, but also French – are more likely to be quoted extensively.[59] In *AK (Article 15(c)) Afghanistan*, the Immigration and Asylum Chamber of the United Kingdom's Upper Tribunal identified as a 'drawback' the fact that it did 'not have certified translations or full transcripts of all the decisions cited to [it]', but noted that it had 'been helpful nevertheless to have translations of some and summaries of others'.[60] Perhaps this explains why some non-English-speaking

suppress (*Mme D*, Case 535458, 7 October 2005). These French cases are cited in J. McAdam, 'Part I: Overview', IARLJ, 'Convention Refugee Status and Subsidiary Protection Working Party: First Report' (7th World Conference, Mexico City, November 2006) 2–13, at 6.

[56] See for example Lambert, Transnational Law, *supra* note 26, at 4–5; and J.C. Hathaway, *The Rights of Refugees under International Law* (Cambridge University Press, 2005) at 1–2.

[57] See many of the examples identified in Section 6.6.

[58] Lambert, Transnational Law, *supra* note 26, at 10.

[59] J.-Y. Carlier and D. Vanheule, 'Where is the Reference? On the Limited role of Transnational Dialogue in Belgian Refugee Law', G. S. Goodwin-Gill and H. Lambert (eds.), *The Limits of Transnational Law: Refugee Law, Policy Harmonization and Judicial Dialogue in the European Union* (Cambridge University Press, 2010) 17–34, at 30–31; H. Lambert and J. Silga, 'Transnational Refugee Law in the French Courts: Deliberate or Compelled Change in Judicial Attitudes?', G.S. Goodwin-Gill and H. Lambert (eds.), ibid., 35–56, at 49. Further underscoring the importance of linguistic accessibility, courts in German-speaking jurisdictions are more likely to reference each other's decisions: see P. Tiedemann, 'The Use of Foreign Asylum Jurisprudence in the German Administrative Courts', G.S. Goodwin-Gill and H. Lambert (eds.), *ibid.*, 57–84, at 78–80.

[60] *AK (Article 15(c)) Afghanistan v. Secretary of State for the Home Department, CG* [2012] UKUT 163 (United Kingdom, Upper Tribunal, Asylum and Immigration Chamber), para. 194. This case also demonstrates that in jurisdictions with adversarial legal systems, judges are typically reliant on the parties carrying out investigation of foreign case law and presenting it to the court: H. Lambert and R. Husain, 'The British Judiciary and the Search

states offer English translations online,[61] and online databases typically provide summaries (and, where possible, judgments) in English.[62] Hélène Lambert proposes additional reasons for why courts in certain jurisdictions may be more commonly cited than others, focusing particularly on the typical length of judgments and the depth of reasoning which is evident in the text. She argues that British judgments more commonly contain references to foreign judgments and are themselves more frequently cited abroad than French cases. British judgments are longer, explicitly draw on binding or persuasive precedents, and carefully explain all steps of the legal reasoning process.[63] Other authors agree that judges in civil law jurisdictions with a tradition of short decisions with little articulated reasoning are typically more limited in their engagement in judicial dialogue,[64] while courts in (usually common law) jurisdictions where judgments are longer and reasoning is given in full are better candidates for 'export'.[65]

There are some jurisdictions, however, whose courts are excluded from the dialogue. The United States and Mexico have enacted complementary protection norms, and yet the decisions of their national courts are simply not referenced in judgments from the states on which this chapter

for Reciprocal Relations with its Continental Partners', G.S. Goodwin-Gill and H. Lambert (eds.), *The Limits of Transnational Law: Refugee Law, Policy Harmonization and Judicial Dialogue in the European Union* (Cambridge University Press, 2010) 125–49, at 142. In contrast, in inquisitorial systems, judges are more likely to conduct such investigations independently of the parties. See further analysis in Section 6.4.

[61] See, for example, the translations available on the website of the German Federal Administrative Court, which has a section dedicated to 'Decisions in Asylum and Immigration Law': www.bverwg.de/informationen/english/federal_administrative_court.php. Hélène Lambert and Raza Husain claim that British authorities are far more likely to consider cases from non-English-speaking jurisdictions when official translations into English are freely available: Lambert and Husain, British Judiciary, *ibid.*, at 141.

[62] See for example European Database of Asylum Law, www.asylumlawdatabase.eu/en.

[63] Lambert, Transnational Judicial Dialogue, *supra* note 33, at 534–35.

[64] See, for example, Carlier and Vanheule, Belgian Refugee Law, *supra* note 59, at 32; Lambert and Silga, Transnational Refugee Law in the French Courts, *supra* note 59, at 52–53. A particularly acute example is Denmark, where judicial review of administrative asylum decisions is not permitted, meaning that very few judicial decisions on asylum cases exist in this jurisdiction. Denmark's reservations to European Community harmonisation directives also limit the applicability of foreign decisions: see J. Vedsted-Hansen, 'The Absence of Foreign Law in Danish Asylum Decisions – Quasi-Judicial Monologue with Domestic Policy Focus?', G.S. Goodwin-Gill and H. Lambert (eds.), *The Limits of Transnational Law: Refugee Law, Policy Harmonization and Judicial Dialogue in the European Union* (Cambridge University Press, 2010) 170–85, at 179–82.

[65] Lambert and Husain, British Judiciary, *supra* note 60, at 143.

focuses.[66] There are some explanations for why judicial dialogue does not extend to courts in these countries. In relation to the United States, it is likely a matter of incommensurability of complementary protection laws, as the American legislation differs significantly from the laws of this chapter's case study jurisdictions. For example, under the relevant paragraphs of the US Code of Federal Regulations,[67] there is a difference between 'affirmative' and 'defensive' tracks of protection, and, while *non-refoulement* is a mandatory obligation, the granting of refugee status is formally discretionary.[68] This fact distinguishes the American system from the more uniform legislative regimes in Canada, Australia, New Zealand and Europe, thus making dialogue with American courts difficult.

The Mexican legislation, the Law on Refugees, Complementary Protection and Political Asylum (*Ley sobre Refugiados, Protección Complementaria y Asilo Político*) (2011, amended 2014), is cast in more similar terms to the laws of the states examined in this chapter. Article 28 confers complementary protection on a claimant whose life is at risk, or who is at risk of torture or other cruel, inhuman or degrading treatment or punishment, in his or her country of origin.[69] In addition, article 13 gives an expansive definition of those who are entitled to refugee protection – a definition that captures many more than Convention refugees. For one thing, it lists not only the five Convention grounds but also gender as a possible basis of persecution. It also extends to individuals 'who

[66] Regrettably, the research for this chapter has not extended to a comprehensive survey of American and Mexican case law on complementary protection. For that reason, no conclusion can be reached as to the whether judges in these jurisdictions engage in dialogue in the reverse direction by referring to decisions from EU member states, Canada, New Zealand and Australia.

[67] Code of Federal Regulations, Title 8 Aliens and Nationality (United States), as last amended 1 January 2012, §§ 208.16, 208.17.

[68] J. McAdam, 'Complementary Protection and Beyond: How States Deal with Human Rights Protection', UNHCR New Issues in Refugee Research Working Paper No. 118 (August 2005) at 13–18.

[69] Law on Refugees, Complementary Protection and Political Asylum (*Ley sobre Refugiados, Protección Complementaria y Asilo Político*), dated 28 January 2011 (then called Law on Refugees and Complementary Protection (*Ley de Refugiados y Protección Complementaria*), as last amended 30 October 2014. This summary of the Mexican law is drawn from N. Dicker and J. Mansfield, 'Filling the Protection Gap: Current Trends in Complementary Protection in Canada, Mexico and Australia', UNHCR New Issues in Refugee Research, Research Paper No. 238 (May 2012) at 13. That research refers to the former version of the law, Law on Refugees and Complementary Protection (2011) (*Ley de Refugiados y Protección Complementaria*).

have fled their country because their lives, safety or freedom have been threatened by generalized violence, foreign aggression, internal conflicts, massive violation of human rights or other circumstances which have seriously disturbed public order'.[70] Given the similarities between the laws in Mexico and the other jurisdictions examined in this chapter, it is surprising that judgments from Australia, Canada, New Zealand or Europe omit any mention of Mexico as another jurisdiction with complementary protection laws. It is difficult to identify the reasons for this exclusion. Possible explanations include that Mexican judgments, written in Spanish, are less accessible to English-speaking judges in the Commonwealth, and that there is no tradition of transnational judicial dialogue with Mexican judges in other contexts. According to Eduardo Ferrer MacGregor and Rubén Sánchez Gil, Mexican courts, eager to demonstrate their independence from foreign influences, rarely explicitly cite decisions from abroad, even when it is clear that they are borrowing legal reasoning or analytical tools.[71] Perhaps the reluctance of Mexican courts to engage in overt judicial dialogue accounts, at least partially, for its exclusion from dialogue between courts in other jurisdictions.

Second, judicial dialogue between judges in Europe, Canada, Australia and New Zealand is not limited to courts at any particular rung of a judicial hierarchy: superior bodies such as the United Kingdom Supreme Court down to primary appellate bodies such as the NZIPT engage in such dialogue with comparable frequency, relative to the number of cases dealing with complementary protection which they hear. Likewise, the decisions which are consulted emanate from courts and tribunals of varying levels of superiority, from the Council of State of the Netherlands to the Refugee Review Tribunal (RRT) of Australia. Despite this variety, decisions of superior courts are typically accorded greater weight and deference.[72] This preference may be due to the general recognition that decisions of senior courts are more authoritative than those of lower courts and tribunals. Hélène Lambert, in a study of cases relating to asylum law (not limited to complementary protection) in Britain and France, also suggests that the spread of international judicial dialogue between courts of differing seniority may not be even, with superior courts being more likely to engage in

[70] This translation is drawn from Dicker and Mansfield, *ibid.*, at 14.

[71] See E.F. MacGregor and R.S. Gil, 'Foreign Precedents in Mexican Constitutional Adjudication', *Mexican L. Rev.* 4:2 (2012) 293–307.

[72] By way of example, in *Al-Sirri*, the Supreme Court of the United Kingdom referred to the decisions of senior appellate courts in Australia, Canada, Germany and New Zealand: see *Al-Sirri (FC)*, *supra* note 24, discussed further in section 6.6.4.

such exchange. She notes that in some inferior appellate bodies, decision-makers are not required to have legal training, and that purely administrative officials without legal backgrounds are less likely to draw on foreign jurisprudence than are judges of senior courts who are comprehensively inculcated into legal culture. She partially attributes the paucity of judicial dialogue in decisions of the French National Asylum Court to this factor.[73] Another explanation for lower courts' more sparing use of foreign decisions is that these bodies must process a high volume of cases at first instance or on direct appeal, and time pressures restrict the attention they can devote to a rigorous assessment of case law from other jurisdictions.[74]

Naturally, foreign cases, whatever their persuasive value, cannot overrule binding domestic precedents or rules of legislative interpretation. There have been instances in which national courts have explicitly rejected the applicability of foreign jurisprudence on the basis that the domestic legislative provisions they are interpreting are not sufficiently alike to their counterparts in other jurisdictions.[75] Indeed, the Federal Court of Australia has described the Australian law on international protection as 'a code in the sense that the relevant criteria and obligations are defined in it and it contains its own definitions'.[76] The Court concluded that in some cases it is impossible to identify 'international standards' forged by domestic courts around the world because '[d]ifferent countries have different systems' and the legislative discrepancies may be too substantial to disregard by applying identical tests.[77] Courts in states which adhere particularly fiercely to dualist conceptions of international law are less likely to incorporate findings from abroad.[78]

[73] Lambert, Transnational Judicial Dialogue, *supra* note 33, at 531–32. See also Lambert and Silga, Transnational Refugee Law in the French Courts, *supra* note 59, at 50–51.

[74] Lambert and Silga, *ibid.*, at 198.

[75] Jane McAdam has pointed to numerous key distinctions between the terms of Australia's Migration Act and foreign equivalents: McAdam, Australian Complementary Protection, *supra* note 53, at 696. For instance, the Migration Act 1958, *supra* note 3, confers complementary protection where 'the Minister is satisfied Australia has protection obligations because the Minister has substantial grounds for believing that, as a necessary and foreseeable consequence of the non-citizen being removed from Australia to a receiving country, there is a real risk that the non-citizen will suffer significant harm': s 36(2)(aa). As McAdam points out, this imposes a convoluted standard of proof that entails multiple independent threshold tests ('satisfied', 'substantial grounds for believing', 'necessary and foreseeable consequence', 'real risk' and 'significant harm') and which is substantially higher than in other jurisdictions where only one or a small number of these thresholds are included (McAdam, at 715).

[76] *Minister for Immigration and Citizenship v. MZYYL*, *supra* note 54, para. 18.

[77] *Ibid.*, paras. 20 and 37.

[78] See for example R. Stern, 'Foreign Law in Swedish Judicial Decision-making: Playing a Limited Role in Refugee Law Cases', G.S. Goodwin-Gill and H. Lambert (eds.), *The Limits*

6.4 The Method behind Judicial Dialogue

National courts are regrettably opaque when it comes to the methodology they employ in selecting, considering and applying case law from foreign jurisdictions. Other chapters in this collection have relied on interviews with national judges to gain insights on the procedures these decision-makers tend to favour.[79] This chapter, based instead on what is evident from written documents, is more limited in the conclusions it can draw on the methods behind judicial dialogue. Nonetheless, it makes two observations: the first concerning the role of the parties to a case in bringing foreign cases to the court's attention, and the second concerning extra-curial opportunities for exchanges between judges.

First, there is no clear pattern in the role played by parties to a case in fostering judicial dialogue. Judgments are frequently silent as to whether foreign cases which they cite were used by the parties in their written or oral submissions, or whether the judges located and considered such cases at their own initiative. Judgments which are explicit about how a foreign case has come to the court's attention exhibit diversity in this regard. For example, in a case concerning the meaning of the term 'particularly serious crime' in article 33(2) of the Refugee Convention, the parties referred the United Kingdom Asylum and Immigration Tribunal to one case of the Federal Court of Australia.[80] In its judgment, the Tribunal considered an additional case from the same Australian court on its own initiative, stating that this was 'for completeness'.[81] In *AK (Article 15(c)) Afghanistan*,[82] the Immigration and Asylum Chamber of the United Kingdom's Upper Tribunal specifically requested that the respondent gather relevant case law from courts and tribunals across the EU and in Switzerland.[83] Some authors posit that courts in countries with adversarial legal systems, typically those with common law traditions, are

of Transnational Law: Refugee Law, Policy Harmonization and Judicial Dialogue in the European Union (Cambridge University Press, 2010) 186–203, at 200–01; Tiedemann, German Administrative Courts, *supra* note 59, at 80–84; and Vedsted-Hansen, Danish Asylum Decisions, *supra* note 64, at 182–84.

79 See e.g. Chapter 4 in this volume.

80 The case to which the parties referred the Tribunal was *Betkoshabeh v. Minister for Immigration and Multicultural Affairs* (1998) 157 ALR 95 (Australia, Federal Court), cited in *IH (s 72; 'Particularly Serious Crime') Eritrea v. Secretary of State for the Home Department* [2009] UKAIT 12 (United Kingdom, Asylum and Immigration Tribunal), paras. 32 and 69–72.

81 *A v. Minister for Immigration and Multicultural Affairs* [1999] FCA 116 (Australia, Federal Court), cited in *IH (s 72; 'Particularly Serious Crime') Eritrea*, *ibid.*, para. 60.

82 *AK (Article 15(c)) Afghanistan*, *supra* note 60.

83 *Ibid.*, para. 194.

more likely to rely on parties to bring foreign case law to their attention.[84] As a general methodological feature, it appears that parties are welcome to, and often do, invoke foreign case law in their submissions, and that judges are inclined to identify additional relevant jurisprudence from abroad when they feel that it would assist them in resolving cases before them.

Second, in the field of complementary protection, a substantial amount of dialogue between judges of different national jurisdictions occurs outside of published decisions. For example, manuals drafted for the purposes of training and setting standards for decision-makers in Australia's RRT and Canada's Immigration and Refugee Board draw extensively on cases from other jurisdictions.[85] The European Chapter of the International Association of Refugee Law Judges (IARLJ), UNHCR and the Council of Europe have all advocated common manuals and training sessions for judges applying asylum law across Europe.[86] Institutional judicial conferences have cultivated transnational colloquy.[87] The IARLJ, which has the constitutional aim of 'further[ing] exchanges and the dissemination of information on international law and practice as it relates to the status of refugees' between judges and quasi-judicial decision-makers,[88] has convened conferences dealing specifically with complementary protection. The IARLJ also commissions working parties comprising 'small transnational groups of judges' to investigate specific aspects of international protection.[89] James Hathaway contends that such conferences provide crucial

[84] Lambert and Husain, British Judiciary, *supra* note 60, at 142. See also the discussion of *AK (Article 15(c) Qualification Directive) Iraq*, *supra* note 60, in Section 6.3.2.

[85] MRT and RRT (Australia), Complementary Protection Training Manual, *supra* note 3; Legal Services, Immigration and Refugee Board (Canada), 'Consolidated Grounds in the *Immigration and Refugee Protection Act*: Persons in Need of Protection – Danger of Torture' (15 May 2002), www.irb-cisr.gc.ca/Eng/brdcom/referencexs/legjur/Documents/ProtectTorture_e.pdf; Legal Services, Immigration and Refugee Board (Canada), 'Consolidated Grounds in the *Immigration and Refugee Protection Act*: Persons in Need of Protection – Risk to Life or Risk of Cruel and Unusual Treatment or Punishment' (15 May 2002), www.irb-cisr.gc.ca/Eng/brdcom/references/legjur/Documents/ProtectLifVie_e.pdf.

[86] Lambert, Transnational Judicial Dialogue, *supra* note 33, at 526; Presidency of the European Union to the General Affairs Council and European Council of the European Union, 'The Stockholm Programme: An Open and Secure Europe Serving and Protecting the Citizens' (2 December 2009), at 70.

[87] Anne-Marie Slaughter identifies conferences as a key forum for judicial dialogue across various areas of law: A.-M. Slaughter, 'Judicial Globalization', *Virginia J. of Int'l L.* 40:4 (2000) 1103–24, at 1120–21.

[88] 'Constitution of the International Association of Refugee Law Judges', preamble, www.iarlj.org/general/iarlj/the-association/constitution/english.

[89] See IARLJ, 'Criteria for Working Parties' (2009), www.iarlj.org/general/52-working-parties/guidelines-and-criteria/379-criteria-for-wp. The working party most relevant for this

opportunities for judges to formulate international protection standards in a way that is 'vigorously collaborative'.[90] Beyond these publicly available sources, it is possible that judges in different jurisdictions engage in private conversations that are never recorded and may not be patent in their judgments, creating a traffic in ideas that is somewhat invisible.[91] While the impact of these extra-curial exchanges is difficult to quantify,[92] it is likely that training manuals, conferences and personal conversations go some way to inuring judges to certain approaches to interpreting and applying their domestic complementary protection provisions. One case which, unusually, sheds light on the role of this informal dialogue is *KH (Article 15(c) Qualification Directive) Iraq*, heard by the United Kingdom Asylum and Immigration Tribunal. This judgment provides a list of resources that were before the Tribunal, including reports from IARLJ conferences and an IARLJ working party on complementary protection.[93] Even in this case, the degree of influence actually exerted by these documents is ambiguous. Further empirical research would assist in determining the impact of dialogue that occurs outside of published decisions.

6.5 The Purpose and Effects of Judicial Dialogue

Domestic judges, within their judgments, are rarely explicit regarding their motivations for drawing on cases concerning complementary protection from other national jurisdictions. It is possible to speculate about judges' various purposes. For example, given the newness of complementary protection laws in most of the countries considered in this chapter, courts may simply have no domestic authorities from which to derive interpretive guidance.[94] Alternatively, foreign cases may fulfil an ornamental purpose, lending an air of authority to a particular finding; this rationale is particularly plausible in judgments which do little more than briefly allude to foreign decisions in which similar issues have been considered. Anne-Marie Slaughter has argued that even cursory references to foreign case law may

chapter is the Convention Refugee Status and Subsidiary Protection Working Party, which presented reports at the 2006 and 2009 global conferences of the IARLJ.

90 Hathaway, Forum for the Transnational Development of Refugee Law, *supra* note 28, at 419.

91 A.-M. Slaughter, 'A Typology of Transjudicial Communication', *Univ. Richmond L. Rev.* 29:1 (1994) 99–138, at 103; and Lambert, Transnational Judicial Dialogue, *supra* note 33, at 533.

92 On the difficulty of measuring the influence of informal channels of communication, see C. McCrudden, 'A Common Law of Human Rights?: Transnational Judicial Conversations on Constitutional Rights', *Oxford J. Legal Studies* 20:4 (2000) 499–532, at 511.

93 *KH (Article 15(c) Qualification Directive) Iraq v. Secretary of State for the Home Department, CG* [2008] UKAIT 23 (United Kingdom, Asylum and Immigration Tribunal), appendix I.

94 Slaughter, Transjudicial Communication, *supra* note 91, at 131.

have such a legitimating effect by giving other branches of government and the public a 'simple demonstration that others have trodden a similar path'.[95]

But this section argues that judges' purpose in engaging in judicial dialogue on questions of complementary protection is more than simply cosmetic. Indeed, many of the judgments which feature in this chapter engage in a deep and thoughtful analysis of a number of foreign cases. Several of them address foreign decisions at length, providing factual context and including extensive quotations. In some such cases, courts consider decisions of numerous bodies across multiple jurisdictions, identifying commonalities and inconsistencies before settling on and justifying their preferred approach.

In making this argument, this section focuses on one overarching purpose underlying judicial dialogue in the field of complementary protection: the pursuit of protection standards which are harmonised between different national jurisdictions. It argues that this purpose encompasses two more specific purposes, which in turn yield two disparate effects. The first sub-purpose, common to many fields of human rights, is to establish a global best practice, with the effect of enhancing protection standards for forced migrants. The second sub-purpose is to make protection standards consistent in order to deter secondary movements of forced migrants. As this section explains, harmonisation is important in the field of international protection because of the expectation that forced migrants will cherry-pick the jurisdiction in which to lodge their protection claims based on which state will provide them with the most favourable treatment. At least in the current political climate in the jurisdictions analysed in this chapter, states are reluctant to offer conditions to forced migrants that are more generous than those provided in other states. For this reason, judicial dialogue can produce a uniform lowering of standards across states with complementary protection regimes. Both of these competing purposes and their effects – the strengthening and the dilution of protection standards – are evident in the case studies provided in Section 6.6.

6.5.1 The Aspiration to Harmonise Complementary Protection Standards

Governments enacting complementary protection laws, as well as courts interpreting and applying them, emphasise their wish to implement consistent standards of protection between different states. Judges have expressed

[95] *Ibid.*, at 118. See also McCrudden, Common Law of Human Rights, *supra* note 92, at 530; Lambert, Transnational Judicial Dialogue, *supra* note 33, at 530.

a belief that judicial dialogue is a tool that will facilitate this harmonisation. The Federal Court of Canada has stated that '[t]here is little doubt that in order to better carry out its mandate, the [Refugee Protection Division of the Immigration and Refugee Board] should keep abreast of international developments and would be well advised to consider … recent decisions of other immigration tribunals'.[96] The Supreme Court of New Zealand emphasised 'the importance of domestic courts endeavouring to develop and maintain a common approach to the meaning of the language of an international instrument which is given effect as domestic law in numerous jurisdictions', before proceeding to consider a line of authorities from the Canadian Federal Court of Appeal and the Court of Appeal for England and Wales.[97] Consistent with this approach, the training manual for Australia's RRT states that, in pointing to international jurisprudence and thus elucidating 'accepted international standards and understandings of the key terms of Australia's complementary protection provisions', it hoped to help Australian decision-makers in interpreting domestic laws and to contribute to a harmonisation of international law.[98] In *AK (Article 15(c)) Afghanistan*, the United Kingdom's Upper Tribunal wrote:

> [I]t seems to us highly desirable that judges in Europe (who have to apply common legal standards set out in EU law and have to have regard to [ECtHR] jurisprudence) should look to each other's decisions as a source of assistance in terms of the application of the relevant law.[99]

The following two subsections contend that this purpose of harmonisation produces two virtually opposing effects, both of which are apparent in the case studies provided in Section 6.6: to bolster standards in favour of applicants for complementary protection, and to weaken those standards.

6.5.2 *Forging a Global Best Practice: Enhancing Standards of Complementary Protection*

Harmonising complementary protection standards can have beneficial effects for forced migrants. In some cases, national courts seeking to

96 *Nagamany v. Canada (Minister of Citizenship and Immigration)*, 2005 FC 1554 (Canada, Federal Court), para. 64.

97 *Attorney General v. Tamil X* [2011] 1 NZLR 721 (New Zealand, Supreme Court), para. 70. The 'international instrument' to which the Supreme Court referred was the Refugee Convention, and specifically its clauses on exclusion from refugee status. This case receives further attention in Section 6.6.4.

98 MRT and RRT (Australia), Complementary Protection Training Manual, *supra* note 3, at 5, 12.

99 *AK (Article 15(c) Qualification Directive) Iraq*, *supra* note 60, para. 194.

bring their interpretations into line with those in other jurisdictions do so with the intention of building a global best practice with their colleagues abroad. This phenomenon is well documented in the literature on judicial dialogue in the area of human rights law. Slaughter contends that there is a fundamental, ideological foundation underpinning judicial dialogue in relation to human rights: that decision-makers across jurisdictions see the enforcement of human rights standards as a common judicial enterprise based on precepts of human dignity that transcend state boundaries.[100] According to Slaughter, judges perceive themselves as engaging in a collective deliberation aimed at eliciting best practice and ensuring that individuals are not arbitrarily denied protections and freedoms based merely on the state in which they find themselves.[101] The principle of universality immanent in human rights law renders this field ripe for courts and tribunals to adopt an international orientation. According to Slaughter,

> The premise of universalism … does not anoint any one tribunal with universal authority to interpret and apply these rights. Collective judicial deliberation, through awareness, acknowledgement, and use of decisions rendered by fellow human rights tribunals, frames a universal process of judicial deliberation and decision.[102]

These benevolent motivations are no less pertinent for complementary protection. Several commentators have lamented that individuals seeking international protection have historically encountered arbitrarily unequal protections based solely on which state happens to be their first arrival point after fleeing persecution.[103] Recognising the importance of developing a more equitable protection regime across national borders, national judges have expressed a concerted intention to draw on jurisprudence from outside their own countries to contribute to a global best practice. For example, the NZIPT has emphasised the intention of the country's legislature that its complementary protection laws should be applied in

[100] Slaughter, Transjudicial Communication, *supra* note 91, at 118, 121–23, 132; and Slaughter, Judicial Globalization, *supra* note 87, at 1123.

[101] Slaughter, Transjudicial Communication, *supra* note 91, at 121. See also McAdam, Australian Complementary Protection, *supra* note 53, at 690–91; B. Gorlick, 'Common Burdens and Standards: Legal Elements in Assessing Claims to Refugee Status', *Int'l J. of Refugee L.*, 15:3 (2003) 357–76, at 358; McCrudden, Common Law of Human Rights, *supra* note 92, at 513; Lambert, Transnational Judicial Dialogue, *supra* note 33, at 520.

[102] Slaughter, *ibid.*, at 121–22.

[103] McAdam, Complementary Protection, *supra* note 7, at 47; Allard, Casualties of Disharmony, *supra* note 33, at 296, 323; Presidency of the European Union, Stockholm Programme, *supra* note 86, at 69.

a way that 'strengthens New Zealand's already highly regarded refugee determination system and reflects best practice internationally'.[104]

The effect of this desire to fortify protections standards by engaging in judicial dialogue is clear in some of the case studies in Section 6.6. In particular, national courts and tribunals have adopted practices and interpretations that have been favourable to applicants for complementary protection in relation to the sequence in which they consider claims for refugee status and complementary protection (Section 6.6.2) and the standard of proof for complementary protection claims (Section 6.6.3).

6.5.3 *Deterring Secondary Movements of Forced Migrants: Diluting Complementary Protection Standards*

The pursuit of consistent standards in relation to complementary protection, facilitated by judicial dialogue, has proven to be a double-edged sword. While on some legal questions, judges have adopted interpretations which are advantageous to applicants for complementary protection, on others, judicial dialogue has been a harbinger of standards which are less favourable to applicants.

Slaughter has observed the potential for such a diminishing effect in relation to human rights norms generally. She comments that transnational judicial exchanges are a means of assuring national governments that states are discharging human rights obligations equally, but that where collective will for upholding these obligations is lacking, standards can be diluted across the board.[105] There are provisions in many international human rights treaties which aim to prevent precisely this outcome, by highlighting that the respective treaties should not be construed as limiting or derogating from any protection offered under domestic law.[106] Nonetheless, if it is true that domestic courts may validate their imposition of higher standards by reference to foreign decisions, then it is equally foreseeable that courts will be inclined to lower standards where lesser protections are the norm elsewhere, in particular concerning

[104] Explanatory Note to Immigration Bill 2009 (New Zealand), cited in *AC (Syria)* [2011] NZIPT 800035 (NZIPT), para. 49.

[105] Slaughter, Transjudicial Communication, *supra* note 91, at 116–17.

[106] See, for example, ICCPR, *supra* note 12, article 5(2); International Covenant on Economic, Social and Cultural Rights (16 December 1966) 993 UNTS 3, entered into force 3 January 1976, article 5(2); Convention for the Protection of Human Rights and Fundamental Freedoms (European Convention on Human Rights, ECHR) (4 November 1950) 213 UNTS 222; 312 ETS 5, entered into force 3 September 1953, article 53.

aspects of complementary protection that are not covered by an international human rights treaty.

While this argument holds water for human rights obligations in general, it is particularly compelling in relation to complementary protection. In this context, judges can engage in judicial dialogue with a political purpose in mind. Even more than other fields of human rights law, national governments (and national populations) are concerned about not shouldering more than their 'fair share' of the perceived international 'burden' of refugee and complementary protection.[107] Despite persuasive research that migrants benefit rather than strain industrialised states' budgets,[108] many governments continue to express urgency about deterring secondary movements of refugees. They insist that having consistent standards of protection will encourage individuals to seek protection in the first country in which they arrive after fleeing persecution, and will deter migrants from picking among states for the jurisdiction in which they will be treated most favourably.[109] Especially in the context of alleged immigration 'crises' that the media and governments exploit and that domestic populations decry,[110] courts are under pressure to extend protections only as far as other states to

[107] McAdam, Complementary Protection, *supra* note 7, at 47. For a more in-depth explanation of how such political concerns can affect judicial reasoning, see Hart, Complementary Protection, *supra* note 45, 180–88.

[108] See, for example, the study by the Bertelsmann Foundation that migrants living in Germany (limited to those without a German passport) on average contribute considerably more to the state's budget (in the form of taxes and social insurance contributions) than they take out (in the form of benefits and other governmental support). In 2012, the surplus that migrants contributed was as high as €12 billion. See H. Bonin, 'Der Beitrag von Ausländern und künftiger Zuwanderung zum deutschen Staatshaushalt' (November 2014), http://ftp.zew.de/pub/zew-docs/gutachten/ZEW_BeitragZuwanderungStaatshaushalt2014.pdf. Over the past decade, research in Australia has similarly indicated that migrants (including humanitarian entrants) have a long-term net benefit on the national economy: see, for example, Access Economics, 'Migrants Fiscal Impact Model: 2008 Update' (11 April 2008) www.immi.gov.au/media/publications/research/_pdf/migrants-fiscal-impact-april-2008.pdf; and R. Parsons, 'Assessing the Economic Contribution of Refugees in Australia' (Multicultural Development Association, June 2013) http://apo.org.au/node/35435.

[109] J. McAdam, 'The European Union Qualification Directive: The Creation of a Subsidiary Protection Regime', *Int'l J. Refugee L.* 17:3 (2005) 461–516, at 462 and 466; McAdam, Regionalizing International Refugee Law, *supra* note 44, at 256.

[110] McAdam, Regionalizing International Refugee Law, *supra* note 44, at 260. Also see for example European governments' responses to undocumented maritime arrivals: G. Legorano and L. Moloney, 'Italian Towns Push Back on Growing Burden of Europe's Migrant Crisis', *Wall Street Journal* (28 April 2015), www.wsj.com/articles/italian-towns-push-back-on-growing-burden-of-europes-migrant-crisis-1430085784; and P. Farrell, 'Could Australia's "Stop the Boats" Policy Solve Europe's

avoid their countries possibly becoming targets for asylum seekers. Judicial dialogue is one means of courts ascertaining that the standards they impose are comparable to those on which courts in other jurisdictions rely.

The drive to suppress secondary movements is especially strong within Europe, where EU initiatives to remove barriers to movement between member states has arguably made it easier for individuals to relocate within the bloc before lodging their protection claim.[111] The EU Qualification Directive espouses as one of its aims 'help[ing] limit the secondary movement of applicants for international protection between Member States, where such movement is purely caused by differences in legal frameworks'.[112] The European Commission has reiterated the need to 'level the EU asylum playing field' and 'ensure that asylum burdens are not felt disproportionately by a few Member States'.[113] The Presidency of the EU has similarly opined that '[c]ommon rules, as well as a better and more coherent application of them, should prevent or reduce secondary movements within the EU'.[114] It is significant for courts and tribunals that the Presidency identified both the formation and the *application* of common rules as facilitating this objective.

To the chagrin of numerous commentators, the EU Qualification Directive has induced some European countries to weaken their legislative protections,[115] despite the Directive's explicit provision permitting

Migrant Crisis?', *Guardian* (22 April 2015), www.theguardian.com/world/2015/apr/22/could-australia-stop-the-boats-policy-solve-europe-migrant-crisis.

111 McAdam, Regionalizing International Refugee Law, *supra* note 44, at 256, 262. José H Fischel De Andrade has expressed this as Europe 'erect[ing] … a fortress against potential refugees': J. H. Fischel De Andrade, 'Regional Policy Approaches and Harmonization: A Latin American Perspective', *Int'l J. of Refugee L.* 10:3 (1998) 389–406, 396. For a more detailed exploration of the factors which make concern about secondary movement especially strong within the EU, see Hart, Complementary Protection, *supra* note 45, at 182–88.

112 EU Qualification Directive, *supra* note 5, preamble para. 13.

113 European Commission, Communication to the Council and the European Parliament, 'Strengthened Practical Cooperation – New Structure, New Approaches: Improving the Quality of Decision Making in the Common European Asylum System' (17 February 2006), at 2, 3 and 6.

114 Presidency of the European Union, Stockholm Programme, *supra* note 86, at 69.

115 McAdam, Regionalizing International Refugee Law, *supra* note 44, at 256. For example, Lambert describes the lowering of the United Kingdom's protections for individuals deemed to have engineered their situation of risk after arriving in the United Kingdom and therefore claiming protection in 'bad faith': H. Lambert, 'The EU Asylum Qualification Directive, its Impact on the Jurisprudence of the United Kingdom and International Law', *Int'l and Comparative L. Quarterly* 55:1 (2006) 161–92, at 172–73. For an overview of other changes to domestic legislation restricting access to protection in response to European harmonisation, see E.R. Thielemann, 'Why Asylum Policy Harmonization Undermines Refugee Burden-Sharing', *European J. Migration and Law* 6:1 (2004) 47–66, at 54.

states to set standards which are more favourable to individuals seeking protection.[116] There has also been evidence of a lowering of standards in terms of judicial application of complementary protection laws. The following section provides examples of aspects of complementary protection which have felt this effect. In particular, courts have adopted standards which are unfavourable to applicants in relation to exclusion from complementary protection (Section 6.6.4), and the interpretation of 'indiscriminate violence' in article 15(c) of the EU Qualification Directive (Section 6.6.5).

It should be noted that, precisely to allay concerns regarding forum-shopping by forced migrants (among other objectives),[117] the EU adopted the so-called Dublin Regulation (2013), now in its third iteration.[118] The Dublin Regulation allocates responsibility for processing individual protection claims by establishing a general rule that the first EU member state in which a person seeking protection arrives must process his or her claim.[119] This means that other EU member states may decline to assess such a claim and request that the member state of first arrival do so instead. Even the Dublin Regulation does not, however, wholly prevent forced migrants from having their protection claims being heard outside of their country of first arrival. The ECtHR has determined on several occasions that one member state is not permitted to return a forced migrant to another member state for processing of the individual's protection claim due to poor conditions or inadequate procedural guarantees in the latter.[120] The CJEU has similarly found that 'Dublin transfers' are impermissible to a member state with 'systemic flaws in the asylum procedure and reception conditions for asylum applicants'.[121] Under the Dublin Regulation itself, there are also special conditions for processing claims of unaccompanied minors and family members of beneficiaries of international protection which prevail over the general rules pertaining to member states of first arrival.[122] As a final point, evidentiary barriers – sometimes apparently

116 EU Qualification Directive, *supra* note 5, preamble para. 14 and article 3.

117 The CJEU explicitly identified reducing asylum 'forum shopping' as an objective of the Dublin Regulation in Joined Cases C-411/10, C-493/10, *NS and Others v. Secretary of State for the Home Department and Others* [2011] ECR I-13905, ECLI:EU:C:2011:865, para. 79.

118 Regulation 604/2013 of the European Parliament and of the Council establishing the criteria and mechanisms for determining the Member State responsible for examining an application for international protection lodged in one of the Member States by a third-country national or a stateless person (recast), OJ L 180/31, 26 June 2013 (Dublin Regulation).

119 *Ibid.*, article 13.

120 *MSS v. Belgium and Greece*, *supra* note 46; *Tarakhel v. Switzerland* (Appl. No. 29217/12), Judgment (Grand Chamber), 4 November 2014, selected for publication 2014.

121 *NS and Others*, *supra* note 117, para. 86.

122 Dublin Regulation, *supra* note 118, articles 8–11.

deliberately created by asylum seekers themselves[123] – can impede a factual assessment of which EU member state a forced migrant first arrived in. Thus, the Dublin Regulation regime does not fully assuage European governments' concerns over asylum 'shopping'. Even with the Dublin Regulation in place, some governments have advocated measures as drastic as suspending free movement between EU member states to curb the secondary movement of forced migrants within the Union.[124]

6.6 Case Studies

This section explores five questions arising under complementary protection laws which have been the subject of extensive dialogue between judges in different national jurisdictions. These case studies illustrate various aspects of the extent, method, purpose and effects of judicial dialogue. For example, they draw attention to why national courts have engaged in horizontal dialogue on these questions, showing why vertical dialogue with regional and international courts could not have provided comprehensive assistance. They shed light on methodological questions such as the role of the parties in bringing foreign case law to a court's attention and the influence of extra-curial resources, such as judicial training manuals and reports from judicial conferences. They also exemplify the disparate effects that judicial dialogue can generate, arguably belying the judges' purpose in engaging in such exchanges.

6.6.1 *Factual Claims about Country-of-origin Information*

As a general principle on the use of authorities, courts around the world typically rely on previous cases to formulate *legal* principles, endeavouring to apply laws consistently between cases irrespective of factual differences between them. It is rarer for courts to rely on *factual* findings from previous decisions, as facts are usually singular to the case before them.

In cases concerning complementary protection, however, domestic courts in different national jurisdictions frequently draw on decisions from other states regarding factual information on country-of-origin conditions and the likely treatment of individuals with certain characteristics if their protection applications are rejected. Such factual conclusions

[123] See, for example, H. Grant and J. Domokos, 'Dublin Regulation Leaves Asylum Seekers with their Fingers Burnt', *Guardian* (7 October 2011), www.theguardian.com/world/2011/oct/07/dublin-regulation-european-asylum-seekers.

[124] See, for example, 'France and Italy Push for Reform of Schengen Treaty', *BBC News* (26 April 2011), www.bbc.co.uk/news/world-europe-13189682.

are considered generalisable between applicants for complementary protection hailing from the same country and with the same characteristics. For example, in *AZ (Iran)*, the NZIPT relied on two decisions of British immigration tribunals which had found that Christian converts who were returned to Iran were not subject to persecution provided that they were not church leaders and did not proselytise, noting that the cases relied on had given serious consideration to information regarding conditions in Iran.[125] In *AK (Article 15(c)) Afghanistan*,[126] the Immigration and Asylum Chamber of the United Kingdom's Upper Tribunal embarked on a particularly elaborate analysis of other states' factual findings regarding whether various parts of Afghanistan satisfied the threshold for indiscriminate violence required by article 15(c) of the EU Qualification Directive. At the direction of the Tribunal, the respondent had requested relevant information from courts and tribunals in fourteen other EU member states and Switzerland, and ultimately the Tribunal incorporated findings from Switzerland, Belgium, Sweden, France, Spain and Germany into its reasoning. In weighing up the conflicting factual findings of courts across these jurisdictions, the Tribunal recognised that, in order to borrow findings of fact from other states, the original findings must be recent, based on comprehensive country-of-origin information, and 'support[ed] ... by clear reasons'.[127]

Courts in other states which are considering whether they can, consistently with their statutory obligations, return an applicant for complementary protection to their country of origin are an obvious source of such factual findings. Indeed, aside from harmonising protection standards, another purpose which judges may harbour is to save court resources: producing in-depth factual assessments of country-of-origin conditions is resource-intensive, and it is simply more efficient to borrow recent, reliable findings from another forum.[128]

[125] *AZ (Iran)* [2012] NZIPT 800237 (NZIPT), para. 48, citing *FS and Others (Iran – Christian converts) Iran v. Secretary of State for the Home Department, CG* [2004] UKIAT 303, paras. 186–90 and *SZ and JM (Christian – FS confirmed) Iran v. Secretary of State for the Home Department, CG* [2008] UKAIT 82 (both United Kingdom, Asylum and Immigration Tribunal). In a different case, the NZIPT referred to a research paper of Australia's RRT which stated that the Methodist Church in Fiji continued to promote discrimination against sexual minorities, despite legal prohibitions on discrimination: *BS (Fiji)* [2012] NZIPT 800041 (NZIPT), para. 91, citing RRT of Australia, Research Response FJ135763 (1 December 2009).

[126] *AK (Article 15(c) Qualification Directive) Iraq*, *supra* note 60.

[127] *Ibid.*, para. 194.

[128] For an analysis of how foreign factual findings are employed in German asylum cases, see Tiedemann, German Administrative Courts, *supra* note 59, at 66. For an analysis of Swedish courts, see Stern, Swedish Judicial Decision-making, *supra* note 78, at 198.

6.6.2 *The Interaction between Protection under the Refugee Convention and Complementary Protection*

One question arising in complementary protection claims is how courts should manage situations in which an applicant may be eligible for different types of protection – protection under international refugee law and complementary protection. This question is especially important in European states, as, under the EU Qualification Directive, beneficiaries of complementary protection are granted fewer entitlements than those assessed to be Convention refugees. Notably, it does not arise in other areas of human rights law, in which courts are not required to assign applicants a single category of human rights entitlements. As a result, horizontal dialogue is more fruitful for domestic judges than vertical dialogue in this area.

In various forums of exchange outside of published decisions, judges have been urged to consider an applicant's eligibility for Convention refugee status as a priority over their entitlement to complementary protection, employing cases from national courts as examples of good and poor practice in this regard. The training manual on complementary protection for Australia's RRT points to cases from New Zealand and Canada that demonstrate the correct order: determining Convention refugee status before eligibility for complementary protection.[129] An operational manual of Canada's Immigration and Refugee Board refers to the same practice in Danish and Swedish tribunals.[130] One report of the IARLJ calls attention to a Canadian case which illustrated this process correctly,[131] while two other IARLJ reports lamented the inconsistent practice of the French *Commission des Recours des Réfugiés* in assessing eligibility for refugee status and complementary protection in that order.[132] Judges now consistently

[129] MRT and RRT (Australia), Complementary Protection Training Manual, *supra* note 3, at 8. This training manual drew on numerous foreign authorities, including *AC (Syria)*, *supra* note 104, para. 45; *AB (Iraq)* [2011] NZIPT 800014, paras. 61–72; *Re IVH* [2004] RPDD No. 57 (Canada, Refugee Protection Division, Immigration and Refugee Board).

[130] Legal Services, Immigration and Refugee Board (Canada), Risk to Life or Risk of Cruel and Unusual Treatment or Punishment, *supra* note 85, at 40–41.

[131] *Re IVH*, *supra* note 129, cited in Reekie, Part III: Canada, *supra* note 52, at 41 n 25. In this case, the Refugee Protection Division, having found the applicant to be a Convention refugee, deemed it unnecessary to consider whether the individual in question was also a person in need of complementary protection.

[132] A report published by the IARLJ noted that in one French case, a Colombian woman was found eligible for complementary protection on the basis that she had been targeted by FARC because she was a member of a landowning, cattle-breeding family. The

assess individuals' eligibility for refugee protection before considering their eligibility for complementary protection, although the impact of these extra-curial sources on informing this practice is difficult to quantify.

6.6.3 *The Standard of Proof for Complementary Protection Claimants*

Establishing credibility is a routine obstacle for applicants for international protection. It is often difficult to prove that a future risk exists for a particular individual in a foreign country, especially as the states in question are frequently unstable, making reliable evidence harder to garner.[133] For that reason, the standard of proof that a protection claim must satisfy is a critical question.

Although the standard of proof for complementary protection is formulated differently between jurisdictions, one common element is that there must be 'substantial grounds' for believing that the person will be at risk of serious harm.[134] In interpreting this standard, some national tribunals have cast doubt on the utility of vertical dialogue with international and regional bodies, where different standards of proof have been employed.[135]

IARLJ criticised the *Commission des Recours des Réfugiés* for failing to consider whether she could qualify as a Convention refugee on the basis that her persecution was on the grounds of political opinion or membership in a particular social group: *Mlle Ricon Perez*, 29 September 2006 (France, *Commission des Recours des Réfugiés*), cited in L. Dufour, 'Part II(B): France – The 1951 Geneva Convention and Subsidiary Protection: Uncertain Boundaries', IARLJ, 'Convention Refugee Status and Subsidiary Protection Working Party: First Report' (7th World Conference, Mexico City, November 2006) 31–35, at 35.

133 See for example Gorlick, Common Burdens, *supra* note 101, at 363; Mandal, Protection Mechanisms, *supra* note 30, at 22; D. Tennent, 'The Contribution of the New Zealand Refugee Status Appeals Authority to International Refugee Jurisprudence: A Submission to both Acknowledge the Contribution of the Authority and to Advocate for its Retention', *Waikato L. Rev.* 15 (2007) 160–89, 168.

134 See Immigration and Refugee Protection Act 2001, *supra* note 9, s 97(1); Migration Act 1958, *supra* note 3, s 36(2)(aa); Immigration Act 2009, *supra* note 11, ss 130, 131; EU Qualification Directive, *supra* note 5, article 2(f).

135 For example, Canada's Immigration and Refugee Board has impugned the suitability of certain UNCAT rulings. The Board stated that the Committee's standard of harm being a 'foreseeable and necessary consequence' is too high, and that in the context of complementary protection it should be sufficient that there is a 'reasonable chance or serious possibility' of the harm arising: Legal Services, Immigration and Refugee Board (Canada), Danger of Torture, *supra* note 85, at 20–21 (citing decisions including UNCAT, *Mutombo v. Switzerland*, Communication No. 13/1993, 27 April 1994, UN Doc. CAT/C/12/D/013/1993; and *EA v. Switzerland*, Communication No. 28/1995, 10 November 1997, UN Doc. CAT/C/19/D/28/1995). Similarly, the training manual for Australia's MRT and RRT has rejected the high standard of proof imposed by UNCAT: MRT and RRT (Australia), Complementary Protection Training Manual, *supra* note 3, at 19.

Where domestic courts have deemed such comparisons inapposite, they have frequently looked to their counterparts in other national jurisdictions for direction.

One contentious issue has been whether the standard of proof in relation to complementary protection is the same as the standard of proof in Convention refugee claims, or should be more onerous given that complementary protection does not share the same history or international recognition as traditional refugee protection. In *obiter* in the case of *AC (Syria)*,[136] the NZIPT addressed this question by surveying domestic jurisprudence from several jurisdictions. It pointed to a decision of the High Court of Australia, which held that applicants for refugee status must prove that there is a 'real chance' of exposure to persecution on a Convention ground, not merely a 'remote chance' that is 'merely assumed' or based on 'mere speculation'.[137] Although the Tribunal approved of this test for Convention refugee applications, it noted that domestic courts had differed on the standard required for complementary protection claims. Whereas courts in the United Kingdom had accepted a 'real chance' standard, Canadian courts had imposed a higher threshold of the 'balance of probabilities'.[138] The Tribunal declined to express a preference for either approach.[139]

The training manual for Australia's RRT likewise canvassed decisions of the United Kingdom's Immigration Appeal Tribunal (which imposed the same 'real chance' standard as applied in Convention refugee claims)[140] and of the Canadian Federal Court of Appeal (which applied the higher 'balance of probabilities' standard).[141] The manual conclusively favoured the United Kingdom's lower threshold.[142] This instance of judicial dialogue exemplifies one purpose behind such exchanges: the pursuit of a global best practice. The leaning that these sources display is in favour of interpreting complementary protection laws advantageously to applicants.

[136] *AC (Syria)*, *supra* note 104.

[137] *Minister for Immigration and Ethnic Affairs v. Guo* (1997) 191 CLR 559 (Australia, High Court), at 572, cited in *ibid.*, para. 112.

[138] *AC (Syria)*, *supra* note 104, para. 132.

[139] *Ibid.*, para. 133.

[140] *Kacaj v. Secretary of State for the Home Department* [2001] INLR 354 (United Kingdom, Immigration Appeal Tribunal), para. 12, cited in MRT and RRT (Australia), Complementary Protection Training Manual, *supra* note 3, at 8.

[141] *Li v. Canada (Minister of Citizenship and Immigration)*, 2005 FCA 1 (Canada, Federal Court of Appeal), paras. 18–28, cited in MRT and RRT (Australia), *ibid.*, at 19.

[142] MRT and RRT (Australia), *ibid.*, at 21.

6.6.4 *Exclusion from Complementary Protection*

The duty of *non-refoulement* – the obligation not to return individuals to countries where they face a risk of torture or other ill-treatment, or where their life is in peril – is absolute.[143] Human rights bodies have found that the obligation permits no derogation, irrespective of whether the individual facing expulsion has engaged in any form of reprehensible conduct.[144]

The granting of refugee status or complementary protection, however, depends on the conduct of the applicant. Under article 1F of the Refugee Convention, refugee status is not available to certain persons, irrespective of the dangers they face in their countries of origin. Article 1F states:

> The provisions of this Convention shall not apply to any person with respect to whom there are serious reasons for considering that:
> (a) he has committed a crime against peace, a war crime, or a crime against humanity, as defined in the international instruments drawn up to make provision in respect of such crimes;
> (b) he has committed a serious non-political crime outside the country of refuge prior to his admission to that country as a refugee;
> (c) he has been guilty of acts contrary to the purposes and principles of the United Nations.[145]

In domestic laws, these so-called exclusion clauses have been extended to applicants for complementary protection.[146]

For the sake of clarity, it is often the case that the *non-refoulement* principle prohibits returning individuals 'excluded' from refugee or complementary protection to their countries of origin, where they are at risk of death, torture or other extreme mistreatment. Rather, the consequence of exclusion is that they may be denied other benefits and entitlements that accompany the status of a refugee or a beneficiary of complementary protection. For example, they may be detained or prosecuted for their crimes in the country in which they lodged their protection claim, and they may not be granted the right to work, seek education or receive welfare payments.

[143] Refugee Convention, *supra* note 1, article 33; CAT, *supra* note 6, article 3; Convention on the Rights of the Child (20 November 1989) 1577 UNTS 3, entered into force 2 September 1990, articles 6 and 37, as interpreted in UN Committee on the Rights of the Child, General Comment No. 6, 1 September 2005, UN Doc. CRC/GC/2005/6, paras. 26-28.

[144] See, for example, *Chahal*, *supra* note 47; UNCAT, *Tapia Paez v. Sweden*, Communication No. 39/1996, 28 April 1997, UN Doc. CAT/C/18/D/39/1996.

[145] Refugee Convention, *supra* note 1, article 1F.

[146] EU Qualification Directive, *supra* note 5, article 17; Immigration and Refugee Protection Act 2001, *supra* note 9, s 101; Migration Act 1958, *supra* note 3, s 36(2C); Immigration Act 2009, *supra* note 11, ss 127, 137(2), 198(1)(c).

While regional and international courts have an extensive jurisprudence on *non-refoulement*, the human rights treaties that they apply do not feature an equivalent to the exclusion clauses. As a result, national courts do not engage in vertical dialogue concerning these clauses. Instead, a key source of guidance for interpretation of these clauses comes from other domestic courts.[147]

Before complementary protection laws were enacted, such exchanges were common in relation to traditional refugee claims. In *Tamil X*,[148] the Supreme Court of New Zealand considered cases from the Canadian Federal Court of Appeal and the Court of Appeal of England and Wales in concluding that a person could be excluded on the basis of joint enterprise liability with a terrorist organisation of which he or she was never a formal member.[149] More recently judicial dialogue has also assisted national courts in applying the exclusion clauses in complementary protection cases.

For instance, in *Al-Sirri*,[150] the Supreme Court of the United Kingdom devoted thorough attention to foreign domestic decisions determining the standard of proof which must be satisfied in order for an applicant to be excluded from refugee status. The Court surveyed cases from Australia's Administrative Appeals Tribunal[151] and Federal Court,[152] Canada's Federal Court of Appeal,[153] Germany's Federal Administrative Court[154] and New Zealand's Court of Appeal.[155] It ultimately determined that there must be

[147] Given that the grounds for exclusion from complementary protection are identical to those in the Refugee Convention, the UNHCR's publications on the interpretation of the clauses (see, for example, UNHCR, Note on the Exclusion Clauses, 30 May 1997, UN Doc. EC/47/SC/CRP.29) may also be persuasive in the context of complementary protection. For a fuller analysis of the issues raised in this subsection, see Hart, Complementary Protection, *supra* note 45, at 191–94.

[148] *Attorney General v. Tamil X*, *supra* note 69, paras. 57–70.

[149] Referring to (at paras. 58 and 64): *Ramirez v. Canada (Minister of Employment and Immigration)* (1992) 89 DLR (4th) 173 (Canada, Federal Court of Appeal), at 180; *Bazargan v. Canada (Minister of Citizenship and Immigration)* (1996) 205 NR 282 (Canada, Federal Court of Appeal), para. 11; and *JS (Sri Lanka) v. Secretary of State for the Home Department* [2010] 2 WLR 17 (United Kingdom, Court of Appeal of England and Wales), para. 38.

[150] *Al-Sirri (FC)*, *supra* note 24.

[151] *W97/164 v. Minister for Immigration and Multicultural Affairs* [1998] AATA 618 (Australia, Administrative Appeals Tribunal), para. 43, cited at *Al-Sirri (FC)*, *ibid.*, para. 72.

[152] *Arquita v. Minister for Immigration and Multicultural Affairs* (2000) 106 FCR 465 (Australia, Federal Court), para. 54, cited at *Al-Sirri (FC)*, *ibid.*, para. 73.

[153] *Ramirez*, *supra* note 149, para. 5, cited at *Al-Sirri (FC)*, *ibid.*, para. 74.

[154] BVerwG, judgment of 31 March 2011, 10 C 2.10 (Germany, Federal Administrative Court), para. 29, cited at *Al-Sirri (FC)*, *ibid.*, para. 74.

[155] *X v. Refugee Status Appeals Authority; Attorney-General (Minister of Immigration) v. Y* [2009] NZLR 73 (New Zealand, Court of Appeal), paras. 77 and 79, cited at *Al-Sirri (FC)*, *ibid.*, para. 74.

'reasonable grounds', based on 'clear and credible evidence', for believing that a person had engaged in conduct falling within the exclusion clauses, and that the standard of proof is certainly lower than 'beyond reasonable doubt' but otherwise should not be compared to domestic analogies.[156]

In *Gurung*,[157] the United Kingdom Immigration Appeal Tribunal referred to cases from Canada, the Netherlands, New Zealand, the United States and Australia in determining whether the reasons for excluding a person should be assessed independently or balanced against the degree of persecution he or she would face in the home country;[158] whether a person's eligibility for refugee status must be assessed prior to the assessment of his or her exclusion from that status;[159] and the standard of proof for exclusion.[160]

In *JS (Sri Lanka)*,[161] the Supreme Court of the United Kingdom drew on a case in which the German Federal Administrative Court had 'helpfully considered' joint enterprise liability in order to conclude that, in the context of complementary protection, formal membership in an organisation is unnecessary for responsibility for an excludable offence to arise.[162] In *ABC (A Minor)*,[163] the High Court of England and Wales considered the separate issue of whether a minor can be excluded from complementary protection for having committed a serious non-political crime. It adopted the approach of the New Zealand Court of Appeal in finding that all of the circumstances of the applicant, including his youth, should be taken into account in assessing whether he should be excluded.[164] The High Court found that this interpretation was 'to be preferred' over competing approaches, including that set out in UNHCR's 'Note on the Exclusion Clauses',[165] on the basis that it better reflected the ordinary meaning of the text of the ground of exclusion contained in both the Refugee Convention

[156] *Al-Sirri (FC)*, *ibid.*, para. 75.

[157] *Gurung v. Secretary of State for the Home Department* [2002] UKIAT 4870 (United Kingdom, Immigration Appeal Tribunal).

[158] *Gonzalez v. Canada (Minister of Employment and Immigration)*, 1994 FC 646 (Canada, Federal Court of Appeal), cited in *ibid.*, para. 18.

[159] *Minister for Immigration and Multicultural Affairs v. Singh* (2002) 209 CLR 533 (Australia, High Court), cited in *Gurung*, *supra* note 157, paras. 64, 69.

[160] *Ramirez*, *supra* note 149, para. 5, cited in *Gurung*, *ibid.*, para. 95.

[161] *JS (Sri Lanka)*, *supra* note 149.

[162] *Ibid.*, paras. 14 and 47–48.

[163] *ABC (A Minor) (Afghanistan) v. Secretary of State for the Home Department* [2011] EWHC 2937 (Admin) (High Court of England and Wales (Administrative Division)).

[164] *Ibid.*, para. 27. The decision cited was *S v. Refugee Status Appeals Authority* [1998] 2 NZLR 291 (New Zealand, Court of Appeal).

[165] UNHCR, Note on the Exclusion Clauses, *supra* note 147.

and the EU Qualification Directive.[166] Addressing yet another facet of the exclusion clauses, the Federal Administrative Court of Germany relied on jurisprudence of the British Immigration Appeal Tribunal and the Supreme Court of Canada to find that 'acts contrary to the purposes and principles of the United Nations' need not involve the use of governmental power, and can be committed by individuals acting in a private capacity.[167]

The interpretation of the exclusion clauses is one example where prolific dialogue between judges in different national jurisdictions has had the effect of entrenching standards which are disadvantageous to applicants. Domestic judges have witnessed their counterparts in other jurisdictions applying these clauses liberally – establishing low thresholds for excluding applicants – and have adopted these standards themselves. Through extensive dialogue, this interpretive trend has spread. To date, judges have not directly explicated their purpose in adhering so closely to the tests adopted in other jurisdictions. This chapter conjectures that they are motivated, at least in part, by an aversion to issuing decisions that may be perceived to render their state a particularly favourable site for applicants to lodge their complementary protection claims.

6.6.5 *Complementary Protection on the Basis of Indiscriminate Violence*

Article 15(c) of the EU Qualification Directive provides that complementary protection should be granted where there is a 'serious and individual threat to a civilian's life or person by reason of indiscriminate violence in situations of international or internal armed conflict'.[168] This article is novel – indeed, it is unique even among complementary protection laws, with most of the countries examined in this chapter specifically excluding complementary protection in cases of indiscriminate violence.[169] For its part, the ECtHR has historically resisted claims that indiscriminate violence, in the absence of an individualised threat, is sufficient to injunct an

[166] *ABC (A Minor) (Afghanistan)*, *supra* note 163, para. 27.

[167] BVerwG, judgment of 14 October 2008, 10 C 48.07 (Germany, Federal Administrative Court), para. 24. This case relied on *KK (Article 1F(c)) Turkey v. Secretary of State for the Home Department* [2004] UKIAT 101 (United Kingdom, Immigration Appeal Tribunal); and *Pushpanathan v. Canada*, 1998 1 SCR 982 (Canada, Supreme Court).

[168] EU Qualification Directive, *supra* note 5, article 15(c). Relevant domestic and regional decisions on international protection on the grounds of indiscriminate violence are explored more fully in Hart, Complementary Protection, *supra* note 45, at 194–200.

[169] Immigration and Refugee Protection Act 2001, *supra* note 9, s 97(1)(b)(ii); Migration Act 1958, *supra* note 3, s 36(2B)(c).

expulsion under article 3 of the European Convention on Human Rights (ECHR).[170] Even in more recent cases in which the Court has speculated that an extreme risk posed by indiscriminate violence may in itself bar an expulsion, it has emphasised that it is interpreting article 3 of its own constitutive human rights instrument (the ECHR) and not article 15(c) of the EU Qualification Directive.[171] The CJEU has highlighted that the EU Qualification Directive's article on indiscriminate violence 'is a provision, the content of which is different from that of Article 3 of the [ECHR], and the interpretation of which must, therefore, be carried out independently'.[172]

In light of the novelty of indiscriminate violence as a basis for international protection, domestic decision-makers in Europe have derived extensive direction from each other regarding the interpretation of this provision. One common issue is the intensity of violence required to meet the threshold of 'international or internal armed conflict', an expression that the EU Qualification Directive does not define. The IARLJ observed that decision-makers in France (the first country in which the Directive was implemented) identified armed conflicts according to the standards of international humanitarian law,[173] and anticipated that other European

[170] See commentary on the difference between the jurisprudence of the ECtHR and the text of the EU Qualification Directive in *KH (Article 15(c) Qualification Directive) Iraq*, *supra* note 93, para. 1, citing *Vilvarajah v. United Kingdom* (Appl. No. 13163/87, 13164/87, 13165/87, 13447/87 and 13448/87), Judgment (Chamber), 30 October 1991, Series A, No. 215. See also *SSH v. United Kingdom* (Appl. No. 60367/10), Judgment (Chamber), 29 January 2013, not reported, paras. 85–87.

[171] *Sufi and Elmi*, *supra* note 50, para. 226.

[172] *Elgafaji*, *supra* note 40, para. 28. In distinguishing between the test for article 3 of the ECHR and the test for indiscriminate violence in article 15(c) of the EU Qualification Directive, *Elgafaji* has been followed by domestic courts: see for example *AMM and Others (Conflict; Humanitarian Crisis; Returnees; FGM) Somalia*, *supra* note 50, paras. 328–37.

[173] Under international humanitarian law, an international armed conflict exists in 'all cases of declared war or of any other armed conflict which may arise between two or more of the High Contracting Parties, even if the state of war is not recognised by one of them', and also in cases of 'partial or total occupation of the territory of a High Contracting Party, even if the said occupation meets with no armed resistance': Geneva Convention for the Amelioration of the Condition of the Wounded and Sick in Armed Forces in the Field (12 August 1949) 75 UNTS 35, entered into force 21 October 1950, article 2. This article is common to all four of the 1949 Geneva Conventions. An armed conflict also exists in situations 'in which peoples are fighting against colonial domination and alien occupation and against racist regimes in the exercise of their right of self-determination': Protocol Additional to the Geneva Conventions of 12 August 1949, and relating to the Protection of Victims of International Armed Conflicts (Additional Protocol I) (8 June 1977) 1125 UNTS 3, entered into force 7 December 1979, article 1(4). The existence of a non-international armed conflict is determined according to the intensity of the violence and

domestic courts would follow suit.[174] Initially, this prediction proved to be prescient. In *KH (Article 15(c) Qualification Directive) Iraq*,[175] the United Kingdom Asylum and Immigration Tribunal adopted the international humanitarian law test for the existence of an internal armed conflict, citing precedents from France, the Netherlands, Sweden and Germany.[176] The Tribunal saw the uniformity of other states' practice in this regard as a forceful reason, in itself, for it to adopt the same test. It stated that '[g]iven that one of the objectives of the Directive is to achieve the application of common criteria throughout the EU, [the consistency of other domestic courts' interpretation of article 15(c)] is not an unimportant matter'.[177] It proceeded to state:

> If … a UK tribunal or court could sensibly construct its own notion of the 'autonomous meaning' of the term 'international or internal armed conflict' without regard to any shared international law framework, then (except accidentally) there would be nothing 'common' about the criteria it devised and no basis to complain about other Member States adopting similarly unilateral notions.[178]

In BVerwG 43.07,[179] perhaps compelled by the same drive for consistency, Germany's Federal Administrative Court relied on *KH (Article 15(c) Qualification Directive) Iraq* as authority for its finding that article 15(c) is animated only by violence meeting the international humanitarian law threshold for an armed conflict.[180]

These cases illustrate that horizontal judicial dialogue concerning article 15(c) had the effect of spreading a strict interpretation disfavouring applicants for complementary protection who are affected by situations of general violence that do not meet the threshold of an international

the level of organisation of the parties: *Prosecutor v. Tadić*, Decision on the Defence Motion for Interlocutory Appeal on Jurisdiction (Trial Chamber), Case No. IT-94-1-AR72, 2 October 1995, para. 70; *Prosecutor v. Limaj, Bala and Musliu*, Judgment (Trial Chamber II), Case No. IT-03-66-T, paras. 83–92.

174 McAdam, Part I: Overview, *supra* note 55, at 8.

175 *KH (Article 15(c) Qualification Directive) Iraq*, *supra* note 93.

176 *Ibid.*, para. 34. The cases cited included *MA*, Case 508193, 22 November 2005 (France, *Commission des Recours des Réfugiés*); Case 200608939/1 LJN BB0917, 20 July 2007 (The Netherlands, Council of State); UM 23-06, September 2007 (Sweden, Migration Court of Appeal); and 2 LB 38/07, 21 November 2007 (Germany, Higher Administrative Court of Schleswig-Holstein).

177 *KH (Article 15(c) Qualification Directive) Iraq*, *supra* note 93, para. 34.

178 *Ibid.*, para. 41.

179 BVerwG 10 C 48.07, *supra* note 167.

180 *Ibid.*, paras. 22 and 24.

or non-international armed conflict, as defined under international humanitarian law.

This trend has, however, been mollified by subsequent cases. The year after the Asylum and Immigration Tribunal handed down its decision in *KH (Article 15(c) Qualification Directive) Iraq*, the English Court of Appeal decided the case of *QD & AH (Iraq)*.[181] This case overturned the Tribunal's previous ruling on the threshold for engaging article 15(c), concluding that the test for determining an internal armed conflict for the purposes of article 15(c) differs from the test for establishing the existence of an armed conflict under international humanitarian law.[182] Notably, the Court of Appeal reached this decision without reference to any foreign national case law: it simply embarked on an orthodox exercise of statutory interpretation of the text of an EU instrument in light of its context and purpose. If anything, this judgment reinforces that horizontal judicial dialogue can have the pernicious effect of diluting protection standards in circumstances where courts, without engaging in such dialogue, may independently reach conclusions more favourable to applicants for complementary protection.[183]

It is also likely that, in contrast to the effect of diluting standards that horizontal judicial dialogue initially engendered, vertical judicial dialogue may enhance protection standards in regard to article 15(c). In *Diakité*, the CJEU found that the test established for whether an armed conflict exists for the purposes of international humanitarian law – including through decisions of the International Criminal Tribunal for the Former Yugoslavia (ICTY) – are not suitable for interpreting article 15(c).[184] In this respect, this decision reflected that of the Court of Appeal in *QD & AH (Iraq)*. The CJEU stated:

> While international humanitarian law is designed, inter alia, to provide protection for civilian populations in a conflict zone by restricting the effects of war on persons and property, it does not ... provide for international protection to be granted to certain civilians who are outside both the

[181] *QD & AH (Iraq) v. Secretary of State for the Home Department* [2009] EWCA Civ 620 (Court of Appeal of England and Wales).

[182] *Ibid.*, paras. 15–18.

[183] The decision in *QD & AH (Iraq)*, *ibid.*, on the independent meaning of 'internal armed conflict' in article 15(c) has since been followed in other British decisions: see for example *AMM and Others (Conflict; Humanitarian Crisis; Returnees; FGM) Somalia*, *supra* note 50, paras. 35 and 337. These subsequent decisions have, like *QD & AH (Iraq)*, not engaged in horizontal judicial dialogue with domestic courts in other jurisdictions to reach their conclusion on the meaning of article 15(c).

[184] *Diakité*, *supra* note 44, paras. 20–35.

> conflict zone and the territory of the conflicting parties. As a consequence, the definitions of 'armed conflict' provided in international humanitarian law are not designed to identify situations in which such international protection would be necessary and would thus have to be granted by the competent authorities of [EU] Member States.... Accordingly, it is not possible ... to make eligibility for subsidiary protection conditional upon a finding that the conditions for applying international humanitarian law have been met.[185]

Departing from the test established by the ICTY which includes an assessment of the intensity and duration of an armed conflict, the CJEU found that the only relevant factor for interpreting article 15(c) was whether there was 'a situation in which a State's armed forces confront one or more armed groups or in which two or more armed groups confront each other'.[186] The CJEU's decisions are persuasive authority in the domestic courts of EU member states. This decision may, if followed by domestic courts, reverse the trend established by previous case law in which domestic courts in various EU jurisdictions lowered protection standards based on the guidance they derived from horizontal judicial dialogue.

6.7 Conclusion

In the field of complementary protection, judicial dialogue is a heterogeneous practice, and yet some patterns are identifiable. First, it is a practice that is widespread, particularly on a horizontal plane between national courts and tribunals, though with some vertical exchanges on certain issues that fall within the purview of international and regional courts and quasi-judicial bodies. It is likely that extra-curial sources play some role in drawing courts' attention to relevant foreign case law. Otherwise, however, the opacity of judges' methodology in selecting foreign or international cases to cite when interpreting complementary protection laws highlights the value of empirical research with judges themselves in understanding these processes. While it is likely that some judges include references to judgments from abroad for ornamental purposes, it is clear that others embark on transnational judicial exchanges with a deeper purpose of harmonising complementary protection laws.

Where this purpose is undergirded by a desire to forge a rights-enhancing global best practice, the effect can be to bolster protection standards. In contrast, where judges are influenced by the current political

185 *Ibid.*, paras. 23 and 26.
186 *Ibid.*, paras. 28 and 32.

climate and their priority is to prevent their state from being 'chosen' by forced migrants allegedly looking for the most favourable treatment, courts can – with the 'support' of foreign jurisprudence – adopt interpretations which are less generous to applicants for complementary protection. This downward spiral may be averted if regional and international bodies assume more proactive roles in monitoring complementary protection standards. The CJEU's role in enhancing standards has already become apparent in relation to the interpretation of article 15(c) of the EU Qualification Directive, while the ECtHR's jurisprudence on family unity, standards of mistreatment and other questions has also had a powerful effect on the assessment of claims for international protection. These and other bodies may perform similar functions going forward.

7

The Construction of Same-Sex Families in Western Europe through Legislative and Judicial Dialogues

The Role of National Legislatures and Supranational Courts

DANIELE GALLO AND MATTEO M. WINKLER*

7.1 Introduction

In the last few decades there have been significant developments in many Western European countries concerning the legal treatment of gay and lesbian persons.[1] Three main models have been adopted:[2] (1) some states grant full marriage equality;[3] (2) others have passed a registration scheme;[4] and (3) others, lacking legislative intervention, still leave it to the courts to determine the level of protection to same-sex couples on

* Although this chapter is a result of the common effort of both authors, sections 7.3 and 7.4 where drafted by Daniele Gallo, while Matteo M. Winkler drafted sections 7.1 and 7.2.

[1] This stands in contrast to developments in Eastern Europe. See *inter alia* A. Bodnar and A. Sledzinska-Simon, 'Between Recognition and Homophobia: Same-Sex Couples in Eastern Europe', D. Gallo, L. Paladini and P. Pustorino (eds.), *Same-Sex Couples before National, Supranational and International Jurisdictions* (Berlin: Springer, 2014) 211–48.

[2] See K. Waaldijk, 'Great Diversity and Some Equality: Non-Marital Legal Family Formats for Same-Sex Couples in Europe', *GenIUS* I:2 (2014) 42–56, at 44 (summarising the current laws and models in force in European countries). On Europe and same-sex couples generally, see *inter alia* K. Waaldijk and A. Clapham (eds.), *Homosexuality: A European Community Issue* (Dordrecht: Martinus Nijhoff, 1993); R. Wintemute, 'International Trends in Legal Recognition of Same-Sex Partnerships', *Quinnipiac L. Rev.*, 23:2 (2004) 577–95; and K. Boele-Woelki and A. Fuchs (eds), *Legal Recognition of Same-Sex Relationships in Europe. National, Cross-Border and European Perspectives*, 2nd ed. (Antwerp: Intersentia, 2012).

[3] The countries that nowadays recognise same-sex marriage are: Belgium, Denmark, Finland (in force from 1 March 2017), France, Iceland, Ireland, Luxembourg, the Netherlands, Norway, Portugal, Spain, Sweden and the United Kingdom.

[4] Andorra, Austria, Belgium, Croatia, the Czech Republic, Cyprus, Estonia, Finland, France, Germany, Greece, Hungary, Italy, Ireland, Liechtenstein, Luxembourg, Malta, the Netherlands, Slovenia, Spain, Switzerland and the United Kingdom. This model refers to domestic partnership adopted in the Scandinavian countries since 1989, before being replaced with the strong model of same-sex marriage. See K. Waaldijk, 'Others May Follow: The Introduction of Marriage, Quasi-Marriage, and Semi-Marriage for Same-Sex Couples

a case-by-case basis.[5] Each model has various implications and effects, and generally delineates the level of acceptance of homosexuality in the respective country.[6] Steps have also been taken at the international level, where the European Court of Human Rights (ECtHR) and the Court of Justice of the European Union (CJEU) have both made important contributions.[7] As Kees Waaldijk observes, in Western Europe, '[t]here seems to be a general trend of progress: where there is legal change it is change for the better. Countries are not all moving at the same time and certainly not at the same speed, but they are moving in the same direction: forward'.[8]

This chapter describes and analyses how the growing recognition of same-sex family rights in Western Europe is connected to a certain degree of dialogue between different nations. We argue that this dialogue was mainly initiated by national legislatures, and this justifies the special focus on legislative dialogues in this chapter. As will be seen, this does not mean that national or regional courts have not played a significant role in this respect; in fact, they have helped to pave the way for these rights by interpreting

in Europe', *New England L. Rev.* 38:3) (2003–2004) 569–89, at 570; I. Curry-Sumner, 'Uniform Patterns Regarding Same-Sex Relationships', *Int'l L. Forum* 7:3 (2005) 186–94, at 192, distinguishes between a 'weak' and a 'strong' registration scheme based on the recognition of property and fiscal rights only, as in the former, or in the extension to same-sex couples of family law rights relating to partnership and children, as in the latter. On the Nordic model, see H. Friðriksdóttir, 'The Nordic Model: Same-Sex Families in Love and Law', Gallo, Paladini and Pustorino (eds.), Same-Sex, *supra* note 1, 161–80.

5 Examples of such unresponsiveness are Italy and Greece. See T. Fidalgo de Freitas and D. Tega, 'Judicial Restraint and Political Responsibility: A Review of the Jurisprudence of the Italian, Spanish and Portuguese High Courts on Same-Sex Couples', Gallo, Paladini and Pustorino (eds.), Same-Sex, *supra* note 1, 287–318; S. Drosos and A. Constantinides, 'The Legal Situation of Same-Sex Couples in Greece and Cyprus', Gallo, Paladini and Pustorino (eds.), Same-Sex, *supra* note 1, 319–42. See also M. Coester, 'Same-Sex Relationships: A Comparative Assessment of Legal Developments Across Europe', *European J. of L. Reform* 4:2 (2002) 585–601, at 591, who discusses the piecemeal regulation model, under which 'the law would take account of social and economic realities, and thereby mitigate hardships which result from the fact that the law puts the long-term partner of a person on the same footing as a stranger'.

6 In particular, as noted by K. Waaldijk, 'Civil Developments: Patterns of Reform in the Legal Position of Same-Sex Partners in Europe', *Canadian J. of Family L.* 17:1 (2000) 62–88, at 65: 'the form[s] chosen will have different kinds of [legal and psychological] effects on the partners, and on the wishes of others to become same-sex partners.'

7 H. Lau, 'Sexual Orientation: Testing the Universality of International Human Rights Law', *University of Chicago L. Rev.* 71:4 (2004) 1689–1720, at 1691 (also pointing out the opposition between human rights universalism and cultural relativism which allows certain states to resist the former).

8 K. Waldijk, 'Standard Sequences in the Legal Recognition of Homosexuality – Europe's Past, Present and Future', *Australasian Gay and Lesbian L. J.* 4 (1994) 50–72, at 51.

and applying the law in a way that supports pro-gay policies. We conclude by finding that there is evidence not only of horizontal dialogues between national legislatures but also of horizontal dialogues between domestic courts, horizontal dialogues between supranational courts (ECtHR and CJEU), as well as vertical dialogues between the latter and domestic courts.[9]

The chapter is structured as follows. In Section 7.2, we analyse the dialogue between legislatures on the protection of same-sex family rights. The discussion centres on the extent of this legislative dialogue (its intensity and frequency), as well as its method as we try to understand through which channels the dialogue has been taking place. Account is also taken of the effects of the legislative dialogue, in particular the extent to which it has favoured the development of rights of same-sex families in Western Europe. Section 7.3 considers the extent, method and effects of the CJEU's and the ECtHR's engagement with jurisprudence and legislation, including dialogues *inter se* and with domestic courts. Section 7.4 offers concluding remarks on the role of judicial and legislative dialogue in promoting the protection of same-sex couples in Western Europe.

7.2 Dialogues between National Legislatures

National legislatures have played an essential role in developing a discourse on the legal recognition of same-sex families in Western Europe. As both common sense and political reality suggest, the reasons for this seem to lie in the fact that, according to European democratic tradition, highly controversial issues are typically resolved by legislatures rather than by courts. In any event, it was at the legislative level that said discourse started in Scandinavia in the 1970s and 1980s.

This section offers a chronological analysis of the extent, method and effects of legislative dialogue on the protection of same-sex couples. As to its extent, national legislatures in charge of drafting bills that protect same-sex couples did so by reference to what has already been done in other countries. The method used, however, differs from nation to nation. In fact, the cross-fertilisation of legal systems *vis-à-vis* the regulation of same-sex couples is limited to nations that have close cultural, historical and/or linguistic relationships, where the level of legal protection enacted ultimately depends on indigenous factors such as the political strength of religious groups, existing social conventions

[9] This chapter does not deal with horizontal dialogue among domestic courts. On horizontal and vertical dialogues, see generally Introduction to this volume, Section 1.2.1.

regarding homosexuality or the political significance of gay and lesbian associations. In culturally close nations, the method of dialogue is simply copying the law of the other country; in other cases, a proper national solution must be found. Finally, as to the effects of such a dialogue, it stimulated a discussion on the issue for all of Western Europe, but with different legislative solutions. In certain cases, due to indigenous factors, the dialogue moved only vertically between international institutions and domestic legislatures.

The first European country that legislated on this issue was Denmark. Following a political debate that lasted almost two decades, the Danish Parliament enacted a Registered Partnership Act in 1989 allowing same-sex couples to register their union and hence obtain the same rights and duties as married couples.[10] As Jens M. Scherpe notes, after Denmark, '[e]very other country contemplating regulating same-sex relationships now had a yardstick against which any suggested regulation would have to be measured'.[11] Indeed, Norway, Sweden and Iceland followed the Danish example, in 1993, 1995 and 1996, respectively; Finland took longer, but a similar law was enacted there in 2002.[12]

Interestingly, this process materialised through both a vertical and a horizontal legislative dialogue. On the one hand, both Denmark and the other Scandinavian countries were stimulated by a resolution adopted by the inter-parliamentary Nordic Council in 1984.[13] In said Resolution, the Council put pressure on the member states to 'study and collect information about the situation of homosexuals in each country, [and] examine the ... possibility of adopting laws to secure the equality of homosexuals and their protection against discrimination'.[14] This Resolution represented a milestone in the progress of same-sex couples' rights in the Nordic

[10] Registered Partnership Act No. 372 of 1 June 1989 (Denmark). See Friðriksdóttir, The Nordic Model, *supra* note 4, at 167. See also W.N. Eskridge and D.R. Spedale, *Gay Marriage: For Better or For Worse? What We've Learned from the Evidence* (Oxford University Press, 2006) 49–61 (describing the final steps of the Registered Partnership Law in Denmark until its approval on 27 May 1989).

[11] J.M. Scherpe, 'The Nordic Countries in the Vanguard of European Family Law', *Scandinavian Studies in Law* 50:1 (2007) 265–87, at 270.

[12] See, respectively, the Registered Partnership Act No. 40 of 30 April 1993 (Norway), the Registered Partnership Act No. 1117 of 23 June 1994 (Sweden); the Registered Partnership Act No. 87 of 12 June 1996 (Iceland); and the Registered Partnership Act No. 950 of 9 November 2001 (Finland).

[13] Nordic Council Resolution 17/1984. The Nordic Council has 87 elected members from Denmark, Finland, Iceland, Norway and Sweden as well as from the Faroe Islands, Greenland and Åland.

[14] H. Fridriksdóttir, The Nordic Model, *supra* note 4, at 164.

countries; it facilitated legislative dialogue on the matter and ultimately served as a justification, in each nation, for legislating on the issue.

On the other hand, the horizontal legislative dialogue on the rights of same-sex couples was facilitated through direct connections at various levels between the members of parliament of the various Nordic countries. For instance, one year after Denmark had passed the Registered Partnership Act, five members of the Norwegian Parliament introduced a bill copying the text of the Danish Act. The identical text of these bills among the various nations concerned is a vivid example of this horizontal dialogue. Contacts were also established between gay and lesbian advocates and associations in the region. It is important to note that even if it does not seem that their role was essential to the approval of domestic partnership laws, they actively participated in the relevant discussions and their advocacy proved to have transnational effects.

The extent and influence of horizontal and vertical dialogue on the rights of same-sex couples in Scandinavia was the result of 'an intricate interaction between legislative changes and shifting popular attitudes'.[15] The following factors contributed to these developments and effects. First, the Danish model proved successful because the outcome satisfied the various actors in society. While to many the battle for same-sex marriage continued,[16] the fact that the institution of domestic partnership was reserved for gays and lesbians accommodated the instinctive fear, felt by the conservatives, that same-sex couples should not be confused with marriage and family. Second, the discourse on same-sex families, *inter alia* through legislative dialogue, found fertile ground in the Nordic countries because they had already repealed their sodomy laws long ago, and had started the process of contemplating laws prohibiting discrimination based on sexual orientation in the workplace and access to housing. Third, it was generally considered unacceptable in Scandinavia to display animus against homosexuality based on religion alone.[17] Fourth, the precedent set by the

[15] J. Rydström, *Odd Couples: A History of Gay Marriage in Scandinavia* (Amsterdam: Amsterdam University Press, 2011) at 112.

[16] G. Johnson, 'Civil Unions, A Reappraisal', *Vermont L. Rev.* 30 (2006) 891–912, at 894.

[17] For most Scandinavians 'it is simply not considered acceptable to declare that one's interpretation of God's intentions is the only acceptable one', as clarified by Eskrigde and Spedale, Gay Marriage, *supra* note 10, at 61 (referring to Denmark). Moreover, '[l]ike Denmark, all of the four Nordic countries have a state church which is not obligated to solemnize same-sex unions under the state's registered partnership law. Therefore, unless individual congregations exercise discretion to give their blessing, same-sex couples can only exchange vows in a civil ceremony. Nevertheless … the Nordic bloc nations have gradually harmonized their registered partnership regimes.' M.Y.K. Lee, *Equality, Dignity, and*

passage of the Danish Act persuaded the parliaments of the surrounding nations to imitate the Danish precedent. At the core of the debate was the need of same-sex couples for security, equality and freedom that typically crosses national borders. Furthermore, the fact that the Danish legal recognition of same-sex couples did not result in a disruption in social cohesion showed other Scandinavian parliaments that the 'slippery slope' argument had been proved wrong.

All in all, it can be concluded that the Danish scheme circulated and was adopted following vertical and horizontal dialogue among the legislatures, the Nordic Council and other political channels that favoured the circulation of the Danish scheme. This resulted in the most advanced protection of same-sex couples worldwide, at least for a decade.

After they had been adopted in the Nordic countries, registered partnership laws 'flowered like azaleas is April'[18] throughout the rest of Western Europe. In 2001, the Netherlands was the first country in the world to put same-sex and straight couples on an equal footing concerning civil marriage.[19] Belgium, having strong historical, cultural and linguistic links with its Dutch neighbour, enacted a similar law in 2003.[20]

It seems reasonable to assume that the success of gay rights advocates in Nordic countries had triggered local gay associations and the political parties sympathetic to their cause to move forward in other countries, thereby facilitating legislative dialogues on the matter. The registered partnership scheme was successful where said associations were considered credible actors in the political debate, as was the case in both the Netherlands and Belgium. In fact, the two countries' family laws had already recognised cohabitation and registered partnerships for both straight and same-sex couples since 1997[21] and 2000 respectively.[22] The existing support for cohabitating couples greatly limited the resistance against an extension

Same-Sex Marriage: A Rights Disagreement in Democratic Society (The Hague: Martinus Nijhoff, 2010) at 17.

18 Eskridge and Spedale, Gay Marriage, *supra* note 10, at 77.

19 See C. Glass, N. Kubasek and E. Kiester, 'Towards a European Model of Same-Sex Marriage Rights: A Viable Pathway for the U.S.', *Berkeley J. of Int'l L.* 29:1 (2011) 132–73, at 142–50 (describing the preparatory path of the law).

20 *Ibid.*, 150–53.

21 See Waaldijk, Others May Follow, *supra* note 4, at 578 (noting that 'the introduction of a registered partnership regime [in the Netherlands happened] along with the model introduced by the Danish legislation in 1989').

22 *Ibid.*, at 583 (discussing the new law enacted in 2000 in Belgium on the registration of cohabiting couples). See also P. Reyniers, 'Same-Sex Couples in France and Belgium: The Resilient Practice of Judicial Deference', Gallo, Paladini and Pustorino (eds.), Same-Sex, *supra* note 1, 249–62, at 255 (discussing Belgian law).

of the institute of civil marriage to same-sex couples. Also, geographical closeness and historical, linguistic and cultural affinity between the two countries were inevitably relevant for reaching positive effects through legislative dialogue. Finally, there was no significant religious opposition which could raise socially acceptable objections against same-sex marriage.[23]

Yet, there are also countries where the horizontal legislative dialogue failed or was non-existent, presumably because of an unfavourable local environment. One example is France, whose 1999 law on *Pacte Civil de Solidarité* (PaCS) – a 'quasi-marriage regime'[24] – was directly initiated through a resolution of the European Parliament which recommended equality of treatment and recognition of gay and lesbian couples by EU member states. In fact, one might even speak of vertical legislative dialogue initiated at the domestic level, as the resolution was promoted and voted for by the political party that led the French government at that time.[25]

The need for vertical dialogue reflects the fact that, unlike in the Nordic countries, gay and lesbian couples in France faced more opposition in having their relationships recognised. It also explains the more limited protection offered by the PaCS. In 1997, the French Supreme Court had ruled that 'just as there can be no marriage between persons of the same sex, neither can there be same-sex cohabitation',[26] thus calling for a legislative intervention. Yet, when the government introduced the PaCS bill one year later, it was concerned about the possibility that the French Parliament could reject the bill. Therefore, a minister felt the need to point out that the PaCS would never be confused with marriage or family: 'there is no celebration, no solemnities, no fidelity, and no intention to found a family. Marriage is fundamentally different'.[27] Despite resistance

[23] See Eskridge and Spedale, Gay Marriage, *supra* note 10, 83–84.

[24] Law No. 999-944 of 15 November 1999, relating to the *Pacte Civil de Solidarité*. See Waaldijk, Others May Follow, *supra* note 4, 570–71.

[25] See Resolution of the European Parliament on Equal Rights for Homosexuals and Lesbians in the European Community, 7 February 1994, OJEC C 61/40 of 28 February 1994. For a mention of the connection between the European Parliament resolution and French legislation on same-sex couples, see C. Richards, 'The Legal Recognition of Same-Sex Couples: The French Perspective', *Int'l & Comp. L. Quarterly* 51:2 (2002) 305–24, at 314.

[26] *Ibid.*, at 313. See also *Vilela v. Mme Weil*, 17 December 1997, 1998 JCP II–10093 (Cour de Cassation (France)).

[27] E. Steiner, 'The Spirit of the New French Registered Partnership Law. Promoting Autonomy and Pluralism or Weakening Marriage?', *Child and Family L. Quarterly* 12:1 (2000) 1–14, at 4.

in both chambers of the French Parliament, the bill was eventually turned into law.[28]

However, unlike the Nordic, Dutch and Belgian laws, the PaCS only established a contractual framework and was also available to opposite-sex couples.[29] Thus, the protection of same-sex couples was not at the core of the law.[30] In fact, the law did not expressly stipulate that the 'couple' concerned actually had to live together, although the *Conseil Constitutionnel* would later interpret it in that sense.[31] Hence, until the law on same-sex marriage (*Mariage pour Tous*) was passed by the Parliament in 2013,[32] France was a typical example of a country that had opted for marriage-like or semi-marriage legislation which expressed a compromise between the willingness to pursue a minimum level of protection for same-sex couples on the one hand and the intention not to confuse the PaCS with marriage and family on the other.

The French example also reinforces the argument made earlier that a horizontal dialogue between legislatures with a positive effect on the protection of same-sex couples' rights is possible only where and when the local environment in the countries involved welcomes a genuine dialogue about homosexuality, and where such dialogue is socially accepted. When religiously or politically inspired opposition is strong, the possible effect of legislative dialogue on the matter is a political compromise that inevitably leads to minimal legislation on same-sex couples. As William N. Eskridge and Darren R. Spedale explain, the social environment that existed in France in 1999 was not supportive enough, and the main reason for the 'partial investment of rights and duties was the strong opposition roused by proposals that looked like same-sex marriage.'[33]

[28] As observed by Richards, *supra* note 25, at 306: 'In this more conservative country, same-sex couples have had to struggle against strong opposition whose arguments are presented in many forms, but the roots of which can be traced to France's religious heritage.'

[29] W.N. Eskridge and D.R. Spedale, Gay Marriage, *supra* note 10, at 80.

[30] Under said law, '[c]ouples who register will obtain most [but not all] of the rights and obligations traditionally associated with marriage in the field of social welfare, housing, tax law and property rights, but [...] significant distinctions will remain in the areas of inheritance and children, as well as in the event of a possible breakdown of the relationship.' Steiner, The Spirit, *supra* note 27, at 1.

[31] *Conseil Constitutionnel*, 9 November 1999, No. 99–419 DC.

[32] Law No. 2013–404 of 17 May 2013 (France), opening marriage to same-sex couples.

[33] Eskridge and Spedale, Gay Marriage, *supra* note 10, at 80 ('the stronge[r] the religion-based opposition to same-sex marriage [was], the more likely a country was to do nothing or to adopt a *marriage-like* institution rather than either same-sex marriage or registered partnership').

Germany is seen in a similar light. In 1993, the German Constitutional Court ruled that the German Constitution did not provide for a right to marry a person of the same sex, exhorting the legislature to step in.[34] In 2001, the *Bundestag* approved a Life Partnership Act (*Lebensgemeinschaftsgesetz*), the constitutionality of which was upheld in 2002 after it had been challenged by the Catholic *Länder.*[35] The Act conferred certain rights to same-sex couples such as hospital visitation, immigration and naturalisation, joint tenancy, inheritance rights, pension and health insurance, as well as some co-parenting rights. Compared to the French PaCS, the German Act was closer to the Nordic registered partnership scheme. However, instead of referring directly to the rights and duties arising out of marriage, the Act contemplated an autonomous regulation of same-sex couples that applied to the latter only. Like the French law, the more restrictive nature of the *Lebensgemeinschaftsgesetz* seems to be directly influenced by a less favourable domestic environment. Thus, the rather limited extent of horizontal legislative dialogue on the issue of same-sex relationships in France and Germany and the existence of stronger local opposition resulted in limited positive effects of such dialogue for the protection of same-sex couples in the two countries.

It appears, however, that the geographical extent of legislative dialogue expanded to Spain in the 2000s. In 2004, the Spanish government succeeded in passing a law that rendered the institution of marriage under the Spanish Civil Code gender-neutral.[36] While members of the Catholic Church organised a rally against the law in Madrid, the government vigorously defended the law, and Prime Minister José Luis Zapatero relied on other countries' legislation to rebut the opposition's main argument: 'We are not the first to adopt such a law', he told the Parliament, 'but I am sure that we will not be the last, many other countries will come after, pushed by two unstoppable forces, liberty and equality'.[37]

[34] German Constitutional Court (BVerfG), Judgment of 4 October 1993, 1 BvR 640/93. See J. M. Scherpe, 'National report: Germany', *American University J. of Gender, Social Policy and L.* 19:1 (2011), 151–86, at 153; and G. Repetto, 'At the Crossroads between Privacy and Community: The Legal Status of Same-Sex Couples in German, Austrian and Swiss Law', Gallo, Paladini and Pustorino (eds.), Same-Sex, *supra* note 1, 263–86, at 267.

[35] German Constitutional Court (BverfG), Judgment of 17 July 2002, 1 BvF 1/01 and 1 BvF 2/01; Scherpe, Germany, *supra* note 11, at 155.

[36] See Ley 13/2005, de 1 de julio, por la que se modifica el Código Civil en materia de derecho a contraer matrimonio (Amending the Civil Code Regarding the Right to Marry), BOE 157, 2 July 2005. For a commentary see C. Martínez de Aguiree Aldaz and P. de Pablo Contreras, 'National Report: Spain', *American University J. of Gender, Social Policy and L.* 19:1 (2011) 289–307, at 291 (discussing the constitutionality of the law); and Glass, Kubasek and Kiester, Towards a European Model, *supra* note 19, at 153–58 (describing the *iter legis*).

[37] Eskridge and Spedale, Gay Marriage, *supra* note 10, at 85.

Apparently, the Spanish population was open and ready to accept the positive effects of horizontal legislative dialogue on same-sex couples' rights. Two factors played a role in this respect. First, homosexuality was already widely accepted in Spanish society, and some regulations on registered same-sex partnerships and cohabitation already existed at the regional level.[38] Second, the law was strongly connected with redressing the persecution of and discrimination against homosexuals during the dictatorship of Francisco Franco with the complicity of the Catholic Church.[39] Hence, when the Popular Party took power in 2011, it did not dare to officially propose to abrogate the law.

Compared to other countries, Spain rejected the Nordic model of registered partnership, opting for the other end of the spectrum with the affirmation of a full marriage model, while France and Germany moved closer to the opposite end, trying to accommodate the requests of religious-based opposition. As a result, the French, German and Spanish laws all reflected typical national environments of acceptance of same-sex couples. For this reason, it also proved difficult to export these laws to other countries without adapting them to the peculiarities of the importing states. The German model, for example, experienced a small diffusion in other German-speaking countries such as Switzerland[40] and Austria,[41] which adopted laws on same-sex couples in 2007 and 2010, respectively, but it did not circulate elsewhere.[42]

This leads us to a first partial conclusion regarding the extent, method and effects of legislative dialogue on the rights of same-sex families in Western Europe. First, the legal recognition of same-sex couples and the protection of their rights have mainly been steered by domestic legislatures. As to the role exercised by the judiciary, it will be discussed in

[38] See E. Roca, 'Same-Sex Partnerships in Spain: Family, Marriage or Contract?', *European J. of L. Reform* 3 (2001) 365–82. On the problem of civil objection by Spanish officers who opposed the law, see S.P. Alvarez, 'Same-Sex Couples Marriage in Spain: Conscientious Objection of Judges and Mayors', *Sri Lanka J. of Int'l L.* 20:1(2008) 53–66.

[39] G. Perez-Sanchez, 'Franco's Spain. Queer Nation?', *University of Michigan J. of L. Reform* 33:3 (2000) 359–403, at 371.

[40] Federal Law on Domestic Registered Union for Homosexual Couples (*Bundesgesetz über die eingetragene Partnerschaft gleichgeschlechtlicher Paare 2004*), of 18 June 2004 (No. 211.231), 2005 AS 5685 (entered into force on 1 January 2007).

[41] Registered Partnership Act (*Eigentragene Partnerschaft-Gesetz – EPG*), No. 135/2009 of 18 December 2009, 135 BGBl 1 (2009) (entered into force on 1 January 2010).

[42] In fact, 'Germany, Austria and Switzerland indeed have a largely common historical and cultural background, which reflects the different regulations concerning the legal treatment of same-sex couples'. Repetto, At the Crossroads, *supra* note 34, at 263.

Section 7.3. Second, concerning the geographical extent of legislative dialogue, it can be concluded that it primarily takes place between parliaments in countries with historical, cultural and/or linguistic links. There is evidence that in these countries, horizontal legislative dialogue on same-sex couples' rights can have positive effects resulting in better legal protection.

As to the method of legislative dialogue, regional organisations can play a role in the promotion of dialogue, as can direct contacts between parliamentarians. Where these conditions are missing, legislative dialogue is likely to be limited or absent, and the recognition and legal protection of same-sex couples depends mostly on the degree of social acceptance of homosexuality. In these countries, room is thus left for a strong opposition by domestic political conservative forces whose influence can result in weaker statutes which reflect a widespread resistance to the recognition of same-sex couples.

7.3 Dialogues between Supranational Courts and National Judges

It is becoming increasingly common now for same-sex couples to rely on courts to protect their rights. Consequently, national and regional European judges, especially ECtHR judges, have produced a considerable body of jurisprudence that has furthered gay and lesbian rights.

This section analyses the extent, method and effects of the CJEU and the ECtHR's engagement in judicial dialogue on the rights of gay couples, in particular the horizontal dialogue between these two regional courts and their vertical dialogue with domestic courts in selected European countries. It takes a particular interest in the role that this judicial dialogue on the protection of same-sex couples' rights has played in the promotion of these rights.

As will be demonstrated, there are two main questions which are important to deal with as far as the protection of same-sex couples' rights through judicial dialogue is concerned: first, whether a positive obligation of European states' national authorities to recognise same-sex couples' rights can be inferred from the CJEU and ECtHR's jurisprudence; and second, how domestic and regional courts, by relying on the principle of non-discrimination, interpret the relevant national and/or supranational legislation in a way that acknowledges core rights of same-sex couples. The courts' approach can indeed have the effect of inducing or even urging lawmakers to take action, that is, to pass new legislation or amend existing laws. Moreover, even if the CJEU and ECtHR have not always been able to enjoin states to provide full equality to straight and same-sex couples,[43] the two European courts, to different degrees, have created an environment more favourable to gay and lesbian couples. This has been done by grounding their reasoning on a flexible interpretation of national and supranational law and by engaging horizontally with each other as well as vertically with domestic courts of (some) Western European states.

7.3.1 *The CJEU's Engagement with External Jurisprudence and Legislation*

Legislative steps taken by the EU have created a protective infrastructure for same-sex couples. These measures certainly helped to develop a genuine discourse about homosexuality and same-sex couples at the European level and, at least indirectly, weakened the strength of national opposition. First, with Council Directive 2000/78/EC of 27 November 2000, Establishing a General Framework for Equal Treatment in Employment and Occupation, the EU banned both direct and indirect discrimination based on sexual orientation in the workplace.[44] The Directive required that any provision or practice that, though formally neutral, puts gays or lesbians at a particular disadvantage had to be 'objectively justified by a legitimate aim and the means of achieving that aim [be] appropriate and necessary'.[45] In addition, the principle of non-discrimination is recognised by the 2000 European Charter of Fundamental Rights (the EU Fundamental Rights Charter), which received binding force through the 2009 Treaty of Lisbon.[46] Of great importance is Council Regulation (EC, EURATOM) 723/2004 of 22 March 2004, amending the Staff Regulations of Officials of the European Communities and the Conditions of Employment of other

[43] See *infra*, Section 7.3.2, on the inexistence of a right to marriage for same-sex couples arising from the ECtHR's case law.

[44] EC Directive 2000/78/EC of 27 November 2000, Establishing a General Framework for Equal Treatment in Employment and Occupation, OJ L 303 of 2 December 2000, 16.

[45] *Ibid.*, article 2(b)(i).

[46] Article 21 of the EU Fundamental Rights Charter states: '1. Any discrimination based on any ground such as sex, race, colour, ethnic or social origin, genetic features, language, religion or belief, political or any other opinion, membership of a national minority, property, birth, disability, age or sexual orientation shall be prohibited. 2. Within the scope of application of the Treaties and without prejudice to any of their specific provisions, any discrimination on grounds of nationality shall be prohibited.' Treaty of Lisbon amending the Treaty on European Union and the Treaty establishing the European Community (13 December 2007), Official Journal C 306 (17 December 2007), entered into force 1 December 2009.

Servants of the European Communities, which dealt with the granting of employment benefits also to officials registered as stable non-marital partners.[47] In requiring justification for the different treatment of homosexuals in any field, including their living together as couples, EU law contributed to spreading a culture of non-discrimination to many other aspects of European homosexual citizens' lives. Following the aforementioned legislative steps, it sounded odd that fiscal or health benefits could be granted to a worker's straight partner but not to a same-sex partner without reasonable justification. The existence of such discrimination challenged the claim that same-sex couples should not be allowed full marital rights or considered as a family.

Yet this process was long and demanding, and is still in progress. As to the role played by the CJEU, a distinction *ratione materiae* could be made between two categories of proceedings: first, cases on the status of EU staff members; and second, references for preliminary rulings concerning employment relationships at national level. While in both groups of cases the CJEU favoured a 'gay-friendly' interpretation of EU law, the difference lies in the fact that the approach adopted by the Court as to EU staff disputes seems to have a greater potential for the recognition of same-sex couples' rights. The reason for this is that in these cases, the CJEU does not need to take account of states' sovereignty to the same extent as in preliminary rulings. We will first deal with preliminary rulings and subsequently with EU staff cases.

In the *Grant v. South West-Trains Ltd* judgment of 1998 – concerning an English woman who was in a relationship with another woman and claimed to have been discriminated against by being refused a travel allowance that the employer granted to opposite-sex cohabiting couples – the CJEU acknowledged the lack of consensus among member states on the issue of same-sex couples, highlighting that 'while in some of them cohabitation by two persons of the same sex is treated as equivalent to marriage, although not completely, in most of them it is treated as equivalent to a stable heterosexual relationship outside marriage only with respect to a limited number of rights, or else is not recognized in any particular way'.[48]

What must be stressed here is that this engagement undertaken by the CJEU *vis-à-vis* the legal framework of the member states did not bring

[47] Council Regulation (EC/EURATOM) 723/2004 of 22 March 2004 amending the Staff Regulations of Officials of the European Communities and the Conditions of Employment of other Servants of the European Communities, OJ L 124, 1.

[48] Case C-249/96, *Grant v. South-West Trains Ltd* [1998] ECR I-6211, ECLI:EU:C:1998:63, para. 32.

about a more progressive protection of same-sex couples' rights. Rather, reference to domestic law and jurisprudence as well as to the ECtHR's case law was used by the CJEU to justify its holding back of a progressive interpretation of EU law. Indeed, the Court observed that the then European Commission of Human Rights considered in its jurisprudence that despite the modern evolution of attitudes towards homosexuality, stable homosexual relationships did not fall – at that time[49] – within the scope of the right to respect for family life under article 8 of the ECHR.[50] Moreover, the CJEU pointed out that according to the European Commission of Human Rights, national provisions which, for the purpose of protecting the family, accord more favourable treatment to married persons and persons of opposite sex living together as husband and wife than to same-sex persons were not contrary to article 14 of the ECHR, which prohibits *inter alia* discrimination on the ground of sex.[51]

In light of these considerations, the CJEU concluded that 'it is for the legislature alone to adopt, if appropriate, measures which may affect that position'.[52] The state of EU law at that time deemed stable relationships between two persons of the same sex not as equivalent to marriages or stable relationships outside marriage between straight persons. Consequently, there was no obligation imposed upon national employers and no violation of the principle of non-discrimination: they were free to treat the situation of a person who has a stable relationship with a partner of the same sex in a different manner than that of a person who is

[49] On the evolution on the matter in the ECtHR's case law, see *infra*, Section 7.3.2.

[50] Article 8 ECHR states: '1. Everyone has the right to respect for his private and family life, his home and his correspondence. 2. There shall be no interference by a public authority with the exercise of this right except such as is in accordance with the law and is necessary in a democratic society in the interests of national security, public safety or the economic well-being of the country, for the prevention of disorder or crime, for the protection of health or morals, or for the protection of the rights and freedoms of others'.

[51] Article 14 ECHR states: 'The enjoyment of the rights and freedoms set forth in [the] Convention shall be secured without discrimination on any ground such as sex, race, colour, language, religion, political or other opinion, national or social origin, association with a national minority, property, birth or other status'. On the issue of marriage according to the ECtHR, see para. 34 of the *Grant* judgment.

[52] *Grant v. South-West Trains Ltd*, *supra* note 48, para. 36. Moreover, the Court maintained that the applicant had not been treated differently because her and her partner's situation was not comparable to that of a straight couple. This is an 'equal misery argument' (C. Denys, 'Homosexuality: A Non-Issue in Community Law?', *European L. Rev.* 24:4 (1999) 419–25, at 423), as the discrimination was excluded '[s]ince the condition imposed by the regulation's undertaking applies in the same way to female and male workers' (*Grant*, para. 28). See also H. de Waele and A. van der Vleuten, 'Judicial Activism in the European Court of Justice – The Case of LGBT Rights', *Michigan State J. of Int'l L.* 19:3 (2011) 639–66, at 658.

married to or has a stable relationship outside marriage with a partner of the opposite sex.

In 2008 the *Tadao Maruko v. Versorgungsanstalt der deutschen Bühnen* case[53] the CJEU applied for the first time the prohibition of discrimination on grounds of sexual orientation in the context of a preliminary proceeding. Surprisingly, this judgment neither referred to the ECtHR's jurisprudence nor took into account the evolution in the legal orders of EU member states concerning the protection of same-sex families. The Court did not take into account the legal developments in the various member states which pushed governments to make changes towards increasing protection for same-sex couples. The Court applied the aforementioned Directive 2000/78/EC in *Maruko* which concerned the social security treatment of a German gay man who sought payment of the pension as survivor after the death of his male partner. His employer claimed that German law conferred such entitlement only to married couples. The applicant maintained that, under the German Social Security Code, registered same-sex partners were put on an equal footing with spouses, as far as social security benefits were concerned. The Court again deferred to the choices made at the domestic level. It highlighted that the German legislature had amended the Social Security Code in 2004 'in view of the harmonization between marriage and life partnership, with regard to the gradual movement towards recognizing equivalence'.[54] According to the EU judges, the Directive, in principle, precluded national legislation under which, after the death of his or her partner, the surviving partner is not granted a benefit equivalent to that granted to a surviving spouse. Although the CJEU made clear that the assessment on whether a surviving partner is in a situation equivalent to that of a spouse was up to the national court,[55] it referred to the argument of the Bavarian Administrative Court in order to favour a flexible interpretation of the term 'equivalent', to be intended to mean 'comparable' rather than 'identical'.[56] The application of the principle of non-discrimination was grounded precisely on that interpretation.

Having said so, the CJEU did not, however, derive an *erga omnes* recognition of rights for the surviving same-sex partner from the Directive, that is, the entitlement to pension benefits in all member states. According to the Luxembourg Court, if the equivalence/comparability between

[53] Case C-267/06, *Tadao Maruko v. Versorgungsanstalt der Deutschen Buhnen* [2008] ECR I-1757, ECLI:EU:C:2008:179, paras. 19–22.

[54] *Ibid.*, para. 69.

[55] *Ibid.*, para. 73.

[56] *Ibid.*, para. 69.

same-sex couples and straight couples did exist in domestic law, the state would be bound to comply with the Directive; if not, the Directive would not apply inasmuch as it does not create an obligation on national authorities to recognise the equality of opposite-sex and same-sex couples. Therefore, in the *Maruko* judgment, the engagement with the domestic legislation (the German Social Security Code) and jurisprudence (the judgment rendered by the Bavarian Administrative Court) brought the Court to recognise same-sex couples' rights. This distinguishes the case from the *Grant* judgment, in which the deference to national law – at that time not containing any provisions from which a substantial equivalence between straight and same-sex couples could be derived – prevented the Court from providing such recognition.

In another case, *Römer*, of 10 May 2011, the CJEU was asked to render a preliminary ruling in respect to a tax deduction available to spouses but not to same-sex registered partners.[57] Again, the Court examined German law and noticed that the post-2004 Social Security Code 'contributed to the gradual harmonization of the regime of registered life partnership with that of marriage'.[58] The CJEU relied on the *Maruko* case[59] to interpret the notion of 'equivalence'[60] flexibly on one the hand, and on the other to state that the denial of the tax deduction represented a direct discrimination based on sexual orientation, since the national court had already decided that the situation at stake was comparable to that of a married person.[61] Interestingly, once again, as had happened in *Maruko*, no references to the evolving ECtHR jurisprudence or developments in national legislation were made.

The two cases, *Maruko* and *Römer*, show that Germany had resolved to grant certain rights to same-sex couples. This was a choice made by the majority of the democratically elected Bundestag. The CJEU recognised the equivalence/comparability of same-sex partnerships and marriage, thus suggesting that *in concreto*, no significant divergences between the two forms of union existed. The CJEU came to this conclusion by relying on a flexible interpretation of the notion of 'equivalence' offered in national jurisprudence, in this case the Bavarian administrative court. This resulted in the Court upholstering, with its supranational *autoritas*, the idea that

[57] Case C-147/08, *Jurgen Römer v. Freie und Hansestadt Hamburg* [2011] ECR I-3591, ECLI:EU:C:2011:286.
[58] *Ibid.*, para. 45.
[59] *Ibid.*, paras. 32, 34–35 and 42.
[60] *Ibid.*, para. 42.
[61] *Ibid.*, para. 45.

the time had come for granting greater equality to same-sex couples. This idea in turn indirectly influenced the German Federal Constitutional Court.[62] After having followed for a number of years a traditional interpretation of the non-discrimination clause in its national legal order and stressing the duty to promote marriage over other forms of partnership, the German Constitutional Court reversed its interpretation and declared that discrimination on the basis of sexual orientation should be encompassed in article 3 of the *Grundgesetz*.[63]

As to the jurisprudence of the CJEU on the staff of the EU, three cases must be considered: *D. v. Council*[64] and *W. v. Commission*,[65] both concerning the issue of employment benefits for same-sex couples; and *Anton Peter Roodhuijzen v. Commission*,[66] which has an indirect, albeit important, relevance for the matter of the legal treatment of gays and lesbians.

At the core of *D. v. Council* and *W. v. Commission* lies the application of the Staff Regulations of EU staff members 723/2004, in particular Annex VII on the grant of the household allowance. The said Regulations in force at the time of each decision were different: this is the main reason why the General Court (*D. v. Council*) and the Civil Service Tribunal (*W. v. Commission*) came to two different conclusions. The reasoning elaborated by both courts is worth being analysed.

In *D. v. Council* of 2001, the Court noted first of all that a stable relationship between partners of the same sex that has only a *de facto* existence was not necessarily equivalent to a registered partnership under a statutory arrangement that produces legal effects comparable to those of marriage (this was also held in *Grant*).[67] On this basis, the Court pointed out that, even though an increasing number of member states have introduced, alongside marriage, statutory arrangements granting legal recognition to various forms of union, 'arrangements for registering relationships between couples not previously recognised in law are regarded in the member states concerned as being distinct from marriage'.[68] The existing situation in the member states reflected a great diversity of laws as well as the absence of any general equalisation of marriage with other forms of

62 German Constitutional Court (BVerfG), Judgment of 7 July 2009, 1 BvR 1164/07.

63 Repetto, At the Crossroad, *supra* note 34, 275.

64 Case C-122/99 and C-125/99 P, *D. v. Council* [2001] ECR I-4139; ECLI:EU:C:2001:304.

65 Case F-86/09, *W. v. Commission* [2010] ECR 125; ECLI:EU:F:2010:125.

66 Case F-122/06, *Anton Peter Roodhuijzen v. Commission* [2007] ECR SC I-A-1-00387 and II-A-1-02167; Case T-58/08 P, *Commission v. Anton Peter Roodhuijzen* [2009] ECR II-3797.

67 *D. v. Council*, *supra* note 64, para. 33.

68 *Ibid.*, paras. 35–36.

statutory union.[69] The Court, therefore, relied on national legal orders of member states to rule that it could not interpret the Staff Regulations in such a way that situations distinct from marriage were treated in the same way as marriage. Moreover, the Court stressed that it was only up to the legislature to adopt measures that would lead EU judges to a different conclusion, 'for example by amending the provisions of the Staff Regulations'.[70] Thus, the Court did not engage with national laws to exclude an infringement of the official's rights in light of EU law. On the contrary, as done in *Grant*, EU judges focused on the protection of family life, simply observing that the EU's refusal to grant a household allowance to one of its officials does not affect the situation of the official in question as regards to his civil status. Subsequently, such refusal 'only concerns the relationship between the official and his employer, does not of itself give rise to the transmission of any personal information to persons outside the [Union] administration'. For this reason, the contested decision did not constitute an interference with the private and family life of the applicant within the meaning of article 8 of the European Convention on Human Rights (ECHR).[71] As to the principle of non-discrimination, enshrined in article 119 TFEU,[72] the Court ruled that the principle of equal treatment could only apply to comparable situations.[73]

As in *Grant*, the dialogue with national laws and jurisprudence as well as with the ECtHR's case law did not lead the Court to strengthen gay and lesbian persons' rights, especially as neither article 8 of the ECHR nor article 119 TFEU were found to be breached. In line with the Court's general aim

[69] *Ibid.*, para. 50.

[70] *Ibid.*, para. 38.

[71] *Ibid.*, paras. 58–60.

[72] Article 119 TFEU provides: '1. For the purposes set out in Article 3 of the Treaty on European Union, the activities of the Member States and the Union shall include, as provided in the Treaties, the adoption of an economic policy which is based on the close coordination of Member States' economic policies, on the internal market and on the definition of common objectives, and conducted in accordance with the principle of an open market economy with free competition. 2. Concurrently with the foregoing, and as provided in the Treaties and in accordance with the procedures set out therein, these activities shall include a single currency, the euro, and the definition and conduct of a single monetary policy and exchange-rate policy the primary objective of both of which shall be to maintain price stability and, without prejudice to this objective, to support the general economic policies in the Union, in accordance with the principle of an open market economy with free competition. 3. These activities of the Member States and the Union shall entail compliance with the following guiding principles: stable prices, sound public finances and monetary conditions and a sustainable balance of payments.' (Consolidated Version of the Treaty on the Functioning of European Union, Official Journal 326 (26 October 2012), TFEU).

[73] *D. v. Council*, *supra* note 64, para. 48.

of 'avoid[ing] stepping on government[s'] and constitutional court's toes simultaneously',[74] EU judges were using a majoritarian activism approach, 'plac[ing] the impact of its judgments on a graduated scale according to the degree to which the majority of Member States were willing to accept them'.[75]

Even though the rights of same-sex couples were not legally protected, the issue was debated at the institutional level and the judgment of the CJEU contributed to this. This debate led to the adoption of the aforementioned Regulation 723/2004.[76] In particular, the new article 1(2) of Annex VII listed a number of conditions according to which the household allowance could be granted to an official registered as a stable non-marital partner.[77] This provision has thus filled the gap that existed in the Staff Regulations, and employment benefits are now also granted to officials registered as stable non-marital partners.[78]

Indeed, this normative change brought the Civil Service Tribunal to explicitly state in the *W. v. Commission* case of 2010 that the Staff Regulations recognise a substantial equivalence between stable non-marital partnerships, including same-sex, and marriage. The case concerned Mr. W., the applicant, who was an EU staff member based in Belgium, held dual Belgian-Moroccan nationality and whose same-sex relationship had been registered in Belgium. He brought an action against the Commission, challenging its refusal to grant him a household allowance on the grounds that he and his partner had access to marriage in Belgium and, therefore, did not satisfy one of the conditions laid down in article 1(2)(c)(iv) of Annex VII. The applicant claimed that he could not legally marry in Belgium due to his Moroccan nationality. More specifically, he pointed out that Moroccan legislation criminalised homosexual

[74] De Waele and van der Vleuten, Judicial Activism, *supra* note 52, at 658.

[75] G. Martinico and O. Pollicino, *The Interaction between Europe's Legal Systems. Judicial Dialogue and the Creation of Supranational Laws* (Cheltenham: Edward Elgar, 2012) at 154.

[76] See also the discussion by M.F. Orzan, 'Employment Benefits for Same-sex Couples: The Case-Law of the CJEU', Gallo, Paladini and Pustorino (eds.), Same-Sex, *supra* note 1, 493–509, at 497.

[77] According to article 1(2)(c)(iv), revised, the household allowance shall be granted to an official who is registered as a stable non-marital partner, provided that (1) the couple produces a legal document recognized as such by a Member State, or any competent authority of a Member State, acknowledging their status as non-marital partners; (2) neither partner is in a marital relationship or in another non-marital partnership; (3) the partners are not related in any of the following ways: parent, child, grandparent, grandchild, brother, sister, aunt, uncle, nephew, niece, son-in-law, daughter-in-law; (4) the couple has no access to legal marriage in a Member State.

[78] M. F. Orzan, Employment Benefits, *supra* note 76, at 497.

acts and, therefore, a marriage in Belgium would have exposed him and his partner to great danger.[79]

For our purposes the case is relevant because the Tribunal relied extensively not only on the EU Charter but, above all, on the ECHR as well as on the case law of the ECtHR to reach a conclusion different than in *D. v. Council*. Indeed, the Tribunal clarified that 'the extension of entitlement to the household allowance to officials registered as stable, non-marital partners, including those of the same sex, reflects the need to protect officials against the administration's interference in the exercise of their right to respect for their family and private life', as recognised in article 7 of the EU Fundamental Rights Charter and in article 8 of the ECHR. Moreover, the Tribunal pointed out that, as with the protection of the rights ensured by the ECHR, 'the rules of the Staff Regulations extending entitlement to the household allowance to officials registered as stable, non-marital partners, including those of the same sex, must be interpreted in such a way as to make those rules as effective as possible, so that the right in question is not theoretical or illusory, but practical and effective'.[80] The effectiveness of the applicable law is a crucial parameter, and to illustrate its meaning, the Tribunal cited a number of ECtHR's judgments. EU judges highlighted that for officials registered as stable, non-marital partners, including those of the same sex, the right to the household allowance 'could prove theoretical and illusory if the notion of "access to legal marriage in a Member State", the absence of which is one of the conditions for such an official to receive the household allowance, were construed in a purely formal sense'. The application of article 1(2)(c)(iv) of Annex VII thus must be subject to verification.[81] According to the Tribunal, the applicant's access to marriage in Belgium could not be considered practical and effective within the meaning of the ECtHR's case law, since the applicant could be exposed, in case of a same-sex marriage, to danger as the legislation in force in Morocco criminalised homosexual acts.[82]

The last case concerning an EU staff member is *Roodhuijzen v. Commission*. In this judgment, the General Court, by confirming the judgment of the Civil Service Tribunal, ruled that, when applying the Staff Regulations, the term 'stable non-marital partnership' pursuant to article 1(2)(c) of the Staff Regulations had to be given an autonomous interpretation, regardless of the national law. It thereby annulled the EU

79 On the case see *ibid.*, 498–99.
80 *Ibid.*, paras. 42–43.
81 *Ibid.*, para. 44.
82 *Ibid.*, paras. 44–45 and 55.

Commission's denial to recognise a same-sex *de facto* partnership between the applicant, who was an official in Eurostat, and his partner. The Court was clear in stating that the issue of whether two persons are non-marital partners cannot be left solely to the discretion of member states,[83] as also ruled by the ECtHR.[84] Despite the fact that the judgment did not concern a same-sex partnership, it is very important for future decisions, since a 'stable non-marital partnership' includes also same-sex relationships. Here the Court successfully dealt with the Staff Regulations' silence in respect to the concepts of 'marriage' and 'spouse', without grounding its reasoning on the staff member's national law.[85] It remains to be seen whether in future cases, employment benefits such as household and retirement allowances will be interpreted covering both heterosexuals and married or registered gay couples.

From the preceding discussion, as to the issue of the engagement of the CJEU with the domestic laws of member states and domestic courts' jurisprudence as well as with the ECtHR's jurisprudence, two approaches can be identified: the first concerns cases in the context of preliminary rulings procedures (*Grant*, *Maruko*, *Römer*); the second regards cases on the status of EU officials (*D. v. Council*, *W. v. Commission*, *Rodhuijsen*). Concerning the former, it can be concluded that the CJEU's deference to the member states' domestic law and jurisprudence is not *per se* an obstacle to the protection of same-sex couples' rights. By observing the changes that have been brought about over the years in the German legal order, and by interpreting these changes in a flexible manner as seen in the *Maruko* and *Römer* judgments, the CJEU moved towards a reading of national law that is best suited to strengthening same-sex couples' rights. The outcome of the engagement depends precisely on the type of guarantees accorded to those couples by national law. However, an analysis of the protection offered in different national legal systems was not conducted in either *Maruko* or in *Römer*, but only in the *Grant* judgment. As to the engagement of the CJEU with the ECHR, more specifically with the ECtHR's case law, the same holds true: indeed, the Court only made an explicit reference to the ECHR

[83] *Roodhuijzen v. Commission*, *supra* note 66, paras. 35–40.

[84] *Ibid.*, para. 84.

[85] For a comparison with the legal recognition of same-sex UN staff members see D. Gallo, 'International Administrative Tribunals and Their Non-Originalist Jurisprudence on Same-Sex Couples: "Spouse" and "Marriage" in Context, Between Social Changes and the *Doctrine of Renvoi*', Gallo, Paladini and Pustorino (eds.), Same-Sex, *supra* note 1, 511–32; and D. Gallo, 'The "New" Law Applicable to LGBTI International Civil Servants in the UN System', *American University Int'l L. Rev.* 30:4 (2015) 649–64.

as interpreted by the ECtHR in *Grant*.[86] This means that a judicial dialogue between the CJEU and the ECtHR did not necessarily lead to a more advanced protection of rights in 1998, as the former employed the latter's case law to deny stable homosexual relationships to fall within the scope of article 8 ECHR. The engagement with the ECtHR's jurisprudence as well as with the different national laws of member states, therefore, serves to justify an approach which is not inclusive *ex se* towards a greater recognition of rights; such recognition would have been admitted only through a flexible – rather than literal – interpretation of EU law.

In the jurisprudence on EU staff, in *D. v. Council* and *W. v. Commission* the CJEU followed the approach adopted in its preliminary rulings, characterised by a strong attention to the will of national legislatures. Yet in the *Rodhuijsen* judgment did the CJEU go further and opt for an autonomous interpretation of EU law. What is important to stress is that the Court, as it had done with regard to references in preliminary rulings in *Grant*, only relied on a comparative analysis of national laws in *D. v. Council*, which is the most 'conservative' amongst the three judgments on the status of EU staff. By contrast, its engagement with the ECtHR's case law led the Court to adopt more progressive decisions in *W. v. Commission* and *Rodhuijsen*.

7.3.2 The ECtHR's Engagement with Jurisprudence and Legislation

The ECtHR case law on same-sex relationships engages with the CJEU as well as with national courts and legislatures. This dialogue contributed to an increased recognition of same-sex couples' rights at the national level.[87] We argue that this process of gradual recognition of rights took place through five steps.

First, the ECtHR recognised that the principle of non-discrimination based on sexual orientation, due implicitly from the combination of article 8 of the ECHR on the right to respect for private and family life and article 14 on non-discrimination, applied to domestic family law. The Court came to this finding in *Salgueiro da Silva Mouta v. Portugal*, concerning a

[86] *Grant v. South-West Trains Ltd*, *supra* note 52, paras. 33–35.

[87] On the ECtHR's case law on same-sex couples' rights, see *ex multis* P. Johnson, *Homosexuality and the European Court of Human Rights* (New York: Routledge, 2013); J. M. Scherpe, 'The Legal Recognition of Same-Sex Couples in Europe and the Role of the European Court of Human Rights', *Equal Rights Rev.* 10 (2013) 83–96; P. Pustorino, 'Same-Sex Couples before the ECtHR: The Right to Marriage', Gallo, Paladini and Pustorino (eds.), Same-Sex, *supra* note 1, 399–408; and F. Crisafulli, 'Same-Sex Couples' Rights (Other than the Right to Marry) Before the ECtHR', *ibid.*, 409–36.

father's right to custody and visitation of his daughter.[88] This right had been denied to him based on the fact that he lived with another man. Through a typically 'corrective dialogue', the Court rejected the idea expressed by the Portuguese courts which ruled on the matter in the national proceedings that homosexuality was an 'abnormality' and that 'children should not grow up in the shadow of abnormal situations'.[89]

Second, the ECtHR held in *Karner v. Austria* that same-sex cohabiting partners must be treated equally to opposite-sex cohabiting couples, and hence they must enjoy the same rights.[90] In particular, the Court rejected the Austrian government's argument that the national measure at issue aimed at protecting the family unit.[91] Interestingly, in *Karner*, the Court granted gay rights associations with an international standing like ILGA-Europe and Stonewall the right to participate as third-party interveners in the proceedings. The Court further recalled what these associations pointed out, namely that 'a growing number of national courts in European and other democratic society required equal treatment of unmarried different-sex partners and unmarried same-sex partners'.[92] In particular, the associations had referred to several recommendations by the European Parliament, the Parliamentary Assembly of the Council of Europe and the European Directive 2000/78. It was thus through the submissions of those associations that the ECtHR engaged with national law and decisions of

[88] *Salgueiro da Silva Mouta v. Portugal* (Appl. No. 33290/96), Judgment (Chamber), 21 December 1999, ECHR 1999-IX, 309.

[89] *Ibid.*, para. 34. See also paras. 35–36, where it is stated that '[i]t is the Court's view that the above passages from the judgment in question, far from being merely clumsy or unfortunate as the Government maintained, or mere *obiter dicta*, suggest, quite to the contrary, that the applicant's homosexuality was a factor which was decisive in the final decision.... The Court is therefore forced to find, in the light of the foregoing, that the Court of Appeal made a distinction based on considerations regarding the applicant's sexual orientation, a distinction which is not acceptable under the Convention'. On the notion of 'corrective dialogue', see also the 'report on practice' of Judge Lopez-Guerra in Chapter 13 of this volume.

[90] *Karner v. Austria* (Appl. No. 40016/98), Judgment (Chamber), 24 July 2003, ECHR 2003-IX, 199, para. 43 (concluding that there had been a violation of article 14 of the ECHR in conjunction with article 8).

[91] In this respect, while the Court accepted the alleged aim as admissible, it noted that 'a broad variety of concrete measures may be used to implement it'. However, in the case at issue, 'the margin of appreciation afforded to States is narrow.... [So] it must also be shown that [the measure contemplated] was necessary in order to achieve that aim to exclude certain categories of people – in this instance persons living in a homosexual relationship ... The Court cannot see that the Government ha[s] advanced any arguments that would allow such a conclusion' (para. 41).

[92] *Ibid.*, para. 36.

domestic courts.[93] Like the CJEU did in *D. v. Council*, the Court assumed a majoritarian activism approach; however, the references to domestic sources resulted in a ruling favouring equal treatment of same-sex couples.

Third, in *Schalk and Kopf v. Austria*,[94] the ECtHR reached two different conclusions concerning the following matters: interpretation of articles 14 and 8 of the ECHR; interpretation of article 12 of the ECHR and the (non-)existence of a right to marry for same-sex couples. As to the interpretation of articles 14 and 8, the Court, besides recognising that the relationship of the Austrian same-sex couple at stake fell within the notion of 'private life' according to article 8, for the first time in its jurisprudence ruled that this relationship also constituted 'family life'.[95] To reach this conclusion, the Court noted that 'a rapid evolution of social attitudes towards same-sex couples ha[d] taken place in many member states'. The Court stressed that a considerable number of member states now afforded legal recognition to same-sex couples. Moreover, it is also highlighted that EU law reflects a growing tendency to include same-sex couples in the notion of 'family'.[96]

As to the interpretation of article 12, and in general concerning the question about the (non-)existence of a right to marry for gays and lesbians, the Court interpreted it in a flexible and dynamic manner. It observed that article 12, by granting the right to marry to 'men and women' and to found a family, distinguished itself from the wording used in all other substantive articles of the ECHR, which states that 'everyone' is granted a given right. The Court went on, however, to stress that the choice of this wording in article 12 must be read in light of the ECHR's historical context as 'in the 1950s[,] marriage was clearly understood in the traditional sense of being a union between partners of different sex'.[97] On the basis of its own case law on transsexuals – in which it had departed from a rigid interpretation of the term 'couple' – the ECtHR recognised, in principle, an inclusive interpretation of article 12, that is, an interpretation that also included

93 *Ibid.*

94 *Schalk and Kopf v. Austria* (Appl. No. 30141/04), Judgment (Chamber), 24 June 2010, ECHR 2010-IV, 409. See also generally *Hämäläinen v. Finland* (Appl. No. 37359/09), Judgment (Grand Chamber), 16 July 2014, selected for publication 2014.

95 *Schalk and Kopf v. Austria*, *supra* note 94, para. 90.

96 *Ibid.*, para. 93. In this regard, see M. Bonini Baraldi, 'EU Family Policies Between "Good Old Values" and Fundamental Rights: The Case of Same-Sex Families', *Maastricht J. of European & Comp. L.* 15:4 (2008) 517–52; L. Hodson, 'A Marriage by Any Other Name? *Schalk and Kopf v. Austria*', *Human Rights Law Review* 11:1 (2011) 170–79.

97 *Schalk and Kopf v. Austria*, *supra* note 94, paras. 54–55.

homosexual relationships, notwithstanding the letter of the norm.[98] In spite of this interpretation, the Court noted that there was no European consensus regarding same-sex marriage, given that at the time, no more than six out of the forty-seven Convention states allowed for same-sex marriage in their domestic laws.[99] In conclusion, the Court found that article 12 did not impose an obligation on the respondent government to grant same-sex couples access to marriage.[100]

Fourth, the inclusion of the relationships of same-sex couples within the notion of 'family life' was reiterated in the judgment *Vallianatos and Others v. Greece*, where the Court added that a lack of cohabitation between the two partners did not deprive the relationship of the stability necessary to form a real couple.[101] We observe in particular that the Court found a violation of article 14 taken in conjunction with article 8 as it recognised a trend towards legal recognition of same-sex relationships in Europe. Going beyond what had already been stated in *Schalk*, the ECtHR relied on that trend to reduce member states' margin of appreciation in enacting legislation which discriminates against same-sex couples.[102] The evolution in the *Vallianatos* judgment lies in the fact that the ECtHR identified, for the first time, a positive obligation of domestic authorities to recognise same-sex couples' rights: if national authorities wish to introduce a registered partnership, they are free – not obliged – to do so, but – when they do – they must offer the same protection to heterosexuals and homosexuals alike.

Finally and most recently, the ECtHR, in *Oliari and Others v. Italy* of 2015,[103] went beyond its findings in *Vallianatos*. The case concerned three gay Italian couples that had challenged Italian courts' decisions to not grant them a right to marry under the Italian Constitution. While the ECtHR did not criticise Italian courts for not recognising a right to marry for homosexual couples, it held that under article 8, national authorities were obliged to 'ensure that the applicants have available a specific legal framework

[98] *Ibid.*, paras. 49 and 51–53. Amongst other relevant judgments on transsexuals in which the Court had developed its progressive jurisprudence see *Christine Goodwin v. the United Kingdom* (Appl. No. 28957/95), Judgment (Grand Chamber), 11 July 2002, ECHR 2002-VI, 1.

[99] *Ibid.*, para. 58.

[100] *Ibid.*, para. 63.

[101] *Vallianatos and Others v. Greece* (Appl. Nos. 29381/09 and 32684/09), Judgment (Grand Chamber), 7 November 2013, ECHR 2013-VI (extracts), 125, para. 73; see also, on this case, Drosos and Constantinides, The Legal Situation, *supra* note 5.

[102] *Vallianatos and Others v. Greece*, *supra* note 101, para. 91.

[103] *Oliari and Others v. Italy* (Appl. Nos. 18766/11 and 36030/11), Judgment (Chamber), 21 July 2015, selected for publication 2015.

providing for the recognition and protection of their same-sex unions'.[104] With the judgment, the Court stated that civil unions/registered partnerships for homosexuals must be introduced in Italy. What has to be stressed is the attention that the Court gave to two elements. The first is the comparative law reasoning, focused on the legal systems of the Council of Europe member states, on the EU Fundamental Rights Charter as well as – quite surprisingly – on the US Supreme Court' decision of 26 June 2015 in the case of *Obergefell et al. v. Hodges, Director, Ohio Department of Health et al*,[105] in which the right to same-sex marriage for US citizens was fully recognized.[106] The second and crucial element on which the Court grounded its judgment is the reference to national court's jurisprudence on the status of same-sex couples in the respondent country as well as on the passive (*rectius*: negligent) behaviour on the part of the legislator. In particular, the deep engagement of the Court with the findings of Italian courts is clear where the Court noted that, 'in the light of domestic courts' conclusions on the matter' that remained unheeded by the legislator, Italy failed to fulfil its positive obligation under article 8.[107] The Court observed that, despite several attempts, the Italian legislature had been inert and unable to enact the relevant legislation. The Court criticised the inaction of the Italian legislature which 'seems not to have attached particular importance to the indications set out by the national community, including the general Italian population and the highest judicial authorities in Italy'.[108] On the basis of this consideration, the Court found that the constant failure of the legislator to take account of the Italian Constitutional Court's pronouncements on the unconstitutionality of the absence of a regulation of the situation of same-sex couples over a significant period of time would potentially undermine the authority of the judiciary and create a situation of legal uncertainty for citizens.[109]

As to the general population, interestingly, the Court noted that there is a social consensus on the legal and thus formal recognition of same-sex couples' rights in the Italian population. In this regard, it relied on official surveys and statistics, which indicate that there is a popular acceptance of homosexual couples, as well as popular support for their protection.[110]

[104] *Ibid.*, para. 185.

[105] US Supreme Court, *Obergefell et al. v. Hodges, Director, Ohio Department of Health et al.*, 26 June 2015, 576 US ___.53-2

[106] *Oliari and Others v. Italy*, *supra* note 103, paras. 53–54 and 65.

[107] *Ibid.*, para. 185.

[108] *Ibid.*, para. 179.

[109] *Ibid.*, para. 184.

[110] *Ibid.*, para. 181.

As to the highest judicial authorities, the Court stressed that the need to recognise and protect homosexual relationships has been expressed by the Italian Constitutional Court and the Court of Cassation.[111] The ECtHR thus engaged in a true dialogue, especially with the Italian Constitutional Court, with regard to judgment No. 138/10 – which concerned the first two applicants in the *Oliari* case – as well as two subsequent cases. Here the ECtHR pointed out, first, that the Constitutional Court repeatedly called for a juridical recognition of the relevant rights and duties of homosexual unions and, second, that such a measure could only be put in place by the parliament.[112] The fact that no legislation had been adopted by the Italian legislature – at the time – notwithstanding the several prayers for intervention expressed by national courts, led the ECtHR to find Italy in violation of article 8. In relation to article 12, the Court confirmed that homosexuals could theoretically be granted the right to marriage, but it reiterated the conclusion it reached in *Schalk*: the question of whether or not to allow same-sex marriage is left to regulation by the national law of the contracting state.[113] Once again the Court based its ruling on comparative arguments, studying the recognition of same-sex marriage in domestic law in Europe. It found that despite the gradual evolution of domestic law on the matter, article 12 does not impose an obligation to grant same-sex couples access to marriage, insofar as there was no European consensus on the matter.[114]

As far as the extent and method of the dialogue with domestic legislatures and judges are concerned, we have seen that the ECtHR grounds its reasoning on EU law as well as the law of the Council of Europe's member states. As to the effects of this dialogue, we observe that it had an impact on the legal protection of same-sex couples at both the international and the national levels. These effects are looked at in more detail in the following analysis.

First, even if the ECHR does not directly provide for a right to marry a person of the same sex, the Court nevertheless interpreted the Convention to mean that marriage includes the right to marry a person of the same sex if the national legislature provides for such a right. To reach that conclusion, the ECtHR used article 9 of the EU Fundamental Rights Charter to

[111] See *inter alia* Judgments No. 138/10 of 12 April 2010 and No. 4/11 of 16 December 2010, both delivered by the Constitutional Court; and Judgments No. 4184/12 of 12 March 2012 and No. 2400/15 of 9 February 2015, both delivered by the Supreme Court of Cassation.

[112] *Oliari and Others v. Italy*, *supra* note 103, para. 180.

[113] *Ibid.*, para. 191.

[114] *Ibid.*, paras. 182–83.

interpret article 12 of the ECHR.[115] By using the EU Charter to help this transversal reading of the ECHR, the Court finally asserted that same-sex marriages in Europe are neither prohibited nor imposed: they are allowed. Second, the ECtHR's jurisprudence influenced national systems to different degrees, including the decisions of domestic courts, who engaged with relevant ECtHR jurisprudence to allow for an enhanced effect in the recognition of same-sex couples' rights. In Italy, for example, domestic courts used the ECtHR's *Schalk* judgment to press for the legal recognition of same-sex couples in Italian law.[116] While it had passed specific legislation under Directive 2000/78,[117] similar to many Eastern European countries and Greece,[118] Italy had not yet enacted any regulation concerning same-sex couples. Given these circumstances, Italian courts resorted to the statement of the ECtHR in *Schalk* that same-sex couples constitute a 'family' under the ECHR, and to acknowledge that an Italian citizen and his same-sex partner, who had been married in Spain, had the right to stay on Italian soil via a permanent resident permit in order to afford them a life as a 'family'.[119] In its *Schalk* judgment, the ECtHR had also confirmed the view that, under the national legislature's discretion, same-sex marriages can be considered 'proper' marriages that are effectively protected by article 12 of the ECHR. Relying heavily on this and other statements of the ECtHR in *Schalk*, in its Decision No. 4184 of 2012, the Italian Supreme Court of Cassation (*Corte di Cassazione*) ruled for the first time on whether two same-sex Italian citizens, married abroad, were entitled to record their marriage certificates at the Italian Civil Registry Office.[120] The judges stressed the need for the Parliament to recognise this new family

115 See *Schalk and Kopf v. Austria*, *supra* note 94, para. 61, where it is affirmed that '[R]egard being had to Article 9 of the [EU] Charter, therefore, the Court would no longer consider that the right to marry enshrined in Article 12 must in all circumstances be limited to marriage between two persons of the opposite sex. Consequently, it cannot be said that Article 12 is inapplicable to the applicants' complaint. However, as matters stand, the question whether or not to allow same-sex marriage is left to regulation by the national law of the Contracting State.'

116 See Fidalgo de Freitas and Tega, Judicial Restraint, *supra* note 5, at 297, noting that 'according to the Italian Supreme Court of Cassation, the ECtHR [in *Schalk*] would have removed the obstacle that prevented the recognition of same-sex marriage, reserving the guarantee of the said right to the free choices by national parliaments'.

117 See Legislative Decree of 9 July 2003, No. 216, 2003 OJ 187 (13 August 2003).

118 In this regard see respectively A. Bodnar and A. Sledzinska-Simon, Between Recognition and Homophobia, *supra* note 1, and Drosos and Constantinides, The Legal Situation, *supra* note 5.

119 See for instance Tribunal of Reggio Emilia, Judgment of 13 February 2012, No. 1401/11.

120 See M.M. Winkler, 'Italy's High Court Rules on Recognition Claim by Same-Sex Couple Married in the Netherlands', *Gay/Lesbian Law Notes* (2012) 108.

status, thus deferring to the legislature to act. With Decision No. 4184, the *Corte di Cassazione* did not grant the request of the petitioning same-sex couple. However, with the inspiration from the ECtHR's *Schalk* judgment, it reaffirmed that the impossibility of recording the same-sex marriage at the Registry Office in Italy was not due to the contrariety of this institution to public order, but to the non-recognisability of the marriage certificate in the Italian legal system. In other words: two Italian same-sex citizens could not register a marriage celebrated abroad, not because that marriage is non-existent or invalid for the Italian legal system, but because same-sex unions are unsuited to give rise to any legal effects therein.[121]

The second part of Decision 4184 was devoted to the interpretation of the right to marriage contained in the Italian Constitution. Decision 4184 stated that in the *Schalk* judgment, the ECtHR did away with the explicit condition underpinning marriage: that only persons of different sexes can get married. In other words, the *Corte di Cassazione* recognised that the ECtHR had removed the obstacle that had prevented the recognition of same-sex marriage in Italian law before, now giving national parliaments a free choice to guarantee the said right to same-sex couples.[122]

As far as Italy is concerned,[123] the effects of the ECtHR's *Oliari* judgment on the domestic legal system have been very remarkable. In particular, pending the finalisation of our chapter, law 76/2016 on the recognition of same-sex civil unions has been finally adopted. It also will be interesting to see whether the judgment will serve as a legal basis to oblige all member states of the Council of Europe to introduce some form of legal recognition of same-sex couples in their domestic law. Issues arising from this judgment will look to whether the ECtHR will, for example, find Russia or Turkey in violation of article 8 ECHR for not having provided for the recognition of same-sex couples in domestic law and whether individual complaints should be brought to Strasbourg by applicants from Turkey or Russia. Or is the Italian case a special one because of the existence of a social consensus *vis-à-vis* same-sex couples' rights, and, above all, because of the active role played by Italian judicial authorities? The Italian judiciary, albeit not recognising a right to conclude a civil union/registered partnership formally under current Italian law, has on several occasions urged the national legislature to adopt appropriate domestic legislation. A

[121] See Fidalgo de Freitas and Tega, Judicial Restraint, *supra* note 5, at 296.

[122] *Ibid.*, at 297.

[123] For further insights on the situation in Italy, see the contributions in A. Schillaci (ed.), *Omosessualità, eguaglianza, diritti* (Rome: Carocci, 2014).

reading of the concurring opinion, where the three judges of the ECtHR[124] deemed it necessary to make clear that Italy is indeed a special case, could reveal, *a contrario*, that the *Oliari* judgment has the potential to produce *erga omnes* effects, thus supporting an interpretation of article 8 aimed at establishing a duty of all Council of Europe member states to legally recognise same-sex couples' rights. In our opinion, however, the most plausible outcome seems to be that such obligations may arise only if the combination of three conditions will be fulfilled: the legislators' inertia, domestic judicial action and social consensus on the need to protect same-sex couples' rights.

Effects of the ECtHR's dialogue with domestic courts and domestic legislatures concerning the protection of same-sex couples' rights can also be observed in Austria. The ECtHR case law had an impact on the Austrian legislature and the Austrian Supreme Court. In the domestic judgments leading to the ECtHR's judgment in *Karner v. Austria*, the applicant succeeded in the first and second domestic instance. The Austrian Supreme Court, however, simply rejected the claim, noting that the legislature had not intended that the tenancy law should also apply to same-sex couples. After the Supreme Court's ruling, the matter was therefore in the hands of the Austrian legislature. In 2004, the Socialist Party, at the time in opposition, declared that it intended to pursue full equality for same-sex couples. When it won the election in 2007, discussions began about a bill that took the Swiss Registered Partnership Act as a model.[125] After a two-year discussion, the bill was presented to the Parliament and approved on 30 December 2009 (*Lebenspartnerschaftsgesetz*, LPG), and entered into force on 1 January 2010.[126] Despite these protection-enhancing effects of the ECtHR's *Karner* judgment, in 2013, the ECtHR returned to the Austrian law. In *X and Others v. Austria* it determined that a lesbian couple, one of whom wanted to adopt the daughter of the other, were a family under article 8 of the ECHR.[127] Furthermore, it held that the couple had a right to enter into a second-parent adoption. It reasoned that because Austrian law

[124] Concurring opinion of Judge Mahoney joined by Judges Tsotsoria and Vehabovi, to *Oliari and Others v. Italy*, *supra* note 103.

[125] The *Registered Partnership Act* was passed on 18 June 2004 and approved by a popular referendum on 5 June 2005. The law entered into force 1 January 2007. See *supra* note 40.

[126] See D. Aichberger-Beig, 'Registered Partnership for Same-Sex Couples', B. Verschraegen (ed.), *Austrian Law. An International Perspective* (Wien: Jan Sramek Verlag, 2010), 61–76, at 68. Registered Partnership Act, *supra* note 41.

[127] *X and Others v. Austria* (Appl. No. 19010/07), Judgment (Grand Chamber), 19 February 2013, ECHR 2013-II, 1.

entitled cohabiting partners of the opposite sex to adopt, same-sex couples must enjoy this right under article 14 of the ECHR as well.[128] The ruling put the LPG into question as it expressly opposed the extension of adoption rights to same-sex registered partners.[129] Finally, and also in 2013, the Austrian Constitutional Court allowed lesbian couples to access medically assisted procreation processes, in spite of the fact that the LPG excluded such access. The Austrian Constitutional Court incorporated the ECtHR's *Schalk* judgment into its ruling and remarked that the LPG's insemination ban amounted to a violation of the Austrian Constitution and the ECHR. It held that it breached both the couples' right to family life and their right to be free from discrimination based on sexual orientation.[130] An effective judicial dialogue thus took place between the ECtHR and Austrian courts.

The ECtHR's judgment in *Schalk and Kopf v. Austria* also had an impact on France, especially on the French legislature. When it began discussing a law on same-sex marriage and adoption by same-sex couples (*Mariage pour Tous*), the French Parliament was influenced by *Schalk* but also by the CJEU's *Maruko* judgment. In the preparatory works, both rulings are cited as a confirmation of the legislature's power to pass such a law. The *Schalk* judgment was furthermore relied on to exclude an *obligation* to do so under the ECHR.[131] The ECtHR case law was also used in order to support the extension of the right to adopt for same-sex couples. Under French law, single persons can adopt. In 2008, the ECtHR ruled that France had breached the ECHR in not considering gays and lesbians adequate potential parents under national adoption law. If gays or lesbians were suitable to be good parents as singles, it became difficult to deny that they could be good parents together.[132] On this basis, the French Parliament expressly referred to the ECtHR ruling to extend the possibility to jointly adopt to same-sex couples. Finally, the government noted that '[m]any countries

[128] *Ibid.*, para. 125: '[h]ad the first and third applicants been an unmarried different-sex couple, the domestic courts would not have been able to refuse the adoption request as a matter of principle.'

[129] *Ibid.*, para. 39. Section 8(4) of the Registered Partnership Act provides as follows: 'Registered partners shall not be allowed to adopt a child jointly, nor shall one registered partner be allowed to adopt the other partner's child.'

[130] Constitutional Court of Austria, *In re Christina Maria B. and Daniela Bauer*, 10 December 2013, G 16/2013, G 44/2013; and the related commentary M. Guerrero, 'Assisted Reproduction in the Shadow of the Past. Austrian Constitutional Court, Judgment of 10 December 2013', G 16/2013 and G/44/2013, *Vienna J. Int'l Const. L.* 8:2 (2014) 224–34.

[131] See French National Assembly, *Projet de Loi Ouvrant le Mariage aux Couples de Personnes de Meme Sexe. Etude d'Impact*, November 2012, Parliamentary Documents, I-4.2.

[132] See *E.B. v. France* (Appl. No. 43546/02), Judgment (Grand Chamber), 22 January 2008, not reported.

experienced the same evolutions as France. Confronted with the same issues, some of them decided to amend their statutes.'[133] As stated earlier, same-sex marriage has been legal in France since 18 May 2013.

7.4 Concluding Remarks

Following from the points made in the preceding sections, some final remarks follow on the limitations and potential of legislative and judicial dialogues in 'putting the rights in action' and guiding legal changes and reforms.

First, as to national legislatures, from the analysis in Section 7.2, it follows that the recognition of same-sex couples' rights can be effectively passed by a process of cross-fertilisation among national legislatures, with the result that those rights can penetrate in different cultural, social and, ultimately, legal traditions. This shows the inherent *vis expansiva* implied in those rights, including values such as equality, legal protection for cohabiting couples and respect for family life. At the same time, however, it must be noted that this transnational diffusion via legislative dialogue can function only if the countries involved in the dialogue have some degree of homogeneity, be it social, political, cultural, religious and/or linguistic.

Second, as to supranational courts, the CJEU's approach is characterised by its deferential attitude *vis-à-vis* national legislatures. Deference to legislatures is an important factor in the ECtHR's jurisprudence as well, with a distinction to be made between cases that concern questions of same-sex marriage on the one hand and same-sex registered partnerships on the other. As to the former, the ECtHR, on the basis of the notion of 'European consensus', fosters the recognition of same-sex couples' rights only if the laws of the respondent state recognises the institution of same-sex marriage: there is no positive obligation imposed upon the state. As to the latter, the ECtHR first of all clarified in *Vallianatos* that if a state decides to introduce a registered partnership scheme for heterosexual couples, this partnership scheme must also be accessible for homosexual couples. Subsequently, in the *Oliari* case, it went further and derived a positive obligation from article 8 ECHR to introduce registered partnerships/civil unions. At least, this positive obligation addresses countries such as Italy, in which the judiciary had urged the legislature to take action and enact legislation. Whether this obligation also addresses other member states of the Council of Europe that have not enacted

[133] *Ibid.*, at 1–3.

laws on the status of same-sex couples remains to be seen. In any event, concerning both the right to marriage and the right to enter into a civil partnership, the fostering of the rights of gays and lesbians is the result of a teleological, systemic and inclusive interpretation of articles 8, 12 and 14 ECHR that has allowed the ECtHR to leave aside a formal constructivist and literal interpretation of its Convention. One of the results of this is the recognition that same-sex persons may, in principle, be entitled to marry according to article 12, although the provision refers explicitly to 'men and women'. The same holds true *mutatis mutandis* for the CJEU when it ruled on the status of EU staff members. The result is that the most recent case law of the CJEU and ECtHR, when faced with the interpretation of relevant EU law and articles of the ECHR in regard to the protection of same-sex couples, strongly favoured the full recognition of same-sex couples' rights.

Third, with regard specifically to the dialogue between the ECtHR and national courts, it must be stressed that whilst the ECtHR recently imposed changes through the denationalisation of family law[134] (*Oliari*), it did so by relying on the approach adopted by high national judicial authorities who pushed for a greater intervention on the part of Italian legislator and questioned legislative inertia. However, the ECtHR also triggered a 'corrective dialogue' with national authorities, which resulted in the Austrian Constitutional Court adopting a bolder approach on the protection of homosexuals, also in relation to the Austrian parliament. Similarly, ECtHR jurisprudence encouraged the Italian Supreme Court and the Italian Constitutional Court to urge the legislator to step in and provide some form of legal recognition to same-sex couples, which has finally been introduced in Italy. This mutual engagement of courts reveals the 'maieutic' force[135] of legal pluralism[136] as well as the

[134] See generally G. de Burca and O. Gerstenberg, 'The Denationalization of Constitutional Law', *Harvard Int'l L. J.* 47:1 (2006) 243–62.

[135] See A. von Bogdandy and S. Schill, 'Overcoming Absolute Primacy: Respect for National Identity under the Lisbon Treaty', *Common Market L. Rev.* 48:5 (2011) 1417–53; on the concepts of legal cosmopolitism and judicial dialogue (and its positive externalities), see M. P. Maduro, 'Courts and Pluralism: Essay on a Theory of Judicial Adjudication in the Context of Legal and Constitutional Pluralism', J.L. Dunoff and J.P. Trachtman (eds.), *Ruling the World: Constitutionalism, International Law, and Global Governance* (Cambridge University Press, 2009) 356–79; C. Focarelli, *International Law as Social Construct. The Struggle for Global Justice* (Oxford University Press, 2012) at 316–21; N. Walker, 'Beyond Boundary Disputes and Basic Grids: Mapping the Global Disorder of Normative Orders', *Int'l J. of Constitutional L.* 6:3–4 (2008) 373–96.

[136] On legal pluralism, see, among others, A. von Bogdandy, 'Pluralism, Direct Effect, and the Ultimate Say: On the Relationship between International and Domestic Constitutional Law', *Int'l J. of Constitutional L.* 6:3–4 (2008) 397–413; M. Delmas-Marty, *Ordering Pluralism. A Conceptual Framework for Understanding the Transnational Legal World* (Oxford University Press, 2009).

intention of national judges to find external legitimation for their rulings. As to France, the ECtHR's case law – and to a minor extent the case law of the CJEU – has been used as a tool to provide a sound legal basis for the adoption of the *Mariage pour Tous* law.

Lastly, it is evident that the challenges implied in the whole legal discourse on same-sex couples, including through legislative and judicial dialogue, is a matter of legitimacy and of balancing of judges' prerogatives with the legislator's main functions. This challenge can increase when supranational institutions like the ECtHR and the CJEU exercise influence on national judicial systems.

However, it must be noted that many questions remain open: What is the proper boundary between judicial activism and judicial recognition of human rights as a remedy to legislators' inertia? Keeping in mind its democratic source, is legislative action always the best tool to confer rights to citizens? To what extent can judges urge the legislator to 'take same sex-couples' rights seriously', including through engagement in judicial dialogue?

Besides enforcing and consequently protecting the law, courts shape the law,[137] and, by doing so, represent an indispensable antidote to populism and act as a fundamental barrier to a dangerous dictatorship of the majority. When rights are at stake and those rights are the result of social and cultural changes, courts, without being overly 'creative'[138] agents of change, should intercept and legally frame the socio-cultural transformations that occur in modern societies. This can happen *inter alia* through courts' careful engagement in judicial dialogue with their international and national counterparts.

The problem with opting for a Scalian originalism and a literal interpretation of the law is that it tends to interpret the law *ex ante*,[139] as something that remains static from the particular moment it was enacted, without considering that concepts such as equality constantly change. It is in this evolution that the universal – rather than immutable – character of human rights actually lies. Indeed, this character can be reinforced by principled dialogue between national and international legislatures and courts enacting laws and rulings on human rights issues, such as the rights of gay and lesbian people.

[137] On this issue see J. Klabbers, A. Peters and G. Ulfstein, *The Constitutionalization of International Law* (Oxford University Press, 2009) at 127.

[138] On the risks deriving from such 'creativity' see M. Cappelletti, *Giudici legislatori?* (Milan: Giuffrè, 1984) at 14; see also J. Waldron, 'The Core Case against Judicial Review', *Yale L. J.* 115:6 (2006) 1346–1403, at 1395.

[139] As demonstrated by J. Rubenfeld, *Freedom and Time – A theory of Constitutional Self-Government* (New Haven: Yale University Press, 2001) at 188.

Reports on Practice: Domestic Judges

8

Engaging in Judicial Dialogue

Some Reflections from the United Kingdom Supreme Court

THE RIGHT HONOURABLE LORD CARNWATH
OF NOTTING HILL

8.1 Introduction

When looking at the United Kingdom Supreme Court's (UK Supreme Court or Supreme Court) engagement in judicial dialogue, it is important to remember by way of background that the Supreme Court as it exists now, although only created in 2009, has a very long tradition of internationalism because it inherited the jurisdiction of the old Appellate Committee of the House of Lords. Internationalism was also a prominent feature of the old Privy Council; in the past, the Judicial Committee of the Privy Council[1] acted as the final court of appeal for the whole of what was then the British Empire. If we go back to the nineteenth century, the Privy Council was probably the most important court in the world in terms of the number of people it affected. It had a long tradition of reconciling common law principles with local legal principles. For example, it contributed to making English law the dominant law throughout the world in matters of mercantile and shipping law. At the same time, it heard appeals from countries as diverse as Canada, India and Australia, paying due regard to the local law of these countries. The UK Supreme Court builds on the Privy Council's internationalist tradition in its contemporary engagement in judicial dialogue with international and foreign national courts.

Today, the UK Supreme Court is required to follow the case law of the Court of Justice of the European Union (CJEU) on European Union

[1] The Judicial Committee of the Privy Council (JCPC) still exists as the court of final appeal for the UK overseas territories and Crown dependencies, and for those Commonwealth countries that have retained the appeal to Her Majesty in Council or, in the case of Republics, to the Judicial Committee. The same judges who sit as the Justices of the UK Supreme Court also sit on the JCPC.

matters and to take account of jurisprudence of the European Court of Human Rights (ECtHR) on human rights matters. The Supreme Court often finds itself in a position where it builds on and develops the great tradition of common law, which is still shared with large parts of the world, but where, at the same time, it has to reconcile this tradition with European principles. Compared to other European apex courts, this puts the UK Supreme Court in a very unusual position.

Against this historical background, I will share some of my experience of our Supreme Court's interaction with foreign and international courts. I will address the courts with which the Supreme Court engages most often, how the Supreme Court finds out about their decisions and the most common reasons that the Supreme Court engages in judicial dialogue.

8.2 The Extent of the Supreme Court's Engagement with Foreign and International Courts

The Supreme Court most frequently engages with the ECtHR and the CJEU, followed by European national courts and courts from prominent Commonwealth members, such as Australian and Canadian courts.

As far as the interaction with the ECtHR is concerned, the United Kingdom was a latecomer to the European Convention on Human Rights (ECHR or the Convention)[2] in terms of incorporation of the Convention into UK law. The United Kingdom was one of the first signatories to ratify the Convention in 1951, but we did not incorporate its provisions into our domestic law until 2000. Until incorporation, the Convention rights were not enforceable by domestic courts. One possible explanation for the United Kingdom's late incorporation was that, before incorporation, UK judges were rather suspicious of the ECHR, feeling that the Convention was fine for everyone else, but that it was irrelevant for the United Kingdom itself. The United Kingdom indeed exported the ECHR to many of the colonies when they gained independence. But somehow we thought that the United Kingdom itself did not need the Convention, and people like Lord Denning were actually quite rude about it.[3] However, I believe a new generation grew up

[2] Convention for the Protection of Human Rights and Fundamental Freedoms (4 November 1950), 213 UNTS 222; 312 ETS 5, entered into force 3 September 1953.

[3] In one case he described the Convention as 'drawn in such vague terms that it can be used for all sorts of unreasonable claims and provoke all sorts of litigation': *Ahmed v. Inner London Education Authority* [1978] QB 36 (Court of Appeal). (Lord Denning was probably

with the recognition that the ECHR and the ECtHR's jurisprudence is actually rather important, including for the effective protection of human rights in the United Kingdom. Many British judges were very pleased when, in 2000, they became able to take the ECHR into their jurisprudence. But we had a lot of catching up to do. The Supreme Court's frequent engagement with ECtHR jurisprudence plays an important role in this respect.

When it comes to foreign national courts, we are far more likely to refer to their judgments when these judgments are available in English, and when they contain fully reasoned decisions. For example, it is not a secret that a lot of the French judgments are very short. By contrast, the decisions of the UK Supreme Court are probably far too long, and one could say the same about some of the Australian or Canadian judgments. However, when the UK Supreme Court is looking for potentially relevant foreign jurisprudence, it is primarily looking for decisions that fully spell out the reasons for their respective conclusions. Such decisions are more likely to be found in the German Constitutional Court or the German Federal Court of Justice than in the French courts, and in Australian and Canadian courts. The decisions of the latter are also relied on because these courts basically speak the same legal language of the common law. Members of the UK Supreme Court also sit on the Judicial Committee of the Privy Council, which remains the court of final appeal for Caribbean countries, and therefore we are less likely to look to these Caribbean countries for guidance.

8.3 Discovering Relevant Foreign and International Cases

There are three main ways that justices of the UK Supreme Court come across relevant cases from other jurisdictions. First, informal contacts with colleagues in other countries are sometimes valuable. An example is an appeal from Mauritius that the Judicial Committee of the Privy Council heard in 2013.[4] In a lot of matters, Mauritius follows the Napoleonic Code. When it came under British rule, part of the deal was that they could keep the Napoleonic Code for those issues for which it was relevant. The case before the UK Supreme Court involved the effect of a cyclone that had

the best-known and most influential English judge of second half of the last century. He presided over the Court of Appeal as Master of the Rolls for 20 years from 1962.)

[4] *General Construction Limited v. (1) Chue Wing & Co Ltd (2) Ibrahim Cassam & Co Ltd (in Liquidation) (Mauritius)*, (per Lord Mance) [2013] UKPC 30.

knocked down a crane, causing damage. The issue was whether that was *force majeure*, and it was to be decided in accordance with the principles of the Mauritian Code, which follows the French Code. We had conflicting decisions of two chambers of the *Cour de Cassation* on the relevant provisions of this Code. And here we were in London, trying to resolve issues arising from the *Cour de Cassation*! Happily, a French contact drew our attention to a more recent decision of a chamber of *Cour de Cassation*, which seeks to reconcile the two conflicting approaches with which we were grappling. Another example of judicial dialogue through informal exchange is the UK Supreme Court's 2013 judgment involving the EU Air Quality Directive.[5] The problem raised by these proceedings was that the limits on nitrogen dioxide imposed by the European Union in order to achieve better air quality, which were set in 1999 and thought to be achievable by (at latest) 2010, for various reasons had not been achieved and were not expected to be achieved for many years – at least not for central London. The UK government effectively took the position that there may be a standard, but that this standard cannot actually be achieved. NGOs brought an action seeking enforcement of the Directive. It was a difficult case for the Supreme Court, involving questions of how far the government would potentially have to go in restricting traffic in central London. But we were sure that other European countries had similar experiences, and through a body called the Association of Councils of State and Supreme Administrative Jurisdictions (ACA), of which I am a member, I made contact with a German and a French counterpart. The German judge of the Federal Administrative Court came back with an example from Munich on a similar issue, which was very helpful.

The second, and most important, means by which we find out about relevant judgments from foreign or international courts depends on the role of advocates in this process. Most of the research on relevant foreign and international judgments is done by the advocates, especially by those that appear before the Supreme Court. If they wish to refer to international law or foreign domestic courts' jurisprudence, they include it in the case list submitted with the case file.

[5] *R (on the application of ClientEarth) v. The Secretary of State for the Environment, Food and Rural Affairs*, (per Lord Carnwath) [2013] UKSC 25. Council Directive 2008/50/EC of 21 May 2008 on ambient air quality and cleaner air for Europe, OJ 2008 No. L152, 11 June 2008, at 1–44. NB: subsequent to the conference on which this article is based, the UK Supreme Court handed down a judgment making orders consequent on the CJEU's judgment in this case: *R (on the application of ClientEarth) v. The Secretary of State for the Environment, Food and Rural Affairs* [2015] UKSC 28.

Third, the Supreme Court has judicial assistants who are occasionally asked to do some extra comparative research. In fact, in the aforementioned case about air pollution, we happened to have a young German judge working with us at the time, completing a clerkship for six months. We asked him to help us with the research, and benefitted from his being able to translate some of the relevant German judgments into English. He produced a note on the relevant judgments from German courts, and we also submitted the note to the parties to the case. It is normal practice that if the Supreme Court comes across relevant foreign or international material in its research, it will be shared with the parties, giving them a chance to comment on it.

All in all, the Supreme Court's use of cases from foreign national courts is not formalised. Most cases are decided under our national law. Nonetheless, foreign jurisprudence may in some cases play an important role for the members of the Court to develop their thinking and reasoning.

8.4 The Motives behind the Supreme Court's Engagement in Judicial Dialogue

The UK Supreme Court relies on judgments of foreign domestic and international courts mainly for resolving the concrete issues before it, as demonstrated by the examples given in the preceding sections. We refer to foreign and international material most frequently in cases where we encounter difficult legal questions, and any help we can get from anywhere is gratefully received in these cases. As well as casting light on difficult problems, recourse to comparative materials can also inspire us to develop the law in new directions, albeit incrementally.

A related motive for engaging in judicial dialogue in these difficult cases, which are often also either politically or socially sensitive, is that we may be looking for some degree of comfort. Judges are by general nature conservative and cautious. If they are asked to 'jump into a new field', it is very comforting for them to find out that other judges whom they respect, wherever in the world, have done the same thing in solving a legal problem and actually rationalised it. There are various areas in which this may occur. One example is the debate about the right to die. Cases concerning this question are pending and will continue to come up before national and international courts.[6]

[6] NB: subsequent to the conference on which this article is based, the UK Supreme Court handed down a judgment in *R (on the application of Nicklinson) v. Ministry of Justice*, (per Lord Neuberger) [2014] UKSC 38, which considered the so-called right to die.

9

Engaging in Judicial Dialogue

The Practice of the German Federal Constitutional Court

ANDREAS PAULUS*

9.1 Introduction

Let me start by highlighting that I agree with what my learned colleague from the UK Supreme Court, Lord Carnwath, states in his contribution on his court's engagement in judicial dialogue with other national, European and international courts[1]: one has to realise that this is a judicial practice that is sometimes a bit murkier in reality than in theory; yet, it works just fine. Using foreign and international sources is a learning experience; we learn from others. And that is what I find distressing with the approaches of some colleagues, for instance from the United States – that they have to pretend, at least, to close their minds and think that they are alone in the world. I think the European experience, for all of us involved in various capacities, is a different one. We can learn from each other because we have similar problems. I think that this is the point of judicial dialogue. It does not mean that we have to subscribe to the respective foreign or international courts' view; it simply means that we look at what others do. And sometimes we realise that their ideas are useful to us.

We received a questionnaire prepared by the organisers of the conference.[2] It is fantastic; and yet it is very difficult to answer for a sitting justice. First, it requires considerable research for which we do not have the time or

* This is a slightly redacted version of an oral presentation given at the academic conference on transnational judicial dialogue on human rights in Oslo, 22–23 June 2013. These views are strictly personal and do not necessarily reflect those of the German Federal Constitutional Court.

1 Report on practice by Lord Carnwath in this volume (Section 8.1).

2 See Annex 1 to this book.

resources. Second, it would also require reporting from our deliberations, which are secret.[3] This makes it even more problematic to write a formal response to the questions posed in the questionnaire.[4] What this contribution gives, instead, are informal responses. These may be just as good, because these responses may better reflect the thinking behind the practice. This piece is thus not very formal, but it follows a certain structure. I make an attempt to show that the German Federal Constitutional Court's (Federal Constitutional Court or *Bundesverfassungsgericht*) exposure to and engagement with material from international courts, European courts and national courts is quite extensive, and very specific to the court in question and the legal effect on its decisions.[5]

9.2 Deference and Its Limits: The European Court of Justice, the European Court of Human Rights and Other International Legal Bodies

9.2.1 European Law and the European Court of Justice

With regard to the German Federal Constitutional Court's relation to the Court of Justice of the European Union (CJEU), the main topic is the right measure of deference. Article 19 of the Treaty of the European Union (TEU) says that the CJEU is the final arbiter of European law.[6] That does not leave much space for domestic courts to go against the grain of the jurisprudence of the EU Court.

The German Federal Constitutional Court derives the authority of the CJEU from the German Constitution (*Grundgesetz*). EU law and German constitutional law are two interlocking systems. Article 23 of the German Constitution provides that Germany, including the Federal Constitutional Court as its judicial organ, does indeed wish to be part of the construction of the European Union, but under certain conditions, that is, for certain

[3] On the secrecy of deliberations, see sect. 30 para. 2, first sentence BVerfGG (Gesetz über das Bundesverfassungsgericht [Federal Constitutional Court Act]), BGBl I S. 1473 (11 August 1993).

[4] But see the report by the XVIth Congress of the Conference of European Constitutional Courts based on a questionnaire: *The Cooperation of Constitutional Courts in Europe. Current Situation and Perspectives*, Vol I (Wien: Verlag Österreich, 2014) 199–234.

[5] For a more extensive presentation, see P.M. Huber and A. Paulus, 'Cooperation of Constitutional Courts in Europe: The Openness of the German Constitution to International, European, and Comparative Constitutional Law', M. Andenæs and D. Fairgrieve (eds.), *Courts and Comparative Law* (Oxford University Press, 2015) 281–99.

[6] Consolidated Version of Treaty on European Union, Official Journal 326 (26 October 2012).

reasons and with certain limitations.[7] The Federal Constitutional Court is adjudicating those conditions and limitations. Or, to put it more positively, it adjudicates those reasons for engagement. Basically, these reasons are: the maintenance of democracy; the observance of the rule of law and human rights; and finally, subsidiarity and federalism. Not everything should go immediately to Europe and be decided at the European level. We are therefore very keen to ensure that the CJEU also observes the limits of its competences. The CJEU is a court with limited competences for a Union with enumerated powers. In fact, as a Federal Constitutional Court, we are ourselves familiar with the strictures of being limited to interpreting and applying a certain law – in our case, German constitutional law. In principle, the Federal Constitutional Court can deal with other substantive law only insofar as this relates to the *Grundgesetz*. As a rule, as long as it is not of constitutional significance, we accept the rulings of the 'regular' courts regarding the interpretation and application of legislation.

Reference to the CJEU's jurisprudence is acceptance of this jurisprudence, as there is recognition of the precedence of EU law even over constitutional law, but this acceptance has certain limits. These limits have been developed in decade-long jurisprudence of the Federal Constitutional Court. The first relevant judgment setting out one of these limitations is a very famous one: *Solange* (as long as).[8] In fact, the *Solange* approach has more recently been adopted by the ECtHR for its own interaction with the CJEU and European law.[9] It effectively means that the EU needs to have an effective system of protection of human rights. In its *Solange I* decision of 1974, the Federal Constitutional Court reserved the right to review European Community (EC) law for its compatibility with the German Constitution and possibly to reject it *as long as* the European Communities did not offer protection of fundamental rights equivalent to that contained in the German Constitution. Taking into account the

[7] Article 23(1) of the German Constitution reads as follows: '(1) With a view to establishing a united Europe, the Federal Republic of Germany shall participate in the development of the European Union that is committed to democratic, social and federal principles, to the rule of law, and to the principle of subsidiarity, and that guarantees a level of protection of basic rights essentially comparable to that afforded by this Basic Law. To this end the Federation may transfer sovereign powers by a law with the consent of the Bundesrat. …' (official translation available at: www.bundestag.de/blob/284870/ce0d03414872b427e57fccb703634dcd/basic_law-data.pdf).

[8] Federal Constitutional Court, Judgment of 29 May 1974, 2 BvL 52/71 (*Solange I*); and Judgment of 22 October 1986, 2 BvR 197/83 (*Solange II*).

[9] *Bosphorus Hava Yollari Turizm v. Ireland* (Appl. No. 45036/98), Judgment (Grand Chamber), 30 June 2005, ECHR 2005-VI, 107, para. 155.

developments in the European Communities and the jurisprudence of the (then) European Court of Justice (ECJ) concerning fundamental rights, in 1986 the Federal Constitutional Court issued its *Solange II* decision. It noted that the standard of protection of fundamental rights had risen substantially at the European level. The *Bundesverfassungsgericht* therefore held that it would no longer review secondary EC law for its compatibility with the fundamental rights in the German Constitution, *as long as* the ECJ (now CJEU) itself would effectively ensure the effective protection of these rights. Thus, today the Federal Constitutional Court says to anybody who comes to it with a claim that the European Union has violated human rights or fundamental freedom: 'Please show us that this is not only the situation in your individual case; you need to show that there is a systematic failure at the level of the EU.' The Federal Constitutional Court has not quite defined what a 'systematic failure' means. Therefore, it is hard for an applicant to argue this, and this is exactly the point, as to the Court should not interfere with the CJEU's jurisprudence when it is unnecessary to do so. But this works only because the CJEU has developed a scheme of protection of fundamental freedoms and human rights of its own. Nowadays, it administers its own EU Charter of Fundamental Rights (the Charter).[10] Admittedly, our Constitutional Court is sceptical of the CJEU's extensive interpretation of the Charter's scope of application with regard to domestic legislation that does not implement EU law, something that was expressed clearly in a recent judgment.[11]

The second argument that the Federal Constitutional Court relies on when determining the limits of accepting CJEU jurisprudence is the *ultra vires* argument. This applies only if the CJEU went beyond the jurisdiction given to it by the member states of the EU in the European Treaties. In general, the Federal Constitutional Court gives the CJEU much leeway because the TEU says that the CJEU is the final arbiter of the limits of EU competences. But we also have to insist that our own constitutional limits need to be respected. The Federal Constitutional Court would be very reluctant to tell the CJEU that it is in plain error, disrespecting our constitutional limits, and it has never done this so far. Our Constitutional Court would only consider this when the case is a very important one, as the *ultra vires* limitation to accepting CJEU decisions is not about secondary legal details or legal niceties. But we reminded the CJEU of those limits

[10] Charter of Fundamental Rights of the European Union, Official Journal C 326, 26 October 2012.

[11] Federal Constitutional Court, Judgment of 24 April 2013, 1 BvR 1215/07, paras. 88–91.

of acceptance when it recently, in the *Åkerberg Fransson* case, rendered a judgment that could be understood to have provided that the Charter also applies in cases where domestic legislation bears only a scant relationship to European law.[12] This is exactly what was not meant to happen when it was decided to limit the Charter's scope of application to the implementation of EU law.

A third limitation to our acceptance of CJEU jurisprudence relates to the constitutional identity of the Federal Republic of Germany as set out in our *Grundgesetz*. If the CJEU were to interfere with this constitutional identity, the respective judgment could not be implemented. In this context, the Federal Constitutional Court once theoretically pointed to the fact that the introduction of a surveillance state would conflict with our understanding of human dignity, the protection of which is central to the German Constitution, and could thus not be accepted.[13] It is impossible to contract out of the protection of human dignity under the present German Constitution; to do so would require a rewriting of the Constitution. However, the identity argument is in conformity with EU law itself; in fact, article 4(2) TEU explicitly provides that '[t]he Union shall respect the equality of Member States before the Treaties as well as their national identities, inherent in their fundamental structures, political and constitutional, inclusive of regional and local self-government.' However, the two Courts interpret 'constitutional identity' with a slightly different emphasis: the CJEU as an invitation for balancing EU and national powers that are relatively broadly defined,[14] whereas the Federal Constitutional Court, in line with articles 23 and 79(3) of the *Grundgesetz*, as an absolute bar to modifications of core constitutional guarantees.[15] Nevertheless, I submit that these are two sides of the same coin: balancing requires a hard core of respect and an area in which compromises appear possible. I am thus confident that any divergences can be bridged with good will on both

[12] Case C-617/10, *Åklagaren v. Åkerberg Fransson* [2014] ECR I-0000, ECLI:EU:C:2013:105, para. 44.

[13] Federal Constitutional Court, Judgment of 2 March 2010, 1 BvR 256/08, 1 BvR 263/08 and 1 BvR 586/08, para. 215.2.

[14] See, e.g. case C-208/09, *Ilonka Sayn-Wittgenstein v. Landeshauptmann von Wien*, [2010] ECR I-13693, ECLI:EU:C:2010:608, para. 83; and case C-36/02, *Omega Spielhallen- und Automatenaufstellungs-GmbH v. Oberbürgermeisterin der Bundesstadt Bonn*, [2004] ECR I-9609, ECLI:EU:C:2004:614, paras. 23 *et seq.*

[15] Federal Constitutional Court, Order for a Preliminary Ruling of 14 January 2014, 2 BvR 2728/13, 2 BvR 2729/13, 2 BvR 2730/13, 2 BvR 2731/13 and 2 BvE 13/13, para. 29 (Outright Monetary Transactions (OMT)); and Judgment of 30 June 2009, 2 BvE 2/08, 2 BvE 5/08, 2 BvR 1010/08, 2 BvR 1022/08, 2 BvR 1259/08 and 2 BvR 182/09.

sides, and that is exactly the attitude required by both European and most domestic laws.[16]

By way of summary, in theory there are limits to the Federal Constitutional Court's acceptance of CJEU jurisprudence. In practice so far, there has been deference. But deference does not exclude 'dialogue' between the Federal Constitutional Court and the CJEU – rather, deference necessitates such 'dialogue' regarding its exercise, but also its limits. One of the results of the recent interpretation of the CJEU's *Åkerberg Fransson* case was to highlight that an effective dialogue with the CJEU requires clarity from both sides. We should not engage in a *dialogue des sourds* (dialogue of the deaf) as the French say. However, I am glad to report the Federal Constitutional Court so far never has had to disregard a judgment by the CJEU due to the CJEU's non-observance of constitutional limits. To avoid this as far as possible also in future, the Constitutional Court has recently referred the decision on the Outright Monetary Transaction program of the European Central Bank to the CJEU.[17]

9.2.2 *The European Court of Human Rights*

In theory, the European Court of Human Rights (ECtHR) falls into the category of an international court which has jurisdiction to interpret and apply international law, in particular the European Convention on Human Rights (ECHR or the Convention).[18] In general, together with many international treaties, the Convention has direct effect in Germany. However, according to German law, the Convention and its interpretation and application by the ECtHR are still subject to the Constitution to a larger extent than EU law. Nevertheless, in practice and whenever possible, we interpret legislation in accord with international law, including the ECHR and the case law of the ECtHR. Two points are to be made in this context: first, there is a constitutional duty of all courts, including the Federal Constitutional Court, to take the judgments of the ECtHR into account.[19] In exceptional cases when the Federal Constitutional Court sees a need to deviate from the ECtHR's jurisprudence, it has to put forward very strong reasoning. Usually, the *Bundesverfassungsgericht* is reluctant to do this. In practice, it is much easier to apply the ECtHR's case law than to wend the

[16] *Ibid.*, Order for a Preliminary Ruling (OMT), *ibid.*, para. 30.

[17] *Ibid.*

[18] Convention for the Protection of Human Rights and Fundamental Freedoms (4 November 1950) 213 UNTS 222; 312 ETS 5, entered into force 3 September 1953.

[19] Federal Constitutional Court, Judgment of 14 October 2004, 2 BvR 1481/04.

difficult way of finding convincing reasons to deviate from it. The reasons for a digression must be constitutional in nature. This in itself severely limits its deviations from ECtHR jurisprudence.

Second, the Federal Constitutional Court held that ECtHR judgments binding on Germany may still have to be 'translated' into our own practice so that they conform to existing German constitutional doctrine. The Court did this, for instance, with regard to preventive detention of convicted criminals, who, after they have served their time in prison, can be held in preventive detention if they still pose a significant threat to the public.[20] Actually, the Constitutional Court largely understands German constitutional law to be a different legal system from the law of the ECHR. It defines and interprets the domestic legal system in line with the ECHR and the ECtHR's interpretation and application of the Convention as far as possible; however, as with the acceptance of the CJEU's jurisprudence, there are limits to how far the Federal Constitutional Court can go in that regard. In the latter case, it is the task of the German parliament to bring domestic legislation in line with Germany's international commitments within the constitutional limits.

9.2.3 International Legal Bodies

As regards international legal bodies in general, the Federal Constitutional Court makes a distinction between decisions or other sources that are binding within Germany's jurisdiction and non-binding pronouncements. As far as binding pronouncements are concerned, they have a function of providing us with normative guidance in the sphere of competence of the particular international body in question. An example would be the judgments of the International Court of Justice (ICJ) regarding the right to consultation with consular officials under article 36 of the Vienna Convention on Consular Relations.[21] Germany has submitted to the jurisdiction of the ICJ; hence, what the ICJ pronounces gives normative guidance, even in cases not involving Germany, that is, cases that are not legally binding on it.[22]

As for non-binding pronouncement, for example of UN human rights treaty bodies, the Federal Constitutional Court may look at them and cite

[20] Federal Constitutional Court, Judgment of 4 May 2011, 2 BvR 2365/09, 2 BvR 740/10, 2 BvR 2333/08, 2 BvR 1152/10 and 2 BvR 571/10.

[21] *LaGrand Case (Germany v. United States of America)*, ICJ Reports (2001), 466; *Case Concerning Avena and Other Mexican Nationals (Mexico v. United States of America)*, ICJ Reports (2004), 12.

[22] Federal Constitutional Court, Judgment of 5 November 2013, 2 BvR 1579/11.

them, but they are not necessarily regarded as authoritative. In 2013, the Federal Constitutional Court referred to non-binding pronouncements in a case regarding student fees,[23] and in 2012 in a case concerning benefits for asylum seekers.[24]

9.3 Foreign Courts: Reference, Not Deference

Another area of the Federal Constitutional Court's 'dialogue' with foreign and international courts is our engagement with decisions of foreign national courts. Here, there is no deference; rather, mere reference. The Federal Constitutional Court attempts to learn from foreign courts in many areas relating to all sorts of issues. However, it is a cherry-picking exercise in which it selects foreign national courts' jurisprudence on the basis of what can be most useful, such as the practice of courts in Europe and jurisdictions with a democratic and liberal background. It is not suitable to cite courts from dictatorships or other authoritarian systems, because the standards that the Federal Constitutional Court applies are different ones. Citation of foreign judgments is often simply a matter of acknowledging the respective court's 'copyright' to ideas expressed in their judgments. We have to cite them when we apply their ideas.

In addition, the European *Verbund* or community of (constitutional) courts[25] is based on a community characterised by common principles and rights. This association leads to mutual acknowledgement and respect for the quality of the legal work of our colleagues in other European countries. The decisions of our own court are at the same time a contribution to the *Verbund*, to this web of legal concepts and their application to social life. Our court learns, and others may learn from us.

9.4 Conclusion

In the end, when engaging with foreign or international material, constitutional courts must be very careful in distinguishing between the levels of authority of foreign and international judgments. This has become very complicated in the twenty-first century for many of us. Certainly, our

[23] Federal Constitutional Court, Judgment of 8 May 2013, 2498 1 BvL 1/08.

[24] Federal Constitutional Court, Judgment of 18 July 2012, 134 1 BvL 10/10 and 1 BvL 2/11.

[25] See A. Voßkuhle, 'The Cooperation between European Courts: The Verbund of European Courts and Its Legal Toolbox', Court of Justice of the EU (eds.), *The Court of Justice and the Construction of Europe: Analyses and Perspectives on Sixty Years of Case-law* (The Hague: Springer, 2013) 81–99.

national constitutions, be they written or unwritten, are both enabling and limiting constitutional or supreme courts in taking into account the insights of foreign and international courts. But as we are part of the EU, the Council of Europe and the international community by the will of our constitutions, the interaction between our courts leads to mutual learning and the development of common ideas on the meaning of twenty-first-century constitutionalism in Europe and beyond.

10

Judicial Dialogue

The Experience of Italy

RAFFAELE SABATO

10.1 Introduction

This brief contribution is intended to offer some insight into Italian courts' experience with engaging in judicial dialogue.[1] It updates and complements an oral presentation that was given at the conference 'Transnational Judicial Dialogue: Concept, Method, Extent and Effects' in Oslo in 2013.[2] To set the scene, we discuss the role of the several Italian courts engaging in dialogue with each other, and in particular the role of the Supreme Court (Section 10.2). We then examine Italian courts' dialogue with European and international courts (Section 10.3). In Section 10.4, two cases handed down by Italian courts are discussed in detail. The cases are meant to demonstrate Italian courts' engagement in judicial dialogue in their mutual relationships at the internal level, as well as with the Italian legislature and with regional and international courts.

10.2 The Role of Italian Courts in Judicial Dialogue under Italy's Recent Legislation

Judicial dialogue among Italian courts has a long tradition. Due to recent legislation, Italian courts have experienced innovation in their mutual relationships and in the role that different courts play, in a system in which the *Corte Suprema di Cassazione* (Supreme Court or Court of Cassation) is at

[1] It is beyond the scope of this contribution to enter into a detailed discussion of the definition of 'judicial dialogue'. See on this topic the Introduction to this volume (Chapter 1), Section 1.2.1.

[2] In the period of time between the conference and the submission of the article, changes in the legal and institutional framework took place at such a level – see e.g. the delivery of the 2014 Judgment of the Italian Constitutional Court (Italian Constitutional Court, Judgment

the top of the judiciary and a separate *Corte Costituzionale* (Constitutional Court) is in charge of judicial review. As a consequence of reforms, dialogue took on new functional goals.

In Italy's tradition, the only function of the judicial hierarchy was to make appeals possible. In fact, in the Italian system, precedents of the same or higher courts do not bind judges. Although consistently applied sequences of judgments are cited as precedents, they only have persuasive authority. In a period in which Italy had to approach the problem of an enormous volume of cases pending before the courts, among other things because the Supreme Court was not given any discretion in selecting its cases, changes were called for. In 2005, the Italian Parliament conferred on the executive the power to issue secondary legislation to ensure uniformity of application of the law, at least within the civil sector of the Supreme Court, with the aim of discouraging litigation. In 2006, a legislative decree introduced a minimal *stare decisis* concept: if a panel of the Supreme Court wished to overrule precedents of the joint chambers, the panel itself could not do so, but would have to refer the case to the same joint chambers.[3] Although judges of the first and second instances were not, strictly speaking, obliged, in subsequent civil cases, to follow the new *stare decisis* rule, the fact that the Supreme Court was (partially) bound by (some of) its precedents introduced an incentive for a more balanced 'domestic' dialogue. In practice, the civil-sector panels of the Supreme Court were forced to either follow the previous decisions of the joint chambers or issue well-reasoned referrals to the joint chambers to persuade them to overrule their precedent. Indirectly, lower judges were also made aware of the importance of precedents, since further legislation (of 2009)[4] allowed appeals before the Supreme Court for reasons of law only

of 22 October 2014, No. 238/2014) in reaction to the International Court of Justice's (ICJ) *Jurisdictional Immunities of the State (Germany v. Italy: Greece intervening)*, ICJ Reports (2012) 99 discussed *infra* – that a significant updating and revision of the text became necessary.

3 The rule is contained in the text of article 374 of the Italian Code of Civil Procedure, as amended by article 8 of Legislative Decree of 2 February 2006, No. 40, issued on the basis of a law delegating the government to issue such decree, of 14 May 2005, No. 80. Italian Code of Civil Procedure (*Codice di Procedura Civile*), Legislative Decree of 28 October 1940, No. 1443.

4 *Ibid.* Reference is made to the new article 360 *bis* of the Italian Code of Civil Procedure, introduced by article 47 of the Law of 18 June 2009, No. 69. The provision was introduced to 'filter' the numerous civil cases that are traditionally brought before the Supreme Court, under the Italian Constitution which provides for an unlimited access of cases to the Court. Interpretation of article 360 *bis* was first provided by the Joint Civil Chambers of the Supreme Court in a decision of 6 September 2010, No. 19051.

if the appeal could show that the decision was inconsistent with previous case law.

The system was reinforced by further legislative changes in 2012,[5] affecting the dialogue first-instance and second-instance civil judges: appeals against first-instance decisions before second-instance judges (usually the courts of appeal) were to be declared inadmissible if the appeal did not clearly show which part of the first-instance decision was inconsistent with the law. Additionally, appellate judges were given discretion to dismiss appeals that, on the basis of a preliminary review, were not deemed as having a reasonable probability of success.

The legislative innovations of 2009 and 2012 gave a powerful impetus to judicial dialogue among Italian courts. They contributed to enhancing the coherence of Italian judicial decisions and the coordination between courts of different instances. The very fact that many decisions of the courts of appeal and the Supreme Court are based on – and have to quote – precedents today in order to declare appeals inadmissible is, in itself, a strong tool for judicial interaction. It is also a prerequisite for a better judicial dialogue with regional and international courts.

In the criminal sector, judicial interaction has traditionally been encouraged by the Supreme Court which, unlike in the civil sector, has been able to render judgments with shorter delays, containing fewer conflicting interpretations.

As a result of the changes in legislation, the Supreme Court and its documentation service – that is, the sector of the Court composed of judges who select decisions to be indexed and who alert when inconsistent interpretations arise – found their role in judicial dialogue strengthened. As we shall see, another strong and sometimes conflicting protagonist in judicial dialogue with regional and international courts is to be found in the country's Constitutional Court.

10.3 Italian Courts' Dialogue with International and European Courts

Like in many other European countries, over the recent decades important developments in the Italian legal practice are due to the increasing interaction between the domestic judiciary and European and other international

[5] The new provisions were contained in the Decree-Law of 22 June 2012, No. 83, article 54, whereby the legislature sought to improve the efficiency of the system of appeals by establishing further 'filters'.

courts. The Italian Constitutional Court, by way of interpretation of constitutional rules, has set up a dominant role for itself in the governance of this type of dialogue, leaving – at least initially – little space to common judges, including the Supreme Court.

At present, the Constitutional Court has construed different legal frameworks for such dialogue, depending on whether the case in question concerns European Union (EU) law (and, therefore, dialogue between domestic judges and the Court of Justice of the European Union [CJEU] in Luxembourg) or international law (which includes the European Convention of Human Rights [ECHR[6]] and therefore dialogue between domestic judges and international courts such as the European Court of Human Rights [ECtHR] in Strasbourg). In the area of EU law, the Constitutional Court has granted common judges wider possibilities for dialogue.

Until 1984, the Constitutional Court prevented common judges from directly disregarding Italian laws if they conflicted with EU law,[7] requiring judges to refer cases in which such a conflict arose to the Constitutional Court. The Constitutional Court recognised article 11 of the Italian Constitution (the Constitution)[8] as the legal basis for allowing Italy's participation in the European Communities (EC). However, since it also held that direct applicability of European law would unduly interfere with the sovereignty of the Italian Parliament, it considered that application of

[6] Convention for the Protection of Human Rights and Fundamental Freedoms (European Convention on Human Rights, ECHR) (4 November 1950) 213 UNTS 222; 312 ETS 5, entered into force 3 September 1953.

[7] On this aspect, see the essay by M. Cartabia, 'The Italian Constitutional Court and the Relationship between the Italian Legal System and the European Community', A.-M. Slaughter, A. Stone Sweet and J. Weiler (eds.), *The European Court and National Courts: Doctrine and Jurisprudence. Legal Change in its Social Context* (Oxford: Hart Publishing, 1998) 133–46, at 133 *et seq.*

[8] Article 11 of the Italian Constitution states: 'Italy rejects war as an instrument of aggression against the freedom of other peoples and as a means for the settlement of international disputes. Italy agrees, on conditions of equality with other states, to the limitations of sovereignty that may be necessary to a world order ensuring peace and justice among the Nations. Italy promotes and encourages international organisations furthering such ends.' The application of this rule to the European Communities showed creativity on the part of the Constitutional Court, since article 11 had been shaped having in mind the movement toward the creation of the United Nations (see the reference to war), at a moment (1947) in which no prospective European Communities existed. Since limitations of sovereignty were already accepted in the Constitution, the interpretation of the Court linking the EU to article 11 has allowed Italy to ratify the European Treaties by ordinary majorities in Parliament, instead of using the much more complex system of constitutional amendment, also allowing the possibility of a referendum. Constitution of the Italian Republic (*La Costituzione della Repubblica Italiana*) (22 December 1947) Official Gazette No. 298, entered into force 1 January 1948.

incompatible European law was possible only if the same Constitutional Court declared domestic law unconstitutional as a consequence of a violation of article 11, that is, the constitutional provision requiring Italy to abide by European community law. By the end of the 1970s, this doctrine became an evident obstacle to judicial dialogue with the CJEU. In 1978, through the *Simmenthal*[9] decision, the Luxembourg Court ruled that a national court may, on its own motion, refuse to apply any provision of national legislation conflicting with EC law. It held that it was not necessary for the court to request or await the prior setting aside of such provisions by legislative or other constitutional means. Therefore, the Italian Constitutional Court had to overrule its previous decisions. This happened in 1984, by a decision[10] in which the Court recognised that EC law has primacy over Italian law. The question of sovereignty was by-passed by the acceptance of the so-called doctrine of competence, establishing that European law is not hierarchically above national law, but has a sphere of competence into which national law cannot enter – this being an accepted 'limitation' to sovereignty in line with article 11 of the Italian Constitution. This allowed common judges – without involving the Constitutional Court – to decide to apply European law instead of national law. However, the Constitutional Court reserved the final word for itself: should European law breach the basic principles of the Constitution or the fundamental rights of individuals, then the Court itself could declare European law inapplicable, by way of introducing a 'counter-limitation' to the applicability of EU law; it would do so by declaring the Italian legislation ratifying the relevant EU Treaty partially unconstitutional.[11] This safeguard has implications for the extent and purpose of Italian courts' engagement in judicial dialogue with regional and international courts.

[9] Case 106/77, *Amministrazione delle Finanze dello Stato v. Simmenthal S.p.A* [1978] ECR 629; ECLI:EU:C:1978:49.

[10] Italian Constitutional Court, Judgment of 5 June 1984, No. 170/1984. This decision was rendered within the well-known *Granital* litigation.

[11] See as an example of this type of decision the judgment of the Italian Constitutional Court of 22 October 2014, *supra* note 2, para. 4.2. It may be interesting to note that the doctrine of 'counter-limitations' to the 'limitation' of sovereignty contained in article 11 was developed by the Italian Constitutional Court on the grounds that the same article 11 does not allow limitations of sovereignty in every case, but only to achieve peace and justice among nations. Therefore, the Constitutional Court declared to have the power – in its view – to exercise control over the possible aberrant use of the sphere of competence allowed to European institutions, in ways that are inconsistent with the main principles of the Constitution. It is clarified below that 'counter-limitations' are much wider (i.e. not limited to the main principles, but to all rules contained in the Constitution; so called 'enlarged counter-limitations') when rules of the ECHR are at stake.

The framework for judicial dialogue concerning legal principles of the ECHR is, at present, comparable with the one applicable to EC law before 1984: dialogue as a conversation between national judges and the ECtHR, as an international court, therefore suffers from many limitations under the principles set by the Italian Constitutional Court. However, an evolution is evident also in this area.

Traditionally, the ECHR has been treated as any other piece of conventional international law. Under article 10 of the Italian Constitution,[12] as interpreted by the Constitutional Court, national judges could not refuse to apply domestic law, even if this law conflicted with the Convention rules as construed by the ECtHR. Like in the approach to EC law before 1984, national courts could only refer such cases to the Constitutional Court. Since, however, the ECHR was domestically irrelevant (its violations by Italy only raised an issue of international liability of the state), Constitutional Court judges could only have domestic law struck down because of its incompatibility with principles of the Italian Constitution, not of the ECHR. The Constitutional Court then created, in the 1990s, a doctrine according to which constitutional principles are usually consistent with the rights as set out in the Convention.[13] Thus, the Constitutional Court was to serve as a guarantor of an integrated system of protection of human rights based on both texts. As a consequence, formal dialogue was limited in scope to vertical dialogue between domestic judges of common courts (including the Supreme Court) and the Constitutional Court, the former only having the possibility to persuade the latter that constitutional rules had to be read consistently with ECtHR case law.

There was, however, another possibility for domestic judges to enter into a more direct but informal dialogue with the ECtHR, which has been resorted to most often in practice. Without starting a dialogue with the Constitutional Court, the domestic judge could enter into such an informal dialogue with the ECtHR by directly using the Convention as a guideline for the interpretation of domestic law. This was possible when no direct and clear conflict existed.

[12] The text of the first paragraph of article 10 of the Italian Constitution, *supra* note 8, provides that '[t]he Italian legal system conforms to the generally recognised principles of international law.' The Italian Constitutional Court has interpreted this rule in the sense that it automatically transposes customary international law, but not treaties, into Italian law. Therefore, only customary law prevails over domestic legislation.

[13] See for references D. Tega, 'La Cedu e l'ordinamento italiano', M. Cartabia (ed.), *I diritti in azione. Universalità e pluralismo dei diritti fondamentali nelle Corti europee* (Bologna: Il Mulino, 2007) 67–90, at 67 *et seq*.

An innovation occurred in the course of the constitutional reform of 2001: article 117 of the Italian Constitution was reformulated so as to provide that the state and the regions exercise their legislative power 'in compliance with the Constitution and with the constraints deriving from EU legislation and international obligations'. This reform set the stage in 2007 for the Constitutional Court to overrule its previous case law and state that the ECHR is placed in an intermediate position between the Constitution and ordinary domestic law.[14] In the event that judges in common courts found domestic legislation to be incompatible with the Convention, it became possible for these judges to refer the case to the Constitutional Court on the basis of the violation of the Convention, and not, as before, of domestic Constitutional rules to be construed in harmony with the Convention. Now, if the Convention were violated, article 117 of the Constitution would be too. The development of 2007 reinforced the ability of the domestic judge to enter into a formal, albeit indirect, vertical dialogue with the Strasbourg Court. This potential for dialogue was strengthened further by the Constitutional Court's recognition that ECHR provisions had to be read as interpreted by the ECtHR. Before raising an issue before the Constitutional Court, common judges were now explicitly granted the power, insofar as possible, to interpret domestic law in consistency with ECtHR case law.

Despite this opening of dialogue possibilities between Italian common courts and the ECtHR, the Constitutional Court retained most of its role as a key actor: even if article 117 of the Italian Constitution would be violated by domestic law that was contradicting the ECHR, the domestic law in question would not be declared unconstitutional if 'counter-limitations' to the accepted 'limitations' to parliamentary sovereignty were touched upon. Differently from what had been stated with reference to the aforementioned 'counter-limitations' doctrine applicable to the transposition of EU law into Italian law, the Constitutional Court introduced another doctrine applicable to possible inconsistencies between Italian law and the ECHR: the doctrine of 'enlarged counter-limitations'. The previous 'counter-limitations' doctrine allowed declaring parts of the Italian legislation transforming EU law into domestic law unconstitutional with reference to the basic (but not all) principles of the Constitution. Under the new 'enlarged counter limitations' doctrine, however, the Constitutional Court reserved for itself the power

[14] The development took place through two judgments of the Italian Constitutional Court, having almost the same content (and therefore called 'Twin Judgments'). Italian Constitutional Court, Judgments of 24 October 2007, Nos. 348–349/2007.

to verify whether the ECHR, as interpreted by the Strasbourg Court, was consistent with *all* other constitutional values. Only then would it declare the domestic law unconstitutional as a result of a direct violation of the ECHR and an indirect violation of article 117 of the Italian Constitution.

The ECHR's ranking halfway between ordinary statutes and constitutional rules became an incentive for increased constitutional review of laws. Italian judges started to raise issues disclosing potential conflicts between domestic legislation and the ECHR as indirect violations of the Constitution. At the same time, they started to extend the dialogue technique of consistent interpretation developed in regard to EU law to the ECHR, so as to avoid referral of cases to the Constitutional Court. In addition, on the basis of the Lisbon Treaty provision on the accession of the EU to the ECHR,[15] some Italian judges suggested (unsuccessfully) that the technique of directly disregarding domestic law that violates EU law could now be applied to the ECHR as well without lower judges having to involve the Constitutional Court.[16] The Constitutional Court, however, maintained its position on the difference of EU law and ECHR law, and, in a decision of 2011,[17] made it even stricter. In this decision it stated that, even after the Lisbon Treaty entered into force, directly disregarding domestic law violating the ECHR without involvement of the Constitutional Court itself was precluded to common judges.

More recently, based on a decision of March 2015,[18] the impact of which is too early to assess, it even seems that the Constitutional Court now wishes to go back to the situation before 2007. More specifically, while it reaffirmed common judges' general obligation to interpret Italian law consistently in light of the ECHR and ECtHR case law, it further stated that,

[15] Article 6(2) TEU as introduced by the Lisbon Treaty. See also article 59 (2) ('the European Union may accede to this Convention, as amended by Protocol No. 14 to the ECHR which entered into force on 1 June 2010'). Treaty of Lisbon amending the Treaty on European Union and the Treaty Establishing the European Community (13 December 2007), Official Journal C 306 (17 December 2007), entered into force 1 December 2009.

[16] See for references the Judgment of the Italian Constitutional Court of 11 March 2011, No. 80/2011.

[17] *Ibid.* On this decision, concerning the interpretation technique suggested by the judges mentioned in the text, and on the attempts of Italian judges to use, with a similar technique, the Charter of Fundamental Rights of the European Union as a 'bridge' to the direct application of the ECHR, see G. Tiberi, S. Ninatti and A. Osti, 'The Legal Importance and Implementation of the Charter of Fundamental Rights in Italy', G. Palmisano (ed.), *Making the Charter of Fundamental Rights a Living Instrument* (Leiden: Brill, 2015) 276–313, at 277 *et seq.*

[18] Italian Constitutional Court, Judgment of 26 March 2015, No. 49/2015. The decision is closely linked to the ECtHR judgment *Varvara v. Italy* (Appl. No. 17475/09), Judgment (Chamber), 29 October 2013, not reported.

when doing so, common judges should nonetheless give priority to a reading of domestic law that is in accordance with the Constitution, which is 'axiologically dominant' over the ECHR. Last, the Italian Constitutional Court declared that common judges are bound by Strasbourg case law only in a limited number of circumstances.[19] Only in these instances should they refer cases to the Constitutional Court for this Court to verify whether the obligation to conform to article 117 of the Italian Constitution or to 'counter-limitations' prevails over ECHR-consistent interpretation.

To conclude this section, we can observe that with this decision new constraints on dialogue between Italian common courts (including the Supreme Court) and the ECtHR have appeared. It will only be possible to assess their extent at a later stage. What seems certain is that common judges are no longer encouraged to creatively raise issues before the Constitutional Court by taking inspiration from ECtHR case law.

10.4 Two Examples of Judicial Dialogue in Italian Courts

Choosing examples from the experience of a country in which judicial dialogue is a complex reality entails an unavoidable degree of arbitrariness. However, examples are the best way to clarify characteristics of Italian courts' engagement in judicial dialogue with various national, regional and international counterparts. Examples also show the ways in which the judiciary – both at the domestic and at the international levels – reacts to action or inaction of its counterparts. Of the two examples chosen, the first relates to the vertical relationships of Italian courts with European Courts, as well as the horizontal relationship between the latter (subsection 10.4.1), whereas the second example concerns Italian courts' engagement in dialogue with the International Court of Justice (ICJ) and foreign domestic courts on an issue of customary international law (subsection 10.4.2). In addition, the question about the role of the Italian legislature in this dialogue appears in both examples.

10.4.1 The Agrati-Scattolon Cases

The so-called *Agrati-Scattolon* cases can serve as an example of a complex judicial dialogue in the area of civil law. The dialogue involved the Italian

[19] Such cases are cases in which (a) the ECtHR has ruled on the specific case pending before them; (b) the case before them concerns an area in which Strasbourg case law is settled; and (c) in areas where a pilot judgment decision is involved. The concept of 'settled' case law of the Strasbourg Court is debatable.

legislature and judges, including the Constitutional Court, and both the ECtHR and CJEU.

In the framework of a nationwide reform, an Italian law of 1999[20] provided that some auxiliary school staff, who had been employed by local authorities, were allowed to ask for the transfer of their work relationship to the central state. The law stated that the transfer involved recognition of previous service at the municipal level for legal and financial purposes. A ministerial decree,[21] based on a trade union agreement, applied the provision of the 1999 law by establishing that the amount of compensation previously acquired in the service with local authorities had to be maintained in the new employment relationship with the state. This gave rise to legal actions brought by a number of employees, including Ms Agrati. They claimed that they should also have their seniority recognised in terms of years served in local administrations, and that therefore their pay should not only be increased to the level previously enjoyed, but they should be supplemented with the seniority bonuses earned by other state employees of the same level of seniority (who, however, had a lower basic pay). The transferred employees further contested that the trade union agreement and the ministerial decree could not derogate from the law adopted in 1999. According to estimates, 80,000–90,000 employees had been transferred. Accepting their claims would cost the Italian state about 600 million Euros, with relevant pay increases for the transferred personnel, who, as an effect of the addition of their original pay and the claimed raise, would earn more than their fellow state employees who had served for the same amount of time. As a consequence, in 2005 the Italian Parliament passed an interpretative law,[22] which reiterated the content of the ministerial decree.

The subsequent judicial dialogue on this topic was initiated by domestic judges, who referred the interpretative law to the Italian Constitutional Court. By a decision of 2007, the Court[23] held that the law of 2005 did not

[20] Law No. 124 of 3 May 1999, article 8(2).

[21] Italian Ministerial Decree of 5 April 2001, Official Gazette 13 April 2001, No. 87.

[22] Article 1(218) of Law No. 266 (2006 Finance Act) of 23 December 2005, concerning the annual and multiannual budget of the state, established that article 8(2) of Law No. 124 of 1999 had 'to be interpreted as meaning that the school auxiliary personnel previously employed with local authorities and transferred to the state shall be integrated in the professional chart of the state in the corresponding positions established on the basis of the full recognition of the remuneration earned at the time of the transfer'.

[23] Italian Constitutional Court, Judgment of 18 June 2007, No. 234/2007. This judgment was issued before the two judgments (the so called 'Twin Judgments'), *supra* note 14, allowing constitutional review of ECHR violations.

violate any constitutional principle. The Italian Court of Cassation entered into the dialogue in 2008: with a first decision,[24] it shared the view of the Constitutional Court and did not raise any new issue. At a later stage, however, the Court of Cassation[25] decided to refer new questions to the Constitutional Court, in particular asking whether the law of 2005 complied with article 117(1) of the Italian Constitution, read in conjunction with article 6 of the ECHR.[26]

The decision of 2009,[27] with which the Constitutional Court entered the formal dialogue initiated by the Court of Cassation, is a landmark decision. The Constitutional Court held again that the law of 2005 did not undermine principles of the Constitution or the ECHR. The 2005 interpretative law established only one of the possible meanings of the interpreted law (of 1999), and consequently, no unfavourable modification of an acquired right had occurred. For this reason, the interpretative law was also coherent with ECtHR case law on article 6 of the ECHR, concerning admissibility of retroactive legislation. By adopting the (retroactive) interpretative law, the legislature had not intended to affect the outcome of pending litigation, but rather wanted to reorganise labour relationships in the public sector effectively. The Court also stated that the specific case offered an example in which, in accordance with several decisions of the ECtHR, states were allowed to legislate retroactively in exceptional circumstances. It found that in this particular occurrence, an overriding reason of 'public utility' or 'general interest' existed: the need to ensure that all employees at the same seniority levels fulfilling similar tasks were treated equally by applying one consistent system of pay increase, in spite of the fact that employees' original statuses differed.

Being unsuccessful in domestic proceedings because of the interpretative law, Ms Agrati and other employees complained before the ECtHR, which subsequently entered the dialogue on the issues in question. In a judgment of 2011,[28] the ECtHR rather surprisingly contradicted the Italian Constitutional Court and ruled that article 6 of ECHR had been violated because there was no reason of public utility or general interest justifying

[24] Court of Cassation, Judgment of 16 January 2008, No. 677/2008.

[25] Court of Cassation, Order of 4 September 2008, No. 400/2008.

[26] For this dialogue technique, based on the joint violation of a constitutional provision and the ECHR, see *supra* note 19.

[27] Italian Constitutional Court, Judgment of 16 November 2009, No. 311/2009.

[28] *Agrati and Others v. Italy* (Appl. Nos. 43549/08, 6107/09 and 5087/09), Judgment (Chamber), 7 June 2011, not reported. Italy's request to take the case to the Grand Chamber, because of the serious inconsistency with previous case law of the same ECHR, was rejected.

the intervention of the legislature in pending cases. The text of the decision was relatively short and did not examine all the reasons given by the Italian Constitutional Court.

In the meantime, upon application of Ms Scattolon, the Tribunal of Venice had brought forward many of the grounds on which the ECtHR judgment *Agrati and Others v. Italy* was later to be based. By an order of 2010,[29] the Venice Tribunal issued a preliminary reference order to obtain an immediately applicable decision of the CJEU, since ECtHR decisions were only binding on the state at the international level and thus were of little immediate use for the employees. The CJEU thus entered the dialogue. The Venice judge asked whether EU Directive 77/187 was applicable to the transfer of public school personnel.[30] The Venice judge also raised an additional question, modelled on the issues that had been examined by the Italian Constitutional Court and that were under scrutiny by the ECtHR. In a landmark decision of 2011,[31] the Luxembourg Court held that domestic legislation, read in the light of the EU law, must ensure that the transition of an employment relationship from one branch in the public administration to the other does not result in less favourable conditions for the employee. It further held that it was for the national court to verify whether the applicant was affected by a loss of salary. On the one hand, the CJEU thus referred only to loss of salary as being incompatible with EU law. On the other hand, it ruled that it was unnecessary to deal with the issues related to the interpretative legislation. Therefore the Luxembourg judges showed their clear-cut view: while compensations must not be jeopardised by the transfer, workers should not take advantage of an obscure provision of the law in order to have compensations unduly increased. As a consequence of the dialogue between the Venice Tribunal and the CJEU, it is undisputed in Italy today that, in order to decide individual cases under the *Agrati-Scattolon* sequence of precedents, it is necessary to determine whether there was a substantial reduction in salary.

The *Agrati-Scattolon* example shows the difficulties that are inherent in judicial dialogue, especially when technical concepts (seniority, bonuses,

29 Tribunal of Venice, order of 26 February 2010, referred to in case C-108/10, *Ivana Scattolon/ Ministero dell'Università e della Ricerca* [2011] ECR I-7491; ECLI:EU:C:2011:542.

30 Council Directive 77/187/EEC of 14 February 1977 on the approximation of the laws of the Member States relating to the safeguarding of employees' rights in the event of transfers of undertakings, businesses or parts of businesses, OJ 1977 No. L061, 5 March 1977.

31 See case C-108/10, *supra* note 29. See also the discussion of this judgment by R. Cosio, 'Il difficile dialogo tra le Alte Corti: il caso Scattolon', *Massimario di giurisprudenza del lavoro* 4:20 (2012) 103–16, at 114–16; F. Gea, 'Transfert d'entreprise entre personnes morales de droit public et ancienneté des salariés transférés', *Revue de droit du travail*, 12 (2011) 701–04.

salary loss) are involved and judges of different countries are familiar with different pay systems. In addition, this example shows how the dialogue can extend to the legislatures: because of an initial interpretation of the 1999 law by the courts in favour of the applicants, retroactive legislation had to be passed. This raised issues on which an extensive multi-level judicial dialogue took place.

As to the contrast between the decisions of the Constitutional Court and the ECtHR, according to Italian observers, if the latter had more accurately considered the domestic case law and the national technicalities of pay systems, it would not have found a violation of article 6 ECHR in *Agrati and Others v. Italy.* Giving domestic authorities a wider margin of appreciation in this case could have led the ECtHR to recognise the general interest on which retroactive legislation was based: to prevent a poorly drafted and obscure piece of legislation from allowing transferred workers to obtain unjustified pay increases. However, one can question whether the Italian Constitutional Court had been genuinely open to dialogue with the ECtHR in its decision of 2009. The Italian Constitutional Court did not follow the relatively strict existing ECtHR case law on the prohibition to introduce retroactive legislation, although it referred to the relevant precedents. Therefore, the Strasbourg judges – unfamiliar with the pay systems of Italy – were reasonably suspicious as to whether a reference to 'public interest' could justify the adoption of retroactive interpretative legislation.

Finally, the ECtHR's judgment was narrowly based only on the formal reinforcement of the ban on retroactive legislation. This distanced the judgment from the complex facts of the cases. The approach of the ECtHR enabled the CJEU to play the role of protagonist in the dialogue, taking advantage also of its rulings' direct applicability in Italian law. The CJEU was more successful in basing its decision on a clearer vision of the interests at stake. This directed the subsequent judicial dialogue to a strengthened Rome-Luxembourg relationship. Italian judges are no longer considering whether the ECtHR's *Agrati* judgment should be applied, since the CJEU's *Scattolon* decision is taking precedence.[32]

10.4.2 The Case of Jurisdictional Immunities of States

A second example showing the degree of complexity of judicial dialogue in which Italian courts are involved can be drawn from a case that arose in a

[32] The Judgments of the Court of Cassation (of 12 October 2011, No. 20980/2011 and of 14 October 2011, No. 21282/2011), issued right after the CJEU had decided the *Scattolon* case,

context that is wider than the European one, as it concerns general customary international law. At the same time, this example involves international legal standards (and judges) and their relationship to domestic law (and judges) not only of one country but of different countries. In the so-called *Jurisdictional Immunities of the State* judgment, decided by the ICJ, an action was brought by Germany against Italy, with Greece intervening.[33] The dispute arose because of Italian court decisions on the content of a rule of non-written customary *ius gentium*, which is subject to continuous change.

The case, and therefore the judicial dialogue on the issue, began with several Italian victims of Nazi-era war crimes seeking justice before Italian courts against Germany as the international successor of the Nazi regime, after they had exhausted every other remedy. One of the victims, Mr Ferrini, had raised his claim before lower Italian courts where it had been dismissed, based on the recognition that Germany was entitled to state immunity under customary international law. However, in a landmark decision of 2004,[34] the Italian Court of Cassation unexpectedly came to the conclusion that the principle of state immunity under international law was not operational when international crimes are involved. In their subsequent judgments, the lower courts of first and second instance thus awarded compensation to Mr Ferrini.

In its reasoning the Italian Court of Cassation gave its view on the content of the principle of state immunity under modern customary law. Arguments included consideration of newly formed *ius cogens* rules, specifically rules on international crimes which, in the Court's opinion, prevailed over the principle of state immunity. The Court also drew an analogy between customary rules on state immunity and the rules on functional immunity of state officials, the latter not being unlimited either. The Court concluded that the principles of sovereign equality of states, on which immunity was based, and the protection of inviolable human rights had to be balanced. The *Ferrini* reasoning was later reaffirmed in several other judgments of the Italian Court of Cassation, in both civil and criminal cases related to war crimes which had been committed in Italy.[35]

supra note 29, followed the CJEU rather than of the Strasbourg judgment. The reason for this was – *inter alia* – that the latter was not final at the time. The later Judgment of the Court of Cassation of 18 July 2012, No. 12357/2012, argued that it was necessary to follow the CJEU's *Scattolon* judgment, even if the ECtHR's *Agrati* judgment, *supra* note 28, had now become final. The Court of Cassation observed that many of the assumptions on which the ECtHR had based its arguments were ill founded.

[33] ICJ, *Jurisdictional Immunities of the State, supra* note 2.

[34] Court of Cassation, Judgment of 11 March 2004, No. 5044/2004.

[35] The most famous cases before the Italian Court of Cassation are those of 29 May 2008, No. 14201/2008 (*Germany v. Mantelli*) and of 21 October 2008, No. 1072/2008 (*Milde v. Italy*).

Furthermore, victims of a massacre by Nazi troops in Greece in 1944 had obtained a ruling against Germany from the Greek Court of Cassation,[36] which Greek ministries and the German judiciary refused to enforce because of German state immunity. However, local courts in Italy declared the judgment enforceable in view of the *Ferrini* precedent, and these decisions were upheld by the Italian Court of Cassation.[37] A villa in Italy owned by a German governmental entity was to be subjected to a legal charge in favour of the Greek plaintiffs. The proceedings were, however, stayed since in the meantime Germany had instituted proceedings against Italy before the ICJ, alleging that Italy had violated its obligation to respect the immunity enjoyed by Germany under international law.

In the case before the ICJ in The Hague, the Italian government was thus called to argue in favour of the view that its judiciary had taken in assessing the content of contemporary customary international law on state immunities. This view had been formed *inter alia* through the Greek and Italian courts' judicial dialogue. Not surprisingly, Germany defended the traditional view on state immunities, and argued in addition that international agreements on reparations had been adopted and implemented which waived the reparation claims of the victims involved in the cases at hand. The Greek government took a prudent standing, underlining that the judgment of the ICJ would have effect also in the Greek legal system.

In 2012, the ICJ held that Italy had violated its obligation to respect the immunity enjoyed by Germany under international law,[38] which was subject to no exceptions even when war crimes were involved. Therefore, state immunity was absolute and could not be balanced against other principles of public international law. As a further consequence, Italy was obliged to annul the decisions of its courts, by means of its own choosing. The enforcement of the Greek judgment in Italy also had to be denied due to Germany's state immunity.

It was then for the Italian legislature to act in a legal situation created by judicial dialogue between Italian, Greek, and German courts as well as the

The judgment of the ICJ cited *supra* note 2 contains a more complete list of cases before Italian courts at the time the ICJ proceedings were initiated.

[36] *Hellenic Areios Pagos, Prefecture of Voiotia v. Federal Republic of Germany*, Judgment of 4 May 2000, No. 11/2000 (Greece, Court of Cassation). The decision is referred to as the *Distomo massacre* case as it concerned a massacre by Nazi troops in the village of Distomo in 1944.

[37] Italian Court of Cassation, Judgment of 20 May 2011, No. 11163/2011.

[38] ICJ, *Jurisdictional Immunities of the State*, *supra* note 2.

ICJ. Through the adoption of a special law in 2013,[39] the Italian parliament expressly denied Italian courts' jurisdiction over cases referred to in the ICJ judgment, including pending proceedings before Italian courts. It also introduced a remedy to remove effects of earlier decisions of Italian courts in the matter that were covered by the *res iudicata* principle.

But the dialogue within the Italian judiciary went on. The Tribunal of Florence, dealing with a case of victims of war crimes, referred new arguments to the Italian Constitutional Court. It questioned the constitutionality of the obligation of the Italian courts to abide by the decision of the ICJ of 3 February 2012 – an obligation flowing from the domestic law of 1957 implementing the Charter of the United Nations,[40] as well as by the special law of 2013. In particular, the Tribunal of Florence argued that without providing any other form of judicial redress for violations of fundamental rights, the law was contrary to the basic principle of judicial protection of fundamental rights guaranteed by the Italian Constitution in articles 2 and 24.

In a historical decision of 2014[41] the Italian Constitutional Court activated its 'counter-limitation' doctrine,[42] and declared the domestic law implementing the Charter of the United Nations – to the limited extent in which it obliged Italian courts to adapt the Italian system to the ICJ decision of 2012 – contrary to articles 2 and 24 of the Constitution. According to the Constitutional Court, foreign states' immunity from jurisdiction cannot be justified when the act to be exempted from liability is a war crime or a crime against humanity, detrimental to the inviolable rights of the person, the protection of which is guaranteed by one of the overriding principles of the Italian Constitution. The Constitutional Court found it unnecessary to determine whether customary international law granted state immunity for war crimes and crimes against humanity. The Court, indeed, recognised that the rule existed in the international sphere because the ICJ deemed it so in its judgment. However, since this rule was conflicting with basic principles of the Italian legal system, article 10 of the Italian

[39] Law No. 5 of 14 January 2013, no. 24, entered into force 30 January 2013, containing rules for the adaptation of the domestic law to the UN Convention on Jurisdictional Immunities of States and their Property (2 December 2004) UN Doc. A/RES/59/38, not yet in force.

[40] Article 1 of Law No. 848 of 17 August 1957 (Implementation of the Charter of the United Nations).

[41] Italian Constitutional Court, Judgment of 22 October 2014, No. 238/2014. The Court's discussion was presided over and the decision drafted by the Court's president, the international and European law professor Giuseppe Tesauro.

[42] See *supra* note 18.

Constitution was not operational in transposing it into the domestic sphere. It recalled that the fundamental principles of the Italian constitutional order and of inalienable human rights constituted a limit to the reception of generally recognised international rules, to which the Italian legal order otherwise conforms ('counter-limitation').

This second example of horizontal and vertical judicial dialogue of Italian courts is interesting as it shows the need to abandon the quest to achieve uniformity through judicial dialogue when fundamental values enshrined in domestic law conflict with external obligations.[43] The *Jurisdictional Immunities* decision of the Italian Constitutional Court is therefore comparable to the *Solange II*[44] decision of the German Constitutional Court or to some decisions of the United Kingdom Supreme Court, clarifying the extent to which domestic courts should recognise international obligations in domestic law when they allegedly conflict with fundamental rights protected in domestic law.[45] It should be noted that such well-reasoned 'rebellions' to uniformity and consistency on the basis of fundamental values enshrined in domestic law or on well-established, reasonable internal processes can be beneficial for the development of international law and jurisprudence of international and regional courts in the future.

In the *Jurisdictional Immunities* decision, the Constitutional Court of Italy takes the lead in this direction. The judgment clearly refers to the 'old times' (the beginning of the 20th century) when the customary rule on state immunity from domestic jurisdiction of other states did not distinguish between *acta iure imperii* and *acta iure gestionis*. It then highlights that Italian (and Belgian) judges - some national pride is implied in the Court's language - started to advocate such a distinction, expressing the

[43] On this see also the commentary, by P. De Sena, 'The Judgment of the Italian Constitutional Court on State Immunity in Cases of Serious Violations of Human Rights or Humanitarian Law: A Tentative Analysis under International Law' *Questions of Int'l L.* (2014) 17–31, available at www.qil-qdi.org.

[44] Federal Constitutional Court (BVerfG, Germany), Judgment of 22 October 1986, 2 BvR 197/83 (*Solange II*). For a discussion of this case, see also the report on practice by Justice A. Paulus in this volume (Chapter 9).

[45] E.g. UK Supreme Court, *Manchester City Council v. Pinnock* [2010] UKSC 45, para.48; and *R v. Horncastle* [2009] UKSC 14, in which the UK Supreme Court convinced the Grand Chamber of the ECtHR to review some aspects of the judgment *Al-Khawaja and Tahery v. the United Kingdom* that had been handed down by the Fourth Section (*Al-Khawaja and Tahery v. the United Kingdom* (Appl. Nos. 26766/05 and 22228/06), Judgment (Grand Chamber), 15 December 2011, ECHR 2011-VI, 191). For a detailed discussion of the interaction between the UK Supreme Court and the ECtHR in this case, see the report on practice by Judge Lopez-Guerra in this volume (Chapter 13).

view that customary law had evolved so as to recognise immunity only for *acta iure imperii*.

The lesson to be learned, therefore, lies in the fact that judicial dialogue – when it does not result in uniformity – nonetheless contributes to the development of the law, especially international customary law based on *opinio iuris*. At some point, there must be somebody – today usually a judge – starting to express such an *opinio*. Others may follow. To paraphrase the words of the Italian Constitutional Court in its decision on *Jurisdictional Immunities*, judicial dialogue fulfils an important purpose even if it does not lead to uniformity. It may have 'the effect of producing a further [development] of the scope of a rule, with an impact in the domestic legal system. At the same time, it can also contribute to a desirable evolution of international law, which is urged by many.'[46]

[46] See *supra* note 41, para. 3.3 of the reasoning (translation by author).

PART II

Judicial Dialogue in the European Court of Human Rights

11

The ECtHR's Engagement with German and Russian Courts' Decisions

Encouraging Effective Cooperation to Secure ECHR Rights

AMREI MÜLLER

11.1 Introduction

The system for the protection of the European Convention on Human Rights (ECHR or the Convention) has often been described as a 'cooperative system' between domestic courts (and other domestic authorities) on the one hand and the European Court of Human Rights (ECtHR or the Court) on the other.[1] States have the primary obligation to 'secure' the rights of the Convention to 'everyone within their jurisdiction',[2] *inter alia* through their courts;[3] while the ECtHR has a subsidiary but complementary responsibility to 'ensure the observance of the engagements undertaken by the High Contracting Parties in the Convention and the Protocols thereto'.[4] The ECtHR shares the task with domestic courts to not only protect the rights of the ECHR, but to also 'elucidate ... and *develop* the rules instituted by the Convention'[5] for ensuring the effective and up-do-date

[1] J. Meyer-Ladewig, *Europäische Menschenrechtskonvention – Handkommentar*, 3rd ed. (Baden-Baden: Nomos, 2011) at 30; D. Harris, M. O'Boyle and C. Warbrick, *The Law of the European Convention on Human Rights*, 3rd ed. (Oxford University Press, 2014) at 764; A. Voßkuhle, 'Multilevel Cooperation of the European Constitutional Courts: Der Europäische Verfassungsgerichtsverbund', *European Constitutional Rev.* 6:2 (2010) 175–198.

[2] Article 1 ECHR; and, among many, *Z. and Others v. the United Kingdom* (Appl. No. 29392/95) Judgment (Grand Chamber), 10 May 2001, ECHR 2001-V, 1, para.103.

[3] Articles 13 and 35(1) ECHR.

[4] Article 19 ECHR.

[5] See e.g. *Ireland v. the United Kingdom* (Appl. No. 5310/71), Judgment (Plenary), 18 January 1978, Series A, Vol. 25, para. 154; *Guzzardi v. Italy* (Appl. No. 7367/76), Judgment (Plenary), 6 November 1980, Series A, Vol. 39, para. 86; *Karner v. Austria* (Appl. No. 40016/98), Judgment (Chamber), 24 July 2003, ECHR 2003-IX, 199, para. 26; and *Konstantin Markin v. Russia* (Appl. No. 30078/06), Judgment (Grand Chamber), 22 March 2012, ECHR 2012-III, 77 (extracts), para. 89 (emphasis added).

rule of (European human rights) law in all member states of the Council of Europe (CoE).[6]

In the 'cooperative system' for the protection of ECHR rights in a constantly changing environment, judicial dialogue in the widest sense between the ECtHR and domestic courts – that is, the ECtHR engaging with and relating to decisions of domestic courts, and domestic courts engaging with and relating to ECtHR jurisprudence in their respective decisions[7] – is a built-in feature at all stages of the individual complaints procedure under the ECHR: at the admissibility stage regarding the interpretation of the exhaustion of the domestic remedies rule;[8] at the merits stage regarding the up-to-date interpretation and effective application of the substantive provisions of the ECHR;[9] and at the implementation stage regarding the execution of ECtHR judgments.[10]

This chapter analyses some aspects of this built-in dialogue feature in the 'cooperative system' at the merits stage[11] of the individual complaints procedure. It asks whether, and if so, how, the ECtHR uses this built-in dialogue feature as a tool to achieve the main purpose of strengthening the collaborative nature of the Convention system, in particular the

[6] The Court made this role of domestic courts clear in *Demir and Baykara v. Turkey* (Appl. No. 34503/97), Judgment (Grand Chamber), 12 November 2008, ECHR 2008-V, 395, para. 86 (emphasis added); and *Kronfeldner v. Germany* (Appl. No. 21906/09), Judgment (Chamber), 19 January 2012, not reported, para. 59; see also E. Bjørge, 'National Supreme Courts and the Development of ECHR Rights', *Int'l J. of Constitutional L.* 9:1 (2011) 5–31, at 9–13; and the speeches by the former and current ECtHR presidents, Sir Nicolas Bratza and Dean Spielmann: Speech by Sir Nicolas Bratza at the High Level Conference on the Future of the Court, Brighton, 20 April 2012, available at www.echr.coe.int/Documents/Speech_20120420_Bratza_Brighton_ENG.pdf, at 3–5; Opening Speech of President Dean Spielmann at the Solemn Hearing of the European Court of Human Rights on the Occasion of the Opening of the Judicial Year, January 2014, available at www.echr.coe.int/Documents/Dialogue_2014_ENG.pdf, at 32.

[7] See also the definition of 'judicial dialogue' set out in the Introduction to this volume (Chapter 1), Section 1.2.1.

[8] In particular the interpretation of article 35(1) ECHR.

[9] In particular the interpretation and application of the articles set out in section I ECHR.

[10] In particular the interpretation of article 46(3)-(5) ECHR.

[11] The decision for this focus should not obscure the fact that dialogue between the ECtHR and domestic courts is also present concerning the interpretation of article 35(1) ECHR and concerning the determination of relevant measures for redress once the Court has found a violation of the ECHR in line with article 46 ECHR. Such dialogue can also contribute to the more effective implementation of the ECHR in line with domestic courts' primary obligations, e.g. through establishing more effective remedies at the domestic level in line with article 35(1) ECHR. Due to space constraints, these interesting questions cannot, however, be covered here.

strengthening of domestic courts' role as the primary actors in this system, which, in turn, will give the ECtHR the space to take on a truly subsidiary role.[12]

Against this background, what *particular* conduct of domestic courts can we expect the ECtHR to encourage through its dialogue with these courts? Expectations can be deduced from and formulated based on the two factors that describe the Court's subsidiary role in securing the rights of the Convention, supported by relevant Articles of the Convention.[13] The first factor is the extent to which domestic courts and other authorities protect the rights of the Convention, which influences the strictness with which the ECtHR chooses to review the conduct of domestic authorities in a particular case (subsidiary role by discretion).[14] The more actively domestic courts and other national authorities enforce and engage with the Convention,[15] the more subsidiary the Court's supervisory role can be. This is in line with the logic of subsidiarity that requires the higher level to act if the lower level is unable or unwilling to effectively fulfil the lower and higher level entities' common task.[16] The second factor that determines the Court's subsidiary role is related to its institutional position as a regional human rights court (subsidiary role by necessity).[17] This is, for example, the case in relation to the ECtHR's fact-finding capacities, in relation to its ability to review national courts' decisions concerning the lawfulness

[12] In the literature, such strengthening of the implementation of the Convention at the domestic level by the ECtHR has also been analysed by J. Christoffersen, *Fair Balance: Proportionality, Subsidiarity and Primarity in the European Convention on Human Rights* (Leiden: Martinus Nijhoff, 2009); and L. Helfer, 'Redesigning the European Court of Human Rights: Embeddedness as a Deep Structural Principle of the European Human Rights Regime', *European Journal of International Law* 19:1 (2008) 125–59. This chapter focuses on the role of dialogue between the ECtHR and domestic courts in this process.

[13] This builds on the analysis of Christoffersen, Fair Balance, *supra* note 12, in particular chapter 3.

[14] *Ibid.*, at 230 *et seq.*; and E. Brems and L. Lavrysen, 'Procedural Justice in Human Rights Adjudication', *Human Rights Quarterly* 35:1 (2013) 176–200, at 195 *et seq.* It should be noted in this context that the conduct of domestic courts is only one factor that might influence the Court's choice of what standard of review it applies. See also the discussion in Section 11.3.

[15] In line with articles 1, 13, 35(1), 46(1) and 52 ECHR.

[16] For the general definition of the principle of subsidiarity, including an analysis of its historical origin, see P. Carozza, 'Subsidiarity as a Structural Principle of International Human Rights Law', *American Journal of International Law* 79:1 (2003) 38–79, at 41 *et seq.*; and H. Petzold, 'The Convention and the Principle of Subsidiarity', R. Macdonald, F. Matscher and H. Petzold (eds.), *The European System for the Protection of Human Rights* (Dordrecht: Martinus Nijhoff, 1993) 41–62.

[17] Christoffersen, Fair Balance, *supra* note 12, at 276 *et seq.*

of a certain measure under *domestic* law, as well as in relation to gaining a full understanding of local circumstances and historical particularities in a specific country. Thus, concerning these issues the ECtHR will necessarily take on a subsidiary role, and is to a large extent dependent on the work of domestic courts (and other domestic authorities) when it decides on a particular case.

Based on these two factors that determine the Court's subsidiary role, it can first be expected that through its dialogue with domestic courts, the Court encourages domestic courts to effectively do what it cannot do itself due to its position as a regional human rights court. Second, it can be anticipated that the ECtHR, through its engagement with the national courts' decisions, will aim to strengthen domestic courts' capacities to remedy alleged violations of the ECHR at the domestic level as effectively as possible. This can, *inter alia*, be done by requiring (or at least encouraging) national judicial review based on the substance of the Convention, and by requiring (or at least encouraging) domestic courts to follow certain procedures in their decisions on the substance of Convention rights that make it more likely that this substance is protected effectively. And third, it can be expected that the Court encourages domestic courts to take part in 'elucidate[ing] … and develop[ing] the rules instituted by the Convention'[18] through their 'evolutive' interpretation of the ECHR and/or of parallel domestic (constitutional) law in 'present-day conditions'.[19] This would help the Court to ensure that its own interpretation of the ECHR remains grounded in the legal and social developments in European states, in particular when a new area of the law of the ECHR is concerned.[20]

To see whether these expectations are supported by the ECtHR's practice, and using the overall analytical framework for this edited volume,[21] the chapter examines the extent, purpose and effects of the ECtHR's dialogue with domestic courts (i.e. its use of and engagement with domestic courts'

[18] See *supra* note 5.

[19] *Tyrer v. United Kingdom* (Appl. No. 5856/72), Judgment (Chamber), 25 March 1978, Series A, Vol. 26, para. 31.

[20] In line with its subsidiary role, the Court prefers to rely on domestic courts' or legislatures' decisions when engaging in evolutive interpretation. This preference is noted by Harris *et al.*, Law of the ECHR, *supra* note 1, at 9–10. It has also been made clear by the former president of the Court, Sir Nicolas Bratza, e.g. in his speech 'Dialogue between Judges: How Can We Ensure Greater Involvement of National Courts in the Convention System?', Strasbourg, 27 January 2012, available at www.echr.coe.int/Documents/Dialogue_2012_ENG.pdf, at 27.

[21] As set out in the Introduction to this volume, Sections 1.2.2–1.2.5.

decisions).[22] The focus is on the ECtHR's engagement with the decisions of domestic courts from the CoE member state that is a direct party to the relevant case before the ECtHR.[23] A more descriptive Section 11.2 asks questions about the *extent* of dialogue i.e. when the ECtHR engages with domestic courts' decisions most frequently, and how it relates to judgments of domestic courts in its own judgments and decisions. With these findings as a basis, Sections 11.3 and 11.4 examine the *purpose* and some of the *effects* of the ECtHR's engagement with domestic courts' decisions. It is in these two parts where a more thorough discussion takes place concerning whether the ECtHR also uses or could use its engagement with domestic court decisions as a (strategic) tool to induce domestic courts to more directly engage with and thus more effectively protect and develop the Convention rights at the domestic level, in line with the three expectations formulated earlier. It also asks whether the ECtHR's engagement with domestic court decisions indeed has these effects. Concluding remarks are offered in Section 11.5.

Before we can begin with the substantive analysis, its limits have to be set out. Due to the exhaustion of domestic remedies rule in article 35(1) ECHR, in the vast majority of cases, a complaint that reaches the ECtHR has been considered by a domestic court before.[24] The Court therefore relates to decisions of the domestic courts from states that are direct parties to the case in almost all its judgments and decisions. With about 18,000 judgments delivered between 1959 and 2014,[25] and even more decisions that might be relevant for answering the questions about the extent, purpose and effect of the ECtHR's use of domestic court decisions, it was necessary to drastically limit the number of cases that are examined in this chapter. The chapter is

22 Note that no separate part is included in this chapter that analyses the *method* of the ECtHR's dialogue with domestic courts as suggested in the Introduction to this edited volume. This is because in the vast majority of cases, the ECtHR gets access to the relevant decisions of domestic courts that considered the complaint before through the case file submitted. Therefore, the Court does not need to develop any particular 'method' to find out about relevant domestic court decisions.

23 Domestic courts' use of the ECtHR's judgments and decisions will only be touched upon in order to explain some aspects of the effects of the ECtHR's own engagement with domestic court decisions (Section 11.4).

24 Exceptions are cases where no effective domestic remedy exists at the national level. See e.g. *Catan and Others v. Moldova and Russia* (Appl. Nos. 43370/04, 8252/05 and 18454/06), Judgment (Grand Chamber), 19 Oct 2012, ECHR 2012-V, 309 (extracts); and *Aslakhanova and Others v. Russia* (Appl. Nos. 2944/06 and 8300/07, 50184/07, 332/08 and 42509/10), Judgment (Chamber), 18 December 2012, not reported, paras. 88–91 and 126.

25 See the statistical overview on the number of judgments delivered by the Court between 1959 and 2014: www.echr.coe.int/Documents/Overview_19592014_ENG.pdf, at 3.

therefore restricted to an analysis of the ECtHR's engagement with decisions of German and Russian courts in the most relevant judgments and decisions that were handed down between 1 January 2011 and 31 December 2013.[26] These two states were chosen because they represent two of the larger but rather different countries of the forty-seven CoE member states. In particular, they differ in regard to the development and effectiveness of their domestic legal and court systems for the protection of fundamental rights.

While the analysis is thus limited and may not capture particular developments in other countries as well as some longer-term trends, the comparison between these countries enables us to analyse whether the condition and stage of development of the domestic system for the protection of ECHR rights, in particular the conduct of domestic courts, influence the ECtHR's use of the domestic courts' decisions (dialogue). This is interesting in regard to the guiding question posed earlier as to whether the ECtHR uses its opportunities to enter into a dialogue with domestic courts with a strategic purpose to strengthen the cooperative elements of the system. Moreover, it promises to show whether the modes of the ECtHR's engagement with domestic courts' decisions to achieve this have similar effects in regard to Germany and Russia.[27]

A further limitation of this chapter is that it does not examine the ECtHR's use of decisions of domestic courts from member states of the CoE that are not parties to the case. This has been analysed elsewhere.[28] The chapter also excludes an inquiry into the Court's use of decisions of foreign domestic courts that are not members of the CoE, or of other international or regional courts or quasi-judicial bodies.[29]

[26] In this period of time, 56 judgments and 27 decisions against Germany and 356 judgments and 126 decisions against Russia were issued. While these judgments and decisions are the basis for the analysis, not all of them are analysed in detail. The focus is on developments that are relevant for the context of this chapter. Sometimes decisions or judgments that were delivered outside the determined period of time are also looked at to highlight some longer-term or more recent trends.

[27] See in particular *infra*, Section 11.4.

[28] See e.g. L. Helfer, 'Consensus, Coherence and the European Convention on Human Rights', *Cornell Int'l L. J.* 26:1 (1993) 133–65; P. Mahoney, 'The Comparative Method in Judgments of the European Court of Human Rights: Reference Back to National Law', G. Cavinet, M. Andenæs and D. Fairgrieve (eds.) *Comparative Law Before the Courts* (London: British Institute of International and Comparative Law, 2004) 135–50, at 139–42; and P. Carozza, 'Uses and Misuses of Comparative Law in International Human Rights: Some Reflections on the Jurisprudence of the European Court of Human Rights', *Notre Dame L. Rev.* 73:5 (1998) 1217–37.

[29] For an analysis of some of these aspects, see the contribution of Judge Nußberger in this volume (Chapter 15). See also the analysis by M. Forowicz, *The Reception of International*

11.2 The Extent of the ECtHR's Engagement with German and Russian Courts' Decisions

Due to the exhaustion of domestic remedies rule, the ECtHR can regularly rely on a decision by a domestic court in its own examination of a complaint. Proceedings before and judgments of domestic courts are commonly summarised in the facts section of each ECtHR judgment. Depending on the particularities of the case in question, the ECtHR then relies on and engages with the proceedings in domestic courts and/or the content of their judgments to a greater or lesser extent when it decides on the admissibility and/or the merits. What follows is an attempt to highlight four areas where the ECtHR does so particularly frequently in its decisions on the merits: when it comes to the facts established by domestic courts and relevant evidence obtained (subsection 11.2.1); when it comes to understanding the interpretation and application of domestic law (subsection 11.2.2); when the ECtHR needs to comprehend historical, social, cultural, religious, and other particularities of the domestic system from which the case originates (subsection 11.2.3); and when it comes to domestic courts' application of material provisions of the ECHR (or equivalent domestic law), including the fair balancing of interests (subsection 11.2.4). The following subsections will give an overview of this extent, and, notably in subsection 11.2.4, of some of the aspects that determine how the Court uses domestic courts' decisions in its own judgments and decisions.

11.2.1 ECtHR's Reliance on the Facts Established and Evidence Obtained by Domestic Courts

As mentioned, the Court has limited fact-finding capacities. Not surprisingly, '[a]s a result, and in line with the principle of subsidiarity, the Court prefers to rely, where possible, on the findings of competent domestic authorities',[30] including national courts. The Court regularly highlights that it is not a fourth-instance court and thus will not normally substitute its own assessment of the facts and evidence with those of the domestic

Law in the European Court of Human Rights (Oxford University Press, 2010); M. Ambrus, 'Comparative Law Method in the Jurisprudence of the European Court of Human Rights in the Light of the Rule of Law' *Erasmus L. Rev.* 2:3 (2009) 353–71; and C. Rozakis, 'The European Judge as Comparatist' *Tulane L. Rev.* 80:1 (2005–2006) 157–279.

30 *Finogenov and Others v. Russia* (Appl. Nos. 18299/03 and 27311/03), Judgment (Chamber), 20 December 2011, ECHR 2011-VI, 365 (extracts), para.237.

courts.[31] While states have a certain freedom to decide on the procedures and methods that allow for effective fact-finding and obtaining of evidence, including under article 6 ECHR,[32] the Court frequently calls on domestic courts to 'sufficiently establish the relevant facts'[33] needed to solve the case before them in light of the ECHR or domestic law interpreted in light of the Convention. It also calls on them to assess and evaluate these facts and evidence in a reasonable, non-arbitrary manner.[34]

In line with its limited capacities in this area, there are many examples concerning both Germany and Russia in which the Court relies on the facts established by domestic courts and evaluates them in a similar way as the domestic courts. For instance, it has used reports by medical and other experts, documents, witness statements, interviews with relevant persons, analyses of local developments, reviews of assurances of foreign domestic courts, and other information obtained by domestic courts (and other domestic authorities).[35] In other cases, the Court criticises domestic courts when they fail to sufficiently obtain

[31] See e.g. *Klaas v. Germany* (Appl. No. 15473/89), Judgment (Chamber), 22 September 1993, Series A, Vol. 269, para. 29; *Suleymanov v. Russia* (Appl. No. 32501/11), Judgment (Chamber), 22 January 2013, not reported, para. 162; *Shakurov v. Russia* (Appl. No. 55822/10), Judgment (Chamber), 6 June 2012, not reported, para. 125; *Giuliani and Gaggio v. Italy* (Appl. No. 23458/02), Judgment (Grand Chamber), 24 March 2011, ECHR 2011-II, 275 (extracts), paras. 179–80; *Sahin v. Germany* (Appl. No. 30943/96), Judgment (Grand Chamber), 8 July 2003, ECHR 2003-VIII, 63, para. 73; *Vidal v. Belgium* (Appl.No.12351/86), Judgment (Chamber), 22 April 1992, Series A, No. 235, para. 33.

[32] See e.g. *Hümmer v. Germany* (Appl. No. 26171/07), Judgment (Chamber), 9 July 2012, not reported, para. 40.

[33] *H.W. v. Germany* (Appl. No. 17167/11), Judgment (Chamber), 19 September 2013, not reported, para. 113.

[34] See e.g. *Khamidov v. Russia* (Appl. No. 72118/01), Judgment (Chamber), 15 November 2007, not reported, para. 170; *Communist Party and Others v. Russia* (Appl. No. 29400/05), Judgment (Chamber), 19 June 2012, not reported, para. 113; *van Kück v. Germany* (Appl. No. 35968/97), Judgment (Chamber), 12 June 2003, ECHR 2003-VII, 1, paras. 46–47; and *Kononov v. Latvia* (Appl. No. 36376/04), Judgment (Grand Chamber), 17 May 2010, ECHR 2010-IV, 35, para. 189.

[35] E.g. *Ahrens v. Germany* (Appl. No. 45071/09), Judgment (Chamber), 22 March 2012, not reported, para. 77; *Axel Springer AG v. Germany* (Appl. No. 39954/08), Judgment (Grand Chamber), 7 February 2012, not reported, paras. 98–99; *Hoffer and Annen v. Germany* (Appl. Nos. 397/07 and 2322/07), Judgment (Chamber), 13 January 2011, not reported, para. 44; *Ostermünchner v. Germany* (Appl. No. 36035/04), Judgment (Chamber), 22 March 2012, not reported, paras. 73 *et seq.*; *Reiner v. Germany* (Appl. No. 28527/08), Judgment (Chamber), 19 January 2012, not reported, para. 89; *Sievert v. Germany* (Appl. No. 29881/07), Judgment (Chamber), 19 July 2012, not reported, paras. 64–65; *Kulevskiy v. Russia* (Appl. No. 20696/12), Decision (Chamber), 20 November 2012, not reported, paras. 36–37; *Communist Party and Others v. Russia*, *supra* note 34, para. 113 *et seq.*; and *Ageyevy v. Russia* (Appl. No. 7075/10), Judgment (Chamber), 18 April 2013, not reported, para. 131.

relevant evidence and/or for fail to clarify essential facts. An example is *H.W. v. Germany*, where the domestic courts prolonged the applicant's preventive detention based on a medical report assessing the applicant's dangerousness that had been prepared more than twelve years before.[36] In *Kasparov and Others v. Russia*, the Court criticised domestic courts for not having established where exactly the applicant had been arrested by the police, even though such clarification was crucial for the outcome of the case.[37]

Even if it criticises domestic courts for insufficiently clarifying facts or obtaining evidence, due to its dependence on domestic courts in this area, the Court nonetheless relies on the facts and evidence established by domestic courts or other authorities. It does so also in cases when it does not follow the domestic court's decision. This involves a re-interpretation or re-assessment of relevant facts by the ECtHR, often when domestic courts failed to consider the presence of an important factor or when the quality (thoroughness, consistency, etc.) of the domestic procedures establishing facts and evidence were insufficient.[38] An example is the judgment *Finogenov and Others v. Russia* which concerned the Russian authorities' handling of the hostage crisis in the 'Dubrovka' (Nord-Ost) theatre in Moscow in 2002. The ECtHR questioned the domestic courts' interpretation of relevant facts and evidence in the case, in particular the domestic courts' findings that the death of a great number of hostages had not been a consequence of the gas that had been used by the Russian authorities when they stormed the beleaguered theatre with the more than 800 hostages inside.[39] In other cases where the facts and evidence are clearly insufficiently established, the ECtHR uses the limited facts

[36] *H.W. v. Germany*, *supra* note 33, paras. 111–113; see also *Ageyevy v. Russia*, *supra* note 35, para. 147, for a similar criticism of domestic courts not consulting medical experts.

[37] *Kasparov and Others v. Russia* (Appl. No. 21613/07), Judgment (Chamber), 3 October 2013, not reported, paras. 63–69 and 88.

[38] *Finogenov and Others v. Russia*, *supra* note 30, para. 238; *Maslova and Nalbandov v. Russia* (Appl. No. 839/02), Judgment (Chamber), 24 January 2008, not reported, paras. 101 *et seq.*; and *Isayeva and Others v. Russia* (Appl. Nos. 57947/00, 57948/00 and 57949/00), Judgment (Chamber), 24 February 2005, not reported, paras. 179 *et seq.*

[39] *Ibid.*, paras. 200 *et seq*; see also other cases where the ECtHR re-evaluated some facts: *Savriddin Dzhurayev v. Russia* (Appl. No. 71386/10), Judgment (Chamber), 25 April 2013, ECHR 2013-III, 133, paras. 159–61 and 165; *Idalov v. Russia* (Appl. No. 5826/03), Judgment (Grand Chamber), 22 May 2012, not reported, paras. 139 *et seq.*; *Ageyevy v. Russia*, *supra* note 35, paras. 44, 48 *et seq.*, 146, 150 and 234; *Schwabe and M.G. v. Germany* (Appl. Nos. 8080/08 and 8577/08), Judgment (Chamber), 1 December 2011, ECHR 2011-VI, 59, para. 105; and *B.B. and F.B. v. Germany* (Appl. Nos. 18734/09 and 9424/11), Judgment (Chamber), 14 March 2013, not reported, paras. 50–51.

available as much as possible,[40] or otherwise (reluctantly) draws *prima facie* conclusions on e.g. the disappearance, death or torture of persons implicating state agents.[41]

In other cases, the Court recognises that domestic courts are unable to obtain the required evidence and facts due to the inactivity of other domestic authorities, or are unable to start criminal or civil proceedings in a particular case. To address this problem, concerning, for instance, alleged violations of articles 2 and 3 ECHR, the Court has set out clear obligations on states to conduct effective investigations into alleged killings, torture and inhumane or degrading treatment that establish relevant facts and ensure accountability of those responsible. These investigative obligations address mainly the police and public prosecutor's offices. But the Court has also slowly widened its jurisprudence on article 13 ECHR, requiring states to establish effective remedies that allow individuals to challenge decisions of investigative authorities, among others decisions concerning fact-finding.[42] For example, in *Aslakhanova and Others v. Russia*, the ECtHR found a violation not only of the procedural (investigative) obligations of article 3 ECHR, but also of article 13 ECHR on grounds that an existing domestic remedy that allows applicants to challenge decisions of investigating authorities to discontinue criminal proceedings had been ineffective in this particular case.[43]

11.2.2 ECtHR's Use of Domestic Court Decisions to Understand National Law

The ECtHR often uses domestic court decisions to understand a particular norm of national law. It has often held that

> [i]t is in the first place for the national authorities, notably the courts, to interpret and apply the domestic law, even in those fields where the Convention "incorporates" the rules of that law: the national authorities

[40] E.g. *Aslakhanova and Others v. Russia*, *supra* note 24, paras. 103 and 106.

[41] See e.g. *Makhauri v. Russia* (Appl. No. 58701/00), Judgment (Chamber), 4 October 2007, not reported, para. 123; *Gandaloyeva v. Russia* (Appl. No. 14800/04), Judgment (Chamber), 4 December 2008, not reported, para. 89; *Akkum and Others v. Turkey* (Appl. No. 21894/93), Judgment (Chamber), 24 March 2005, ECHR 2005-II, 247, para. 211; *Toğcu v. Turkey* (Appl. No. 27601/95), Judgment (Chamber), 31 May 2005, not reported, para. 95; and *Varnava and Others v. Turkey* (Appl. No. 16064/90), Judgment (Grand Chamber), 18 September 2009, ECHR 2009-V, 13, para. 184.

[42] Note, however, that these remedies do not need to be judicial remedies in all cases; for details see Harris *et al.*, Law of the ECHR, *supra* note 1, at 771–73.

[43] *Aslakhanova and Others v. Russia*, *supra* note 24, para. 153.

> are, in the nature of things, particularly qualified to settle the issues arising in this connection.[44]

As indicated by the quote, the ECtHR's need to understand domestic law is particularly pressing in areas where the Convention requires it to determine whether a measure taken by the state had been 'lawful' under national law.[45]

In cases where the Court uses domestic court decisions to comprehend a particular norm of domestic law, it frequently does not only rely on domestic courts' decisions that were handed down on the particular case before the ECtHR, but also on other decisions of domestic courts, including precedents, applying and interpreting a particular provision of domestic law that is relevant for solving the case before it.[46] For example, in the case *Heinisch v. Germany*, the ECtHR summarises various decisions of the German Federal Constitutional Court (FCC) and the Federal Labour Court not directly issued in the *Heinisch* case, in order to understand the provisions of the German Labour Code that were relevant for the *Heinisch* case.[47] An example from Russia is the case *Communist Party and Others v. Russia* where the Court relied on decisions of various domestic courts to comprehend Russian electoral law.[48] In *Konstantin Markin v. Russia*, the ECtHR used the Russian Constitutional Court's (RCC) interpretation of

[44] *Winterwerp v. the Netherlands* (Appl. No. 6301/73), Judgment (Chamber), 24 October 1979, Series A, Vol. 33, para. 46. Among the many relevant cases against Germany and Russia, see *Mork v. Germany* (Appl. Nos. 31047/04 and 43386/08), Judgment (Chamber), 9 June 2011, not reported, para. 37; *Wasmuth v. Germany* (Appl. No. 12884/03), Judgment (Chamber), 17 February 2011, not reported, para. 53; and *H.W. v Germany*, *supra* note 33, para. 65; *Soltysyak v. Russia* (Appl. No. 4663/05), Judgment (Chamber), 10 February 2011, not reported, para. 58; and *Hromadka and Hromadkova v. Russia* (Appl. No. 22909/10), Judgment (Chamber), 11 December 2014, not reported, para. 160. See also Harris *et al.*, Law of the ECHR, *supra* note 1, at 506.

[45] E.g. under articles 2(2), 5(1), 6(1) and (2), 7, 8(2)-11(2) and 12 ECHR.

[46] This is in line with the fact that the ECtHR also recognised unwritten judge-made law as 'law'. See *Sunday Times v. the United Kingdom* (Appl. No. 6538/74), Judgment (Plenary), 26 April 1979, Series A, Vol. 30, para. 47.

[47] *Heinisch v. Germany* (Appl. No. 28274/08), Judgment (Chamber), 21 July 2011, ECHR 2011-V, 229 (extracts), para. 34; see also *Aydin v. Germany* (Appl. No. 16637/07), Judgment (Chamber), 27 January 2011, not reported, para. 57; *Hümmer v. Germany*, *supra* note 32, para. 27; *Litwin v. Germany* (Appl. No. 29090/06), Judgment (Chamber), 3 November 2011, not reported, paras. 19, 20 and 47; *Radu v. Germany* (Appl. No. 20084/07), Judgment (Chamber), 16 May 2013, not reported, para. 113; *Wasmuth v. Germany*, *supra* note 44, para. 27.

[48] *Communist Party and Others v. Russia*, *supra* note 34, para. 47; other examples are *Kotov v. Russia* (Appl. No. 54522/00), Judgment (Grand Chamber), 3 April 2012, not reported, paras. 52–59; and *Pyatkov v. Russia* (Appl. No. 61767/08), Judgment (Chamber), 13 November 2012, not reported, paras. 63 and 95.

the relevant Russian law setting out the rights of (male) military personnel to find that this law was rather inflexible when it was applied to 'exceptional circumstances'.[49] The ECtHR also uses domestic court decisions to understand recent changes to domestic law, or new laws that have been adopted only recently.[50]

Only in cases where domestic courts clearly misapplied a domestic legal provision, the ECtHR will (reluctantly) re-interpret domestic law and/or find a violation of the relevant Convention article because a domestic law lacked the 'quality of law'. For example, in many cases concerning pre-trial detention in Russia, the Court found that the provisions of Russian law governing detention pending trial as interpreted and applied by lower domestic courts fall short of the 'quality of law'.[51]

11.2.3 Reliance on Domestic Decisions to Understand Domestic Particularities

Another way the ECtHR makes use of the domestic courts' decisions in its own judgments is when it needs to better understand the local conditions in a particular country. Questions concerning the history of, as well as the social, cultural and religious developments within a particular society have to be taken into account in certain complaints raised before the Court. Due to its position as a regional court that prevents it from being in 'direct and continuous contact with the vital forces'[52] of all forty-seven CoE member states, the ECtHR relies on the decisions of domestic courts to build up its understanding of these developments and local conditions. As with the establishment of facts and the application of domestic law, the Court reserves itself a right to re-evaluate these developments and the weight they should be given in a particular case.

An example of where the ECtHR followed the domestic courts' taking account of their country's historical context is *Peta Deutschland v. Germany*. In this case, German courts had prohibited the planned publication of several posters of the animal welfare group *Peta Deutschland*,

49 *Konstantin Markin v. Russia* (GC), *supra* note 5, paras. 145 *et seq.*

50 E.g. *Gracia Cancio v. Germany* (Appl. No. 19488/09), Decision (Chamber), 29 May 2012, not reported.

51 Among many cases concerning Russia, see *Tsarenko v. Russia* (Appl. No. 5235/09), Judgment (Chamber), 3 March 2011, not reported, paras. 60–61; *Pyatkov v. Russia, supra* note 48, paras. 89–90; and *Ageyevy v. Russia, supra* note 35, para. 180 *et seq.*

52 The Court uses this phrase frequently in this context, see e.g. *Animal Defenders International v. United Kingdom* (Appl. No. 48876/08), Judgment (Grand Chamber), 22 April 2013, ECHR 2013-II, 203, para. 111.

interfering with the group's right to freedom of expression. The posters compared the treatment of animals in factory farms with the treatment of concentration camp inmates, and included photographs that showed animals in those farms alongside naked and emaciated concentration camp inmates. Noting that this case indeed had to be solved in light of Germany's history,[53] the ECtHR followed the reasoning of domestic courts.[54]

In other cases, the Court did not follow the domestic court's taking account of the historical and social context. In *Konstantin Markin v. Russia* the Grand Chamber rejected the Russian government's and RCC's arguments that denying a right to parental leave to Russian service*men* could be justified with the fact that historically it had been primarily women who cared for children.[55] Similarly, in *Anchugov and Gladkov v. Russia*, the Court did not accept the arguments of the Russian government[56] that the constitutional ban on voting rights for prisoners was justified in Russia in particular because it had been in place since the beginning of the nineteenth century.[57] The Court thus only takes on domestic court's arguments concerning historical, social, religious, cultural and legal particularities as long as they are compatible with the effective and up-to-date protection of Convention rights. In *Konstantin Markin*, the Court rejected the domestic courts' arguments with reference to the fact that states are prohibited from imposing 'traditional gender roles and stereotypes',[58] referring also to the CoE's aim to promote gender equality and its strong stand against discrimination based on sex.[59] Similarly, in *Anchugov and Gladkov v. Russia* the Court rejected the domestic courts' and government's reference to 'traditions' by highlighting that universal suffrage had become the basic principle governing the right to vote in a democratic state in the twenty-first century.[60]

53 *Peta Deutschland v. Germany* (Appl. No. 43481/09), Judgment (Chamber), 8 November 2012, not reported, para. 49.

54 The decisions by the relevant domestic courts, including the FCC, are summarised in *ibid.*, paras. 10–19. Other cases where the Court took Germany's historical context into account are *Göbel v. Germany* (Appl. No. 35023/04), Judgment (Chamber), 8 December 2011, not reported, paras. 47 and 25; and *Hoffer and Annen v. Germany*, *supra* note 35, paras. 46 *et seq.*; in *Appel-Irrgang and Others v. Germany* (Appl No. 45216/07), Decision (Chamber) 6 October 2009, ECHR 2009-IV, 397, at 11, the ECtHR heavily relied on the Berlin legislature's and courts' knowledge of the social circumstances in Berlin.

55 *Konstantin Markin v. Russia* (GC), *supra* note 5, paras. 142–43.

56 *Anchugov and Gladkov v. Russia* (Appl. Nos. 11157/04 and 15162/05), Judgment (Chamber), 4 July 2013, not reported, paras. 87–88.

57 *Ibid.*, para. 103.

58 *Konstantin Markin v. Russia* (GC), *supra* note 5, paras. 127 and 142.

59 *Ibid.*, paras. 49–62 and 142.

60 *Anchugov and Gladkov v. Russia, supra* note 56, paras. 94, 96 and 103.

11.2.4 *Relating to Domestic Courts' Interpretation and Application of Substantive Law*

In many cases the ECtHR also relates to and makes use of the domestic courts' reasoning in decisions on material law in its own judgments and decisions – conduct that is in line with the principle of subsidiarity.[61] Whether the ECtHR chooses a strict or weak standard with which it reviews the domestic courts' decision, and whether it follows or rejects all or some of the domestic courts' arguments or decisions in this dialogue on substantive law questions, depends on many factors, some of which shall be highlighted here. First, the extent to which domestic courts take account of the ECHR as well as relevant jurisprudence of the ECtHR (subsection 11.2.4.1); second, whether or not domestic courts followed certain procedures in coming to their decision on a question of material law (subsection 11.2.4.2); third, the thoroughness of the domestic courts' reasoning in their own decisions (subsection 11.2.4.3); and fourth, the relevance of the case for the 'elucidat[ion] ... and develop[ment] of the rules instituted by the Convention'[62] (subsection 11.2.4.4). These frequently interrelated factors were chosen to be looked at closer here and in Section 11.3 because they are particularly important to understand the alleged purpose of the ECtHR's dialogue with domestic courts to strengthen these courts' role in securing ECHR rights.

11.2.4.1 Domestic Courts Taking Account of the ECHR and the ECtHR's Jurisprudence

In cases concerning Germany and Russia, the degree to which the domestic court engages with the provisions of the Convention and relevant ECtHR jurisprudence is an important factor that determines the ECtHR's mode of dialogue with domestic courts – that is, whether the Court approves or rejects the reasoning of domestic courts. Relatedly, it can influence the strictness of the review the ECtHR chooses to apply,[63] including the

[61] There are some exceptions where the Court engages very little or not at all with the arguments of the domestic courts in their application and interpretation of the ECHR and/or parallel domestic law. An example is *Hermann v. Germany* (Appl. No. 9300/07), Judgment (Grand Chamber), 26 June 2012, not reported. The Court's non-engagement with the FCC's reasoning in this case has been rightly criticised in the dissenting opinion to the judgment.

[62] See *supra* note 5.

[63] See e.g. *Von Hannover v. Germany* (No.2) (Appl. Nos. 40660/08 and 60641/08), Judgment (Grand Chamber), 7 February 2012, ECHR 2012-I, 351, para. 107; *MGN Limited v. the United Kingdom* (Appl. No. 39401/04), Judgment (Chamber), 18 January 2011, not reported, paras. 150 and 155; *Palomo Sánchez and Others v. Spain* (Appl. Nos. 28955/06,

width of the margin of appreciation it decides to leave domestic courts to balance certain interests in cases that require a proportionality analysis, that is, cases that concern alleged violations of rights protected under articles 8–11 and 14 ECHR, article 1 P-1 and article 2 P-4.

Examples concerning Germany are *M v. Germany* and *Von Hannover v. Germany (No. 1)* on the one end and *Von Hannover v. Germany (No. 2)* and later cases concerning preventive detention in Germany[64] on the opposite end. In the first two cases, the Court found a violation of article 5(1) and article 8 ECHR, respectively. In both cases, one important reason for the ECtHR to reject the findings and reasoning of domestic courts was the fact that they did not take sufficient account of the relevant ECHR provisions as well as established ECtHR jurisprudence. In *M. v Germany*, the fact that the German courts did not review whether the applicant's preventive detention beyond a ten-year point was justified under any of the subparagraphs of article 5(1)(a)-(f) ECHR, but solely under relevant German law, contributed to the Court rejecting the reasoning of the domestic courts.[65] In *Von Hannover v. Germany (No. 1)*, the fact that the German courts did not take account of the ECHR and relevant ECtHR jurisprudence on articles 8 and 10 ECHR contributed significantly to the Court's finding that the German authorities had acted outside their margin of appreciation.[66] By contrast, in *Von Hannover v. Germany (No. 2)* the ECtHR explicitly commended domestic courts for applying domestic law in light of the ECHR and the ECtHR's jurisprudence. In addition, it praised domestic courts for having changed their previous approach to balancing journalists' right to freedom of expression and the public's right to be informed on the one hand and the right to privacy of well-known public figures on the other, in light of *Von Hannover (No. 1)*.[67] The Court

28957/06, 28959/06 and 28964/06), Judgment (Grand Chamber), 12 September 2011, ECHR 2011-V, 145, para. 57. See also the observations by Brems and Lavrysen, Procedural Justice, *supra* note 14, at 195 *et seq*.

[64] E.g. *Glien v. Germany* (Appl. No. 7345/12), Judgment (Chamber), 28 November 2013, not reported; *S. v Germany* (Appl. No. 3300/10), Judgment (Chamber), 28 June 2012, not reported; and *G. v. Germany* (Appl. No. 65210/09), Judgment (Chamber), 7 June 2012, not reported.

[65] *M. v. Germany* (Appl. No. 19359/04), Judgment (Chamber), 17 December 2009, ECHR 2009-VI, 169, paras. 96–105; see also *Schwabe and M.G. v. Germany*, *supra* note 39, paras. 77 and 79.

[66] See in particular the summary of the position of the FCC in the judgment, where the Court observes that this position was based on criteria set out in German law only: *Von Hannover v. Germany (No. 1)* (Appl. No. 59320/00), Judgment (Chamber), 24 June 2004, ECHR 2004-VI, 1, paras. 54 and 72.

[67] *Von Hannover v. Germany (No. 2)*, *supra* note 63, paras. 124–25; see also *Batuzov v. Germany* (Appl. No. 17603/07), Decision (Chamber), 22 May 2012, not reported.

reiterated that it would need 'strong reasons to substitute its view for that of the domestic courts' where domestic courts had undertaken 'the balancing exercise … in conformity with the criteria laid down in the Court's case law'.[68]

Similar patterns can be observed concerning Russia, even though there are only few cases where the ECtHR commended Russian courts for taking sufficient account of the ECHR and relevant ECtHR jurisprudence. Examples are *Makarenko v. Russia* on the 'positive' end and *Tsarenko v. Russia* and *Khlyustov v. Russia* on the 'negative' end. In *Makarenko v. Russia*, a case involving defamation, the ECtHR did not find a violation of article 10 ECHR. It observed that:

> In assessing the necessity of the interference [with the applicant's right to freedom of expression], it is also important to examine the way in which the domestic courts dealt with the case, and in particular whether they applied standards which were in conformity with the principles embodied in Article 10 … A perusal of the judgments by the Justice of the Peace, the Leninskiy District Court and the Smolensk Regional Court … reveals that they fully recognised that the present case involved a conflict between the right to freedom of expression and protection of the reputation or rights of others, a conflict they resolved by weighing the relevant considerations.[69]

Based on this, the Court further noted that it was 'satisfied that the reasons adduced by the national courts for convicting the applicant were relevant and sufficient within the meaning of its case-law'.[70]

By contrast, in other cases involving Russia, the ECtHR criticised lower domestic courts for failing to follow instructions by the RSC or the RCC to solve particular types of cases by applying not only domestic law, but by also taking into account the ECHR and relevant ECtHR jurisprudence.[71] For example, in *Tsarenko v. Russia*, the Court observed that neither the

[68] *Ibid.*, para. 107; for a similar observation, see *Peta Deutschland v. Germany*, para. 47; and the judgments cited *supra* note 63.

[69] *Makarenko v. Russia* (Appl. No. 5962/03), Judgment (Chamber), 22 December 2009, not reported, para. 155.

[70] *Ibid.*, paras. 156–57; see also *OOO 'Vesti' and Ukhov v. Russia* (Appl. No. 21724/03), Judgment (Chamber), 30 May 2013, not reported, para. 67. However, in this judgment the ECtHR also voiced some criticism of domestic courts for not determining whether the relevant statements of the applicant constituted factual allegations or value judgments in line with the ECtHR's jurisprudence on defamation (para. 64); and *Aleksey Ovchinnikov v. Russia* (Appl. No. 24061/04), Judgment (Chamber), 16 December 2010, not reported, paras. 53–56.

[71] See e.g. *Tsarenko v. Russia, supra* note 51, paras. 60–61; *Pyatkov v. Russia, supra* note 48, paras. 89–90; *Ageyevy v. Russia, supra* note 35, paras. 104, 231–32; and *Khlyustov v. Russia* (Appl. No. 28975/05), Judgment (Chamber), 11 July 2013, not reported, paras. 95 and 100.

lower courts nor the Russian government in its submissions to the ECtHR followed the strict instructions of the RCC to interpret relevant provisions of the Russian Code of Criminal Procedure on pre-trial detention in light of article 5 ECHR.[72] In this case, through their broad interpretation of the Code, the Russian lower courts had prolonged the applicant's pre-trial detention again and again, far beyond the period of eighteen months permitted for individuals accused of particularly serious offences.

In other cases concerning Russia, the ECtHR did not agree with the way in which Russian courts applied the ECtHR's jurisprudence. An example is *Anchugov and Gladkov v. Russia*,[73] a case concerning article 32(3) of the Russian Constitution imposing a blanket ban to vote on all convicted prisoners serving their prison sentence, and its compatibility with the Convention and ECtHR case law. Domestic courts argued that the case before them had to be distinguished[74] from the case *Hirst v. the United Kingdom (2005)*,[75] a finding with which the ECtHR did not agree.[76] This and other cases[77] show that the ECtHR will not endorse all references of domestic courts to the ECHR and the ECtHR's jurisprudence, and that thus not all engagement of domestic courts with the ECHR/ECtHR case law will result in the ECtHR following the reasoning of the domestic court in a particular case, or giving it a broader margin of appreciation when balancing different interests. It is the quality and up-to-datedness of the domestic courts' engagement as well as its conformity with Convention principles and rights that are decisive for the Court in choosing how it, in turn, relates to the decision of domestic courts – that is, into what sort of dialogue it enters with them.

11.2.4.2 Domestic Courts Following Certain Procedures

Another factor that determines whether the ECtHR approves or rejects a domestic court's decision, and that influences the strictness with which it scrutinises that decision, is the procedure that the domestic court followed in coming to its decision on the interpretation and application

[72] *Ibid.*, paras. 60–61; and *Pyatkov v. Russia*, *supra* note 48, paras. 89–90. For a similar finding concerning articles 2(2) and (4) P-4, see *Khlyustov v. Russia*, *supra* note 71, paras. 91 and 100–02.

[73] *Anchugov and Gladkov v. Russia*, *supra* note 56, para. 23.

[74] *Ibid.*

[75] *Hirst v. the United Kingdom (No.2)* (Appl. No. 74025/01), Judgment (Grand Chamber), 6 October 2005, ECHR 2005-XI, 187, para. 82.

[76] *Anchugov and Gladkov v. Russia*, *supra* note 56, paras. 101–09.

[77] See e.g. *Savriddin Dzhuraev v. Russia*, *supra* note 39, para. 172; and *Konstantin Markin v. Russia* (GC), *supra* note 5, para. 141.

of a material provision. When domestic courts consider the arguments and interests of all parties involved and/or concerned by the case, and when they include all parties in the proceedings, the ECtHR is more likely to approve the decision of domestic courts, *inter alia* through giving domestic courts a wider margin of appreciation in their decisions on questions of material law. In *Shtukaturov v. Russia* the ECtHR has noted this explicitly:

> [T]he Court reiterates that, whilst Article 8 of the Convention contains no explicit procedural requirements, 'the decision-making process involved in measures of interference must be fair and such as to ensure due respect of the interests safeguarded by Article 8'.... The extent of the State's margin of appreciation thus depends on the *quality of the decision-making* process. If the procedure was seriously deficient in some respect, the conclusions of the domestic authorities are more open to criticism.[78]

These procedural requirements are particularly prominent in article 8 ECHR,[79] but are not limited to this article.[80]

Examples concerning Germany are *Enke v. Germany* on the 'positive' end and *Anayo v. Germany* on the 'negative' end. In the decision *Enke v. Germany*, the applicant father complained that giving custody over his child exclusively to the child's mother violated his rights under article 8

[78] *Shtukaturov v. Russia* (Appl. No. 44009/05), Judgment (Chamber), 27 March 2008, ECHR 2008-II, 353, para. 89 (citations omitted, emphasis added). See also sources cited *supra* note 63.

[79] This is clear from the formulation used by the Court frequently in cases concerning article 8 ECHR that it cannot determine whether the reasons domestic authorities adduced to justify an interference into a parent's right to family life were 'sufficient' without 'at the same time determining whether the decision-making process, seen as a whole, was fair and provided the applicant with the requisite protection of his interests safeguarded by Article 8'. See e.g. *Anayo v. Germany* (Appl. No. 20578/07), Judgment (Chamber), 21 December 2010, not reported, para. 65; *T.P. and K.M. v. the United Kingdom* (Appl. No. 28945/95), Judgment (Grand Chamber), 10 May 2001, ECHR 2001-V, 119, para. 72; and *Sommerfeld v. Germany* (Appl. No. 31871/96), Judgment (Grand Chamber), 8 July 2003, ECHR 2003-VIII, 137, para. 66.

[80] E.g. procedural obligations under article 2 ECHR (*McCann and Others v. the United Kingdom* (Appl. No. 18984/91), Judgment (Grand Chamber), 27 September 1995, Series A, Vol. 324, para. 161); article 3 ECHR (*Assenov and Others v. Bulgaria* (Appl. No. 24760/94), Judgment (Chamber), 28 October 1998, Reports 1998-VIII, para. 102); article 4 ECHR (*Rantsev v. Cyprus and Russia* (Appl. No. 25965/04), Judgment (Chamber), 7 January 2010, ECHR 2010-I, 65, para. 288); article 8 ECHR (*Craxi v. Italy (No. 2)* (Appl. No. 25337/94), Judgment (Chamber), 17 July 2003, not reported, para. 74); article 10 ECHR (*Özgür Gündem v. Turkey* (Appl. No. 23144/93), Judgment (Chamber), 16 March 2000, ECHR 2000-III, 1, paras. 133–34); and article 14 ECHR (*Nachova and Others v. Bulgaria* (Appl. Nos. 43577/98, 43579/98, 43577/98 and 43579/98), Judgment (Grand Chamber), 6 July 2005, 2005-VII, 1.).

ECHR. The fact that the procedures before the domestic courts were very inclusive – that is, they took thorough account of the interests of everyone involved – was the most important factor contributing to the Court finding the case inadmissible: the Court noted that the applicant had been directly involved in the proceedings, he had had the right to appeal decisions of lower courts, the domestic courts had considered relevant expert advice, and they had had regard to the whole family situation, including in particular to the best interests of the child.[81] It concluded that 'the domestic courts' procedural approach was fair and based on sufficient material'. It thus held that the domestic courts had acted within their margin of appreciation in deciding on the relevant questions of material law.[82] In *Anayo v. Germany*, by contrast, the ECtHR found a violation of article 8 ECHR based first and foremost on the fact that the domestic court had not considered whether allowing contact between young twins and their biological father was not only in the biological father's interest but also in the twins' best interest.[83]

An example from Russia, containing both positive and negative examples of domestic courts following the required inclusive procedures, is the case *Ageyevy v. Russia*, which involved domestic courts' revocation of the adoption of two children by the applicant couple. The first decision that the ECtHR reviewed was the domestic courts' decision to approve an order to temporarily remove the children from their parents after one of the children had been rushed to hospital with severe burn injuries, resulting in the initiation of a criminal investigation against the parents. The ECtHR observed that in their review of the removal order, the domestic courts had correctly involved the parents in the decision-making process, giving 'due consideration to all the relevant circumstances of the case and carefully assess[ing] the impugned order'. It also observed that 'before the courts the applicants were represented by counsel and were fully able to state their case and to contest any evidence in the case file they considered

[81] *Enke v. Germany* (Appl. No. 545/08), Decision (Chamber), 9 October 2009, not reported, at 6–7.

[82] *Ibid.*, 7; and similar findings in *Ahrens v. Germany*, *supra* note 35, paras. 77 *et.seq.*; *Aydin v. Germany*, *supra* note 47, paras. 61–63; *Siebenhaar v. Germany* (Appl. No. 18136/02), Judgment (Chamber), 3 February 2011, not reported, para. 43 *et seq.*; and *Appel-Irrgang and Others v. Germany*, *supra* note 54.

[83] *Anayo v. Germany*, *supra* note 79, para. 71; see also *Elsholz v. Germany* (Appl. No. 25735/94), Judgment (Grand Chamber), 13 July 2000, ECHR 2000-VIII, 345, paras. 52–53; *Zaunegger v. Germany* (Appl. No. 22028/04), Judgment (Chamber), 3 December 2009, not reported, paras. 58–62; *Schneider v. Germany* (Appl. No. 17080/07), Judgment (Chamber), 15 September 2011, not reported, para. 104; and *Görgülü v. Germany* (Appl. No. 74969/01), Judgment (Chamber), 26 February 2004, not reported, paras. 48–50.

false'.[84] The Court thus did not find a violation of article 8 ECHR on account of the removal of the children into public care.[85] The ECtHR came to the opposite finding concerning the domestic courts' decision to revoke the adoption of the two children even though the parents had been acquitted in the criminal procedures. The ECtHR held that when reviewing the revocation, domestic courts had ignored the interests of the parents and the children.[86] Among other things, the domestic courts had never questioned the children about how they had been treated by their parents.[87]

In other cases, the ECtHR commended domestic courts for following other procedures, for example for conducting a comparative review of domestic law and jurisprudence in CoE member states to establish whether a European consensus existed on a certain question. In *Stübing v. Germany*, in the course of the domestic proceedings, an expert report had been prepared, containing a comparative analysis of whether incest was criminalised in different member states of the CoE.[88] The ECtHR used this in its own judgment to find that there was no European consensus on the matter.[89] Thus, it seems that it was among other things the fact that the domestic courts had conducted a comparative analysis that resulted in the Court lowering its standard of review in this case. This contributed to the Court leaving domestic courts a broader margin of appreciation in their decision on material law, that is, whether the applicant's conviction for incest corresponded to a 'pressing social need'.[90]

11.2.4.3 Thoroughness of Domestic Courts' Reasoning

A factor that is very much related to the two factors mentioned in the preceding section and that also influences the Court's decision as to how it

[84] *Ageyevy v. Russia*, *supra* note 35, para. 131. See also *Communist Party and Other v. Russia*, *supra* note 34, paras. 85–88; *Rytchenko v. Russia* (Appl. No. 22266/04), Judgment (Chamber), 20 January 2011, not reported, paras. 41–44; and *Dmitriy Ryabov v. Russia* (Appl. No. 33774/08), Judgment (Chamber), 1 August 2013, not reported, paras. 51–52.

[85] *Ibid.*, para. 132.

[86] *Ibid.*, para. 151; for similar findings of the Court on the inadequateness of domestic court procedures, see *Idalov v. Russia* (Appl. No. 5826/03), Judgment (Grand Chamber), 22 May 2012, not reported, para. 162; and *Kasparov and Others v. Russia*, *supra* note 37, para. 63.

[87] *Ibid.*, para. 150; and *Shtukaturov v. Russia*, *supra* note 78, where the Court noted that the applicant's 'participation in the decision-making process was reduced to zero' (para. 91). Similarly, see *Kiyutin v. Russia* (Appl. No. 2700/10), Judgment (Chamber), 10 March 2011, ECHR 2011-II, 29, paras. 73–74.

[88] *Stübing v. Germany* (Appl. No. 43547/08), Judgment (Chamber), 12 April 2012, paras. 19 and 33.

[89] *Ibid.*, paras. 28–30 and 66.

[90] *Ibid.*, para. 60.

makes use of, rejects or approves of the domestic court's judgment, and/or lowers the strictness of its review, is the thoroughness of the domestic court's reasoning. There are many examples in which it seems that the diligence with which the domestic courts brought forward their reasons for a particular decision influences the Court's use of the domestic decision in its own judgment. The Court has formulated this very clearly in *K.A. v. Finland*, a case concerning the taking into institutional care of the applicant parents' children. Here, the Court required that 'relevant and sufficient' reasons had to be given for such a decision – that is, reasons that were

> capable of convincing an objective observer that the measure is based on a careful and unprejudiced assessment of all evidence on file, with the distinct reasons for the care measure being stated explicitly. The reasoning adopted should reflect the careful scrutiny which the competent organs can be expected to carry out in a matter of such magnitude by weighing the various evidence militating in favour and against the care measure.[91]

One example from the cases concerning Germany is *Peta Deutschland v. Germany*. The Court commended the domestic courts for their careful examination of the case, giving 'relevant and sufficient reasons' for their decision.[92] It relied to a large extent on the arguments brought forward by domestic courts in its own review and evaluation as to whether the civil injunctions against the applicant association were a proportionate means to protect the plaintiffs' personality rights, finding that domestic courts had not overstepped their margin of appreciation.[93]

There are also cases concerning Russia where the Court commended domestic courts for delivering well-reasoned decisions, and where it therefore did not find that an interference with the applicants' rights was disproportionate. For example, in *Dmitriy Ryabov v. Russia*, the ECtHR recognised that the domestic courts had 'adduced relevant reasons to justify their decisions restricting the applicant's parental rights',[94] and had considered 'sufficient material to reach a reasoned decision'.[95] Likewise, in

[91] *K.A. v. Finland* (Appl. No. 27751/95), Judgment (Chamber), 14 January 2003, not reported, para. 103.

[92] *Peta Deutschland v. Germany*, *supra* note 53, paras. 49 and 51.

[93] *Ibid.*; see also *Hoffer and Annen v. Germany*, *supra* note 35, para. 49; *Siebenhaar v. Germany*, *supra* note 82, paras. 45–47; *Aydin v. Germany*, paras. 61 and 63; *Von Hannover v. Germany (No. 2)*, *supra* note 63, paras. 124–26; and *Dojan and Others v. Germany* (Appl. Nos. 319/08, 2455/08, 7908/10, 8152/10 and 8155/10), Decision (Chamber), 13 September 2011, not reported, 15–16.

[94] *Dmitriy Ryabov v. Russia*, *supra* note 84, paras. 49 and 52.

[95] *Ibid.*, para. 54.

Amirov v. Russia, a case concerning article 5(3) ECHR, the ECtHR observed that domestic courts had displayed special diligence in forwarding 'relevant and sufficient reasons' for keeping the applicant in pre-trial detention.[96] In *Shikuta v. Russia* the ECtHR noted in addition that the domestic courts had 'carefully balanced the interests of justice against the applicant's right to liberty'.[97] Unlike in many other cases against Russia involving article 5(3) ECHR,[98] the ECtHR did not find violations in these cases, thus confirming domestic courts' reasoning and findings.

By contrast, in many other cases the ECtHR has criticised domestic courts for not giving 'relevant' and 'sufficient' reasons for their decisions. For example in *Tsikakis v. Germany*, the Court disapproved the shallow reasoning of the regional domestic court that had decided that the applicant was not allowed to see and spend time with his child, who lived with his mother, for the coming two years. In particular, the ECtHR observed that the regional court had not explained why there were no possibilities to coerce the mother into more cooperation, for example through the imposition of a fine for non-cooperation. Moreover, the ECtHR noted that the domestic court did not give any reasons why it thought that the mother would, within the coming two years, change her position and become more cooperative.[99] The domestic court giving insufficient reasons for their decisions contributed to the Court's finding that the domestic court's finding on questions of material law (article 8 ECHR) were outside their margin of appreciation.[100]

In many cases concerning Russia, the ECtHR has criticised the schematic reasoning patterns of national courts that failed to take account of the individual circumstances of each case, for example when deciding on whether pre-trial detention can be justified under article 5(3) ECHR. In *Dirdizov v. Russia*, this critique is clearly summarised:

> Each time, having found a violation of Article 5 § 3 …, the Court noted the *fragility of the reasoning* employed by the Russian courts to authorise an applicant's remaining in custody. From case to case it pointed out the following major defects in the courts' argumentation: reliance on the gravity

96 *Amirov v. Russia* (Appl. No. 51857/13), Judgment (Chamber), 27 November 2014, not reported, paras. 103–13; see also *Bordikov v. Russia* (Appl. No. 921/03), Judgment (Chamber), 8 October 2009, not reported, paras. 91–94; and *Buldashev v. Russia* (Appl. No. 46793/06), Judgment (Chamber), 18 October 2011, not reported, paras. 97–99.

97 *Shikuta v. Russia* (Appl. No.45373/05), Judgment (Chamber), 11 April 2013, para. 47.

98 See the judgments discussed *infra*, text accompanying notes 201 and 102.

99 *Tsikakis v. Germany* (Appl. No. 1521/06), Judgment (Chamber), 10 February 2011, not reported, para. 80.

100 *Ibid.*, para. 81.

> of the charges as the primary source to justify the risk of the applicant's absconding; reference to the applicant's travel passport, his financial resources and the fact that his alleged accomplices are on the run as the basis for the assumption that the applicant would follow suit; a suspicion, in the absence of any evidentiary basis, that the applicant would tamper with witnesses or use his connections in state bodies to obstruct justice, and a failure to thoroughly examine the possibility of applying another, less rigid, measure of restraint, such as bail.[101]

In *Dirdizov*, for instance, in their reasoning why the applicant should be kept in pre-trial detention, domestic courts did not take account of the fact that the applicant was seriously ill and could not receive adequate medical treatment in pre-trial detention. Similarly, in *Idalov v. Russia*, the ECtHR criticised the Russian courts for 'using stereotyped formulae without addressing specific facts' when applying article 5(3) ECHR.[102] In other cases, the ECtHR criticised the domestic courts for not giving reasons why the applicants had to be kept in metal cages during their appearance in court even though there was no sign of them being dangerous;[103] for imposing automatic travel bans on individuals who were refusing to pay an obligation without considering the individual circumstances of the person concerned and without justifying why such a travel ban would be effective in the particular case;[104] for not adducing 'compelling and objective arguments to show' that the protection of public health required 'the applicant's exclusion from residence on account of his health status';[105] or more generally, for giving 'unconvincing' reasons for decisions.[106] In addition, the ECtHR often does not follow Russian courts' lines of argument when these courts fail to conduct a proportionality analysis in cases that involve restrictions of rights.[107]

[101] *Dirdizov v. Russia* (Appl. No. 41461/10), Judgment (Chamber), 27 November 2012, not reported, para. 108.

[102] *Idalov v. Russia (GC), supra* note 39, para. 147; see also *Pyatkov v. Russia, supra* note 48, paras. 107 *et seq.*; and *Khodorkovskiy v. Russia* (Appl. No. 5829/04), Judgment (Chamber), 31 May 2011, not reported, para. 202.

[103] *Svinarenko and Slyadnev v. Russia* (Appl. Nos. 32541/08 and 43441/08), Judgment (Chamber), 11 December 2012, not reported, para. 67; this finding has been confirmed by the Grand Chamber in *Svinarenko and Slyadnev v. Russia* (Appl. Nos. 32541/08 and 43441/08), Judgment (Grand Chamber), 17 July 2014, not reported, para. 137.

[104] *Khlyustov v. Russia, supra* note 71, paras. 95–100.

[105] *Kiyutin v. Russia, supra* note 87, para. 72.

[106] *Ageyevy v. Russia, supra* note 35, para. 149.

[107] *Avilkina and Others v. Russia* (Appl. No. 1585/09), Judgment (Chamber), 6 June 2013, not reported, para. 51; also *Khlyustov v. Russia, supra* note 71, para. 101; *Ageyevy v. Russia, supra* note 35, para. 238; and the dissenting opinion by judges Rozakis, Steiner and Spielmann to *Kamaliyevy v. Russia* (Appl. No. 52812/07), Judgment (Chamber), 3 June 2010, not reported, paras. 5 and 6.

11.2.4.4 Relevance of the Case for the Elucidation and Development of the Law of the Convention

Another factor that determines the ECtHR's use of domestic court decisions is the relevance of the case for the elucidation and development of the law of the ECHR in 'present-day conditions'. After all, the Court's judgments also serve 'to elucidate, safeguard and develop the rules instituted by the Convention',[108] and the Court relies *inter alia* on decisions of domestic courts to fulfil this task, notably when a relatively new area of human rights protection is concerned. Two types of cases can be distinguished in this context: first, cases where the ECtHR takes on a domestic court's progressive argument in the interpretation of the Convention (or of domestic constitutional law, sometimes interpreted in light of the Convention), thereby 'distributing' the domestic court's interpretation to other CoE member states; second, cases where the ECtHR takes on a case mainly because the issue and the manner in which it was decided by domestic courts includes questions of law that are of great importance for the development of the law of the ECHR as a whole, concerning all member states of the CoE.

From among the cases analysed in this chapter, the judgments *Heinisch v. Germany* and *Vinter and Others v. the United Kingdom* can serve as examples for the first. In *Heinisch v. Germany*, the Court did not follow the domestic courts in this particular case. However, it used earlier decisions of the FCC and the Federal Labour Court to advance some aspects of the protection of whistle-blowers in its jurisprudence. Based on its earlier case law, one factor in the Court's balancing exercise of Ms Heinisch's right to freedom of expression against her employer's right to the protection of its reputation and business interests was the question as to whether Ms Heinisch could have used other channels as an alternative to the bringing of a criminal complaint in order to disclose the illegal conduct and wrongdoing of her employer. It is this criterion that the Court clarified with reference to the decision of the Federal Labour Court. It used the Federal Labour Court's decision to establish that internal channels for raising concerns with the employer about unlawful conduct of the employer had to be used only if redress could legitimately be expected. In particular, if an employer failed to remedy an unlawful conduct even though the employee had previously drawn its attention to that practice, the employee was no longer bound by a duty of loyalty towards his/her employer.[109] Thus, the

[108] See *supra* note 5.

[109] *Heinisch v. Germany*, *supra* note 47, paras. 72–73.

Court used the Federal Labour Court's decisions to further develop a small aspect of its jurisprudence on the protection of whistle-blowers.[110] In *Vinter and Others v. the United Kingdom*,[111] the FCC's (progressive) interpretation of the German Basic Law, containing provisions equivalent to those of the ECHR[112] (and judgments of the Italian Constitutional Court[113]), influenced the ECtHR's 'evolutive' interpretation of the ECHR in a judgment concerning a state other than Germany. The FCC's and the Italian Constitutional Court's judgments contributed to the Court's finding that all prisoners, including those serving life sentences, 'should be offered the possibility of rehabilitation and the prospect of release if that rehabilitation is achieved'.[114] In coming to this conclusion, the Court highlighted the arguments made by the German and Italian Constitutional Courts not only in the section where it summarised relevant comparative and international law[115] but also in the section on substantive findings.[116]

An example of the second type of case, important for the development of the law of the ECHR as a whole, is the judgment in *Konstantin Markin v. Russia*. Here, the Court observed that it would take on the case *inter alia* because it involved an issue of general interest relevant not only for Russia but also for many other member states of the CoE which discriminate against male military personnel when it comes to granting parental leave.[117] In this context, the ECtHR referred to the purpose of the Convention system as a whole, which is to 'provide individual relief' but whose 'mission is also to determine issues on public-policy grounds in the common interest, thereby raising the general standards of protection of human rights and extending human rights jurisprudence throughout the community of the Convention States'.[118] It can be assumed that in *Konstantin Markin*,

110 The ECtHR later relied on this small aspect in *Rubins v. Latvia* (Appl. No.79040/12) Judgment (Chamber), 13 January 2015, para. 88. See also the more general observation by A. Voßkuhle, president of the FCC, that the ECtHR has taken on doctrinal legal concepts that have been developed by the FCC throughout its existence: A. Voßkuhle and R. Gerhardt, 'Wir Leben in einem Europäischen Gerichtsverbund – Die Rechtsprechung des BVerfG zu den Grundrechten wird weltweit rezipiert' (2015) 48:2 *Zeitschrift für Rechtspolitik* 61–62.

111 *Vinter and Others v. United Kingdom* (Appl. Nos. 66069/09, 130/10 and 3896/10), Judgment (Grand Chamber), 9 July 2013.

112 Relevant judgments of the German courts are summarised in *ibid.*, paras. 69–71.

113 Relevant judgments of the Italian Constitutional Court are summarised in *ibid.*, para. 72.

114 *Ibid.*, para. 114.

115 See *supra* notes 112 and 113.

116 *Vinter and Others v. the United Kingdom* (GC), *supra* note 111, para. 117.

117 *Konstantin Markin v. Russia* (GC), *supra* note 5, para. 90.

118 *Ibid.*, para. 89.

the (conservative) argumentation of the RCC that was followed by the government in its submissions to the Court contributed significantly to the ECtHR's finding of a violation of articles 8 and 14 ECHR, as well as to its decision to address the 'important question of general interest'[119] raised by the case.[120]

11.3 Purpose of the ECtHR's Engagement with German and Russian Courts' Decisions

After this review of the Court's practice, the following section examines the question about the ECtHR's purpose of engaging with the domestic courts' decisions. In Section 11.5, the discussion moves to an evaluation of whether this purpose has been achieved by analysing some of the effects of this engagement. As will be shown, it seems that this purpose is mainly to strengthen the cooperation between the ECtHR and domestic courts for the implementation of Convention rights, in particular to strengthen domestic courts' primary role in this regard. In line with observations in the introduction, three inter-related purposes of the ECtHR's engagement with domestic court decisions are highlighted here: the purpose of compensating for the limits of the ECtHR's own capacities (subsection11.3.1); the purpose of encouraging domestic courts to take on a stronger role in enforcing Convention rights at the domestic level, for example through inducing them to more directly consider the ECHR/ECtHR jurisprudence, and by inducing them to follow certain procedures and to deliver well-reasoned judgments (subsection 11.3.2); and the purpose of encouraging domestic courts to, where necessary, develop the law of the Convention (subsection 11.3.3).

11.3.1 Compensating for the Limits of the ECtHR's Capacities

In particular, the extent of the ECtHR's engagement with domestic court decisions discussed in Sections 11.2.1–11.2.3 can be explained with the ECtHR's limited capacities that derive from its institutional position as a regional court. The purpose of the ECtHR's engagement in this area is to compensate for these limited capacities.

119 *Ibid.*, para. 90.

120 The Court did not, for example, follow arguments of the RCC that giving parental leave to military servicemen would have a negative effect on the fighting power and operational effectiveness of the armed forces (paras. 113, 128 and 144) and that it contradicted the traditional role that women played in child care (paras. 116, 127, 132 and 139–43).

11.3.1.1 Facts and Evidence

First, this purpose is reflected in (a) the circumstance that the Court relies on the facts and evidence established by German and Russian courts in all cases reviewed for this chapter, no matter what Convention right the case is concerned with, and no matter whether or not domestic courts have interpreted the facts in light of the Convention and the ECtHR's jurisprudence; and (b) in the circumstance that the Court normally does not wish to substitute its own assessment of the facts and evidence with those of the domestic courts, often referring to its limited and subsidiary role in this area. At the same time, the Court deliberately attempts to encourage domestic courts to sufficiently establish all facts that are relevant to solve the case at hand. Its encouragement of domestic courts to duly assess and interpret all factors and evidence of importance through its use of domestic court decisions also reveals this purpose. The examples of cases given in Section 11.2.1 show that this is done by the Court pointing out to domestic courts both when they did well in sufficiently establishing all relevant facts and evidence and evaluated them in a reasonable, non-arbitrary manner, and when they failed to do so.

Another mode for the Court to underline this purpose is through establishing direct *obligations* under articles 2 and 3 ECHR to effectively investigate alleged killings and allegations of torture.[121] More recently, the Court broadened its jurisprudence on article 13 ECHR, encouraging domestic courts to review the conduct of domestic investigative authorities. Even if the ECtHR does not directly require states to establish effective *judicial* remedies in this area,[122] the Court highlighted that a judicial domestic remedy in Russian law against arbitrary decisions of investigating authorities not to open or to discontinue investigations into alleged killings or into allegations of torture were generally well in line with article 13 ECHR.[123] Its findings of violations of procedural obligations under articles 2 and 3 as well as of article 13 ECHR in *Aslakhanova and Others v. Russia*, where this particular remedy under Russian law had been ineffective,[124] suggests

[121] Generally, see Harris *et al.*, Law of the ECHR, *supra* note 1, at 214 *et seq.* and 275 *et seq.*

[122] *Kaya v. Turkey* (Appl. No. 22729/93), Judgment (Chamber), 19 February 1998, not reported, para. 106; see also Harris *et al.*, Law of the ECHR, *supra* note 1, at 771–73 and 779–80.

[123] See *Trubnikov v. Russia* (Appl. No. 49790/99), Decision (Chamber), 14 October 2003, para. 2, analysing the relevant domestic remedy that exists in Russian law against the arbitrary exercise of powers by an investigating authority. In general, the ECtHR found it to be in conformity with article 13 ECHR.

[124] See e.g. *Aslakhanova and Others v. Russia*, *supra* note 24, para. 153; similarly, see *Musayev and Others v. Russia* (Appl. Nos. 57941/00, 58699/00 and 60403/00), Judgment (Chamber),

that the Court wants to strengthen domestic courts in their review powers to ensure that obligations to conduct effective investigations are complied with by domestic investigating authorities. This is supported by the Court's more general findings of violations of states' procedural investigative obligations under article 2 ECHR, but also a violation of article 13 ECHR in other cases where 'the criminal investigation into the deaths was ineffective and the effectiveness of any other remedy that may have existed … is consequently undermined'.[125] However, in its rather detailed instructions to Russian authorities as to how to improve the domestic system for the investigation into disappearances (alleged violations of articles 2 and 3 ECHR) in *Aslakhanova and Others v. Russia*, the Court did not recommend a stronger role for domestic courts to review the activities of other domestic investigating authorities for their conformity with articles 2 and 3 ECHR.[126] This could have been expected against the background of the above observations and the ECtHR's alleged purpose to make up for its own limited capacities through its interaction with domestic courts.

11.3.1.2 Understanding National Law

Second, the purpose of the ECtHR's engagement with domestic court decisions to make up for its own limited capacities is reflected in its reliance on domestic courts' interpretation and application of national law and its general reluctance to find a violation of the ECHR because domestic courts have not interpreted and applied domestic law 'correctly'. The review of the cases mentioned earlier in the section suggests that through its use of domestic courts' decisions that apply and interpret relevant domestic law, the Court encourages domestic courts to also highlight relevant earlier domestic case law – including precedents – that are relevant for understanding the actual scope of domestic law.[127] Moreover, the ECtHR's distinct criticism of, for example, Russian lower courts when they do not apply domestic law in line with the instructions of the RCC in the

26 July 2007, not reported, paras. 173–75; and *Khashiyev and Akayeva v. Russia* (Appl. Nos. 57942/00 and 57945/00), Judgment (Chamber), 24 February 2005, not reported, para. 183.

125 *Musayev and Others v. Russia, supra* note 124, para. 175; see also *Khashiyev and Akayeva v. Russia, supra* note 124, paras. 183–86; *Aslakhanova and Others v. Russia, supra* note 24, para. 153.

126 *Aslakhanova and Others v. Russia, supra* note 24, paras. 210 *et seq.*; the recommendations were made in the context of the Court's determination of the consequences which may be drawn from article 46 ECHR for Russia in light of the numerous previous findings about the lack of proper investigations into allegations of disappearances in Chechnya.

127 See e.g. the discussion of *Heinisch v. Germany* and *Communist Party and Others v. Russia* in Section 11.3.2.

area of pre-trial detention[128] can be understood to reflect this purpose, calling on Russian courts to improve their performance. Domestic courts' faithful application of national law is essential for the functioning of the Convention system as a cooperative system.

11.3.1.3 Understanding Domestic Local Conditions

Third, the purpose of the ECtHR's engagement with domestic court decisions to make up for its own limited capacities is reflected in its attempts to encourage national courts to bring out historical, social, religious, cultural, legal and other particularities in their decisions that are relevant for deciding the case at hand. The cases mentioned in Section 11.2.3 indicate that the Court is doing this by highlighting when a reference to such particularities is justified in light of the effective and up-to-date protection of Convention rights, through its use of the respective domestic court's decision.

11.3.2 Encouraging the Implementation of Convention Rights by Domestic Courts

Another important purpose that we can discern in the ECtHR's engagement with the decisions of domestic courts is the purpose of encouraging domestic courts to take on an active role in enforcing the rights under the Convention at the domestic level in line with their primary obligation under the ECHR. Notably the jurisprudence discussed in subsections 11.2.4.1 – 11.2.4.3 reveals this purpose. The Court may limit the strictness with which it reviews decisions made and measures taken by domestic authorities, *inter alia* by awarding domestic courts a broader margin of appreciation, and/or by less likely finding a violation of the Convention for other reasons, when domestic courts (a) actively engage with the Convention and ECtHR jurisprudence, (b) follow certain procedures in their decision-making processes, and/or (c) deliver well-reasoned judgments. This can constitute an 'incentive'[129] that the ECtHR offers to domestic courts to take on such an active role.

In addition to the examples given in subsections 11.2.4.1 – 11.2.4.3, the Court's reaction to the FCC taking direct account of the ECtHR's earlier judgments on preventive detention in *Kronfeldner v. Germany* makes this clear. In this judgment, the ECtHR highlighted that by instructing

[128] Among many other similar cases, *Pyatkov v. Russia*, *supra* note 48, paras. 89–90.

[129] See the speech of the president of the ECtHR, Dean Spielmann, of 20 March 2014, noting that the margin of appreciation is 'neither a gift nor a concession … but instead an *incentive* to national courts to conduct the requisite Convention review', at 12, available at www.echr.coe.int/Documents/Speech_20140320_London_ENG.pdf (emphasis added).

domestic criminal courts to apply the German Criminal Code's provisions on preventive detention in line with the ECtHR's earlier judgments on this matter, the FCC's judgment 'reflect[ed] and assum[ed] the joint responsibility of the State Parties and this Court [the ECtHR] in securing the rights set forth in the Convention'.[130]

At the same time, the ECtHR's differentiated engagement with the judgments of domestic courts reveals the purpose of ensuring a more effective implementation of the Convention at the domestic level through improving domestic courts' performance. The case *Ageyevy v. Russia* analysed in subsection 11.2.4.2 can be taken as an example of the ECtHR's differentiated approach. The case involved the review of different domestic court decisions on various aspects of the revocation of the applicants' adoption of two children, and the Court did evaluate each of these decisions separately, underlining aspects that satisfied procedural requirements under article 8 ECHR as well as aspects that failed to do so.[131] The same can be observed in regard to different domestic courts that decide on the same case and give more or less 'relevant' and more or less 'sufficient' reasons for their decisions, as mentioned in subsection 11.2.4.3. The case *Dirdizov v. Russia* can be recalled in this context where the Court particularly welcomed the judgment of the Tatarstan Supreme Court, which had given good reasons for why the applicant could no longer be held in pre-trial detention.[132] At the same time, the Court criticised lower domestic courts for their schematic patterns of reasoning used not only in the decisions on the lawfulness of Mr. Dirdizov's pre-trial detention but also in numerous other decisions on keeping individuals in pre-trial detention.[133] With this type of emphasis, the ECtHR also strengthens and encourages the work of 'good' domestic courts through its engagement with national court decisions. It might hope to rely on and cooperate with these 'good' courts for the effective implementation of the Convention in the future.[134]

[130] *Kronfeldner v. Germany*, *supra* note 6, para. 59. It should be noted, however, that the ECtHR does not go so far as to require the *direct* application of ECHR or a 1:1 incorporation of its jurisprudence into member states' domestic law in regard to all articles of the Convention. A good example to illustrate this is another case concerning preventive detention in Germany, where the Court agreed with the FCC's finding that 'a schematic alignment of the meaning of the constitutional notion of "penalty" to that under the Convention was not mandatory if, in substance, the minimum standards set by the Convention were complied with' (*Glien v. Germany*, *supra* note 64, para. 124).

[131] See *Agayevy v. Russia*, *supra* note 35.

[132] *Dirdizov v. Russia*, *supra* note 101, para. 109.

[133] *Ibid.* paras. 108–09; and *Khlyustov v. Russia*, *supra* note 71, para. 95.

[134] This tendency has been observed in regard to domestic courts concerning countries not studied in this chapter, e.g. the cooperation between the ECtHR and the Constitutional Tribunal of Poland. See W. Sadurski, 'Partnering with Strasbourg: Constitutionalisation of

11.3.3 Encouraging Evolutive Interpretation by Domestic Courts

As highlighted in the introduction, domestic courts and the ECtHR also share the task to 'elucidate … and develop the rules instituted by the Convention'[135] in 'light of present-day conditions'.[136] This reveals another purpose of the ECtHR's engagement with domestic courts' decisions: to encourage national courts to engage in dynamic interpretation of the Convention or domestic law in light of the Convention where this is necessary to ensure up-to-date protection. The judgments discussed in subsection 11.2.4.4 reflect this purpose. They show that the ECtHR takes on domestic courts' dynamic interpretation of the Convention or of parallel domestic law in its own judgments,[137] and that the ECtHR points out to domestic courts when they *should* have engaged in such progressive interpretation.[138]

In addition, the Court reminds states that through the 'evolutive' interpretation of the Convention they can contribute to the effective and up-to-date protection of ECHR rights not only within their own country but also at the European level, beyond their national borders. First, this can be inferred from the ECtHR's pronouncement in *Kronfeldner v. Germany*, where the Court held that the FCC's approach to interpret the provisions of the Basic Law (German Constitution) in light of the Convention and the jurisprudence of the ECtHR in a progressive manner demonstrated the FCC's 'continuing commitment to the protection of fundamental rights not

the European Court of Human Rights, the Accession of Central and East European States to the Council of Europe, and the Idea of Pilot Judgments' (2009) 9:3 *Human Rights Law Review* 397–453.

135 See the judgments cited *supra* note 5.

136 See the judgments and academic literature cited *supra* notes 6 and 19.

137 See the judgment *Heinisch v. Germany, supra* note 47. Earlier cases on the protection of whistle-blowers concerned whistle-blowers who had been employed in the public sector and were the only persons who knew about illegal conduct or wrongdoing at their workplace (e.g. *Guja v. Moldova* (Appl. No. 14277/04), Judgment (Grand Chamber), 12 February 2008, ECHR 2008 II, 1, para. 72; *Marchenko v. Ukraine* (Appl. No.4063/04), Judgment (Chamber), 19 February 2009, not reported, para. 46). While Ms Heinisch had also been employed by a state-owned company providing care for the elderly, this was the first case before the ECtHR in which it had to balance Ms Heinisch's right to freedom of expression by signalling illegal conduct or wrongdoing on the part of her employer against the company's right to protection of its reputation and commercial interests, *inter alia* through requiring loyalty from its employees, in a private-law employment relationship.

138 See the judgment *Konstantin Markin v. Russia* (GC), *supra* note 5, paras. 89–90, discussed in subsection 11.2.4.4; and *Svinarenko and Slyadnev v. Russia* (GC), *supra* note 104, paras. 122–39.

only on [a] national, but also on [a] European level'.[139] Second, decisions of domestic courts can influence the ECtHR finding that a 'European consensus' exists on a certain question.[140] Through their contribution to the shaping of a 'European consensus' by employing a dynamic interpretation of the Convention, domestic courts can influence the development of European human rights law.[141] This possibility can be an additional incentive for domestic courts to actively engage with Convention rights and ECtHR jurisprudence, and to interpret the Convention dynamically in areas where this is required in light of 'present-day conditions'. Domestic courts' active involvement in the development of the law of the Convention can strengthen the cooperative elements of the Convention, enabling the ECtHR to keep the interpretation and application of the ECHR grounded in the legal and social developments in CoE member states.[142]

11.4 Effects of the ECtHR's Engagement with German and Russian Courts' Decisions

All three identified purposes of the ECtHR's engagement with the decisions of domestic courts can arguably contribute to strengthening the Convention system as a 'cooperative system'. This last section tentatively analyses whether some or all of the three alleged purposes of the Court's engagement with the decisions of domestic courts are achieved, if not immediately, then in the longer term through continuous interaction between the ECtHR and German and Russian courts. First, we examine whether the ECtHR's engagement with domestic courts' decisions indeed has the effect of helping the ECtHR to reduce the limitations of its capacities that flow from its position as a regional court. In other words, do German and Russian courts 'listen' to the ECtHR and improve their fact-finding capacities, their diligence in applying domestic law and their capacities in highlighting relevant historical realities and social developments as a result of the ECtHR's encouragements (subsection 11.4.1)? Second, it is studied whether the ECtHR's use of domestic court decisions results

[139] *Kronfeldner v. Germany*, *supra* note 6, para. 59.

[140] It should be noted, however, that most of the time the ECtHR relies on domestic legislation and less so on decisions of domestic courts when it establishes the existence of a 'European consensus'.

[141] See the discussion of *Vinter and Others v. United Kingdom*, *supra* note 111.

[142] This is also clear from the ECtHR's attempt to encourage domestic courts to highlight relevant historical, social, cultural or religious particularities of their country in their decisions, as was pointed out in subsection 11.3.1.3.

in domestic courts taking on a more active role in the enforcement of the Convention, in line with their primary obligation in this regard (subsection 11.4.2). And third, it is examined whether the Court's engagement with domestic courts' decisions indeed encourages these courts to highlight relevant social and legal developments ('present-day conditions') in their judgments, including through the progressive interpretation of the Convention and/or parallel domestic constitutional law (subsection 11.4.3). To achieve these aims, this section does, to an extent necessary and possible, analyse developments at the domestic level in Germany and Russia.[143]

11.4.1 Do German and Russian Courts 'Compensate' for the ECtHR's Limited Capacities?

The question arises of whether the ECtHR's use of domestic court decisions as analysed in subsections 11.2.1–11.2.3 and 11.3.1 indeed enables the ECtHR to make up for its limited capacities in fact-finding as well as in understanding domestic law and national particularities that are relevant for making a decision.

11.4.1.1 Diligent Fact-Finding and Obtaining of Evidence?

Concerning the sufficient establishment of relevant facts and evidence, as well as their comprehensive evaluation by domestic courts, one can observe that some domestic courts improved their capacities in this area, arguably also in reaction to the Court's use of these domestic courts' earlier decisions. In the early 2000s, for example, German courts were criticised by the ECtHR for not asking for independent psychological expert advice that would help them to evaluate children's statements in child custody cases,[144] and would enable them to pay due regard to the interests of children in

[143] A caveat has to be made in this regard. This chapter can neither analyse all potential effects of the ECtHR's engagement with domestic courts' decisions comprehensively nor establish clear causalities between the ECtHR's engagement and the domestic courts' subsequent conduct. The analysis is limited to highlighting some legal effects that are apparent from the judgments examined in this chapter; it excludes a comprehensive analysis of the use of the ECHR/ECtHR jurisprudence in German and Russian court decisions that were never brought before the ECtHR.

[144] *Elsholz v. Germany* (Appl. No. 25735/94), Judgment (Grand Chamber), 13 July 2000, ECHR 2000-VIII, 345, para. 52; and *Sahin v. Germany*, where the ECtHR Chamber judgment had criticised domestic courts for basing their decisions on incomplete and vague statements that the child had made to a psychologist concerning her relationship with her father: *Sahin v. Germany* (Appl. No. 30943/96), Judgment (Chamber), 11 October 2001, not reported, paras. 46–48. This was, however, not considered problematic by the Grand

these cases, in particular when one parent opposed contact between the child and the other parent. In more recent child custody judgments against Germany, the ECtHR has not criticised this anymore.[145] This might *inter alia* be due to the ECtHR-influenced jurisprudence of the FCC, demanding that lower courts take due account of the wishes of children in such cases, if necessary with the help of psychological expert opinions.[146]

Concerning Russian courts' fact-finding and evaluation of these facts, there are positive and negative developments to observe. In a 2013 statement in which the RSC instructed lower courts on the application of the ECHR and relevant ECtHR jurisprudence, the RSC reminded lower courts that it was 'essential' that they establish all relevant facts concerning violations of Convention rights, and include them in the case file.[147] At the same time, there remain many cases where the ECtHR criticises Russian courts for not sufficiently establishing or not evaluating all relevant facts before them. Prominent examples are Russian courts' decisions about the extradition of individuals to countries where these individuals run the risk of being exposed to torture or inhuman or degrading treatment. Despite the ECtHR's rather explicit criticism, it seems that not much has improved in Russian courts' conduct in this area. For example, in *Savriddin Dzhuraev v. Russia* of April 2013, the Court once more found a violation of article 3 ECHR based *inter alia* on the fact that the Russian courts had ignored the evidence produced by the applicant that he ran a real risk of being tortured by Tajik authorities if he was extradited to that country,[148] even though the ECtHR had seriously criticised domestic courts for this in several similar cases in 2010.[149]

11.4.1.2 Faithful Application of National Law?

Another question is whether the Court's engagement with the way in which domestic courts interpret and apply national law has the desired

Chamber judgment that came to a different conclusion on this point: *Sahin v. Germany* (Appl. No. 30943/96), Judgment (Grand Chamber), 8 July 2003, ECHR 2003-VIII, 63, paras. 70–78.

[145] See e.g. *Kuppinger v. Germany* (Appl. No. 62198/11), Judgment (Chamber), 15 January 2015, not reported; and *B.B. and F. B. v. Germany*, *supra* note 39, para. 50.

[146] See the discussion by K.-P. Horndasch, 'Das Recht des Kindes auf Umgang', *Familie Partnerschaft Recht* (2012) 18:5 208–12, at 210.

[147] RSC, Resolution of the Plenum of 27 June 2013, No. 21.

[148] *Savriddin Dzhuraev v. Russia*, *supra* note 39, paras. 161 and 165.

[149] *Khodzhayev v. Russia* (Appl. No. 52466/08), Judgment (Chamber), 12 May 2010, not reported, para. 104; *Gaforov v. Russia* (Appl. No. 25404/09), Judgment (Chamber), 21 October 2010, not reported, para. 122–27; *Khaydarov v. Russia* (Appl. No. 21055/09), Judgment (Chamber), 20 May 2010, not reported, paras. 113–14; and *Iskandarov v. Russia* (Appl. No. 17185/05), Judgment (Chamber), 23 September 2010, not reported, para. 133.

effect that domestic courts apply and interpret domestic law faithfully in subsequent cases, thereby improving their primary role in this area. This concerns the conduct of Russian courts in particular. Here, the pattern is similar as in regard to fact-finding obligations. In the aforementioned 2013 instruction to lower courts, the RSC reminded domestic courts that they are required to identify the legal basis in Russian law for any restriction of ECHR rights in their decisions, and to ensure that the restriction foreseen in domestic law pursued a legitimate aim.[150] On the other hand, concerning the Court's criticism of Russian lower courts for not applying and interpreting relevant domestic law in line with the instructions of the RCC in their decisions on prolonging pre-trial detention,[151] it seems that little improvement can be observed. Despite the ECtHR having criticised domestic courts for not applying and interpreting domestic law in this area correctly, starting with the judgment *Korchuganova v. Russia* (2006),[152] the Court had to repeat this criticism most recently in January 2015 when adopting its judgment *Yuriy Rudakov v. Russia.*[153]

11.4.1.3 Highlighting Relevant Domestic Particularities?

In regard to Russia,[154] it can also be asked whether domestic courts, through the ECtHR's engagement with their decisions, developed their awareness as to which local historical, social, religious and other particularities they should highlight and can rely on when handing down decisions involving fundamental rights. Recent judgments from the RSC and the RCC on the constitutionality and Convention-compatibility of regional and federal laws restricting LGTB rights in Russia are an indication that the RSC and the RCC did not listen carefully to the ECtHR's Grand Chamber judgments in *Konstantin Markin v. Russia* and *Anchugov and Gladkov v. Russia* discussed in subsection 11.2.3. Several regional laws prohibiting public activities that 'propagate' homosexuality ('non-traditional sexual relationships') among minors and the punishment of such activities with administrative fines[155] were found to be in line with the Russian Constitution,

[150] RSC, Resolution of the Plenum of 27 June 2013, No. 21, para. 5.

[151] The repeated instructions of the RCC are summarised again in the ECtHR's more recent judgment on this issue, *Yuriy Rudakov v. Russia* (Appl. No. 48982/08), Judgment (Chamber), 15 January 2015, not reported, paras. 49–53.

[152] *Korchuganova v. Russia* (Appl. No.75039/01), Judgment (Chamber), 8 June 2006, not reported, para. 51.

[153] *Yuriy Rudakov v. Russia, supra* note 151, para. 64.

[154] This issue is not usually a problem in judgments concerning Germany. Therefore, this section concentrates on the developments in Russia.

[155] For a summary of the relevant regional laws, see M. Issaeva and M. Kiskachi, 'Immoral Truth vs. Untruthful Morals? Attempts to Render Rights and Freedoms Conditional upon

articles 10 and 14 ECHR and articles 19 and 26 ICCPR by the RCC and the RSC. Both courts held that the restriction on the right to freedom of expression was proportionate as it aimed to protect the intellectual, moral and psychological integrity of children.[156] Among other things, the RCC observed that the legislator had acted within its discretion when adopting the relevant laws as it had harmonised the protection of individuals' rights to freedom of expression with the beliefs about the values of family, motherhood, fatherhood and childhood as predominant in 'the special *historical* conditions' of Russian society.[157] It upheld this finding even after the UN Human Rights Committee had found relevant regional laws to be inconsistent with articles 19 and 26 ICCPR.[158] In addition, the RCC and RCS did not pay attention to ECtHR judgments establishing that 'particularly weighty reasons need to be advanced' to justify discrimination based on sex[159] or sexual orientation,[160] and that reasons given for difference in treatment based *solely* on sexual orientation will always amount to discrimination.[161]

11.4.2 Do German and Russian Courts More Actively Implement Convention Rights?

To evaluate whether the ECtHR's engagement with domestic court decisions results in building more effective remedies for alleged Convention violations at the domestic level, an attempt is made to establish whether the ECtHR's use of domestic courts' decisions indeed encourages domestic courts to solve more fundamental rights cases before them through

Sexual Orientation in Light of Russia's International Obligations' *Russian L. J.* 2:1 (2014) 82–105, at 85–88. Since July 2013, Federal Law No.135-FZ also 'protects' children from information propagating the negation of traditional family values at the level of federal law.

156 RCC, Ruling of 19 January 2010, No. 151-O-O; Ruling of 24 October 2013, No. 1718-O; and RSC, Ruling of 15 August 2012, No. 1-APG12-11.

157 RCC, Ruling of 24 October 2013, No. 1718-O, para. 2.1.

158 HRC, *Fedotova v. Russia*, Communication No.1932/2010, 30 November 2012, UN Doc. CCPR/C/106/D/1932/2010, para. 10.6.

159 *Konstantin Markin v. Russia* (GC), *supra* note 5, para. 127.

160 E.g. *Kozak v. Poland* (Appl. No. 13102/02), Judgment (Chamber), 2 March 2010, not reported, para. 92.

161 *Ibid.* para. 92; *E.B. v. France* (Appl. No. 43546/02), Judgment (Grand Chamber), 22 January 2008, not reported, paras. 91 and 93; *S.L. v. Austria* (Appl. No.45330/99), Judgment (Chamber), 9 January 2003, ECHR 2003-I, 71 (extracts), para. 37; *Smith and Grady v. the United Kingdom* (Appl. Nos. 33985/96 and 33986/96), Judgment (Chamber), 27 September 1999, ECHR 1999-VI, 45, paras. 89 and 94; and *Karner v. Austria* (Appl. No. 40016/98), Judgment (Chamber), 24 July 2003, ECHR 2003-IX, 199, paras. 37 and 41.

directly or indirectly interpreting and applying the ECHR and ECtHR jurisprudence (subsection 11.4.2.1);[162] and whether they indeed follow better procedures and deliver better reasoned judgments (subsection 11.4.2.2).[163]

11.4.2.1 More Domestic Judicial Review Based on ECHR/ ECtHR Jurisprudence in Germany and Russia?

In subsection 11.2.4.1 it was observed that if a domestic court engages with the Convention and the ECtHR's jurisprudence in its own judgments, the ECtHR is more likely to follow the decision of the domestic court and/ or to limit the strictness of its review, *inter alia*, by giving the domestic authorities a wider margin of appreciation in deciding on a question of material law. This fits with the observations in subsection 11.4.2 that one of the purposes of the Court's engagement with domestic court decisions is to incentivise national courts to take on a more proactive role in their interpretation and application of the Convention, in order to strengthen the Convention system as a cooperative system. A tentative look at recent developments concerning Convention-related judgments of domestic courts in Germany and Russia will show whether the ECtHR's engagement with the decisions of domestic courts indeed has this effect. In particular, the question can be asked as to whether the Convention's position in domestic law has been strengthened,[164] whether domestic courts are more willing to solve cases involving human rights questions in light of the Convention and/or the ECtHR's jurisprudence,[165] and whether individuals'

[162] As suggested in sections 11.2.4.1, 11.2.4.2 and 11.3.2 *supra*.

[163] As suggested in sections 11.2.4.3 and 11.3.2 *supra*.

[164] So far, the ECtHR has not established a state obligation under the ECHR to directly incorporate the Convention into domestic law in its jurisprudence. See relevant judgments: *James and Others v. the United Kingdom* (Appl. No. 8793/79), Judgment (Plenary), 21 February 1986, Series A, Vol. 98, paras. 84–86; *The Holy Monasteries v. Greece* (Appl. Nos. 13092/ 87 and 13984/88), Judgment (Chamber), 9 December 1994, Series A, Vol. 301-A, para. 90; *McCann and Others v. the United Kingdom* (Appl. No. 18984/91), Judgment (Grand Chamber), 27 September 1995, Series A, Vol. 324, para. 153; and *Christine Goodwin v. the United Kingdom* (Appl. No. 28957/95), Judgment (Grand Chamber), 11 July 2002, ECHR 2002-VI, 1 para. 113.

[165] The ECtHR has so far not held that there is a *general* obligation of domestic courts to review individual complaints in line with the substance of the ECHR. From the Court's current interpretation of relevant articles 6 and 13 ECHR, outside specific contexts, domestic courts' powers to review alleged violations of the Convention can be restricted by domestic law or general policies. See also the analysis by Christoffersen (2009), Fair Balance, *supra* note 12, at 375–76; and Harris *et al.*, The Law of the ECHR, *supra* note 1, at 769–71 and 774–82. However, under some articles of the Convention, the ECtHR requires review in line with the substance of these articles, e.g. concerning article 5(4) ECHR.

rights to complain about an alleged violation of the ECHR or domestic law read in light of the ECHR before domestic courts are reinforced.

As far as Germany is concerned, the ECtHR's use of domestic courts' decisions seems to have contributed to domestic courts' greater engagement with the ECHR and the ECtHR's case law, and thus to a strengthening of the Convention's position in domestic law. This is exemplified in particular in German courts' reactions to the ECtHR's use of German courts' decisions in *Von Hannover v. Germany (No. 1)*[166] and in the first judgment on preventive detention, *M v. Germany*.[167] In *M v. Germany* the ECtHR had noted that domestic courts had not examined whether the applicant's preventive detention beyond a ten-year period was justified under any subparagraph of article 5(1) ECHR other than subparagraph (a), 'because they [the domestic courts] were not required to do so under the provisions of the German Basic Law'.[168] Moreover, it does not seem that the domestic courts, including the FCC, had made their decision on the compatibility of the German Criminal Code's provisions on preventive detention with the Basic Law in light of article 5(1)(a) ECHR and relevant ECtHR jurisprudence. In its eventual reaction to *M. v. Germany*, the FCC not only followed the ECtHR's arguments and declared the relevant provisions of the German Criminal Code unconstitutional, thereby overruling its earlier jurisprudence on the matter, but also clarified that all German courts were obliged to interpret German law, including the Basic Law, in line with the ECHR and ECtHR jurisprudence. The FCC clarified that judgments of the ECtHR would take (*de facto*[169]) precedence over domestic law including the Constitution,[170] and that domestic courts were thus bound to follow them,[171] except in a

166 *Von Hannover v. Germany (No. 1)*, *supra* note 66, 24 June 2004.

167 *M v. Germany*, *supra* note 65.

168 *Ibid.* para. 102.

169 Formally, in the hierarchy of domestic sources of German law, the ECHR only has the rank of an ordinary federal law and thus stands below the German Constitution.

170 FCC, Judgment of 4 May 2011, 2 BvR 2365/09, 2 BvR 740/10, 2 BvR 2333/08, 2 BvR 1152/10 and 2 BvR 571/10, paras. 82 and 88.

171 *Ibid.*, paras. 89–90. The FCC substantiated its reasoning with reference to the Basic Law's 'openness to international law', and to the Basic Law's general aim to avoid conflicts between national and international law. See also M. Andenæs and E. Bjørge, 'National Implementation of ECHR Rights', A. Føllesdal, B. Peters and G. Ulfstein (eds.), *The European Court of Human Rights in a National, European and Global Perspective* (Cambridge University Press, 2014) 181–262, at 234; and the analysis by Behnsen, commenting on responses to *Von Hannover v. Germany (No. 1)*: A. Behnsen, 'Das Recht auf Privatleben und die Pressefreiheit – Die Entscheidung des Europäischen Gerichtshofs für Menschenrechte in der Sache *Hannover ./. Deutschland*', *Zeitschrift für ausländisches öffentliches Recht und Völkerrecht* 65:1 (2005) 239–55, at 251.

very limited number of exceptional cases.[172] The FCC thereby clarified and narrowed the position that it had adopted in earlier jurisprudence in 2004 in its response to *Görgülü v. Germany*.[173] In this response, the FCC had recognised that domestic courts and other authorities should 'take account' of the ECHR and ECtHR jurisprudence in their decisions, but had also held that domestic courts were not bound to follow this jurisprudence as long as they gave good reasons for it.[174] The ECtHR recognised and welcomed the FCC's clarified and ECHR-friendly response to *M. v. Germany* in its later judgments on preventive detention.[175]

Individuals' right to invoke the substance of their ECHR rights before German courts has also been strengthened. This is another effect that can at least partly be attributed to the ECtHR's use of German court decisions in its judgments. In the FCC reactions to the ECtHR's judgments

[172] *Ibid.*, paras. 93–94. The exceptions are: (a) cases that involve 'multipolar fundamental rights relations' ('mehrpolige Grundrechtsverhälnisse'), i.e. cases in which different rights of different individuals have to be weighed against each other. The FCC argues that in these types of cases, it can happen that if the scope of one person's right is broadened by ECtHR jurisprudence, this might at the same time limit the scope of another person's right. In such a case, the domestic courts might still come to different conclusions than the ECtHR; and (b) cases where following the ECtHR 'no longer seems justifiable according to recognised methods of statutory and constitutional interpretation'. It is somewhat unclear when this is the case, but most commentators agree that it will only be so when a judgment of the ECtHR would conflict with the absolute core content of the Basic Law. Exception (b) therefore seems to be a theoretical possibility only. This is observed e.g. by T. Groh, 'Nächster Halt: Karlsruhe – Endstation: Straßburg. Die Bedeutung des BVerfG und des EGMR für die Entscheidung umgangsrechtlicher Streitigkeiten', *Familie Partnerschaft Recht* 15:4 (2009) 153–56, at 154–55; and J. Meyer-Ladewig and H. Petzhold, 'Die Bindung deutscher Gerichte an Urteile des EGMR' *Neue Juristische Wochenschrift* 58:1(2005) 15–21, at 19. See also the analysis by A. Zimmermann, 'Grundrechtsschutz zwischen Karlsruhe und Straßburg', *Schriftenreihe der Juristischen Gesellschaft zu Berlin*, Heft 190 (2012) at 31–32.

[173] *Görgülü v. Germany, supra* note 83.

[174] FCC, Judgment of 14 October 2004, 2 BvR 1481/04, paras. 31–32. This approach has been criticised in the literature as opening the floodgates for lower courts to disregard ECtHR jurisprudence. See e.g. H. Cremer, 'Zur Bindewirkung von EGMR-Urteilen – Anmerkungen zum *Görgülü*-Beschluss des BVerfG vom 14.10.2004' (2004) 31:22 *Europäische Grundrechtezeitschrift* 683–700, at 694; C. Tomuschat, 'The Effects of the Judgments of the European Court of Human Rights According to the German Constitutional Court' (2010) 11:5 *German Law Journal* 513–26, at 522–25. See also the analysis by Zimmermann, Grundrechtsschutz, *supra* note 172, at 30; and H. Sauer, 'Die Neue Schlagkraft der Gemeineuropäischen Grundrechtsjudikatur – Zur Bindung Deutscher Gerichte an die Entscheidungen des Europäischen Gerichtshofs für Menschenrechte', *Zeitschrift für ausländisches öffentliches Recht und Völkerrecht* 65:1 (2005) 35–69, at 45.

[175] See *supra* note 139; and *S. v Germany* (Appl. No.3300/10), Judgment (Chamber), 28 June 2012, not reported, para. 115; *G. v Germany* (Appl. No.65210/09), Judgment (Chamber), 7 June 2012, not reported, para. 45 *et seq.*; and *Glien v. Germany, supra* note 64, paras. 42 *et seq*.

concerning preventive detention, the FCC clarified that individuals could complain about alleged violations of the Convention before the FCC when domestic law had not been interpreted in conformity with the Convention, including when domestic law had been interpreted in disregard of relevant ECtHR jurisprudence.[176] In *Von Hannover (No. 2)* the ECtHR commended this development. It noted that the FCC had 'undertaken a detailed analysis of the Court's case-law in response to the applicants' complaints that the Federal Court of Justice had disregarded the Convention and the Court's [the ECtHR's] case-law'.[177] Such strengthening of individuals' rights to invoke the Convention and the ECtHR's jurisprudence before domestic courts is well in line with the principle of subsidiarity and the primary obligations of states to provide effective remedies at the domestic level, and is likely to contribute to a further strengthening of the cooperation between German courts and the ECtHR in the enforcement of Convention rights in Germany. The establishment of a judicial remedy for overly long criminal and civil proceedings that allegedly violate article 6(1) ECHR in German law in reaction to *Sürmeli v. Germany*[178] and *Rumpf v. Germany*[179] can be seen in the same light.[180]

Similarly, in the aforementioned ruling of June 2013, the RSC reminded all Russian courts of their obligation to apply Russian law in light of the

[176] FCC, Judgment of 4 May 2011, *supra* note 170, paras. 87 and 89. See also Zimmermann (2012), Grundrechtsschutz, *supra* note 172, at 31–32; Cremer, Bindewirkung, *supra* note 174, at 698; and O. Klein, 'Straßburger Wolken am Karlsruher Himmel. Zum geänderten Verhältnis zwischen Bundesverfassungsgericht und Europäischem Gerichtshof für Menschenrechte seit 1998' *Neue Zeitschrift für Verwaltungsrecht* 29:10 (2010) 221–25, at 224.

[177] *Von Hannover v. Germany (No. 2)*, *supra* note 63, para. 125.

[178] *Sürmeli v. Germany* (Appl. No. 75529/01), Judgment (Grand Chamber), 8 June 2006, ECHR 2006-VIII, 179, where the Court found a violation of the reasonable time requirement in article 6(1) ECHR, as well as of article 13 ECHR, since no effective remedy existed for overly long judicial proceedings before domestic courts.

[179] *Rumpf v. Germany* (Appl. No. 46344/06), Judgment (Chamber), 2 September 2010, not reported. In this pilot judgment, the ECtHR directly asked Germany to include an effective domestic remedy for overly long court proceedings in domestic law.

[180] Since 3 December 2011, German law contains a remedy in respect of the length of criminal and civil proceedings: The Act on Protracted Court Proceedings and Criminal Investigations was published in the *Federal Law Gazette* – Part I, 2011, at 2302 *et seq.* on 2 December 2011 and entered into force the next day. This has also been recognised by the ECtHR; see e.g. *Taron v. Germany* (Appl. No. 53126/07), Decision (Chamber), 29 May 2012, not reported, para. 44. For a discussion, see C. Steinbeiß-Winkelmann, 'Rechtsschutz bei überlangen Gerichtsverfahren – Zum Neuen Gesetzentwurf der Bundesregierung' *Zeitschrift für Rechtspolitik* 43:7 (2010) 205–09.

ECHR and to follow the ECtHR's jurisprudence.[181] It observed that to ensure the effective protection of the rights of the Convention, domestic courts should take Strasbourg jurisprudence into account, including those against state parties other than Russia.[182] Moreover, it held that the non-application of the ECHR and/or relevant ECtHR jurisprudence could result in higher courts squashing the decisions of lower courts.[183] However, in December 2013, the RCC made a slightly more ambiguous pronouncement on the role of domestic courts giving effect to ECtHR judgments that contradict domestic Russian law and/or earlier judgments of the RCC.[184] In a decision relating to the implementation of the ECtHR's Grand Chamber judgment *Konstantin Markin v. Russia*, the RCC held that lower courts were obliged to reopen proceedings in cases where the ECtHR had found a domestic Russian law and/or an earlier judgment of Russian courts to contradict the ECHR, as required by relevant provisions of the Russian Code of Civil Procedure.[185] At the same time, however, it held that lower courts were obliged to defer to the RCC if they could not resolve such a case by enforcing a judgment of the ECtHR without at the same time disregarding provisions of domestic law as interpreted by the RCC.[186] As observed by Grigory Vaypan, this in effect means that the RCC narrowed the number of cases in which lower domestic courts would directly apply the Convention, as the RCC declared itself exclusively competent to assess whether Russian law was consistent with the ECHR.[187] In addition, the RCC left the question open in which (exceptional) situations it might give preference to municipal Russian law and/or its own interpretation of this law, even if the ECtHR had found that the relevant municipal law and/or the RCC's interpretation contradicted the ECHR.[188] It made some ECHR-friendly observations, such as that a refusal to implement ECtHR judgments would not be an option for lower courts

[181] RSC, Resolution of the Plenum of 27 June 2013, No. 21. With this resolution, it reminded lower domestic courts of an earlier decision with a similar content that it had adopted in 2003: RSC, Resolution of the Plenum of 10 October 2003, No. 5.

[182] RSC, Resolution of the Plenum of 27 June 2013, No. 21, paras. 2 and 3.

[183] *Ibid.*, para. 16.

[184] RCC, Judgment of 6 December 2013, No. 27-P.

[185] *Ibid.*, para. 3.

[186] *Ibid.*, para. 3.1.

[187] G. Vaypan, 'Acquiescence Affirmed, Its Limits Left Undefined: The *Markin* Judgment and Pragmatism of the Russian Constitutional Court *vis-a-vis* the European Court of Human Rights' *Russian L. J.* 2:3 (2014) 130–40, at 133.

[188] The RCC observed that it would, 'within the limits of its competence', determine 'possible constitutional means of implementation of the judgments' of the ECtHR if a provision of domestic law was found to be inconsistent with the Russian Constitution/the ECHR by

reviewing the case,[189] and that it was willing to deviate from its own earlier judgments should the ECtHR find those judgments contradicting the ECHR.[190] These indicate that the RCC will aim to interpret Russian law in harmony with the Convention and relevant ECtHR jurisprudence in the future and avoid open confrontation with the ECtHR. However, unlike the German FCC, the RCC did not define (very) narrow exceptional situations in which it (or lower Russian courts) might deviate from ECtHR jurisprudence.[191] Instead, it adopted an *ad hoc* and case-by-case approach to solving tensions between the ECHR as interpreted by the ECtHR and domestic law and/or the RCC's judgments, and it limited lower courts' role in this process.

Beyond these decisions of the RCC and RSC that explicitly deal with the relationship between Russian law and the ECHR and domestic courts' role in enforcing the Convention, the record of Russian courts (including the RCC and RSC) in interpreting and applying Russian law in light of the Convention is mixed.[192] There have been decisions in which the RCC has effectively interpreted and applied domestic law in light of the Convention and relevant ECtHR jurisprudence,[193] and where it has confirmed that

the ECtHR. See RCC, Judgment of 6 December 2013, No 27-P, para. 3.2 (last sentence). (Note: the RCC seems to conflate its review of domestic law for compatibility with the Russian Constitution and with the Convention.)

189 *Ibid.*, para. 3.2. The RCC also reiterated its earlier pronouncements that ECtHR judgments were binding on Russian courts, and that the ECHR has become part of Russian law (para. 2). See the discussion of earlier judgments by A. Burkov, 'Russia', L. Hammer and F. Emmert (eds.), *The European Convention on Human Rights and Fundamental Freedoms in Central and Eastern Europe* (The Hague: Eleven, 2012) 425–77, at 435–36.

190 *Ibid.*, para. 3.2.

191 See *supra* note 172.

192 See e.g. the detailed analyses by A. Trochev, 'All Appeals Lead to Strasbourg? Unpacking the Impact of the European Court of Human Rights on Russia' *Demokratizatsiya: The Journal of Post-Soviet Democratization* 17:2 (2009) 145–78; Burkov, Russia, *supra* note 189, at 425–77; А. Бурков, 'Как применить гарантии Европейской конвенции о защите прав человека и основных свобод в судах России', *Права человека. Практика Европейского суда по правам человека* 4 (2012) 34–39; А. Бурков, 'Применение Конвенции о защите прав человека и основных свобод в российских судах общей юрисдикции' *Права человека. Практика Европейского суда по правам человека* 8 (2010) 30–46; V. Starzhenetskii, 'Assessing Human Rights in Russia: Not to Miss the Forest for the Trees' *Rev. of Central and East European L.* 37:2–3 (2012) 349–458, at 351–52; B. Bowring, 'Russia and Human Rights: Incompatible Opposites?' *Göttingen J. of Int'l Law* 1:2 (2009) 257–78, at 272; and M. Issayeva, I. Sergeeva and M. Suchkova, 'Enforcement of the Judgments of the European Court of Human Rights in Russia: Recent Developments and Current Challenges' *Sur – Int'l J. on Human Rights* 8:15 (2011) 67–90.

193 See e.g. the more recent judgment: RCC, Judgment of 22 April 2013, No. 8-P, which has been judged cautiously positive by А. В. Должиков, 'Правосубъектность граждан

individuals under Russian jurisdiction are able to argue cases based on the ECHR and ECtHR jurisprudence before Russian courts.[194] In other judgments, the RCC ignored relevant ECtHR jurisprudence, and there have also been judgments of the RCC that misinterpret the arguments of the ECtHR.[195] While the RSC's references to the ECHR and ECtHR jurisprudence remain relatively rare,[196] and its role model function for lower courts is therefore limited,[197] it has issued a number of circular letters to lower courts on how to interpret and apply domestic law correctly in light of relevant ECtHR jurisprudence against Russia.[198] There is great variation in the extent to which lower courts in the regions of the Russian Federation engage with the ECHR, ranging from some courts rejecting the binding force of the ECHR and ECtHR jurisprudence to others embracing and applying it effectively.[199]

в избирательном судопроизводстве', *Вестник Балтийского федерального университета им. И. Канта* 9 (2013) 21–29; and RCC, Judgment of 10 October 2013, No. 20-P, where the RCC effectively followed the Grand Chamber's findings in *Anchugov and Gladkov v. Russia*, to an extent relevant to the case before the RCC (unlike the ECtHR's *Anchugov and Gladkov*, No. 20-P involved questions of the right to stand for elections, not the right to vote). See also other 'positive' RCC judgments discussed by Burkov, Russia, *supra* note 189, at 435–36 and 454; Starzhenetskii, Assessing Human Rights, *supra* note 192, at 315; Trochev, All Appeals, *supra* note 192, at 158; and Bowring, Incompatible Opposites, *supra* note 192 at 272.

194 RCC, Judgment of 5 February 2007, No. 2-P; and the analysis by Burkov (2012), Russia, *supra* note 189, at 435.

195 Trochev (2009), All Appeals, *supra* note 192, at 158; K. Koroteev and S. Golubok, 'Judgment of the Russian Constitutional Court on Supervisory Review in Civil Proceedings: Denial of Justice, Denial of Europe', *Human Rights Law Review* 7:3 (2007) 619–32; Bowring (2009), Incompatible Opposites, *supra* note 192, at 272. Recent examples are decisions of the RCC on the constitutionality of the Federal Law curtailing NGO activities (RCC, Judgment of 8 April 2014, No. 10-P; several decisions on the constitutionality of regional and federal laws restricting LGTBI rights (RCC, Ruling of 19 January 2010, No. 151-O-O; and Ruling of 24 October 2013, No. 1718-O); as well as cases that were later brought before the ECtHR, such as *Konstantin Markin v. Russia*: RCC, Ruling of 15 January 2009, No. 187-O-O. In this judgment, the RCC ignored relevant ECtHR jurisprudence.

196 Burkov, Russia, *supra* note 189, at 455–61, also observing that the quality of the RSC's references to the ECHR is not very high; Trochev, All Appeals, *supra* note 192, at 159–60.

197 Burkov, Russia, *supra* note 189, at 459.

198 Trochev (2009), All Appeals, *supra* note 192, at 160. They can be accessed at the RSC's website: www.vsrf.ru/second.php.

199 Burkov (2012), Russia, *supra* note 189, at 460–61; and Trochev (2009), All Appeals, *supra* note 192, at 160–61. Reasons for these variations are numerous. Among them are the closeness of regional courts to law enforcement agencies, the limited incentives lower courts have to apply the ECHR (they do not face any repercussions if they do not interpret and apply domestic law in conformity with the Convention), the activities of NGOs in a particular region, and the fact that many lower courts are overloaded with work and

The area of detention is an example of how the ECtHR's attempts to encourage domestic courts' more direct engagement with the ECHR/ECtHR jurisprudence through its own use of Russian domestic courts' decisions have had limited success so far in relation to lower courts.[200] ECtHR judgments concerning Russia and involving article 5 ECHR regularly refer to numerous other judgments handed down by the Court, criticising Russian courts for not taking account of this article as well as relevant ECtHR jurisprudence when, for example, deciding on prolonging the pre-trial detention of an individual.[201] Lower courts fail to apply the relevant provisions of the Russian Code on Criminal Procedure in light of article 5(3) ECHR and the relevant case law of the ECtHR. The RCC had already in 1996 and 1998 given instructions to domestic courts to interpret the Russian Code of Criminal Procedure in conformity with article 5(3) ECHR.[202] Thus, in this situation it does not seem that the ECtHR's engagement with domestic court decisions, differentiating between the 'correct' decisions of the RCC and the 'wrong' decisions of many lower courts, has the effect that lower courts are more likely to follow the 'correct' decisions of the RCC or to generally take more account of the ECHR and relevant ECtHR jurisprudence in their decisions.[203] It can be hoped that the aforementioned 2013 RSC instructions to lower courts will

therefore have little time and resources to understand and engage with the ECHR and relevant ECtHR jurisprudence. See the analysis by Trochev, *supra* note 192, at 156, 157 and 161; and A. Burkov, 'How to Improve the Results of a Reluctant Player: The Case of Russia and the European Convention on Human Rights', S. Flogiatis, T. Zwart and J. Fraser (eds.), *The European Court of Human Rights and its Discontents – Turning Criticism into Strength* (Cheltenham: Edward Elgar, 2013) 147–57, at 154–55.

200 See also the observations by Trochev (2009), All Appeals, *supra* note 192, at 161; and analysis by В. Н. Русинова, 'Актуальные проблемы обеспечения свободы и неприкосновенности личности', *Вестник Российского государственного университета им. И. Канта* 9 (2009) 45–54, at 46–48.

201 *Korchuganova v. Russia, supra* note 152, para. 51; *Sherstobitov v. Russia* (Appl. No. 16266/03), Judgment (Chamber), 10 June 2010, not reported, para. 113; *Shukhardin v. Russia* (Appl. No. 65734/01), Judgment (Chamber), 28 June 2007, not reported, para. 67; *Nakhmanovich v. Russia* (Appl. No. 55669/00), Judgment (Chamber), 2 March 2006, not reported, para. 79; *Khudoyorov v. Russia* (Appl. No. 6847/02), Judgment (Chamber), 8 November 2005, ECHR 2005-X, 301 (extracts), para. 142; *Tsarenko v. Russia, supra* note 51, paras. 60–61; and *Pyatkov v. Russia, supra* note 48, para. 89.

202 See the reference to the relevant decisions of the RCC in *Tsarenko v. Russia, supra* note 51, para. 60; and *Yuriy Rudakov v. Russia, supra* note 152, paras. 49–53.

203 The same can be concluded from *Ageyevy v. Russia, supra* note 35, para. 104, where the ECtHR noted that domestic courts in this case did not follow the detailed instructions of the RCC to lower courts to ensure that the right to privacy received sufficient protection (honour, dignity and reputation), in line with ECtHR jurisprudence.

increase these courts' willingness and capacity to improve in this and other areas – something which is more likely if the RSC and RCC would better monitor and sanction the non-implementation of their instructions to lower courts.[204]

11.4.2.2 Better Procedures and Reasoning in German and Russian Court Decisions?

As analysed in subsections 11.2.4.2 and 11.2.4.3, another way the ECtHR uses domestic courts' decisions in order to encourage those courts to enforce the Convention more directly at the domestic level is through its comments on the procedures that domestic courts followed, and on the quality of their reasoning. Also in this context, the ECtHR may limit the strictness of its review of domestic court decisions, including, where relevant, by giving domestic courts a wider margin of appreciation in their decisions on material provisions of the ECHR/parallel domestic law. The question we try to answer next is thus whether this indeed encourages German and Russian courts to follow certain procedures and to deliver better-reasoned judgments in fundamental rights cases.

Procedures and proportionality analyses have been improved in German court decisions, in particular regarding article 8 ECHR cases that require a balancing of interests of several individuals involved, usually the interests of biological and legal mothers and fathers and their children, and sometimes the interests also of foster or adoptive parents. In particular, judgments mentioned in subsection 11.2.4.2 had the effect that German courts are now giving greater weight to biological fathers' rights to have contact with or receive (joint) custody of their children who were born out of wedlock, and who may have another legal father.[205] In reaction to *Zaunegger v. Germany*, the FCC declared provisions of the German Civil Code unconstitutional which established that biological fathers not living with their child's mother could only obtain custody over their children

[204] That this is a major problem underlying the non-implementation of the ECHR/ECtHR jurisprudence by lower courts is noted by Burkov, Russia, *supra* note 189, at 451–52; and Trochev, All Appeals, *supra* note 192, at 156 and 160.

[205] It is widely recognised that the ECtHR had considerable influence in this area, including through its use of German court decisions. See e.g. C. Campbell, 'Mehr Rechte für Väter von nicht-ehelichen Kindern' *Neue Juristische Wochenschrift – Spezial* 9:19 (2012) 580–81; D. Kloster-Harz, 'Gesetz zur Stärkung der Rechte des leiblichen, nicht rechtlichen Vaters auf Umgang und Auskunft – Umsetzung der Rechtsprechung des EGMR durch den deutschen Gesetzgeber' *Zeitschrift für Familienrecht und Familienverfahrensrecht* 5:15 (2013) 337–39; and C. Brückner, 'Väterrechte vor dem Europäischen Gerichtshof für Menschenrechte', *Familie Partnerschaft Recht* 11:5 (2005) 200–04.

born out of wedlock with the mother's consent.[206] The FCC ordered the legislator to change the respective provisions, and the lower courts to interpret the respective provisions in light of the *Zaunegger* judgment as long as no legislative changes had been made.[207] The ECtHR's finding of a violation of article 8 ECHR in *Zaunegger v. Germany*, *Anayo v. Germany* and *Schneider v. Germany* were all based on provisions of the German Civil Code, the application of which resulted in a situation where German courts were unable to strike a fair balance between the rights to family and private life of biological and legal fathers and mothers and their children.[208] The law prevented them from taking due account of the rights of biological fathers, and of children's rights to have contact with their biological fathers, as long as this was not detrimental to their best interests.[209] In July 2013, the changed provisions of the German Civil Code entered into force,[210] and German courts are developing criteria that allow them to determine on a case-by-case basis how the rights of biological and legal fathers and mothers and their children are to be balanced.[211] Earlier, the FCC had initiated similar changes to relevant German law in response to the judgment *Keegan v. Ireland*,[212] allowing domestic courts to take account of biological fathers' rights in adoption procedures.[213]

In addition to this effect, we can observe another potential effect of the ECtHR's engagement with German court procedures and decisions on the subsequent conduct of German courts. This effect is the FCC's inclination to conduct its own comparative analyses on how a certain issue is regulated in different CoE member states, and to rely on the outcome in its reasoning. Such comparative analyses are, of course, only conducted in areas where ECHR law is unclear or developing.[214]

206 FCC, Judgment of 21 July 2010, 1 BvR 420/09. See also the discussion by H. Küpper, 'The Decisions of the European Court of Human Rights and their Implementation in Germany' *Vienna Journal on International Constitutional Law* 5:2 (2011) 200–10, at 207–08.

207 *Ibid.*, para.74.

208 *Zaunegger v. Germany*, *supra* note 83, para. 44; *Anayo v. Germany*, *supra* note 79, para. 70; *Schneider v. Germany*, *supra* note 83, para. 100.

209 German law was based on the assumption that it would automatically be in the best interest of children to not have contact with their biological fathers when the mother opposed such contact.

210 Gesetz zur Stärkung der Rechte des leiblichen, nicht rechtlichen Vaters, vom 4. Juli 2013 (BGBl. I S. 2176).

211 See the analysis by Kloster-Harz, Gesetz zur Stärkung, *supra* note 205, at 339; and Horndasch, Das Recht des Kindes, *supra* note 146.

212 *Keegan v. Ireland* (Appl. No. 16969/90), Judgment (Chamber), 26 May 1994, Series A, Vol. 290.

213 Brückner (2005), Väterrechte, *supra* note 205, at 203.

214 See *Stübing v. Germany* (Appl. No. 43547/08), Judgment (Chamber), 12 April 2012, not reported, para. 30.

The ECtHR's encouragements of Russian domestic courts to improve their procedures as well as to deliver better-reasoned judgments, including through the application of the principle of proportionality, also seem to have some positive effects. In the aforementioned 2013 instructions to lower courts, the RSC reminded lower courts to 'always *justify* the need to limit human rights and fundamental freedoms on the basis of findings of fact'.[215] It further 'called courts' attention to the fact that restrictions to human rights and fundamental freedoms are permitted only if there are relevant and sufficient grounds for such restrictions, and if a balance is established between the legitimate interests of the person whose rights or freedoms are limited, and the legitimate interests of other persons, the state and society'.[216] Likewise, there are indications that some lower courts provide sufficient reasons, for example when they justify the extension of detention pending criminal proceedings.[217] This has been recognised by the ECtHR in several judgments of 2014.[218] At the same time, concerning article 5(3) ECHR alone, there remain many cases also before the ECtHR where the Court, including the Grand Chamber,[219] repeatedly criticised Russian courts for their schematic patterns of reasoning, failing to take account of the individual circumstances of the person in pre-trial detention and failing to come forward with a convincing justification of why continued pre-trial detention was necessary.[220]

The RCC has, at least in two judgments, relied on the European consensus doctrine. This is an indication that the ECtHR's engagement with Russian and other domestic courts' decisions may have influenced the RCC's procedures and encouraged it to look beyond the borders of the Russian Federation to examine how a certain issue is regulated elsewhere, and to rely on these findings in its interpretation and application of Russian law in light of the ECHR. In the first judgment of 2009, the RCC

215 RSC, Resolution of the Plenum of 27 June 2013, No. 21, para. 8 (emphasis added).

216 *Ibid.* (author's translation).

217 The RSC has also required this of lower courts; see RSC, Resolution of the Plenum of 19 December 2013, No. 41; and Resolution of the Plenum of 29 October 2009, No. 22.

218 See e.g. *Zimin v. Russia* (Appl. No. 48613/06), Judgment (Chamber), 6 February 2014, not reported, paras. 33–42; *Amirov v. Russia* (Appl. no. 51857/13), Judgment (Chamber), 27 November 2014, not reported, paras. 109–10; *Sigarev v. Russia* (Appl. No. 53812/10), Judgment (Chamber) 30 October 2014, not reported, para. 51–57; and *Shikuta v. Russia* (Appl. No.45373/05), Judgment (Chamber), 11 April 2013, not reported, paras. 46–48.

219 *Idalov v. Russia* (Grand Chamber), *supra* note 39, para. 147.

220 *Dirdizov v. Russia*, *supra* note 101, para. 108, referring to a great number of other cases against Russia where the ECtHR found that domestic courts had failed to provide sufficient and relevant grounds for keeping an applicant in pre-trial detention. For an analysis of the reasons for this, see e.g. Trochev, All Appeals, *supra* note 192, at 157 and 161.

had relied on a clear trend in Europe and general international law that classifies the imposition of the death penalty as inhuman and degrading treatment. Based on this, the RCC held that reintroducing the death penalty into Russian law after a ten-year moratorium would breach Russia's international obligations.[221] The second judgment was handed down by the RCC on 22 April 2013[222] and concerned the question of whether voters had a right to challenge infringements of their electoral rights before Russian courts. It had come up in the aftermath of the Russian State Duma elections in December 2011. In many cases, observers had noted a dramatic difference in the number of votes reported in the central state automatic counting system and the number of votes that had been recorded by district election commissions in their final protocols.[223] Voters, observers and members of district election committees had challenged these irregularities before Russian courts. These courts, including the RSC,[224] rejected the complaints, holding that individual voters' rights had not been affected by the irregularities, as the right to participate in elections was limited to submitting a paper ballot to the voting boxes. Only political parties could challenge irregularities in the counting and reporting of election results before domestic courts. These arguments were followed by the representative of the Russian president, the lower and upper houses of the parliament, the Ministry of Justice and the Procurator's Office, when the complaint reached the RCC.[225] Relying on relevant ECtHR jurisprudence, a comparative analysis of the situation in sixteen other European and member states of the Commonwealth of Independent States (CIS) with a system of proportional representation and PACE resolutions, the RCC rejected these arguments.[226] It held that individual voters had a legitimate interest that their vote in support of one or another political party or candidate were counted up correctly, and that therefore the 'active electoral right' was not limited to the right to come to an electoral district and cast a vote freely. The right also included the process of counting votes and obtaining a correct final result which reflected the real will of the electorate.

[221] RCC, Ruling of 19 November 2009, No. 1344-O-R.

[222] RCC, Judgment of 22 April, No. 8-P.

[223] The differences were always in favour of Putin's ruling party *Yedinaya Rossiya* ('United Russia').

[224] RSC, Ruling of the Appeals Chamber of 9 November 2012, No. 14-KF-12–560.

[225] See the summary of the processes that led to the RCC's judgment by A. Burkov, 'Voter – Is He a Trembling Creature, or Has He the Right?', 24 November 2013, available at www.sutyajnik.ru/articles/484.html; see also Должиков, Правосубъектность, *supra* note 193.

[226] RCC, Judgment of 22 April 2013, No. 8-P, para. 2.2; see also the analysis by Должиков, Правосубъектность, *supra* note 193, at 25.

Voters should have the right to check the validity of the counting process, including through initiating review procedures before domestic courts (within certain limits).[227]

11.4.2.3 Do German and Russian Courts, Where Necessary, Contribute to the Evolutive Interpretation of the Convention?

Last, we can ask whether the ECtHR's engagement with domestic courts' decisions as described in subsections 11.2.4.4 and 11.3.3 indeed has the effect that domestic courts, where necessary, engage in the dynamic interpretation of the Convention or parallel domestic constitutional law in light of 'present-day conditions'.

The judgment in *Stübing v. Germany* indicates that the FCC is ready to engage in evolutive interpretation of German law in light of the ECHR, even though in this particular case it decided not to declare the relevant provision of the German Criminal Code unconstitutional. Among other things, it relies on the fact that there was no European consensus on the question of whether it was necessary to criminalise incest to protect public health and morals.

There are other FCC judgments that also indicate that the FCC has recognised its role in contributing to the development of ECHR rights, or, most frequently, the rights enshrined in the German Constitution in light of the ECHR.[228] The FCC does so either through evolutive interpretation of the Basic Law/ECHR,[229] or by calling on the legislature to examine whether domestic legislation securing fundamental rights is still up-to-date and in line with more recent social developments. An example of the former is a 2013 decision of the FCC on same-sex couples' right to second-parent adoption.[230] In this decision, the FCC held that the term 'parents' used in article 6(2) of the Basic Law should be understood as not only

[227] RCC, Judgment of 22 April 2013, No. 8-P, para. 2.3; despite the largely Convention-conforming findings of the RCC, the applicants challenged certain subsequent findings of the RCC that unduly limit the right to complain about irregularities in electoral processes in Russian courts, before the ECtHR. The case is pending before the ECtHR (*Davydov and Others v. Russia* (Appl. No. 75947/11), communicated on 18 March 2014).

[228] The role of German courts, including of the FCC, in concretising and thereby developing open legal provisions is discussed by H. Cremer, '"Caroline II – Zwischenschritt auf dem Weg zu einem Kooperationsverhältnis Straßburg-Karlsruhe?" – Eine kurze Stellungnahme' *Zeitschrift für ausländisches öffentliches Recht und Vökerrecht* 74:2 (2014) 215–22, at 221.

[229] For more details, see also C. Grewe, 'Vergleich zwischen den Interpretationsmethoden europäischer Verfassungsgerichte und des Europäischen Gerichtshofs für Menschenrechte' *Zeitschreift für ausländisches öffentliches Recht und Völkerrecht* 61:2 (2001) 459–73, at 469.

[230] FCC, Judgment of 19 February 2013, 1 BvL 1/11, 1 BvR 3247/09.

covering opposite-sex parents but also same-sex parents. In coming to this conclusion, it observed that when the Constitution had been adopted in 1949, the term 'parents' clearly meant a mother and a father of a child.[231] However, in light of changed social circumstances and the increased recognition of same-sex partnerships in German legislation, today the term 'parents' should be understood to include parents of the same sex.[232] It is possible that the ECtHR will rely on this FCC judgment in judgments against states other than Germany in the future when it moves on to strengthen the rights of same-sex couples. An example for the latter means of contributing to the development of ECHR rights in Germany is an FCC decision of 2003 concerning the rights of biological fathers to access their children. In this decision, the FCC had asked the legislature to evaluate whether the assumptions underlying the provisions of the German Civil Code that automatically gave sole custody over a child born out of wedlock to the mother, and did not give the child's father a right to request joint custody against the will of the mother, were still reflecting reality.[233] These two examples show that the FCC can contribute to the evolutive interpretation of the ECHR, even if it does so rather indirectly, by interpreting provisions of the Basic Law progressively, or by evaluating whether legislation aimed to protect fundamental rights reflects present-day realities.[234] To what extent the FCC has been inspired to do so by the ECtHR's use of the FCC's decisions in its judgments is difficult to say.

Apart from the judgment adopted by the RCC on the right to vote mentioned earlier where the RCC did not clearly engage in evolutive interpretation, but relied on the European consensus doctrine that is regularly associated with evolutive interpretation, there are few indications that Russian courts feel encouraged by the ECtHR to engage in such interpretation. The reason for this might be that the Russian judiciary focuses first and foremost on bringing domestic law into line with existing ECtHR jurisprudence, and less on contributing to the progressive development of the law of the ECHR through evolutive interpretation.[235] After all, the CoE itself recognised that the legal order of the Russian Federation did not meet the standards of

[231] *Ibid.*, para. 55.

[232] *Ibid.*

[233] FCC, Judgment of 29 January 2003, 1 BvL 20/99 and 1 BvR 933/01; see also Campbell, Mehr Rechte, *supra* note 205, at 580.

[234] Interpretation of domestic law in light of present-day conditions is common also at the Federal Court of Justice. See: T. Fischer and R. Gerhardt, 'Rechtsprechung ist in einem Weiteren Sinn auch Rechtspolitik' *Zeitschrift für Rechtspolitik* 74:2 (2014) 58–61, at 58.

[235] This assumption seems to be shared also by the president of the RCC, Valery Zorkin; see V. Zorkin, 'Interaction between National and Supranational Justice in Modern Times: New

the Convention when the country joined the CoE in 1996,[236] and Russia is still in the process of reforming its legal system. Wojciech Sadurski has also observed this in regard to other Eastern European member states of the CoE.[237] In addition, following a long tradition of positivistic, text-based application of law, it is only slowly that the Russian courts are getting accustomed to the practice of teleological interpretation of domestic law and the ECHR,[238] as well as the notion of legal precedent.[239] Lastly, until recently, the ECtHR did not require that Russian applicants raise their complaint before the RCC or RSC before they submit it in Strasbourg. It did not consider proceedings before the RCC and RSC an effective remedy that needs to be exhausted in line with article 35(1) ECHR.[240] Many Russian cases on which the ECtHR has decided have therefore not been considered by the RSC or RCC before, including cases where the RSC or RCC could potentially have engaged in evolutive interpretation.[241] Consequently, compared to the FCC, the RSC and RCC have had fewer opportunities to show their willingness to engage in evolutive interpretation of the ECHR/the Russian Constitution, something that may, however, change with a recent decision of the ECtHR (at least for civil cases).[242]

Prospects', O. Chernishova and M. Lobov (eds.), *Russia and the European Court of Human Rights: A Decade of Change. Essays in Honour of Anatoly Kovler* (Oisterwijk: Wolf Legal Publishers, 2013) 27–38, at 38.

[236] See the analysis by Burkov (2012), Russia, *supra* note 189, at 425–27; and L. Mälksoo, 'Concluding Observations: Russia and European Human Rights-Law: Margins of the Margin of Appreciation', *Rev. of Central and East European L.* 37:2–3 (2012) 359–69, at 363.

[237] W. Sadurski, *Constitutionalism and the Enlargement of Europe* (Oxford University Press, 2012), at 49–50; see also Voßkuhle and Gerhardt, Wir Leben, *supra* note 110, at 61, making a similar observation.

[238] On this, see e.g. the analysis by Т.К. Примак, Г.В. Казакова, К.А. Орлова, 'Проблемы толкования правовых норм в деятельности судебных органов' *Вестник Балтийского федерального университета им. И. Канта* 9 (2014) 35–43.

[239] Starzhenetskii (2012), Assessing Human Rights, *supra* note 192, at 351; and W. Pomeranz and M. Gutbrod, 'The Push for Precedent in Russia's Legal System', *Rev. of Central and East European L.* 37:1 (2012) 1–30.

[240] *Denisov v. Russia* (Appl. No. 33408/03), Decision (Chamber), 6 May 2004, not reported; *Berdzenishvili v. Russia* (Appl. No. 31697/03), Decision (Chamber), 29 January 2004, ECHR 2004-II, 317 (extracts). The main reason for this finding was the fact that Russian law did not set any time limits for lodging complaints before the RCC and RSC, undermining the principle of legal certainty. After the Russian legislature reformed the relevant provisions of the Russian Code of Civil Procedure, the ECtHR has recognised that for civil cases, applicants need to bring their case to the RSC to comply with the exhaustion of domestic remedies rule (*Abramyan and Yakubovskiye v. Russia* (Appl. Nos. 38951/13 and 59611/13), Decision (Chamber), 12 May 2015, not reported).

[241] Lower courts generally do not engage in evolutive interpretation to the same extent as apex courts.

[242] *Abramyan and Yakubovskiye v. Russia, supra* note 240, paras. 93–103.

11.5 Concluding Remarks

The analysis in this chapter reveals that the ECtHR uses the built-in dialogue feature of the Convention system with the overarching *purpose* to strengthen the cooperative elements of that very system between itself and domestic courts for the effective safeguarding of the rights of the Convention. First, the Court does so by encouraging domestic courts to effectively fulfil certain tasks that it cannot fulfil itself because of its limited capacities due to its position as a regional human rights court. Second, the ECtHR achieves this by encouraging domestic courts to take on a stronger role in enforcing the rights of the Convention at the domestic level. This is clear from the fact that the ECtHR uses the strictness of its review as an 'incentive', that is, as a tool to 'reward' domestic courts for their direct engagement with the Convention/ECtHR jurisprudence, for following relevant procedures and for giving thorough reasons for their decisions. Third, the ECtHR accomplishes this by encouraging domestic courts to not shy away from engaging in evolutive interpretation where this is necessary for the effective protection of Convention rights in light of 'present-day conditions'. Concerning the *effects* of this dialogue with domestic courts, the analysis showed that the ECtHR is successful with this approach when it comes to strengthening German courts as primary actors in the cooperative system. The effects on Russian courts in this regard are more mixed.

Finally, an attempt should be made to tentatively answer the question raised in the introduction as to whether the ECtHR has adopted different modes of 'dialoguing' with German and Russian courts, given the different stages of development of the German and Russian judicial system. It seems that the ECtHR has not done so. It scrutinises all domestic courts' procedures and decisions, and highlights problematic and positive elements concerning both German and Russian courts. It is clear that there are more problematic elements to note in Russian court decisions than in German court decisions. However, the analysis revealed that the Court is ready to highlight good arguments and conduct by Russian courts in its dialogue, even if other elements in the relevant decision are insufficient. Any perceived difference in treatment of German and Russian court decisions by the ECtHR results from the degree to which Russian and German courts secure the Convention rights themselves through the many different modes of engagement with the ECHR and ECtHR jurisprudence highlighted in this chapter, fulfilling their primary implementation obligations under the Convention.

12

Encouraging Judicial Dialogue

The Contribution of Human Rights NGOs' Briefs to the European Court of Human Rights

LAURA VAN DEN EYNDE

12.1 Introduction

As underlined by the editor of this volume and by other contributors, much remains to be explored as to 'how judges learn about foreign law developments'.[1] This chapter lifts the veil on one of the ways[2] via which judges – in this context, judges of the European Court of Human Rights (ECtHR or the Court) – learn about foreign legal material: the contributions made by *amici curiae*, or 'friends of the court'. The hypothesis that ECtHR judges find inspiration to look at the jurisprudence of other courts in *amicus curiae* briefs stems from judgments directly indicating that comparative elements were brought by *amici*,[3] from statements of the judges themselves and from scholarly literature.[4] The hypothesis is thus

[1] R. Black and L. Epstein, '(Re-)Setting the Scholarly Agenda on Transjudicial Communication', *Law & Social Inquiry* 32:3 (2007) 789–807, at 805.

[2] Among the interesting avenues which could also be explored is the possibility for the Court to *request* comparative analysis, for example from universities or expert centres. Despite the potential advantages of such a mechanism, the Court has not used this possibility so far.

[3] For example, in *Sheffield and Horsham v. the United Kingdom* (Appl. Nos. 22985/93 and 23390/94), Judgment (Grand Chamber), 30 July 1998, Reports 1998-V, para. 35, the Court explicitly said to have examined the comparative study submitted by Liberty. In *Christine Goodwin v. the United Kingdom* (Appl. No. 28957/95), Judgment (Grand Chamber), 11 July 2002, ECHR 2002-VI, 1, paras. 55–57, the Court mentioned the 'updated' information brought by this NGO. See also *Mamatkulov and Askarov v. Turkey* (Appl. Nos. 46827/99 and 46951/99), Judgment (Grand Chamber), 4 February 2005, ECHR 2005-I, 293, para. 98.

[4] However, some authors, while discussing the phenomenon of judicial dialogue, do not even list *amicus curiae* participation as one of the avenues through which judges could be encouraged to look and maybe cite cases from other jurisdictions. See, for examples, R. Nickel, 'Transnational Borrowing Among Judges: Towards a Common Core of European and Global Constitutional Law?', R. Nickel (ed.), *Conflict of Laws and Laws of Conflict in Europe and Beyond – Patterns of Supranational and Transnational Juridification* (Antwerp: Intersentia, 2010) 239–62, at 248–53; and G. Canivet, 'La Pratique du Droit Comparé par les Cours Suprêmes. Brèves Réflexions sur le Dialogue des Juges dans les Expériences Françaises

the following: briefs which try to inform and/or to influence the Court by engaging in comparative legal analyses and by referring to various international, regional and domestic court decisions can encourage the Court to have this 'dialogue'. This contribution empirically examines whether, and in what form, *amici* indeed bring this information in their briefs to the ECtHR, and whether traces of the comparative references of the briefs can be found in the Court's judgments. An exploration of the briefs' content and their influence on the judgments helps to explain one of the methods through which ECtHR judges become aware of foreign decisions. It also seeks to provide answers to questions asked in this volume regarding the impact of the Court's use of *amicus curie* briefs on the extent, methods and purposes of the ECtHR's engagement in judicial dialogue.

This chapter focuses on the briefs submitted by human rights non-governmental organisations (NGOs) to the Grand Chamber of the ECtHR. This topic is particularly relevant, as no empirical work has yet examined the content of the briefs and drawn the link with the practice of the ECtHR's judicial dialogue. While some studies have closely examined the role of civil society organisations before the ECtHR, they do not focus on the comparative material that their briefs bring before the Court.[5] Most authors who assert that *amici* play an important role base their findings on a small number of cases, often those that are most frequently cited; or they only rely on the references in the judgments.

This chapter adopts the following structure. Section 12.2 sets out the research methodology relied on in this chapter. Based on a short overview of the existing literature, Section 12.3 briefly examines some aspects of the extent, method and purpose of the ECtHR's engagement with judicial dialogue. Section 12.4 presents the findings from the briefs' analysis in three subsections. In the first, a general picture is drawn, which shows the recent increase in *amicus*' participation before the Grand Chamber and highlights the number of briefs which look at comparative material in conjunction with relevant Convention articles (subsection 12.4.1). The references to international or foreign judgments are counted and classified according to whether they emanate from international or regional jurisdictions or

et Européenne: en Commentaire de l'Article de Sir Basil Markesinis et Jörg Fedtke: Le Juge en Tant que Comparatiste', *Tulane L. Rev.* 80:11 (2005) 221–45, at 226. The reason why they do not mention *amicus curiae* briefs stems probably from the particular angle they are writing from and the practices of other courts.

[5] L. Hodson, *NGOs and the Struggle for Human Rights in Europe* (Oxford: Hart Publishing, 2011) and R. Cichowski, 'Civil Society and the European Court of Human Rights', J. Christoffersen and M. Madsen (eds.), *The European Court of Human Rights between Law and Politics* (Oxford University Press, 2011) 77–97.

from Council of Europe (CoE) member states or non-member states (subsection 12.4.2). The next subsection (12.4.3) analyses methodological concerns in the briefs, namely whether the briefs provide some insights about the way *amici* proceeded to select and gather the comparative material. Section 12.5 inquires as to whether comparative references in the briefs are also found in the case law and, more generally, links the analysis to the previous discussion in Section 12.3 concerning the extent, method and purpose of the ECtHR's engagement in judicial dialogue. Concluding remarks are offered in Section 12.6.

12.2 Research Methodology

The first step was to collect the *amicus curiae* briefs and analyse their content.[6] Written comments can be submitted to the ECtHR by 'any State or person concerned not party to the proceedings'.[7] This chapter, however, focuses on interventions by one of the largest and most prolific type of intervener: NGOs dedicated to the promotion and protection of human rights.[8] A broad definition of the term 'NGO' has been adopted[9] in order to include, among others, law school clinics and research centres. For four reasons, the analysis is also limited to briefs submitted to the Grand Chamber, which is composed of seventeen judges, compared

[6] For a detailed account on how the briefs were found, see L. Van den Eynde, 'An Empirical Look at the Amicus Curiae Practice of Human Rights NGOs before the European Court of Human Rights', *Netherlands Quarterly of Human Rights* 31:3 (2013) 271–314, at 278–79.

[7] Convention for the Protection of Human Rights and Fundamental Freedoms (ECHR) (4 November 1950) 213UNTS 222, entered into force 3 September 1953, article 36(2). This article provides two different situations: one where the Court invites an *amicus curiae* submission (this is rare) and one where a third party seeks to provide information to the Court on its own initiative. Acceptance of such briefs is 'at the discretion of the President of the Court'; R. Mackenzie, 'The Amicus Curiae in International Courts: Towards Common Procedural Approaches?', T. Treves *et al.* (eds.), *Civil Society, International Courts and Compliance Bodies* (The Hague: T.M.C. Asser Press, 2005) 295–311, at 303.

[8] Of course, each NGO defends its own vision of what 'human rights' entail, sometimes emphasising a specific interpretation of a right.

[9] That is, groups that are private (i.e. not established by a government or an intergovernmental agreement), independent and non-profit, and not founded by or controlled by a government and which have as a primary concern the promotion and/or protection of human rights. Groups whose primary goal is not the defence of human rights, such as professional associations, have been excluded; see also the definition of Peter Macalistair-Smith in P. Macalistair-Smith, 'Non-Governmental Organizations, Humanitarian Action and Human Rights', U. Beyerlin *et al.* (eds.), *Recht Zwischen Umbruch und Bewahrung: Völkerrecht, Europarecht, Staatsrecht: Festschrift für Rudolf Bernhardt* (Berlin: Springer, 1995) 477–502, at 477.

to the chambers, which are composed of seven judges.[10] First, the Grand Chamber decides on cases that raise the most important and leading legal questions[11] and plays a special role in safeguarding a unified interpretation of the Convention. Second, the Grand Chamber's comparative analyses are more developed than those made by other formations of the Court.[12] Third, as will be shown in this chapter, the ratio of *amicus* participation is highest before the Grand Chamber. And fourth and finally, it was necessary to limit the number of analysed briefs in a chapter of limited scope.

At the time of writing (August 2015), the Grand Chamber has delivered 388 judgments and decisions in total.[13] NGOs' submissions were collected until January 2014 and NGOs had submitted interventions in seventy-five of the Grand Chamber cases, which is 19.3 per cent.[14] This is much higher than the ratio obtained when all the Court's judgments are considered, as *amici curiae* were found to have participated in only 1.2 per cent of the ECtHR's proceedings.[15] In those 75 cases before the Grand Chamber, 127 briefs were submitted between 1994 and 2014.

10 Rules 24 and 25 of the Rules of the European Court of Human Rights (1 June 2015).

11 See articles 30 and 43 ECHR; and J. Sikuta and E. Hubalkova, *European Court of Human Rights: Case Law of the Grand Chamber 1998–2006* (The Hague: T.M.C. Asser Press, 2007).

12 F. Tulkens, S. Van Drooghenbroeck and F. Krenc, 'Le Soft Law et la Cour Européenne des Droits de l'Homme: Questions de Légitimité et de Méthode', *Revue Trimestrielle des Droits de l'Homme* 91 (2012) 433–89, at 473. See also L. Burgorgue-Larsen, 'Les Interventions Eclairées devant la Cour Européenne des Droits de l'Homme ou le Rôle Stratégique des Amici Curiae', Collectif, *La Conscience des Droits - Mélanges en l'Honneur de Jean-Paul Costa* (Dalloz, Paris, 2011) 67–81, at 74; L. Hennebel, 'Le Rôle des Amici Curiae devant la Cour Européenne des Droits de l'Homme', *Revue Trimestrielle des Droits de l'Homme* 71 (2007) 641–68, at 658.

13 According to the research tool HUDOC: <hudoc.echr.coe.int/eng#{%22documentcollectionid2%22:[%22GRANDCHAMBER%22]> (last accessed 5 August 2015). I extracted the Grand Chamber judgments and decisions (when it exceptionally rules on admissibility) and eliminated the cases repeated on the list, which often concern preliminary objections or pecuniary damage awards. The percentage is higher if the third-party interventions made before the former plenary Court are taken into account (such as the cases *Soering v. the United Kingdom* (Appl. No. 14038/88), 7 July 1989, Series A, Vol. 161; *Sunday Times v. the United Kingdom and Observer and Guardian Newspapers v. the United Kingdom* (Appl. No. 13166/87), 26 November 1991, Series A, Vol. 217; and *Lingens v. Austria* (Appl. No. 9815/82), 8 July 1986, Series A, Vol. 103).

14 The cases which received the most attention are *A, B and C v. Ireland* (Appl. No. 25579/05), Judgment (Grand Chamber) 16 December 2010, ECHR 2010-VI, 185; *Lautsi and Others v. Italy* (Appl. No. 30814/06), Judgment (Grand Chamber), 18 March 2011, ECHR 2011-III, 61 (extracts); *X. and Others v. Austria* (Appl. No. 19010/07), Judgment (Grand Chamber) 19 February 2013, ECHR-II, 1; *Center of Legal Resources on behalf of Valentin Câmpeanu v. Romania* (Appl. No. 47848/08), Judgment (Grand Chamber), 17 July 2014, selected for publication 2014; and *S.A.S. v. France* (Appl. No. 43835/11), Judgment (Grand Chamber), 1 July 2014, selected for publication 2014.

15 See Van den Eynde, An Empirical Look, *supra* note 6.

The briefs have been coded to track the following information: the coding records from which organisation(s) the brief emanates and when it was submitted (columns 2–3 of the table in the Appendix). The latter shows the increase in the number of briefs submitted, and this might explain why the process of the ECtHR's judicial dialogue has accelerated in recent years.[16] Regarding the extent of 'dialogue' in the briefs, the coding records which Convention article(s) is (are) discussed in the briefs and whether the briefs contain comparative legal material (columns 5–6). If a brief does contain such material, the table records the references to judgments of other jurisdictions, indicating which international or regional court[17] are cited (columns 7–10), and in case the judgment comes from a national court, the country of origin is recorded (columns 11–12). A distinction has been drawn between case law from the Council of Europe member states and non-member states. This approach follows the distinction made by Hanneke Senden between the internal and the external component of comparative interpretation: the internal component means that the comparative study limits itself to a comparison between the countries that fall within the jurisdiction of the Court, that is, the contracting states to the ECHR.[18] The external component refers to the use of sources that are not covered by the first component.[19] It has been decided not to record references to judicial decisions of the respondent member state.[20]

Subsection 12.4.3 examines whether the briefs contain a methodological component, in particular whether they justify the selection of courts they cite. Finally, in order to uncover some aspects of a brief's influence on the extent of the ECtHR's judicial dialogue, the last column of the table links the references found in the briefs with those found in the respective ECtHR judgments. A restrictive approach has been adopted, and only the exact

[16] E. Voeten, 'Borrowing and Nonborrowing among International Courts', *The Journal of Legal Studies* 39:2 (2010) 547–76, at 558.

[17] References to the Human Rights Committee have also been included, although it is a quasi-judicial body. The references to other UN treaty bodies are not examined in this contribution. For a classification, see C. Romano, 'The International Judiciary in Context', *The Project on International Courts and Tribunals*, www.pict-pcti.org/publications/synoptic_chart/synop_c4.pdf.

[18] H. Senden, *Interpretation of Fundamental Rights in a Multilevel Legal System: An Analysis of the European Court of Human Rights and the Court of Justice of the European Union* (Cambridge: Intersentia, 2011), at 115. She includes references to international documents, but I limit the analysis to references to national courts outside the CoE.

[19] *Ibid.*

[20] Although this is the place where dialogue most often takes place, it would be difficult to draw conclusions from the briefs as to whether they 'just' want to explain the domestic situation or if they want to encourage judicial dialogue.

same references in the briefs and in the judgments were counted. This implies that some of the *amici's* comparative material influence might be missed, and in this regard a few methodological caveats must be stressed. First it must be recalled that cross-citations within the ECtHR's case law are not perfect indicators of judicial dialogue,[21] especially since non-quotation at the ECtHR is apparently quite frequent.[22] Moreover, the influence could also come from other sources than the *amicus curiae* briefs, as the ECtHR judges may have received this information from their own research division or from the parties to the case. Finally, even if the same comparative material is referred to in a brief and the respective judgment of the ECtHR, there might be different uses of it: for example, a foreign or international case can only be mentioned in a footnote in the brief, but is extensively analysed in the ECtHR judgment, and vice versa.

Section 12.5 presents these findings and quotes a few briefs and judgments by way of illustration.

[21] As Cesare Romano wrote, 'The task of empirically validating hypotheses in this field is laborious and complex. First, it is difficult to find incontrovertible empirical evidence of jurisprudential dialogue. We know that judges (or the clerks who help in the drafting of their judgments) read cases of other courts. ... What we cannot exactly gauge is what impact any given major judgment of one court has on specific cases considered by other courts'; C. Romano, 'Deciphering the Grammar of the International Jurisprudential Dialogue', *New York University J. of Int'l L. and Politics* 41:4 (2009) 755–87, at 762. Focusing on citations can thus be misleading: the citation of a foreign court does not necessarily mean that foreign ideas were really a decisive consideration for the outcome of a case; M. Gelter and M. Siems, 'Networks, Dialogue or One-Way Traffic? An Empirical Analysis of Cross-Citations between Ten of Europe's Highest Courts', *Utrecht L. Rev.* 8:2 (2012) 88–99, at 89. The study of external citations may also exaggerate external influence or underestimate transnational influence if courts (willingly or not) conceal such influences; Voeten, Borrowing, *supra* note 16, at 548. A link can be made with 'acculturation' which Goodman and Jinks describe as 'the process by which actors adopt the beliefs and behavioral patterns of the surrounding culture, without actively assessing either the merits of those beliefs and behaviors or the material costs and benefits of conforming to them'; R. Goodman and D. Jinks, 'International Law and State Socialization: Conceptual, Empirical and Normative Challenges', *Duke L. J.* 54:4 (2005) 983–98, at 992–93. For a discussion on the relationship between citation and influence on judges, see N. Duxbury, *Jurists and Judges: An Essay on Influence* (Oxford: Hart Publishing, 2001).

[22] ECtHR judges explicitly acknowledge the possibility that comparative law affects the judgment but does not appear in the judgment at all; K. Dzehtsiarou and V. Lukashevich, 'Informed Decision-Making: The Comparative Endeavours of the Strasbourg Court', *Netherlands Quarterly of Human Rights* 30:3 (2012) 272–98, at 279. See, for example, for an acknowledgment of a 'hidden background influence', the research on the German Constitutional Court conducted by B. Bryde, 'The Constitutional Judge and the International Constitutionalist Dialogue', *Tulane L. Rev.* 80:1 (2005) 203–19, at 207 and on Italian courts G. Ferrari and A. Gambaro, 'The Italian Constitutional Court and Comparative Law. A Premise', *Comparative L. Rev.* 1:1 (2010) 1–22.

12.3 The Extent, Method and Purpose of the ECtHR's Engagement in Judicial Dialogue

Before turning to an analysis of the briefs, this section shortly presents the state of the art regarding the ECtHR's engagement in judicial dialogue, its extent, method and purpose. This serves to frame the debate but also to locate the shortcomings identified by the doctrine.

As Christopher McCrudden wrote, the comparative method is 'explicitly built into the fabric of judicial decision-making in the European context'.[23] The Court itself clarified in *Demir and Baykara v. Turkey* that

> in defining the meaning of terms and notions in the text of the Convention, [the Court] can and must take into account elements of international law other than the Convention, the interpretation of such elements by competent organs, and the practice of European States reflecting their common values. The consensus emerging from specialised international instruments and from the practice of Contracting States may constitute a relevant consideration for the Court when it interprets the provisions of the Convention in specific cases.[24]

It is thus clear that 'the legal system of the Convention is not a watertight, self-sufficient system. It is in constant dialogue with other legal systems'.[25] Nonetheless, the precise extent of judicial dialogue at play before the European Court is difficult to assess. As the introduction to this book makes clear, the concept of judicial dialogue is understood in different ways, and dialogue may take place in various forms and settings. Finding evidence of dialogue through cross-references to international or foreign material entails methodological challenges including empirical studies that possibly underestimate its real extent, especially if the focus of the research is on references to *judicial decisions* – as it is in this chapter.[26] Thus far, only a few empirical analyses are available. A study by Erik Voeten

[23] C. McCrudden, 'Common Law of Human Rights? Transnational Judicial Conversations on Constitutional Rights', *Oxford J. of Legal Studies* 20:4 (2000) 499–532, at 522.

[24] *Demir and Baykara v. Turkey* (Appl. No. 34503/97), Judgment (Grand Chamber), 12 November 2008, ECHR-V, 395, para. 85. The Court also added that 'it is not necessary for the respondent State to have ratified the entire collection of instruments that are applicable in respect of the precise subject matter of the case concerned. It will be sufficient for the Court that the relevant international instruments denote a continuous evolution in the norms and principles applied in international law or in the domestic law of the majority of member States of the Council of Europe and show, in a precise area, that there is common ground in modern societies'; *Ibid.* para. 86.

[25] C. Rozakis, 'The European Judge as Comparatist', *Tulane L. Rev.* 80:1 (2005) 257–79, at 268.

[26] See Section 12.2 *supra*.

concluded, among other things, that 'the ECtHR rarely cites other courts in majority judgments, although ECtHR judges do so regularly in separate opinions' suggesting that 'judges are aware of external jurisprudence but are cautious in their explicit reliance on it'.[27] His findings on numerical references to foreign judgments are mentioned in the next section when the same references in the briefs are analysed.

Questions can also be posed about the method through which ECtHR judges learn about foreign case law. It is perplexing that so much has been written on the use of foreign law by judges but so little on how judges acquire this information.[28] Judges usually have libraries at their disposal, but they predominantly receive their information from the submission of the parties.[29] The situations in which claimants themselves[30] or lower courts refer to foreign sources of law to support their arguments seem an obvious trigger for courts to cite foreign case law. ECtHR judges can also be informed by their own internal services. The Registry, composed of lawyers, administrative and technical staff and translators, provides legal and administrative support to the Court in the exercise of its judicial functions.[31] Within the Registry, there is a Research Division that can conduct comparative research.[32] Yet, its analyses are often limited to the situation

[27] Voeten, Borrowing, *supra* note 16, at 549. He searched for references to US case law, the Supreme Court of Canada, the South African Constitutional Court, the IACHR, the United Nations Human Rights Committee, the Committee Against Torture (CAT), the ICTY, the ICTR, the WTO, the ICJ, the Permanent Court of International Justice (PCIJ) and the CJEU; *ibid.*, at 557–58.

[28] A. von Brünneck, 'Constitutional Review and Legislation in Western Democracies', C. Landfried (ed.) *Constitutional Review and Legislation: An International Comparison* (Baden-Baden: Nomos, 1988) 219–61, at 229.

[29] *Ibid.*, at 230.

[30] The Rules of the Court stipulate which factual or legal information has to be produced by the parties, the reaction of the Court if it is felt that the information is not adequate; R. Wolfrum, 'The Taking and Assessment of Evidence by the European Court of Human Rights', S. Breitenmoser *et al.* (eds.), *Human Rights, Democracy and the Rule of Law* (Baden-Baden: Nomos, 2007) 915–24, at 916. The most relevant provisions on the taking and assessment of evidence are contained in the Rules 44A, 44C, 44D, 45, 46, 47, 54, 58, 59, 60 of the Rules of the Court as well as in its Practice Direction. Needless to say, the fact that claimants bring up what they consider to be relevant foreign sources of law provides no guarantee that the Court will pick up and reaffirm their relevance or explicitly deal with them in the merits; A. Hallo de Wolf and D. Wallace, 'The Overseas Exchange of Human Rights Jurisprudence: The US Supreme Court in the European Court of Human Rights', *Int'l Criminal Justice Rev.* 19:3 (2009) 1–21, at 5.

[31] There are currently some 640 staff members of the Registry – 270 lawyers and 370 other support staff. They are required to adhere to strict conditions as to their independence and impartiality; website of the ECtHR, www.echr.coe.int/Pages/home.aspx?p=court/howitworks.

[32] Dzehtsiarou and Lukashevich provide a detailed account of the procedure: 'A summary of the research report produced upon a request of a Judge-Rapporteur is often included

in member states, and the extent to which the Court relies on these resources is not clear. Kanstantsin Dzehtsiarou and Vasily Lukashevich state that the reports on comparative law are 'not publicly available', and that it is not clear 'whether such reports are prepared in a particular case or not'.[33] Further, Françoise Tulkens, Sébastien Van Drooghenbroeck and Frédéric Krenc point out that '[i]t is illusory to believe that the Court, as Dworkin's Hercule, would have, in every case before it, the time and resources needed to navigate this ocean of sources'.[34] Such writings, as well as other statements by the judges or by NGOs, allow us to assume that NGOs' briefs are an influencing factor on cross-citations in the ECtHR's case law.[35]

Regarding the use of the comparative law in its adjudication, the Court has been criticised for not clarifying the method it uses in general, and in particular in the context of applying the margin of appreciation. There are two forms of criticism in this regard. The first are normative considerations,[36] and the second are more methodological considerations: it has been argued, *inter alia*, that in the Court's case law, comparisons are carried out randomly, that they are superficial and that comparative material is interpreted arbitrarily.[37] Judges who compare have been accused of

in the judgment and entitled "law in Contracting States,"' "comparative and international law" or "relevant comparative law and material"'; Dzehtsiarou and Lukashevich, Informed Decision-Making, *supra* note 22, at 292. On the question as to whether the ECtHR may rely on or point to foreign sources out of its own volition, see Hallo de Wolf and Wallace, Overseas Exchange, *supra* note 30, at 5. According to Wolfrum, '[q]uestions of law need not be raised by the parties, the ECtHR can examine them proprio motu'; Wolfrum, Taking and Assessment of Evidence, *supra* note 30, at 919.

33 Dzehtsiarou and Lukashevich, Informed Decision-Making, *supra* note 22, at 280.

34 Tulkens, Van Drooghenbroeck and Krenc, Soft Law, *supra* note 12, at 473 (my translation). See also Senden, Interpretation of Fundamental Rights, *supra* note 18, at 261.

35 See also the discussion in Section 12.5 *infra*, which enlarges upon this aspect.

36 They evolve on the relevance of granting the majority a rule-making power in the field of human rights, the paradox of this mechanism in the context of an international judicial control and the risk of a lowering of the standards; see for more European Court of Human Rights, 'Dialogue Between Judges' (2008), www.echr.coe.int/Documents/Dialogue_2008_ENG.pdf; E. Örücü, *Judicial Comparativism in Human Rights Cases* (United Kingdom National Committee of Comparative Law, 2003) at 239; P. Carozza, 'Uses and Misuses of Comparative Law in International Human Rights: Some Reflections on the Jurisprudence of the European Court of Human Rights', *Notre Dame Law Review* 73:5 (1998) 1217–38, at 1236.

37 M. Ambrus, 'Comparative Law Method in the Jurisprudence of the European Court of Human Rights in the Light of the Rule of Law', *Erasmus L. Rev.* 2:3 (2009) 353–71, at 354. In addition, it has been observed that in some cases the Court examines the countries' general direction concerning the disputed issue, while in other cases it requires that the member states' approach be comparable in terms of concrete provisions or measures; *ibid*, 365.

'citational "cherry-picking"',[38] and the Court itself has been blamed for almost never saying which method of comparison it applied and which countries it surveyed.[39] In subsection 12.4.3, this contribution inquires whether briefs score better in this regard, and whether they could improve the Court's record in this context.

There are many purposes for engaging in judicial dialogue,[40] and it is sometimes difficult to identify the purposes of references to foreign material. ECtHR judges in particular explain that the presentation of comparative research helps them to see the problem at stake from another angle, to have a broader spectrum of possible solutions to a particular legal problem and to assist them in interpreting the Convention.[41] H. Senden identifies the following purposes of comparative law in the interpretation phase: to resolve an unresolved interpretative question and to adopt a

[38] B. Flanagan and S. Ahern, 'Judicial Decision-Making and Transnational Law: A Survey of Common Law Supreme Court Judges', *Int'l and Comp. L. Quarterly* 60:1 (2011) 1–28, at 22. Carozza is of the opinion that 'the only characteristics of the Court's comparative method on which virtually all commentators have agreed are its lack of depth, rigor, and transparency'; Carozza, Uses and Misuses, *supra* note 36, at 1225.

[39] Carozza, *ibid.*, at 1225. See, in the same direction, M. Delmas-Marty, *The European Convention for the Protection of Human Rights: International Protection versus National Restrictions*, C. Chodkiewics (ed.), *International Studies in Human Rights* (Dordrecht: Martinus Nijhoff, 1992) at 305.

[40] Brian Flanagan and Sinéad Ahern surveyed about forty common law judges about the considerations which might justify the citation of comparative material in the interpretation of domestic rights. Respondents rated these answers as the most important: 'a) It provides an additional source of impartial guidance (such as precedent), thus facilitating objectivity in judicial interpretation; b) It provides an additional source of legal authority, thus increasing the chances that a legal authority can be found to match what you already believe to be the best result from a policy perspective; c) It assists the work of establishing enlightened approaches to rights in emerging democracies'. Answers that have not been listed as the most important are: 'd) The gains to your state's international standing from a visible judicial engagement with foreign ideas and attitudes; e) It provides an additional factual source, thus enabling the court to make more accurate predictions as to the effects of challenged laws and rights; f) The importance of upholding comity between judges internationally; and g) It demonstrates that the judicial review of legislation for compatibility with rights also happens in other respectable democracies'; Flanagan and Ahern, Judicial Decision-Making, *supra* note 38, at 19–20. See also H. Koh, 'International Law as Part of Our Law', *American J. of Int'l L.* 98:1 (2004) 43–57.

[41] K. Dzehtsiarou, 'Consensus from Within the Palace Walls', *UCD Working Papers in Law, Criminology and Socio-Legal Studies Research Paper no. 40/2010I*, available at www.ssrn.com/abstract=1678424. See also C. Kakouris, 'L'Utilisation du Droit Comparé par les Tribunaux Nationaux et Internationaux', *Revue Hellénique de Droit International* 47 (1994) 31–45, at 33. According to Örücü, 'By surveying the words used in resorting to foreign cases, it becomes obvious that foreign law is used transnationally as an interpretative source rather than a source of direct application'; Örücü, Judicial Comparativism, *supra* note 36, at 237.

new interpretation, to argue that a specific interpretation should not be adopted or to show a textual difference.[42] The ECtHR also relies on comparative arguments when 'determining the latitude a state has for defining whether a certain limitation to the right is necessary ... mainly in the form of searching for a common European standard'.[43] This raises the thorny question of consensus, where the Court looks for the existence of rights-enhancing practices and policies among the contracting states.[44] When these practices achieve a certain measure of uniformity, what has been labelled as 'consensus', the Court raises the standard of rights-protection to which all states must adhere.[45] Concretely, the Court analyses the degree to which common practices or policies can be discerned among the contracting states and measures the behaviour of the respondent state against the practices of all other states.[46] Where a majority of states have expanded the scope of a right guaranteed by the Convention or broadened the class of individuals to whom it applies, the Court is more likely to find that a domestic law or policy which restricts such an expanded right violates the Convention.[47] Conversely, where there is an absence of consensus, the margin of appreciation enjoyed by the national authorities will be correspondingly wide.[48] But the Court also establishes the existence or absence of a consensus by relying on international treaties, judgments of international courts, judgments of extra-European legal orders and soft law.[49] The requirements for establishing a consensus standard are thus 'loose',[50] and this is criticised.[51] The analysis of the briefs offers the opportunity to inquire whether the briefs also use comparative legal material to serve a

[42] Senden, Interpretation of Fundamental Rights, *supra* note 18, at 226–39.

[43] Ambrus, Comparative Law Method, *supra* note 37, at 356.

[44] L. Helfer, 'Consensus, Coherence and the European Convention on Human Rights', *Cornell Int'l L. J.* 26:1 (1993) 133–65, at 134.

[45] For example, on the issue of a European standard, see *Dudgeon v. the United Kingdom* (Appl. No. 7525/76), 22 October 1981, Series A, Vol. 45, L. Helfer, 'Lesbian and Gay Rights as Human Rights: Strategies for a United Europe', *Virginia J. of Int'l L.* 32:1 (1991), 157–212 at 173.

[46] Helfer, *ibid.*, at 164.

[47] *Ibid.*

[48] European Court of Human Rights, Dialogue Between Judges, *supra* note 36, at 7.

[49] L. Wildhaber, A. Hjartarson, and S. Donnelly, 'No Consensus on Consensus? The Practice of the European Court of Human Rights', *Human Rights L. J.*, 33:7–12 (2014) 248–63, at 253–55.

[50] G. Letsas, *A Theory of Interpretation of the European Convention on Human Rights* (Oxford University Press, 2007) at 77–78.

[51] See among others I. de la Rasilla del Moral, 'The Increasingly Marginal Appreciation of the Margin-of-Appreciation Doctrine', *German L. J.* 7:6 (2006) 611–24, at 618.

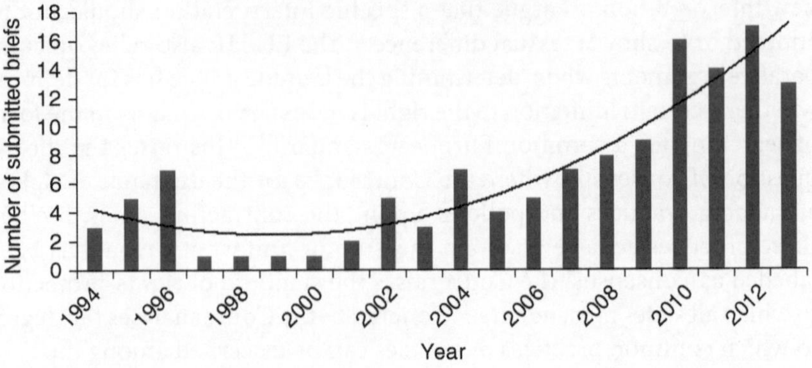

Figure 12.1 Number of NGO interventions before the Grand Chamber per year

variety of purposes, which would be in line with the Court's purposes of using this material.

12.4 Analysis of the Briefs: Citations of International and Foreign Cases and Methodology

12.4.1 Findings: The General Picture

As mentioned earlier, human rights NGOs have submitted 127 *amicus curiae* briefs in 75 cases before the Grand Chamber. They were submitted by eighty-three different groups.[52]

An increase in the number of judgments with external citations over time has been observed.[53] At the same time, the number of briefs submitted to the Court has also increased over time (see Figure 12.1), suggesting links between the two elements.

Little scholarly research has been conducted on the use of comparative material in relation to the interpretation of the different provisions of the Convention. One of the exceptions in this regard is the work of Hanneke Senden, according to whom this method had been invoked for various Convention rights. She observes that there is no clear trend evidencing

[52] For a typology of these groups, see Van den Eynde, An Empirical Look, *supra* note 6, at 282–87.

[53] Voeten, Borrowing, *supra* note 16, at 558. He notes, however, that this increase has not kept pace with the overall increase in judgments.

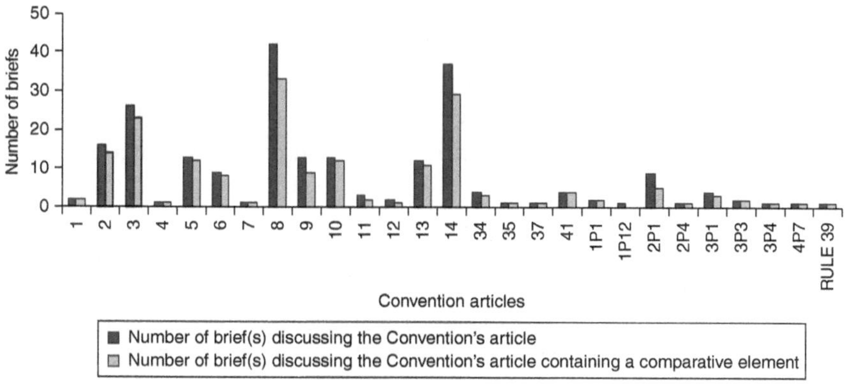

Figure 12.2 Breakdown of total number of briefs discussing provision of the Convention and relative numbers of briefs introducing comparative elements

that the comparative method is mainly used in specific types of cases.[54] However, she notes that article 8 'is overrepresented in the case law on comparative interpretation'[55] and speculates that it is due to its broad character. The analysis of the briefs yields a similar result: comparative material is brought forward in regard to the interpretation of various rights.[56] In addition to article 8, article 14 is also referred to very often, which is unsurprising, as in most cases these articles are considered together.

Out of the total of 127 analysed briefs, 105 briefs mention international or comparative law in one way or another.[57] This amounts to a very high ratio of 82 per cent of the briefs, which already allows us to confirm the hypothesis that briefs bring comparative material to the Court. *Amicus* participation is one of the methods through which judges learn about foreign law and case law, which can presumably contribute to increasing the extent of the ECtHR's dialogue.

Figure 12.2 shows, in dark grey, the total number of briefs discussing each of the Convention's articles, and in light grey the briefs which contain an international or comparative component.

Various degrees of comparative exercises can be observed in the briefs: it is the main focus of some, while others just mention a single

[54] Senden, Interpretation of Fundamental Rights, *supra* note 18, at 240.
[55] *Ibid.*
[56] I recorded the focus – or the foci – of the brief, not of the case in which it was submitted.
[57] See the fifth column in the Appendix.

foreign norm. It is not always easy to know 'what … an argument based on the comparison of laws'[58] is, but for the context of this chapter, a single reference to international or comparative law suffices to qualify the brief positively in this column. Some briefs contain comparative law material only by citing foreign laws and no case law. In order to provide a more comprehensive picture, these briefs are also counted in the light grey columns. However, the following discussion and its findings and the table in the Appendix only analyse and record references to international and foreign case law.[59]

The following is an excerpt of a brief that primarily provides a comparative analysis. It comes from the Helsinki Foundation for Human Rights, submitted in the case of *N. v. the United Kingdom:*

> In our intervention we would like to submit our analysis of three different legal regimes which had to deal with the issue of expulsion of the HIV-infected (or a person having death threatening illness) to the country where he / she may not obtain a treatment prolonging or sustaining a life. In particular, we covered in our research Poland, Germany and France.[60]

Another example is to be found in the brief submitted by the NGO JUSTICE in the case of *Al-Khawaja and Tahery v. the United Kingdom*, explicitly disagreeing with the comparative analysis made by the national court:

> JUSTICE submits that the Supreme Court's analysis of the comparative common law was, at best, a partial one. On the available evidence, it is simply not possible to say – as the Supreme Court claimed – that other common law jurisdictions would not also find a criminal conviction based solely or to a decisive extent on hearsay to breach their respective constitutional guarantees of a fair trial. By way of illustration, JUSTICE provides further analysis of the relevant law in Australia, Canada and New Zealand

[58] M.-C. Ponthoreau, 'L'Argument Fondé sur la Comparaison dans le Raisonnement Juridique', P. Legrand (ed.) *Comparer les Droits, Résolument* (Paris: Presses Universitaires de France, 2009) 537–60, at 539–40.

[59] This limitation was chosen on the one hand to specifically assess the contribution of NGOs to *judicial* dialogue, and on the other hand to narrow down the presentation of findings. This may have a particular bearing on the evaluation of the extent to which the comparative material brought forward in the briefs influences the Court's search for a consensus, as the Court often relies more on legislation than on jurisprudence from different member states of the CoE when establishing the (non-)existence of a European consensus. Except for the UN Human Rights Committee (see *infra*), decisions of quasi-judicial bodies have not been counted.

[60] Brief of the "Helsinki Foundation for Human Rights" in *N. v. the United Kingdom* (Appl. No. 26565/05), Judgment (Grand Chamber), 27 May 2008, ECHR 2008-III, 227, at 2.

> and sets out the relevant position in three other major common law jurisdictions: Hong Kong, Ireland and South Africa.[61]

Sometimes, it also appears that the permission granted to submit written comments specifically delineates the role of the *amicus* to the input of a comparative analysis:

> Liberty ... welcomes the opportunity to submit its comments on certain specific issues relevant to this case as set out in the permission of the President ... limited to a comparative study of the position of civil servants in member States with respect to article 10 of the Convention and to an analysis of relevant case-law developed under other relevant international and national human rights instruments including within the framework of the ILO.[62]

Finally, it should be stressed that the large majority of briefs mention a vast array of sources, emanating from the national, regional and international levels. Strikingly, they also refer to many non-binding instruments, considering them as part of a larger breeding ground.[63]

12.4.2 References to International and Foreign Judgments and Decisions

12.4.2.1 International Courts

It is natural that briefs rely on international standards, as the ECtHR has confirmed that the Convention forms part of public international law.[64] The Court has also reiterated that the Convention should, as far as possible, be interpreted in harmony with other rules of international law.[65] It has been said that the contribution of the *amici* in this field is very important,

[61] Brief of "Justice" in *Al-Khawaja and Tahery v. the United Kingdom* (Appl. Nos. 26766/05 and 22228/06), Judgment (Grand Chamber), 15 December 2011, ECHR 2011, 191, para. 42.

[62] Brief of "Liberty" in *Ahmed and Others v. the United Kingdom* (Appl. No. 22954/93), Judgment (Chamber), 2 September 1998, Reports 1998-VI, at 2. This is not a Grand Chamber case. The dissenters noted: 'We are inclined to agree with the Canadian Supreme Court, quoted by Liberty in its submission to the Court, which held that public servants cannot be silent members of society ...'; (emphasis added) Joint Dissenting Opinion of Judges Spielmann, Pekkanen and Van Dijk.

[63] See also Tulkens, Van Drooghenbroeck and Krenc, Soft Law, *supra* note 12.

[64] L. Wildhaber, 'The European Convention on Human Rights and International Law', *Int'l and Comp. L. Quarterly* 56:2 (2007) 217–31, at 220.

[65] *Ibid.* Such an interpretation has sometimes been justified by article 31 of the Vienna Convention on the Law of Treaties, which calls upon 'the context' to interpret the text, but also calls upon 'the ordinary meaning of the words'; J.-F. Flauss, 'Du Droit International Comparé des Droits de l'Homme dans la Jurisprudence de la Cour Européenne des Droits de l'Homme', *Publications de l'Institut Suisse de Droit Comparé* 43 (2002) 159–82, at 160.

not only because they bring international law to the Court's attention but also because it is a way to fight the risk of compartmentalisation and fragmentation of international law.[66]

Christos Rozakis claims that 'the international legal order is frequently reflected in the decisions and judgments of the EC[t]HR'.[67] However, regarding an eventual judicial dialogue, Erik Voeten found that 'the ECtHR is similarly sparse in citing other international courts. ICJ case law is cited just five times in the main part of majority judgments, two of which came in interstate cases … In the period under analysis *(i.e. 1959–2006)*, ICTY case law is cited in one judgment (*Al-Adsani v. the United Kingdom*) in support of a finding of no violation'.[68]

The same picture emerges from the briefs. While many rely on international standards, citing a variety of instruments and decisions of quasi-judicial bodies, the ICJ is only mentioned in ten briefs. The statutes of the International Criminal Tribunals for the former Yugoslavia and Rwanda and the ICC as well as the Charter of the International Military Tribunal at Nuremberg have been cited, but only a few references to these courts and tribunals' case law are included.[69]

12.4.2.2 The United Nations Human Rights Committee (UN HRC)

Although a quasi-judicial body, it has been decided to include the UN HRC in the analysis, as it focuses on the protection of roughly the same rights as the ECtHR.[70] The references to the body charged of monitoring the implementation of the International Covenant on Civil and Political Rights (ICCPR) have been interpreted narrowly: only references to decisions on individual communications have been counted, not the references to general comments or concluding observations.[71]

[66] H. Ascensio, 'L'Amicus Curiae devant les Juridictions Internationales', *Revue Générale de Droit International Public* 105:4 (2001) 897–930, at 924.

[67] Rozakis, The European Judge, *supra* note 25, at 274.

[68] Voeten, Borrowing, *supra* note 16, at 565. See also M. Forowicz, *The Reception of International Law in the European Court of Human Rights* (Oxford University Press, 2010).

[69] See, for example, the reference to the judgment of *USA v. POHL and Others*, 13 January 1947 of the Trials of the War Criminals before the Nuremberg Military Tribunals under Control Council Law No. 10, cited in the brief of "the European Center for Law and Justice" in *Gross v. Switzerland* (Appl. No. 67810/10), Judgment (Grand Chamber), 30 September 2014, selected for publication 2014.

[70] For more, see M.-A. Eissen, 'The European Convention on Human Rights and the United Nations Covenant on Civil and Political Rights: Problems of Coexistence', *Buffalo L. Rev.* 22:1 (1972) 181–216.

[71] It can be expected that the references to these documents as well as other UN material in general would substantially increase the count.

Thirty-two briefs mention the UN HRC (see eighth column of the table in the Appendix), which is the highest number compared to the references to other courts and tribunals. The dialogue (or absence of dialogue) between the two bodies needs further analysis. It is currently receiving more attention,[72] in particular because of the ECtHR judgment *Shingara Mann Singh v. France*[73] and the HRC's View *Ranjit Singh* v. *France*.[74]

References were also found to the Committee on the Elimination of Racial Discrimination, the Committee against Torture, the Committee on the Rights of the Child, the Committee on the Elimination of Discrimination against Women and the Committee on Economic, Social and Cultural Rights.[75]

12.4.2.3 Regional Courts: The Court of Justice of the European Union and the Inter-American Court of Human Rights

The following discussion concerns what has been called 'horizontal networks' of judicial dialogue[76] and analyses the mentioning in briefs of case law from two regional courts: the Court of Justice of the European Union (CJEU) and the Inter-American Court of Human Rights (IACtHR). No reference has been found to the African Court on Human and Peoples' Rights, which issued its first judgment on the merits only recently.

The relationship between the two European systems has been copiously studied,[77] as there are indeed many overlaps of competences. Whilst

[72] A. Buyse, 'Straatburgse Echo's in Genève? De Invloed van de EHRM-Jurisprudentie op het VN-Mensenrechtcomité', *Nederlands Tijdschrift voor Mensenrechten (NTM/NJCM-Bull.)* 35:7 (2010) 741–53; A. Buyse, 'Tacit Citing – The Scarcity of Judicial Dialogue between the Global and the Regional Human Rights Mechanisms in Freedom of Expression Cases', T. McGonagle and Y. Donders (eds.), *The United Nations and Freedom of Expression and Information: Critical Perspectives* (Cambridge University Press, 2015) 443–65.

[73] *Shingara Mann Singh v. France* (Appl. No. 24479/07), Judgment (Chamber) 13 November 2008, not reported.

[74] HRC, *Ranjit Singh v. France*, Communication No. 1876/2009, 27 September 2011, UN Doc. CCPR/C/102/D/1876/2009 (2011), para. 8.4. See also F. Tulkens and S. Van Drooghenbroeck, 'The Domestic Courts' Response to Divergent Views Among International Human Rights Bodies: Thoughts Prompted by the *Singh v. France* Cases', A. Alen *et al.* (eds.), *Liberae Cogitationes, Liber Amicorum Marc Bossuyt* (Antwerp, Intersentia, 2013) at 735–54.

[75] As the number of these references is quite low and the details would overburden the presentation, they are not referenced in the Appendix. For more information, please contact the author, who has the relevant material on file.

[76] L. Burgorgue-Larsen, 'De l'Internationalisation du Dialogue des Juges. Missive Doctrinale à l'attention de Bruno Genevois', R. Badinter *et al.* (eds.), *Le Dialogue des Juges. Mélanges en l'Honneur du Président Genevois* (Paris: Dalloz, 2009) 95–130, at 98–99.

[77] See, among many, E. Bribosia, L. Scheeks and A. Ubeda de Torres, *L'Europe des Cours. Loyautés et Résistances, Collection "Penser le Droit"* (Brussels: *Bruylant*, 2010), at 332; and Sir

it has been said that there is a 'constant dialogue between the CJEU and the European Court of Human Rights',[78] and that there are 'abundant instances of regular exchanges' between the two courts,[79] Voeten found that the CJEU case law was used only eight times as an aid to interpret the ECHR, mostly in an innocuous manner.[80] A similarly low number of twenty references to the CJEU are found in the briefs. What is interesting is that some briefs refer to the CJEU in cases against non–EU member states, such as against Russia[81] and Switzerland.[82]

The human rights mechanism and instruments of the American continent receive a lot of attention in the briefs. As a prominent partner in the ECtHR's dialogue, the IACtHR has been called 'the closest ally of the EC[t]HR in the protection of the human rights at a regional level, which has been a source of inspiration for the Court in many instances'.[83] For a few years, it was only the Inter-American organs which made reference to the ECtHR's jurisprudence,[84] and not vice versa. Laurence Burgogue-Larsen

N. Bratza, 'The European Convention on Human Rights and the Charter of Fundamental Rights of the European Union: A Process of Mutual Enrichment', A. Rosas *et al.* (eds.), *The Court of Justice and the Construction of Europe: Analyses and Perspectives on Sixty Years of Case-law* (The Hague: T.M.C. Asser Press, 2013) 167–81.

78 A. Hamann and H. Ruiz Fabri, 'Transnational Networks and Constitutionalism', *Int'l J. of Constitutional L.* 6: 3–4 (2008) 481–508, at 498.

79 In *Bosphorus Hava Yolları Turizm ve Ticaret Anonim Şirketi v. Ireland* (Appl. No. 45036/98), Judgment (Grand Chamber), 30 June 2005, ECHR 2005-VI, 107, the Court made an important clarification about the relationship between the Convention and community law, by saying that the protection of fundamental rights in the latter, 'unless manifestly deficient', could be considered equivalent to that of the ECHR; in Wildhaber, The European Convention, *supra* note 64, at 230.

80 Voeten, Borrowing, *supra* note 16, at 565.

81 Briefs of "the Human Rights Training Institute of the Paris Bar Association" in *Sergey Zolothukin v. Russia* (Appl. No. 14939/03), Judgment (Grand Chamber), 10 February 2009, not reported; and of "the Human Rights Centre of Ghent University" in *Konstantin Markin v. Russia* (Appl. No. 30078/06), Judgment (Grand Chamber), 22 March 2012, ECHR 2012-III, 77 (extracts). See for more on this issue E. Bribosia and S. Van Drooghenbroeck, 'Emprunts et Migrations Entre le Droit de l'Union Européenne et Celui du Conseil de l'Europe', *Traductions et Droits Européens, Enjeux d'une Rencontre* (Facultés Universitaires Saint-Louis, Bruxelles, 2009) at 133–79.

82 Brief of "Justice" in *Nada v. Switzerland* (Appl. No. 10593/08), Judgment (Grand Chamber), 12 September 2012, ECHR 2012-V, 213.

83 Rozakis, The European Judge, *supra* note 25, at 276.

84 H. Gros-Espiell, 'La Convention Américaine et la Convention Européenne des Droits de l'Homme: Analyse Comparative', *Recueil des Cours de l'Académie de Droit International de la Haye*, t. 218, 6 (1989) 167–412. See also G. Neuman, 'Import, Export, and Regional Consent in the Inter-American Court of Human Rights', *European J. of Int'l L.*, 19:1 (2008) 101–23. The ECtHR quotes it mainly in cases which concern article 2 (right to life) and 3 (prohibition of torture, inhuman and degrading treatment); Rozakis, The European Judge, *supra* note 25, at 276.

observes that 'today, the transcontinental dialogue appears more balanced',[85] and that the Strasbourg universe is now familiar with the Inter-American human rights jurisprudence. According to the coding, it has been found that jurisprudence of the Inter-American Court has been cited in twenty-nine briefs.

12.4.2.4 Cases from Contracting States

As outlined earlier, the ECtHR looks not only to the respondent state's legal system but also to those of other Council of Europe member states. It 'usually resorts to such dialogue whenever new issues are submitted to it for which no established case supports a secure solution, or when the Court feels that developments in the European continent call for a change to its established case law'.[86] This is also strongly linked to the issue of consensus.[87]

Forty-eight briefs mention case law[88] from other CoE countries. Figure 12.3 shows which countries (other than the respondent state) have been pointed at in the briefs:

The clear pattern arising from these figures is that the countries most often cited by the *amici* are the founding members of the Council of Europe, which some have called 'a club of largely like-minded West European countries which share much of their legal and political culture and traditions'.[89]

12.4.2.5 Cases from Non-Contracting States

This subsection looks at the references to case law from jurisdictions located outside the Council of Europe. The ECtHR has referred to the

[85] L. Burgorgue-Larsen, 'Conclusions. Pour une Coopération Interrégionale Renforcée', *Clôture du Congrès International: Les Cours Régionales des Droits de l'Homme. Pratiques Juridictionnelles et Politiques Jurisprudentielles* (Strasbourg: Council of Europe Publishings, 20 December 2009) 1–4, at 2 (my translation). See also L. Hennebel, 'Les Références Croisées entre les Juridictions Internationales des Droits de l'Homme', in *Le Dialogue des Juges. Actes du Colloque Organisé le 28 avril 2006 à l'Université Libre de Bruxelles* (Brussels, Bruylant, 2007) 31–76 and Voeten, Borrowing, *supra* note 16, at 562.

[86] Rozakis, The European Judge, *supra* note 25, at 271.

[87] A. Heringa, 'The Consensus Principle – The Role of "Common Law" in the ECHR Case Law', *Maastricht J. of European and Comp. L.* 3:2 (1996) 106–45, at 108.

[88] The database (Appendix) does not distinguish between decisions by Supreme Courts, lower courts, administrative courts, etc.

[89] W. Sadurski, 'Partnering with Strasbourg: Constitutionalisation of the European Court of Human Rights, the Accession of Central and East European States to the Council of Europe, and the Idea of Pilot Judgments', *Human Rights L. Rev.* 9:3 (2009) 397–453, at 400.

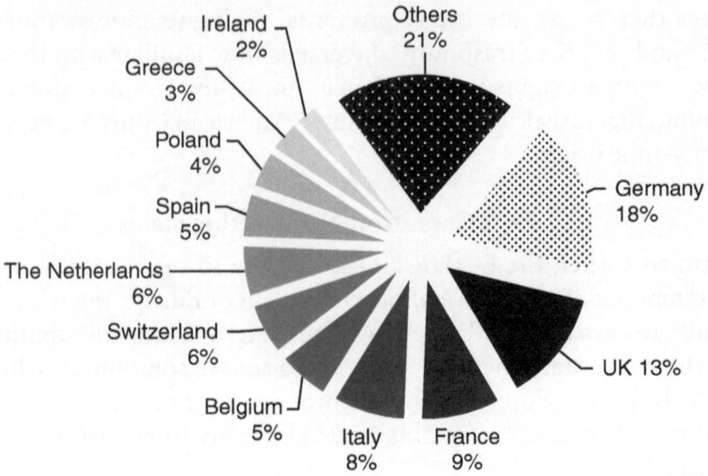

Figure 12.3 References to case law from other contracting states

decisions of the highest courts of various non-member countries.[90] This type of dialogue takes place in a very 'open' space, where judges 'engage in judicial conversations on the basis of a spontaneous opening to the judicial world in its entirety'.[91] As Rozakis notes,

> the dialogue with foreign jurisdictions leads to a real 'globalization' of the EC[t]HR functions in the sense that it brings within the EC[t]HR's consideration laws and experiences relating directly to societies other than European ones and consequently to mentalities, customs and morals which are linked with conceptions not necessarily intended in the conscience of those applying them to operate as ecumenical principles or values.[92]

According to Rozakis, the most frequent interlocutor of the ECtHR has been the US Supreme Court.[93] Jean-François Flauss confirms the

[90] C. Zoethout, 'The Dilemma of Constitutional Comparativism', *Zeitschrift für ausländisches öffentliches Recht und Völkerrecht* 71:4 (2011) 787–806, at 789.

[91] Burgorgue-Larsen, De l'Internationalisation du Dialogue des Juges, *supra* note 76, at 98–99.

[92] Rozakis, The European Judge, *supra* note 25, at 276.

[93] According to Flauss, while the case law of the US Supreme Court has often been taken into account by the ECtHR, its influence has been limited. The ECtHR started to use US Supreme Court jurisprudence in the 1980s to support its interpretation of the Convention. US jurisprudence had more of a reinforcing or strengthening role. The Court's engagement has become more recurrent and visible in the last fifteen years, first in the dissenting opinions, then also in the judgments. Today, US Supreme Court jurisprudence, if sufficiently established, can influence the interpretation of the European Convention; J.-F. Flauss, 'La Présence de la Jurisprudence de la Cour Suprême des Etats-Unis d'Amérique dans le Contentieux Européen des Droits de l'Homme', *Revue Trimestrielle des Droits de l'Homme* 62 (2005) 313–31, at 316. See *also* E. Zoller,

important American influence, partly due to the activism of NGOs, which 'tend more and more to invoke the US Supreme Court case law. This attitude is not surprising, as the large majority of NGOs is Anglo-Saxon and a few even have their main seat in the US'.[94] The Canadian jurisprudence has been equally if not more influential than US jurisprudence. It even played a major role in establishing violations of the Convention in several judgments. One example is *Hirst v. United Kingdom (No. 2)*,[95] in which the UK legislation preventing prisoners from voting was found in breach of the Convention. The Grand Chamber confirmed the Chamber finding, which, in its evaluation of the legitimate aim of the restriction and its proportionality, referred to Canadian case law, which found similar measures in breach of the Canadian Charter of Rights and Freedoms.[96]

The same tendencies observed in the Court's jurisprudence are present in the briefs, in which those countries have prominent places. Fifty briefs mention case law from outside the Council of Europe, and Figure 12.4 shows which countries have been cited.

According to Voeten, when the ECtHR relies on the judgments of foreign constitutional courts, 'it does so only in cases involving the United Kingdom and uses decisions only from other common-law jurisdictions that were already cited by the U.K. courts'.[97] This observation does not hold for the briefs, which in many instances mention common law judgments in cases against civil law countries. However, it is noticeable that the references to cases from civil law jurisdictions – for example, Brazil or Colombia – have not (yet) been made in cases concerning the United Kingdom or Ireland.

12.4.3 *Methodological Concerns in the Briefs*

This subsection examines the methodological component of the briefs, focusing in particular on considerations related to the selection of jurisdictions to compare and collect data.[98]

'Le Dialogue des Juges de la Cour Européenne des Droits de l'Homme et de la Cour Suprême des Etats-Unis sur les Droits Fondamentaux', *Les Petites Affiches* 112 (4 June 2008) 26–32.

94 Flauss, *ibid.* at 326 (my translation).

95 *Hirst v. the United Kingdom (No.2)* (Appl. No. 74025/01), Judgment (Grand Chamber), 6 October 2005, ECHR 2005-IX, 187.

96 *Ibid.*, paras. 35–37, 75 and 80; and *Hirst v. the United Kingdom (No. 2)* (Appl. No. 74025/01), Judgment (Chamber), 30 March 2004, not reported.

97 Voeten, Borrowing, *supra* note 16, at 561.

98 However, most of the time, it is difficult to distinguish precisely between these different elements.

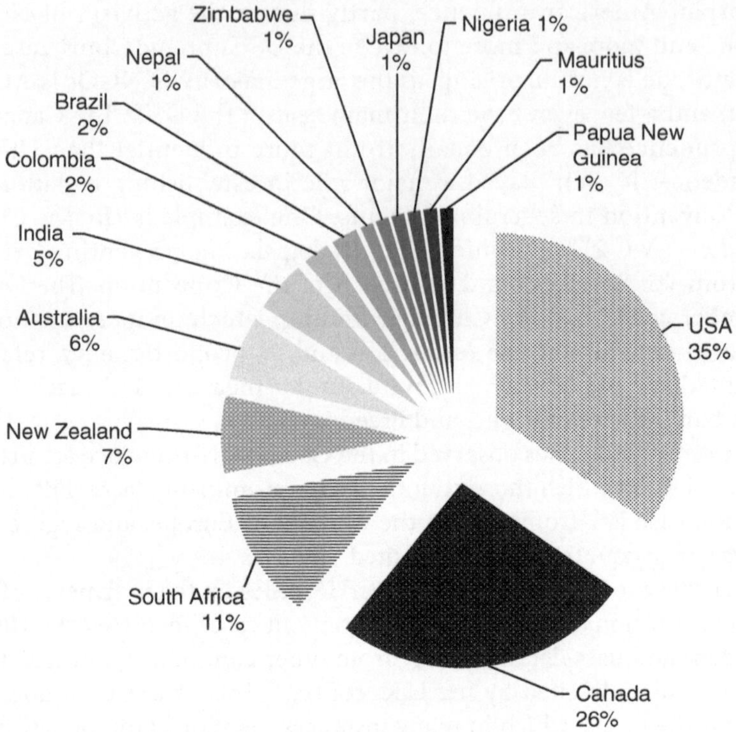

Figure 12.4 References to case law from non-contracting states

To recall, many authors deplore the unsystematic character of case selection[99] in the ECtHR's comparative undertakings, and the so-called 'cherry-picking' is one of the most common criticism.[100] It has been suggested that third-party interveners can play a vital role in this field, as they have different resources than the Court. An advantage of NGOs is that 'they focus on a particular legal issue and can be considered experts in the area of their activity. Furthermore, they are not subordinate to the Contracting Parties and for that reason they can independently assess national laws and practice'.[101]

Thus, the content of the briefs mentioning other states' jurisprudence (the two last columns in the table in the Appendix) were first scrutinised

[99] R. Hirschl, 'The Question of Case Selection in Comparative Constitutional Law', *American J. of Comp. L.* 53:1 (2005) 125–56, at 129.

[100] Dzehtsiarou and Lukashevich, Informed Decision-Making, *supra* note 22, at 289–90.

[101] *Ibid.*, at 296.

to find some explanation as to why those specific countries were cited. Indeed, in the comparative enterprise, a 'global community of courts does not ... include all courts from all countries'.[102] It appears that briefs citing international judgments or decisions of member states or non-member states seldom articulate a justification for the selection of those materials. With the exception of a few 'good practices' which are detailed *infra*, the briefs do not score much better than the Court does. But NGOs are not primarily comparatists. And as they often want to strategically advocate for a particular interpretation, it is to be expected that the briefs 'cherry-pick' to a certain extent.[103]

I agree with Senden that the comparative analysis of 'internal' sources within the CoE requires different justifications than for the 'external' materials.[104] However, as alluded to in the case of *Demir and Baykara*,[105] the Court does not seem to think that this distinction is relevant. Regarding the 'internal component', it has been argued that

> the ECtHR should be extra careful in the selection and representation of laws in the final judgment because inadequate representation may reduce the legitimising potential of comparative law. The persuasive use of comparative analysis is essentially linked to establishing the presence or absence of a European consensus about a legal issue. Consequently, any such attempt to persuade will largely depend on the ability of the Court to show that a conclusion as to a consensus has a reliable empirical basis.[106]

Regarding the briefs, this aspect is of course strongly dependent on whether the NGO tries to establish the existence or absence of a consensus.

102 A.-M. Slaughter, 'A Global Community of Courts', *Harvard Int'l L. J.* 44:1 (2003) 191–291, at 194.

103 In addition, it is true that, as a consequence of the immense volume of material available to the comparatist, comparative law is almost necessarily unsystematic; J. Hill, 'Comparative Law, Law Reform and Legal Theory', *Oxford J. of Legal Studies* 9:1 (1989) 101–15, at 111. On the challenges of this information density, see D. Gerber, 'Globalization and Legal Knowledge: Implications for Comparative Law', *Tulane L. Rev.* 75:4 (2001) 949–75, at 950; and Flanagan and Ahern, Judicial Decision-Making, *supra* note 38, at 954.

104 Senden, Interpretation of Fundamental Rights, *supra* note 18, at 260.

105 *Demir and Baykara v. Turkey*, *supra* note 24.

106 Dzehtsiarou and Lukashevich, Informed Decision-Making, *supra* note 22, at 289–90; S. Van Drooghenbroeck notes that in the most recent practice, the Court's analysis of the present day conditions is less systematically done through studies of comparative national law than of the analysis of 'indications' provided in various European and international instruments. This is maybe because of the difficulty of conducting a thorough analysis of the legislation of all forty-seven contracting states. S. Van Drooghenbroeck, 'Les Frontières du Droit et le Temps Juridique: la Cour Européenne des Droits de l'Homme Repousse les Limites', *Revue Trimestrielle des Droits de l'Homme* 79 (2009) 811–49, at 831. He argues

For example, arguing that there was a consensus on the issue raised in *Finci v. Bosnia and Herzegovina*, the "AIRE Centre" explained:

> The intervenors have considered the legal systems of all of the Member States of the Council of Europe concerning the withdrawal of the right to stand office. We focus on the most prominent and representative of these systems which form the basis of a European consensus, including the post-Second World War practice in Western Europe, post-communist regimes in Central and Eastern Europe and criminal statutes throughout the CoE.[107]

A brief not pursuing this aim does not have the same constraints. For example, the Greek Helsinki Monitor exposed the Greek situation in a case against Turkey because 'Greece is another State party to ICERD, which also has a special similar law ... that punishes incitation to racial discrimination, hatred or violence, and expression of racially offensive ideas',[108] and a Greek court had pronounced itself on the same issue.

Another explanation as to why briefs point to some jurisdictions is that they seek to complete a comparative analysis performed by a domestic court and/or in the respective government's submission to the Court:

> The German Federal Government has already performed a limited comparative analysis of the privacy regimes of different contracting member states ... dealing in particular with Germany and the UK. The Organisations' written comments therefore focus upon Greece, Hungary, Italy, the Netherlands, France, Poland and Sweden ... and explain how the equivalent balance is drawn in New Zealand, which the Organisations submit provides a useful and appropriate comparator outside the CoE but against a broadly analogous legal and social context.[109]

Except for these few examples,[110] no reason is given to why the briefs often limit themselves to the 'old club' of contracting states, as Figure 12.3 shows.

that because the Court takes the liberty to look at a variety of instruments, this should be accompanied by the responsibility to sufficiently justify why and to what extent this particular element has been considered.

107 Brief of the "AIRE Centre" in *Finci v. Bosnia and Herzegovina* (Appl. Nos. 27996/06 and 34836/06), Judgment (Grand Chamber), 22 December 2009, not reported.

108 Brief of the "Greek Helsinki Monitor" in *Aksu v. Turkey* (Appl. Nos. 4149/04 and 41029/04), Judgment (Grand Chamber), 15 March 2012, ECHR 2012-1, 447.

109 Brief of "the Media Legal Defence Initiative", "the International Press Institute", "the World Association of Newspapers and News Publishers" in *Von Hannover v. Germany (No. 2)* (Appl. No. 40660/08), Judgment (Grand Chamber), 7 February 2012, ECHR 2012-I, 399 and *Axel Springer AG v. Germany* (Appl. No. 39954/08), Judgment (Grand Chamber), 7 February 2012, not reported.

110 See also the Brief of "Transgender Europe" in *Hämäläinen v. Finland* (Appl. No. 37359/09), Judgment (Grand Chamber), 16 July 2014, selected for publication 2014, at 2–4, explaining why it focuses on the thirty-one Member States of the Council of Europe that deal with

Various explanations could be given: the information from these countries could simply be more readily available to NGOs (they are located in these countries, or have branches or contacts there), and/or there are lower language barriers concerning these countries.[111] Another simple reason is that many of the 'new' CoE member states have less extensive case law to rely on. Yet another reason might stem from a more strategic choice by NGOs: maybe those countries 'speak better' to judges, and the Court must also be careful that the decision speaks to its audience. These results must indeed be seen in parallel with the fact that, in Grand Chamber cases, the United Kingdom is by far the state which sees the largest number of third-party interventions against it. Wojciech Sadurski suggests that 'there may be a legitimate feeling among many of the Western European states, especially among their executive branches and bureaucracies, that they have not much to learn from the other European states (and certainly not from the recently democratised ones) in the domain of human rights'.[112] However, the numbers of cross-references to judgments from Eastern European courts might increase quickly as some Constitutional Courts from previous Communist authoritarian states (the Polish Constitutional Tribunal, the Czech Constitutional Court, the Romanian Constitutional Court) are building 'a strong alliance with the ECtHR in order ... to pursue their ideological visions of progressive development of human rights'.[113] This could be furthered by briefs taking on some of these Eastern European courts' judgments in their comparative analysis.

Regarding the 'external' component – that is, references to foreign jurisdictions as set out in Figure 12.4 – there are again briefs which are silent about their choice of jurisdictions, others which mention in a loose manner 'comparable jurisdictions'[114] or 'other democratic societies'[115] and some which develop the justification more extensively.[116]

legal gender recognition and explains that it will compare more in detail those Member States that reserve marriage to different-sex couples.

111 C. L'Heureux-Dubé, 'The Importance of Dialogue: Globalization and the International Impact of the Rehnquist Court', *Tulsa L. J.* 34:1 (1998) 15–40, at 21.

112 Sadurski, Partnering with Strasbourg, *supra* note 89, 433.

113 *Ibid.*, at 438.

114 Brief of the "Committee on the Administration of Justice", "Liberty" and "British-Irish Rights Watch" in *John Murray v. the United Kingdom* (Appl. No. 18731/91), Judgment (Grand Chamber), 8 February 1996, Reports 1996-I.

115 Brief of the "FIDH", "ILGA–Europe", the "BAAF" and the "APGL" in *E.B. v. France* (Appl. No. 43546/02), Judgment (Grand Chamber), 22 January 2008, not reported.

116 See for examples (although they were submitted in Chamber cases and not Grand Chamber cases) a reference to 'other democratic societies with good human rights records'; Brief of the "FIDH" *et al.* in the case of *Gas and Dubois v. France* (Appl. No. 25911/07), Judgment

According to some critics 'simply categorizing countries as "large, prosperous, [and] rights-enjoying democracies" is insufficient to successfully and systematically determine which countries are suitable sources of persuasive authorities for courts and which are not'.[117] As McCrudden says, 'Not surprisingly, the type of political regime from which foreign judicial decision arises markedly affects the likelihood of its being cited. In the main, it is the judiciaries of liberal democratic regimes that cite each other'.[118] A survey conducted by Brian Flanagan and Sinéad Ahern asked 'which traits ... other jurisdictions [must] possess to justify their citation in a judgment about domestic rights'. A large majority of the surveyed judges (81 per cent) indicated that a democratic form of government was a prerequisite for the citation of the law of another jurisdiction in a judgment about domestic rights.[119] With very few exceptions, the briefs follow the same pattern. For Rex Glensy, 'the first push towards referencing other democracies is purely instinctive'.[120] According to him, we believe that genuine liberal democracies are legitimate originators of persuasive authority and thus potential partners of a dialogue 'because we tend to accept the legitimacy and guidance of those who look most like ourselves'.[121]

Similarly to the above, the analysis of the briefs does not allow to clearly articulate why American and Canadian judgments make 61 per cent of all foreign cases cited in NGOs' *amicus curiae* before the ECtHR and why the picture is not more diverse globally. The reasons for this might be similar to the explanations usually advanced by the judges who adopt foreign precedents in constitutional law cases.[122] Clearly, the fact that most of the

(Chamber), 15 March 2012, ECHR 2012-II, 245, para. 10. In another brief, a reference to the New York Court of Appeal was justified 'because it has confronted this question (of the eviction of the surviving same-sex partner)'; Brief of "ILGA-Europe", "Liberty" and "Stonewall" ubmitted in *Karner v. Austria* (Appl. No. 40016/98), Judgment (Chamber), 24 July 2003, ECHR_2003-IX, 199, at 2–3.

117 Statement of Professor Ramsey during the *Legislative Hearing on H.R. Res. 568 before the Subcommittee on the Constitution of the House Comm. on the Judiciary, 108th Congress, 2nd. Session, 2004*, cited by R. Glensy, 'Which Countries Count? *Lawrence v. Texas* and the Selection of Foreign Persuasive Authority', *Virginia J. of Int'l L.* 45:2 (2005) 357–449, at 404.

118 McCrudden, Common Law, *supra* note 23, at 517. See also B. Ackerman, 'The Rise of World Constitutionalism', *Virginia L. Rev.* 83:4 (1997) 771–97.

119 Flanagan and Ahern, Judicial Decision-Making, *supra* note 38, at 21. These were the options: 'Please mark as many as appropriate: a) none in particular, b) they must be democratic, c) they must be a 'common law' jurisdiction, d) they must speak the same language, e) they must have close historical links (such as colonial associations), f) other.'

120 Glensy, Which Countries Count, *supra* note 117, at 413–14.

121 *Ibid.*

122 See P. Tripathi, 'Foreign Precedents and Constitutional Law', *Columbia L. Rev.* 57:3 (1957) 319–47, at 343. He mentions the maturity of the systems, the cultural admiration for

countries cited belong to the common law world offers some explanation (different status of courts' decisions, of legal reasoning, etc.).[123] Similarly, there is no doubt that the accessibility and language factors play a role. Indeed, in general, the degree of knowledge and access to external jurisprudence remains very uneven.[124] One should not forget the large presence of Anglo-Saxon NGOs[125] that are active before the Court, which is *inter alia* due to the tradition of allowing *amicus curiae* in domestic jurisdictions in these countries. Moreover, the fact that many NGOs are part of networks 'that transfer information and other resources across borders'[126] might also influence the NGOs' choices for comparative material. These networks often bear a strong Western European imprint. Jackie Smith and Dawn Wiest found that participation in international NGOs and transnational social movement organisations varies dramatically across countries, particularly outside the core of the global economy.[127]

Correspondingly, some scholars have warned that judicial dialogue by the ECtHR and/or dialogue initiated by NGOs should not be Western-centric (or, in our case, common law–centric).[128] Discussing American constitutional jurisprudence – but equally valid for the European

specific nations, the cultural and educational background of judges (and thus in our cases, of the lawyers working on the amicus curiae brief), etc.

[123] See C. Saunders, 'Judicial Engagement with Comparative Law', T. Ginsburg and R. Dixon (eds.), *Comparative Constitutional Law* (Cheltenham: Edward Elgar, 2011) 571–98.

[124] B. Genevois, 'L'Inspiration Réciproque des Jurisprudences des Juridictions Suprêmes Nationales et Internationales en Matière de Droits Fondamentaux', *Les Petites Affiches* 112 (2008) 15–20, at 20 (my translation).

[125] G. Dutertre, 'La Pratique de la Tierce Intervention devant la Cour à la Lumière de la Convention et du Règlement Intérieur', E. Decaux and C. Pettiti (eds.), *La Tierce Intervention Devant la Cour Européenne des Droits de l'Homme et en Droit Comparé* (Brussels: Bruylant, 2008) 103–14, at 104.

[126] P. van Tuijl, 'NGOs and Human Rights: Sources of Justice and Democracy', *J. of Int'l Affairs* 52:2 (1999) 493–512, at 494; and M. Keck and K. Sikkink, *Activists Beyond Borders: Advocacy Networks in International Politics* (Ithaca: Cornell University Press, 1998).

[127] J. Smith and D. Wiest, 'The Uneven Geography of Global Civil Society: National and Global Influences on Transnational Association', *Social Forces* 84:2 (2005) at 621–52.

[128] In the same vein, Jean du Bois de Gaudusson emphasises how complex the participation of the supreme courts of developing countries is in the dialogue between judges. To date, the case law developed by Northern and developed countries is hardly influenced by jurisprudence from the South; J. du Bois de Gaudusson, 'La Complexité de la Participation des Cours Suprêmes des Pays en Voie de Développement au Dialogue des Juges', *Les Petites Affiches* 112 (2008) 22–25 (my translation). See also H. Buxbaum, 'From Empire to Globalization … and Back? A Post-Colonial View of Transjudicialism', *Indiana J. of Global Legal Studies* 11:1 (2004) 183–89. For a counter-position, see B. Markesinis, *Juges et Universitaires Face au Droit Comparé: Histoire des Trente-cinq Dernières Années* (Paris: Dalloz, 2006) at 44–45.

context – David Fontana believes a more inclusive dialogue would be desirable, because there is 'a growing number of citizens [that] come from parts of the world whose traditions are not reflected in traditional American constitutional law'.[129] Also in Europe, less Western-centric judicial dialogue could be used as a strategy of inclusion. Reem Bahdi suggests that transnational judicial reference to courts of non-Western cultures could also send the message that transjudicialism is a 'shared enterprise'.[130] This could also enhance the relevance of European human rights jurisprudence at the global level.

Regarding data collection of comparative material from CoE member and non-member states, methodological information found in the briefs is even scarcer. Today, many judgments, especially from the highest courts, are available online. Nonetheless, accuracy cannot always be guaranteed. Only a very low number of briefs seem to have provided some explanation of their methodologies relating to data gathering on comparative material.

First, the brief of "Liberty" in *Sheffield and Horsham v. the United Kingdom* explained that:

> The research was carried out during July, August and September 1997. A questionnaire, a sample of which is found at Appendix C, was sent to relevant Government agencies, Consuls and Embassies, Universities, academics, lawyers and other practitioners and appropriate Non-Government Organisations. The questionnaire was also posted on the Internet. The responses were constructive and timely. These were followed up with telephone conversations to confirm details and, where necessary, additional legal research was carried out. The contact and reference point for each country can be found at Appendix B. Liberty was able to identify the position relating to transsexual and transgendered people in all of the Council of Europe member States at that time. Additional research was undertaken in key Commonwealth jurisdictions and in a number of other countries including the United States. The results can be found in full at Appendix A.[131]

Second, the brief of "Article 19" and "Interights" in *Goodwin v. the United Kingdom* observed:

> The present comments are based in large part on the statements of legal experts from seven European countries published in 1993 in a book edited

[129] D. Fontana, 'Refined Comparativism in Constitutional Law', *UCLA Law Review* 49:2 (2001) 539–623, at 616.

[130] R. Bahdi, 'Globalization of Judgment: Transjudicialism and the Five Faces of International Law in Domestic Courts', *Geo. Wash. Int'l L. Rev* 34:3 (2002) 555–603, at 599.

[131] Brief of "Liberty" in *Sheffield and Horsham v. the United Kingdom*, *supra* note 3. See also Brief of "Liberty" in *Goodwin v. the United Kingdom*, *supra* note 3.

> by ARTICLE 19 titled *Press Law and Practice: Press Freedom in European and Other Democracies*, supplemented by information published in August 1993 in *The ARTICLE 19 Freedom of Expression Handbook*. In preparing these comments we contacted the contributors to our books and other legal experts to ascertain whether there had been any significant legal developments in the intervening months, and the information they supplied is also included. The seven European countries whose law and jurisprudence are herein discussed are Austria, France, Germany, the Netherlands, Norway, Spain and Sweden.[132]

Finally, some briefs also mention case law that does not support their argument, and even if it is mainly for the sake of showing how isolated those cases are, such practice works towards completeness in the NGOs' surveys and could contribute to refute the criticisms of cherry-picking.[133] Another manner of avoiding criticism is to admit the brief's limits. A brief of the NGO "Article 19" states, for example, that '[o]ur discussion does not purport to be comprehensive but rather illustrative'.[134]

The healthy call for increased attention to methods in comparative law studies[135] could also apply to the *amicus curiae* briefs. And as it seems correct to request from the comparatists that they expose their choices, so too could it be expected from the *amici* presenting comparative law.[136]

12.5 The Briefs' Impact on the Extent, Method and Purpose of the ECtHR's Dialogue

In this last section an attempt is made to tentatively assess the impact that the ECtHR's use of the briefs has on the extent, method and purpose of the ECtHR's dialogue with other international and domestic courts. The analysis also aims to link the discussion in Section 12.3 with what has been stated in Section 12.4.

Coming back to the framework suggested by the editor, the extent of judicial dialogue might be influenced by *amicus curiae* briefs. First,

[132] Brief of "Article 19" and "Interights" in *William Goodwin v. the United Kingdom* (Appl. No. 17488/90), Judgment (Grand Chamber), 27 March 1996, Reports 1996-II, at 1 and 17.

[133] Indicated 'to be departed from' (TBDF) in the Appendix.

[134] Brief of "Article 19" in *Sunday Times v. the United Kingdom (No 2)* and *Observer and Guardian Newspapers v. the United Kingdom*, supra note 13.

[135] Gerber, Globalization, *supra* note 103, at 950. See also Carozza, Uses and Misuses, *supra* note 36, at 1225.

[136] Ponthoreau, L'Argument Fondé sur la Comparaison, *supra* note 58, at 539–40. In addition, according to Gerber, the information should present four characteristics: be 1) sufficient in scope, 2) efficiently organised, 3) readily available and 4) action oriented; Gerber, Globalization, *supra* note 103, at 959.

in parallel with the statement that the phenomenon of cross-citations is accelerating, a similar trend of increasing *amicus* participation over *time* has been observed. Regarding the *type of issue*, the analysis of the briefs' content has shown that the input of comparative material in third-party interventions is made in all kinds of cases, but in particular on the issues of private and family life and non-discrimination, which match the observations made regarding the Court's use of comparative elements. Concerning the *spatial component* and the *material*, the briefs rely on a large set of national, regional and international binding and non-binding sources, and supply the Court with case law from various courts. *Amici* encourage dialogue in all directions. Although judicial autarchy and self-reference are the default posture of courts,[137] the briefs do not hesitate to encourage the Court to look at other continents. Some parallel patterns in the briefs and the ECtHR's case law can be discerned: the case law that receives the most attention comes from the UN HRC, the IACtHR and the United States. The ICJ and the CJEU are cited infrequently. Similarly, when national courts are cited, there is a strong inclination for courts from states belonging to the 'club' of original contracting parties to the CoE or for the jurisprudence of common law courts of Western liberal democracies. The two landscapes of comparative elements – in the briefs and in the Court's judgments and decisions – thus present strong similarities. But it was also observed that regarding some references, the briefs dare to go further. Sometimes they, for instance, cite CJEU judgments in cases involving states outside the European Union or judgments originating from common law jurisdictions in cases involving civil law countries. It thus remains to be observed whether the extent of judicial dialogue in those directions will change in the future, including towards a greater inclusion of jurisprudence originating from Eastern European domestic courts.

To test these findings further, an additional query was made: the observation of whether any of the references found in the briefs (and exposed in columns 7–12 of the Appendix) were made in the respective judgment of the ECtHR as well (as indicated in the final column of the Appendix). As explained earlier, a restrictive approach was adopted for the purpose of the present study: only the exact same references in the briefs and in the cases were counted,[138] and if the foreign case law was mentioned only in the

[137] Romano, Deciphering the Grammar, *supra* note 21, at 758.

[138] It is, however, not distinguished whether they were found in majority or dissenting opinions.

paragraph summarising the third interveners' submission, the reference was not counted.[139]

To recall, among the 127 analysed briefs, 105 mention at least one international or foreign legal document. Among these 105 briefs, 38 contain a reference to international or foreign case law which is subsequently found in the Grand Chamber judgment. This means that more than a third of the briefs (36.1 per cent) bringing comparative material to the Court find an echo in the Court's jurisprudence. This is a high ratio. However, the influence of NGOs' briefs must be cautiously stated, especially because the possible influence of the *amici* does not take place in a vacuum, and other independent elements play into the dynamic of cross-citation. For example, ECtHR judges may have received this information from their own research division in the Registry or from the parties. Finally, even if the same judgment is referred to, there might be different uses of it. Sometimes a case is only mentioned in a footnote in the brief, but then extensively analysed in the respective ECtHR judgment and vice versa; sometimes the same case is mentioned in a brief and in the respective judgment of the ECtHR, but for different reasons.[140]

The presence of comparative material in the briefs and the correlations between its manifestation in the briefs and in the case law allows us to presume that *amici* influence the extent of the judicial dialogue at the ECtHR. Of course, causal influences between the briefs and the judgments remain to be comprehensively studied: are the *amici*, through their written briefs, encouraging the judges to import law or are the judges, through their use of comparative materials, encouraging the *amici* to present it?[141] The measurement of influence would be facilitated if judges would locate

[139] See, for example, the case of *R. v. Borden* of the Supreme Court of Canada, 1994, referred to in the *amicus* brief of the "Fédération Internationale des Droits de l'Homme" in *D.H. and Others v. Czech Republic* (Appl. No. 57325/00), Judgment (Grand Chamber), 13 November 2007, ECHR 2007-IV, 241, which is mentioned in para. 173 of the case as part of the summary of the FIDH's intervention.

[140] For example, the brief of "Redress" in *Varnava and Others v. Turkey* (Appl. No. 16064/90), Judgment (Grand Chamber), 18 September 2009, ECHR 2009-V, 13, refers to paragraph 15 of HRC, *Irene Bleier Lewenhoff and Rosa Valino de Bleier v. Uruguay*, Communication No. 30/1978, 29 March 1982, UN Doc. CCPR/C/15/D/30/1978 at 109 to support the affirmation that 'a victim is also entitled to satisfaction and guarantees of non-repetition, which should include effective measures aimed at the cessation of continuing violations'; Brief of "Redress" in *Varnava, ibid.* at 5. The Court cites the same case, but its paragraph 14 which says that '[i]n a number of cases, the HRC has found that a breach of Article 6 of the Covenant has occurred, but has been unable to make a final decision in that regard in the absence of confirmation of death'; case of *Varnava and Others v. Turkey*, ibid. para. 100.

[141] Black and Epstein, (Re-)Setting the Scholarly Agenda, *supra* note 1, at 805.

the source of the comparative information, as is the practice before other courts.[142] However, this tentative conclusion on the influence of NGO briefs on the extent to which the ECtHR engages in dialogue is confirmed by scholars and ECtHR judges. Tulkens, Van Drooghenbroeck and Krenc wrote that 'the comparative law analysis delivered by others, may in fact, have a decisive impact. This impact is particularly noticeable when NGOs, specialised in the matters at stake in the case and having considerable resources to map in an accurate and reliable way the external sources likely to be relevant, join the proceedings as third-party interveners'.[143] According to them, '[i]t is clear that in practice, references to external sources are richer and more numerous when third-party interventions are allowed'.[144] Dzehtsiarou and Lukashevich, who have interviewed ECtHR judges, report that most of them 'indicated a positive appreciation of third parties' reports'.[145] Judge Spielmann (now president of the ECtHR), for example, points out that judges 'rely more on the Research Division[,] but if what the Research Division report provides is confirmed by NGOs then it is very important'.[146] Finally, it could also be argued that even if the precise impact on the extent of judicial dialogue is difficult to measure, briefs containing comparative elements might generally influence the 'posture of openness' of the Court towards external sources, or, in the words of Vicki Jackson, a posture of engagement.[147]

Regarding the method related to judicial dialogue, two aspects need to be distinguished: one concerns the manner in which judges become aware of comparative material; the other concerns the method accompanying the use of comparative material in the Court's analysis. This chapter provides a clear answer to the first aspect: more than 80 per cent of the *amicus*

[142] See, for example, the famous case of *Lawrence v. Texas* in which Justice Kennedy cited three ECtHR case and indicated 'See Brief of Mary Robinson *et al.* as Amici Curiae 11–12', US Supreme Court, *Lawrence v. Texas*, 26 June 2003, 539 US 558.

[143] Tulkens, Van Drooghenbroeck and Krenc, Soft Law, *supra* note 12, at 473 (my translation); Olivier De Schutter had already written in 1996 that briefs contained, among others, comparative elements, but had only a small quantity of cases to observe; O. De Schutter 'Sur l'Emergence de la Société Civile dans le Droit International: le Rôle des Associations Devant la Cour Européenne des Droits de l'Homme', *European J. of Int'l L.* 7:3 (1996) 372–410, at 396.

[144] Tulkens, Van Drooghenbroeck and Krenc, Soft Law, *supra* note 12, at 473.

[145] Dzehtsiarou and Lukashevich, Informed Decision-Making, *supra* note 22, at 296. See also K. Dzehtsiarou, *European Consensus and the Legitimacy of the European Court of Human Rights* (Cambridge University Press, 2015).

[146] *Ibid.*

[147] For more on this, see V. Jackson, *Constitutional Engagement in a Transnational Era* (Oxford University Press, 2010).

briefs sent to the Grand Chamber contain comparative elements. Thus, relying on *amicus curiae* briefs is certainly part of the method through which ECtHR judges learn about relevant case law from international and domestic courts. The second aspect raises the question of whether the briefs contribute to the Court making its choices more open as to which comparative material it relies on, and thus whether this could help to address the criticism of 'cherry-picking'. In the context of the ECtHR, the criticism of not clearly disclosing its comparative method is most frequently voiced when the Court establishes the existence or non-existence of a consensus. The *amicus curiae* briefs might help the Court in this regard: some contain extensive and detailed appendices with surveys and/ or precise information as to how data was collected.[148] This explicit and detailed methodological information in the briefs could be taken on by the ECtHR in its judgments to make the Court's comparative methods more transparent. So far, this has not happened in regard to the good practices in the briefs mentioned earlier in the chapter. If briefs themselves would increasingly lift the curtain on their data-gathering and data selection methods, this could not only strengthen the quality of the briefs but also increase the added value of NGOs' participation in the ECtHR's comparative engagements.

We now move to consider whether the ECtHR's use of comparative material from the *amicus curiae* briefs contributes to the ECtHR achieving some of the alleged purposes of its engagement in judicial dialogue. As it has been suggested,[149] the purposes of the ECtHR's engagement in judicial dialogue are various. As the references to foreign case law in the judgments pursue different objectives, so do these references in the *amicus curiae* briefs, as already evidenced in excerpts from various briefs set out earlier in the chapter. The following paragraphs contain more excerpts which illustrate how the use of briefs can contribute to achieving some of the ECtHR's alleged purposes of engagement with foreign and international material. However, as a caveat, it must be said that it is difficult to routinely establish the exact purpose of the ECtHR's and/or the briefs' use of comparative material, since most of the time there is no explicit indication in this regard, neither in the briefs nor in the Court's judgments. Moreover, often different purposes overlap. Therefore, a case-by-case analysis is indicated.[150]

[148] See the examples given *supra*, subsection 12.4.3.

[149] See the discussion *supra* Section 12.3.

[150] An evaluation of the ECtHR judges' practice of referring to external documents is difficult to generalise; see D. Staes, 'The Use of Documents Other Than the European Convention on

There are examples of the ECtHR's use of the comparative material brought forward in the briefs to establish the existence of a 'consensus' on a particular question concerning the interpretation of the ECHR. A famous example is the *amicus curiae* brief submitted by Amnesty International in the case of *Soering v. the United Kingdom*,[151] decided by the then Plenary Court. The Court concluded (using the NGO's words) that there was a 'virtual consensus in Western European legal systems that the death penalty is, under current circumstances, no longer consistent with regional standards of justice'.[152] Another often cited example is the *Goodwin v. the United Kingdom* case,[153] in which the Court found an international trend towards legal recognition following gender re-assignment, relying on the survey on this issue that had been submitted by the NGO Liberty.[154] Thus, in both cases the ECtHR used the comparative analyses submitted by NGOs for the purpose of establishing the existence of a European consensus, allowing it to progressively develop the law of the ECHR concerning article 3 and article 8 of the ECHR, respectively. At the same time, the comparative material highlighted by the *amici* ensured that the Court's progressive interpretation remained grounded in the changing social and political circumstances in CoE member states. It thereby contributed to achieving one of the main purposes of the European consensus doctrine as such – that is, provide 'a response to the legitimacy challenges made against evolutive interpretation'.[155]

The case of *A. and Others v. the United Kingdom*[156] is an example of the use of foreign judgments for other purposes: to show that there are alternative policy options, which might be less rights-restrictive, and to clarify the requirements to meet Convention standards. In this case, a practice aimed at protecting national security was to be made compatible with the United Kingdom's obligations under article 5(4) of the ECHR. The applicants had *inter alia* complained that the procedure before the Special Immigration Appeals Commission – that decided on their indefinite

Human Rights and Its Protocols before the European Court of Human Rights: Reflections from and upon a Users' Perspective', *Human Rights and Int'l Legal Discourse* 2 (2014) 186–214, at 212.

151 *Soering v. the United Kingdom*, *supra* note 13.

152 *Ibid.*, para. 102.

153 *Christine Goodwin v. the United Kingdom*, *supra* note 3.

154 *Ibid.* para. 84.

155 K. Dzehtsiarou, 'European Consensus and the Evolutive Interpretation of the European Convention on Human Rights', *German L. J.* 12 (2011) 1730–45.

156 *A. and Others v. the United Kingdom* (Appl. No. no. 3455/05), Judgment (Grand Chamber), 19 February 2009, ECHR 2009-II, 137.

detention under UK anti-terrorism legislation – had been unfair because the evidence (intelligence information) against them had not been fully disclosed to them for reasons of 'national security'. The issue at stake had already involved some back-and-forth between different jurisdictions and the involvement of NGOs. In the case of *Chahal v. the United Kingdom*,[157] the ECtHR examined the British special advocates system – a system of appointing security-cleared advocates to defend detainees in cases involving material that could not be disclosed for reasons of national security – for its compatibility with article 5(4) of the ECHR.[158] Five NGOs intervened, through three *amicus curiae* briefs (see Appendix). In this case, the Court condemned the system and explained that it

> attaches significance to the fact that, as the intervenors pointed out ... in Canada a more effective form of judicial control has been developed in cases of this type. This example illustrates that there are techniques which can be employed which both accommodate legitimate security concerns about the nature and sources of intelligence information and yet accord the individual a substantial measure of procedural justice.[159]

Here, the Court used the *amici's* comparative information to show that there are other existing practical solutions that are more compatible with the requirements of the ECHR than the British solution is. However, it did not directly recommend the United Kingdom to adopt the less rights-restrictive Canadian alternative, nor did it express an opinion of whether all aspects of the Canadian model conformed to the Convention. The United Kingdom responded by creating a new system. It found inspiration in the Canadian model but left aside the protections of detainees' procedural rights it entailed. A few years later, the Canadian Supreme Court, in *Charkaoui v. Minister of Citizenship and Immigration*,[160] ruled unanimously that the Canadian procedure violated the Canadian Charter of Rights and Freedoms. It also considered the British system and quoted the *Chahal* case. Although the British model was criticised, it was subsequently adopted by the Canadian Parliament, continuing the 'race to the bottom'. Meanwhile in the United Kingdom, judges again scrutinised the

[157] *Chahal v. the United Kingdom* (Appl. No. 22414/93), Judgment (Grand Chamber), 15 November 1996, ECHR 1996-V.

[158] See for more on this D. Jenkins, 'There and Back Again: The Strange Journey of Special Advocates and Comparative Law Methodology', *Columbia Human Rights L. Rev.* 42:2 (2011) at 279–355.

[159] *Chahal v. the United Kingdom, supra* note 157, para 130.

[160] Supreme Court of Canada, *Charkaoui v. Canada (Minister of Citizenship and Immigration)* [2007] 1 SCR 350.

procedure. When it reached Strasbourg (under the name *A. and others v. the United Kingdom*), the organisations Liberty and Justice both submitted *amicus curiae* briefs. The brief presented by the latter explained the initial misunderstanding of the situation in Canada[161] and alerted the Court about the changes that had been made in Canada and the critical arguments which had been formulated by the Canadian Supreme Court. It describes the procedure at that time and devotes a part to the case of *Charkaoui v. Minister of Citizenship and Immigration.*[162] This judgment of the Canadian Supreme Court received attention in the ECtHR's judgment *A and Others v. the United Kingdom* under the heading 'Other materials concerning non-disclosure of evidence in national security cases'. Two paragraphs of McLachlin CJ were quoted by the Court, highlighting that the right of a person whose liberty was in jeopardy to know the case against him, could never be limited by national security concerns to the extent that this right was 'effectively gutted'.[163] The Court did not once again refer to this finding of the Canadian Supreme Court and the NGO's elaborations in the merits part of the judgment. Nonetheless, it can be assumed that the Canadian Supreme Court's arguments contributed to the Court clarifying that the use of undisclosed evidence and special advocates were only compatible with article 5(4) of the ECHR when the allegations in the material open to the applicant were sufficiently detailed to enable an effective challenge.[164]

There are several examples of where the Court used comparative material highlighted by the *amici* to assist its reasoning and develop its interpretation of the Convention's provisions. This is among the purposes for which the ECtHR engages in transnational judicial dialogue. One example is the case of *Konstantin Markin v. Russia.*[165] It involved the differential treatment of fathers and mothers in the military and their rights to parental leave. The Court used comparative material in its argumentation, which had also been brought forward by a brief. The Human Rights Centre of Ghent University submitted that '[t]here is a rich body of materials that is developed by both international organizations and international courts

[161] The brief states: 'Given the weight that was attached in *Chahal* to the Canadian example of using security-cleared counsel, however, we think it is important to clarify what the Canadian experience actually has been. In fact, it appears that our fellow NGO intervenors in *Chahal* may have inadvertently misapprehended the position in Canada in 1996'; brief of "Justice" in *A. and Others v. the United Kingdom, supra* note 156, para. 13.

[162] *Ibid.* paras. 42–47.

[163] *A. and Others v. the United Kingdom, supra* note 156, para. 111.

[164] *Ibid.*, para. 220.

[165] *Konstantin Markin v. Russia* (GC), *supra* note 81.

acknowledging and addressing the link between gender stereotypes and gender inequality'.[166] The brief then mentioned, among others, the CJEU case *Roca-Álvarez* v. *Sesa Start España ETT*[167] which 'condemned the perpetuation of "a traditional distribution of the roles of men and women by keeping men in a role subsidiary to that of women in relation to the exercise of their parental duties" '.[168] The Court devoted a few paragraphs to outline the facts and the reasoning of this case in the 'relevant international and comparative material' section of its judgment.[169] Ultimately the Court noted that it 'agrees with the applicant and the third party that [the difference in treatment between servicemen and servicewomen] has the effect of perpetuating gender stereotypes and is disadvantageous both to women's careers and to men's family life'.[170] The interveners reported being satisfied that their participation had been recognised and that the Court relied on some of their arguments.[171] It can even be assumed that the foreign and comparative material contributed to the Court's decision to overrule[172] its own earlier judgment in *Petrovic v. Austria*.[173] Judge Pinto de Albuquerque, in his concurring opinion emphasised that, 'As a result of this wide international consensus [on the right to parental leave] in European and universal human rights law and international labour law, the approach taken by the Court in the case of *Petrovic v. Austria* is manifestly outdated'.[174] In this judgment of 1998, the Court had held that a distinction on the basis of sex with respect to parental leave allowances did not violate article 14 of the ECHR because at the material time there was no European consensus in this field, as the majority of contracting states did not provide for parental leave or related allowances for fathers.[175]

166 Brief of "the Human Rights Centre of Ghent University" in *Konstantin Markin v. Russia, ibid.*

167 Case C-104/09, *Roca-Álvarez v. Sesa Start España ETT SA*, [2010] ECR I-8661; ECLI:EU:C:2010:561.

168 Brief of "The Human Rights Centre of Ghent University" in *Konstantin Markin* v. *Russia, supra* note 81, at 7 and *Roca-Álvarez* v. *Sesa Start España ETT SA, supra* note 167, para. 36.

169 *Konstantin Markin v. Russia, supra* note 81, paras. 67–70

170 *Ibid.*, para. 141.

171 A. Timmer, 'Gender Justice in Strasbourg', *Strasbourg Observers*, 22 March 2012, www.strasbourgobservers.com/2012/03/22/gender-justice-in-strasbourg/.

172 *Konstantin Markin v. Russia, supra* note 81, paras. 139 and 140.

173 *Petrovic v. Austria* (Appl. No. 20458/92), Judgment (Chamber), 27 March 1998, Reports 1998-II.

174 Partly Concurring, Partly Dissenting Opinion of Judge Pinto de Albuquerque, *Konstantin Markin v. Russia, supra* note 81.

175 *Petrovic v. Austria, supra* note 173, paras. 39–43.

Another example of the ECtHR relying on comparative material brought forward by an *amicus* brief for the purpose of supporting its interpretation of a particular Convention right is the judgment in *Gäfgen v. Germany.*[176] The same reference to a foreign case in an *amicus curiae* brief can be observed in the subsequent judgment of the ECtHR. Here, the organisation Redress Trust mentioned various cases in which the respective courts had held that threats of torture constitute torture. Among others, the brief quoted extracts of the recent Inter-American Court of Human Rights' judgment in *Maritza Urrutia v. Guatemala.*[177] In the 'public international and comparative law and practice' section of the facts, the Grand Chamber referred to this case and emphasised some extracts on the legal qualification of torture.[178] Then, under its analysis of the alleged violation of article 3 and more particularly regarding the legal qualification of the treatment at stake in this case, the Court wrote:

> Having regard to the relevant factors for characterising the treatment to which the applicant was subjected, the Court is satisfied that the real and immediate threats against the applicant for the purpose of extracting information from him attained the minimum level of severity to bring the impugned conduct within the scope of Article 3. It reiterates that according to its own case-law … which also refers to the definition of torture in Article 1 of the United Nations Convention against Torture … and according to the views taken by other international human rights monitoring bodies … *to which the Redress Trust likewise referred*, a threat of torture can amount to torture, as the nature of torture covers both physical pain and mental suffering. In particular, the fear of physical torture may itself constitute mental torture.[179]

The Court thus admits that a threat of torture can amount to torture. It bases this conclusion on its own case law, an international source and the views of human rights monitoring bodies, explicitly stressing that the intervening NGO likewise referred to these authorities. The comparative material here reinforced its interpretation of the scope of article 3.[180]

[176] *Gäfgen v. Germany* (Appl. No. 22978/05), Judgment (Grand Chamber), 1 June 2010, ECHR 2010-IV, 247.

[177] IACtHR, *Maritza Urrutia v. Guatemala*, Judgment, 27 November 2003, Series C, No. 103 mentioned in the brief of "Redress Trust" in the case of *Gäfgen v. Germany, supra* note 176, para. 14 of the brief.

[178] *Ibid.*, para. 66 of the case.

[179] *Ibid.* para. 108 (emphasis added).

[180] Ultimately, in the particular circumstances of the case, the Court found that the method of interrogation to which the applicant was subjected was sufficiently serious to amount

In other cases, the comparative material brought forward by the briefs contributed to strengthening the dissenters' arguments, who for their part wished to use this material to confirm and/or develop their interpretation of the Convention. An example here is the dissenting opinion to the ECtHR judgment *Mouvement raëlien suisse v. Switzerland*,[181] a Grand Chamber case about the protection of the freedom of expression involving, among others, the issue of 'hyperlinks' in a website. According to the organisation Article 19,

> the decisions of the Swiss authorities and the Chamber's judgment reflect[ed] an inadequate understanding of the nature and function of hyperlinks. They fail[ed], moreover, to adequately explain why a website whose content is itself lawful may nonetheless be penalised on account of the unlawful content of a third party's website for which it is not responsible.[182]

The brief then provided a technical definition of a 'hyperlink', referring to a judgment from the High Court of England and Wales[183] and mentioning the decision of a Californian Superior Court to emphasise the important role of hyperlinks to impart ideas on the Web.[184] The brief continued by citing a judgment of the British Columbia Supreme Court, which was pending before the Canadian Supreme Court at the time of submission (September 2011).[185] At the time of deliberation by the Grand Chamber, the Canadian Supreme Court had decided the case, and two dissenting opinions to *Mouvement raëlien suisse v. Switzerland* referred to the Canadian case.[186] The majority judgment did not find a violation of article 10 of the ECHR. However, the dissenters cited the Canadian case

to inhuman treatment prohibited by Article 3, but that it did not reach the level of cruelty required to attain the threshold of torture; *ibid.* para. 108 of the case.

181 Brief of "Article 19" in *Mouvement raëlien suisse v. Switzerland* (Appl. No. 16354/06), Judgment (Grand Chamber), 13 July 2012, ECHR 2012-IV, 373 (extracts).

182 *Ibid.* para. 13.

183 *Research in Motion UK Ltd v. Inpro Licensing SARL and Others*, 2 February 2006, England and Wales High Courts (Patents Courts) [2006] EWHC 70 (Pat), cited in the Brief of "Article 19" in *Mouvement raëlien suisse* v. *Switzerland, supra* note 181, para. 14.

184 *Ibid*, para. 15. The referred case is *DVD Copy Control Association Inc. v. A.T. McLaughlin*, 21 January 2004, No. CV 786804 (Supreme Court of California).

185 Brief of "Article 19" in *Mouvement raëlien suisse v. Switzerland, supra* note 181, para. 16. The referred case is *The Crookes v. Wikimedia Foundation* [2008] BCSC 1424 (British Columbia Supreme Court) and the brief provides the link to its electronic version.

186 Supreme Court of Canada, *Wayne Crookes, et al. v. Jon Newton* [2011] 3 SCR 269. See Joint Dissenting Opinion of Judges Sajó, Lazarova Trajkovska and Vučinić and Dissenting Opinion of Judge Pinto de Albuquerque in *Mouvement raëlien suisse v. Switzerland, supra* note 181.

to emphasise the neutral content of hyperlinks, the difficulty of controlling them and the danger if they were subjected to traditional publication rules. The dissenters thus quoted foreign peers who had already dealt with cases involving these new technologies to better grasp their implications and to support their finding of a violation of the Convention.[187]

In summary, most probably, the comparative material brought forward in *amicus* briefs increases the extent to which the ECtHR engages in transnational judicial dialogue. This also confirms that reliance on *amicus curiae* briefs is one of the methods that the ECtHR has at its disposal to find out or confirm relevant comparative material that it can use in its own judgments. Concerning other aspects of the Court's methodology when choosing the foreign or international jurisprudence with which to engage, it was suggested that the ECtHR could rely on briefs to a greater extent to make its choices more transparent. To this end, the briefs themselves could improve in clarifying the methodology they use for choosing the comparative material in their submissions. The ECtHR's reliance on comparative material highlighted by NGO submissions can also help it to achieve the various purposes of engagement in judicial dialogue. The examples in this section showed that comparative material brought forward by NGOs can have a role in establishing the (non-)existence of a European consensus on a certain matter, suggesting alternative policies which are less rights-restrictive or strengthening the interpretation of a Convention provision.

12.6 Conclusion: NGOs as Messengers … Whose Messages Find an Echo

'Judicial dialogue' lies on a terrain that has been deeply changed by globalisation.[188] One of the open questions about this practice concerns the manner in which judges learn about foreign legal material. This chapter set out to explore one of the *methods* through which the ECHR becomes aware of foreign and international jurisprudence, and it analysed the contribution that NGOs in their third-party interventions can make in this regard. The empirical analysis of the briefs submitted by human rights NGOs to the Grand Chamber of the ECtHR revealed a strong presence of comparative materials in their arguments. NGOs can thus indeed be considered

[187] Mouvement raëlien suisse v. Switzerland, *supra* note 181, Joint dissenting opinion of Judges Sajó, Lazarova Trajkovska and Vučinić.

[188] M. Ferrarese, 'When National Actors Become Transnational: Transjudicial Dialogue between Democracy and Constitutionalism', *Global Jurist* 9:1 (2009) 1305 *et seq.*

'messengers'[189] of a specific type of information which can lead the Court to engage in judicial dialogue. A subsequent comparison of the references found in the briefs and in the concerned cases concluded that more than a third of the submitted briefs suggesting the Court to look elsewhere by citing cases from other courts find an echo in the judgments.

This confirms that the *amici curiae* and in particular the comparative material brought forward in their submissions can influence the *extent* to which the ECtHR engages in dialogue. The analysis also showed that the ECtHR's use of comparative material submitted in *amicus curiae* briefs can help the Court to achieve the alleged *purposes* of its engagement in transnational judicial dialogue. Potentially, it can also contribute to the Court clarifying the *methodology* it applies when deciding which foreign and international jurisprudence to engage with. While this chapter did not go into the larger question of the *effect* of judicial dialogue, the argumentative techniques of *amici* referring to foreign judgments can be seen as one potential *effect* of the ECtHR's dialogue, as the influence can go both ways. It would now be interesting to compare the briefs submitted before other courts, and explore to what degree interveners adjust their interventions to the preferences and discourse of these courts and if transnational legal mobilisation practices can be observed. In this regard, we note that some *amicus curiae* briefs underline the leading role the Court has played[190] and could thus act as a model for other courts or institutions.[191]

This chapter thus adds one piece to the puzzle on how ideas migrate and how judicial dialogue might be fuelled. Moreover, this chapter contributes to the analysis of NGOs' work towards the activity of the ECtHR

189 This expression is borrowed from W. Osiatynski, 'Paradoxes of Constitutional Borrowing', *Int'l J. of Constitutional L.* 1:2 (2003) 244–68, at 255.

190 See, for example, the brief of "Liberty", the "AIRE Centre" and the "Joint Council for the Welfare of Immigrants" in *Chahal v. the United Kingdom, supra* note 157, that explains that article 3 of the ECHR is absolute and that limitations and derogations are not permitted, and 'The Convention in this respect has become a model for later human rights treaties' (para. 2.3). After citing international and foreign examples, the *amici* argue that there is no justification for departing from the Court's constant jurisprudence; para. 2.4.

191 See, for example, the brief submitted by the "AIRE Centre" in *Hirsi Jamaa v. Italy*, on the obligations of States regarding interception of migrants at sea. Arguing that the EU Charter of Fundamental Rights is binding on all Member States but that 'the CJEU has not yet had the opportunity to rule on the matter', that there is a lacuna in EU law regarding the applicability of EU asylum acquis to such interceptions, and that the ECtHR case law already had a significant impact on the EU's legislative process, it insists that '[a] clear judgment from this Court will provide invaluable assistance to all Contracting Parties and the European institutions'; Brief of the "AIRE Centre" in *Hirsi Jamaa v. Italy* (Appl. No. 27765/09), Judgment (Grand Chamber), 23 February 2012, ECHR 2012-II, 97, at 10.

in general. This is important, as the evolution of the Convention system was – and continues to be – critically linked to a dynamic interaction between civil society and the ECtHR.[192] The development of human rights jurisprudence is not only increasingly influenced by a judicial dialogue[193]; it is also a dialogue involving civil society organisations. It will be interesting to follow the extent to which the globalised agenda and working methods of NGOs parallel a 'globalisation' of references.

Acknowledgments

I would like to thank the organisers of the Conference on Transnational Judicial Dialogue: Concept, Method, Extent, Effects, held in Oslo on 21–22 June 2013, and all of its participants for fruitful discussions. I am particularly grateful to Yonatan Lupu, Erik Voeten and Amrei Müller for their comments. Any mistakes are mine alone.

[192] Cichowski, Civil Society, *supra* note 5, at 77.
[193] L'Heureux-Dubé, The Importance of Dialogue, *supra* note 111, at 16.

Appendix: Cases Analysed

1. Number	2. Name of the case	3. Name of intervener(s)	4. Year of intervention	5. HR / article concerned
1	A. AND OTHERS v. THE UK	Justice	2008	5+6
2	A. AND OTHERS v. THE UK	Liberty	2008	5
3	A., B. and C. v. IRELAND	Center for Reproductive Rights and the University of Toronto International Reproductive and Sexual Health Law Programme	2008	2+3+8+11
4	A., B. and C. v. IRELAND	European Centre for Law and Justice	2008	2+8
5	A., B. and C. v. IRELAND	Pro Life Campaign	2009	2
6	A., B. and C. v. IRELAND	Alliance Defense Fund, European Centre for Law and Justice, the Society for the Protection of the Unborn Children	2009	8
7	AKDIVAR AND OTHERS v. TURKEY	Amnesty International	1996	35
8	AKSU v. TURKEY	Greek Helsinki Monitor	2008	8+14+34
9	AL-JEDDA v. THE UK	Liberty and Justice	2009	5
10	AL-KHAWAJA v. UK	Justice	2010	6
11	AYDIN v. TURKEY	Amnesty International	1996	3+13
12	BAYATYAN v. ARMENIA	Amnesty International, Conscience and Peace Tax Conscience, Friends World Committee for Consultation (Quakers), International Commission of Jurists, War Resister's International	2010	4+9
13	BLECIC v. CROATIA	Interights	2005	8+1P1
14	BOSPHORUS v. IRELAND	Institut de formation en droits de l'homme du barreau de Paris	2004	1+1P1
15	CARSON AND OTHERS v. THE UK	Age Concern and Help the Aged	2008 and 2009	8
16	CENTRE FOR LEGAL RESOURCES ON BEHALF OF V. CAMPEANU v. ROMANIA	Bulgarian Helsinki Committee	2011	34

6. International or comparative analysis?	7. ICJ	8. HRC	9. CJUE	10. IACtHR	11. Case law of contracting states: which countries	12. Case law of non-contracting states: which countries	13. At least one common reference in the brief and in the case
1	0	0	0	0	0	Canada	1
1	0	1	1	0	0	New Zealand, India	0
1	0	1	0	0	Germany, Italy, Portugal, Slovakia, Spain	0	0
1	0	0	0	0	Poland	USA	0
0	0	0	0	0	0	0	0
1	0	0	0	0	Poland, Germany, Spain	0	0
1	0	0	0	1	0	0	1
1	0	1	0	0	Greece	0	0
1	0	0	1	0	0	0	1
1	0	0	0	0	Ireland	USA, Australia, Canada, New Zealand, South Africa	1
1	0	0	0	0	0	USA	0
1	0	1	0	1 To be departed from (TBDF)	0	0	1
1	1	0	1	0	UK	South Africa	0
1	1	1	1	0	France	0	1
0	0	0	0	0	0	0	0
0	0	0	0	0	0	0	0

(*continued*)

1. Number	2. Name of the case	3. Name of intervener(s)	4. Year of intervention	5. HR / article concerned
17	CENTRE FOR LEGAL RESOURCES ON BEHALF OF V. CAMPEANU v. ROMANIA	Euroregional Center for Public Initiatives (Romania)	2011	2+3+5+8+14
18	CENTRE FOR LEGAL RESOURCES ON BEHALF OF V. CAMPEANU v. ROMANIA	Human Rights Watch	2011	2+5+14
19	CENTRE FOR LEGAL RESOURCES ON BEHALF OF V. CAMPEANU v. ROMANIA	Mental Disability Advocacy Centre	2011	2+3+34
20	CENTRO EUROPA 7 s.r.l v. ITALY	Open Justice Initiative	2010	10
21	CHAHAL v. THE UK	Liberty, AIRE Centre, Joint Council for the Welfare of Immigrants	1996	3+13
22	CHAHAL v. THE UK	Amnesty International	1996	8+13
23	CHAHAL v. THE UK	JUSTICE	1996	13
24	CHAPMAN v. THE UK, COSTER v. UK, SMITH v. UK, BEARD v. UK, LEE v. UK	European Roma Rights Center	2000	8+14
25	CHRISTINE GOODWIN v. THE UK and I. v. THE UK	Liberty	2002	8
26	D.H. AND OTHERS v. THE CZECH REPUBLIC	Interights, Human Rights Watch	2006	14
27	D.H. AND OTHERS v. THE CZECH REPUBLIC	International Step by Step Association, Roma Education Fund, European Early Childhood Research Association	2006	2P1+14
28	D.H. AND OTHERS v. THE CZECH REPUBLIC	Minority Rights Group International, European Network against Racism, European Rome Information Office	2006	14+2P1
29	D.H. AND OTHERS v. THE CZECH REPUBLIC	Fédération Internationale des droits de l'homme	2006	2P1+14
30	DEL RIO PRADA v. SPAIN	The International Commission of Jurists	2013	7

6. International or comparative analysis?	7. ICJ	8. HRC	9. CJUE	10. IACtHR	11. Case law of contracting states: which countries	12. Case law of non-contracting states: which countries	13. At least one common reference in the brief and in the case
0	0	0	0	0	0	0	0
1	0	0	0	0	0	0	0
1	0	1	0	1	Ireland	Canada	0
1	0	0	0	0	France, Germany	0	0
1	0	1	0	0	0	South Africa	0
1	0	0	1	0	0	0	0
1	0	0	1	0	0	0	0
1	0	0	0	0	0	0	0
1	0	1	0	0	0	Australia, New Zealand, USA	1
1	0	0	1	1	Germany, Switzerland, UK, the Netherlands	Canada, USA	0
0	0	0	0	0	0	0	0
1	0	0	0	0	0	0	0
1	0	0	0	0	France	Canada, USA	0
1	0	0	0	1	France, the Netherlands	0	0

(*continued*)

1. Number	2. Name of the case	3. Name of intervener(s)	4. Year of intervention	5. HR / article concerned
31	DE SOUZA RIBEIRO v. France	Groupe d'Information et de Soutien des Immigrés (GISTI); La Ligue des droits de l'homme et du citoyen; le Comité Inter Mouvements Auprès des Evacués (Cimade)	2012	13+8
32	E.B. v. France	Fédération internationale des Ligues des Droits de l'Homme (FIDH); European Region of the International Lesbian and Gay Association (ILGA–Europe); British Association for Adoption and Fostering (BAAF); and Association des Parents et futurs parents Gays et Lesbiens	2005	8+14
33	EL-MASRI v. MACEDONIA	The Redress Trust	2011 & 2012	3+5+13
34	EL-MASRI v. MACEDONIA	Amnesty International and the International Commission of Jurists	2011	3+5+13
35	EL-MASRI v. MACEDONIA	Interights	2011	5
36	FERNANDEZ MARTNEZ v. SPAIN	ECJL (European Centre for Law and Justice)	2010	9
37	FERNANDEZ MARTNEZ v. SPAIN	Chair for Law and Religions of the Université Catholique de Louvain and the American Religious Program of the Ethics and Public Policy Center	2010	9
38	FINCI v. BOSNIA AND HERZEGOVINA	AIRE Centre	2008	3P1+14
39	FINCI v. BOSNIA AND HERZEGOVINA	The Open Society Justice Initiative	2007	14+3P1+1P12
40	GAFGEN v. GERMANY	Redress Trust	2009	3+6
41	GROSS v. SWITZERLAND	European Centre for Law and Justice	2012	2+3+8
42	GROSS v. SWITZERLAND	Dignitas	2012	8
43	GROSS v. SWITZERLAND	Americans United for Life	2012	2+3+8
44	GROSS v. SWITZERLAND	Alliance Defending Freedom (ADF)	2013	2+3+8
45	H.L.R. v. FRANCE	Rights International	1996	3
46	HAMALAINEN v. FINLAND	Transgender Europe	2013	8

6. International or comparative analysis?	7. ICJ	8. HRC	9. CJUE	10. IACtHR	11. Case law of contracting states: which countries	12. Case law of non-contracting states: which countries	13. At least one common reference in the brief and in the case
0	0	0	0	0	0	0	0
1	0	0	0	0	0	Canada, USA, South Africa	0
1	0	1	0	1	England, Wales	0	1
1	0	1	0	1	0	USA	1
1	1	1	0	0	0	0	1
1	0	1	0	0	Germany	0	0
1	0	1	0	0	Germany, Italy, Norway, Belgium	USA	0
1	0	0	0	0	Czech Republic, Lithuania	0	0
0	0	0	0	0	0	0	0
1	0	1	0	1	0	South Africa	1
1	0	0	0	0	0	0	0
0	0	0	0	0	0	0	0
1	0	0	0	0	0	USA	0
1	0	0	0	0	Germany, UK, the Netherlands	Canada	0
1	0	1	0	1	Italy, UK	0	0
1	0	0	0	0	Austria, Germany, Luxembourg, Switzerland	0	1

(continued)

1. Number	2. Name of the case	3. Name of intervener(s)	4. Year of intervention	5. HR / article concerned
47	HAMALAINEN v. FINLAND	Amnesty International	2013	14
48	HERRMANN v. GERMANY	European Centre for Law and Justice	2011	9
49	HIRST v. THE UK (No. 2)	AIRE Centre	2005	3P3+10+14
50	HIRST v. THE UK (No. 2)	The Prison Reform Trust	2005	3P3
51	HIRSI JAMAA AND OTHERS v. ITALY	AIRE Centre, Amnesty International and FIDH	2010	3
52	HIRSI JAMAA AND OTHERS v. ITALY	Columbia Law School Human Rights Clinic and many other clinics and individuals	2010	3
53	HIRSI JAMAA AND OTHERS v. ITALY	Human Rights Watch	2010	3
54	JANOWIEC AND OTHERS v. RUSSIA	Human Rights Centre "Memorial" (Moscow), European Human Rights Advocacy Centre (London), Essex Transitional Justice Network School of Law (Essex)	2012	2+3
55	JANOWIEC AND OTHERS v. RUSSIA	Public International Law and Policy Group	2012	3+41
56	JANOWIEC AND OTHERS v. RUSSIA	OSJ	2012	2+3+5+13
57	JANOWSKI v. POLAND	Rights International	1998	10
58	JERSILD v. DENMARK	Human Rights Watch (NY based)	1994	10
59	JEUNESSE v. THE NETHERLANDS	Defence for Children the Netherlands	2013	8
60	JEUNESSE v. THE NETHERLANDS	Immigrant Council of Ireland	2013	8 + 3P4
61	JOHN MURRAY v. THE UK	Committee on the Administration of Justice, Liberty and British-Irish Rights Watch	1995	6
62	JOHN MURRAY v. THE UK	Amnesty International	1995	6+14
63	JOHN MURRAY v. THE UK	Justice	1995	6
64	KINGSLEY v. THE UK	Liberty	2001	41
65	KONSTANTIN MARKIN v. RUSSIA	Human Rights Centre of Ghent University	2011	14
66	KURIC v. SLOVENIA (formerly MAKUC v. SLOVENIA)	Open Society Initiative	2007	8+13+14

6. International or comparative analysis?	7. ICJ	8. HRC	9. CJUE	10. IACtHR	11. Case law of contracting states: which countries	12. Case law of non-contracting states: which countries	13. At least one common reference in the brief and in the case
1	0	1	0	1	0	Nepal	1
0	0	0	0	0	0	0	0
1	0	0	0	0	0	0	0
1	0	0	0	0	0	Canada, South Africa	1
1	1 (PCIJ)0		1	0	0	0	1
1	0	0	0	0	0	USA (TBDF)	1
1	1	1	0	1	0	USA (TBDF)	1
1	0	0	0	1	0	0	0
1	0	0	0	1	0	0	0
1	0	1	0	1	0	0	0
1	0	0	0	1	UK	USA, Australia, India, Canada	0
1	0	0	0	0	0	USA	0
1	0	0	1	0	0	0	0
1	0	0	0	1	0	0	1
1	0	0	0	0	Italy	Canada, USA, Australia	1
1	0	0	0	0	0	USA	0
0	0	0	0	0	0	0	0
1	1	0	0	1	0	0	0
1	0	0	1	1	0	0	1
1	0	0	0	1	0	0	0

(*continued*)

1. Number	2. Name of the case	3. Name of intervener(s)	4. Year of intervention	5. HR / article concerned
67	KURIC v. SLOVENIA (formerly MAKUC v. SLOVENIA)	Peace Institute – Institute for Contemporary Social and Political Studies, and Legal Information Centre of Non-Governmental Organisations	2007	13+14
68	KURIC v. SLOVENIA (formerly MAKUC v. SLOVENIA)	The Equal Rights Trust	2007	8+14
69	LAUTSI v. ITALY	Associazone Nazionale del libero Pensiero	2010	9
70	LAUTSI v. ITALY	Greek Helsinki Monitor (! Intervened in both instances)	2009	9
71	LAUTSI v. ITALY	Alliance Defense Fund (on behalf of 32 members of the European Parliament)	2010	2P1, 41
72	LAUTSI v. ITALY	European Centre for Law and Justice	2010	9+2P1
73	LAUTSI v. ITALY	International Commission of Jurists; Interights and Human Rights Watch.	2010	2P1
74	MAKARATZIS v. GREECE	Institut de formation en droits de l'homme du barreau de Paris	2004	2
75	MAMATKULOV AND ASKAROV v. TURKEY	International Commission of Jurists	2004	3
76	MAMATKULOV AND ASKAROV v. TURKEY	Human Rights Watch, Aire Centre	2004	RULE 39
77	McCANN AND OTHERS v. THE UK	Amnesty International	1994	2
78	McCANN AND OTHERS v. THE UK	Liberty, Committee on the Administration of Justice, Inquest, and British-Irish Rights Watch	1994	2
79	MOCANU and OTHERS v. ROMANIA	The Redress Trust	2013	3
80	MOUVEMENT RAELIEN SUISSE v. SWITZERLAND	Article 19	2011	10
81	N. v. THE UK	Helsinki Foundation for Human Rights	2007	3+8
82	NACHOVA AND OTHERS v. BULGARIA	Open Society Justice Initiative	2004	2+13+14
83	NACHOVA AND OTHERS v. BULGARIA	Interights	2004	14

6. International or comparative analysis?	7. ICJ	8. HRC	9. CJUE	10. IACtHR	11. Case law of contracting states: which countries	12. Case law of non-contracting states: which countries	13. At least one common reference in the brief and in the case
0	0	0	0	0	0	0	0
1	0	0	0	1	UK	Canada	0
0	0	0	0	0	0	0	0
1	0	0	0	0	Switzerland, Germany	0	1
1	0	0	0	0	0	USA	0
0	0	0	0	0	0	0	0
1	0	1	0	0	UK, Italy, Spain, France, Switzerland, Germany, Macedonia	Canada, Colombia, USA	1
1	0	0	0	0	0	0	0
1	0	1	0	0	UK, Germany	USA, Canada	1
1	1	1	0	1	0	Canada	1
1	0	0	0	0	0	0	0
1	0	1	0	1	0	0	0
1	1	0	0	1	UK, the Netherlands	0	1
1	0	0	0	0	UK, Germany, Belgium	USA, Canada	1
1	0	0	0	0	Poland, Germany, France	0	0
1	1	0	0	0	Germany	0	0
1	0	0	1	1	Switzerland, UK	India, Canada, USA, New Zealand, South Africa, Australia	0

(*continued*)

1. Number	2. Name of the case	3. Name of intervener(s)	4. Year of intervention	5. HR / article concerned
84	NACHOVA AND OTHERS v. BULGARIA	European Roma Rights Centre	2004	14
85	NADA v. SWITZERLAND	Justice	2010	13
86	O'KEEFFE v. IRELAND	European Centre for Law and Justice	2012	3+2P1
87	ORSUS v. CROATIA	Interights	2009	6+14+2P1
88	ORSUS v. CROATIA	Greek Helsinki Monitor	2009	3+2P1+14
89	S. AND MARPER v. THE UK	Privacy International	2006	8
90	S. AND MARPER v. THE UK	Liberty	2006	8+14
91	S.A.S. v. FRANCE	Amnesty International	2013	9+10+14
92	S.A.S. v. FRANCE	Human Rights Centre of Ghent University	2012	8+9+10
93	S.A.S. v. FRANCE	Article 19	2013	9+10+14
94	S.A.S. v. FRANCE	Liberty	2012	8+9+10+14
95	S.A.S. v. FRANCE	Open Society Initiative	2012	8+9+10+14
96	S.H. AND OTHERS v. AUSTRIA	European Centre for Law and Justice	2011	8+14
97	S.H. AND OTHERS v. AUSTRIA	Aktion Leben	2011	8+12+14
98	S.H. AND OTHERS v. AUSTRIA	Hera ONLUS – SOS Infertilita (Italy)	2011	8
99	SAADI v. THE UK	Centre for Advice on Individual Rights in Europe ("AIRE Centre"), the European Council on Refugees and Exiles ("ECRE") and Liberty	2007	5 + 2P4
100	SANOMA v. THE NETHERLANDS	Open Society Initiative, Committee to Protect Journalists, Media Legal Defence Initiative, ARTICLE 19, Guardian News and Media Limited	2009	10
101	SAUNDERS v. THE UK	Liberty	1995	6
102	SENATOR LINES Gmbh v. 15 EU MEMBER STATES	Fédération Internationale des Ligues des droits de l'homme	2003	1
103	SENATOR LINES Gmbh v. 15 EU MEMBER STATES	International Commission of Jurists	2003	34
104	SERGEY ZOLOTUKHIN v. RUSSIA	Human Rights Training Institute of the Paris Bar Association	2008	4P7

6. International or comparative analysis?	7. ICJ	8. HRC	9. CJUE	10. IACtHR	11. Case law of contracting states: which countries	12. Case law of non-contracting states: which countries	13. At least one common reference in the brief and in the case
1	0	1	1	1	the Netherlands	USA	0
1	0	0	1	0	Germany, UK	Canada	1
0	0	0	0	0	0	0	0
1	0	0	0	0	Germany	USA	0
0	0	0	0	0	0	0	0
1	0	0	0	0	0	USA	0
1	0	1	1	0	Germany	Canada	1
1	0	1	0	0	0	0	0
0	0	0	0	0	0	0	0
1	0	1	0	0	Spain, Russia, Belgium	Canada, USA	1
1	0	0	0	0	UK	0	0
1	0	0	0	0	France, Italy, the Netherlands	0	1
0	0	0	0	0	0	0	0
0	0	0	0	0	0	0	0
1	0	0	0	0	Italy	0	0
1	0	1	0	0	Malta (TBDF), Serbia (TBDF), Montenegro (TBDF), Greece (TBDF)	0	1
1	0	0	0	0	UK, Ireland, Portugal, Belgium, Germany, Lithuania,	Canada, New Zealand	0
1	0	0	0	0	Italy, Spain	South Africa	1
1	0	0	0	0	0	0	0
1	0	0	1	0	0	0	0
1	0	1	1	0	Germany, Belgium, France, Italy	0	1

(*continued*)

1. Number	2. Name of the case	3. Name of intervener(s)	4. Year of intervention	5. HR / article concerned
105	SHEFFIELD AND HORSHAM v. THE UK	Liberty	1997	8+12+14
106	SINDICATUL 'PASTORUL CEL BUN' v. ROMANIA	The Becket Fund for Religious Liberty and the International Center for Law and Religion Studies	2012	9+11
107	SINDICATUL 'PASTORUL CEL BUN' v. ROMANIA	European Centre for Law and Justice	2010	11
108	SITAROPOULOS AND GIAKOUMOPOULOS v. GREECE	Hellenic League for Human Rights	2011	3P1
109	SODERMAN v. SWEDEN	Human Rights Centre of Ghent University	2013	8
110	STAFFORD v. THE UK	Justice	2001	5
111	STANEV v. BULGARIA	Interights	2010	5+8
112	TAHSIN ACAR v. TURKEY	Amnesty International	2002	37
113	TARAKHEL v. SWITZERLAND	The AIRE Centre, Amnesty International and ECRE	2014	3
114	TARAKHEL v. SWITZERLAND	Defence for Children the Netherlands	2013	3+8
115	V. v. THE UK and T. v. THE UK	Justice	1999	3+5+6
116	VALLIANATOS & MYLONAS v. GREECE, C.S. & OTHERS v. GREECE	FIDH, ICJ, AIRE CENTRE & ILGA-EUROPE	2011	8+14
117	VARNAVA AND OTHERS v. TURKEY	Redress Trust	2008	41
118	VO v. FRANCE	Center for Reproductive Rights	2003	2
119	VON HANNOVER v. GERMANY & AXEL SPRINGER AG v. GERMANY	Media Legal Defence Initiative, the International Press Institute, the World Association of Newspapers and News Publishers	2010	8+10
120	WILLIAM GOODWIN v. THE UK	Article 19 and Interights	1995	10
121	X. v. LATVIA	Reunite International	2013	8

6. International or comparative analysis?	7. ICJ	8. HRC	9. CJUE	10. IACtHR	11. Case law of contracting states: which countries	12. Case law of non-contracting states: which countries	13. At least one common reference in the brief and in the case
1	0	0	1	0	Switzerland	0	1
1	0	0	0	0	0	USA	0
0	0	0	0	0	0	0	0
1	0	0	0	0	0	0	0
0	0	0	0	0	0	0	0
1	0	0	0	0	0	0	0
1	0	0	0	0	0	USA	0
1	0	1	0	1	0	0	0
1	0	0	1	0	0	0	1
1	0	0	1	0	0	0	1
1	0	0	0	0	0	Canada	0
1	0	1	0	0	Hungary	USA, Canada, Brazil, Colombia	0
1	1	1	0	1	0	0	1
1	0	0	0	0	Germany, France, Austria, the Netherlands	Canada, USA, South Africa	1
1	0	0	0	0	Greece, Italy, Netherlands, France, Poland, Sweden	New Zealand	0
1	0	0	0	0	Germany, Netherlands, Norway, Sweden	India, Zimbabwe, Japan, Nigeria, Mauritius, Papua New Guinea	0
1	0	0	0	0	0	0	0

(*continued*)

1. Number	2. Name of the case	3. Name of intervener(s)	4. Year of intervention	5. HR / article concerned
122	X. AND OTHERS v. AUSTRIA	Fédération Internationale des ligues des Droits de l'Homme, International Commission of Jurists (ICJ), International Lesbian, Gay, Bisexual, Trans and Intersex Association Europe (ILGA-Europe), British Association for Adoption and Fostering (BAAF), Network of European LGBT Families Associations (NELFA), and European Commission on Sexual Orientation Law (ECSOL)	2012	8+14
123	X. AND OTHERS v. AUSTRIA	European Centre for Law and Justice	2012	8+14
124	X. AND OTHERS v. AUSTRIA	Amnesty International	2012	8+14
125	X. AND OTHERS v. AUSTRIA	Alliance Defending Freedom, Fédération Pro Europa Christiana, Oesterreichische Gesellschaft zum Schutz von Tradition, Familie und Privateigentum, Freunde kinderreicher Familien in Oesterreich	2012	8+14
126	X., Y. AND Z. v. THE UK	Rights International	1996	8+14
127	YUMAK AND SADAK v. TURKEY	Minority Rights Group International (MRG)	2007	3 P1

6. International or comparative analysis?	7. ICJ	8. HRC	9. CJUE	10. IACtHR	11. Case law of contracting states: which countries	12. Case law of non-contracting states: which countries	13. At least one common reference in the brief and in the case
1	0	0	0	1	UK, Belgium, Germany	USA, South Africa, Brazil	0
0	0	0	0	0	0	0	0
1	0	1	0	1	0	0	0
0	0	0	0	0	0	0	0
1	0	0	1	0	Belgium, Spain, France, Poland, Portugal, Switzerland, Greece, Finland, Romania, UK	USA (TBDF)	0
1	0	0	0	1	0	0	0

Reports on Practice: ECtHR Judges

13

Dialogues between the Strasbourg Court and National Courts

LUIS LÓPEZ GUERRA

13.1 Types of Dialogue between Courts

Since article 35(1) of the European Convention on Human Rights (ECHR or the Convention)[1] provides that the European Court of Human Rights (ECtHR or the Court or the Strasbourg Court) will only accept applications after all domestic remedies have been exhausted, the Court's task consists almost exclusively of addressing complaints about judicial decisions or judgments allegedly causing or confirming violations of Convention rights. In many cases, those judgments were rendered by the highest courts of Convention member states.

In deciding the cases brought before it, the Court has established patterns for interpreting the Convention. Article 32(1) ECHR provides that the jurisdiction of the Court extends to all matters concerning the interpretation and application of the Convention, and the Court's judgments are binding on the parties to the case.[2] Therefore, these patterns become *res interpretata*, that is, guidelines that national courts must use in applying Convention provisions, and/or the interpretation of domestic law in light of the ECHR.[3]

Nevertheless, the binding *res interpretata* effect of the Court's interpretations does not mean that national courts must apply Strasbourg case law mechanically. The ECHR provides a common standard of human rights, but individual states may certainly supplement this standard with higher levels of human rights protection.[4] Furthermore, in a more general sense,

[1] Convention for the Protection of Human Rights and Fundamental Freedoms, 213 UNTS 222, entered into force 3 September 1953.

[2] Article 46(1) ECHR.

[3] A. Bodnar, '*Res Interpretata*: Legal Effect of the European Court of Human Right's Judgments for Other States Than Those Which Were Party to the Proceedings', Y. Heack and E. Brems (eds.), *Human Rights and Civil Liberties in the 21st Century* (Dordrecht: Springer, 2014) 223–62.

[4] Article 53 ECHR reads: 'Nothing in this Convention shall be construed as limiting or derogating from any of the human rights and fundamental freedoms which may be

the Court has defined the Convention as a 'living instrument',[5] whose application must protect human rights against the background of changing and evolving challenges. National courts, using their margin of appreciation, are usually the first to be faced with new problems that may require introducing nuances or even reappraising Strasbourg Court case law.

In that regard, four different situations may arise concerning the Court's interaction with domestic courts. First, and most frequently, national courts apply Strasbourg Court case law without reservation, and the Court then confirms their decisions (confirmative dialogue). Second, while accepting the binding force of Strasbourg case law, national courts may sometimes apply it incorrectly. In such cases the Strasbourg Court may correct those erroneous interpretations (corrective dialogue). Third, national court judgments may depart from Strasbourg's decisions, suggesting that its case law should be modified or even reconsidered (dialogue with discrepancy). Finally, there are occasions where national courts accept and apply ECtHR jurisprudence while nonetheless pointing to its alleged discrepancies. In these cases, the Strasbourg Court may not yet have had the opportunity to react to the domestic courts' criticism (proposed dialogue).

In these four situations, dialogues between national courts and the Strasbourg Court are played out in a series of interactions that generally follow a certain chronological order: (a) the Court establishes a pattern of interpretation in its decision concerning a national court's judgment; (b) in a subsequent case the national court takes the Strasbourg Court's interpretation into account when rendering its judgment; and (c) the Strasbourg Court reacts to the national court's application of its case law.

13.2 Confirmative Dialogue: *Coban v. Spain* and *Von Hannover v. Germany (No. 2)*

In the most frequent and simple type of dialogue between courts, the Strasbourg Court confirms that a national court has applied its case law correctly, and thus declares the application inadmissible by means of a short letter to the applicant. In such cases it may appear that there is no express dialogue – at best, it may be deemed an implied dialogue.

ensured under the laws of any High Contracting Party or under any other agreement to which it is a Party'.

[5] For instance, *Tyrer v. the United Kingdom* (Appl. No. 5856/72), Judgment (Chamber), 25 April 1978, Series A, Vol. 26, para. 31.

But genuine dialogue may arise in this type of confirmative situation if the Strasbourg Court expressly assesses the national court's judgment in a Committee or Chamber decision or judgment. Such pronouncements are important to confirm national courts' correct application of the Convention for future cases, as well as to encourage domestic courts' active engagement with the ECHR and the ECtHR jurisprudence.

A good example can be found in the Court's 2006 decision in *Coban v. Spain*.[6] In a previous 1998 judgment in *Valenzuela Contreras v. Spain*,[7] the Court ruled that Spain had violated article 8 of the Convention concerning the right to private and family life, since Spanish legislation on the interception of telephone calls (article 579 of the 1988 Criminal Procedure Act) was clearly insufficient to guarantee this Convention right in cases involving wiretapping. Thus, the violation of article 8 ECHR derived from a lack of quality and precision in Spanish law.

Later, in its decision in *Coban*, the Court accepted the Spanish courts' subsequent application of Strasbourg case law on this matter. While the language of the aforementioned article 579 was found insufficient in terms of Convention requirements, the Court underscored that in their application of Strasbourg case law on article 8 ECHR, the Spanish courts had actually added extra conditions for obtaining judicial authorisation to intercept communications under the Criminal Procedure Act, thus effectively filling the gaps in Spanish law. For that reason, in *Coban v. Spain*, the ECtHR did not accept the applicant's complaint that Spanish law provided inadequate protection. It held that deficiencies in the written law had been remedied by the Spanish courts' uniform application of Strasbourg case law. Indeed, *Coban* confirmed that Strasbourg case law had been correctly applied, citing several judgments in that regard of the Spanish Constitutional Court and Supreme Court.[8]

The 2012 case of *Von Hannover v. Germany (No. 2)*[9] provides another interesting example of dialogue between courts in which Strasbourg confirmed the correctness of national courts' application of its case law. In its previous 2004 judgment in *Von Hannover v. Germany (No. 1)*, the Court considered that, despite the fact that the right to privacy of relevant public figures may

[6] *Coban v. Spain* (Appl. No.17060/02), Decision (Chamber), 25 September 2006, not reported.

[7] *Valenzuela Contreras v. Spain* (Appl. No. 27671/95), Judgment (Chamber), 30 July 1998, ECHR 1998-V, 1924.

[8] *Coban v. Spain*, *supra* note 6, paras. 3 and 4.

[9] *Von Hannover v. Germany (No. 2)* (Appl. Nos. 40660/08 and 60641/08), Judgment (Grand Chamber), 7 July 2012, ECHR 2012-I, 351.

be restricted, the German courts had violated article 8 ECHR by allowing the publication of photos of famous persons.[10]

In *Von Hannover v. Germany (No. 2)* the Court then examined how the German courts had applied the case law established in *Von Hannover (No. 1)*.[11] Instead of the previous, rather inflexible 'relevant public figures' approach, a system of gradual protection for public figures had been developed by the German courts, taking into account the circumstances of each case when determining the level of protection to be afforded to a famous individual's personal privacy.[12] This was the position adopted by the German Federal Court of Justice (citing the *Von Hannover (No. 1)* judgment),[13] and confirmed by the German Constitutional Court.[14] The Constitutional Court declared that there were different legitimate ways of interpreting German constitutional provisions governing privacy. If German courts had previously (in 1999) accepted the constitutionality of the 'relevant figure' principle, they might also, within the Constitution, adopt the principle of 'gradual protection'.[15] In *Von Hannover (No. 2)*, the ECtHR confirmed that this approach met the requisites of article 8 ECHR, likewise agreeing that publication of photos of public figures may be justified by the accompanying text.[16]

13.3 Corrective Dialogue: *Al Skeini v. the United Kingdom*

Another type of dialogue entails the Court's criticism of a national court's application of Strasbourg case law. A prime example is the dialogue maintained with the UK courts concerning the extension of the ECtHR's jurisdiction. The 2011 judgment in *Al Skeini and Others v. the United Kingdom* addressed claims brought by Iraqi citizens against UK authorities for the deaths of their family members by British troops occupying Iraq.[17] The UK courts dismissed those claims based on their interpretation of

10 *Von Hannover v. Germany (No. 1)* (Appl. No. 59320/00), Judgment (Chamber), 24 June 2004, ECHR 2004-VI, 1.

11 *Von Hannover v. Germany (No. 2)*, *supra* note 9, paras. 27–53 and 114–26.

12 In this case, the German courts also considered that the publication of photographs affecting one's privacy could be justified when accompanied by text reporting on current events closely related to those photos.

13 Federal Court of Justice (BGH, Germany), Judgment of 6 March 2006, VI ZR 51/06.

14 Federal Constitutional Court (BVerfG, Germany), Judgment of 26 February 2008, 1 BvR 1602/07, 1 BvR 1606/07 and 1 BvR 1626/07.

15 *Ibid.*

16 *Von Hannover v. Germany (No. 2)*, *supra* note 9, paras. 117–18 and 126.

17 *Al-Skeini and Other v. the United Kingdom* (Appl. No. 55721/07), Judgment (Grand Chamber), 7 July 2011, ECHR 2011-IV, 99.

the Strasbourg case law in *Bankovic and Others v. Belgium and Others*[18] concerning a NATO warplane bombing of a Serbian television building in Belgrade. The British courts considered that, pursuant to the ECtHR's *Bankovic* decision, member states to the ECHR are only obliged to ensure observance of the Convention principles within the area under their jurisdiction, understood as the area subject to their 'effective control'.[19] Occupied Iraq was not deemed to fall within this definition, since it was not subject to the 'effective control' of the British authorities. Furthermore, the British courts maintained that jurisdiction cannot be 'parcelled' or divided according to subject matter.[20]

In *Al Skeini*, the Strasbourg Court disagreed with the UK courts' application of its *Bankovic* decision. According to the Court, 'effective control' by any state authority (in this case by the United Kingdom) over a given territory (in this case Iraq) can be assessed with respect to any of the different areas of the state's activities. In the case at hand, the United Kingdom had assumed caretaker responsibility in a part of Iraq in one of those areas of activity (public security), and therefore, the Court deemed the state had jurisdiction over such matters. As a consequence, the United Kingdom was obliged to conform to Convention mandates in all aspects concerning public security. Thus, the UK courts' argument that jurisdiction cannot be 'parcelled' was not accepted, and their application of the *Bankovic* case law was considered erroneous by the Strasbourg Court.[21]

13.4 Dialogue and Discrepancy

A different type of dialogue appears when national courts make express reference to Strasbourg Court case law but state that they do not or will not

[18] *Bankovic and Others v. Belgium and Others* (Appl. No. 52207/99), Judgment (Grand Chamber), 12 December 2001, ECHR 2001-XII, 333.

[19] Divisional Court, *R(Al-Skeini and others) v. Secretary of State for Defence* [2004] EWHC 2911 (Admin); Court of Appeals, *Al-Skeini & Ors, R (on the application of) v. Secretary of State for Defence* [2005] EWCA Civ 1609; and House of Lords, *Secretary of State for Defence v. Al-Skeini & Ors* [2007] UKHL 26.

[20] House of Lords, *Secretary of State for Defence v. Al-Skeini & Ors* [2007] UKHL 26, paras. 127–29.

[21] *Al-Skeini and Other v. the United Kingdom* (GC), *supra* note 17, para. 137. It can, of course, also be argued that in *Al Skeini*, the ECtHR itself deviated from the approach it had taken in *Bankovic*. See e.g. A. Nußberger, 'The Concept of Jurisdiction in the Jurisprudence of the European Court of Human Rights', *Current Legal Problems* 65:241 (2012), especially at 262 *et seq*.

apply it to a specific case. There may be different motives for this departure. It may be that ECtHR case law is not wholly adequate for solving the specific conflict brought before the national court and therefore requires review or adaptation. Or the national court may consider the Strasbourg Court's case law on a given matter incorrect, and may want to signal that it should be reversed. In a third possibility the national court may severely criticise the Court's case law, while nevertheless applying it by imposition, because of its binding effect.

In some cases the national courts' resistance to applying Strasbourg Court case law has prompted the Court to modify its position, and sometimes significantly so. This is obviously not frequent, but neither is it exceptional, and in such cases there is a genuine dialogue between courts.

13.4.1 *'Slight' Rectification of the Court's Case Law:* Scoppola v. Italy (No. 3)

The 2012 judgment in *Scoppola v. Italy (No. 3)*[22] provides an example of how a national court's criticism may prompt a slight change in the Court's case law. Previously, commencing with *Hirst v. United Kingdom (No. 2)*,[23] the Court had stated that a generalised policy denying prisoners voting rights violated article 3 of Protocol I (P-I) to the ECHR that recognises the right to free elections. This judgment has been the subject of much criticism in the United Kingdom.

The *Scoppola* case concerned the Italian practice of disenfranchisement following criminal conviction. The Italian *Corte di Cassazione* expressly took into account the *Hirst* case law, but considered that it was not applicable.[24] It reasoned that since disenfranchisement only affected prisoners whose sentence exceeded three years, there was no general policy in Italy denying prisoners the right to vote.

Not surprisingly, the United Kingdom participated as a third party in the *Scoppola* proceedings. In an initial Chamber judgment, the Court found a violation of article 3 P-I, following its precedent in *Hirst*.[25] However,

[22] *Scoppola v. Italy (No. 3)* (Appl. No. 126/05), Judgment (Grand Chamber), 22 May 2012, not reported.

[23] *Hirst v. the United Kingdom (No. 2)* (Appl. No. 74025/01), Judgment (Chamber), 30 March 2004; confirmed by the Grand Chamber in *Hirst v. United Kingdom (No. 2)* (Appl. No. 74025/01), Judgment (Grand Chamber), 6 October 2005, ECHR 2005-IX, 187.

[24] Court of Cassation (*Corte di Cassazione*, Italy), Judgment of 17 January 2006, No.788/2006.

[25] *Scoppola v. Italy (No. 3)* (Appl. No. 126/05), Judgment (Chamber), 18 January 2011, not reported.

when the case was referred to the Grand Chamber, this position was subsequently revised. According to the Grand Chamber, to be compatible with article 3 P-I, disenfranchisement of prisoners does not necessarily have to be imposed by an individualised judicial decision after considering the accused's specific circumstances. It suffices that the denial of the right to vote is not automatically imposed on all persons serving custodial sentences. Thus, establishing (non-individualised) legal distinctions, for instance based on the severity of the sentence, does not violate a prisoner's voting rights. In the Italian case, the Grand Chamber took into account that the denial of voting rights was not imposed on all prisoners, but rather based on the length of their sentences.[26] Furthermore, the Grand Chamber recognised that in Italy, prisoners may be rehabilitated and have their voting rights reinstated.[27]

13.4.2 'Significant' Rectification: Al Khawaja and Tahery v. the United Kingdom

In its 2011 Grand Chamber judgment in *Al-Khawaja and Tahery v. the United Kingdom*,[28] the Strasbourg Court changed its previous position, taking into account the reasoning of the UK national courts in similar cases with respect to the Court's earlier case law on the matter. In this case, in the initial 2009 Chamber judgment,[29] the Court ruled that the United Kingdom had violated article 6 ECHR, protecting the right to a fair trial, by imposing a sentence based on hearsay evidence not confirmed by witnesses examined at trial by the accused. The United Kingdom asked that the case be referred to the Grand Chamber, and a five-judge panel granted that request.

While the case was pending before the Grand Chamber, the UK courts had several opportunities in similar cases to comment on the Chamber judgment.[30] For example, in the 2009 case of *The Crown v. Horncastle and*

[26] *Scoppola v. Italy (No.3)* (GC), *supra* note 22, paras. 102 and 104.

[27] Judge David Thór Björgvinsson wrote a dissenting opinion, rejecting the Grand Chamber's radical reversal of the *Hirst* precedent. See *ibid.*, dissenting opinion of Judge David Thór Björgvinsson.

[28] *Al-Khawaja and Tahery v. the United Kingdom* (Appl. Nos. 26766/05 and 22228/06), Judgment (Grand Chamber), 15 December 2011, ECHR 2011-VI, 191.

[29] *Al-Khawaja and Tahery v. the United Kingdom* (Appl. Nos. 26766/05 and 22228/06), Judgment (Chamber), 20 January 2009, not reported.

[30] The ECtHR's Grand Chamber judgment (*Khawaja and Tahery v. the United Kingdom*, *supra* note 28) lists the following relevant UK cases: Court of Appeal, *R. v. Sellick and Sellick* [2005] EWCA Crim 651; House of Lords, *R. v. Davis* [2008] UKHL 36; Court of

Others, the UK Supreme Court upheld a sentence based on the witnesses' written declarations, which were read aloud at trial without the accused having the possibility of cross-examining those witnesses.[31] Departing from Strasbourg case law, the UK Supreme Court ruled that in certain cases a sentence can legitimately be based exclusively on circumstantial or hearsay evidence. In those specific cases, the Supreme Court deemed it justified to depart from the Strasbourg Court case law set out in the *Al-Khawaja* Chamber judgment.[32]

When the Grand Chamber ruled on *Al-Khawaja and Tahery*, it took into account the UK Supreme Court's departure and revoked the inflexible rule set out in the Chamber judgment. The Court considered that a sentence based solely on circumstantial evidence could be admissible under the Convention if countervailing circumstances were present that would compensate the fact that the defence was not able to examine the witnesses for the prosecution.[33] In his concurring opinion, the (then) Judge with respect to the United Kingdom, Sir Nicholas Bratza, acknowledged the important role that the UK Supreme Court's opinion had played when the Grand Chamber reconsidered the initial Chamber judgment.[34]

13.5 Proposed Dialogue: Criticism by National Courts

A separate type of dialogue between courts arises when national courts accept and apply the Strasbourg Court's case law while criticising its content and pointing out its alleged deficiencies. This has been the case on at least one occasion with respect to the Spanish national courts. Their criticism has been directed toward Strasbourg case law addressing criminal cases in which, after the accused was acquitted at trial, the appeals court revoked the acquittal and sentenced the accused without a hearing.

The origin of this peculiar dialogue can be found in the Strasbourg case law on article 6(1) ECHR with respect to due process, requiring that all

Appeal, *R. v. Horncastle and Others* [2009] EWCA Crim 964; and UK Supreme Court, *R v. Horncastle and Others* [2009] UKSC 14.

31 UK Supreme Court, *R v. Horncastle and Others* [2009] UKSC 14.

32 *Ibid.*, paras. 91 and 113–15.

33 *Al-Khawaja and Tahery v. the United Kingdom* (GC), *supra* note 28, para. 147. The Court took account of the UK Supreme Court's detailed arguments highlighting the practical difficulties with applying the Chamber's general rule in the domestic setting. See also the discussion by Lord Kerr, 'The Need for Dialogue between National Courts and the European Court of Human Rights, S. Flogaitis, T. Zwart and J. Fraser (eds.), *The European Court of Human Rights and Its Discontents – Turning Criticism into Strength* (Cheltenham: Edward Elgar, 2013) 104–15, at 106–08.

34 *Ibid.*, concurring opinion by Judge Bratza.

judicial decisions in criminal cases must be based on evidence examined during a public hearing. A court must decide on the facts only after evidence has been examined, with the required intervention of the accused.[35] In that regard, the Court has repeatedly stated in cases concerning Spain that when a person is acquitted at trial, the appeals court cannot decide on questions of fact and cannot reverse the acquittal without a public hearing in which the accused has the opportunity to be heard.[36] However, when the appeals court decides only on questions of law, it is not necessary to hear the accused.[37]

This confirmation of the principle of public examination of evidence at all levels has been progressively accepted in the Spanish Constitutional and Supreme Court's case law. But the Spanish Supreme Court has applied this principle while at the same time expressing much criticism of Strasbourg's position in that regard. The Spanish Supreme Court maintains that requiring examination of evidence at the appeals stage undermines the significance of first-instance criminal trials and, in effect, requires proceedings to be repeated at two levels.[38] This dialogue is certainly incomplete, or perhaps it should merely be considered an attempt at dialogue on the part of the Spanish courts. To date, the Strasbourg Court has not addressed this criticism.

[35] This is established jurisprudence since the judgment *Ekbatani v. Sweden* (Appl.No.10563/83), Judgment (Plenary), 26 May 1988, Series A, Vol. 134.

[36] For example, see *Igual Coll v. Spain* (Appl. No. 37496/04), Judgment (Chamber), 10 March 2009, not reported.

[37] For example, see *Bazo González v. Spain* (Appl. No.30643/04), Judgment (Chamber), 16 December 2008, not reported.

[38] See, for instance, the criticism in the Spanish Supreme Court, Judgment of 19 July 2012, STS 670/2012 (Rapporteur: Alberto Jorge Barreiro). But the Supreme Court has followed the case law of the ECtHR consistently on the matter. See Judgments of 25 January 2012, STS 406/2012; of 11 October 2012, STS 757/2012; and of 29 May 2013, STS 474/2013, among many others. For a discussion of this problem, see also M. D. Martinez, 'Guarantees of Due Process in Criminal Appeal Procedure', *Revista de Derecho Politico* 87:27 (2013), available at http://e-spacio.uned.es/fez/eserv.php?pid=bibliuned:DerechoPolitico-2013-87-6005&dsID=Documento.pdf.

14

The ECtHR's Use of Decisions of Domestic Courts from States Not Involved in the Case and of Other Council of Europe Bodies

ERIK MØSE

14.1 Introduction

I have been asked to address the topic of the European Court of Human Rights (ECtHR or the Court) and its use of decisions of domestic courts other than in the country directly concerned, as well as decisions of other Council of Europe (CoE) bodies. We have been provided with a useful questionnaire, and its systematic approach is generally followed in this chapter.[1]

The formulation of the title calls for a few comments. First, the word 'decisions' of domestic courts of course includes judgments. Second, the ECtHR's 'use' of domestic court decisions covers both references in the comparative law section of the Court's judgments and the reasons in the law part. Third, the formulation 'states not involved in the case' excludes judgments and other national decisions rendered as part of the exhaustion of domestic remedies – an admissibility criterion under the Convention. What matters in our context are, therefore, judgments by courts in other CoE member states and in countries outside that organisation. Finally, the expression 'other Council of Europe bodies' covers institutions established directly by that organisation's Statute of 1949 (such as the Committee of Ministers) and treaty-based bodies (for instance, the European Committee for the Prevention of Torture). In what follows, the decisions mentioned in the title will also be briefly referred to as 'comparative material'.

14.2 How Does the Court Find Out about Relevant Comparative Material?

There is a wealth of institutional knowledge about comparative material within the Court, based on its fifty-five years of existence. Some of

[1] See Annex 2 to this volume.

this material has been referred to in previous case law and is therefore relatively easy to access, for instance through the Court's case law search engine (hudoc[2]). Furthermore, the Court's judges and staff from the CoE's forty-seven member states have a lot of experience from a variety of legal fields.

In cases under consideration, the parties' submissions focus on the Court's own case law (or of the former European Commission of Human Rights), but it is not unusual that they contain references to comparative material. Furthermore, when third parties have been granted leave to appear before the Court, their observations often include such material. In particular, written submissions of human rights NGOs frequently invoke decisions of other international human rights bodies – but this discussion falls outside the scope of this chapter.[3]

However, the Court is constantly faced with new issues which require an in-depth analysis. It cannot rely solely on institutional knowledge or submissions from the involved parties and third parties. In 2004, the Court established a Research Division. It is attached to the Office of the Jurisconsult and includes lawyers and other staff. A list of its research reports from 2004 to October 2015 amounts to ninety-one pages, covering a variety of issues, including convention case law, comparative law and international law. The division plays a very important role, and the quality of its work is impressive.

The main task of the Research Division is to assist the Grand Chamber, but it also provides reports in complex Chamber cases. The comparative law reports give the judges a basis for their assessment as to whether there is an evolving trend or consensus within the Council of Europe member states. A very brief summary of such material is often included in the comparative law section of the judgments.

For administrative and budgetary reasons, it is not possible to include all forty-seven CoE member states in the comparative research conducted in each case. Normally, the survey is limited to around thirty to thirty-five countries. However, when selecting them the Court seeks to achieve a representative sample which reflects the different legal traditions in the member states of the organisation. Furthermore, the judges and the staff working on the specific case often have information about the situation in CoE states that is not included in the survey.

[2] See: www.hudoc.echr.coe.int.

[3] The ECtHR's use of decisions from other international courts and quasi-judicial bodies is discussed by Judge Nußerger in Chapter 15 of this volume. As regards the specific significance of NGO contributions, see Chapter 12 by Laura Van den Eynde in this volume.

14.3 Domestic Court Decisions in CoE Member States That Are Not Parties to the Case

When the Court needs to know the legal situation in CoE member states that are not parties to the case, its judgment will usually not refer specifically to domestic decisions from those countries – neither in the comparative law section nor in the reasoning. What matters to the Court is the general legal situation in a state, not whether that situation is the result of statutory acts, administrative regulations or domestic judgments. This is in line with the principle that states are free to select how they implement the requirements of the Convention at the domestic level. Consequently, when the parties or the third parties have referred to judgments in other European states, it is quite possible that such decisions will not be visible in the Court's judgment or only be mentioned very briefly.

However, it does happen that the Court refers to judgments in other CoE member states. Two recent examples may be illustrative. In *Vinter and Others v. the United Kingdom*,[4] in which the Grand Chamber did not accept a life sentence without any possibility of review, reference was made to decisions by the German and Italian Federal Constitutional Courts. And in *S.A.S. v. France*,[5] the Grand Chamber mentioned (conflicting) decisions by the highest courts in Belgium, Spain and The Netherlands before reaching the conclusion that the general prohibition against wearing the burka in public was not a violation of the European Convention on Human Rights (ECHR or Convention).[6] In *S.A.S. v. France*, the domestic decisions were mentioned in the comparative law section, not in the reasoning. Furthermore, it does not follow from the judgments that the decisions had any impact on the Court's reasoning or result.[7] This is the normal situation. But, for instance, in *Vinter v. the United Kingdom*, the Court explicitly referred to the two constitutional courts also in its reasoning, the aim being to illustrate the commitment in some states to both the rehabilitation and prospect of eventual release of prisoners with a life sentence.[8]

[4] *Vinter and Others v. the United Kingdom* (Appl. Nos. 66069/09; 130/10 and 3896/10), Judgment (Grand Chamber), 9 July 2013, ECHR 2013-III, 317 (extracts).

[5] *S.A.S. v. France* (Appl. No. 43835/11), Judgment (Grand Chamber), 1 July 2014, selected for publication 2014.

[6] Convention for the Protection of Human Rights and Fundamental Freedoms (European Convention on Human Rights, ECHR) (4 November 1950) 213 UNTS 222; 312 ETS 5, entered into force 3 September 1953.

[7] SAS v. France, *supra* note 5, paras. 41–52.

[8] *Vinter and Others v. the United Kingdom, supra* note 4, paras. 69–72 and 117.

It may be asked whether the Court accords similar weight to the decisions of domestic courts from all CoE member states when evaluating whether there is a European trend or consensus. The practical importance of this question should not be exaggerated. As mentioned earlier, it is – from a Convention perspective – the general legal situation in a country that matters, not whether it is based on legislation or case law. Having said that, it should be emphasised that the CoE is based on the principle of equality of states, and the Court does not take into account the size or geographical location of a certain country. In my view, it is the substance and persuasive force of a domestic decision which determines its impact, not the jurisdiction within which it has been rendered. The impact of a judgment from a European state will depend on a concrete evaluation.

14.4 Domestic Court Decisions Outside the CoE

The situation is different with respect to the ECtHR's references to decisions of domestic courts in states that are not members of the CoE. They are mentioned more frequently than domestic decisions of CoE member states' courts that are not direct parties to the case, and this is not a new trend.[9] Already the former Commission used such comparative material. In *X v. the United Kingdom* (1980),[10] a case concerning the question of abortion, the Commission referred to the US Supreme Court's ruling in *Roe v. Wade*[11] in its reasoning. The ECtHR has continued this practice.

Some judgments mention extra-European judicial decisions in the comparative law section, but they do not rely on them in the reasoning. Some examples can be given here:

- *Morris v. the United Kingdom* (2002),[12] which involved questions about court martials and their compatibility with article 6(1) of the Convention. Reference was made to judgments of the Canadian Supreme Court.
- *Appleby and Others v. the United Kingdom* (2003)[13] concerned the distribution of leaflets in a private shopping mall. Case law from the United

[9] See, for instance, C. Rozakis, 'The Interaction between the European Court of Human Rights and the Other Courts', World Conference on Constitutional Justice, Cape Town, 22–24 January 2009.

[10] *X. v. the United Kingdom* (Appl. No. 8416/78), Decision (Commission), 13 May 1980, D.R. 19, 250, para. 14.

[11] US Supreme Court, *Roe v. Wade*, 22 January 1973, 410 US 113.

[12] *Morris v. the United Kingdom* (Appl. No. 38784/97), Judgment (Chamber), 26 February 2002, ECHR 2002-I, 387, paras. 33–35.

[13] *Appleby and Others v. the United Kingdom* (Appl. No. 44306/98), Judgment (Chamber), 6 May 2003, ECHR 2003-VI, 185, paras. 26–30 and 46.

States and Canada was mentioned in the comparative law part but not considered decisive in the reasoning.

- *Gäfgen v. Germany* (2010)[14] concerned the question of evidence obtained in breach of article 3 of the Convention. Decisions of the US and South African Supreme Courts were cited in the ECtHR's judgment.
- *Al-Khawaja and Tahery v. the United Kingdom* (2011)[15] was about the possible violations of articles 6(1) and (3)(d) ECHR in cases in which domestic courts accorded substantial weight in their findings to previous witness statements that were read out in court but not repeated by the witness in person in court (due to the witness's death), and where the defendant and his lawyers therefore did not have the chance to cross-examine the witness in court. Decisions from Scotland, Ireland, Australia, Canada, Hong Kong, New Zealand, South Africa and the United States were referred to in the ECtHR's judgment.
- *Vinter v. the United Kingdom* (2012)[16] concerned the question of the compatibility of life imprisonment with release only possible in the event of terminal illness or serious incapacitation with article 3 of the Convention. Reference to the highest courts of Germany, Canada, South Africa, the United States as well as Mauritius, Namibia, Hong Kong and New Zealand can be found in the ECtHR's judgment.
- *Sabanchiyeva v. Russia* (2013)[17] involved the finding of a violation of article 8 of the Convention on the basis of a statutory ban on returning bodies of terrorists to their families for burial. The Court mentioned a judgment of the Israeli High Court.

There are fewer judgments where the Court, in its reasoning, explicitly accords weight to judicial decisions from states outside the CoE. Illustrations are:

- *James and Others v. the United Kingdom* (1986),[18] a judgment that concerned article 1 of Protocol I to the ECHR and the leasing of property. The judgment made reference to a decision by the US Supreme Court.

[14] *Gäfgen v. Germany* (Appl. No. 22978/05), Judgment (Grand Chamber), 1 June 2010, ECHR 210-IV, 247, paras. 73–74.

[15] *Al-Khawaja and Tahery v. the United Kingdom* (Appl. Nos. 26766/05 and 22228/06), Judgment (Grand Chamber), 15 December 2011, ECHR 2011-VI, 191, paras. 63–87.

[16] Vinter and Others v. UK, *supra* note 4, paras. 56–73.

[17] *Sabanchiyeva and Others v. Russia* (Appl. No. 38450/05), Judgment (Chamber), 6 June 2013, ECHR 2013-III, 1 (extracts), para. 92.

[18] *James and Others v. the United Kingdom* (Appl. No. 8793/79), Judgment (Plenary), 21 February 1986, Series A, Vol. 98, para. 40.

- *Christine Goodwin v. the United Kingdom* (2002)[19] concerned the rights of transsexuals under articles 8 and 12 of the Convention. In its reasoning, the Court relied on case law from Australian and New Zealand courts.
- *Pretty v. the United Kingdom* (2002)[20] is about a possible right to assisted suicide under articles 2, 3 and 8 ECHR. In its judgment, the ECtHR highlighted comparable reasons in a decision by the Canadian Supreme Court.
- *Allan v. the United Kingdom* (2002),[21] concerning the accused's right to keep silent, sought guidance in a decision by the Canadian Supreme Court.
- *Hirst v. the United Kingdom (No. 2)* (2005),[22] about prisoners' voting rights under article 3 of Protocol I to the Convention, engaged with a ruling by the Canadian Supreme Court.

It follows from this non-exhaustive overview that references to judicial decisions from non-CoE countries cover many areas and hence a variety of Convention rights. It is not unusual for the Court to include such rulings in the comparative law part of the judgment, but it rarely uses them explicitly in its reasoning. The weight placed on these domestic decisions depends on the particular case. They may be used as an argument in favour of or against finding a violation. My own experience is that such decisions may carry some weight for individual judges as well when they are mentioned only in the comparative law part and not in the part of the ECtHR's judgment where reasons are given for the decision.

It is noteworthy that the Court mainly refers to the decisions of the Supreme Courts of the United States, Canada and South Africa, as well as courts in Australia and New Zealand. The reason may be that decisions from these institutions are easily accessible and that the language does not present a problem. Another explanation could be that courts from the common law area may be of particular interest in British cases (of which there are many examples amongst the cases previously mentioned).

It may be asked in general why the ECtHR should refer to decisions of domestic courts in states that are not members of the Council of Europe. In

[19] *Pretty v. the United Kingdom* (Appl. No. 2346/02), Judgment (Chamber), 29 April 2002, ECHR 2002-III, 155, para. 66.

[20] *Christine Goodwin v. the United Kingdom* (Appl. No. 28957/95), Judgment (Grand Chamber), 11 July 2002, ECHR 2002-VI, 1, para. 84.

[21] *Allan v. the United Kingdom* (Appl. No. 48539/99), Judgment (Chamber), 5 November 2002, ECHR 2002-IX, 41, para. 51.

[22] *Hirst v. the United Kingdom (No. 2)* (Appl. No. 74025/01), Judgment (Grand Chamber), 6 October 2005, ECHR 2005-IX, 187, paras. 75 and 80.

my view such references may support the legal argumentation and hence strengthen the judgment; they may inspire the reflection of the Court, irrespective of whether the domestic decision is mentioned in the reasoning or in the comparative law part; they show the parties or third parties that their arguments that are based on such decisions have been taken into account; and they indicate more generally that the Court is aware of the complexity of the issues and of important legal developments elsewhere.

14.5 References to Documents of Other CoE Bodies

According to the Statute of the CoE, dated 5 May 1949, the organs of the organisation are the Committee of Ministers (CoM) and the Parliamentary Assembly (PACE).[23] Over the years, these organs have each adopted an impressive number of resolutions and recommendations covering many different fields, such as pre-trial detention, fair trial and freedom of expression. Some of them are based on or influenced by the case law of the Court.

Such instruments are mentioned very frequently in the Court's judgments, both in the comparative law part of the judgment and in its reasoning. Using them forms part of everyday judicial life in the ECtHR. This is not surprising. The recommendations and resolutions promote the core values of the CoE: human rights, democracy and the rule of law. They have been adopted by the two highest organs of the organisation after thorough discussions, and thus reflect broad consensus of the CoE's member states. These values also form the basis of the Convention. The documents emerging from CoM and PACE, not all of which are legally binding, express the collective will of the member states. They thus contain arguments of considerable weight, for instance when the Court is exploring whether there exists a trend or consensus.

It falls outside the scope of this chapter to consider the Court's use of the many binding conventions that have been adopted by the CoE. As of October 2015, the European Treaty Series listed 217 such instruments (conventions and protocols).[24] However, in the present context it is important to recall that some of these conventions established bodies (committees) which are tasked with supervising or applying their respective instrument. Their decisions or guidelines are frequently applied in the Court's case law.

[23] Statute of the Council of Europe (5 May 1949), CETS No. 001, entered into force 3 August 1949.

[24] Available at www.coe.int/en/web/conventions/full-list.

An obvious illustration is the Committee for the Prevention of Torture (CPT), established under the European Convention for the Prevention of Torture and Inhuman or Degrading Treatment or Punishment (1987).[25] Its reports can be specific (issued after the Committee's visits in individual countries) or general (containing an analysis of recurring problems). They are particularly relevant for the ECtHR when it comes to interpreting and applying article 3 of the Convention. Many ECtHR judgments about overcrowding in institutions where persons are deprived of their liberty have made use of the CPT's reports, including in the reasoning part of the respective judgments. One example is the pilot judgment in *Ananyev v. Russia*, a case concerning structural problems in Russia with respect to pre-trial detention.[26]

Another example of a body established within the CoE is the European Commission for Democracy through Law (the Venice Commission), which was created by the Committee of Ministers in 1990. Its activities in the field of building and strengthening democratic institutions, on questions of constitutional law and the organisation of elections have often been referred to by the Court. There are also several judgments where the ECtHR engages with documents of the European Commission against Racism and Intolerance (ECRI), the Consultative Council of European Judges (CCJE), the European Commissioner for Human Rights and the CoE's Bioethics Committee.

14.6 Concluding Observations

It follows from the preceding overview that the ECtHR uses various types of material, but not all in the same way. Decisions of national courts from states that are directly involved in a case under consideration are of particular relevance. They are scrutinised within the context of the Convention's system of supervision. When the Court decides whether the individual's complaint is admissible, it has to consider whether domestic remedies have been exhausted and also whether the application has been sent within six months after the last domestic decision has been adopted. Furthermore, the national court's reasoning will be crucial in the Court's determination on the merits (violation or not). For these reasons, there

[25] European Convention for the Prevention of Torture and Inhuman or Degrading Treatment or Punishment (26 November 1987) CETS No. 126, entered into force 1 February 1989.

[26] *Ananyev and Others v. Russia* (Appl. Nos. 42525/07 and 60800/08), Judgment (Chamber), 10 January 2012, not reported, paras. 56 and 144. The judgment also contains several references to decisions by CoE bodies other than the CPT.

is an ongoing judicial dialogue between the Court and the highest courts in the CoE member states. The more convincing reasons adduced at the national level, the less likely it is that the ECtHR will conclude that there has been a violation of the Convention. On the other hand, once the Court has found a breach, this will have an impact on the development of the national court's future jurisprudence.

Specific judgments by courts in other CoE member states play a very modest role in the Court's judgments. It is the general legal situation in a country that matters when the Court seeks to clarify whether there are any emerging trends. On the other hand, decisions from national judiciaries outside the CoE are used more frequently and more directly. They are mostly mentioned in the comparative law section of the judgment, but there are examples where they form part of the reasoning as support for the Court's conclusion.

Of particular relevance to the ECtHR are decisions by the CoE statutory bodies (CoM and PACE) as well as reports, opinions or guidelines from CoE human rights bodies (such as the CPT, the Venice Commission and ECRI). These bodies all seek to promote the ideals of the organisation, which also underpin the Convention, and some of them have specific knowledge within the fields covered by certain Convention rights. Decisions by such bodies carry considerable weight.

The Court also refers to many other sources, such as other human rights conventions, general international law and international criminal law. These fall outside the scope of this chapter. It is not possible to give any general answer as to the relative weight of all these norms and decisions, as this will depend on the particular circumstances of each case.

The use of the various decisions of other courts and bodies discussed here reflects the methodology of the Court – the relevance and weight of those legal arguments. However, it can also be seen as a sort of 'judicial dialogue', understood in a wider sense. This is an interesting topic, but it should not be forgotten that the Court decides about 80,000 cases every year. More than 90 percent of them are inadmissible, and many judgments contain no references to the types of decisions discussed here. Consequently, the dialogue described in this chapter takes place within a small part of the Court's total workload. This does not mean that this topic is not important, but rather that it should be seen in perspective.

15

The ECtHR' Use of Decisions of International Courts and Quasi-Judicial Bodies

ANGELIKA NUßBERGER

This short contribution concentrates on the European Court of Human Rights' (ECtHR or the Court) use of decisions of international courts and quasi-judicial bodies.[1] It aims to supplement the contributions of Judges Luis López Guerra and Erik Møse to shed more light on 'what we are doing' and 'why we are doing what we are doing' when our Court engages in judicial dialogue.

15.1 References to Decisions of International Courts and Quasi-Judicial Bodies in the ECtHR's Judgments

Judges at the ECtHR have a clearly defined task: to ensure the observance of the engagements undertaken by the High Contracting Parties in the European Convention on Human Rights (ECHR or Convention)[2] and the Protocols thereto, and thus to adjudicate potential human rights violations in individual cases.[3] The interpretation of the Convention – necessary for fulfilling this task – is thus not an academic exercise or *l'art pour l'art*. That is why, as a rule, the ECtHR refers to decisions of international courts and quasi-judicial bodies only when the material is relevant for deciding the case.

The starting point in international law is the Vienna Convention on the Law of Treaties (VCLT),[4] which states in article 31(3)(c) that account has to be taken of 'any relevant rules of international law applicable in the

[1] By 'quasi-judicial bodies' the organisers of the conference meant international and regional bodies that have judicial functions but cannot issue binding judgments, e.g. the UN human rights treaty bodies.

[2] Convention for the Protection of Human Rights and Fundamental Freedoms (4 November 1950) 213 UNTS 222; 312 ETS 5, entered into force 3 September 1953.

[3] Articles 19 and 34 ECHR.

[4] Vienna Convention on the Law of Treaties (23 May 1969) 1155 UNTS 331; 8 ILM 679 (1969), entered into force 27 January 1980.

relations between the parties'.[5] This principle has often been stressed by the Court, for example, in *Sabeh El Leil v. France*:

> The Convention … cannot be interpreted in a vacuum. The Court must therefore be mindful of the Convention's special character as a human rights treaty, and it must also take the relevant rules of international law into account.[6]

Therefore, first and foremost, we have to identify the 'relevant rules of international law' in every given case.

In this context, I also want to point to distinctions that should be made. First, as noted by my colleague, Judge Erik Møse,[7] there is a ladder of court judgments: those rendered by a single judge,[8] a committee,[9] a Chamber,[10] and finally the Grand Chamber.[11] Approximately 95 per cent of the cases sent to the Court are decided by a single judge or by a committee. All these cases do not form part of what is called 'judicial dialogue', as they are decided without giving any or very few reasons.[12] The remaining 5 per cent of the cases relevant to this research are just the tip of the iceberg. It is above all the Grand Chamber which has a comprehensive approach to each case and engages in the search for all potentially relevant international material. This does also happen for chamber judgments, but only if required by the specific questions raised.

Further, it matters in which part of the judgment international legal material is found: under the heading 'Relevant international law' or under the heading 'The law'. In the former we give a comprehensive overview of relevant norms adopted within the Council of Europe (CoE) or other international organisations as well as of relevant judgments and decisions. This basically serves the same purpose as the documentation of the national law applied in a specific case. The idea is to explain the basis for our legal analysis. It may be compared to the bibliography in a research work, as it shows what material has been used. Judges do not always agree on what has to be included and what can be left out. According to one

5 Article 31(3)(c) VCLT.

6 *Sabeh El Leil v. France* (Appl. No. 34869/05), Judgment (Grand Chamber), 29 June 2011, not reported, para. 48.

7 See Judge Erik Møse's report on practice (Chapter 14) in this volume.

8 Article 27 ECHR.

9 Aricle 28 ECHR.

10 Article 29 ECHR.

11 Aricle 31 ECHR.

12 This is mainly due to the backlog of clearly inadmissible cases the Court was confronted with as a consequence of the long delay of the entry into force of Protocol No. 14 of the

school of thought, the material quoted should be restricted to what will be directly used and quoted in the legal analysis. Others argue that even the material consulted but not relied upon should be included. The 'real' dialogue, however, takes place when international legal material is included in the part of the judgment under the heading 'The law'. This is the essential part of the judgment which concerns the interpretation and application of the Convention.

Last but not least, it might be helpful to make a further distinction. Sometimes findings of international bodies are not relevant for the interpretation of the Convention based on judicial dialogue, but only for fact-finding in a given case. The necessity of 'fact-finding' depends on the subject matter. It is important in cases where it is controversial what has happened, especially in interstate cases. As a rule, it is also relevant for extradition and expulsion cases in which it is important to get detailed information about the situation in the country to which the person is going to be expelled. We very much rely on findings of the United Nations High Commissioner for Refugees (UNHCR), the Council of Europe Commissioner for Human Rights and also on much NGO material. To quote from the judgment in *Samsam Mohammed Hussein v. the Netherlands and Italy* about whether or not to transfer a person to Italy,

> In determining whether it has been shown that the applicant runs a real risk of suffering treatment proscribed by Article 3 if transferred to Italy, the Court will examine the issue in the light of all the material placed before it or, if necessary, material obtained *proprio motu*.[13]
>
> Taking into account the reports drawn up by both governmental and non-governmental institutions and organisations on the reception schemes for asylum seekers in Italy.[14]

Reading and evaluating these reports is a precondition for deciding such cases. It is true that usually fact-finding is done by the national courts. But in specific circumstances, such as in expulsion and extradition cases where we have to assess future risks, we may have to complement the fact-finding done on the national level. We take into account all information we can get in order to understand the situation in the country in which the applicant alleges to be confronted with risks to life and health. This fact-finding, in

ECHR. The Court is currently working on a new system providing at least short motivations for single-judge cases.

[13] *Samsam Mohammed Hussein and Others v. the Netherlands and Italy* (Appl. No. 27725/10), Judgment (Chamber), 2 April 2013, not reported, para. 69.

[14] *Ibid.*, para. 78.

the form of a dialogue, is different from what we are talking about here: specific judicial dialogue.

15.2 Searching for the Relevant Material

How do we find the material we quote and rely on? The legal assessment is part of the Court's duty; especially, it is the duty of the *rapporteur* to identify all relevant material. Hence, comparative and international material can be adduced even if it is not mentioned by the parties. We can distinguish between 'inside material' and 'outside material'. 'Inside material' is what we collect by our own means, with the help of the Registry and the Research Division, a process already described by Judge Erik Møse.[15] If we have a specific case touching upon international law, we can make a request for research on international law, not only comparative law. One example is the *Kurić* case, where research on international law was conducted on the topic of change of citizenship in situations of state succession.[16] If the research results turn out not to be helpful for the case at hand, they can always be left out.

The question is also how far our specific personal knowledge as judges comes into play. All judges have had a life prior to joining the ECtHR. Some of us were working for international bodies; for instance, Judge Erik Møse was a judge at the International Criminal Tribunal for Rwanda, Judge Boštjan Zupančič was on the United Nations Committee against Torture, and I was member of the Committee of Experts on the Application of Conventions and Recommendations of the International Labour Organization. So naturally, we bring with us some sort of expert knowledge in international law and check whether it is helpful for the analysis of the case.

Thus, to conclude on 'inside material', the approach in this respect is the most comprehensive one: we look at all the material we can get. To quote Judge Mark Villiger, we want to 'make possible a decision which, in one form or another, will be as informed as possible; will have as high a quality as possible; will be as objective, fair and wise as possible; and will come about as efficiently as possible'.[17]

[15] Report on practice by Judge Erik Møse in this volume (Chapter 14).

[16] *Kurić and Others v. Slovenia* (Appl. No. 26828/06), Judgment (Grand Chamber), 26 June 2012, ECHR 2012-IV, 1.

[17] M. Villiger, 'The Dialogue of Judges', C. Hohmann-Dennhardt, P. Masuch and M. Villiger (eds.), *Grundrechte und Solidarität, Durchstzung und Verfahren – Festschrift für Renate Jäger* (Kehl: N.P. Engel, 2010) 195–209, at 197.

I see a difference here in regard to 'outside material', the material that is brought in from the parties and third-party interveners. This is because they naturally select material with a view to win the case, lobby for some decision or promote a certain international body. By way of example, we have now an interesting case pending that concerns home births. While it is not prohibited for women in the Czech Republic to give birth at home, midwives are not allowed to assist them. The case pending before our Chamber[18] concerns the question whether or not such prohibition is acceptable under article 8 of the Convention. The Czech government quotes as relevant international legal material documents of the World Health Organization and the UN Committee on Economic, Social and Cultural Rights on the reduction of child mortality. For their part, the applicants refer to a report on the Czech Republic issued by the Committee on the Elimination of All Forms of Discrimination against Women criticising the situation in hospitals in the Czech Republic where women's wishes are often not respected. We are certainly aware of the fact that parties are partial and do not provide us with international and comparative material unless this helps to further their cause. We, on the contrary, collect such material with the aim of gaining the most comprehensive perspective possible.

15.3 Selection of Relevant Material

At first glance, it may seem that we mostly consider material in the realm of civil and political rights, because these are the rights which constitute the main subject matter the Court has to deal with in relation to the Convention. But we also have extensive quotations of case law of international bodies dealing with social questions. An example is the judgment *Demir and Baykara v. Turkey* which contains several references to the ILO Expert Committee and the European Committee on Social Rights.[19]

It might also appear logical that we quote European bodies more often than extra-/non-European bodies. Here the answer is 'yes'. We first have a look at the work of the different bodies of the CoE, for example the Venice Commission, the European Committee on Torture and the Human Rights Commissioner. Yet, sometimes, we also quote material from the

[18] The case has been decided in the meantime: *Dubská and Krejzová v. Czech Republic* (Appl. Nos. 28859/11 28473/12) Judgment (Chamber), 11 December 2014, selected for publication 2014.

[19] *Demir and Baykara v. Turkey* (Appl. No. 34503/97), Judgment (Grand Chamber), 12 November 2008, ECHR 2008-V, 333.

Inter-American system. One example is *Gäfgen v. Germany* where the Court had to decide whether the threat of torture also falls under article 3 of the Convention.[20] Here, under the heading 'The law' we quoted from the case *Maritza Urrutia v. Guatemala* rendered by the Inter-American Court of Human Rights:

> [The ECtHR] reiterates that according to its own case-law ... which also refers to the definition of torture in Article 1 of the United Nations Convention against Torture ... and according to the views taken by other international human-rights monitoring bodies ... to which the Redress Trust likewise referred, a *threat of torture* can amount to torture, as the nature of torture covers both physical pain and mental suffering. In particular, the fear of physical torture may itself constitute mental torture.[21]

We have also considered findings from the African Commission on Human and Peoples' Rights. In *Sitaropoulos v. Greece* concerning voting rights of expatriates, the ECtHR noted the African Commission's interpretation of article 13 of the Charter on Human and Peoples' Rights in light of the UN Human Rights Committee's General Comment on Article 25 of the International Covenant on Civil and Political Rights:

> Article 13 § 1 of this Charter is worded as follows: "Every citizen shall have the right to participate freely in the government of his country, either directly or through freely chosen representatives in accordance with the provisions of the law." ... Taking the view that this provision was similar in substance to Article 25 of the International Covenant, the African Commission on Human and Peoples' Rights interpreted Article 13 of the Charter in the light of the Human Rights Committee's General Comment on Article 25. It therefore held that any conditions applicable to the exercise of Article 25 rights should be based on objective and reasonable criteria established by law (see *Purohit and Moore v. The Gambia*, Communication no. 241/2001, § 76).[22]

So the Court follows a comprehensive approach with respect to international legal material. Of course, specialised bodies have special knowledge which may be important to us. I have already mentioned the UNHCR and the Committee against Torture. There is no catalogue of criteria clearly defining what can be looked at and what has to be excluded.

[20] *Gäfgen v. Germany* (Appl. No. 22978/05), Judgment (Grand Chamber), 1 June 2010, ECHR 2010-IV, 247.

[21] *Ibid.*, para. 108 (emphasis added); and para. 66 (quoting from the case of *Maritza Urrutia v. Guatemala*, Inter-American Court of Human Rights, Series C, No.103, Judgment (Merits, Reparations and Costs), 27 November 2003.

[22] *Sitaropoulos and Giakoumopoulos v. Greece* (Appl. No. 42202/07), Judgment (Grand Chamber), 15 March 2012, ECHR 2012-II, 279, paras. 30–31.

Nevertheless, the 'legal value' always has to be carefully assessed, taking into account not only the characteristics of the source but also the context in which it was elaborated and applied.

It is difficult to answer the question about the number of references to decisions of international courts or quasi-judicial bodies that have been deliberately left out by the ECtHR despite being mentioned by the parties or members of the Court. The secrecy of the deliberations in the ECtHR does not allow me to provide any details in this regard. Still, I can give you an indirect answer. Quite often you can find additional international legal material quoted in dissenting or concurring opinions. If that material is not included in the main judgment, you might guess that it was suggested to be taken up but ultimately was not integrated. Indeed, judges may be more outspoken in these opinions; sometimes there are extensive quotes, which may constitute a form of dialogue not included in the judgment.

But there might be a rational criterion for not referring to a particular source, namely that we do not include redundant information. Often several bodies provide the same information. For example, in the judgment *Siliadin v. France* concerning forced labour, ILO instruments on forced labour were quoted, and not material stemming from the European Committee on Social Rights.[23] It was perhaps not done on purpose, but it would not have had any added value.

15.4 Criteria for Engaging in a Transnational Judicial Dialogue

There is no clear-cut catalogue of criteria defining when and how and with which international court/quasi-judicial body to engage in a transnational judicial dialogue. As explained earlier, several distinctions can be made: between material coming from European and non-European bodies; between binding judgments and non-binding opinions; between judicial bodies, quasi-judicial bodies, and political bodies; between state bodies and non-governmental bodies; and between ratified treaties and non-ratified treaties. Yet, concerning the question of including or excluding specific material, these distinctions are not necessarily decisive. The Court has quite a holistic approach and tries to get a complete picture of the relevant tendencies and differences in international law. This was already evident in a very early and influential judgment, *Marckx v. Belgium*, in which the Court founded its innovative approach on conventions that had

[23] *Siliadin v. France* (Appl. No. 73316/01), Judgment (Chamber), 26 July 2005, ECHR 2005-VII, 289.

not yet come into force.[24] Another famous example is *Demir and Baykara v. Turkey*:

> [I]n searching for common ground among the norms of international law the Court has never distinguished between sources of law according to whether or not they have been signed or ratified by the respondent State ...[25]

The most important aspect for the decision on citing or not citing international legal material is rather in how far the quotation helps in finding an answer to the concrete question raised by the case before the Court. It would be of no use to quote general rules on general topics such as equality between men and women when we are dealing with the specific problem of parental leave or retirement age. On the contrary, we will be tempted to quote reports concerning the respondent state when they touch upon the specific problem with which the Court is confronted. One example in this context is *De Souza Ribeiro v. France*, where we took into account the concluding observations of the UN Human Rights Committee on the fourth periodic report of France.[26] Reports or judgments concerning third countries will be less interesting.[27] Nevertheless, they might be helpful as illustrations for general tendencies.[28]

15.5 Purpose of References

As concerns the main purpose of references to international legal material, we can distinguish between two sorts of questions that have to be answered: (1) questions of general international law inherent in the cases brought before the Court, and (2) innovative questions of human rights law.

In the first category we are confronted with questions of international law as such. There are three subcategories. First, there might be parallel procedures brought before our Court and before other international bodies or jurisdictions. The most famous example is the case

[24] *Marckx v. Belgium* (Appl. No. 6833/74), Judgment (Plenary), 13 June 1979, Series A, Vol. 31, para. 41.

[25] *Demir and Baykara v. Turkey*, *supra* note 19, para. 78.

[26] *De Souza Ribeiro v. France* (Appl. No. 22689/07), Judgment (Grand Chamber), 13 December 2012, ECHR 2012-VI, 139.

[27] But see *supra* note 21 (quoting supervisory bodies on other countries than Germany).

[28] See e.g. the comprehensive quotations on equality between men and women in child-raising in *Konstantin Markin v. Russia* (Appl. No. 30078/06), Judgment (Grand Chamber), 22 March 2012, ECHR 2012-III, 1, paras. 49–70 (quoting not only UN and Council of Europe documents but also EU documents and jurisprudence of the CJEU).

Georgia v. Russia (No. 2) where we were confronted with an inter-state complaint.[29] At the same time the International Court of Justice (ICJ) was also called upon to decide on similar problems in connection with the interpretation of the Convention against Racial Discrimination.[30] Other examples of parallel and subsequent procedures are *Prince Hans-Adam II of Liechtenstein v. Germany*[31] and the case concerning the massacre in Distomo.[32] In such cases it is crucial to avoid any discrepancies in decision-making. This is also secured by important procedural safeguards.

By way of example, I want to point to an interesting Chamber decision where the Court declined to deal with a case because it had already been brought before the Committee on Freedom of Association of the International Labour Organization.[33] Relying on article 35(2)(b) of the Convention,[34] the Court declared the application inadmissible because the case was being dealt with by another international body.[35] References to procedures before other international adjudicatory bodies thus serve the aim of transparency of international decision-making.

A second subcategory concerns cases where the ECHR has to be interpreted in the light of more specific international treaties. The Court is called upon to take into account not only the relevant treaties but also their practical application. International child abduction cases might serve as an example. While we deal with such cases under the very general provision of 'right to family life' (article 8 of the Convention), the 1980 Hague Child Abduction Convention provides for much more detailed

[29] *Georgia v. Russia* (No. 2) (Appl. No. 38263/08), Judgment (Chamber), 13 December 2011, not reported.

[30] *Application of the International Convention on the Elimination of All Forms of Racial Discrimination (Georgia v. Russian Federation)*, ICJ Reports (2011) 70.

[31] *Prince Hans-Adam II of Liechtenstein v. Germany* (Appl. No. 42527/98), Judgment (Grand Chamber), 12 July 2001, ECHR 2011-VIII, 1. See also *Certain Property (Liechtenstein v. Germany)*, ICJ Reports (2005) 6.

[32] *Sfountouris and Others v. Germany* (Appl. No. 24120/06), Judgment (Chamber), 31 May 2011, not reported; see also *Jurisdictional Immunities of the State* (*Germany v. Italy: Greece intervening*), ICJ Reports (2012) 99.

[33] *The Professional Trades Union for Prison, Correctional and Secure Psychiatric Workers and Others (POA and Others) v. the United Kingdom* (Appl. No. 59253/11), Judgment (Chamber), 21 May 2013, not reported.

[34] Article 35(2)(b) ECHR: 'The Court shall not deal with any application submitted under Article 34 that … is substantially the same as a matter that has already been examined by the Court or has already been submitted to another procedure of international investigation or settlement and contains no relevant new information.'

[35] See *supra* note 33, para. 27 ('The Court recalls that the purpose of this provision is to avoid a plurality of international proceedings relating to the same cases.').

provisions.[36] In deciding such cases in a consistent manner it is necessary to take into account all relevant material, for example the Explanatory Report on the Hague Convention.[37] The two Grand Chamber judgments *Neulinger Shuruk v. Switzerland*[38] and *X. v. Latvia*[39] are good examples for this approach.

The same is true for a third subcategory: cases which have not been dealt with by another international court but which concern questions of general relevance in international law. Examples here are *Sabeh El Leil v. France* concerning the scope of immunity of a state in labour disputes;[40] *El Masri v. Macedonia* on international responsibility for rendition;[41] and *Stichting Mothers of Srebrenica and Others v. the Netherlands*, concerning immunity enjoyed by the United Nations.[42] We are, of course, dedicated to the aim of ensuring consistency in international law. If we deal with general concepts of international law, such as state immunity or jurisdiction, we do take a very close look at whatever is decided by other international bodies. Undoubtedly, there is an intense reflection on other sources of international law.

The second category of cases concerns human rights problems in which we are called upon to develop our case law further and to consider innovative approaches. For this group, international law serves more as a source of inspiration. In deciding on the development of our case law we might look at judgments of international courts as well as decisions of international quasi-judicial bodies giving answers to similar problems.

Such material can also be of great value for defining the 'European consensus', an element vital for defining the margin of appreciation left to the member states in deciding on a specific problem. This has been the Court's practice since the adoption of the judgment *Marckx v. Belgium*, in which the Court referred to two Conventions that had not yet entered into force.

[36] Hague Convention of 25 October 1980 on the Civil Aspects of International Child Abduction, 1343 UNTS 89, entered into force 1 December 1983.

[37] E. Pérez-Vera, 'Explanatory Report on the 1980 Hague Child Abduction Convention', HCCH Publications (1982).

[38] *Neulinger and Shuruk v. Switzerland* (Appl. No. 41615/07), Judgment (Grand Chamber), 6 July 2010, ECHR 2010-V, 117.

[39] *X. v. Latvia* (Appl. No. 27853/09), Judgment (Grand Chamber), 26 November 2013, ECHR 2013-VI, 319.

[40] Sabeh El Leil v. France, *supra* note 6.

[41] *El-Masri v. the Former Yugoslav Republic of Macedonia* (Appl. No. 39630/09), Judgment (Grand Chamber), 13 December 2012, ECHR 2012-VI, 263.

[42] *Stichting Mothers of Srebrenica and Others v. the Netherlands* (Appl. No. 65542/12), Judgment (Chamber), 11 June 2013, ECHR 2013-III, 255.

As a more recent illustration it is worth quoting the *Bayatyan* case against Armenia about conscientious objection, in which the Court has held:

> The Court would further point out the equally important developments concerning recognition of the right to conscientious objection in various international fora [equally important to developments in domestic law in CoE member states]. The most notable is the interpretation by the UNHRC of the provisions of the ICCPR (Articles 8 and 18), which are similar to those of the Convention (Articles 4 and 9). Initially the UNHRC adopted the same approach as the European Commission, excluding the right of conscientious objection from the scope of Article 18 of the ICCPR. However, in 1993, in its General Comment No. 22, it modified its initial approach and considered that a right to conscientious objection could be derived from Article 18 of the ICCPR inasmuch as the obligation to use lethal force might seriously conflict with the freedom of conscience and the right to manifest one's religion or belief. In 2006 the UNHRC explicitly refused to apply Article 8 of the ICCPR in two cases against South Korea concerning conscientious objectors and examined their complaints solely under Article 18 of the ICCPR, finding a violation of that provision on account of the applicants' conviction for refusal to serve in the army for reasons of conscience.[43]

So when considering European consensus, we take into account not only comparative law, as noted by Judge Erik Møse,[44] but also international law in order to find out general tendencies and developments.

While we may look to international law for an innovative approach, we do not necessarily always follow it. For instance, in *Sitaropoulos v. Greece*, while confronted with far-reaching different approaches to granting voting rights to expatriates, the judges of the Grand Chamber nevertheless unanimously held that the restrictive regulation in Greek law did not violate the Convention; the Grand Chamber based its argument on the finding that there was no common approach in international law.[45] Further, in *Stichting Mothers of Srebrenica v. the Netherlands* concerning the relationship between immunity and *jus cogens*, the Court held:

> International law does not support the position that a civil claim should override immunity from suit for the sole reason that it is based on an allegation of a particularly grave violation of a norm of international law, even

[43] *Bayatyan v. Armenia* (Appl. No. 23459/03), Judgment (Grand Chamber), 7 July 2011, ECHR 2011-IV, 1, para. 105.

[44] Report on practice by Judge Erik Møse in this volume (Chapter 14).

[45] Sitaropoulos v. Greece, *supra* note 22, para. 75.

> a norm of *ius cogens*. In respect of the sovereign immunity of foreign States this has been clearly stated by the ICJ in *Jurisdictional Immunities of the State (Germany v. Italy: Greece intervening)*, judgment of 3 February 2012, §§ 81–97. In the Court's opinion this also holds true as regards the immunity enjoyed by the United Nations.[46]

The minority in *Al-Adsani v. The United Kingdom* saw this differently.[47] But that was before the ICJ judgment had been adopted.

15.6 Main Effect of the ECtHR's References to International Courts' and Quasi-Judicial Bodies' Decisions

The influence of international courts' and quasi-judicial bodies' decisions on the ECtHR's jurisprudence varies according to the problem the Court is confronted with. When the Court has to take a stand on questions of international law, the information on decisions in the field of international law obviously plays a decisive role as shown for example in the judgment *Sabeh El Leil v. France*.[48] Consistency and harmony of international law is the primary aim.

On the contrary, when the Court is confronted with a new problem of human rights law, it assumes a leading role. Even if it takes note of how others decide, decisions of other bodies would not necessarily have a decisive influence, but constitute one argument among others. In *Demir and Baykara v. Turkey*, the Court held:

> The consensus emerging from specialised international instruments and from the practice of Contracting States *may constitute* a relevant consideration for the Court when it interprets the provisions of the Convention in specific cases.[49]

In the judgment in *National Union of Rail, Maritime and Transport Workers (RTM) v. the United Kingdom*, the Court explains that it does not feel obliged to follow the expert bodies' opinions:

> [T]he Court considers that the negative assessments made by the relevant monitoring bodies of the ILO and European Social Charter are not of such persuasive weight for determining whether the operation of the statutory ban on secondary strikes in circumstances such as those complained of in

46 *Stichting Mothers of Srebrenica v. the Netherlands*, *supra* note 42, para. 158.

47 *Al-Adsani v. the United Kingdom* (Appl. No. 35763/97), Judgment (Grand Chamber), 21 November 2001, ECHR 2001-XI, 79.

48 *Sabeh El Leil v. France*, *supra* note 6.

49 *Demir and Baykara v. Turkey*, *supra* note 19, para. 85.

the present case remained within the range of permissible options open to the national authorities under Article 11 of the Convention.[50]

15.7 Formal or Informal Meetings with Judges from Other International Courts and Quasi-Judicial Bodies

ECtHR judges have regular meetings with the judges of the Court of Justice of the European Union, but they also have a lot of meetings in different formats and not on a regular basis. To give a few examples: for the solemn opening of the judicial year in 2013, we invited Judge Theodor Meron, President at the International Criminal Court for the Former Yugoslavia. He gave a speech on human rights standards in the jurisprudence of international criminal courts and tribunals, in which he noted parallel developments in the jurisdictions.[51] Some of our judges visited the American Court of Human Rights in 2012. The South American colleagues then came to Strasbourg in 2014 for a study tour. We also had a visit of the South African Development Community (SADC) Tribunal, which had been dissolved in 2011. More recently, the ECtHR was visited by the Myanmar Human Rights Commission. During all these meetings the exchange on common problems and approaches is most fruitful.

15.8 Concluding Remarks on the Impact of Legal Material Coming from Different Sources

In conclusion, I want to stress that we distinguish between references to decisions of national courts from states that are directly involved in the case, references to national courts' decisions that are not directly involved in the case (from other CoE member states and non-member states), and references to other international courts' and quasi-judicial bodies' decisions. Concerning national court decisions, we are called upon to apply the Convention, to make an assessment on the basis of the Convention and to have the famous 'last word' on the violation or non-violation of the Convention. Judge Luis López Guerra has rightly described this as a reciprocal dialogue.[52]

[50] *National Union of Rail, Maritime and Transport Workers (RTM) v. the United Kingdom* (Appl. No. 31045/10), Judgment (Chamber), 8 April 2014, not reported, para. 98.

[51] T. Meron, 'Human Rights Standards in the Jurisprudence of International Criminal Courts and Tribunals', Opening of the Judicial Year, 25 January 2013, European Court of Human Rights, Strasbourg, France, available at: www.echr.coe.int/Documents/Speech_20130125_Meron_ENG.pdf.

[52] Report on practice by Judge Luis López Guerra in this volume (Chapter 13).

Case law of non-European courts might be used for comparative purposes, but as a rule, it is not surprising if the US Supreme Court or the Supreme Court of Canada decides a question differently. This does not create any problems, for them or for us. We never deny that we can have very different opinions and approaches. The death penalty is a famous example. The European standard is so different from many other countries in the world that we do not have to be 'upset' if cases are decided in the opposite way. There is no need for justification.

On the contrary, the decisions of international courts and quasi-judicial bodies are important for our work. I believe that we, as the ECtHR, have a specific responsibility in this respect and have to be aware of the ongoing developments in international law. International law has to be taken into account. I think it is urgent and necessary that we are open and responsive, and that we see ourselves as part of a network within which international law is being formed. This is an essential feature of international law and gives credibility to the whole system. Hence, if different standards are promoted across the globe, it is necessary to provide good explanations for those standards. For example, there might not yet be a consolidated rule,[53] or the European standard might be considered to be higher.

It is interesting to note that the 'official dialogue' between the judgments handed down by the different courts and the decisions adopted by the different quasi-judicial bodies is superseded by a sort of 'unofficial dialogue' based on the dissenting and concurring opinions of judges who comment extensively on the respective positions and take inspirations from them.

International law has to develop in a consistent manner. What is called 'dialogue' between the different jurisdictions forms an important part of this process. As in real life, dialogue can always be of a different quality. The more pertinent it is what somebody says, the more attentively you will listen. Also, if comments are completely opposite to your own views, you might be interested to understand why this is; at the same time you might not always find it necessary to contradict those comments and start a controversial debate. That is how I would describe the ECtHR's approach to a transnational judicial dialogue: it can have different degrees of intensity, from a very intense exchange to a friendly diplomatic smile.

[53] Cf. *Sitaropolous v. Greece, supra* note 22.

PART III

Normative and Theoretical Appraisals

16

From Judicial Dialogue to Cosmopolitan Norms

Enhancing Democracy in Globalised States

CLARA MARSAN-RAVENTÓS

16.1 Introduction

The traditional chain of accountability through elected representatives by which internal justice is achieved in constitutional democracies is challenged by globalisation processes. Important decisions are taken and rules that affect individuals are made at regional or international levels without these individuals being able to influence these decisions. Against this background of relocation of power beyond state borders, this chapter looks at the practice of transnational judicial dialogue by national courts. It analyses the purpose and effects of such dialogue in order to answer whether this practice can help to redress this increasing democratic deficit of states and the hollowing out of decision-making and law-making processes within the state. The chapter relies on the theory of cosmopolitanism - a normative theory which defends a more accountable global order both forged and sustained by transnational judicial dialogue.

Section 16.2 sets out the democratic deficit problem which affects states and examines how globalisation has aggravated this deficit. Section 16.3 highlights how cosmopolitanism provides analytical tools to address this democratic deficit problem affecting states. Cosmopolitanism helps us rethink national and international institutions and processes to provide new remedies to tackle these democratic deficit–related problems within states. Section 16.4 focuses on the role of domestic and international courts and their engagement in transnational judicial dialogue in this process of rethinking along cosmopolitan lines. Domestic judges are in a strategic position to reform national democracies in order to address the increasing democratic deficit, and thus to contribute to the effective functioning of these democracies in today's globalised world. In particular, domestic courts' use of foreign and international jurisprudence is a way to draw new normative solutions from the cosmopolitan legal order. Judges are thus able to enrich the national legal framework, which can contribute to perfecting democratic processes at the national and international levels. This chapter's central thesis is that judges, through their engagement in judicial dialogue, are in a privileged position to open the national legal framework to international and transnational influences, while ensuring that these opening processes provide internal justice. By doing so they can contribute to the making of cosmopolitan norms and ensure the democratic accountability of globalised decision-making processes. Domestic judges should deliver transparent rulings in which they openly acknowledge their engagement in dialogue. Transparency creates awareness of the dialogue between different legal frameworks, and allows this dialogue to contribute to the making of cosmopolitan norms. Transparency also legitimises domestic judicial institutions in the eyes of the people who live under their jurisdiction. Judicial dialogue will be accepted if it enhances delivery of justice at the domestic level, for instance when it is used to find new interpretations to a given norm.

16.2. The Challenges Faced by Constitutional Democracies in the Age of Globalisation

This section highlights some of the unsolved problems of constitutional democracies (subsection 16.2.1) and shows that the practical consequences of these problems are amplified through changes taking place in the globalised world (subsection 16.2.2). A particular emphasis is placed on how states' autonomy to adopt and change their legal order is compromised.

16.2.1 The Infinite Imperfection of Constitutional Democracies and the Role of Courts in Alleviating It

Today, national democracies are built within constitutional structures. Constitutions systemise the rule of law and the democratic principles of the state, which seek to provide a framework of justice and liberty to its citizens. So perceived, democracy is the conjunction of institutions and processes that legitimise the state's power structure, where power ultimately stems from the people. Such 'government of the people' is usually equated to the majority rule imposed by electoral systems; that is, a *demos* is in government through their elected representatives.

Yet, when trying to measure the 'peoples'' involvement in government, the unavoidable question arises: Which individuals are able to participate in government by crafting or changing a constitution, as well as by designing the policies and laws of the polity? In other words, who is part of a 'people' or *demos* in each polity? From a constitutional theory perspective it is the constitution, through nationality (citizenship), that determines whether an individual is part of the polity or not. Thus, a *demos* is composed of the citizens of a constitutionalised jurisdiction that coincides with the borders of a nation-state. These citizens with rights and obligations belong to the 'governing people'. As the sovereign people, citizens have the exclusive right to decide who the people are: they are able to include and exclude people from the group that will govern the nation. One can nonetheless ask: Are today's sovereigns ('the people') able to found and change their democratic constitution? Are they able to delimit the 'people' and thus decide which individuals (citizens) are in or outside the polity? In theory they should, but reality is rather different. Not only is a 'people' often deprived of a direct influence to craft their constitution because they are born at a time when the constitutional structures have already been established; they are too unable to define themselves as a political unit of citizens. These two problems are connected to the fact that the 'people' is an abstraction particularly difficult to shape. In practice, the people can never decide who the people are in a material sense,[1] which means that most of the time only 'intermediaries' (usually elected representatives) will have the sovereign power to decide on the constitutional structure. We cannot even use borders to define a 'people', since borders are established as a result of wars and/or international agreements. They do not necessarily reflect the will of a given people to establish a sovereign state in that precise region.[2] As a result, the impossibility to have a clear and yet dynamic definition of 'a people' suggests that there are difficulties to empowering every single person (in particular non-citizens who lack the right to vote) subjected to the polity's norms through the right to political participation. Moreover, the imprecise definition of 'a people' suggests that the very constitutional structure may fall short of ensuring that all the people who are subjected to this structure and its basic norms can also be crafters and owners of this structure and its norms.[3] As I will explain, this and the effects of globalisation lead to the misrepresentation

[1] 'Democratic theory or constitutionalist doctrines do not provide us with good reasons as to why the social extension of the people should be what it empirically is (cf. Habermas 1996, 139f.).' C. Offe, 'Homogeneity and Constitutional Democracy', V.E. Richard and N. Stehr (eds.), *Governing Modern Societies* (University of Toronto Press, 2000) 177–211, at 151.

[2] See, for instance, the state borders inherited through the decolonisation period and the conflicts between ethnical groups that have existed since.

[3] There may be individuals who are subject to the state's laws but who do not belong to the 'governing people' (citizens) and who have fewer or no rights and obligations – for instance,

of individuals within the state. If this is so, the constitution and state laws will probably not reflect the moral and political choices of those parts of the population that are bound by the constitution but not fully included in it or able to change it, excluding them as full citizens. The two democratic deficits identified here (first, the impossibility to influence one's constitution and, second, the impossibility to have constitutional systems that are inclusive with all individuals subjected to them) turn contemporary democracies into infinite or perpetually imperfect systems. Since it is difficult to imagine each and every individual living within a state empowered as a *de facto* sovereign, democracy will never be fully achieved (and is thus infinitely imperfect). Yet, there are possibilities to alleviate these imperfections, and judges are essential actors to count on for that.

In every constitutional democracy voters – comprised only of a part of the population, excluding for instance underage, convicted individuals, non-citizens, individuals with a certain gender or ethnicity, etc. – give a mandate to a particular group of people who, in turn, will determine both the content of the law and who is bound by the law. Such a privileged group of people (usually members of the executive and legislative branches of government) can change the content of the constitution (constitutional reform) as well as impose a particular authoritative reading of the constitutional order (law-making and legal interpretation). The latter is also performed by the judiciary. Courts regularly interpret the meaning of the law in particular cases, including the meaning of constitutional norms. Often, courts' interpretations of constitutional norms will have no impact on the inclusiveness of norms and, hence, on their democratic pedigree. Yet, on other occasions, judicial interpretations can have a significant impact on the definition of the constitutional order and the 'inclusiveness effect' of its norms. This turns judicial decisions into milestones of the state's democratic pedigree; that is, judges simultaneously define the legal order and the *demos*, for judges are permanently choosing a given view of the legal system over competing ones and thus making the legal order more or less open to all individuals bound by state norms. In particular, the judicial has emerged as the state branch that is able to open up the legal order to the changes of the society when legislation (or, more importantly, the constitution) is unable to provide such flexibility. Thus, judicial review has been regarded by some as the chance to gain that

they do not have voting rights. The chain of accountability to these individuals is thus broken. It should be noted that I am not defining the people morally or ethnically but constitutionally, i.e. who is able to (re)define the constitution is a member of 'the people'.

'exception' or 'constitutional reading' that was previously excluding their interests – that is, the court is adding certain moral or religious codes or customs as possible readings of the normative structure while others are rejected or ignored.[4] If people are bound by laws that do not take into account their preferences (from moral, religious, ethnic, cultural or other perspectives), each of these individuals can become, from a legal perspective, a 'non-person.'[5] As a result, they cannot be said to be part of the *demos*, or ultimately to hold membership within the sovereign united people. From this, it can be seen that when a state's institutions, including the judiciary, make or interpret the law, this process goes far beyond ensuring respect for the rule of law. Therefore, to ensure the functioning of a constitutional democracy, state institutions have a duty to make sure that an *inclusive* reading of the constitutional order and law is privileged. This addresses internal claims for more rights by those who feel misrepresented (e.g. undocumented immigrants) or who do not wish to be represented (aspirations for independence within the state), and allows for the greatest possible representation of the people who are bound by the decisions of these state institutions. It is important to highlight such internal function. Moreover, with globalisation and the increase in so-called judicial dialogue, I argue later on that courts could take on the same role that they are playing at the national scale to ensure an inclusive reading of the constitution also at a transnational scale.

The fact that most states are democratic constitutions does not mean that all share the same degree of 'democratic imperfectness'. Many elements, such as how old a constitution is, whether it is easy or not to modify the constitution, whether citizens are involved in such renewal, whether judicial review is allowed, or whether the system is made of a small and homogenous society, directly affect the chances of having a more or less inclusive and thus democratic system. Yet, most of the time we will see how those living under a constitution struggle to adapt it as much as possible to their will. As John Elster observed, the paradox of representative democracies is that 'each

[4] Examples are decisions as to whether marriage is an institution open to same-sex couples or whether exceptions to the obligation to wear a helmet can be accepted based on e.g. freedom of religion. An example of the latter is the exception granted to Sikhs not to take off their turbans to wear helmets. These examples show how a particular interpretation will help to build up a more or less inclusive legal order by allowing specific groups (gay couples or Sikhs) to feel part of the legal order by having their particular circumstances taken into account or not.

[5] Or the people's 'political death,' as Nancy Fraser would coin, taking Hannah Arendt's work into consideration. N. Fraser, 'Reframing Justice in a Globalizing World', *New Left Review* 36 (2005) 69–88, at 76.

generation wants to be free to bind its successors, while not being bound by its predecessors'.[6] While constitutions are only meaningful if they are established to remain, a durable constitution has to adjust to avoid becoming a tyrant structure that oppresses a sovereign society in permanent evolution. It will be argued that courts (in particular through judicial dialogue) are key to allow such stable but flexible constitutions (through 'detachment' and 'continuity', as explained in subsection 16.4.2.1) by offering inclusive interpretation of the law and the 'people' through adjudication.

I will now discuss how globalisation challenges state power. Non-national decisions affect nationals through transnational economic, governmental or legal processes, and intensify the problems arising from constitutional democracies' intrinsic imperfections. In the following, I highlight some of these aggravations, focusing on constitutional democracies' decreasing capacities to provide justice and to decide on their national legal frameworks.

16.2.2 Globalisation Aggravating Constitutional Democracies' Problems

Globalisation not only aggravates the democratic deficit of the state; it also exposes that the Westphalian paradigm - which describes the international arena as a sum of fully sovereign, powerful and autonomous states - is no longer accurate. One of the many effects of globalisation is that sovereignty is now shared between many governmental and non-governmental global actors. Important state functions such as national law-making processes and policy-making are shared with actors that are not members of the polity. As a result, the authority of the state's *demos* has decreased to a great extent.

The analysis of globalisation's effects on states has taken a number of different forms. Some authors have approached it through culture,[7] others through law (studying in particular the exportation of constitutionalism),[8]

[6] J. Elster, *Ulysses and the Sirens. Studies in Rationality and Irrationality* (Cambridge: Cambridge University Press, 1979) at 94.

[7] Arguing that globalisation is a tool for the imposition of particular cultural practices on people around the globe. See, for instance, J. Tully, 'On Law, Democracy and Imperialism', S. Tierney and E. A. Christodoulidis (eds.), *Political Theory and Public Law* (London: Ashgate, 2008) 69–102; see also T. Risse, 'Social Constructivism Meets Globalization' and J. Tomlinson, 'Globalization and Cultural Analysis', D. Held and A. McGrew (eds.), *Globalization Theory. Approaches and Controversies* (Cambridge: Polity Press, 2007) 126–47 and 148–70 respectively.

[8] G. Palombella and N. Walker (eds.), *Relocating the Rule of Law* (Portland: Hart Publishing, 2009). See also Likosky who argues that 'national constitutions are developed and

or even through sociological and economic approaches to globalisation.[9] Regardless of their chosen perspective, to a varying degree, all analysts recognise a risk of imposing foreign law, economic systems or social practices through global interaction.[10] The risk lies in the erosion of the sovereignty connected to a national 'people' and the homogenisation process caused by globalisation.

Looking in particular at the changes that national legal structures undergo through globalisation processes, many authors identify different ways in which law is involved in this global interaction.[11] Some observe that globalisation can involve the expropriation of control of a polity through law, depriving its people of their sovereignty, for example when a polity comes under belligerent occupation.[12] On other occasions, the law-making process of indigenous government may be substituted by conditional agreements that invite a state to make legal changes at the domestic level.[13] There are also examples of a less direct influence on domestic law

applied to countries around the world as if they were countries within a single country.' M. Likosky (ed.), *Transnational Legal Processes, Globalisation and Power Disparities* (London: Butterworth, 2002), at foreword vii.

9 The sociological approach analyses globalisation through an anthropological lens. We can find many contributors of the 'law and society' approach in the School of Law of the University of Wisconsin (e.g. D. Trubek). S.F. Moore or S.E. Merry are further examples. S.E. Merry, 'From Law and Colonialism to Law and Globalization: A Review Essay on Martin Chanock, Law, Custom, and Social Order: The Colonial Experience in Malawi and Zambia', *Law and Social Inquiry* 28:2 (2003) 269–90, at 10. The economic approach associates globalisation with a particular economic system that is being spread – namely, capitalism: see B. de Sousa Santos, *La reinvención del estado y del estado plurinacional* (Bolivia: Alianza Internacional CENDA-CEJIS-CEDIB, 2007).

10 Be it through friendly or unfriendly mechanisms as we will later see in this section.

11 Nicolaidis and Kleinfeld have derived four abstract types describing the role of law in globalisation processes: bottom-up and top-down mechanisms, and from coercive diplomacy to enmeshment diplomacy. The four different mechanisms of influence have an impact upon different segments of the institutional and social structure of the polity (civil servants, civil society, government, the judiciary, etc.). R. Kleinfeld and K. Nicolaidis, 'Can a Post-colonial Power Export the Rule of Law? Elements of a General Framework', Palombella and Walker (eds.), Relocating, *supra* note 8, at 152.

12 Clear examples are the control of Germany after the Second World War or, more recently, of Afghanistan or Iraq by occupying powers. See also the discussion by U. Mattei, 'Patterns of African Constitution in the Making', M. Likosky (ed.), Transnational Legal Processes, *supra* note 8, at 275–76.

13 An example here is the collaboration between the EU and African, Caribbean and Pacific (ACP) countries put in place by the Cotonou Agreement. This agreement between the EU and the ACP countries has the main purpose of redressing poverty and ensuring sustainable development. Another example is provided within the EU's accession process of new member states. From Spain, Greece and Portugal, to the more recent accessions in Eastern Europe, the respective states had to change their constitutions and legal order substantively

and law-making processes. Among them is the 'assistance' that is given to polities to (re)construct their national legal systems. This is often done by international organisations such as the World Trade Organization (WTO) in economic matters, or the Council of Europe (CoE) in matters relating to human rights and democracy. This influence may be less evident, but is nonetheless very effective. For instance, many judges and lawyers have been trained by these organisations. Finally, a fourth type of influence on states' legal orders through international interaction in a globalised world is a non-institutionalised one. This is the influence of private corporations that are able to produce significant legal changes inside a particular polity. Most of the time, this is achieved through a mediator placed within the affected polity that has influence on its internal law-making processes (members of parliament or judges).[14]

Accordingly, states are no longer seen as autonomous in the design of their democratic order. Nancy Fraser has argued that such 'heteronymous states' fail to maintain the chain of democratic accountability and, ultimately, are unable to provide a framework of justice to their citizens. If that is the case, should we favour a global perspective where the state, while remaining an important actor, is no longer the place where justice is best upheld, and thus look for a different structure to substitute the Westphalian format (first option)? Or should we continue to view the state as the best functional unit in which individual justice can be provided (second option)?

The first option – to move beyond a state-centred system – reveals a sceptical attitude towards the continued capacity of states to provide a normative framework of socio-political and economic justice. This option is supported by Fraser. She proposes the building of a system of representation beyond the state, encompassing all actors that interact in the global sphere to ensure their accountability: a 'meta-political democracy'.[15] It is

in order to comply with the requirements of the EU. We can see the influence of the EU particularly well in the case of Spain. The persistent resistance of the Spanish political class to engage in constitutional reform has been given up only to recognise the EU in the Spanish constitution (through the modification of article 13.2 of the Spanish Constitution – reform of 27 August 1992). Even then, the political class tried to persuade the Spanish Constitutional Court that no reform was necessary. V. Ferreres Comella, 'Una defensa de la rigidez constitucional', *Cuadernos de filosofía del derecho* 23 (2000), 29–48, at 32. A second reform was due to the pressure of the EU within the context of the economic crisis in 2011 to ensure economic stability (reforming article 135 of the Spanish Constitution).

[14] Pharmaceutical companies or technological corporations are among the big multinationals criticised for their role in exercising undue pressure on governments to adopt favourable laws that benefit these corporations.

[15] N. Fraser, Reframing Justice, *supra* note 5, at 86.

attractive to call for the application of the all-affected principle worldwide, that is, a principle that would ensure that everyone has the possibility to have a say in any matter that influences him/her.[16] Yet, how is it possible to articulate a system of representation based on this principle on a global scale when, as I have argued in subsection 16.2.1, it is not even put into practice within democratic states? If we have problems delimiting within the state who the 'real' sovereign is, how can we ever locate an authority on a global scale? Such a global authority seems implausible and undesirable. It seems implausible because we seem to be moving towards a more multilateral world. And it seems undesirable because if there is something that can be learned from colonialism and globalisation, it is that there is a plurality of polities in the world. These polities should not be forced into one structure, but rather, we should aim to find the appropriate mechanisms to let them coexist with their different political models.

Therefore, the second option seems to be more plausible. Today, the state-centred framework remains an optimal legal structure from which representation and agency can be organised and exercised, even when we are dealing with global matters. It might be that in the future another structure will be more suitable, but for now, the costs of abandoning the organisational framework that the state provides seem too high. In addition, a system of representation beyond the state would burden the people, as they would face a decrease of democratic accountability through the elimination of national democratic institutions and procedures. States are still the most prominent actors in the international arena, and individuals still live and function primarily within states. In fact, globalisation points to the need to reinvent the state from within and the role it should play in a globalised world.

This brings us to the second option introduced earlier: today we have to attach 'the maintenance of multicultural dialogue' to the Westphalian label, as opposed to the homogenisation and hegemony that globalisation brings.[17] The updating of the Westphalian paradigm will be performed best by looking at global interactions and their consequences through the lens of cosmopolitanism. I argue that such reinvention of the state in accordance with cosmopolitan theory will help redress what Fraser calls 'misrepresentation' and the democratic deficit described in subsection 16.2.1. Such reinvention will, without any doubt, affect the state's institutional design,

[16] For more on this principle applied in a transnational sphere, see J. Karlsson, *Affected and Subjected – The All-Affected Principle in Transnational Democratic Theory* (Berlin: Wissenschaftszentrum für Sozialforschung, 2006).

[17] de Sousa Santos, La Reinvención, *supra* note 9.

and domestic courts will play an important role in these reinvention processes. They can help to rebuild the link between states and individuals, and between national and global authorities. This can happen through the courts' inclusive interpretation and application of domestic and foreign and international law, and in particular through their engagement in judicial dialogue with their foreign national and international counterparts.

To explain this further, in Section 16.3 I argue that cosmopolitanism is an optimal theoretical model for understanding how globalised states can be reinvented in such a way that authority is returned to individuals, and the above-discussed problems of misrepresentation are addressed. I then move to show that judicial dialogue plays an important role in this process (Section 16.4). This, in turn, also furthers our understanding about the desired purposes and effects of transnational judicial dialogue.

16.3 Cosmopolitanism's Answer to the Problems of Constitutional Democracies in a Globalised World

First I introduce the notion of cosmopolitan democracies, the functioning of which should be guided by cosmopolitan norms (subsection 16.3.1). I then further explain the qualities of cosmopolitan norms, in particular what distinguishes them from norms of public international law and their role in a cosmopolitan democracy (subsection 16.3.2), before I elaborate further on the question of how the establishment of cosmopolitan democracies can address the problems related to misrepresentation (subsection 16.3.3).

16.3.1 Introducing the Notion of Cosmopolitan Democracies

Cosmopolitan approaches to globalisation do not suggest establishing an overriding global authority that simply disempowers the state. The cosmopolitan perspective that is adopted in this chapter is one that sees globalisation as an opportunity to build a multilevel structure of power beyond the state. It does not advocate replacing the state structure, but promotes the establishment of an order in which the different levels can co-exist and benefit from mutual cross-fertilisation. For the state to be able to represent its people effectively and provide justice, it must be ensured that states keep their capacity to resist any global power that unduly limits its abilities to represent its people and ensure individual justice. The way in which Heinz Klug depicts the new democratic South Africa as a globalised state exemplifies this. In Klug's words, one has to go beyond the concept of 'globalizing constitutionalism'[18] – which focuses on the exportation of constitutional models as a form of contemporary imperialism – and 'understand the specifics of its [constitutionalism's] incorporation into particular national legal systems'.[19] Klug thus stresses that in today's globalised states, the crafting of a national constitution is determined neither only by national powers nor only by global actors. Instead, it is a blending process wherein the national actors involved are able to use international or transnational sources in order to develop ideas on what a constitution could look like. From this perspective, globalisation allows the forging of new norms that are neither purely internal nor a pure imposition from the international sphere. As argued here, such (mixed) norms can be of a cosmopolitan character. The fact that most states are constitutional states has been key to the forging of a cosmopolitan understanding of constitutional matters (e.g. the allocation of power within the state, institutional design and human rights).[20] It is this area in which judicial dialogue occurs most often, and thus promotes the building of a cosmopolitan normative space through the constitutional lexicon.

The state that takes advantage of globalisation to increase internal democracy would fit with the type of cosmopolitan democracy that is developed in the writings of David Held. The notion of cosmopolitan democracy suggests mechanisms to be put in place within the state to secure democratic representation while taking account of the fact that states have to constantly relate to external actors at different levels of power in a globalised world.[21] In Held's account of cosmopolitanism, the main points of conversion between the diverse trends within cosmopolitan theories are '(i) egalitarian individualism, (ii) reciprocal recognition, and (iii) impartialist reasoning'.[22] In this reduction, one can recognise the core of Kant's *Perpetual Peace*, where 'hospitality' between peoples

[18] In the context of South African political reconstruction, Klug has defined 'globalizing constitutionalism' as follows: 'Even if we accept the empirical evidence that more and more nations have adopted written constitutions with bills of rights and have empowered their courts to uphold these new characters as the supreme law of the land, it is not self-evident that the outcome, or even the meaning of these new institutions, is the same in all these societies.' H. Klug, *Constituting Democracy: Law, Globalism and South Africa's Political Reconstruction* (Cambridge University Press, 2000) at 3.

[19] *Ibid.*

[20] On this, see the discussion by H. P. Glenn, 'Cosmopolitan Sources I: Constitutionalism', H.P. Glenn (ed.) *The Cosmopolitan State* (Oxford University Press, 2013) 203–13, at 203.

[21] D. Held, 'The Changing Contours of Political Community: Rethinking Democracy in the Context of Globalization', R.V. Ericson and N. Stehr (eds.), *Governing Modern Societies* (University of Toronto Press, 2000) at 57.

[22] D. Held, *Cosmopolitanism. Ideals and Realities* (Cambridge: Polity Press, 2010) at 15.

is key to understanding the Kantian cosmopolitan constitution.[23] Kant's 'hospitality' can be defined as the right of every human being to be treated with respect everywhere, regardless of state borders. Most followers of Kantian thought see human beings as universally equal: everyone deserves an equal treatment from a moral and legal perspective.[24] In cosmopolitan democracies, justice should thus be delivered to individuals rather than to citizens.

I will now move to further describe the qualities of cosmopolitan norms. I will do so through Seyla Benhabib's work. Benhabib has focused on understanding how the core idea that 'law is made by the sovereign' can apply in the global context where states take the form of cosmopolitan democracies. Looking at the nature of these norms will enable us to see the effects of judicial dialogue, for dialogue will contribute to the building of cosmopolitan norms. Ultimately, understanding the nature of cosmopolitan norms helps me to show how the judiciary's work can contribute to addressing the problem of misrepresentation that was identified earlier in this chapter. This is because the creation of cosmopolitan norms through judicial dialogue can contribute to the building of a cosmopolitan space that can provide individuals with a new *locus* where they can seek justice, and thus partially overcome the shortfalls of national democracy.

16.3.2 *The Nature of Cosmopolitan Norms*

Reforming states into cosmopolitan democracies with the help of cosmopolitan norms addresses the representation problem. Cosmopolitan norms are called to play a role at the supranational level, and therefore it is helpful to look at their relationship (if any) with norms of public international law (PIL). Benhabib has argued that PIL norms differ from cosmopolitan norms, and that it is necessary to show the existence of the latter. I will argue that cosmopolitan norms are in the making, but they are not an autonomous category. Their existence depends on a constant check with other categories of norms, be it PIL or national norms. Nonetheless, certain norms have attributes that escape both PIL's or national norms' logic. It is these different types of emerging norms that can be called 'cosmopolitan'.

[23] I. Kant, *Project for a Perpetual Peace: A Philosophical Essay* (London: Vernor and Hood, 1796).

[24] See e.g. G. Brock, 'Rethinking Cosmopolitanism versus Non-Cosmopolitanism Debate: An Introduction', G. Brock (ed.), *Cosmopolitanism versus Non-Cosmopolitanism: Critiques, Defenses, Reconceptualizations* (Oxford University Press, 2013) 1–31.

In her work, Benhabib uses the European Convention on Human Rights (ECHR)[25] and the EU Charter of Fundamental Rights[26] as examples of laws falling under the category of cosmopolitan norms.[27] As texts that have been approved by states within international organisations that are bound by PIL, it might appear awkward to move them into another normative category, the category of cosmopolitan norms. Why would it nonetheless be possible to argue that these texts reflect cosmopolitan norms? What are the qualities of cosmopolitan norms?

One of the characteristics of these cosmopolitan norms is, following Benhabib, the fact that they are not merely treaties among states that regulate inter-state matters, but norms that 'bind and bend'[28] the state's sovereignty in regard to the way in which states relate to the individuals under their jurisdiction. This implies that states cannot invoke their sovereign power to not comply with human rights law, or to not apply these treaties within their territory. In short, Benhabib argues that states are no longer free to ignore certain international agreements only because states have the sovereign right to do so. PIL scholarship and practice has over the last decades recognised that the classical state-based approach does not describe today's complex reality. Moreover, PIL has gradually focused also on regulating actors other than states, such as individuals or non-state actors, as agents that influence the creation of PIL norms and are protected by them. As a result, what differentiates cosmopolitan norms from PIL norms is the fact that state sovereignty is no longer sufficient to avoid complying with certain obligations. Most authors who work with cosmopolitanism agree that one of the most prominent examples of norms that transgress the classical state-centred realm of PIL are human rights.[29] In Rainer Bauböck's words,

> [T]he human rights revolution after 1945 is certainly the most important cosmopolitan achievement so far. It overturned the previous conception of states as the exclusive subjects of international law and normatively disconnected rights from national membership.[30]

[25] Convention for the Protection of Human Rights and Fundamental Freedoms (4 November 1950) 213 UNTS 222; 312 ETS 5, entered into force 3 September 1953.

[26] Charter of Fundamental Rights of the European Union, Official Journal C 326, 26 October 2012.

[27] S. Benhabib, *Another Cosmopolitanism* (Oxford University Press, 2008), at 15, 16 and 71.

[28] *Ibid.*, at 15–16.

[29] See for example K. Traisbach, 'The Individual in International Law' (Irmgard Coninx Foundation, the Social Science Research Centre Berlin & Humboldt University, 2006) available at www.irmgard-coninx-stiftung.de/fileadmin/user_upload/pdf/archive/Knut_Traisbach.pdf.

[30] R. Rauböck, 'Political Community Beyond the Sovereign State, Supranational Federalism, and Transnational Minorities', S. Vertovec and R. Cohen (eds.) *Conceiving Cosmopolitanism. Theory, Context, and Practice* (Oxford University Press, 2002) 110–36, at 115.

Beyond international human rights treaties, there are national norms, national and international jurisprudence, advocacy, practice, scholarship and so on that converges in the making of a normative space in the area of human rights. It is therefore difficult to assign human rights exclusively to the realm of PIL.

Returning to Kant's notion of hospitality protected by cosmopolitan norms, human rights appeal to the state not only as actor and recipient of a particular law (a PIL norm) but also as a political entity that 'frames' (organises and protects) all individuals under the jurisdiction of the state. Within the last example the state is obliged by cosmopolitan norms as a layer that accompanies PIL's obligations. Individuals are also addressees of cosmopolitan norms – they are compelled to embrace this hospitality and act in kind; that is, not only states have a duty to individuals, but all individuals are bound by these obligations towards fellow human beings. Benhabib uses Kant's ideas to propose a new understanding of sovereignty beyond the state. In this post-national scenario, cosmopolitan norms bridge 'a conceptual and juridical space for a domain of rights-relations that would be binding on non-state actors as well as state actors when they come into contact with individuals who are not members of their own polities'.[31] Benhabib argues that individuals 'own' these cosmopolitan norms, regardless of their citizenship or their state of residence. This forges a cosmopolitan order (of human rights) that is directed to states and individuals. As a result, when states refuse to respect and protect *cosmopolitan* human rights, they lose their right to do as they please.[32] In reality, many states can do (and do) as they please regardless of international human rights norms. However, to some extent states are held accountable internationally, even if only through the criticism voiced by other nations and/or by civil society. Held has also put it plainly: 'The first principle [of cosmopolitanism] is that the ultimate units of moral concern are individual human beings, not states or other particular forms of human association'.[33] This idea is common to many different cosmopolitan schools. Regardless of whether we hold a strong cosmopolitan view of the world (e.g. that there is a global constitution)[34] or a very thin cosmopolitan view of the world

[31] Benhabib, Another Cosmopolitanism, *supra* note 27, at 24. She proposes to see this change through international human rights norms and, in particular, through three notions: crimes against humanity, humanitarian interventions and transnational migration.

[32] *Ibid.*, at 27–31.

[33] Held, Cosmopolitanism, *supra* note 22, at 69.

[34] E.-U. Petersmann, 'The WTO Constitution and Human Rights', *Journal of Int'l Economic L.* 3:1 (2000) 19–25.

(residual constitutionalism),[35] as Posner suggests, all those accepting the cosmopolitan ideal to some degree agree on one element: that aliens have at least some rights,[36] and those rights are cosmopolitan norms by definition because they are not directly linked to the relationship between an individual and a state through nationality, nor are they necessarily part of an international treaty (PIL). They are constantly redefined by a bulk of legal interpretations the sources of which are national laws and jurisprudence as much as international treaties and jurisprudence.

16.3.3 Cosmopolitan Democracies Redressing Misrepresentation and Connected Problems

This brings us back to the question of how to redress the problems experienced by misrepresented individuals in a globalised world. This approach to cosmopolitanism offers interesting options in this regard. Under cosmopolitanism, the obligation to promote and protect human rights would not come from the fact that individuals share an association (i.e. membership in the same legal order) or from international human rights treaties, but from the equality of all human beings that allows them to enjoy those rights. Instead of presenting human rights as imposed norms, a cosmopolitan reading appeals to the logic of transnational dialogue on human rights and their incorporation into local systems *inter alia* through their blending with existing domestic law.

These qualities allow judges to deliver justice for individuals within states, if all involved actors (in particular judges) are aware of the cosmopolitan qualities of these norms as well as the process of their making. In order to build a true cosmopolitan legal order that allows for a redress of democratic misrepresentation, individuals have to be able to enjoy the benefits of the incorporation of international and transnational norms and practices into their national legal order. To achieve this, people must first be able to acknowledge the origin of these (cosmopolitan) human rights norms and practices, which means that authorities (e.g. judges) must be transparent when it comes to the incorporation of transnational norms, principles and practices into the local legal framework. Secondly, the incorporation of transnational practices into the national order must be justified by the fact that such incorporation enhances local justice. If these

[35] E.A. Posner, 'Boumediene and the Uncertain March of Judicial Cosmopolitanism,' *Public L. and Legal Theory Working Paper Series* (University of Chicago Press, 2008) at 10–11.

[36] *Ibid.*

two conditions were met, a cosmopolitan legal order could progress and contribute to redressing the increasing inability of states to provide justice at the domestic level.[37]

I can illustrate this through the example that I will be using later on, the case of human rights and new technologies. Currently, the framework of regulations in this area is fragmented. Individuals are to a large extent affected by decisions that escape the control of national authorities and thus the reach of national accountability mechanisms. For instance, a given privacy regulation in state A will have no impact when Internet content providers are in other jurisdictions, although citizens from state A will access that Internet content. To be effective, norms regulating this field have to undergo permanent changes to keep up with technological developments, they have to involve private entities in the regulatory process and they must be able to be challenged and enforced in a transnational domain. We thus have an example of how democratic oversight can be weakened if individuals cannot see their rights respected in the world of the Internet. We will later see that there have been many important judicial decisions relating to human rights and new technologies. These decisions have built transnational consensus, for each ruling has taken into consideration rulings from other courts. Such consensus has influenced state regulators, regional actors with regulatory powers such as the EU and the conduct of private companies. Within states, such rulings have provided justice in an area that is dominated by the activities of non-state actors. As a result, justice has returned to the state through the interpretation of national law together with transnational and international regulations and practices. This has helped to give answers to challenging questions within states. At the same time, these decisions have informed other global actors too, and invited them to consider the reading that a particular national authority has given to a certain notion, e.g. the 'right to oblivion' or 'to be forgotten' (in connection with the right to receive and impart information and the right to private life) at a certain point in time.[38]

The question can now be posed about the mechanisms and institutions that we have today to promote cosmopolitan norms in order to smooth

[37] Of course, many cosmopolitanists will not agree on the need of such awareness. Jeremy Waldron, for instance, claims that cosmopolitan norms are built with the contribution of many different disciplines through the multi-layered interaction of world citizens. J. Waldron, 'Cosmopolitan Norms', Benhabib (ed.), Another Cosmopolitanism, *supra* note 27, 83–101, at 98.

[38] Case C-131/12, *Google Spain SL, Google Inc. v. Agencia Española de Protección de Datos, Mario Costeja González*, [2014], ECR I-0000; ECLI:EU:C:2014:317.

out the problem of misrepresentation and inability to provide justice to individuals within states. Earlier, the establishment of an overarching international authority was discarded.[39] Therefore, we need to turn to the multiple authorities that currently exist at the national and global levels (state and non-state authorities), first and foremost the globalised states and their organs.

This brings us finally to the role of domestic courts and their engagement in transnational judicial dialogue in this process: national courts as strategically well-placed actors that can be decisive in the transformation of the national and international legal orders into a cosmopolitan legal order, and thereby the transformation of states into cosmopolitan democracies. Judges can contribute to the crafting of a cosmopolitan legal order that ensures a given set of norms to all human beings within the borders of their jurisdiction. Moreover, domestic courts can reinforce the state's authority to rule on a given matter of national and international interest in line with cosmopolitan norms. What we have to consider next is whether courts are adequately equipped to help to make cosmopolitan norms as well as ensure their implementation, first and foremost through engagement in transnational judicial dialogue.

16.4 The Role of Judicial Dialogue in Building Cosmopolitan Democracies

To answer these questions, this section first introduces the changing role of domestic courts in globalised states, including their potential to enhance democracy. This will further clarify why it is reasonable to rely on domestic courts to further the creation of cosmopolitan democracies and cosmopolitan norms (subsection 16.4.1). Second, the nature of transnational judicial dialogue is elaborated on, and it is explained why domestic courts' engagement in transnational judicial dialogue can indeed contribute to the creation of cosmopolitan norms (subsection 16.4.2). Third, concrete examples are given of how domestic courts' engagement in judicial dialogue indeed can help to redress states' democratic misrepresentation problem as well as their decreasing capacity to provide justice through their contribution to forge cosmopolitan norms that govern cosmopolitan democracies (subsection 16.4.3).

Supreme and constitutional courts are the paradigmatic institutions to study here, since they have the capacity to impose a particular reading of

[39] See subsection 16.3.1.

the constitution of the respective polity as explained in subsection 16.2.1.[40] When these courts select an interpretation from competing ones, they are privileging an interpretation of the norms involved in the case and determining the scope of national justice: they are defining whether a bigger or smaller part of the population will feel included as members of the polity through the interpretation privileged by the decision. Courts are also able to insert interpretations that have been provided by other national or international courts. Here is where the possibilities to forge legal arguments that bridge national and transnational perspectives may contribute to the forging of cosmopolitan norms, as is further explained in the following sections.

16.4.1 Domestic Courts' Authority to Become Global Players

It is not by chance that Polibus referred to the magistrate who was in charge of interpreting the law as *cosmopoli*.[41] As will be shown in detail here, we can also observe today how judges contribute to the making of a cosmopolitan legal order when they engage in transnational judicial dialogue. But how can judges help to enhance cosmopolitan *democracy* within globalised states if, traditionally, the judiciary is the least democratic branch in the national legal order? I will not be able to enter into the complex debate around the democratic pedigree of the judiciary, but I will mention some relevant findings. I should start with national judges' and courts' authority. In the last four decades, the judiciary has strengthened its reputation as a reliable institution of the globalised state. This is due to its capacity to answer core constitutional questions through developing and even changing the constitution in order to adapt it to the demands of the globalised society. Two processes exemplify this phenomenon: the national judiciaries' roles in processes of political transitions and their roles in increasingly judicialised states and international society.

Concerning the first example, an analysis of how Central and Eastern European countries and South Africa have proceeded through political transition reveals two common elements in these transition processes.

[40] I thus leave the door open to include any judicial institution that would fit within the profile of a court that is able to provide an authoritative reading of the constitution into our analysis.

[41] M. Giangiulio, 'Ordinamenti pubblici e comunità politica in magna grecia. Ancora sui regimini a numero fisso', A. D'Atena and E. Lanzillotta (eds.), *Da Omero alla Costituzione europea: Costituzionalismo antico e moderno* (Roma: Tored, 2003) 13–31, at 20.

First, the participation of global entities played a considerable role in the transition processes, in particular the CoE and the EU. Second, in many of these countries, a supreme or constitutional court has been one of the main institutions that led the socio-political change.[42] In many Central and Eastern European countries, no constituent assemblies had been held in the transition of the respective polities. Instead, active high courts often articulated the basic political and social contours of the new polities, particularly in the area of fundamental rights and liberties.[43] The case of South Africa is also indicative for the pivotal role that high courts can play in the crafting of 'new' norms. Since the judiciary had for a long time been a hostage of the apartheid government, many people expected a societal scepticism towards the new South African Constitutional Court, but the new democratic judicial structure turned out to be very popular. This has been attributed to the South African Constitutional Court's active participation in the articulation of fundamental rules for the new polity.[44]

Moreover, it can be argued that the progressive judicialisation within and between states as a consequence of globalisation has empowered domestic courts, while the executive or legislative branches have in some situations become less able to act. A 'judicialised world' seems to be an answer to the increasing limitations faced by national legislative and executive branches due to the loss of some of their autonomy as domestic policymakers. By contrast, domestic courts are still able to update the constitutional framework of a particular polity with considerable autonomy.[45]

[42] See, for instance, the well-documented role of Taiwan's Constitutional Court, which 'has been praised by many for facilitating Taiwan's relatively smooth and rapid transition to democracy, and for proving itself a strong guardian of individual rights and freedoms'. D.S. Law and W. Chang, 'The Limits of Global Judicial Dialogue', *Washington L. Rev. Association*, 86:523 (2011) 523–77, at 548.

[43] U. K. Preuss, 'The Exercise of Constituent Power in Central and Eastern Europe', M. Loughlin and N. Walker (eds.), *The Paradox of Constitutionalism: Constituent power and Constitutional Form* (Oxford University Press, 2007) 211–29, at 228; see also, K.L. Scheppele, 'Democracy by Judiciary. Or, Why Courts can be More Democratic than Parliaments', M. Krygier, W. Sadurski and A. Czarnota (eds.), *Rethinking the Rule of Law after Communism* (Budapest: CEU Press, 2005) 25–60, at 25; R. Uitz, *Constitutions, Courts, and History: Historical Narratives in Constitutional Adjudication* (Budapest: Central European University Press, 2005); and W. Sadurski *et al.* (eds.), *Spreading Democracy and the Rule of Law?: The Impact of EU Enlargement on the Rule of law, Democracy and Constitutionalism in Post-communist Legal Orders* (Dordrecht: Springer, 2006).

[44] See the observation by Klug: '[U]nderstanding the "new faith" in the judiciary must be sought in the particular dynamics of the democratic transition'. Klug, Constituting Democracy *supra* note 18, at 47.

[45] As Joakim Nergelius observes, 'The increased powers for courts gives, in combination with a lack of power and authority for political bodies throughout the world, new

An example can be found in Finland. In March 2000, for the first time in its history, Finland adopted a single formal constitution, which through its section 106 (*expressis verbis*) gave domestic courts the power to review the constitutionality of ordinary laws. Finland had never felt the need before to have a body other than the elected representatives that controlled the constitutionality of the law.[46] It is reasonable to argue that with this change in its constitution, Finland reacted to the ever-increasing international pressure on the independence of the Finnish polity. Its 'new' review powers enabled the Finnish Supreme Court to also review the constitutionality of EU law implemented in Finland. The two events of becoming part of the EU in 1995 and setting up a mechanism for the judicial control of constitutionality of laws in 2000 seem to correlate. They reflect the aim to strengthen the protection of the fundamental values of the Finnish constitution through the state branch that remains more autonomous vis-à-vis the EU: the judiciary.[47]

It seems, then, that many courts have made up for their lack of democratic pedigree with an authority that comes from placing individuals at the centre of interpretative bargains between competing understandings of multi-level norms. Are all judges involved in this 'push' towards judicialisation? Clearly, international tribunals and quasi-judicial bodies are involved because they interpret international, regional and often national norms.[48] However, at the centre of this analysis are national courts. I aim

perspectives on the old discussion regarding the separation of powers.' J. Nergelius, 'North and South: Can the Nordic States and the European Continent Find Each Other in the Constitutional Area – or are They too Different?', M. Scheinin (ed.), *The Welfare State and Constitutionalism – Nordic Perspectives* (Copenhagen: Nordic Council of Ministers, 2001), 79–94, at 79. See also N. Walker, 'Beyond Boundary Disputes and Basic Grids: Mapping the Global Disorder of Normative Orders', *Int'l J. of Constitutional L.* 6:3–4 (2008) 373–96, at 394.

46 Nordic countries are small, rather homogeneous and have traditionally entered into a limited number of compromises with international organisations. This assured the functioning of a free but socially controlled legislative and executive. J. Husa, *Nordic Reflections on Constitutional Law: A Comparative Nordic Perspective* (Frankfort: Peter Lang, 2002); Á. T., Árnason, 'Constitutionalism: Popular Legitimacy of the State?', M. Scheinin, Welfare State, *supra* note 45.

47 This follows the patterns established by the two decisions of the German Constitutional Court (BVerfG): Judgment of 29 May 1979, Judgment of 29 May 1974, 2 BvL 52/71 (*Solange I*) and Judgment of 22 October 1986, BvR 197/83 (*Solange II*). With these decisions, the Court wished to avoid the possibility that German obligations under EU law would undermine the protection offered under the German constitution (in particular human rights) standards. See also the report on practice by Justice A. Paulus in this volume (Chapter 9).

48 Since human rights are *par excellence* the norms that would fit into the cosmopolitan project, the ECtHR would be one of the institutions to study in detail. This is strengthened

to point out that national courts have also been responsible for the judicialisation of international relations. In addition, I will show how, through judicial dialogue, these domestic courts are able to craft cosmopolitan norms.

16.4.2 The Nature of Judicial Dialogue: Extent and Method

Judicial dialogue[49] is founded on the 'sympathetic consideration'[50] that courts have given to other courts' decisions. National courts 'consult a system-external source on the basis that there exists some ground of common understanding or affinity for taking that external source seriously'.[51]

Is judicial dialogue triggered out of respect and admiration for other judges' decisions? Is it a move that follows when the necessary piece for the judge's reasoning in a particular case cannot be found within the domestic legal order? Is it a mixture of both – convenience and admiration? Or is it also a question of availability? After all, not every court decision is available worldwide.[52]

Other contributors in this book describe the considerable extent to which domestic courts engage in judicial dialogue in different countries and regions of the world, and the context in which judicial dialogue is triggered.[53] In addition, there may be cases in which domestic courts use but do not directly cite foreign and international material in their judgments.

by the fact that the ECtHR's jurisprudence has far-reaching influence on the shaping of national and international human rights norms. Another example is provided by the CJEU. The CJEU addressed problems arising from the lack of human rights provisions in the founding treaties by borrowing member states' human rights jurisprudence and doctrine.

49 Also known as the migration of constitutional ideas; judicial borrowing; judicial cosmopolitanism or judicial use of comparative law. See A.-M. Slaughter, 'Judicial Globalization', *Virginia J. of Int'l L.* 40:4 (2000) 1103–24; J. Waldron, 'Foreign Law and the Modern *Ius Gentium*', *Harvard L. Rev.* 119:1 (2005) 129–47; S. Choudhry, 'Migration as a New Metaphor in Comparative Constitutional Law', S. Choudhry (ed.), *The Migration of Constitutional Ideas* (Cambridge University Press, 2006) 1–36; and M. Tushnet, 'The Possibilities of Comparative Constitutional Law', *Yale L. J.* 108:6 (1999) 1225–1309, at 1304.

50 Walker, Boundary Disputes, *supra* note 45, at 384.

51 *Ibid.* Such migration has fierce opponents (e.g. originalists such as Justice Scalia from the US Supreme Court) who, in a nutshell, reject the use of foreign and international material because this material has no authority within the United States. Another judge, Posner, swings between rejecting it and at the same time demanding global consensus – a sort of American perspective in the world. R.A. Posner, *How Judges Think* (Cambridge, MA: Harvard University Press, 2008), at 347–68.

52 See also Slaughter's remark that '[i]ndividual courts are often thus quite particular about when they borrow and from whom'. Slaughter, Judicial Globalization, *supra* note 49, at 73.

53 See in particular Chapters 2, 3 and 4 in this volume.

As David S. Law and Wen-Chen Chang put it, 'failure to cite foreign law does not denote failure to consider foreign law'.[54] In other words, judicial dialogue is not about citing, but about the actual use of comparative law. This recognition is key, especially for understanding the relationship between judicial dialogue, cosmopolitanism and the redress of the democratic deficit affecting constitutional democracies. It also helps to explain the existence of disguised dialogue ('indirect dialogue')[55] when foreign norms and argumentation are presented as national legal reasoning based on a particular national legal doctrine.[56] Judicial dialogue takes place to different degrees within each state, and when it happens, it might be evident or it might be disguised. From the perspective taken here, the purpose of judicial dialogue is to contribute to the making of a cosmopolitan legal space and the transformation of current constitutional democracies into cosmopolitan democracies. I will therefore argue in the following sections that in order to reach such purpose, first, the use of judicial dialogue has to increase and, second, 'indirect dialogue' has to gradually disappear in order to become a direct dialogue.

I can exemplify these ideas by returning to the discussion of the development of the protection of human rights in the Internet society. This example vividly shows how domestic courts' engagement in judicial dialogue can avoid the erosion of state authority and at the same time contribute to accepting that more and more actors, including non-state actors, craft multi-level norms. As described, the evolution of communication and information technologies has created many regulatory challenges for states and supranational organisations. The approach to regulate the Internet with the aim to protect the human rights to privacy or freedom of expression has taken neither a bottom-up nor a top-down approach. Instead, multiple actors are contributing to regulating the Internet. Among these actors are domestic and regional courts, which have a considerable influence on the making of 'Internet law' and policy. The German

[54] Law and Chang highlight that the Taiwan Constitutional Court is very active in the use of foreign law and jurisprudence, although that is not necessarily evident through citation of foreign material, but rather through the legal culture of Taiwan. Law and Chang, Judicial Dialogue, *supra* note 42, at 560. Another example is the practice of the French *Cour de Cassation*, which never cites foreign authorities due to sovereignty principles but will extensively use comparative law in its work. See Posner, Judges, *supra* note 51, at 212.

[55] See the introduction to this volume, subsection 1.2.1.

[56] As Bobek puts it, judicial dialogue exists but it is not always evident. Normally such dialogue takes place on the basis of national doctrine, where national scholarship has introduced foreign legal reasonings. M. Bobek, *Comparative Reasoning in European Supreme Courts* (Oxford University Press, 2013), at 193.

and Spanish constitutional courts have set important precedents in the construction of a right to informational self-determination.[57] The CJEU has joined these efforts *vis-à-vis* data privacy through its invalidation of the EU Data Retention Directive.[58] Through such collaboration, courts are building a cosmopolitan space covering the area of human rights and new technologies. They are also offering an opportunity to individuals to claim certain rights that the legal order under which they find themselves has not provided yet. Often, this is possible through the migration of foreign and international legal ideas into the national legal order through judicial dialogue.

16.4.2.1 Judicial Dialogue, Authority and National Autonomy

However, critical questions can be asked about this role of national courts. Are judges forcing the entrance of external normative interpretations to diminish national authority? Is the judges' engagement in judicial dialogue giving legal effect to the influence of public and private external actors?[59] These questions reflect the type of arguments that are made against judicial dialogue. Most of them revolve around the issue of authority and sovereignty, since judicial dialogue could diminish rather than strengthen national authority. I will start by arguing that domestic courts' engagement in judicial dialogue does not involve a loss of authority. After all, domestic judges are strongly committed to internal legality and will only use external sources that do not jeopardise state's authority. Many would still raise the objection that courts are the 'least democratic branch' and, therefore, that courts should not attempt to innovate in any sense, be it in the national or transnational sphere. This section aims to provide the theoretical background to support active judges and, in particular, the need to stimulate transnational judicial dialogue.

[57] The first example dates back from 1983: Federal Constitutional Court (BVerfG, Germany), Judgment of 15 December 1983, 1 BvR 209/83, 1 BvR 269/83, 1 BvR 362/83, 1 BvR 420/83, 1 BvR 440/83 and 1 BvR 484/83. For a detailed study of this jurisprudence, see C. Marsan Raventós, 'Data Retention and Security in Europe: Towards a New Right to Digital Privacy,' C. M. Akrivopoulou and N. Garipidis (eds.) *Human Rights and Risks in the Digital Era: Globalization and the Effects of Information Technologies* (Hershey: IGI Global, 2012) 46–66.

[58] Joined Cases C-293/12 and C-594/12, *Digital Rights Ireland and Seitlinger and others v. Minister for Communications, Marine and Natural Resources and others* [2014] ECR I-0000; ECLI:EU:C:2014:238, invalidating the EU Data Retention Directive (Council Directive 15 March 2006 on the retention of data generated or processed in connection with the provision of publicly available electronic communications services or of public communications networks and amending Directive 2002/58/EC, OJ L 105, 13 April 2006).

[59] S. Choundhry, Migration, *supra* note 49.

To find an answer to these questions and to highlight further how domestic courts' engagement in transnational judicial dialogue can redress the problems connected to misrepresentation, the work by John Hart Ely can be recalled. Ely stresses that what makes national courts important players in a democracy is not their expertise, but their perspective.[60] This special 'perspective' of courts, and its value for a democracy, can be viewed alongside the idea that judges embody detachment and continuity.[61] Domestic courts' perspective describes the need of any legal institution to find a middle way between acting within and maintaining the legal framework by which it is established and which it is meant to uphold (continuity); and to answer societal demands to ensure that the legal framework reflects recent developments, something that can sometimes only be achieved by the judiciary through looking outside the domestic legal framework (detachment).[62] Detachment refers to the capacity of the judiciary to decide when the constitutional framework is not sufficient to provide a satisfactory solution to a certain problem and, hence, to decide when there is a need to incorporate a new interpretation or reading of the legal matter at stake.[63] By identifying these moments, courts contribute to the redefinition of the legal order without disrupting it, which gives a chance to ensure effective representation of those individuals who felt excluded from the available interpretations until then. Due to the global judicialisation processes mentioned earlier, courts are able to redefine the legal order by bringing in solutions adopted in other legal settings. On the other hand, I have referred to 'continuity' or to 'non-disruption', which is part of the judiciary's perspective. A domestic court's role can never be to provide legal answers solely based on norms that lack authority within the respective domestic legal order. In addition, continuity captures the judiciary's capacity to act as the historical memory of the community – something that is also relevant to ensure effective identification of a society with

[60] J.H. Ely, *Democracy and Distrust: A Theory of Judicial Review* (Harvard University Press, 1980), at 102.

[61] The current author has coined this metaphor in her PhD dissertation. C. Marsan Reventós, *Recovering Constituent Power: The Constituent Role of Judges in Globalised States* (Florence: European University Institute, 2010).

[62] This issue is also discussed by Bruce Ackermann for the American context: B.A. Ackerman, 'The Storrs Lectures: Discovering the Constitution', *The Yale L. J.* 93:6 (1984) 1013–72, at 1020.

[63] This is clearly the scenario that Ely calls 'exit strategy', where the judiciary offers a solution to the plaintiff that could not have been reached without references to foreign or international material. Ely, Democracy and Distrust, *supra* note 60, at 179. Ackerman also depicts 'detachment'. Ackerman, Storr Lectures, *supra* note 62, at 1062.

its constitutional order. The judiciary body itself incorporates a sense of being present over long periods of time, as opposed to the discontinuity of governments and legislative bodies.[64] However, continuity also refers to the way the legal arguments are built and presented by the judiciary, including through its engagement in transnational judicial dialogue. When domestic courts engage in judicial dialogue, they not only mediate between the constitutional structure and the transnational legal orders; they present this interaction as a legal reasoning that fits within the domestic constitutional order. Justice John L. Murray clearly states:

> The national judge, remaining true to his or her constitutional principles, is the filter through which universally discussed ideas enlighten, but do not determine, the interpretation of his or her own constitution, in which must always be found the essential ingredients for the justification of his or her judicial conclusions.[65]

This can be illustrated with a return to the example provided earlier on the Internet and the human rights to privacy and freedom of expression. In this area, domestic judges have innovated when they speak about 'the right to informational self-determination', 'Internet data privacy' or '*habeas* data.' Such innovations have not emerged from nowhere. They are the result of mediation and incorporation of transnational approaches to human rights and new technologies that come from different sources: national and international courts, the UN,[66] as well as doctrine and agreements emerging from fora that include the EU, the CoE and private actors, such as the Internet Governance Forum.[67] Ideas are taken from the outside to allow domestic courts to fulfil their 'detachment' function, but are phrased in the language of domestic law to ensure the 'continuity' function that domestic courts have to adhere to. But judicial dialogue also enables judiciaries to share competing and complementary interpretations from different national settings. In line with the qualities of cosmopolitan norms set out earlier, this contributes to the design of a cosmopolitan legal order but, instead of being a cosmopolitan frame crafted by a universal authority (top-down), it is crafted from

[64] A.M. Bickel, *The Least Dangerous Branch: The Supreme Court at the Bar of Politics* (Indianapolis: Bobbs-Merrill, 1962) at 31.

[65] J.L. Murray, 'Judicial Cosmopolitanism' *Judicial Studies Institute J.* 8:2 (2008) 1–17, at 16.

[66] See e.g. the 2013 annual report submitted by special rapporteur Frank la Rue: HRC, Human Rights Council, 23rd Session. Promotion and Protection of all human rights, civil, political, economic, social and cultural rights, including the right of development: Report of the Special Rapporteur on the promotion and protection of the rights to freedom of opinion and expression, Frank La Rue, 17 April 2013, UN Doc A/HRC/23/40.

[67] For more information about the Multistakeholder Platform, see www.intgovforum.org

legal norms in different national and transnational settings on a voluntary basis, elaborated through a complementary approach.

Judicial dialogue is not one of the aspects of globalisation by which states lose autonomy, because *national judges* decide what foreign and international material to use. Moreover, they decide how to understand the foreign and international material, how to blend it into the national legal order and, finally, whether the arguments in the foreign sources should be taken on or not.[68] The authority question remains important but not as a challenge to state authority. Rather, as Mattias Kumm has put it, what is interesting in relation to the authority of dialoguing courts is how multiple national and international, public and private authorities involved will react to the dialogue of these courts.[69] This engagement in judicial dialogue encourages rejecting or integrating a borrowed reasoning, which informs all interested actors about the national court's particular interpretation and application of a particular norm. These particular interpretations inform and update the cosmopolitan legal framework. From this perspective, judicial dialogue is thus a tool to make visible that state authorities and non-state actors are continuously complementing each other in the making of common notions – something that I am calling a cosmopolitan legal framework.[70]

16.4.3 A Purpose for Judicial Dialogue: Redressing Misrepresentation and Injustice within States by Building Cosmopolitan Democracies

We have seen that judicial dialogue has two purposes. One describes an internal process by which a national court uses foreign material in order

[68] For example the two normative concepts *ubuntu* (in Zulu) and *jinkaku* (in Japanese) are examples of how such processes can also take place outside the judicial context. The two concepts symbolise how external material and ideas expressed therein are received, processed and transformed within the state. The result of this interaction with the external is a creative one and thus not an imposition.

[69] Kumm has stressed that the study of the dialogue between courts shows the importance of the area, the interests at stake, etc., but that it 'falls short conceptually' because it cannot reflect the 'graduated claims of authority that various doctrinal frameworks have built into them. The really interesting question concerns the structures of graduated authority built into doctrinal frameworks: who needs to look at what and give what kind of consideration to what is being said and done.' M. Kumm, 'Democratic Constitutionalism Encounters International Law: Terms of Engagement', Choudhry, Migration, *supra* note 49, 256–93, at 292.

[70] The second part of the story of the concepts *ubuntu and jinkaku* is that, because they have been studied outside the state frame, the national concept that emerged from the blending of external and internal legal materials has become global too. In a manner, they prove that globalisation is not only about homogenisation and universality.

to enhance the interpretation of internal norms. The other involves the crafting of cosmopolitan norms through the blending of national and international/transnational legal materials. Yet, to achieve this double purpose effectively, judicial dialogue has to be encouraged and become evident. The internal legal system has to promote such dialogue by putting the necessary means in place to make the system and the governed society into a more cosmopolitan system and society. This could involve establishing a duty for individuals holding certain positions, such as judges and law clerks, to know foreign law. As Justice Murray argues in this context, 'knowledge of the law of other countries is a duty.'[71] Society should not only tolerate the engagement with foreign and international material but actively encourage it.

The two purposes of judicial dialogue also hint at the possibility that judicial dialogue can contribute to providing enhanced justice to individuals within states under their national jurisdictions. To illustrate this effect, I draw on Neus Torbisco's work on the role of courts as defenders of the rights of national minorities. Torbisco observes that, increasingly, minorities are not living under a legal framework that reflects values that are important to them, be they religious, cultural or social. Even courts that have traditionally been able to protect minorities effectively may fail to provide certain groups with the justice they seek.[72] Torbisco analyses different judgments of the ECtHR concerning Muslim religious symbols (headscarves), in particular *Dahlab v. Switzerland*[73] and *Leyla Sahin v. Turkey*,[74] to illustrate her arguments. She shows that the ECtHR has been unable so far to provide an interpretation of the ECHR concerning this question that the Muslim community is looking for. The reason for this is that the ECtHR's judgments usually understand and evaluate the headscarf and questions related to it from a non-Muslim perspective.[75]

In this context, judicial dialogue could contribute to a 'vision' of the headscarf that is as much 'Muslim' as it is 'non-Muslim' and that would attain a cosmopolitan status. A cosmopolitan 'vision' of the headscarf

[71] J.L. Murray, Cosmopolitanism, *supra* note 65, at 5

[72] N. Torbisco Casals, 'Identity Conflicts, Human Rights and the Crisis of Multiculturalism in Europe: From Politics to the Courts', *GRITim Working Paper Series*, 21 (2014) 3–52, at 42, available at www.upf.edu/gritim.

[73] *Dahlab v. Switzerland* (Appl. No. 42393/98) Decision (Chamber), 15 February 2001, ECHR 2001-V, 447.

[74] *Leyla Şahín v. Turkey* (Appl. No. 44774/98), Judgment (Grand Chamber), 10 November 2005, ECHR 2005-XI, 115.

[75] N. Torbisco Casals, Identity Conflicts, *supra* note 72, at 43.

would bring the 'vision' of Muslim and non-Muslin perspectives together in a compromise that represents and unites both perspectives and their communities. The cosmopolitan framework would become more representative than the national one, and would be able to provide justice to a greater number of people. In addition, the supranational decision would be a source for further rulings on these matters at the national level. The effects of producing inclusive transnational norms will benefit individuals within a particular state as much as they will benefit individuals in other states. Human rights standards are constantly redefined, involving different judiciaries at the transnational and international levels. A supranational, cosmopolitan set of norms recognises that values are directly linked to individuals rather than to states or specific nations.[76]

From this perspective, judicial dialogue constitutes an additional forum[77] to debate competing opinions. Judicial dialogue is valuable, first, because it exposes the competing interests that exist within a society or across societies, and because it values each of these interests. As Klug has signalled, the space provided by the court is able to '[keep] alive these alternative possibilities and [seek] justice in each particular case that presents itself within [the court's] jurisdiction'.[78] Second, judicial dialogue makes it possible that supranational norms and reasoning are accommodated in the internal legal order without being perceived as imperialistic or as amounting to undue harmonisation. The internal accommodation is achieved through an appropriation of a legal idea which, from that moment of appropriation, will be shared among different jurisdictions. This brings us to 'democratic iterations'.

In order to enhance democracy within globalised states, the constitutional order has to be flexible enough to adapt to the changes affecting societies in an increasingly borderless world. When judges interpret internal norms taking into account external judicial decisions (and the norms associated with those decisions), they are transforming the original norm. By recognising the authority and value of the foreign source, the internal norm that is being interpreted changes with the accommodation of the international perspective into the national constitutional order. Moreover, as

[76] Or as Posner puts it, 'judicial cosmopolitanism is the view that judges have a constitutional obligation to protect the interests of noncitizens'. Posner, Boumediene, *supra* note 35, at 3.

[77] I do not propose that the court should substitute other fora, but rather complement them. In fact, political fora that allow discussion through democratic and accountable mechanisms seem to us the best place where these core societal issues would be best addressed.

[78] Klug, Constituting Democracy, *supra* note 18, at 161 and 177. In similar terms, Victor Ferreres acknowledges that judicial interpretation is a way to keep plural societies open; see Ferreres, Rigidez constitucional, *supra* note 13, at 124–28.

Benhabib rightly notes, '[i]teration is the reappropriation of the "origin"; it is at the same time its dissolution as the original and its preservation through its continuous deployment'.[79] This means that when a court borrows a foreign reasoning, the court recognises the foreign source as an authority.[80] Through this national accommodation, the original normative idea is no longer foreign, but internal. Thus, democratic iterations describe the effects of judicial dialogue: a cross-fertilisation of different legal orders and, ultimately, the crystallisation of shared legal reasoning in a cosmopolitan framework.

Through judicial dialogue as a mechanism to bring forth democratic iterations, the meaning of every borrowed norm or concept is enhanced by each different contextualisation. Judicial authorities must share certain values in order to engage in a dialogue, but they also have to maintain their distinctiveness by contextualising what is shared in each polity. If this transformation continues, we can observe a judicial reasoning that is borderless and that enhances its authority the more it is used. This is the successful forging of a cosmopolitan legal order through judicial dialogue. It contains reasoning with authority that is transnational, that is not accepted through imposition, but by sympathetic consideration. In other words, while in a Westphalian state domestic judicial decisions only have authority within the borders of a certain state, through judicial borrowing judges enhance the authority of domestic decisions and give them influence beyond the national sphere.

If we consider the examples of the cases on religious symbols, it seems reasonable to assume that if the ECtHR considered the perspective of courts based in Muslim countries, its reasoning could become more inclusive of the values of the Muslim community in the CoE's member states.[81] This does not mean that the outcome of the ruling would change. It is not about changing the final answer of the court and thus shifting burdens between 'winners' and 'losers', majorities or minorities. It is about the richness of the argument forged by judges and how such richness signals that the court has taken into account the claims of all those involved in the dispute. Judicial dialogue thus helps judiciaries to be more inclusive, which in

[79] *Ibid.*

[80] Not an authority from the perspective of being hierarchically subdued to the foreign court, but an authority in the sense that the borrowed reasoning is work emanating from a peer that is valued, a 'recognised colleague'. Concerning some issues, foreign courts are better placed to understand a certain question (e.g. the meaning of the headscarf is not as well understood in societies that hardly have a Muslim community as in societies where Muslims are in the majority).

[81] For a similar argument, see Chapter 5 by A.O. Amoloye-Adebayo in this volume.

turn transforms the nature of the national democracy into a more inclusive one. In other words, such effect will also enhance the richness in legal argumentation in accordance with societal sensibilities.[82]

In the aforementioned scenarios, the judiciary cannot be seen through the lens of the classic separation of powers where the judiciary has only two institutional partners with whom to engage in a dialogue (the legislative and executive). The judiciary also engages in a direct dialogue with other judiciaries, governments and institutions, while at the same time still communicating with the people and their elected representatives. Globalisation has highlighted the need to have judiciaries as autonomous voices, voices to which many listen carefully and engage with through judicial dialogues.[83]

16.5 Concluding Remarks

This chapter has provided a bulk of arguments to stress the positive effects that judicial dialogue can have on the health of our democracies. It has suggested that judicial dialogue should be encouraged and rendered evident ('indirect dialogue' should be turned into 'direct dialogue'). It is central for the purpose and effects of judicial dialogue that courts are transparent when using foreign case law. Transparency will help to show how engagement with foreign and international material is authorised by internal legal orders, and that it is needed to answer open questions in particular cases. Transparency will thus give legitimacy to and further foster the practice of judicial dialogue.

Rather than providing a case-by-case study of the extent, method and effects of single instances of judicial dialogue, I have analysed the effects of such dialogue from the perspectives of democracy and constitutional theory. Since the heteronomy of states is a fact that seems unlikely to change in the near future, collaborative theories in policy-making, legislative practices and adjudication seem to be the best choice in a world

[82] As Torbisco argues, the problem that Muslim communities have with ECtHR judgments concerning headscarves is not that headscarves are prohibited in certain settings, but that the judicial reasoning classifies headscarves as an item that can offend fellow citizens. Torbisco, Identity Conflicts, *supra* note 72, at 43.

[83] The fact that actors other than the elected representatives can transform the constitutional order is not new; in Roman times, constitutional structures were safeguarded and developed by magistrates and jurists. In today's global era, this should happen also through the involvement of civil society, academics and other public and private actors. For the Roman example, see C.H. McIlwain, *Constitutionalism Ancient and Modern* (Ithaca: Cornell University Press, 2005) at 53.

where power is shared between states, private parties and international organisations. Cosmopolitanism offers a theoretical approach to such collaboration and this chapter encourages us to rethink national institutions as agents that should contribute to the making of a cosmopolitan order. When reopening the institutional debate as to how institutions can participate in this cosmopolitan project, careful attention should be given to courts, which are already in a strategic position to inform cosmopolitan norms through the adjudication of national and transnational/international norms. In particular, their access to foreign judicial reasoning should enrich the national legal order. In other words, together with other methods such as academic research and policy-making, judicial dialogue offers an opportunity to discuss the contours of domestic norms regulating ever more complex societies. Such debates are key, as they help to render inclusive judicial decisions that address the rising national complexity. The decisions can consider values emanating from a varying number of communities or individuals. The extent to which communities' and individuals' values have been considered will in turn determine the degree to which these communities and individuals feel represented by the legal framework governing the state. In this context, it has to be highlighted that cosmopolitan norms are not generated by courts alone. They are generated by the whole national legal order that backs the judges' decisions before and after they have engaged in transnational legal reasoning. Without such backing, domestic judges would be deprived of authority and lack the persuasive force to forge any norm that could be assimilated into the building of a cosmopolitan legal order. Thus, the creation of cosmopolitan norms and cosmopolitan democracies needs cosmopolitan judges as much as it needs cosmopolitan nations.

I conclude this chapter by highlighting the advantages of having domestic judges mediate between the constitutional order and other constitutional orders, between different international norms and their interpretations and, ultimately, between all these norms and cosmopolitan values. First, such judges give visibility to an important question that has to be discussed, and generate the social debate around it. Before, during and after a judicial decision is taken, debates take place, and many different actors can directly (through litigation) or indirectly (through publications, political statements, public demonstrations, etc.) participate in it. Second, that the debate takes place in the courtroom where arguments are considered in accordance with rational, legal methods gives yet one more perspective that enriches the social debate. The court does not become a substitute for political fora, but complements the debate in these fora.

Third, judges offer the latest but not the last meaning of the constitution. It is thus possible to continue the debate, and the court's position might not be the one that will finally prevail. This way judicial dialogue finds a better anchorage in a separation-of-powers system in which the judiciary is not in charge of crafting the law. Fourth, the elaboration of a set of common values or norms (in particular human rights norms) through domestic judges cannot be presented as an imposition of foreign ideologies on a particular *demos*, because the crafting of cosmopolitan values is done precisely through the involvement of national judges within states and happens on a voluntary basis. Fifth, engaging judges in finding answers to difficult questions can help the executive and legislative powers to tackle problems that they would not be able to address otherwise due to the delicate political nature of the question. Judges regularly have to solve the case before them and thus provide an answer.[84] As a result, establishing judicial institutions that are obliged to deal with a particular question ensures that social demands find a forum in which they receive due attention. I cannot but support Jed Rubenfeld's observations in this context, when he states that constitutionalism as democracy 'cannot exist without judicial review'.[85]

I have argued that judicial dialogue does not happen every day and in every court. Engagement in such dialogue is also limited by the disposition of judges to engage in dialogue and their capacity to access other courts' decisions. Yet, the fact that the judiciary plays a prominent role at the global level predicts that judicial dialogue will increase. The processes leading to the creation of cosmopolitan norms through judicial dialogue will increase in parallel. This will help to remedy the mis-framing or democratic deficit that affects many constitutional democracies due to globalisation processes.

[84] An example is the 'Catalan issue' in Spain. The question about the extent to which a people has a right to decide on whether it wishes to belong to a particular state can (and has to) be discussed in political fora. So far this question has been dealt with manly through the interventions of the Spanish Constitutional Court (e.g. Constitutional Court of Spain, Decision on the Catalan Statute, STC 31/2010, 28 June 2010).

[85] J. Rubenfeld, *Freedom and Time: A Theory of Constitutional Self-government* (Yale University Press, 2001) at 172.

17

Dialogue or Interaction?

A Non-Cosmopolitan Reading of Transjudicial Communication

LUCA PASQUET

17.1 Introduction

When discussing transjudicial communication, scholars oscillate between two extremes. On the one hand, many of them appear satisfied with the simple finding that courts of different legal regimes interact. These scholars interpret the notion of 'judicial dialogue' in a broad way, encompassing both informal contacts among judges (such as conferences or exchanges of e-mails) and literal quotations of foreign judgments.[1] A distinctive element of this approach is the quantification of inter-court relations,[2] although, studying this frequency (extent) alone cannot complement a lack of clarity in the definition of judicial dialogue.

On the other hand, there are scholars who put forward grand theories to attribute some general meaning to what otherwise could be seen as a mere episodic occurrence or a normal judicial practice carrying with it no special implications. This scholarship depicts transjudicial communication as a process able to strengthen the unity of the international legal system[3] in order to reinforce the separation of powers on a global

[1] Law and Chang have for instance, ironically suggested that the whole debate on the so called judge-to-judge dialogue is actually based 'on the unexceptional and inconsequential claim that judges enjoy a growing range of opportunities to socialize over cocktails and have also learned to e-mail one another'. See D.S. Law and W.-C. Chang, 'The Limits of Global Judicial Dialogue', *Washington L. Rev.* 86:3 (2011) 523–78, at 535. See also E. Lazega, 'Mapping Judicial Dialogue Across National Borders: An Explanatory Network Study of Learning from Lobbying among European Intellectual Property Judges', *Utrecht L. Rev.* 8:2 (2012) 115–28.

[2] See, among others, M. Gelter and M. Siems, 'Network, Dialogue or One Way Traffic? An Empirical Analysis of Cross-Citations between Ten of Europe's Highest Courts', *Utrecht L. Rev.* 8:2 (2012) 88–99; and D. Zaring, 'The Use of Foreign Decisions by Federal Courts: An Empirical Analysis', *J. of Empirical Legal Studies* 3:2 (2006) 297–331.

[3] See, for instance, W. Burke-White 'International Legal Pluralism', *Michigan J. of Int'l L.* 25:4 (2004) 963–80, at 973.

level,[4] to generate a transnational rule of law, advancing human rights and democracy[5] and even to develop some sort of cosmopolitan law in a Kantian or neo-Kantian sense.[6] In this light, the concept of judicial dialogue seems to refer to collaboration rather than mere communication; a process leading somewhere rather than the mere occurrence of communicational events.

Indeed, judicial dialogue is often theoretically apprehended from the standpoint of a liberal-cosmopolitan discourse revolving around concepts such as legal integration and the development of a universal (or global) rule of law. In this sense, 'judicial dialogue' is not understood as simple communication, but as a process which is meaningful and noteworthy in that it goes in a certain direction, specifically toward more legal integration and (perhaps) a 'global rule of law'. This is particularly evident when considering, for instance, the writings of Anne-Marie Slaughter on transjudicial communication or the more recent attempts to read court-to-court communication through the lenses of a Habermasian or neo-Kantian idea of cosmopolitanism.[7] Undoubtedly, these strands of scholarship do not exhaust the ways in which judicial dialogue can be and has been theoretically captured. Nevertheless, I think that the aforementioned approaches should be regarded as the most influential and representative of the debate on judicial dialogue, at least as far as the theoretical appraisal of the phenomenon is concerned. Most importantly, this theoretical background is often taken for granted, so that even authors not subscribing to any particular theoretical conceptualisation of judicial dialogue may find it natural to share the assumptions of a liberal-cosmopolitan approach, thinking, for instance, that more interaction will necessarily lead to more integration. After all, even the linguistic expression 'judicial dialogue', the label chosen to designate the phenomenon we are discussing, is strongly evocative of ideas particularly congenial to a liberal-cosmopolitan reading of transjudicial communication.

In this respect, the main message of my contribution is that all this does not go without saying. Judicial dialogue as influentially conceptualised by Slaughter and other authors is the product of a particular historical and cultural context that still determines the way in which we look at

[4] A.-M. Slaughter, 'A Typology of Transjudicial Communication', *University of Richmond L. Rev.* 29:1 (1994) 99–137, at 135.

[5] *Ibid.*, at 125–26 and 134–35.

[6] In this volume, see Chapter 16 by C. Marsan-Raventós.

[7] See Slaughter, A Typology, *supra* note 4; of the same author see also 'A Global Community of Courts', *Harvard Int'l L. J.* 44:1 (2003) 191–219.

court-to-court interaction. There exists, however, different ways of looking at transnational legal communication that should equally be taken into account when explaining the extent, method, purpose and effects of this practice. Setting out some of these alternative ways will constitute the main objective of the second part of this chapter.

The first part of this chapter situates the 'judicial dialogue' approach of Slaughter in a historical and theoretical context (Section 17.2). First, I emphasise the impact of a certain 'cosmopolitan eschatology' on the concept of judicial dialogue put forward by Slaughter. Second, by doing so, I will historically situate Slaughter's enterprise in a period – the 1990s and early 2000s – of great expectations and optimism as to the capacity of international law and globalisation to unite the world. Third, 'judicial dialogue' will be presented as a project having a distinct liberal and Euro-American flavour (subsections 17.2.1–17.2.3). All these circumstances have played a role in shaping the conception of judicial dialogue that is still prevalent today, including our understanding of its extent, method, purpose and effects. Yet, today's social context appears significantly different from that of the 1990s, and we may ask whether a model developed two decades ago can still be regarded as valid.

The second part of the chapter proposes a reading of transjudicial communication inspired by the legal pluralist scholarship, in an attempt to provide an account of judicial dialogue that is removed from the liberal-cosmopolitan narrative referred to earlier (Section 17.3). As far as the concept of judicial dialogue is concerned, transjudicial communication will not be presented as a form of collaboration among like-minded judges or as a process of integration having discernible effects. Rather, it will be described as a form of interaction, the extent of which can be explained regardless of the willingness of the court to 'dialogue' with its counterparts, and whose effects are contingent or even random (subsections 17.3.1–17.3.3 and 17.3.6).

Two additional questions will then be discussed. The first regards the methodology, or the perspective we may decide to take when observing transnational legal communication. The traditional 'judicial dialogue' approach focuses exclusively on the role of courts, reiterating the traditional deference of lawyers to judges. However, I contend that judicial activity could be better understood and socially contextualised by broadening the scope of analysis, including other actors' and other types of interaction (subsection 17.3.4). This can allow us *inter alia* to identify further factors that determine the extent of judicial dialogue on certain issues involving particular courts. The second question concerns the 'purpose' of transjudicial communication. In this regard, I argue that the choice as to whether or not to quote external sources of authority depends more on the necessity of convincing a given audience than on the consistency with abstract (and purportedly universal) cosmopolitan principles (subsection 17.3.5). In the concluding section, the main arguments are summarised (Section 17.4).

17.2 An Idealistic Cosmopolitan Approach to Transjudicial Communication

17.2.1 Starting from the Word 'Dialogue'

'Judicial dialogue' is a label used by scholars to designate the interactions occurring among courts and judges of different national and international regimes.[8] One first temptation could be to dismiss it as being just a label, just one of the many possible ways human beings can name an aspect of the world, something which we do not need to analyse further. Yet, often labels are carefully chosen to convey a certain message, a function they usually perform admirably. Linguistic expressions are evocative of images and symbols which play a role in shaping our understanding of the concept or phenomena they nominate. As shown by François Ost, for instance, the fact of speaking of 'sources of law' has a special significance, since the image of the source (rather than, say, a cave, a root or a factory) has strongly influenced the way in which Europeans have thought and still think of the law.[9] This certainly applies to 'judicial dialogue', which, just like the expression 'source of law', is a metaphor, an 'indicator and desire of the mind'[10] able to unveil our assumptions and the way in which we look at the world.[11] To use the label 'dialogue' rather than saying 'communicational episodes' is thus anything but neutral.

In order to understand exactly what the expression in question evokes, one should start from the meaning of the word 'dialogue', which can be

[8] See for instance Slaughter, A Typology, *supra* note 4, at 103–22.

[9] See F. Ost, 'Conclusions générales', Y. Cartuyvel *et al.* (eds.), *Les Sources du Droit Revisitées: Théorie des Sources du Droit IV* (Bruxelles: Anthémis – FUSL, 2013) 865–997, at 867–76.

[10] In Italian: 'Metafore Come Spie e Desideri Della Mente', M. Fumagalli Beonio Brocchieri, *Le Bugie di Isotta. Immagini della Mente Medievale* (Bari: Laterza, 2002) at 13.

[11] See U. Eco, 'Metaphor, Dictionary and Encyclopedia', *New Literary History* 15:2 (1984) 255–71, at 270, according to whom 'the metaphor is the tool that permits us to understand the encyclopedia better'; see also generally P. Ricoeur, *La Métaphore Vive* (Paris: Editions du Seuil, 1975), presenting the metaphor as the principle which revives our perception of the world.

understood in two rather different ways. One possible reading follows the definition of 'dialogue' we normally find in dictionaries. In this light, 'the tendency in English is to confine the sense [of the word 'dialogue'] to a conversation between two people'.[12] A second possible reading follows the notion of 'encyclopaedia-like representations of linguistic expressions' illustrated, among others, by Eco.[13] According to the latter, every word represents a concept commonly related to a universe of ideas, stories, images, that is a part of 'our world knowledge'.[14] From this perspective, 'dialogue' is not understood as a simple 'conversation', but is instead linked to a number of morally significant concepts such as tolerance, good will, dialoguing attitudes, mutual engagement, mutual understanding, ecumenism, and inter-cultural dialogue.

This understanding is captured, for instance, by the definition of dialogue we find in the *Concise Companion to the Jewish Religion*, which, for obvious reasons, focuses on the context of inter-faith dialogue:

> a discussion and conversation between two parties holding different views on some matters of high significance but who believe that it is fruitful for them to talk to one another and thus come fairly to understand why the other sincerely holds to his opinion, as well as to assist one another in the furtherance of the aims they have in common.[15]

In sum, the concept of 'dialogue' can be taken to refer to (at least) two different ideas. On the one hand - following the dictionary – 'dialogue' can be conceived of as a simple exchange of messages between two or more parties. In this respect, it is a synonym for direct 'communication'. On the other hand – following an encyclopaedia-like representation – 'dialogue' can refer to a unifying process, or at least to a factor of integration, which implies some degree of mutual understanding, the capacity to identify common problems, and the willingness to engage in a discussion perceived as fruitful by the parties. This second understanding is also related to certain human attitudes – for example, tolerance and openness – which are normally regarded as having positive moral connotations.

[12] J. Cresswell (ed.), *The Oxford Dictionary of Word Origins*, 2nd ed. (Oxford University Press, 2009); see also A. Stevenson (ed.), *Oxford Dictionary of English*, 3rd ed. (Oxford University Press, 2010) defining 'dialogue' as 'a discussion between two or more people or groups'.

[13] See U. Eco, Metaphor, *supra* note 11, at 255: 'a dictionary-like representation should concern a merely linguistic competence, while an encyclopedia-like representation should take into account, as it is commonly said, the whole of our world knowledge'; see also, more generally, J. Haiman, 'Dictionaries and Encyclopedias', *Lingua* 50:4 (1980) 329–57.

[14] *Ibid.*

[15] L. Jacobs (ed.), *A Concise Companion to the Jewish Religion* (Oxford University Press, 1999).

This ambiguity is somewhat reflected in the scholarly debate on 'judicial dialogue'. Some authors take the expression to refer to the simple occurrence of communication among judges of different regimes. Others interpret it in a fairly idealistic way, writing about the existence of a global community of judges sharing a common identity, values and a commitment towards the establishment of a 'global rule of law' that determines the extent, method, purpose and effects of 'judicial dialogue'. This said, the latter and more idealised of these visions seems to be the most influential and illustrative of the ways in which scholars have understood transjudicial communication. Indeed, the most well-known conceptualisation of judicial dialogue, put forward by Slaughter, depicts judicial communication as a unifying dynamic that has the effect of strengthening a global community of judges and a process of collective deliberation.[16] This reading has so deeply shaped our understanding of the phenomenon that it is actually very difficult to conceive of transjudicial communication in complete isolation from certain ideas and assumptions characterising Slaughter's vision. Thus, although not all international law scholars would subscribe to Slaughter's reconstruction, many of them would take for granted the idea that judicial dialogue, especially its purpose and desired effects, is inherently linked to themes such as the rule of law, democracy, legitimacy and fundamental (civil and political) rights.[17] More recent attempts to look at transjudicial communication in the light of the Habermasian theme of cosmopolitanism also confirm the impact of liberal-cosmopolitan approaches and ideas in the debate on transjudicial communication.[18]

In the end, the 'judicial dialogue' metaphor seems particularly well suited to giving a sense of this idealistic, liberal-cosmopolitan sensitivity. It immediately and instinctively conveys the idea of collaboration, a constructive conversation among people willing to listen to each other. Hence, when using this expression, we convey a powerful hidden message,

[16] See Slaughter, A Typology, *supra* note 4, at 119; of the same author see also: A Global Community, *supra* note 7, in particular at 204.

[17] See for instance A. Paulus, 'National Courts and the International Rule of Law – Remarks on the Book by André Nollkaemper', *Jerusalem Rev. of Legal Studies* 4:1 (2012) 5–18; F. Fontanelli, G. Martinico and P. Carrozza (eds.), *Shaping Rule of Law through Dialogue. International and Supranational Experiences* (Europa Law Publishing, Groningen, 2010); and M.A. Waters, 'Mediating Norms and Identity: The Role of Transnational Judicial Dialogue in Creating and Enforcing International Law', *Georgetown L. J.* 93:2 (2005) 487–574.

[18] In this regard, see generally S. Benhabib, 'The Future of Democratic Sovereignty and Transnational Law', European University Institute, Max Weber Programme Lecture Series (2012).

able to forge the way we think of transnational interactions. Judges who 'dialogue' are judges who share an understanding of the purpose and desired effects of 'dialogue' (e.g. a professional identity, a commitment to the rule of law, etc.).

17.2.2 'For Ye Are All One in the Global Community of Courts': Judicial Dialogue as a Cosmopolitan Prophecy of Global Integration

As seen in the previous section, even though it is often taken as a neutral technical expression, the notion of 'judicial dialogue' is strongly evocative of a particularly idealistic account of transjudicial communication that was first elaborated by Slaughter. In the next pages I will argue that such an understanding of court-to-court relations is the product of a precise historical, cultural and social context, as well as the outcome of an intellectual and political project having a distinct liberal flavour. In order to culturally and historically contextualise this endeavour, the present section briefly discusses the influence of a certain cosmopolitan eschatology, internalised by international lawyers, on the elaboration of the idea of 'judicial dialogue'. In addition, it argues that in order to understand Slaughter's enterprise, one should locate it in the atmosphere of generalised optimism about the future of international law that followed the end of the Cold War.

As shown by authors such as Jacob Taubes,[19] different forms of messianic thought and eschatological beliefs (regarding the final events of history and the destiny of humanity)[20] have strongly influenced several fields of Western culture, from philosophy to politics. International law is certainly not immune from this dynamic: international lawyers have formulated their own prophecies and are waiting for the fulfilment of these predictions, living in that 'suspended time' – a time in which every present happening is read in light of the final event to come – which characterises every eschatological perspective.[21] In particular, they have traditionally conceived of history as a process leading somehow inevitably to world integration and some form of legal unity. One could think for instance

[19] See generally J. Taubes, *Occidental Eschatology* (Stanford University Press, 2009); and J. Taubes, *La Teologia Politica di San Paolo* (Milano: Adelphi, 1997) 105–74.

[20] Eschatology is a branch of theology whose object of study are the beliefs related to the final events of history and the ultimate destiny of humankind. See M. Riedl, 'Eschatology', M.C Horowitz (ed.), *New Dictionary of the History of Ideas: Communication of Ideas to Futurology II* (New York: Charles Scribner's Sons, 2005) retrieved 20 May 2013 from Encyclopedia.com: www.encyclopedia.com/doc/1G2-3424300248.html.

[21] V. Westhelle, *Eschatology and Space: The Lost Dimension in Theology Past and Present* (New York: Palgrave Macmillan, 2012) at 58.

of the 'cosmopolitan dream of the international legal community',[22] the Kantian idea of a 'Universal History with a Cosmopolitan Purpose'[23] which international lawyers of the twentieth century have internalised to the point of conceiving, in the words of Martti Koskenniemi, of an 'historical trajectory that would lead to the liberation of individuals enjoying human rights in a global federation under the rule of law'.[24]

More recently, the debate on globalisation has often revolved around the idea of an inevitable historical tendency towards the global integration of different legal orders and traditions. For instance, in the 1990s and at the beginning of the 2000s, the spread of the Internet was understood as leading to global uniform regulation, independent from the territorial and functional fragmentation of the old pre-digital law.[25] Similarly, it was predicted that the growing number of international commercial transactions would have induced a natural convergence of legal orders, especially in allegedly value-free areas of law, less exposed to the fragmenting effects of national legal cultures.[26]

The notion of 'judicial dialogue' is exactly at the point of intersection of these two narratives: a Kantian cosmopolitan internationalism and a vision of globalisation as a unifying process. It is strongly influenced by the two visions and cannot be separated from them. What is more, the model of 'judicial dialogue' – proposed, among others, by Slaughter – offers its own particular prediction of universal integration. We are not dealing with a simple process of 'communication' among judges, but with a transjudicial 'dialogue' that has the purpose and effect of creating a global community of courts over time. The prophecy is one of convergence, uniformity and integration, even of unity. Its core idea is that of a 'collective judicial deliberation',[27] which would be taking place in 'the presumption of an integrated system'.[28]

[22] See D. Kennedy, 'One, Two, Three, Many Legal Orders: Legal Pluralism and the Cosmopolitan Dream', *New York University Rev. of Law & Social Change* 31:3 (2007) 641–60, at 641.

[23] I. Kant, 'Idea for a Universal History with a Cosmopolitan Purpose', H. Reiss (ed.), *Political Writings* (Cambridge University Press, 1991) 41–53.

[24] M. Koskenniemi, 'The Fate of Public International Law: Between Technique and Politics', *Modern Law Review* 70:1 (2007) 1–30, at 2–3.

[25] See the discussion in T. Schultz, 'Carving up the Internet: Jurisdiction, Legal Orders, and the Private/Public International Law Interface', *European J. of Int'l L.* 19:4 (2008) 799–839; see also F. Ost, 'Mondialisation, Globalisation, Universalisation: S'arracher Encore et Toujours à l'état de Nature', C.-A. Morand (ed.), *Le droit Saisi par la Mondialisation* (Bruxelles: Bruylant, 2001) 5–36.

[26] See the discussion in R. Michaels, 'Two Paradigms of Jurisdiction', *Michigan J. of Int'l L.* 27:4 (2005–2006) 1003–70, at 1004–05.

[27] Slaughter, A Typology, *supra* note 4, at 119.

[28] Slaughter, A Global Community, *supra* note 7, at 204.

Although it is maintained that the new transjudicial 'dialogue' will provide space for pluralism and differentiation, it is also clear that 'this pluralism is not unbounded [but] operates within a framework of common fundamental values',[29] since 'common constraints bind courts participating in this form of communication'.[30] In other words, it is a limited pluralism, a differentiation which is only tolerated as far as it takes place within a general overarching structure and a shared value system. The model is that of a federation, or of a community of states (e.g. the EU).[31] But the idea of a limited legitimate differentiation is also typical of a particular view of public international law, according to which special regimes are allowed to exist and to differentiate themselves from general international law, provided that they pay due respect to the latter.[32] Be that as it may, international lawyers have clearly recognised the unifying purpose and effect of the judicial dialogue discourse and have even resorted to it as a possible therapy against the 'disease' of the last decades – fragmentation – 'for it has the potential to preserve the unity of the international legal system'.[33]

Furthermore, this predicted effect focuses on traditional cosmopolitan values such as the rule of law and universal human rights. Not only would the courts involved in this kind of dialogue 'conceive of themselves as servants of the law',[34] but the transjudicial communication would also have the effect of 'spread[ing] ... [the] enhanced protection of universal human rights',[35] considered 'the core of judicial identity in many different courts'.[36] From this point of view, the judicial dialogue model can be seen as one of the updated versions of the old Kantian cosmopolitan dream of the international legal community. While international lawyers no longer speak of a universal political federation, they at least try to federate national courts. 'Imagine a world of regular and interactive transjudicial communication'[37] – Slaughter wrote – 'it is a vision of a global community of law'.[38]

29 *Ibid.*, at 217.
30 Slaughter, A Typology, *supra* note 7, at 118.
31 See A.-M. Slaughter, 'Judicial Globalization', *Virginia J. of Int'l L.* 40:4 (1999–2000) 1103–24, at 1108.
32 See for instance the report of the ILC, Fragmentation of International Law: Difficulties Arising from the Diversification and Expansion of International Law: Report of the Study Group of the International Law Commission finalized by M. Koskenniemi, 13 April 2006, UN Doc. A/CN.4/L.682, 85–100, paras. 159–93.
33 Burke-White, International Legal Pluralism, *supra* note 3, at 973.
34 Slaughter, A Typology, *supra* note 4, at 125–26.
35 *Ibid.*, at 122. Note, however, that Slaughter and other post–Cold War liberal authors mainly promote civil and political rights as 'universal', less so economic, social and cultural rights.
36 *Ibid.*, at 134.
37 *Ibid.*, at 132.
38 Slaughter, Judicial Globalization, *supra* note 31, at 1114.

None of this is surprising if one thinks that Slaughter began conceptualising judicial dialogue in the last decade of the twentieth century, a historical period deeply marked by the end of the Cold War and therefore particularly propitious to a Kantian reading of history. To quote Koskenniemi,

> [T]hen came 1989 and all the enthusiasm about a global rule of law – human rights, trade, environment, criminal law, sanctions and world police. The end of the Cold War was understood – especially in Europe – as a removal of obstacles on the way to history's natural progress towards a universal federation.[39]

It is therefore no coincidence that Slaughter identified the end of the Cold War, the emergence of new democracies and the growing number of supranational tribunals among the causes or 'catalysts' of the increased extent in the occurrence of judicial dialogue.[40] One could even ask if the 'growing sense of participation in a common enterprise' to which Slaughter often refers[41] is not, in the end, a simple sign of the times in which the author was writing.

17.2.3 Judicial Dialogue as a Liberal Project

The context described in the preceding section helps to understand some of the features of the Slaughterian concept of 'judicial dialogue'. Yet, this conceptualisation is not just the consequence of the eschatological expectations tacitly internalised by international lawyers. Rather, it is a political project having a clear Western-liberal connotation and taking the form of the self-fulfilling prophecy.

Certainly, it is often difficult to say where description ends and prediction begins. Scholars often describe present phenomena in light of a future development. It is even more difficult to trace a line between predictions and projects. For instance, it would be hard to tell whether the expected and inevitable proletarian revolution evoked by Karl Marx was a simple prediction or a call to arms.[42] Yet, every prophecy implies a 'suspended

[39] Koskenniemi, The Fate, *supra* note 24, at 3.

[40] Slaughter, Judicial Globalization, *supra* note 31, at 1117; of the same author, see also: A Typology, *supra* note 4, at 129–32.

[41] See for instance Slaughter, A Global Community, *supra* note 7, at 218.

[42] See for instance K. Marx and F. Engels, *The Communist Manifesto* (Martin Lawrence: London, 1930) 42: 'Before all, therefore, the bourgeoisie produces its own gravediggers. Its downfall and the victory of the proletariat are equally inevitable'.

time' in which, while waiting for the fulfilment of the prophecy, people act 'as if' (*comme si*) the predicted event was an inevitable reality.[43] As shown by Jacob Taubes,[44] this opens the problem of the political relevance of the prediction. Political projects often take the form of self-fulfilling prophecies.

This kind of social process is not alien to international law: many institutions and legal doctrines came to life in the suspended time of the 'world federation', not to speak of the inexorable process of European integration.[45] Scholarly approaches can similarly convey political projects. It has, for instance, been maintained that a 'constitutionalist reconstruction of international law [may] influence the process of law-making by the relevant social actors [and] help to promote a multi-level, genuinely, global constitutionalism'.[46] That is to say: a constitutional reconstruction of international law will constitutionalise international law. A certain description of society itself has an impact on society; by describing society, we are changing it.

Similarly, Slaughter's writings on judicial dialogue do not simply describe interactions among judges belonging to different regimes, but propose a clear vision of what the purposes and effects of legal globalisation should be: 'a network of courts self-consciously communicating with one another around the world' strengthening the principle of separation of powers, the rule of law and the protection of human rights (mainly civil and political rights) on a global level.[47] This is a vision of judicial globalisation that is *inter alia* a fundamental component of Slaughter's New World Order.[48] It is also an idea that has important 'potential consequences' (effects), whose existence the author explicitly acknowledges and uses as

[43] Westhelle, Eschatology and Space, *supra* note 21, at 58 and 101, according to which eschatology would be a discourse of 'suspension of time in a *nunc aeternum*'.

[44] Taubes, La Teologia Politica, *supra* note 19, at 105–74.

[45] The expression 'Etats Unis d'Europe' has been used by Victor Hugo in his famous speech 'Un jour viendra': 'Un jour viendra où l'on verra ces deux groupes immenses, les Etats-Unis d'Amérique, les Etats-Unis d'Europe placés en face l'un de l'autre, se tendant la main pardessus les mers, échangeant leurs produits, leur commerce, leur industrie, leurs arts, leurs génies, défrichant le globe, colonisant le désert, améliorant la création sous le regard du Créateur, et combinant ensemble, pour en tirer le bien-être de tous, ces deux forces infinies, la fraternité des hommes et la puissance de Dieu', available at www.nobel-paix.ch/paix_p1/eu-europ.htm. See also P. Rolland (ed.), *L'Unité Politique de l'Europe, Histoire d'une Idée: Les Grands Textes* (Bruxelles: Bruylant, 2006).

[46] A. Peters, 'Compensatory Constitutionalism: The Function and Potential of Fundamental International Norms and Structures', *Leiden J. of Int'l L.* 19:3 (2006) 605–10.

[47] Slaughter, A Typology, *supra* note 4, at 135.

[48] A.-M. Slaughter, *A New World Order* (Princeton: Princeton University Press, 2004) at 65–102.

a means of persuasion.[49] Concerned actors are therefore told how they should act in order to realise the vision.

A project also needs to distinguish itself from alternative visions, pointing to one direction when the road forks. In 1997, Gunther Teubner wrote that two alternative accounts of globalisation would confront each other: on the one hand, Clinton's idea of a 'Pax Americana which will globalize the rule of law', on the other hand a 'Global Bukowina' in which 'civil society itself will globalize its legal orders', distancing itself from political power.[50] It is certainly not difficult to guess where the idea of judicial dialogue conceptualised by Slaughter is to be located in this debate. To quote Slaughter, 'the leading alternative to liberal internationalism is "the new medievalism", a back-to-the-future model of the twenty-first century. Where liberal internationalists see a need for international rules and institutions to solve states' problems, the new medievalists proclaim the end of the nation-state'.[51] A certain preference goes therefore to the liberal Pax Americana.

The judicial dialogue project has indeed a distinct Western-liberal flavour. Many of Slaughter's arguments revolve around the idea of 'objectively identifiable differences between liberal and non-liberal states'.[52] From this perspective, the spread of liberal democracy is presented as an important condition for the establishment of a global community of law, and the 'commitment to and understanding of the rule of law [as the] minimum common ground' without which any transjudicial communication would be impossible.[53] Moreover, the European legal experience in the fields of human rights and constitutional law is generally presented as a model to be followed by non-Western states in view of their 'democratisation'. As an illustration, it is maintained that 'the courts of fledgling democracy, might look to the opinions of courts in older and more established democracies as a way of binding its country to this existing community of states'.[54] The EU system is similarly presented as the model of judicial community par excellence, to be followed on a global scale.[55]

[49] Slaughter, A Typology, *supra* note 4, at 132: 'consider some of the potential implications of this vision …'.

[50] G. Teubner, 'Global Bukowina: Legal Pluralism in the World Society', G. Teubner (ed.) *Global Law without a State* (Brookfield: Dartmouth, 1997) 3–30, at 3.

[51] A.-M. Slaughter, 'The Real New World Order', *Foreign Affairs* 76:5 (1997) 183–97, at 183.

[52] A.-M. Slaughter, 'International Law and International Relations: A Dual Agenda', *American J. of Int'l L.* 87:2 (1993) 205–39, at 232.

[53] Slaughter, A Typology, *supra* note 4, at 125–26.

[54] *Ibid.*, at 134.

[55] Slaughter, Judicial Globalization, *supra* note 31, at 1108: 'it is a dialogue of constitutionalism within a national-supranational framework that is potentially adoptable and adaptable by courts around the world'.

Having said this, the expression 'political project' does not have a negative connotation. As noted by Koskenniemi, modern public international law is itself a political project and the result of a clear political strategy.[56] To say that 'judicial dialogue' is a political project simply means that the scholarly approach at issue proposes a clear view of how international actors should behave in the near future. However, to conceive of scholarly approaches as projects – as opposed to simple theoretical explanations of social reality – can be helpful to realise that they are always conceived in a particular cultural and historical context, as a reaction to other discourses, and with a particular purpose to achieving certain effects. They come, in other words, with a universe of related ideas and assumptions, and are all but neutral. By using the expression 'judicial dialogue', therefore we inevitably imply that judges are 'engaging in a dialogue' on the basis of a liberal-cosmopolitan common vision of the rule of law.

Moreover, the idea of judges around the world sharing a common identity, the same fundamental values and a certain commitment towards the rule of law and certain human (civil and political) rights is particularly attractive to most international lawyers. The cosmopolitan project, and its related ideas are in fact deeply rooted in their DNA. Mario Prost, for instance, maintains that the 'idea of international law … as an instrument of liberal-humanitarian reform [would constitute the] corporate self-consciousness' of international law's societal body.[57] Slaughter's basic premise of a common commitment of national and international judges towards a liberal emancipatory project therefore touches upon the very identity of the profession.

17.3 A Non-Cosmopolitan Approach to Transjudicial Communication

17.3.1 Changing Perspective: 'Taking a Break from the Cosmopolitan Dream'

Despite the attractiveness of the 'judicial dialogue' project, the Slaughterian premises referred to in the preceding section can be challenged on different grounds. First, and as advocated by some authors, one can stress that 'what divides judges around the world now seems important again, and what they share seems less significant'.[58] Such a critique

[56] Koskenniemi, The Fate, *supra* note 24, at 1.

[57] M. Prost, 'All Shouting the Same Slogans: International Law's Unity and the Politics of Fragmentation', *Finnish Yearbook of Int'l L.* 17 (2006) 1–29, at 6.

[58] P.B. Stephan, 'Courts on Courts: Contracting for Engagement and Indifference in International Judicial Encounters', *Virginia L. Rev.* 100:1 (2014) 17–109, at 105.

concerns a change of the social perception of globalisation and suggests that Slaughter's claims, including her explanations of the extent, purpose and desired effects of transnational judicial communication, could today appear less realistic than twenty years ago. The predictions of uniformity from the 1990s seem to have been disproved by later evolutions. As pointed out by Koskenniemi, 'the new developments in the law did not point to unity',[59] but to fragmentation. Similarly, Teubner and Andreas Fischer-Lescano have described a 'fragmented, rather than uniform globalization'[60] in which 'global law [is fragmenting] along sectoral lines'.[61] At the same time, the present context does not seem particularly favourable to a liberal-cosmopolitan interpretation of international relations.[62] While the EU is experiencing the worst economic and political crises of its history, non-liberal states such as China and Russia are growing in wealth and power, showing that influence is not necessarily linked to a liberal conception of the rule of law. Moreover, after more than a decade marked by illegal military interventions, extraordinary renditions and Guantanamo, the word 'democratisation' might have lost much of its appeal.[63] Finally, with the Ukrainian crisis, the planet might seem closer to a second Cold War than to the realisation of a pax euro-americana. In short, the world seems today more divided and less willing to 'dialogue' than twenty years ago. It is therefore legitimate to ask whether a theoretical model developed in the optimism of the 1990s can still be regarded as valid in the years of the great disillusion with international law, international institutions and globalisation.

These considerations are also relevant with respect to the debate on the effects of judicial communication. The idealistic cosmopolitan approach to judicial dialogue suggests that a consistent resort to 'dialogue' among courts could finally lead to some specific results such as more human rights, more democracy, more legitimacy and more legal unity.[64] Admittedly,

59 Koskenniemi, The Fate, *supra* note 24, at 4.

60 Teubner, Global Bukowina, *supra* note 50, at 3.

61 A. Fischer-Lescano and G. Teubner, 'Regime-Collisions: The Vain Search for Legal Unity in the Fragmentation of Global Law', *Michigan J. of Int'l L.* 25:4 (2004) 999–1046, at 1000 and 1009.

62 Stephan, Courts on Courts, *supra* note 58, at 112.

63 To the point that, according to a poll realised by WIN/Gallup in sixty-five different countries, the liberal-democratic United States was considered 'the greatest threat to peace in the world'. See in this respect the official webpage of the 'end of the year survey' 2013, providing information on the methodology used and the results of the poll: www.wingia.com/en/services/about_the_end_of_year_survey/global_results/7/33/.

64 See for instance Slaughter, A Typology, *supra* note 4, at 134–35.

following the traditional liberal cosmopolitan narrative of progress, such outcomes could be seen as natural developments following the normal course of history, only needing a little help to be fully realised. It may thus be normal to think that if judges sharing a liberal-cosmopolitan ethos started to entertain a regular dialogue, the natural consequence could only be the realisation of the values they share. However, the developments of the last fifteen years may prompt observers to take another view, in which history may equally be seen as a contingent process which goes in any direction (also towards a fragmented globalisation) and therefore nowhere in particular. Once one removes oneself from the cosmopolitan narrative of progress, it is hard to see why the practice of judicial dialogue should necessarily lead to some specific effects. After all, judicial dialogue may very well have random effects.

In any event, there is a second and more fundamental objection which can be moved against the Slaughterian approach described earlier. That is, to constantly focus on what judges have (or do not have) in common is reassuring, but might not be the best way to understand the extent, method purpose and effect of court-to-court communication. Slaughter's account of judicial dialogue revolves around the idea of unity: judges can engage in dialogue because of the cultural unity of their professional community (extent) and they must engage in dialogue in order to reinforce and nourish such unity (purpose and effect). As we have seen, such a view certainly gives the sense of an *esprit de corps*, allowing the lawyers of our complex (and perhaps fragmented) legal world to place their hopes in the professional community of judges. However, it may be misleading, since it concentrates on a factor – cultural unity – which might not be determinant to explain the extent of transjudicial communication. After all, interaction could take place regardless of professional unity, and without necessarily having the effect of integrating the transnational legal space. I think therefore that the question to ask is not whether courts are different from or similar to each other, but whether a common ground of shared beliefs and commitments is a necessary condition for communication to occur at all, or a useful factor to explain the extent to which interaction happens. In this regard, I argue that it is possible to give an account of the extent of the interactions taking place among courts of different regimes without also assuming that judges would be performing their function on the presumption of an integrated system – a global community of judges sharing a professional identity, certain common values and the same commitment towards the rule of law.

To be sure, there is at least one strand of scholarship – legal pluralism – which describes the extent of transnational legal communication while nonetheless emphasising the differences existing in the legal realm and refusing unity as a normative category that allegedly determines the purpose and effects of this communication. From this point of view, communication and diversity are not irreconcilable; fragmentation, cultural differences and conflicting rationalities do not seem to hinder legal interaction. It is therefore conceivable to look at judicial interactions from a different angle. A pluralist perspective that – to quote David Kennedy – allows us to 'take a break from the cosmopolitan dream',[65] that is, from 'the project of elaborating, celebrating and adumbrating a normative humanist universalism'.[66] Such an observational standpoint is free from those liberal-cosmopolitan encrustations in which, consciously or unconsciously, we often wrap the concept of transjudicial communication. It is healthy to change perspective from time to time.

In the following pages, therefore, I discuss some (alternative) aspects of the extent, method, purpose and effect of transjudicial communication, seeking inspiration from the literature on legal pluralism. In particular, I focus on insights provided by Teubner and Niklas Luhmann's writings on global law and politics. Indeed, their theoretical model appears particularly suitable to describing processes of transnational communication, for three main reasons.

First, the society described by Luhmann is not confined to the territory of nation-states, but is rather a 'world society', transnational in nature, just like the kind of interactions we want to analyse.[67]

Second, in this society 'there is no top, there is no centre'.[68] It is not observable from a meta-level which allows a unitary vision of society, but only from the perspective of one of the social systems (economy, law, sport, science, education, etc.) composing it.[69] Moreover, Luhmann does not subscribe to the view that a universal rationality inherent in human nature exists. Rather, he maintains, there exists different social rationalities, one for each of the social systems (for instance, economic growth

[65] Kennedy, One, Two, Three, Many Legal Orders, *supra* note 22, at 654.

[66] *Ibid.*, at 641.

[67] See T. Murphy, 'From Subject to System: Some Unsystematic Systems-Theoretic Thoughts on Race Equality and Human Rights', M. King and C. Thornhill (eds.), *Luhmann on Law and Politics: Critical Appraisals and Applications, Oñati International Series in Law & Society* (Oxford: Hart Publishing, 2006) 55–74, at 59–61.

[68] N. Luhmann, *Die Gesellschaft der Gesellschaft* (Frankfurt am Main: Suhrkamp, 1997) at 803: 'ohne Spitze und ohne Zentrum'.

[69] In this respect, see, among others, A.F. Müller, 'Some Observation on Social Anthropology and Niklas Luhmann's concept of Society', M. King and C. Thornhill (eds.), *supra* note 67, 165–86, at 167 and 179.

vs. the preservation of the environment).[70] These rationalities have, it is asserted, penetrated the legal discourse, fragmenting it along sectorial lines. Therefore, this approach seems particularly appropriate if we want to prescind from the Slaughterian assumptions referred to earlier in the chapter.

Third, even following different rationalities, different social systems can constrain and limit each other's rationality by means of interaction and mutual irritation. They can thus find an equilibrium – a *modus vivendi* – and co-evolve accordingly.[71] Most importantly, courts of different regimes following radically different social rationalities can nevertheless observe each other and interact.

At this point, however, it is important to clarify that Luhmann principally dealt with the interactions among different social systems. It is mainly Teubner who adapted the Luhmanian model to the interactions among transnational legal regimes, justifying this shift by the fact that transnational legal regimes are connected in particular to certain sectors of society and therefore follow the specific rationality of certain social systems.[72] In this respect, I will thus principally follow Teubner's insights.

Finally, a terminological warning: transjudicial communication is not necessarily, and not primarily, a collaboration among like-minded judges sharing a common understanding of the purpose and desired effects of this communication. To better convey this idea, in the following pages I avoid using the expression 'judicial dialogue', replacing it with 'interaction'. This choice is aimed at bypassing the inevitable semantic ambiguity of the word 'dialogue', which always carries with it a moral and value-related dimension ('a man of dialogue', 'keep the dialogue open', etc.). Moreover, the word 'interaction' presents the major advantage of not evoking the image of a conversation between human beings. It therefore allows a certain distance to be taken from the lawyerly habit of anthropomorphising courts, associating with them typical human attitudes. Additionally, it allows to better describe those situations in which courts simply incorporate external sources of authority, without directly addressing other courts. Finally,

70 See, for instance, C. Thornhill, 'Luhmann's Political Theory: Politics After Metaphysics? The Gentleman's House (1964)', M. King and C. Thornhill (eds.), *supra* note 67, 75–100, at 75–82.

71 A.F. Müller, Some Observations on Social Anthropology, *supra* note 67, at 174–75.

72 See generally Fischer-Lescano and Teubner, Regime-Collisions, *supra* note 61; see also G. Teubner and P. Korth, 'Two Kinds of Legal Pluralism: Collision of Transnational Regimes in the Double Fragmentation of World Society', M. Young (ed.), *Regime Interaction in International Law: Facing Fragmentation* (Oxford/New York: Oxford University Press, 2010), 23–54.

while 'dialogue' normally evokes a certain temporal continuity (people with common problems seeking a solution together), an 'interaction' can be episodic, subject to chance or completely accidental.

17.3.2 *Mutual Observation in a Radically Fragmented Legal World*

As noted earlier, it is important to observe that for certain authors, cultural uniformity is not the principal element to understanding the purpose and extent of transjudicial communication. Fischer-Lescano and Teubner, for instance, describe a global legal world in which different transnational regimes follow their own particular rationality (protection of human rights/free market/protection of intellectual property/access to medical assistance), seeking to enhance it as far as possible. There is neither a common point of reference to be followed nor a meta-regime to put order into chaos. Nonetheless, this is also a world in which 'judges from very different regimes entered into mutual observation of other regimes'.[73]

In the absence of a clear hierarchy – such as a meta-regime, a global supreme court or another kind of third-party forum – our legal world is characterised by 'a sequence of decisions within a variety of observational positions in a network; a process in which network nodes mutually reconstruct, influence, limit, control and provoke one another'.[74] The observer is always situated and observes the world according to their own rationality (an observational position), but mutual observation takes place nonetheless. In this way – building upon other regimes' judicial decisions – the legal regime creates its own external points of reference in a complex, polycentric legal world. This is what Teubner and Fischer-Lescano have defined as 'uncertainty absorption in a process of iterative connection of legal decision to legal decision'.[75]

While Slaughter has never evoked either the existence or the necessity of a universal centralised system of coordination, she has nevertheless replaced it with a kind of universal judicial rationality, symbolised by a shared commitment towards the rule of law and human rights. The courts she describes enter into a process of spontaneous interaction and mutual observation just as the courts described by Teubner, but they do so by assuming the existence of a common moral and political horizon. The purpose of dialogue is to strengthen this common moral and political

[73] Fischer-Lescano and Teubner, Regime-Collisions, *supra* note 61, at 1042.
[74] *Ibid.*, at 1018.
[75] *Ibid.*, at 1039–40.

horizon, and this also drives the extent of dialogue between like-minded courts. This is the main difference with the model of interaction proposed by Teubner, in which each regime is guided by its own rationality (peace and security, liberalisation of trade, etc.), which in turn is only limited by its social environment (e.g. the need to preserve its influence and authority). Rather than following the same light, transnational legal regimes each navigate according to their own system of positioning. This notwithstanding, they all take note of what happens around them, including what the other regimes are doing.

From a Slaughterian perspective, coordination and communication are possible because particular logics and interests are counterbalanced by shared values and goals. Additionally, the universal horizon of a global community of judges somehow limits the particularistic tendencies of individual courts. In this view, it is fundamental to preserve a common ground among different actors; it is a precondition for communication. 'Dialogue' among similar actors has precisely this purpose. By contrast, a Luhmanian perspective asserts that particular logics can only be limited by other particular rationalities, by other autonomous systems, and by the pressure exerted by the social environment on the system itself.[76] No rationality can claim to represent the whole of society and the universal good. When this happens – take, for instance, politics in totalitarian states and religion in theocracies – it is more pathology than achievement.[77] Moreover, 'dialogue' in the idealistic sense described in the preceding sections does not make sense in the context of a polycentric international or transnational legal space, because there is no neutral space where a common rationality among different systems and regimes can be negotiated or agreed. Regimes can only unilaterally react to external solicitations, and in turn eventually internalise external logic when pushed to do so by their environment.

As to moral values, they are simply unable to provide an external, neutral common ground, a bridge among regimes that influences the extent of their interaction. Luhmann does not deny the existence of shared values at the global level. It would indeed be hard to deny that peace is generally considered a 'good thing'. However, he points out that moral values can be used to justify basically anything and its contrary. As it has been observed, '"good" and "evil" are principally void of content.... Everyone can choose

[76] *Ibid.*, at 1037–38.

[77] G. Verschraegen, 'Human Rights and Modern Society: A Sociological Analysis from the Perspective of Systems Theory', 29 *J. of L. and Society* 29:2 (2002) 258–81, at 271.

the programme that favours his or her own interests and opinions, while despising those who do not adhere to the same programme'.[78] Moral values can be translated in the particular language of any regime and be used to justify and enhance every kind of rationality. Arguments referring to peace can, for instance, be used – and often are used – to justify war: *si vis pacem para bellum*. In a less radical way, the value of peace can be translated into the language of culture and education to justify, for instance, the establishment of the United Nations Educational, Scientific and Cultural Organisation (UNESCO). In fact, the preamble of the Organisation's statute states that 'since wars begin in the minds of men, it is in the minds of men that the defences of peace must be constructed'.[79] From this point of view, it is hard to think that moral values could ever provide a clear guidance for courts on a global level that shape the extent, purpose and desired effects of their interaction. To share values means to share very little. To say that human rights are something good or fundamental does not mean that they are considered more fundamental than other values (trade liberalisation or security).

The absence of a common ground, however, does not prevent interactions from taking place. The latter could, for instance, take the form of collisions (the use of different systems of geolocalisation may well lead to such an epilogue) or that of imitation. And none of them implies collaboration, agreement, or the establishment of a 'dialogue' as a precondition. Courts of different systems necessarily interact, because today, legal communication is transnational in nature. This is a fact we all experience, as lawyers and as human beings living in a globalised society. We continuously receive and transmit pieces of information that have their origin in national legislation and courts, regulatory authorities, professional associations, arbitral tribunals, EU law, international courts, UN bodies, private standards, and so on.

17.3.3 Re-Entry and Constructive Misunderstanding

As mentioned earlier, mutual observation among different regimes and courts is inevitable today, because of the transnational nature of various human activities and the overlapping of multiple authorities in what has been called 'multilevel governance'.[80] As a matter of fact, different legal

[78] Müller, Some Observation on Social Anthropology, *supra* note 69, at 179.

[79] Constitution of the United Nations Educational, Scientific and Cultural Organization, (16 November 1945) 4 UNTS 275, entered into force 4 November 1946.

[80] See, for instance, G. Marks, and L. Hooghe 'Unravelling the Central State, but How? Types of Multi-Level Governance', *American Political Science Rev.* 23:2 (2003) 233–43;

authorities and regimes address the same subjects, or regulate the same activity. Whatever their moral, ideal and cultural divergences, judges therefore have good reason to observe each other closely. Yet, interaction is not reduced to mere observation. Rather, different regimes can exert pressure on each other and prompt the reaction of their counterparts, which may eventually modify their internal structure by internalising external logics.

The main point is that transnational regimes are autonomous, but not isolated. They are exposed to the normative expectations and reactions of their social environment, which includes, for instance, the pressure exerted by public opinion, but also by other legal authorities and regimes.[81] Thus, regimes (and their courts) observe their environment and try to minimise its disappointment by readjusting their own internal structure or logic (for instance, in the form of a new jurisprudence) whenever they perceive that their environment's normative expectations have been frustrated to an extent which puts the regime's authority into peril. In doing so, regimes and their courts may even be pushed to internalise external rationalities.[82] This is the so-called process of re-entry, through which a regime internally reproduces what it has observed in its environment. We could say that this is the Teubnerian counterpart to the notion of cross-fertilisation.[83]

However, it is important to note that a re-entry is not a simple transposition. Rather, it always implies a reconstruction, a translation in the language of the new regime. Yet, as we know, translations always look different from the original.[84] The Eiffel Tower can be reproduced in detail in Las Vegas, but it will never look like the one in the Champs de Mars. This is why we can speak of constructive misunderstanding. Courts adopting doctrines or solutions elaborated in other regimes always do it out of the original context, bringing into a national system a doctrine elaborated by an international court, or into a common law country the solutions

Y. Papadopoulos, 'Problems of Democratic Accountability in Network and Multilevel Governance', *European L. J.* 13:4 (2007) 469–86; A. von Bogdandy and P. Dann, 'International Composite Administration: Conceptualizing Multi-Level and Network Aspects in the Exercise of International Public Authority', A. von Bogdandy *et al.* (eds.), *The Exercise of Public Authority by International Institutions* (Berlin: Springer, 2010) 883–912; R.A. Wessel and J. Wouters. 'The Phenomenon of Multilevel Regulation: Interactions between Global, EU and National Regulatory Spheres', *Int'l Organizations L. Rev.* 4:2 (2008) 259–91.

81 See Fischer-Lescano and Teubner, Regime-Collisions, *supra* note 61, at 1037–38.

82 See Tornhill, Luhmann's Political Theory, *supra* note 70, at 132–35.

83 See Fischer-Lescano and Teubner, Regime-Collisions, *supra* note 61, at 1030–31; and Teubner and Korth, Two Kinds, *supra* note 72, at 12.

84 See G. Teubner, 'The Anonymous Matrix: Human Rights Violations by "Private" Transnational Actors', *Modern Law Review* 69:3 (2006) 327–46, at 337.

elaborated in a country of civil law tradition. To reproduce thus means to reinterpret and to re-contextualise. In this process of evolution by reproduction, the court plays a central role.

The most obvious example of re-entry is the decision of the European Court of Justice (now Court of Justice of the European Union (CJEU)) to establish a system of human rights guarantees in response to the *Solange I* jurisprudence of the German Constitutional Court.[85] This is a typical case in which a regime was irritated by another regime and prompted to partially internalise an external rationality. As we know, the *Solange* doctrine has influenced the jurisprudence of different courts and has been interpreted in many different ways. A solution which originally concerned the relationship between a national court and the CJEU[86] has successively been applied to the relations between the European Court of Human Rights (ECtHR) and the CJEU,[87] between national courts and the ECtHR,[88] and – as maintained by some authors – even between the CJEU and the United Nations Security Council in *Kadi*.[89] This rapid diffusion proves the capacity

[85] Federal Constitutional Court (BVerfG, Germany), Judgment of 29 May 1974, 2 BvL 52/71 (*Solange I*). For a comment, see A. Reinisch, 'Conclusion', A. Reinisch (ed.), *Challenging Acts of International Organizations before National Courts* (Oxford University Press, 2010) 263–65; N. Lavranos, 'The Solange-Method as a Tool for Regulating Competing Jurisdictions Among International Courts and Tribunals', *Loyola of Los Angeles Int'l and Comparative L. Rev.* 30:3 (2008) 275–334; A. Tzanakopoulos, 'Judicial Dialogue in Multi-level Governance: The Impact of the *Solange* Argument', O.K. Fauchald, A. Nollkaemper (eds.), *The Practice of International and National Courts and the (De-) Fragmentation of International Law* (Oxford: Hart Publishing, 2012) 185–215; and M. Milanovic, 'Norm Conflict in International Law', *Duke J. of Comparative and Int'l L.* 20:1 (2009–2010) 102–31.

[86] *Solange I*, *supra* note 85; Federal Constitutional Court (BVerfG, Germany), Judgment of 22 October 1986, 2 BvR 197/83 (*Solange II*); Italian Constitutional Court, *Frontini v. Ministro delle Finanze*, Judgment of 27 December 1973, No. 183/1973.

[87] See *Matthews v. the United Kingdom* (Appl. No. 24833/94), Judgment (Grand Chamber), 18 February 1999, ECHR 1999-I, 251, para. 32; *M and Co. v. Federal Republic of Germany* (Appl. No. 13258/87), Decision (Commission), 9 February 1990, D.R., Vol. 46, 138; *Bosphorus v. Ireland* (Appl. No. 45036/98), Judgment (Grand Chamber), 30 June 2005, ECHR 2005-VI, 107; *Waite and Kennedy v. Germany, Beer and Regan v. Germany* (Appl. Nos. 26083/94, 28938/95), Judgment (Grand Chamber), 18 February 1999, ECHR 1999-I, 393.

[88] See, for instance, Italian Constitutional Court, Judgment of 24 October 2007, No. 349: 'The Constitutional Court, before proceeding to make its judgment on alleged unconstitutionality, ensures that the norm of international law does not conflict with the constitutional regime, or at least that it does not offer a lesser degree of protection than can be derived from the Constitution.' (author's translation); (in Italian: 'la Corte costituzionale, prima di procedere al giudizio sulla asserita illegittimità costituzionale, verifica che la norma internazionale non contrasti con la disciplina costituzionale o comunque non offra una tutela minore rispetto a quella deducibile dalla Costituzione').

[89] According to Tzanakopoulos, Judicial Dialogue, *supra* note 85, at 208 the *Kadi* judgment of the ECJ (now CJEU) would be 'the ECJ's *Solange I* in response to the UN's exercise of

for adaptation of the different regimes that have adopted a *Solange*-like solution. It also shows that the 'equivalent protection' mechanism is particularly well suited to a world characterised by the co-existence of a plurality of legal regimes. In fact, such a mechanism allows different regimes to interact, mutually provoking and influencing each other and to find an equilibrium by internalising each other's rationality.

This being said, in this entire process we do not see much 'dialogue' in the idealistic sense described earlier. We do not see people coming together in a spirit of openness to find a shared solution to an issue they all perceive as a problem. Instead, we see interaction. We see a regime which provokes or even threatens another regime, and a court which is urged to react. The reasons that prompted the CJEU to include human rights norms in its legal arsenal did not have much to do with the cosmopolitan spirit of its judges, who did not seem very concerned with human rights before *Solange I*. Rather, the CJEU was committed to bringing an untenable political situation to an end, that is, to enhance the authority of its regime.[90] The lack of a 'dialogue' based on shared values, however, did not prevent the interactions and their effects described earlier from taking place.

This is a clear case of adaptation to the social environment triggered by an external irritation. Like living organisms that develop new defences against a virus they encounter for the first time, legal regimes and authorities detect the threats coming from their social environment and react to them. Luhmann used to describe the process of social adaptation by telling a historical anecdote: when nomadic populations of Central Asia domesticated horses, attaining increased mobility and military superiority, they forced sedentary populations to build fortifications and change their political system.[91] In this respect, it is interesting to note that while nobody would say that Genghis Khan was 'engaging in a dialogue' with the city of Beijing under siege, we nevertheless label the German Constitutional Court/CJEU interaction triggered by *Solange I* as 'dialogue'. We are too used to conceiving of judges as 'inevitable defenders of ordered liberty'[92] – as priests of the global rule of law – to realise that, even without war horses, judges of different regimes may interact more or less like nomadic hordes and fortified cities.

governmental authority without adequate fundamental rights safeguards'. See joined cases C/402/05 P and C-415/05 P, *Kadi and Al Barakaat International Foundation v. Council et al.* [2008] ECR I-6351, ECLI:EU:C:2008:461.

90 See in this regard Tzanakopoulos, Judicial Dialogue, *supra* note 85, at 195–96.

91 N. Luhmann, *A Sociological Theory of Law* (London: Routledge, 1985); the example is also described by Müller, Some Observation on Social Anthropology, *supra* note 69, at 174.

92 Stephan, Courts on Courts, *supra* note 58, at 113.

Having said this, it is necessary to offer a clarification before additional considerations are made. In the previous pages, I have often referred to the comparison between courts of different regimes following clearly different logics as a decidedly pointed example of how interaction takes place also in the absence of a shared goal, and an ideal common ground between judges. Yet, such an example does not exhaust the typology of possible interactions between courts. It is clear, for instance, that national supreme courts cannot always be associated with a precise functional logic. Be that as it may, my intent here is to stress the importance of the relationship between a court and the normative expectations of its social environment. In the case of the functional regimes referred to earlier in the chapter, the main point is that, whatever the divergences or the similarities among judges, functional regimes are generally expected and even required to follow a specific logic. Were they to give up this task entirely, they would frustrate the expectations of their environment: after all, what is the point in having a specialised institution if it does not enhance its functional rationality? Similarly, even when it is impossible to associate a court with a specific institutional logic, the court's environment will nonetheless have normative expectations that judges will try not to disappoint, in order to defend their authority. To this end, courts will (a) either refer to the decisions of foreign courts, (b) avoid to do so, (c) or take a stance of defiance toward another court or regime. As highlighted further in subsection 17.3.5, the decision of a court to address one of its counterparts or to explicitly reject the decision of another court and thus enter into a conflicting relationship with it mostly depends on the way in which courts perceive the normative expectations of their environment. The abstract convergence of ideas and values between judges of different courts (their 'elective affinities') may play less of a role.

17.3.4 Non-Transjudicial Processes of Legal Decision-Making: Why Focus Only on Court-to-Court Interactions?

If the social environment of a court can influence the latter's decision-making, such an environment is not limited to other courts, but extends to a broader number of actors and social interactions. Judicial decisions can in fact be the point of arrival or the triggering factor of different transnational processes of decision-making, which do not necessarily involve other courts and therefore do not concern transjudicial communication. By focusing exclusively on court-to-court relations and on the similarities amongst judges, we lose sight of these non-judicial transnational legal processes and of how they may influence the extent and effects of transjudicial interaction. We forget, in other words, that judicial decisions are just a small portion of a larger 'ongoing process of articulation, adaptation, re-articulation, absorption, resistance, deployment, and on and on'.[93]

This idea is shared by certain scholars. The view that 'relatively spontaneous, unchoreographed interactions among private parties, mid-level bureaucrats, and NGOs seemingly inadvertently spark a process which ultimately produces law' is, for instance, at the core of Koven Levit's bottom-up approach to international law-making.[94] A similar view is expressed by Teubner and Fischer-Lescano, according to whom 'an arena for a plurality of law-making mechanisms' would be established at the periphery of the diverse legal regimes, while courts would occupy the centre of each regime.[95]

The point to be stressed is that these bottom-up or centre – periphery interactions are not confined within the borders of states, but often take place on a transnational basis, following the global dimension of many sectors of society (global economic transactions, global religions, global scientific community, the global college, etc.). Just as governments are no longer the only state organs participating in international relations, courts are no longer the only actors taking part in transnational legal communication. The process and its effects are decentralised, and it can happen that actors other than courts notice a foreign judgment or another piece of legal communication before national courts do, or even, when national courts ignore it, in their place. At the same time, non-judicial transnational processes can determine the extent and effects of some transjudicial interaction.

As an illustration, we can take the process triggered by the judgment on religious circumcision rendered by the Cologne *Landgericht* on 7 May 2012. In short, the court held that male circumcision for religious reasons was to be considered an illegal practice causing bodily harm in the sense of article 223 of the German Penal Code. Such a practice was also considered in breach of the fundamental rights of the child to physical integrity and self-determination under article 2 (1) and (2) of the German *Grundgesetz*.[96] The judgment is interesting, especially for the consequences

[93] P.S. Berman, 'A Pluralist Approach to International Law', *Yale J. of Int'l L.* 32:2 (2007) 301–30, at 329.

[94] J.K. Levit, 'Bottom-Up International Lawmaking: Reflections on the New Haven School of International Law', *Yale J. of Int'l L.* 32:2 (2007) 393–420, at 409.

[95] Fischer-Lescano and Teubner, Regime-Collisions, *supra* note 61, at 1012–13.

[96] Judgment on male circumcision for religious reasons, District Court of Cologne, Judgment of 7 May 2012, 151 Ns 169/11.

it sparked beyond the borders of Germany. Soon after the decision, the Zurich children's hospital and the hospital of St. Gallen suspended the performance of circumcisions, pending 'evaluations of legal and ethical considerations'.[97] Spokespersons of the Zürich children's hospital explained that, even if Switzerland was not 'directly affected by the Cologne ruling',[98] the German decision had sparked a debate on how to reconcile the rights of the children to physical integrity and self-determination and the right of parents to religious freedom. Martin Kilias, professor of Criminal Law and Criminal Procedure at the University of Zürich, declared that the Cologne judgment was 'a point of ignition for a debate which had been brewing for some time [and that Swiss hospitals had] absolutely taken the right decision'.[99] Meanwhile, in Austria, the governor of Vorarlberg ordered state-run hospitals of the region to stop circumcision 'until the legal situation is clarified'.[100]

In mid-August 2012, the two Swiss hospitals resumed surgeries, announcing that 'the future circumcisions would be examined on a case by case basis, subject to consideration for children's welfare'.[101] It was also announced that both parents would have to give written consent to the procedure. In Austria, the situation was resolved by the official intervention of the Federal Justice Minister Beatrix Karl, who reassured doctors of the Austrian federal state of Vorarlberg that they could 'perform the religious practice without risking charges'.[102]

Finally, in September 2012, at the 21st session of the UN Human Rights Council, the International Humanist and Ethical Union – an NGO with special consultative status – submitted a written statement,[103] in which it followed the reasoning of the *Landgericht* of Cologne and expressed 'concerns regarding the lawfulness and human rights implications of

97 See S. Douez, 'Legal Experts Divided Over Circumcision', *Swissinfo* (26 July 2012), www.swissinfo.ch.

98 See 'Hospitals in Austria and Switzerland Suspend Circumcision', *The Telegraph* (25 July 2012), www.telegraph.co.uk.

99 S. Douez, Legal Experts Divided, *supra* note 97.

100 See 'Swiss Hospitals Rescind Circumcision Ban', *The Times of Israel* (12 August 2012), www.timeofisrael.com; Hospitals in Austria, *supra* note 98.

101 Hospitals in Austria, *ibid.*

102 See 'Austrian Justice Minister Rules Doctors May Resume Circumcision', *Haaretz* (30 July 2012), www.haaretz.com.

103 UN Human Rights Council, 21st Session. Agenda Item 4: Human Rights Situations that require the Council's Attention. Written Statement Submitted by the International Humanist and Ethical Union, a Non-governmental Organization in Special Consultative Status. Ritual Circumcision of Male Children, 30 August 2012, UN Doc. A/HRC/21/NGO/21.

non-consensual circumcision carried out solely on religious grounds'.[104] It therefore suggested the postponement of the genital cutting and a replacement of the circumcision by a symbolic ritual.[105]

The fact that two important Swiss public hospitals, the governor of an Austrian region and an NGO have taken important administrative and political measures following a German judgment not binding on them shows that processes of 'authoritative' persuasion concern not only judges but also other state officials and decision-makers in general. Such a communication therefore works on a multi-level basis, that is, not only among national courts but also among national courts and other foreign or transnational actors. In this light, the importance of a common professional identity, and its relevance for explaining the extent of transnational judicial dialogue should be put into perspective.

What is more, these peripheral interactions, by amplifying the effect of the original foreign judgment, may ultimately prompt other national or supranational courts to adopt a certain solution. In such a case, it would be inaccurate to attribute such an outcome (effect) exclusively to the capacity of the judge to 'engage in a dialogue' with his/her counterparts. The limit of the judicial dialogue approach is precisely that it takes into account only judicial decisions, losing sight of a much broader legal decision-making process that can also determine the extent and effects of transjudicial processes. As a consequence, judges are described almost as hermits living in isolation from society, yet in constant telepathic contact with their colleagues around the globe.

These considerations have to do with methodological choices. Given its structure, the notion and scholarly project of 'judicial dialogue' entails a precise choice to zoom into judges, excluding other relevant actors and dynamics from the picture. This is understandable. Lawyers have traditionally shown a deferential attitude towards judges, perceiving them as a primary source of authority, just like an ancient Greek would have seen the oracle of Delphi, treating judgments like holy writs containing some invisible truth to be found through a process of rationalisation. As Judge Bedjaoui once put it when addressing an audience of international law scholars, '*vous nous faites parfois plus intelligents que nous sommes. Vous nous faites découvrir une profondeur dans nos jugements que nous ne soupçonnions pas tant!*'.[106] Lawyers may therefore find it natural to

[104] *Ibid.*, at 3.

[105] *Ibid.*, at 5.

[106] 'You sometimes make us out to be more intelligent than we are. You make us discover a depth in our judgment that we did not suspect was so great!' (author's translation).

focus exclusively on oracle statements, thus avoiding any mixing of the judge with the NGO, the sacred with the profane. Yet this is just one of the possible choices, with its consequences and blind spots for understanding the extent and wider effects of transjudicial and non-transjudicial communication.

17.3.5 External Dimension vs. Internal Dimension

In the previous sections, I have observed that the scholarly project designated by the label 'judicial dialogue' tends to read court-to-court communication in isolation from other social interactions that may influence legal decision-making. In this section, I stress that such a reading tends to focus on what courts have in common rather than on the specific relationship between each court and the social environment in which it operates. As I briefly discuss, this approach risks underestimating the relationship between a court and its specific audience as a factor explaining (at least in part) the extent and effects of courts' engagement in transjudicial communication.

In order to explain this engagement, the judicial dialogue model generally focuses on an external dimension: a common framework of values and shared professional practices somehow transcending the single court and the individual judge. This idea is epitomised by the concept of the global community of courts. The vision of a community of individuals sharing the same professional commitment is reminiscent of the notion of 'community of practice', developed in the field of cognitive anthropology[107] and then adapted to linguistics[108] and international relations.[109] Communities of practice 'are groups of people who share a concern or a passion for something they do and learn how to do it better as they

M. Bedjaoui, 'La Multiplication des Tribunaux Internationaux ou la Bonne Fortune du Droit des Gens', Société Française pour le Droit International (ed.), *Colloque de Lille: La juridictionnalisation du Droit International* (Paris: Pédone, 2002) 529–45, at 531.

107 In this respect, see E. Wenger, *Communities of Practice: Learning, Meaning and Identity* (Cambridge University Press, 1998); E. Wenger, R. McDermott and W. M. Snyder, *A Guide to Making Knowledge: Cultivating Communities of Practice* (Boston: Harvard Business School Press, 2002).

108 See for example J. Holmes and M. Meyerhoff, 'The Community of Practice: Theories and Methodologies in Language and Gender Research', *Language in Society* 28:2 (1999) 173–83.

109 In this regard, see E. Adler, 'Communities of Practice in International Relations', E. Adler, *Communitarian International Relations: The Epistemic Foundations of International Relations* (New York: Routledge, 2005) 3–29.

regularly interact'.[110] More specifically, such communities are groups having a particular 'identity defined by a shared domain of interest',[111] as well as the context in which its members develop a 'shared practice'.[112]

It would be pointless to contest the very existence of such a community of practice among colleagues sharing common problems. However, it is worth asking to what extent communities of practice are a necessary factor of unity and harmonisation that drives transnational judicial communication rather than one of division and fragmentation. It is, for instance, clear that, by their very nature, communities overlap. In this sense, Emanuel Adler emphasises that 'people simultaneously participate in various overlapping communities whose boundaries are sometimes indistinct'.[113] This may ultimately imply a multiplication of identities rather than a convergence towards a single global one. Judges are members of a global community of judges, but also of a community of national judges, international judges, constitutional judges, national criminal law judges, EU law judges, trade law judges, human rights judges, and so forth. The broadest community does not replace the others, but co-exists with them. Moreover, there is no reason to think that the broadest community should exert a greater influence on its members than any of the other communities (quite the contrary, if one thinks that practices are internalised through daily interaction).[114] Furthermore, for an irony of sorts, the concept of 'community of practice' is also the theoretical ground on which Harlan Grant Cohen explains the fragmentation of international law, observing multiple legal communities,[115] while Slaughter sees only a 'global community of law'.[116]

An alternative approach consists in concentrating on the particular reasons prompting each court to take a certain decision and to adopt (or not to adopt) the solutions elaborated by the courts of other regimes, as well as the distinct purposes of each court engaging in this practice. Teubner, for instance, does not focus on shared practices, but on particular

[110] E. Wenger, *Communities of Practice, A Brief Introduction* (2006), available at www.ewenger.com/theory.

[111] *Ibid.*

[112] *Ibid.*

[113] E. Adler, Communities of Practice, *supra* note 109, at 6; see also H. G. Cohen, 'Finding International Law, Part II: Our Fragmenting Legal Community', *New York University J. of L. and Politics* 44:4 (2012) 1049–1108, at 1064.

[114] See, for instance, Wenger, Communities of Practice, *supra* note 109.

[115] Cohen, Finding International Law, *supra* note 113, at 13–17.

[116] Slaughter, Judicial Globalization, *supra* note 31, at 1114.

rationalities.[117] From this perspective, the way in which courts decide cases and react to external solicitations depends mainly on the logic and purpose of the regime to which they belong. Additionally, the fact that judges share the same professional practices and legal skills does not prevent them from promoting different purposes and following different discourses. In this view, professional proximity cannot cancel differences existing at the level of rationality and institutional policy. For example, the International Court of Justice (ICJ) is a court that is mainly concerned with inter-state disputes, and whose main clients are states. It is therefore not surprising that it prioritises the interests of sovereign states over other conflicting interests, such as human rights. It was therefore clear to most that such a court could never accept a *Ferrini*-like solution,[118] declaring that the *jus cogens* character of certain prohibitions trumps sovereign immunity.[119] The outcome of *Germany v. Italy* was easy to guess, not because of the 'cosmopolitan spirit' of the ICJ, but due to its default preferences.[120]

Admittedly, one could argue that the effect of transjudicial communication on this judgment was easy to predict because the *Ferrini*-solution was particularly unconvincing. In this respect we have to recall that, according to the judicial dialogue model, the spreading of a solution envisaged by a certain court depends largely on its persuasiveness.[121] Now, one way to look at the problem is to present persuasiveness as an almost objectively and universally observable characteristic of the solution proposed: if courts have so much in common and pursue the same objectives, then they will find the same arguments and solutions persuasive. However, this view would fail to see that different courts could find different arguments to be persuasive. In this perspective, one could recall that in 2001 the Grand Chamber of the ECtHR rejected the hypothesis of a 'human rights exception' to state immunity by just nine votes to eight.[122] The fact that half

117 In particular, he does not ask how operations are carried out, but which social rationality they serve. See, for instance, R. Michaels, 'Global Legal Pluralism', *Annual Rev. of L. and Social Science* 5 (2009) 1–35, at 7: 'instead of communities, [Teubner] views discourses at the bases of legal pluralism'.

118 See Court of Cassation (Italy), Judgment of 11 March 2004, No. 5044/2004.

119 See *Jurisdictional Immunities of the State (Germany v. Italy, Greece intervening)*, 3 February 2012, ICJ Reports (2012), 99. For a discussion of this judgment as well as the Italian Constitutional Court's *Ferrini* judgment, see the report on practice by Judge Raffaele Sabato in this volume (Chapter 10).

120 *Ibid.*

121 See, for instance, Slaughter, A Typology, *supra* note 4, at 124–25; of the same author, see also Judicial Globalization, *supra* note 31, at 1111; and A Global Community, *supra* note 7, at 200–01.

122 *Al-Adsani v. the United Kingdom* (Appl. No. 35763/97), Judgment (Grand Chamber), 21 November 2001, ECHR 2001-XI, 79. For a comment, see E. Bates, 'The *Al-Adsani* Case,

of the judges voted in favour of such an exception shows that the argument was convincing to them. Therefore, the question to be asked is: persuasive to whom? The *Ferrini*-argument was certainly unconvincing in the eyes of the ICJ because of the particular logic and institutional sensitivity of the latter, but it was not objectively unpersuasive. The rationality and purpose of the regime and the particular sensitivity of the court therefore often make the difference that determines the extent and effects of transjudicial interaction.

If the existence of radically different rationalities (e.g. peace and security vs. human rights) plays a relevant role in regard to the communication occurring between international or transnational autonomous regimes, the same is not true for holistic legal orders such as domestic systems. Yet, in both cases, the fact that different regimes have different environments is significant in explaining the extent of transjudicial 'dialogue'. According to Luhmann, the social system and its environment are mutually constituted.[123] This means that every system has a certain view of the world that surrounds it and attributes a certain relevance to certain elements of it rather than others. Different systems and different regimes therefore have different visions of the world – or even see different worlds. This implies that courts have different audiences, for example that judges will address different people and attribute a special significance to some actors rather than others. For instance, we may suppose that the ICJ will look especially to states and UN organs, while the ECtHR will probably attribute a particular importance to individuals. This is particularly relevant for two reasons. The first is that, as we have seen, the environment can have an impact on the regime, especially by provoking changes in its structure and logic. The second is that when someone justifies something, they always do so by addressing an audience or having such an audience in mind.[124] We always measure the persuasiveness of an argument (and assumptions about its possible effects) against an image of our audience: Will the reader find it persuasive? This is particularly true for judges. Different environments,

State Immunity and the International Legal Prohibition on Torture', *Human Rights Law Review* 3:2 (2003) 193–224.

[123] See B.R. Hornung, 'The Theoretical Context and Foundations of Luhmann's Legal and Political Sociology', M. King and C. Thornhill (eds), *supra* note 67, 187–216, at 198–99; Müller, Some Observation, *supra* note 69, at 174; Fischer-Lescano and Teubner, Regime-Collisions, *supra* note 61, at 1037–38.

[124] See in this regard C. Perelman and L. Olbrechts-Tyteca, *The New Rhetoric: A Treatise on Argumentation* (Notre Dame, Indiana: University of Notre Dame Press, 1969) 18–19: 'since argumentation aims at securing the adherence of those to whom it is addressed, it is, in its entirety, relative to the audience to be influenced'.

therefore, can also lead to different decisions with regard to the use of foreign and international material.

There is also another factor to be taken into account in this context. Judges are *bricoleurs*: they assemble the different materials they have at hand in order to make their case. The concept of *bricolage*, described as the assembly of something new from whatever is at hand, was first elaborated by Claude Levi-Strauss to explain the process of mythopoesis among primitive people.[125] Numerous authors later referred to this idea in order to describe the reasoning process followed by judges in deciding cases.[126] Arthur Leff, for instance, referred to *bricolage* as the process 'by which judges … bend concepts or rules to serve diverse purposes rather than create new ones more particularly crafted to the job at hand'.[127] As the concept of *fictio juris* illustrates, judges always innovate by pretending they are not – that is, by bending the existing material they have at hand. In order to justify a certain choice, and solve particular problems, judges could therefore potentially assemble any element able to persuade their audience and achieve the desired effect with their decision. External decisions and sources of authority are naturally included in the range of possible material usable by the *bricoleur*, and the Internet has obviously enlarged the range of available materials. However, following this model, cases are not selected for their abstract consistency with a certain principle. Instead, their main value seems to reside in the fact that they are at hand and they happen to be functional to support a certain claim. In this light, the so-called cherry-picking attitude seems more a structural feature of judicial reasoning than an exceptional pathology. The discretion of the judge-*bricoleur* is, however, limited by the expectations of his/her environment and the characteristics of their audience. Judges do not primarily write and engage in transjudicial communication for making a case in the abstract, but rather to persuade a specific audience and to achieve a particular effect. The process of *bricolage* is always tailored to an audience, and consequently limited by the latter.

125 See C. Levi-Strauss, *The Savage Mind*, translated from the French by G. Weidenfield and Nicholson Ltda. 1962 (University of Chicago Press, 1966) at 17.

126 See, for instance, R.J. Krotoszynski, '"I'd Like to Teach the World to Sing (in Perfect Harmony)": International Judicial Dialogue and the Muses – Reflections on the Perils and the Promises of International judicial Dialogue', *Michigan L. Rev.* 104:6 (2006), 1321–60, at 1334; M.V. Tushnet, 'The Possibilities of Comparative Constitutional Law', *Yale L. J.* 108:6 (1999) 1225–1310, at 1238; and N.E.H. Hull, 'Networks & Bricolage: A Prolegomenon to a History of Twentieth-Century American Academic Jurisprudence', *American J. of Legal History* 35:3 (1991) 307–23, at 317–19 (regarding lawyers in general).

127 A.A. Leff, 'The Leff Dictionary of Law: A Fragment', *Yale L. J.* 94:8 (1985) 1855–2252, at 2212.

17.3.6 *Inevitability and Contingency*

While the previous sections have mainly dealt with the purpose and extent of judicial dialogue, the present one is principally concerned with its effects. The main argument that I put forward in this regard is that the fact that different courts address each other does not in itself have any specific consequence or effects. As we have seen, although different actors continuously observe each other, they react to external solicitations in various ways, according to their different characteristics, sensibilities and the normative expectations of their audiences. As a result, the effects of a global judicial interaction appear highly contingent and unpredictable. This obviously contradicts the Slaughterian prediction that connecting judges around the world in a global network would result in 'collective transjudicial deliberations', implying some inevitable effects,[128] such as 'the spread and enhanced protection of universal human rights'.[129]

In this respect, the process of transjudicial communication does not seem to be directed towards achieving any particular purpose or effect: it is neither inherently human rights friendly nor necessarily anti–human rights. *Kadi*[130] shows that in certain situations the best way to protect human rights is to assume a 'parochial stance', reading one's own legal order in complete isolation from other regimes. Moreover, the fact that many courts would be referring to the human rights–related jurisprudence of their counterparts (as highlighted by Slaughter)[131] does not prove much. The point is not how much courts are quoting, but what decision (or paragraph) they are quoting, and with what purpose and effect. In fact, not only are decisions restricting human rights available for quoting just as much as the decisions more favourable to human rights, but the same decision can be used to justify different outcomes.

Clearly, not all human rights–related judgments referring to comparative material have the effect of enhancing human rights protection. For instance, European courts normally approach the problem of the relationship between the immunity of international organisations and the right to an effective remedy in very different ways, to the extent that while some of them are reviewing the immunity in light of the European Convention

128 Slaughter, A Typology, *supra* note 4, at 132–35.

129 *Ibid.*, at 134.

130 *P. Kadi and Al Barakaat International Foundation v. Council and Commission*, *supra* note 89.

131 Slaughter, A Typology, *supra* note 4, at 130.

on Human Rights or of their constitutional law, others are not willing to review the immunity at all.[132] Moreover, as Cedric Ryngaert has noted, these different tendencies 'appear to be transnational in nature, which implies that, within one jurisdiction, different tendencies are at work at the same time'.[133] Human rights are only one of the several discourses that are continuously communicated in our world society, just one of the conflicting rationalities that judges have to take into account.[134] The relations between fundamental rights and other conflicting rationales are set in different ways, more or less suitable to enhancing human rights protection. More importantly, all of these compromises are available for transjudicial communication, published on databases and ready to be quoted by *bricoleur* judges in increasingly more places around the world.

Whatever the benefits of collective intelligence may be, judicial decisions are not the outcome of a sophisticated software programmed to enhance human rights protection or to reach any other effect. And no inevitable progress of history will favour the achievement of any of them. Judicial interaction works in all directions and does not preclude any possible effect. There are no inevitabilities in the process of transjudicial communication. Instead, the effects of the process are always eminently contingent, depending on social and individual preferences, national and international political pressures, the mood of public opinion and countless other variables. In other words, everything could have gone differently, and everything could always be otherwise.

17.4 Conclusion

Metaphors are desires of the mind, and judicial dialogue is no exception. We (Western international law scholars) would like to see judges around the world sharing our (Western) liberal values and engaging in a mutual enterprise to strengthen human rights and the rule of law. In some historical periods, we may even think we are witnessing the materialisation of these dreams. This is, after all, the natural consequence of a certain kind of eschatological perspective deeply internalised by lawyers. While waiting for the materialisation of the cosmopolitan dream, we read all events and social phenomena as signs confirming the inevitable fulfilment of the prophecy. This is what I have called the idealistic cosmopolitan approach

[132] C. Ryngaert, 'The Immunity of International Organizations Before Domestic Courts: Recent Trends', *International Organizations L. Rev.* 7:1 (2010) 121–48, at 136.

[133] *Ibid.*

[134] Teubner, Global Bukowina, *supra* note 50, at 3–4.

to transjudicial communication. Often, our analysis and explanation of the extent, method, purposes and effects of this transnational judicial communication are intentionally or unintentionally tainted by this approach.

Yet it suffices to follow Kennedy's suggestion to 'take a break'[135] from the cosmopolitan dream of international law to see reality in a different light. From this non-cosmopolitan point of view, judges do not dialogue for the purpose of finding shared solutions to shared problems, nor is the extent to which dialogue occurs inevitably determined by shared values and purposes. Rather, courts interact. They observe each other, exert pressure on their counterparts and sometimes reproduce the solutions developed by others in different contexts. These operations do not require common moral ground or a particular form of cultural unity, as Slaughter seems to imply. Instead, even courts of regimes following different social rationalities can interact, just like nomadic hordes and fortified cities mutually exert pressure on each other.

Significant to understanding the purpose of transjudicial interaction (i.e. the reason why a court decides to address or quote one of its counterparts' decisions) is the relationship between a court and its environment, or audience. This chapter suggested that judges are *bricoleurs*; they use everything they have at hand – including external or foreign judicial decisions – to make their case and persuade their audience. The very decision to refer to external sources and the extent of the references can, in this light, be explained by the simple fact that judges have to be convincing in their interpretation and application of relevant law. It may even be conjectured, in this regard, that Google and electronic databases have played a more important role in enhancing the extent of cross-referencing among different courts than the willingness of judges to enhance the legitimacy of transnational law or to build a global rule of law.

In addition, the decision to refer to foreign judicial decisions can be driven by the court's willingness to react to normative expectations of its social environment. An external decision may, for instance, be the pretext to justify a *revirement jurisprudentiel* that appears to be strongly required by a given environment, but which national or internal case law do not envisage or would not permit. Pressure to change may also come from other courts, as in the *Solange* case. Yet, external pieces of communication will only be taken into account to the extent that the senders are perceived as authoritative or relevant by the deciding court – that is, that they are part of the environment constituted by the latter. Different courts may in

135 *Supra* note 65.

fact have very different perceptions as to what actors are to be taken into account and what audience is to be persuaded.

These considerations are also relevant in understanding the extent of transjudicial communication. In fact, the extent to which the judge-*bricoleur* can use foreign and international material finds a limit in his or her audience, or social environment and their normative expectations. The *bricolage* activity of the judge has the purpose of persuading a particular audience with given characteristics, rather than meeting abstract criteria of legitimacy or persuasiveness. As noted before, a court's social environment may push towards a change that requires an external point of reference for the court; in this case, the audience is the element that prompts the judge to find a justification in foreign case law. Yet, it is also possible that the audience reacts negatively to the decision of the judge that refers to a foreign decision, thus setting a limit to the extent of dialogue. Therefore, judges' choices concerning their use of foreign and international material can only be understood by locating and defining their audiences. It is indeed the audience that determines the persuasiveness and the acceptability of a particular reference to foreign legal materials. Nevertheless, since speakers and their audiences mutually influence each other, judges can, to a certain extent, contribute to shaping the normative expectation and the sensitivity of their audiences.

This leads us to the question of the methodology to follow in analysing transnational legal communication – a methodology that allows us to uncover these and further factors that determine the extent, purpose and effects of transjudicial interaction. In this respect, it might be helpful to focus on the audience of the court, or the social environment of the regime, rather than exclusively on the role of judges. In other words, the question is not only what the judge is quoting in his or her decision, not only who the judge has met and what values he or she shares, but to whom the judge is speaking and who reads the decision. Traditionally, international lawyers have approached this question in the light of a limited court-to-court perspective.[136] And since the question determines the answer, they have observed that judges are talking to each other, and so they conjectured that it might be so because of a common professional sensitivity (as maintained by Slaughter).[137] Yet, courts do not operate in a social vacuum. Enlarging the scope of the analysis, we note, for instance, that courts are just one of the actors involved in a complex transnational process of legal

[136] See *supra* notes 34–36.
[137] *Ibid.*

communication, and that judgments are often the consequence – the triggering factor or the intermediary stage – of a broader legal process which does not necessarily involve other judges, but is relevant nonetheless.

A final word shall be added to the desired or expected effects of transjudicial communication. Unless one assumes the existence of a common framework of values able to clearly orient the action of courts (presumption we have rejected for the reasons exposed in subsection 17.3.2), it is difficult to ascribe specific consequences to the consistent resort to judicial dialogue. Opposite effects can be justified on the basis of different foreign decisions, sometimes even on the basis of the same judgment. As far as human rights are concerned, it is evident that judges looking at the decisions of their counterparts will find both good arguments to make human rights prevail over conflicting interests and good arguments to limit the application or the effects of human rights. Transjudicial communication is always multidirectional; it continuously transmits an indefinite number of compromises among different contrasting rationalities and discourses, each of which has a chance to be selected and replicated by other courts. In this context, the spread of a given solution depends on an infinity of variables such as the personal experiences and sensitivity of the judges, the preferences of their audience, the mood of public opinion, the institutional framework in which the judges operate and, as noted earlier, the idea a court may have as to the composition of its relevant audience. It can be said that transjudicial communication at the time of the Internet does not orient the flux of possible solutions towards a given end such as the strengthening of democracy and human rights. Rather, it multiplies the possible outcomes. It is not a stream flowing in one direction (as the idealistic approaches tend to depict it), but an ocean where different currents, pointing in different directions, are at play at the same time. As often happens with complex processes, the effects are contingent and even random.

18

Conclusion

AMREI MÜLLER

The contributions to this book reveal that the practice of judicial dialogue on human rights is widespread in domestic and international courts around the world. Aided by the common framework for this volume, this concluding chapter offers a comparative summary of the various chapters' main findings on the extent, method, purpose and effect of judicial dialogue on human rights.[1] Particular emphasis is placed on the question about the overall effect of judicial dialogue on the protection of human rights. The findings from all contributions help to address the overarching questions posed in Chapters 16 and 17: Do courts' judicial dialogues aim to enhance the protection of human rights and improve the democratic credentials of democracies in a globalised world? If so, do such dialogues actually help to secure the rule of (human rights) law at the domestic and international level? Or are the courts' dialogues instead random exercises, driven by various factors which lead to unpredictable outcomes, that might enhance or undermine human rights?

18.1 Domestic Courts, Judicial Dialogue and Human Rights

18.1.1 Extent

With the exception of Nigerian and Malaysian *Sharīʿah* courts, all domestic courts that have been studied in this volume have increased their judicial dialogues on human rights, however defined, over the years. Much of this increase occurred when and because international human rights treaties were transformed into domestic law, when fundamental rights were given a stronger position in domestic constitutional law or when apex courts in the respective countries reinforced the weight of international human rights treaties in domestic jurisprudence. In Latin America, incorporation

[1] The framework is set out in the introduction to this edited volume, Section 1.2. All the following footnotes refer to the respective chapters and contributions by judges in this volume.

of international human rights treaties into domestic law at the level of domestic constitutions began in the mid-1990s, spreading among countries in the region. This started a far-reaching process of horizontal dialogue on human rights between domestic courts within and outside the region.[2] After the fall of the Iron Curtain, Poland and other Eastern European countries adopted new constitutions, inspired by international human rights treaties. They also opened up to the influence of international law, giving human rights treaties a strong position in domestic law and leading domestic courts to actively interpret and apply domestic law in light of international human rights law.[3] Even if not correlated to the incorporation of international human rights treaties into domestic law, increased engagement in judicial dialogue by the Canadian Supreme Court also appears linked to an enhanced position of human rights in domestic law due to adoption of the Canadian Charter of Rights and Freedoms in 1982.[4] Analyses from Germany, Italy and the United Kingdom also highlight that the weight highest courts accord to international human rights treaties and the case law of international courts can influence the extent that domestic courts in the respective countries engage in vertical and horizontal dialogue.[5]

By contrast, Nigeria and Malaysia have not integrated international human rights treaties into the domestic legal order in a way that allows *Sharīʿah* courts to refer to ratified international human rights treaties. Therefore, unlike in Latin America, Canada and Eastern Europe, domestic bills of rights or incorporated international human rights treaties do not induce judicial dialogue in Malaysian and Nigerian *Sharīʿah* courts with foreign domestic or international courts applying similar provisions of national constitutional law and/or international human rights treaties.

From this we can conclude that domestic courts' engagement in judicial dialogue increases both with the level of incorporation of international human rights treaties and with the willingness of domestic courts to interpret domestic constitutional law in light of international human rights law. This is so even when the 'importing' and 'exporting' courts do not apply the same international human rights treaty directly, but when domestic law is interpreted in light of international human rights law, or when the 'importing' court relies on decisions from an 'exporting' country that

[2] Chapter 3, Section 3.2.

[3] Chapter 2, subsection 2.2.1.

[4] Chapter 4, subsection 4.2.2.

[5] Reports on practice by Judges Paulus (Chapter 9), Lord Carnwath (Chapter 8) and Sabato (Chapter 10).

has ratified the same international human rights treaties as the 'importing' country. In the latter cases, even if the 'exporting' court bases its decision on domestic law, the 'importing' court may take on the 'exporting' court's decision. This is done based on the assumption that the domestic law applied by the 'exporting' court is in line with relevant international human rights treaties that have been ratified by both the 'exporting' and 'importing' states. In these situations, international human rights treaties serve as conduits for dialogue – a phenomenon that is particularly prominent in South America, but also in Eastern Europe and other member states of the Council of Europe (CoE).[6]

The case of judicial dialogue on complementary protection discussed in Chapter 6 further highlights that the existence of common domestic legal concepts can induce horizontal dialogue between domestic courts, whereas courts in states that deviate from these commonalities are little involved or entirely excluded from this dialogue. At the same time, the analysis reveals that the absence of a clear international regulation of a matter can foster horizontal dialogue: this is the case when the subject matter requires a cross-national, concerted response, and where an international or regional court is absent that would induce vertical dialogue on all relevant questions concerning complementary protection.[7]

Even in cases where the applicable law is not conducive to domestic courts' engagement in dialogue, this does not need to prevent all dialogue. Chapter 5 points to the possibility that dialogue between *Sharīʿah* courts applying different schools of Islamic law and between *Sharīʿah* courts and international human rights courts could develop in the future. Such dialogue could be based on certain provisions of the applicable Islamic law that are formulated in an open fashion, inviting interpretation in light of schools of Islamic law other than the one applied by the 'importing' court, and in light of international human rights law as interpreted by regional and international human rights courts and quasi-judicial bodies. For this to happen, and irrespective of the outcome for the protection of human rights, judges on these *Sharīʿah* courts would need to open up to such a possibility and carefully move towards a more dynamic interpretation and application of their respective law.[8]

The extent of dialogue is also determined by the degree to which lawyers in a particular country accept foreign material. Neither South American,

[6] Chapter 3, subsection 3.6.3; Chapter 2, subsection 2.2.4.
[7] Chapter 6, Section 6.3.
[8] Chapter 5, Section 5.4.

Eastern European nor Canadian judges nor the domestic judges from Germany, Italy and the United Kingdom who contributed to this volume questioned that, in principle and within certain limits, the engagement with foreign and international material can improve the quality of their decisions. Heated controversies about the legitimacy of engagement in judicial dialogue, as take place in the US Supreme Court, are absent in the domestic courts studied in this volume. On the contrary, as Judge Paulus formulated in his contribution, many European apex courts engage in mutual interaction as a matter of course, based on the assumption that this leads to 'mutual learning and the development of common ideas on the meaning of 21st century constitutionalism in Europe and beyond'.[9] This approach seems shared by South American and Canadian judges.[10] This is confirmed also by the fact that domestic judges studied in this volume rely on comparative material in majority, dissenting and concurring opinions with most references to foreign and international material being made in majority opinions. Not covered by this trend are, however, the decisions of Nigerian and Malaysian *Sharīʿah* courts, a fact that is attributed to the 'ideological barriers'[11] established by the different schools of Islamic law that these courts apply.

Confirming earlier research, domestic courts analysed in this book cite mainly decisions of courts in Western liberal democracies, with the (Western) European apex courts, the US Supreme Court, as well as Australian and Canadian courts leading the way. South American courts, in addition, increasingly engage in dialogue with each other, a tendency that can also be observed among Eastern European courts. This is particularly so in cases that touch on human rights issues that are common to the respective region, for example forced disappearances and amnesty laws in South America, or where domestic courts face similar challenges related to the transformation process from authoritarian to democratic systems in Eastern Europe.[12]

Which foreign courts are cited is commonly determined by cultural, legal, linguistic, historical and political ties. This is clear in the inter-regional horizontal dialogue between South American courts and the dialogue between Latin American courts and the Spanish Constitutional Court.[13] The Canadian Supreme Court relies most frequently on decisions

[9] Chapter 9 by Judge Paulus.

[10] Chapter 3, Sections 3.2 and 3.3.3; Chapter 4, subsection 4.3.1.2.

[11] Chapter 5.

[12] Chapter 3, subsection 3.3.4; Chapter 2, subsections 2.4.1 and 2.4.3.

[13] Chapter 3, subsection 3.3.5.

of other Commonwealth states, even though the adoption of the Canadian Charter of Rights and Freedoms also resulted in increased referencing to US Supreme Court decisions and to European Court of Human Rights (ECtHR) case law.[14] National judges, moreover, have confirmed that language, the detail and thoroughness of reasoning of the cited courts' judgments and the degree of similarity between the legal questions to be solved are decisive factors that influence their decisions of whether or not a foreign or international material is cited.[15] The Canadian and UK supreme courts predominantly cite decisions of foreign courts available in English, with the Canadian Supreme Court also relying on decisions available in French.[16] Inter-Latin American dialogue is facilitated by the common Spanish/Portuguese languages; and Polish courts rely on foreign judgments not only in English but also those available in German, due to the fact that many Polish judges have a good command of German.[17] Chapter 7, analysing legislative dialogues on the protection of same-sex couples' rights, reveals that social, cultural and linguistic similarities are an important driver for dialogues between parliaments as well.[18]

Different rights and issues attract varying numbers of foreign citations in the domestic courts studied in this book. Not surprisingly, often decisions on specific aspects of a human right the scope of which is unclear and/or on rights that are affected by social, cultural, scientific, technological, medical or other developments include the most references to foreign and international material. In Latin America this concerns cases on freedom of expression, war crimes, forced disappearances and rights of LGTBI people.[19] In Canada, cases that require delicate balancing between different rights, or between individual rights and public interests engender the most references to foreign and international material, something that can also be observed in Polish and other Eastern European courts' dialogue.[20] In Canada, this often involves the interpretation and application of the general limitation clause in the Canadian Charter of Rights and Freedoms that requires Canadian courts to review whether limitations to fundamental rights are necessary 'in a free and democratic society'.[21] The

[14] Chapter 4, subsection 4.3.1.1.

[15] See in particular Chapter 8 by Lord Carnwath and observations in Chapter 6, subsection 6.3.2.

[16] Chapter 8; Chapter 4, subsection 4.3.1.1.

[17] Chapter 2, subsection 2.2.4.

[18] Chapter 7, Section 7.2.

[19] Chapter 3, subsection 3.3.4.

[20] Chapter 2, subsection 2.4.3; Chapter 4, subsection 4.3.4.

[21] Charter 4, Section 4.1.

strong prominence of vertical judicial dialogue in the area of complementary protection offered to migrants who do not qualify as refugees under the UN Refugee Convention is, among other things, also due to the fact that this area of law is affected by constant developments. The circumstances that cause individuals to flee and seek protection abroad are constantly changing.[22] Frequently, it is in these 'difficult' cases affected by changing circumstances that domestic courts engage with foreign and international material thoroughly in their reasoning. In other words, they go beyond making superficial references to foreign or international material.

By contrast, the analysis reveals that decisions interpreting and applying rights that are concretised in detail in domestic legislation are less likely to refer to foreign and international material. An example mentioned in the analysis of Latin American courts and Eastern European courts' dialogue is due process rights, which are additionally often strongly influenced by the historical particularities of a specific domestic legal system.[23] Moreover, domestic courts engage in dialogue usually only on questions of law, most often questions concerning substantive law. An exception is the judicial dialogue on findings of fact in complementary protection cases, in particular on country-of-origin information.[24] It is due to the specificity of the subject area that factual conclusions are considered generalisable when they concern individuals who come from the same country or region, and who face similar threats of persecution in their home country due to their similar personal circumstances.

In addition to the factors already mentioned, further shared factors emerge from the analysis that explain the extent to which domestic courts engage in judicial dialogue on human rights or refrain from doing so. The first factor is regional integration processes promoted *inter alia* by regional human rights courts that facilitate horizontal and vertical judicial dialogue of domestic courts. Polish and other Eastern European courts' wish to bring domestic law into line with EU law and ECtHR jurisprudence has greatly increased these courts' engagement in judicial dialogue with the Court of Justice of the European Union (CJEU), the ECtHR and domestic apex courts in member states of the CoE and the EU.[25] Similar processes, facilitated *inter alia* by the Inter-American Court of Human Rights (IACtHR), can be observed in Latin America.[26] Chapter 7, in addition, reveals that legislative

[22] Chapter 6.
[23] Chapter 2, subsection 2.2.2; Chapter 3, subsection 3.3.4.
[24] Chapter 6, subsection 6.6.1, and Chapter 15 by Judge Nußberger.
[25] Chapter 2, subsections 2.4.1 and 2.4.2.
[26] Chapter 3, Section 3.2.

dialogues on the rights of same-sex couples have been promoted through regional organisations, as has happened through initiatives of the Nordic Council and the EU.[27] The role of regional organisations encouraging horizontal and vertical dialogue seems particularly important in cases where the religious, socio-cultural or political environment is not conducive to trigger such dialogue otherwise. This is also clear from the analysis of domestic courts' horizontal dialogue on complementary protection which, at times, has attained new momentum in EU member states through the involvement of the CJEU (e.g. on the question of granting complementary protection to persons fleeing situations of generalised violence).[28]

Second, parallel non-judicial transnational processes can have a positive influence on the extent of domestic courts' engagement in dialogue. This is particularly so in regard to dialogue on questions that are politically or socially charged, as the example of dialogues on the protection and promotion of LGTBI rights shows. In these areas, transnational legislative dialogues can facilitate transnational judicial dialogues, and networks of civil society organisations (e.g. gay and lesbian associations) can give further pushes to the practice.[29]

Third, strong ideological divergences, in particular those based on religious, social and political factors, between 'importing' and 'exporting' courts are a clear obstacle to judicial dialogue. This emerges most prominently from Chapter 5 on Malaysian and Nigerian *Sharī'ah* courts' non-engagement in judicial dialogue. Ideological factors prevent dialogue not only between *Sharī'ah* courts and non-*Sharī'ah* courts but also between *Sharī'ah* courts that apply different schools of Islamic law.[30] Similarly, Chapter 3 reports a drop in Venezuelan courts' engagement in judicial dialogue at a time when the Venezuelan government became more critical of the influence of the Inter-American Commission on Human Rights (IACHR) and the IACtHR, eventually resulting in Venezuela's withdrawal from the American Convention on Human Rights (ACHR).[31] Examples to the contrary are effective judicial and legislative dialogues on the rights of same-sex couples in countries where the social and political environment is supportive of such dialogue, and where this dialogue is thus picking up on shifting social attitudes towards homosexuality.[32]

27 Chapter 7, Section 7.2.
28 Chapter 6, subsection 6.6.5.
29 Chapter 7, Sections 7.2 and 7.5.
30 Chapter 5, Section 5.3.
31 Chapter 3, subsection 3.3.1.
32 Chapter 7, Section 7.4.

18.1.2 Method

The analysis reveals that domestic courts around the world use similar methods to discover relevant domestic and international material, but that preferences for a particular method vary from court to court and from judge to judge. Often, it is not entirely clear how exactly domestic judges have learned about foreign or international jurisprudence, as this is not made explicit in the judgments. Some comparative findings are summarised here nonetheless.

First, judges and their assistants in all domestic courts analysed in this book regularly conduct their own comparative research, with the exception of Malaysian and Nigerian *Sharīʿah* courts. This method of finding relevant foreign and international material is particularly prominent in the Canadian Supreme Court, in the UK Supreme Court, in South American courts and in the domestic courts that engage in horizontal dialogue with foreign domestic courts on questions relating to the concept of complementary protection offered to migrants. This comparative research is, however, not conducted systematically, let alone formalised or institutionalised. The contributions from domestic judges to this book and the results from interviews with judges of the Canadian Supreme Court summarised in Chapter 4, rather, indicate that judges' personal interests and affinities to comparative law and to a specific legal system play an important role in determining the extent to which comparative research is conducted, and on which jurisdictions this research focuses.[33] An exception is, of course, European apex courts' research on the jurisprudence of the CJEU and the ECtHR, which is conducted more systematically due to this jurisprudence being legally binding on these courts. Not surprisingly, all chapters and contributions covering domestic courts indicate that research on comparative material by judges themselves has been greatly facilitated by the establishment of electronic databases as well as the translation of important domestic judgments into English.

Second, for many domestic judges, participation in regional and international networks of judges has a considerable influence on their degree of knowledge about decisions made by their colleagues in other countries, in regional and international human rights courts and in quasi-judicial bodies. This is particularly so in South America, where these networks are very strong, and judges' interaction has led to spreading knowledge about

33 Reports on practice by Lord Carnwath (Chapter 8) and Judges Sabato (Chapter 10) and Paulus (Chapter 9); Chapter 4, subsection 4.3.1.2.

landmark cases of South American apex courts to an extent that they 'cannot be ignored'[34] by South American judges. Networks give participating judges opportunities to learn about important developments in each other's jurisprudence. They provide fora for conferences, seminars or other face-to-face meetings, prepare collections and summaries of important decisions of domestic courts and develop training manuals on a particular area of law. Especially Chapter 6 identifies the latter as an important source of relevant comparative material for judges applying complementary protection legislation.[35] Chapter 7 highlights that legislative dialogue on the protection of LGTBI rights can profit from the knowledge that is shared between parliamentarians who are connected through regional organisations such as the EU, the CoE or the Nordic Council.[36]

Third, submissions by the parties to the case as well as *amicus curiae* interventions are another important source for judges to learn about relevant international and foreign jurisprudence. Judges from the common law jurisdictions such as Canada and the United Kingdom have identified both submissions of the parties and the *amici* briefs as a particularly relevant source of comparative material[37]; these submissions are among the sources through which Polish judges also gain access to comparative material.[38] They alert judges not only to primary sources such as foreign or international case law but also to secondary sources such as academic analyses of foreign and international law and jurisprudence.

Last, the reliance on personal contacts between judges in different countries, sometimes established through aforementioned networks, is also important when judges wish to find out about relevant comparative and international material. Contributions from the United Kingdom and South America report directly on personal contacts as a source of information on comparative material.[39] In addition, Chapter 7 indicates that personal contacts between parliamentarians can drive legislative dialogues on the protection of human rights. This has been the case in regard to the spreading of early laws protecting same-sex couples in Scandinavia.[40]

[34] Chapter 3, subsection 3.6.4.

[35] Chapter 6, Section 6.4.

[36] Chapter 7, Section 7.2.

[37] Chapter 4, subsection 4.4.2; Lord Carnwath's report on practice (Chapter 8); and Chapter 10, concerning the ECtHR.

[38] Chapter 2, Section 2.3.

[39] Chapter 8; Chapter 4, subsection 4.4.1.

[40] Chapter 7, Section 7.2.

18.1.3 Purpose

Chapters identify a range of motives (purposes) for domestic judges to take part in judicial dialogue or to refrain from doing so. The most common among them, highlighted in all chapters and judges' reports on practice, is the aim to find new ideas and persuasive arguments that help to solve difficult legal problems, in particular when comprehensive domestic material is missing. In these situations, foreign and international decisions serve as sources of inspiration and reflection that can contribute to developing the law in a new direction. Relatedly, domestic judges often wish to add authority to a particular decision by showing a wider audience that others have come to similar conclusions. This is particularly relevant in cases where the legal questions raised are socially, ethically or politically challenging. In addition to the examples mentioned earlier,[41] examples are the UK Supreme Court's extensive references to foreign and international material in judgments concerning a possible 'right to die'; South American courts' engagement in dialogue with other South American courts concerning questions of amnesty laws in the region; and the Polish Constitutional Court's decision on the legality of shooting down a passenger airliner hijacked to commit illegal acts of terrorism. In a Canadian context, this aim to add authority to a judgment through dialogue is particularly important in cases where earlier precedents are reconsidered. In all these cases, engagement with foreign and international decisions can give a 'degree of comfort'[42] to the judges themselves who have to make decisions on challenging questions to which there are no easy answers. Furthermore, it can reassure both individuals directly affected by the decision and wider society that judges make these decisions after careful consideration of relevant arguments in which 'all potential sources of enlightenment'[43] have been taken into account. Reassurances to individuals are particularly relevant also for the dialogue on refugee and complementary protection, since these decisions can potentially have serious consequences for individuals if they are sent back to their home country as a result of said decisions. As Chapter 6 reveals, complementary protection cases therefore often entail domestic courts engaging in 'deep and thoughtful analysis of a number of foreign cases' before they settle on a solution.[44]

[41] See *supra*, subsection 18.1.1.

[42] See Lord Carnwath's report on practice (Chapter 8).

[43] Chapter 4, subsection 4.5.1.

[44] Chapter 6, Section 6.5.

However, as the previously summarised discussion about the extent of judicial dialogue indicates, 'sources of enlightenment' from jurisdictions with similar historical, ideological and political features are given most attention. This links to another related purpose of most South American and Eastern European courts' engagement in dialogue: their wish to relate to judges, courts, other states or regional organisations that share similar legal views on the protection of human rights. An example would be a judgment in which the Polish Supreme Court noted explicitly that not taking diligent account of the ECtHR's jurisprudence was 'obviously against the interest of the State',[45] as this would jeopardise the desire to become closely affiliated with the EU and the CoE and the rule-of-law standards these organisations promote. Broader efforts to ensure that judicial dialogue harmonises the protection of human rights in domestic law with developments in regional and international human rights law are also connected to this purpose. In South America, this is directly required of domestic courts due to their expanded constitutional mandate, obliging them to actively interpret and apply regional and international human rights treaties as part of their countries' constitutions. This entails a need for domestic judges to keep up with developments in international and regional human rights jurisprudence.[46] Eastern European courts also engage in dialogue on human rights with the aim to synchronise protection offered by domestic, regional and international provisions.[47]

The analysis in the chapters seems to confirm that at least some courts and individual judges wish to achieve a broader purpose of contributing to the development and strengthening of common constitutional principles and human rights law through engagement in dialogue, if not at the global level then at the regional level. Polish and other Eastern European courts identifying common 'European standards' on which they base their decisions;[48] the President of the German Constitutional Court referring to a European *Verfassungsgerichtsverbund* (comprising national constitutional courts, the ECtHR and the CJEU) that is involved in the development of common European constitutional principles;[49] and the Italian

[45] Decision of the Polish Supreme Court of 11 of January 1995, Ref. No III ARN 75/04, discussed in Chapter 2, subsection 2.4.1.

[46] Chapter 3, subsection 3.6.3.

[47] Chapter 2, Section 2.4.2.

[48] *Ibid.*, subsection 2.4.1.

[49] As noted in the report on practice by Judge Paulus (Chapter 9), referring to A. Voßkuhle, 'The Cooperation between European Courts: The *Verbund* of European Courts and Its Legal Toolbox', Court of Justice of the EU (eds.), *The Court of Justice and the Construction of Europe: Analyses and Perspectives on Sixty Years of Case-law* (Springer: The Hague, 2013) 81–99.

Constitutional Court refusing to give effect to the International Court of Justice (ICJ)'s judgment on jurisdictional immunities in Italy referring to the need to give priority to the protection of fundamental rights set out in the Italian Constitution[50] can hint at those broader purposes. Likewise, the fact that progressive South American judges who are 'willing to go beyond interpretations of domestic law that are based exclusively on the plain text of the respective national provision when an effective protection [of human rights] requires them to do so'[51] established strong networks to achieve this indicates that at least some South American judges also aim to contribute to the development of strong regional South American and international human rights law. Last, Canadian judges stating that engaging in dialogue on human rights means 'to demonstrate established or emerging patterns informing human rights jurisprudence throughout the world'[52] shows that the thought of engaging in dialogue for the purpose of contributing to the progressive development of *international* human rights law is not alien to Canadian judges either. This is supported by the fact that progressive Canadian judgments on human rights have become a source of inspiration for other domestic apex courts and the ECtHR.[53]

Another purpose of engaging in dialogue that has been highlighted in several chapters is the purpose of bringing out and defending differences between domestic solutions and solutions found elsewhere. This is most prominently stressed in Chapter 5 as one possible purpose that a potential dialogue between Nigerian and Malaysian *Sharīʿah* courts and, for example, the ECtHR could have. In a context where such dialogue is so far hampered by ideological divergences, the first steps in such a dialogue could aim at pointing out the reasons for why in some areas Islamic prescriptions are different from those of international or European human rights law. This could, in turn, feed into a global dialogue on international human rights law, enabling courts like the ECtHR to develop a better understanding of Islamic law – something the ECtHR has been lacking in the eyes of some critics.[54]

[50] As discussed in the report on practice by Judge Sabato (Chapter 10).

[51] Chapter 3, Section 3.5.

[52] Chapter 4, Section 4.6.

[53] *Ibid.*, subsection 4.5.2.

[54] See e.g. E. Brems, 'Face Veil Bans in the European Court of Human Rights: The Importance of Empirical Findings', *J. of L. and Policy* 22:2 (2013–14) 517–51; T. Kayaoglu, 'Trying Islam: Muslims before the European Court of Human Rights', *J. of Muslim Minority Affairs* (2014) 34:4, 345–64; and C. Belelieu, 'The Headscarf as a Symbolic Enemy of the European Court of Human Rights' Democratic Jurisprudence: Viewing Islam through a European Legal Prism in Light of the *Sahin* Judgment', *Columbia J. of European L.* 12:2 (2006)

The analysis in this book also shows that the Brazilian and the Canadian Supreme Courts, as well as courts in Eastern Europe, Italy, Germany and the United Kingdom, have used their engagement with foreign and international material for the purpose of justifying solutions that differ from those reached by the court that is cited. They do so pointing to the particularities in domestic legal orders, to underlying principles of these legal orders,[55] and/or to attitudes of the societies under their jurisdiction with which their decisions have to resonate.[56] It can lead to an enhanced protection of human rights in some cases. In others, it can prevent the domestic standard of protection being brought in line with a higher international standard.

Other purposes of dialogue are more specific to particular domestic courts, or to a specific subject area. South American courts, for example, at times seem to engage in dialogue with the aim to protect their independence against the executive power. This purpose can be achieved in particular through the strong networks of judges in the region supporting such dialogue independently from executive relations between the respective countries.[57] An example of a specific purpose of dialogue due to the specific subject matter can be found in national courts' dialogue on complementary protection. This dialogue is strongly geared towards harmonising protection standards offered to migrants in different countries with the sub-purpose of deterring secondary movements of migrants. At the same time, dialogue on matters of fact (country-of-origin information) in complementary protection cases has the clear purpose of saving time and money required to collect the relevant country-of-origin information.[58] Another specific purpose of dialogue is reported from Poland: the (unsuccessful) attempt of the Polish Constitutional Court to widen its own competences through a reasoning based on references to foreign laws setting out the (broader) competences of constitutional courts in other European countries.[59]

573–623. This would not necessarily entail that the ECtHR comes to different conclusions on questions touching on the Islam, but it might lead to judgments that are better reasoned, in the eyes of Muslims as well.

[55] See e.g. Chapter 2, subsection 2.4.5 (concerning the Polish Constitutional Court's decision on defamation) and Chapter 3, subsection 3.6.4 (concerning the Brazilian Supreme Court's decision on amnesties).

[56] See e.g. the judgments of the Russian Constitutional Court discussed in Chapter 2 (subsection 2.4.5) and in Chapter 11 (Section 11.4).

[57] Chapter 3, Section 3.4.

[58] Chapter 6, subsection 6.6.1.

[59] Chapter 2, subsection 2.4.4.

18.1.4 *Effects*

Chapters reveal varying effects of domestic courts' engagement in judicial dialogue which are often closely connected to the purposes for such dialogue. As far as the *legal* effects of references to foreign and international material on domestic courts' decisions are concerned, these effects depend on whether this material emanates from a domestic or an international court, and, in regard to the latter, whether or not the citing domestic court has submitted to the jurisdiction of the respective international court. Judgments from regional integration courts or human rights courts such as the CJEU, the ECtHR and the IACtHR are binding on domestic courts in states parties to the respective treaties that these regional courts enforce, and therefore these judgments are given greater legal weight in decisions of these domestic courts. In fact, as seen in the contributions by German, UK and Italian judges as well as Chapter 2 on Eastern European courts, European apex courts rarely reject following judgments of the CJEU or the ECtHR, even judgments that were issued against states other than their own. Decisions of foreign domestic courts do not have binding force for the domestic courts by which they are considered. They are relied on as sources of inspiration, and are thus engaged with most often in the parts of judgments where decisions are reasoned and justified.

The effects of dialogue on decisions of domestic courts vary depending on the subject matter and on the court that cites the foreign and international material. Some effects appear in many domestic courts discussed in this volume.

Judicial dialogue can have a specific effect on the interpretation and application of domestic law in a particular case which, in turn, can contribute to the development of domestic law. This can lead to the closing of gaps in domestic law, as examples of Latin American courts' judicial dialogue indicate.[60] Also cases have been reported where Russian courts' dialogue with the ECtHR led to the closing of gaps in Russian law.[61] Other examples from South America indicate that dialogue helped to overcome anachronisms in domestic constitutional law through the respective domestic courts engaging extensively with developments in foreign constitutional law and international human rights law.[62]

[60] Chapter 3, subsection 3.6.1.
[61] Chapter 2, subsection 2.4.2.
[62] Chapter 3, subsection 3.6.2.

In other cases, dialogue has the effect of encouraging comprehensive reasoning on difficult legal questions. This is frequently the case in aforementioned judgments that raise difficult social, moral or ethical questions, politically charged questions or where dynamic solutions are needed.[63] In these cases, the exact legal impact of the foreign or international material on the outcome of the case is hard to determine, other than that the references to this material stimulated the thinking of the judges and the reasoning of the court. In some cases, domestic courts might have come to the same conclusion had they based their reasoning solely on domestic law, while in others the engagement with foreign and international material influenced the direction of the judicial reasoning to a considerable extent. Depending on the aforementioned purposes that dialoguing domestic courts wish to attain, foreign or international courts' reasoning is either embraced or rejected. The rejection element and its purpose of helping the 'importing' court to highlight particularities in the domestic law it applies and interprets or to justify its particular line of reasoning are most evident in Chapter 5 on the practice of Nigerian and Malaysian *Sharī'ah* courts, in the Canadian Supreme Court's frequent rejection of arguments or solutions offered by the US Supreme Court, as well as in European apex courts pointing out the rare occasions in which they would consider not to follow jurisprudence of the ECtHR, CJEU or the ICJ.

This hints at the fact that domestic courts' engagement in judicial dialogue can have both a 'harmonising' and a 'fragmenting' effect for human rights law, depending on the case. This, in turn, can lead to an enhanced or diminished protection of human rights. A harmonising effect of protection standards through judicial dialogue leading to either enhanced protection or the deterioration of such protection can be observed in the analysis of selected domestic courts' dialogue on complementary protection in Chapter 6. In this area, harmonisation of protection standards through dialogue is driven by the desire to deter secondary movements of migrants. In some instances, extensive horizontal dialogue on complementary protection led to the enhanced protection of human rights of migrants. In others, it led to lowering the protection standard offered to migrants. Horizontal dialogue leading to a downward spiral towards lower protection has sometimes been stopped through the intervention of the CJEU issuing a more favourable judgment. One such instance is also an example where a regional court has been able to bring an end to horizontal dialogue which was detrimental to ensuring the effective protection of human rights.[64]

[63] See *supra*, section 18.1.1.
[64] Chapter 6, subsection 6.6.5.

Many examples of domestic courts' dialogue in Eastern Europe, Latin America and Canada indicate that, by and large, this dialogue has harmonising effects and at the same time enhances the protection of human rights in the respective countries. This is particularly clear in South America, where judges have spread the 'constitutional block doctrine' to all countries studied in Chapter 3 through horizontal judicial dialogue. The 'constitutional block doctrine' gives international human rights treaties a strong position in domestic constitutional law, at a level on par with the domestic constitutions.[65] In many Eastern European countries, domestic courts' dialogue that brought domestic law in line with European and international human rights standards led to the enhanced protection of individual rights in these countries.[66] Chapter 7 on the protection of same-sex couples' rights also highlights that overall, legislative and judicial dialogues on these rights had positive, harmonising effects, resulting in better legal protection of same-sex couples in the studied jurisdictions.[67]

Instances of domestic courts' rejecting a solution offered by a foreign national or international court can also result in enhanced protection of human rights in the respective jurisdiction. Examples are the Canadian Supreme Court's rejection of US jurisprudence on the death penalty[68] and the Italian Constitutional Court's rejection to give effect to the ICJ's judgment on jurisdictional immunities in the Italian legal order.[69] Other judgments of European apex courts adopted in their dialogue with the ECtHR and the CJEU, setting out (narrower or wider) limits of their willingness to follow jurisprudence of these courts, can either lead to better or worse protection of fundamental rights in the jurisdiction of the respective courts. This depends on how strictly these limits are construed by the respective courts and on their application to specific cases.[70]

18.2 The ECtHR, Judicial Dialogue and Human Rights

Contributions to this book focus on one regional human rights court's engagement in judicial dialogue: the ECtHR. They reveal that the extent, method, purpose and effects of the ECtHR's dialogue with domestic courts

[65] Chapter 3, Section 3.2.
[66] Chapter 2, subsections 2.4.1 and 2.4.2.
[67] Chapter 7, Section 7.4.
[68] Chapter 4, subsection 4.5.1.
[69] Report on practice by Judge Sabato (Chapter 10).
[70] See the discussion of the relevant Eastern European cases in Chapter 2, subsection 2.4.5; of the German Constitutional Court's decisions in Chapter 9; of decisions of the Italian Constitutional Court in Chapter 10; and of UK cases in Chapter 13.

from inside and outside the membership of the CoE, with other CoE bodies as well as with other international and regional human rights courts and quasi-judicial bodies sometimes differs from the extent, method, purpose and effect of domestic courts' dialogue. This is due to the position of the ECtHR as a regional court. In other areas there are great similarities.

18.2.1 Extent

In the vast majority of cases that make it to Strasbourg, the ECtHR engages in extensive dialogue with various national and international actors, first and foremost with domestic courts that have ruled on the case before. This is due to the exhaustion of domestic remedies rule in the European Convention on Human Rights (Convention or ECHR).[71] The extent of the ECtHR's dialogue with domestic courts from states that are party to the case is partly determined by necessities that derive from its position as a regional human rights court. This position does not allow the ECtHR to accomplish certain tasks that can be accomplished by domestic courts. These include fact-finding, the application and interpretation of domestic law and gaining a comprehensive understanding of local circumstances, including those shaped by historical, social, religious and cultural particularities of a country or region. It is therefore in these areas that the ECtHR relies on material brought to it by domestic courts in almost every case, resulting in extensive dialogue. However, the ECtHR also relies on domestic courts' findings on material law in its own judgments, in particular when domestic courts have applied and interpreted the ECHR and ECtHR jurisprudence in their decisions; when they have followed certain procedures leading to their findings on substantive law; when domestic courts offer thorough reasons for their decisions; and when the case at hand concerns areas of European human rights law that are unclear and thus developing.[72] Also in cases where domestic courts have applied the ECHR and well-established ECtHR jurisprudence incorrectly, or in the very rare cases where domestic courts bring forward well-founded arguments why they refuse to give effect to an ECtHR judgment issued earlier, dialogue between domestic courts and the ECtHR will occur.[73]

[71] Article 35(1) ECHR.

[72] Chapter 11, subsection 11.2.4.

[73] Report on practice by Judge López Guerra (Chapter 13), Sections 13.3 and 13.4.

Concerning the extent of the ECtHR's dialogue with domestic courts of CoE member states that are not direct parties to the case, this dialogue is most prominent when it comes to cases in which the ECtHR has to determine whether a 'European consensus' exists on a certain question. However, in many of these cases, the ECtHR relies on domestic laws in these states, not on judgments of domestic courts. The ECtHR's main interest in this context is to establish the general legal situation in CoE member states.[74] Decisions of domestic courts that are not members of the CoE are referred to by the ECtHR quite frequently as well. As is the case with domestic courts' engagement in dialogue summarised earlier, due to linguistic, political and legal affinities, the ECtHR mainly refers to decisions of apex courts in the United States, Canada, South Africa, Australia and New Zealand.[75] Similarly, references to documents emanating from various CoE bodies are numerous in the ECtHR's judgments and decisions, and thus the dialogue between the ECtHR and these bodies is extensive. This is not surprising, given that these CoE entities promote similar values as the ECtHR and the Convention it applies.[76] The extent of the ECtHR's references to material from other regional and international courts as well as quasi-judicial bodies seems more limited, concentrating on areas where there is clear overlap between the subject matter dealt with by the 'exporting' entity. These are often cases involving questions of general international law, or areas of human rights law that are developing, and where innovative solutions are thus required.[77] At the same time, a wide range of material is considered by the ECtHR, emanating from regional and international courts and organisations that go beyond adjudicating and protecting civil and political rights.[78] Chapter 12 reveals that NGOs' *amicus curiae* briefs alerting the ECtHR to comparative material largely match these patterns concerning the 'sources' of the comparative material mentioned.[79] For example, the analysis highlights that most briefs that contain comparative material concern article 8 of the Convention. This is explained by the fact that it is this article that raises the most questions that require an innovative response, due to its broad character and the fact that the notions of 'family life' and 'private life' undergo constant changes.[80]

[74] Report on practice by Erik Møse (Chapter 14), Section 14.3.
[75] *Ibid.*, Section 14.4.
[76] *Ibid.*
[77] Report on practice by Judge Nußberger (Chapter 15), Sections 15.1 and 15.5.
[78] *Ibid.*, Section 15.3.
[79] Chapter 12, Sections 12.4.2 and 12.5.
[80] *Ibid.*, subsection 12.4.1.

18.2.2 Method

As with domestic courts' dialogue, one can ask how the ECtHR finds out about the relevant material from the various courts and other entities with which it engages. Relevant decisions of domestic courts that have considered the case before are regularly supplied with the case file so that no additional research concerning these courts is required. Judgments and decisions from other domestic, regional or international courts, as well as relevant material of other entities, are obtained from the parties to the case; from the ECtHR's Research Division; by relying on the individual knowledge of the ECtHR judges, some of whom have worked at other international courts or organisations before; by building on comparative material that has been used in earlier judgments of the ECtHR or the former European Commission on Human Rights; and through formal and informal meetings between ECtHR judges and other national and international judges.[81] Chapter 12 confirms that submissions by NGOs are also a widely relied-on source of discovery of relevant international and national comparative material.[82]

18.2.3 Purpose

When it comes to the ECtHR's purpose of engaging in dialogue, distinctions have to be drawn between the purpose of engaging with domestic courts from states that are parties to the case and the purpose of engaging with other domestic, regional and international courts and other entities.

At least some of the purposes of the ECtHR's dialogue with the domestic courts from the state that is party to the case seem to be 'strategic'. Such strategic dialogue aims to enable domestic courts to correctly apply and interpret the Convention (or domestic law in light of the Convention), and thus to ensure that domestic courts effectively safeguard Convention rights of the individuals under their jurisdiction. As highlighted in Chapter 11, there is evidence that the ECtHR aims, through its dialogue with domestic courts, to (1) compensate for its own limited capacities; (2) encourage domestic courts to take on a stronger role in enforcing Convention rights at the domestic level, for example through inducing them to more directly consider the ECHR/ECtHR jurisprudence and by encouraging them

[81] Chapter 15, Sections 15.2 and 15.7; Chapter 14, Section 14.2.
[82] Chapter 12, Section 12.5.

to follow certain procedures and to deliver well-reasoned judgments; and (3) encourage domestic courts, where necessary, to actively develop the law of the Convention through dynamic interpretation.[83] The Court tries, *inter alia*, to achieve this purpose by using the margin of appreciation as an 'incentive';[84] by directly confirming to domestic courts that they correctly followed the ECtHR's earlier jurisprudence; and, where necessary, by alerting domestic courts to the fact that they incorrectly applied the ECHR and/or the ECtHR's earlier jurisprudence.[85] In necessarily very rare cases, the purpose of the ECtHR's dialogue is to correct its own earlier jurisprudence through engagement with judgments of domestic courts that set out the reasons for why they refuse to follow earlier ECtHR jurisprudence. This can be the case when the implementation of earlier ECtHR judgments turns out to be very difficult in practice, and/or where the ECtHR has misunderstood the rationale of specific provisions in domestic law that it has criticised in earlier judgments.[86]

The purposes of the ECtHR's dialogue with other domestic, regional and international courts and other entities are numerous, and some are similar to the purposes of domestic courts' engagement in judicial dialogue summarised in the preceding sections. Among the latter is to get access to sources of inspiration, in particular when it comes to solving 'difficult' cases in which the state of European human rights law is in flux, and to ensure the adoption of well-informed and well-reflected decisions.[87] As a regional human rights court whose jurisprudence affects all forty-seven member states of the CoE, the ECtHR strives to get as comprehensive an overview as possible before making decisions in cases that may require a dynamic approach.

Among the purposes that are more specific to the ECtHR's engagement in dialogue as a regional court are the need to make sure that cases under consideration by another court or quasi-judicial body are rejected,[88] and to ensure that ECtHR jurisprudence develops in harmony with the pronouncements of other CoE organs and entities, with more specialised treaties and their interpretation by relevant international bodies, and with general international law.[89] This analysis can also flow into

[83] Chapter 11, Section 11.3.

[84] *Ibid.*

[85] Report on practice by Judge López Guerra (Chapter 13), Sections 13.2 and 13.3.

[86] See the examples brought by Judge López Guerra, *ibid.*, Section 13.4.

[87] Reports on practice by Judge Nußberger (Chapter 15), Sections 15.2 and 15.5; and by Judge Møse (Chapter 14), Section 14.4.

[88] In line with article 35(2)(b) ECHR.

[89] Chapter 15, Section 15.5.

the Court's assessment as to whether a 'European consensus' exists on a certain question.[90]

Many of these purposes of the ECtHR's dialogue are supported through the comparative material brought forward in *amicus curiae* briefs, in particular when it comes to the establishment of a European consensus, the showing of alternative ways to protect the rights of the Convention (providing comparative material as a source of inspiration), and possibilities to use comparative material to progressively interpret the Convention.[91]

18.2.4 *Effect*

The ECtHR's dialogue with domestic courts from states that are parties to the case has numerous effects on these domestic courts and other domestic actors. They vary depending on the case at hand as well as on the respective domestic system with which the ECtHR is interacting. Some general effects can nonetheless be summarised. First, Chapter 11 reveals that the ECtHR's dialogue with domestic courts can increase domestic courts' diligence when it comes to fact-finding and the consistent application of national law as required by some articles of the Convention.[92] Second, the ECtHR's dialogue can lead domestic courts to more effectively enforce ECHR rights at the domestic level by solving relevant cases with reference to the ECHR and/or relevant ECtHR jurisprudence, by following inclusive procedures and by delivering better reasoned judgments. The extent to which this effect is attained depends, *inter alia*, on the general level of compatibility of the respective domestic legal system (including the functioning of the judiciary) with the standards of the Convention. Third, there is evidence that the ECtHR's dialogue with some domestic courts has encouraged these courts to engage in the evolutive interpretation of the ECHR (or parallel domestic constitutional law) in cases that involve issues affected by rapid social, cultural, technological, medical or other changes.[93] Overall, these effects of the ECtHR's dialogue are well in line with the principle of subsidiarity that characterises the cooperative relationship between the ECtHR and domestic courts when it comes to securing the rights of the Convention in the various member states of the CoE. Dialogue with domestic courts from states that are party to the case

[90] Chapter 12, Section 12.3.

[91] *Ibid.*, Section 12.5.

[92] See e.g. articles 5(1), 8(2)-11(2) ECHR.

[93] Chapter 11, Section 11.4; report on practice by Judge López Guerra (Chapter 13), Sections 13.2 and 13.3.

can, in rare cases, also have the effect of the ECtHR changing its previous jurisprudence on a certain question.[94] By and large, the analysis of the situation in Germany and Russia in Chapter 11 concludes that the ECtHR's dialogue with domestic courts in states that are parties to the case has a positive effect on the level of protection of human rights in the respective countries, as it strengthens domestic courts' capacities to enforce the ECHR.

Among the effects of dialogue with other domestic, regional and international courts, quasi-judicial bodies and other entities is the harmonisation of the ECtHR's jurisprudence with developments in general international law as well as the proactive and dynamic interpretation of the rights of the Convention in light of present-day conditions, following or rejecting the inspiration drawn from 'external' material. Especially in regard to the dynamic interpretation of the ECHR, as a human rights court, the ECtHR assumes a leading role, resulting in a situation where it not always adheres to the findings of other international or regional courts, quasi-judicial bodies or other entities touching on similar questions. Concerning questions of general international law, and driven by the prime desire to ensure harmony in the development of general international law, the ECtHR seems less likely to reject findings by international courts (e.g. the ICJ).[95] Generally, however, it is rare that 'external' material has a decisive influence on the outcome of the ECtHR's findings – its effect being rather one as a source of inspiration that can radiate into various segments of the judgment, including the concurring and dissenting opinions.[96]

18.3 Judicial Dialogue – Aimed at Enhancing the Rule of Human Rights Law or More Random?

Finally, it remains to be considered what these findings on the extent, method, purpose and effects of domestic courts' and the ECtHR's dialogue tell us in regard to the question of whether overall, judicial dialogue is conducive to enhancing the rule of human rights law in the countries studied in this volume and at the international level. Relatedly, does this dialogue contribute to the forging of a cosmopolitan human rights law that will help to resolve the difficulties faced by parliamentary

[94] Chapter 13, Sections 13.4 and 13.5.
[95] Report on practice by Judge Nußberger (Chapter 14), Section 14.6.
[96] Report on practice by Judge Møse (Chapter 15), Section 15.4.

democracies in a globalised world with effectively representing and ensuring justice to their people, as argued in Chapter 16? Or are the effects on human rights protection of this dialogue unpredictable and random, due to the many varying judicial and non-judicial factors influencing domestic and international court's dialogue in every single instance, as suggested in Chapter 17?

The answers to these two questions remain inconclusive. The discussion in Chapter 16 suggests that there are instances where dialogue might indeed lead to the development of relevant domestic and international law that enhances the protection of individual rights and improves the ability of democracies to effectively represent their citizens. This dialogue may be driven by judges who share certain cosmopolitan values.[97] On the other hand, arguments made and examples given in Chapter 17 indicate that the effects of courts' engagement in dialogue (or rather, their interaction[98]) is influenced by a large number of factors. Judges' shared values are only one factor, which can be complemented or overlaid by other factors, such as parallel non-judicial dialogue processes, (non-human rights) interests of those who judges see as their primary audience, power relationships, judges' (random) knowledge about foreign law and access to information, a court's wider social environment, misunderstandings and so forth.[99]

Overall, the dialogues concerning international human rights treaties and fundamental rights in domestic constitutions studied in this book enhance the protection of human rights in the particular jurisdictions, and can also have a positive influence on the development of regional and international human rights law. The effects of Latin American courts' horizontal dialogues, and of Polish, other Eastern European and Canadian courts' horizontal and vertical dialogues, support the former claim, and so does the ECtHR's extensive engagement with domestic courts in countries that are parties to the respective case. In addition, the resistance of domestic courts to give effect to judgments coming primarily from non-human rights courts (but also the ECtHR) in their domestic legal order can uphold human rights protection within the jurisdiction of the relevant domestic court. In the long term, this can also lead to positive developments in international human rights law. The Italian Constitutional Court's opposition to give effect to the ICJ's judgment on jurisdictional

[97] Chapter 16, subsections 16.3.3 and 16.4.2, giving the example of judicial dialogue on the right to privacy in a digital age.

[98] Chapter 17.

[99] *Ibid.*

immunities is the latest example of this sort. The Italian Constitutional Court directly indicated that it wished to induce a change in the law on immunities, a change that makes this law more protective of individual rights.[100] Should this type of interaction be called 'dialogue'? As Pasquet reminds us, it might rather be the latest example of one regime (ICJ) being irritated by another regime (Italian Constitutional Court).[101] The longer term effects of this 'irritation' on the development on the law of immunities and human rights will become clearer only in the future.

The analysis also reveals that judicial dialogue is particularly important to ensure sustained progress in the development of human rights law in areas affected by social, cultural, technological, medical or other changes. Threats to peoples' ability to enjoy their human rights are subject to constant change. In the words of Daniele Gallo and Matteo Winkler, it is in the capacity of human rights to adapt to changing circumstances, in their capacity to *evolve* 'that the universal – rather than immutable – character of human rights actually lies'. They observe further that it is 'this character [that] can be reinforced by principled dialogue between national and international legislatures and courts … on human rights issues'.[102]

These overall findings on the rights-enhancing effect of judicial dialogue lead us to consider whether dialogue should be extended to further areas of human rights law, as well as to national and international courts whose primary task is not to secure human rights. Such dialogue could, for example, lead to a stronger protection of economic, social and cultural rights, something that is called for in a world affected by financial and economic crises,[103] or a more constructive understanding of the relationship between Islamic law and international human rights law. To achieve this, courts must open up to consider new sources: (Western) European apex courts and the ECtHR could draw on Latin American jurisprudence on economic, social and cultural rights; and *Sharī'ah* courts in Nigeria and Malaysia could engage with international human rights treaties and jurisprudence, be it only to heighten other courts' understanding of the reasons why some matters are regulated differently under Islamic law. The result would be a more inclusive dialogue on *all* human rights, which could further enhance their effective implementation and development.

[100] Discussed by Judge Sabato (Chapter 10).
[101] Chapter 17, subsection 17.3.3.
[102] Chapter 7, Section 7.4.
[103] See e.g. A. Nolan (ed.), *Economic, Social and Cultural Rights after the Global Financial Crisis* (Cambridge University Press, 2014).

Annex 1

Transnational Judicial Dialogue: Concept, Method, Extent and Effects

OSLO, 21–22 JUNE 2013

Guiding Questions to National Judges

The ERC project 'MultiRights', the ECRP project 'International Law through the National Prism: the Impact of Judicial Dialogue' and the Norwegian Centre of Excellence 'PluriCourts' host the conference *'Transnational Judicial Dialogue: Concept, Method, Extent and Effects'* on 21–22 June 2013 at the University of Oslo. In addition to the presentation of selected academic papers, roundtable discussions with national judges and judges at the European Court of Human Rights (ECtHR) will be held covering the actual practice of several domestic courts and the ECtHR. Together with judges from other domestic courts, you have kindly agreed to sit on a panel covering domestic courts' judicial dialogue. With this document, we aim to provide you with some additional background information on the projects and the conference and, most importantly, to give you some guidance as to what questions we would like you to discuss during your panel.

Synopsis

The conference will explore the practice of transnational judicial dialogue on issues involving international law by and between domestic and international courts.[1] It seeks to examine whether, how, when and why courts engage in such dialogues; and what the effects are of this practice. In particular, the conference aims to clarify the concept and extent of court-to-court dialogue, the process itself, its limits and possibilities, as well as any influence it may have on the international legal order further

[1] By international courts we mean all international and regional courts that can issue binding judgements, but also international and regional quasi-judicial bodies, like the UN human rights treaty bodies, which can only give 'recommendations'.

down the line. The conference also seeks to address how transnational judicial dialogues occur in different regions of the world and in various fields of law. However, a particular emphasis is put on the European region as well as on human rights/constitutional law (excluding EU law). This regional and thematic focus is reflected in the judges' panels: it is planned to hold one panel discussion with three domestic judges from Germany, Italy and the United Kingdom and another one with three judges from the ECtHR.

Background

Domestic and international courts and tribunals across the world play an important and increasing role in giving effect to international law. National courts take into account judgments by international courts and quasi-judicial bodies, but international courts may also rely on judgments by national courts. Furthermore, national judges may look at how their colleagues in other states have construed international law. There is evidence that such a transnational judicial dialogue takes place in and between various jurisdictions.

While the concept and definition of transnational judicial dialogue will in itself be part of the issues to be discussed at the conference, for the purpose of this document and the following questions we adopt a broad working definition of what we mean by transnational judicial dialogue by domestic courts: any reference by national courts to a decision of a foreign domestic or international court involving international law. With this broad definition we aim to cover all aspects of national courts' references to the decisions of foreign domestic or international courts involving international law, even if there is no 'dialogue' in the true sense of the word that involves an on-going 'conversation' between different courts on a question of law during which the courts oppose or support each other. In other words, it can also include a mere reference to a decision of a foreign domestic court or to a decision of an international court or quasi-judicial body. Moreover, we aim to cover cases in which a domestic court refers to a decision of a foreign domestic court, even if this foreign domestic court did not apply international law directly, but where the impact of international law is visible on the foreign domestic court's decision, e.g. through interpretation of domestic law in the light of international law (e.g. the European Convention on Human Rights (ECHR)).

Questions to National Judges

In line with what has been said above, when you are preparing your answers to the following questions, we would encourage you to focus on issues concerning human rights; however, relevant examples from other fields of international law are also welcome. The questions relate to the scope and process, the obstacles to, and the aims and effects of transnational judicial dialogue by your court. They cover your court's dialogue with the ECtHR, with international courts other than the ECtHR and with foreign domestic courts. Some overlap between the questions is unavoidable.

We hope that your answers to all or some of the questions during the panel discussion – together with the academic papers presented at the conference and ensuing discussions – will help establish best practices, allowing domestic and international courts to arrive at sound responses to shared problems, as well as helping us articulate normative perspectives for assessing judicial dialogues. You are welcome to put your main focus on questions that are particularly relevant to your domestic context. However, as we are interested in the aims and effects of your court's judicial dialogue we would be especially grateful for answers to the questions in section II.

I. The scope and process of your court's engagement in transnational judicial dialogue

The following questions aim to first get an overview of the frequency with which your court engages in transnational judicial dialogue. Second, they aim to establish if there are any criteria that your court applies when deciding as to whether, when and with which foreign domestic or international court to engage in transnational judicial dialogue. You are welcome to give specific examples whenever relevant. Questions under 1. and 2. are furthermore separated into questions 1) concerning your court's dialogue with international courts other than the ECtHR and foreign domestic courts and 2) with the ECtHR.

1. Has your court ever referred to decisions of foreign domestic courts and/or decisions of international courts (excluding the ECtHR) that concern a question of international law? If so, when and with what frequency? And how does your court find out about the foreign/international decisions it uses?
   1.1 Does engagement in transnational dialogue depend on whether foreign/international decisions have been brought forward by the

parties to the case, and/or are the cases brought forward by members of your court?

1.2 Are you aware of cases in which decisions of foreign and/or international courts have been raised by the parties and/or members of the court, and in which it was decided not to refer to such decisions in the judgement? If so, why?

1.3 If not raised by the parties to the case, how does your court find out about relevant decisions of foreign domestic and international courts?

1.4 Are references to foreign and international decisions always made explicit in the final judgements of your court?

1.5 Are there certain subjects/issues within human rights law that are more prone to becoming subject to court-to-court dialogue by your court? If so, why?

1.6 Does your court engage with foreign and/or international judges other than through reference to foreign/international decisions, e.g. through formal or informal judges' meetings?

2. Concerning in particular the extent of your court's interaction with the ECtHR:

   2.1 Does your court routinely refer to the ECHR and jurisprudence of the ECtHR?

   2.2 If so, how does your court find out about the relevant ECtHR judgments and decisions? And does it also take account of ECtHR case-law that concerns countries other than your own?

   2.3 Are there certain subjects/issues within human rights law/domestic constitutional law where you would pay particular attention to the ECtHR's jurisprudence? For example, in regard to fundamental rights questions concerning which states' margin of appreciation is likely to change in the near future?

   2.4 Are regular meetings taking place between your court and judges of the ECtHR/your country's judge at the ECtHR?

3. How does your court decide with which foreign domestic or international courts to engage in transnational judicial dialogue on international law?

   3.1 Are the decisions of certain foreign domestic and/or international courts more prone to be considered by your court? Does your court, for example, show a preference for decisions of foreign domestic courts from the same region or similar legal system? Concerning international courts, is there a preference for referring to the decisions of the ECtHR compared to decisions from other international/regional courts and (quasi-)judicial bodies? If so, why?

3.2 In cases concerning *inter alia* the ECHR, has the ECtHR's practice of taking account of a so-called 'European consensus' in cases that involve difficult balancing of different interests prompted your court to pay heightened attention to legal developments in other member states of the Council of Europe and the decisions of their (highest) courts?

3.3 Concerning in particular UN Human Rights Treaty Bodies, are documents (General Comments, Concluding Observations, Views) of some treaty bodies more prone to be cited than others? If so, which are the ones most likely to be taken into account? Why?

4. What are the obstacles to your court engaging in transnational judicial dialogue?

4.1 Are there barriers in domestic (constitutional) law? If so, which?

4.2 Are there practical obstacles, for example limited access to foreign and international judgements/commentaries, language barriers, etc.? Has your court taken its own initiatives to encourage foreign domestic or international courts to refer to your judgments, for example by translating important judgments into English and/or other languages; or by establishing direct contact with judges from national and/or international courts?

4.3 Are there 'political' obstacles to transnational judicial dialogue, e.g. related to the important role accorded to national parliaments in a democratic system in the decision-making processes on issues involving a strong public interest?

5. As a 'conclusion' to this set of questions, could you please make an attempt to discern any criteria from your court's practice that are employed when deciding when and with which national or international court, and how to engage in transnational judicial dialogue? If applicable, you can differentiate between interaction between your court and international courts other than the ECtHR and domestic courts on the one hand and interaction between your court and the ECtHR on the other hand.

II. The aims and effects of your court's engagement in transnational judicial dialogue

The following questions seek to establish what the potential aims and effects of your court's engagement in transnational judicial dialogue are. You are welcome to give specific examples whenever relevant.

1. When referring to decisions of foreign domestic courts and international courts, do you aim to influence the interpretation and application of domestic and/or international law in your country? If so, how (you are welcome to focus in particular on the ECHR here)? Or does your court refer to decisions of foreign national or international courts for merely 'decorative' purposes?
2. Do you see transnational judicial dialogue as a catalyst for developing international law, in particular (European) human rights law; or rather as a strategy to avoid the application of international law?
3. Concerning in particular the ECtHR, do you engage in transnational judicial dialogue with the ECtHR with the aim to assert your court's interpretation of the ECHR/domestic law in light of the ECHR if it differs from the ECtHR's interpretation? Or is it rather your aim to ease and/or prevent any tensions or conflicting interpretations of the ECHR when engaging in judicial dialogue with the ECtHR? Are there examples of your court engaging in judicial dialogue with the ECtHR for the purpose of promoting a particular progressive interpretation of the ECHR not only in your own country but in other member states of the Council of Europe as well?
4. If your court has initiated a judicial dialogue with other domestic courts, the ECtHR or international courts other than the ECtHR, e.g. in form of regular formal or informal meetings of judges, what is the concrete aim and effect of this initiative?
5. Did recourse to transnational judicial dialogue by your court ever result in any tensions with your national parliament on the interpretation and/or application of a particular domestic law or the ECHR?

Thank you very much for taking the time to consider these questions. We look forward to the panel discussions in Oslo in June!

Annex 2

Transnational Judicial Dialogue: Concept, Method, Extent and Effects

OSLO, 21–22 JUNE 2013

Guiding Questions to Judges at the European Court of Human Rights

The ERC project 'MultiRights', the ECRP project 'International Law through the National Prism: the Impact of Judicial Dialogue' and the Norwegian Centre of Excellence 'PluriCourts' host the conference *'Transnational Judicial Dialogue: Concept, Method, Extent and Effects'* on 21–22 June 2013 at the University of Oslo. In addition to the presentation of selected academic papers, roundtable discussions with national judges and judges at the European Court of Human Rights (ECtHR) will be held covering the actual practice of several domestic courts and the ECtHR.

Together with other judges at the ECtHR, you have kindly agreed to sit on a panel covering the ECtHR's engagement in transnational judicial dialogue. With this document, we aim to provide you with some additional background information on the projects and the conference and, most importantly, to give you some guidance as to what questions we would like you to discuss during your panel.

Synopsis

The conference will explore the practice of transnational judicial dialogue on issues involving international law by and between domestic and international courts.[1] It seeks to examine whether, how, when and why courts engage in such dialogues; and what the effects are of this practice. In particular, the conference aims to clarify the concept and extent of court-to-court

[1] By international courts we mean all international and regional courts that can issue binding judgements, but also international and regional quasi-judicial bodies, like the UN human rights treaty bodies, which can only give 'recommendations'.

dialogue, the process itself, its limits and possibilities, as well as any influence it may have on the international legal order further down the line. The conference also seeks to address how transnational judicial dialogues occur in different regions of the world and in various fields of law. However, a particular emphasis is put on the European region as well as on human rights/constitutional law (excluding EU law). This regional and thematic focus is reflected in the judges' panels: it is planned to hold one panel discussion with three domestic judges from Germany, Italy and the United Kingdom and a separate one with three judges from the ECtHR.

Background

Domestic and international courts and tribunals across the world play an important and increasing role in giving effect to international law. National courts take into account judgments by international courts and quasi-judicial bodies, but international courts may also rely on judgments by national courts and other international courts and quasi-judicial bodies. Furthermore, national and international judges may look at how their colleagues in other states or at international courts have construed international law. There is evidence that such a transnational judicial dialogue takes place in and between various jurisdictions.

While the concept and definition of transnational judicial dialogue will in itself be part of the issues to be discussed at the conference, for the purpose of this document and the following questions we adopt a broad working definition of what we mean by transnational judicial dialogue of the ECtHR: any reference by the ECtHR to a decision of a national[2] or other international court or quasi-judicial body. With this broad definition we aim to cover different aspects of the ECtHR's references (I) to the decisions of domestic courts from countries directly involved in the case; (II)

[2] It is of course questionable whether any (routine) reference by the ECtHR to domestic law and domestic court decisions of the country directly involved in a particular case should fall under the definition of 'judicial dialogue' since, not surprisingly, such references are found in almost every judgment of the ECtHR. However, some aspects of the ECtHR's engagement with domestic courts from countries that are direct parties to a case constitute good examples of judicial dialogue. Examples are cases where national courts from countries directly involved in a case engage in a longer 'conversation' with the ECtHR, either because they show resistance to following the ECtHR's jurisprudence, or because they adopt and further develop the ECtHR's interpretation of the Convention, which is then taken up by the ECtHR. Concerning dialogues between the ECtHR and domestic courts from states that are direct parties to the case, we are only interested in this type of 'real' dialogue where a case/issue goes back and forth between the ECtHR and the domestic court.

to decisions of other domestic courts (including from states not members of the Council of Europe); and (III) to decisions of international courts/quasi-judicial bodies. Concerning the latter two categories, this can even include cases where there is no 'dialogue' in the true sense of the word that involves an on-going 'conversation' between the ECtHR and other courts on a question of law during which the two courts oppose or support each other. In other words, it can also include a mere reference to a decision of a domestic court not directly involved in the case or to a decision of an international court or quasi-judicial body.

Questions to ECtHR Judges

The questions below relate to the ECtHR's use of decisions belonging to the three categories referred to in the preceding paragraph. The questions cover the scope, process, aims and effects of the ECtHR's engagement in judicial dialogue. Some overlap between questions is unavoidable.

We hope that your answers to all or some of the questions during the panel discussion – together with the academic papers presented at the conference and ensuing discussions – will help establish best practices, allowing domestic and international courts to arrive at sound responses to shared problems, as well as helping us articulate normative perspectives for assessing judicial dialogues.

I. *The ECtHR's use of domestic courts' decisions from states directly involved in the case*

The ECtHR routinely refers to national courts' decisions from the country that is directly involved in the case. The main reason for this seems to be the ECtHR's subsidiary role in securing the implementation of the European Convention on Human Rights (ECHR) in the member states of the Council of Europe (CoE). While the exact use of decisions of the domestic court depends first and foremost on the alleged violation of the ECHR and the circumstances of the case, the following questions aim to shed more light on certain aspects of the national court's decisions that might influence the manner in which the ECtHR relates to and uses the domestic court's decisions. You are welcome to give specific examples whenever relevant.

1. Is the degree to which the domestic court directly engages with the Convention relevant for how the ECtHR uses the domestic court's decision in its own review?

2. Are there cases where domestic courts have come up with a particularly progressive interpretation of the Convention or a particular legal concept/principle that the ECtHR has taken on and thereby 'spread' to other member states of the CoE?
3. What role do the procedures that domestic courts have followed when deciding a particular case (e.g. ensuring full participation of the parties in the court proceedings, thoroughness of argumentation, conducting a comparative analysis as to whether a 'European consensus' exists on the particular question of the interpretation of the ECHR) play in how the ECtHR uses decisions of the domestic court? Does it influence the width of the margin of appreciation the ECtHR gives to domestic authorities in their decisions on material questions?
4. In addition to decisions by domestic courts, to what extent does the ECtHR take account of domestic parliamentary debates, including the quality of the democratic process, concerning a particular human rights question? If so, why?
5. What do you consider the deeper aims and purposes of taking decisions of national courts as important factors in your own deliberations? For instance, is it more driven by necessity, i.e. because the ECtHR can rarely conduct its own investigations/fact-finding? Or is the aim to encourage national courts to engage more directly with the Convention? Do you aim to send 'soft' signals to national courts as to what they should do to secure ECHR rights more effectively?
6. As an ECtHR judge of one particular country, do you have regular meetings with domestic judges from your own country? What influence, do you think, such meetings have on the domestic judges' awareness of the ECHR and the ECtHR's jurisprudence?

II. *The ECtHR's use of decisions of other domestic courts and other CoE-bodies*

1. ECtHR's references to decisions of domestic courts from CoE member states that are not direct parties to a case and to documents from other bodies of the CoE:
   1.1 When and with what frequency does the ECtHR refer to domestic courts' decisions from CoE member states that are not direct parties to the case? When does it refer to documents of other bodies of the CoE (e.g. the Parliamentary Assembly (PACE), the

Committee of Ministers (CoM), and the European Commission for Democracy through Law (Venice Commission))?

1.2 How does the ECtHR find out about these decisions/documents? Do they have to be raised by the parties to the case, by single judges of the ECtHR, or does the ECtHR conduct its own research to find relevant decisions?

1.3 Are you aware of cases in which decisions of domestic courts have been raised by the parties and/or members of the court, and in which it was decided to not refer to such decisions in the judgement? If so, why?

1.4 What role do domestic courts' decisions play in the ECtHR's evaluation of the existence of a 'European consensus' on a particular question concerning the interpretation of the ECHR? Does the ECtHR regularly take account of the legal situation, including relevant domestic courts' decisions, in all member states of the CoE? How does it find out about it, and are there any practical obstacles? When evaluating whether a 'European consensus' exists, does the ECtHR accord similar weight to laws/decisions of domestic courts from all CoE member states? What role do documents from other CoE-bodies play in establishing whether there is a 'European consensus'? Are documents from different bodies accorded similar weight?

1.5 What do you consider the main purpose of referring to domestic courts' decisions from CoE member states that are not direct parties to the case and/or to documents of other CoE-bodies? For instance, do you see it as a catalyst for developing the law of the ECHR? Is it for reasons of increasing the ECtHR's legitimacy?

1.6 What do you consider is the main effect of the ECtHR's references to domestic courts' decisions from CoE member states that are not direct parties to the case and/or documents from other CoE-bodies? Is it possible to approximately weigh their influence on the ECtHR's interpretation of the ECHR and the development of the law of the ECHR? If so, how?

2. ECtHR's reference to domestic courts' decisions from states that are not CoE members:

2.1 When and with what frequency does the ECtHR refer to decisions of domestic courts in countries not member of the CoE?

2.2 How does the ECtHR find out about these decisions? Do they have to be raised by the parties to a case, by single judges of the ECtHR, or does the ECtHR conduct its own research to find relevant decisions? If so, how?

2.3 Are you aware of cases in which decisions of domestic courts from non-CoE member states have been raised by the parties and/or members of the court, and in which it was decided to not refer to such decisions in the judgement? If so, why?

2.4 Are decisions from some domestic courts of non-members of the CoE more prone to be considered by the ECtHR than others? If so, which? And why?

2.5 Concerning the four foregoing questions, could you please make an attempt to discern any criteria from the ECtHR's practice that are employed when it decides when, how, and with which domestic court of a non-member state of the CoE to engage in transnational judicial dialogue?

2.6 What do you consider the main purpose of referring to decisions of domestic courts from states that are non-members of the CoE? For instance, do you see it as a catalyst for developing the law of the ECHR?

2.7 What do you consider is the main effect of the ECtHR's references to domestic courts' decisions from non-CoE member states? Is it possible to approximately weigh their influence on the ECtHR's interpretation of the ECHR and the development of the law of the ECHR, and if so how? Can you give specific examples of where such a reference had an influence on the final judgment of the ECtHR?

III. *The ECtHR's use of decisions of international courts and quasi-judicial bodies*[3]

1. When and with what frequency does the ECtHR refer to decisions of international courts and quasi-judicial bodies?
2. How does the ECtHR find out about the relevant decisions of international courts and quasi-judicial bodies? Do they have to be raised by the parties to a case, by single judges of the ECtHR, or does the ECtHR conduct its own research to find relevant decisions? If so, how?
3. Are decisions from some international courts and quasi-judicial bodies more prone to be considered by the ECtHR than others? If so, why?
4. Are you aware of cases in which decisions of international courts or quasi-judicial bodies have been raised by the parties and/or members

[3] By 'quasi-judicial bodies' we mean international and regional bodies that have judicial functions but cannot issue binding judgments, e.g. the UN human rights treaty bodies.

of the court, and in which it was decided not to refer to such decisions in the judgement? If so, why?

5. Concerning the four foregoing questions, could you please make an attempt to discern any criteria from the ECtHR's practice that are employed when it decides when, how, and with which international court/quasi-judicial body to engage in transnational judicial dialogue?
6. What do you consider the main purpose of referring to decisions of international courts and quasi-judicial bodies? For instance, do you see it as a catalyst for developing the law of the ECHR and/or international human rights law? Or do you sometimes use references for the purpose of delineating the development of the law of the ECHR from e.g. developments in 'global' human rights law as developed by the UN human rights treaty bodies?
7. What do you consider is the main effect of the ECtHR's references to international courts' and quasi-judicial bodies' decisions? Is it possible to approximately weigh their influence on the ECtHR's interpretation of the ECHR and the development of the law of the ECHR? If so, how? Can you give specific examples of where such a reference had an influence on the final judgment of the ECtHR?
8. Does the ECtHR hold regular formal or informal meetings with judges from other international courts or quasi-judicial bodies? If so, what are the aims and effects of such meetings?

In conclusion, two more general questions:

1. With respect to the first two categories involving decisions of domestic courts, to what extent may the approach of the ECtHR judge be influenced by his or her perspective on the relationship between the international and the national legal orders, e.g. in terms of 'monism' or 'dualism', and perhaps relatedly to his or her legal background in common law or civil law?
2. With respect to all three categories, could you try to compare the findings from the above questions? I.e. are there any considerable differences in the extent, purpose and effect of the ECtHR's references to (I) decisions of national courts from states that are directly involved in the case, (II) to national courts' decisions that are not directly involved in the case (from other CoE member states and non-member states), and (III) to other international courts and quasi-judicial bodies' decisions. If so, what are the main reasons for such differences?

Thank you very much for taking the time to answer our questions. We look forward to the panel discussions in Oslo in June!

SELECT BIBLIOGRAPHY

Adjami, M., 'African Courts, International Law, and Comparative Case Law: Chimera or Emerging Human Rights Jurisprudence?', *Michigan Journal of International Law* 24:1 (2002) 103–169.

Ahdieh, R.B. 'Between Dialogue and Decree: International Review of National Courts', *New York University Law Review* 79 (2004) 2029–2163.

Alford, R., 'In Search of a Theory for Constitutional Comparativism', *University of California Law Review* 52:3 (2005) 639–715.

'Misusing International Sources to Interpret the Constitution', *American Journal of International Law* 98:1 (2004) 57–69.

Ambrus, M. 'Comparative Law Method in the Jurisprudence of the European Court of Human Rights in the Light of the Rule of Law', *Erasmus Law Review* 2:3 (2009) 353–371.

Andenæs, M. and D. Fairgrieve (eds.), *Courts and Comparative Law* (Oxford: Oxford University Press, 2015).

Arnold, R. (ed.), *The Universalism of Human Rights, Ius Gentium: Comparative Perspective on Law and Justice* (Berlin: Springer, 2013).

Bahdi, R., 'Globalisation of Judgment: Transjudicialism and the Five Faces of International Law in Domestic Courts', *George Washington International Law Review* 34 (2002) 555–588.

Bederman, D. J., 'Diversity and Permeability in Transnational Governance', *Emory Law Journal* 57:1 (2007) 201–233.

Benhabib, S., *Another Cosmopolitanism* (Oxford: Oxford University Press, 2008).

Benvenisiti, E. and Downs, G., 'Towards Global Checks and Balances', *Constitutional Political Economy* 20:3–4 (2009) 366–387.

'The Democratising Effects of Transjudicial Coordination', *Utrecht Law Review* 8:2 (2012) 158–171.

Berman, P. S., 'A Pluralist Approach to International Law', *Yale Journal of International Law* 32:2 (2007) 301–330.

Bingham, T. H., *Widening Horizons: The Influence of Comparative Law and International Law on Domestic Law* (Cambridge: Cambridge University Press, 2010).

Black, R. and Epstein, L., '(Re-)Setting the Scholarly Agenda on Transjudicial Communication', *Law and Social Inquiry* 32:3 (2007) 789–807.

Bobek, M., *Comparative Reasoning in European Supreme Courts* (Oxford: Oxford University Press, 2013).

Bohmer, M., 'Use of Foreign Law as a Strategy to Build Constitutional and Democratic Authority', *Revista Jurídica de la Universidad de Puerto Rico* 77: 411 (2008) 411–432.

Bratza, N., 'The European Convention on Human Rights and the Charter of Fundamental Rights of the European Union: A Process of Mutual Enrichment', A. Rosas *et al.* (eds.), *The Court of Justice and the Construction of Europe: Analyses and Perspectives on Sixty Years of Case-law* (The Hague: T.M.C. Asser Press, 2013) 167–181.

Brock, G. (ed.), *Cosmopolitanism versus Non-Cosmopolitanism: Critiques, Defenses, Reconceptualizations* (Oxford: Oxford University Press, 2013).

Brok, R., *Coercing Virtue: The Worldwide Rule of Judges* (Cambridge, MA: Aei Press, 2003).

Bryde, B., 'The Constitutional Judge and the International Constitutionalist Dialogue', *Tulane Law Review* 80:1 (2005) 203–219.

Buergenthal, T., 'Modern Constitutions and Human Rights Treaties', *Columbia Journal of Transnational Law*, 36:1–2 (1998) 211–223.

Burke-White, W., 'International Legal Pluralism', *Michigan Journal of International Law* 25:4 (2004) 963–980.

Buxbaum, H., 'From Empire to Globalization … and Back? A Post-Colonial View of Transjudicialism', *Indiana Journal of Global Legal Studies* 11:1 (2004) 183–189.

Calabresi, S. and Dotson Zimdahl, S., 'The Supreme Court and Foreign Sources of Law: Two Hundred Years of Practice and the Juvenile Death Penalty Decision', *William and Mary Law Review* 47:3 (2005) 743–909.

Canivet, G., Andenæs, M. and Fairgrieve, D. (eds.), *Comparative Law Before the Courts* (London: British Institute for International and Comparative Law, 2004).

Carozza, P., 'Uses and Misuses of Comparative Law in International Human Rights: Some Reflections on the Jurisprudence of the European Court of Human Rights', *Notre Dame Law Review* 73:5 (1998) 1217–1237.

Cartabia, M., 'Europe and Rights: Taking Dialogue Seriously', *European Constitutional Law Review* 5:1 (2009) 5–31.

Chang, W.-C., 'The Convergence of Constitutions and International Human Rights: Taiwan and South Korea Comparisons', *North Carolina Journal of International Law and Commercial Regulation* 36:3 (2011) 593–625.

Choudhry, S. (ed.), *The Migration of Constitutional Ideas* (Cambridge: Cambridge University Press, 2006).

'Globalization in Search of Justification: Toward a Theory of Comparative Constitutional Interpretation' *Indiana Law Journal* 74:3 (1999) 819–892.

Christoffersen, J., *Fair Balance: Proportionality, Subsidiarity and Primarity in the European Convention on Human Rights* (Leiden: Martinus Nijhoff, 2009).

Claes, M. and de Visser, M. 'Are You Networked Yet? On Dialogues in European Judicial Networks', *Utrecht Law Review* 8:2 (2012) 100–114.

Clark R., Feldbrugge, F. and Pomorski, S. (eds.) *International and National Law in Russia and Eastern Europe, Essays in Honor of George Ginsburgs* (The Hague: Martinus Nijhoff, 2001).

Claydon, J., 'International Human Rights Law and the Interpretation of the Canadian Charter of Rights and Freedoms', *Supreme Court Law Review* 4 (1982) 287–302.

Coester, M., 'Same-Sex Relationships: A Comparative Assessment of Legal Developments Across Europe', *European Journal of Law Reform* 4:2 (2002) 585–601.

Cohen, H. G., 'Finding International Law, Part II: Our Fragmenting Legal Community', *New York University Journal of Law and Politics* 44:4 (2012) 1049–1108.

Danilenko, G. M., 'Implementation of International Law in CIS States: Theory and Practice', *European Journal of International Law* 10:1 (1999) 51–69.

de Burca, G. and Gerstenberg, O. 'The Denationalization of Constitutional Law', *Harvard International Law Journal* 47:1 (2006) 243–262.

Delmas-Marty, M., *Ordering Pluralism. A Conceptual Framework for Understanding the Transnational Legal World* (Oxford: Oxford University Press 2009).

The European Convention for the Protection of Human Rights: International Versus National Restrictions (Dordrecht: Martinus Nijhoff, 1992).

Dorsen, N. 'The Relevance of Foreign Legal Materials in US Constitutional Cases: A Conversation between Justice Antonin Scalia and Justice Stephen Breyer', *International Journal of Constitutional Law* 3:4 (2005) 519–541.

Dunoff, J. L. and Trachtman, J. P. (eds.), *Ruling the World: Constitutionalism, International Law, and Global Governance* (Cambridge: Cambridge University Press, 2009).

Duxbury, N., *Judges and Jurists: An Essay on Influence* (Oxford: Hart Publishing, 2001).

Dzehtsiarou, K. *European Consensus and the Legitimacy of the European Court of Human Rights* (Cambridge: Cambridge University Press, 2015).

Dzehtsiarou, K. and Lukashevich, V., 'Informed Decision-Making: The Comparative Endeavours of the Strasbourg Court', *Netherlands Quarterly of Human Rights* 30:3 (2012) 272–298.

Egede, E., 'Bringing Human Rights Home: An Examination of the Domestication of Human Rights Treaties in Nigeria', *Journal of African Law* 51:2 (2007) 249–284.

Fauchald, O. K. and Nollkaemper, A. (eds.), *The Practice of International and National Courts and the (De-)Fragmentation of International Law* (Oxford: Hart Publishing, 2012).

Ferrarese, M. R., 'When National Actors Become Transnational: Transjudicial Dialogue between Democracy and Constitutionalism', *Global Jurist* 9:1 (2009) 1–31.

Ferrari, G. and Gambaro, A., 'The Italian Constitutional Court and Comparative Law. A Premise', *Comparative Law Review* 1:1 (2010) 1–22.

Fischel De Andrade, J. H., 'Regional Policy Approaches and Harmonization: A Latin American Perspective', *International Journal of Refugee Law* 10:3 (1998) 389–406.

Fischer-Lescano, A. and Teubner, G., 'Regime-Collisions: The Vain Search for Legal Unity in the Fragmentation of Global Law', *Michigan Journal of International Law* 25:4 (2004) 999–1046.

Flanagan, B. and Ahern, S., 'Judicial Decision-Making and Transnational Law: A Survey of Common Law Supreme Court Judges', *International and Comparative Law Quarterly* 60:1 (2011) 1–28.

Flogiatis, S., Zwart, T. and Fraser, J. (eds.), *The European Court of Human Rights and its Discontents – Turning Criticism into Strength* (Cheltenham: Edward Elgar, 2013).

Føllesdal, A., Peters, B. and Ulfstein, G. (eds.), *The European Court of Human Rights in a National, European and Global Perspective* (Cambridge: Cambridge University Press, 2014).

Fontana, D., 'Refined Comparativism in Constitutional Law', *UCLA Law Review* 49:2 (2001) 539–623.

Fontanelli, F., Martinico G. and Carrozza P. (eds.), *Shaping Rule of Law through Dialogue. International and Supranational Experiences* (Groningen: Europa Law Publishing, 2010).

Forowicz, M., *The Reception of International Law in the European Court of Human Rights* (Oxford: Oxford University Press, 2010).

Frankenberg, G., 'Comparing Constitutions: Ideas, Ideals and Ideology – Towards a Layered Narrative', *International Journal of Constitutional Law* 4:3 (2006) 439–459.

Gallo, D., Paladini, L. and Pustorino, P. (eds.), *Same-Sex Couples before National, Supranational and International Jurisdictions* (Berlin: Springer, 2014).

Gelter, M. and Siems, M., 'Citations to Foreign Courts – Illegitimate and Superfluous, or Unavoidable? Evidence from Europe', *American Journal of Comparative Law* 62:1 (2014) 35–86.

'Language, Legal Origins, and Culture before the Courts: Cross-Citations between Supreme Courts in Europe', *Supreme Court Economic Review* 21:1 (2013) 215–269.

'Networks, Dialogue or One-Way Traffic? An Empirical Analysis of Cross-Citations between Ten European Supreme Courts', *Utrecht Law Review* 8:2 (2012) 88–99.

Gerber, D., 'Globalization and Legal Knowledge: Implications for Comparative Law', *Tulane Law Review* 75:4 (2000) 949–975.

Ginsburg, T. and Dixon, R. (eds.), *Comparative Constitutional Law* (Cheltenham: Edward Elgar, 2011).

Glensy, R., 'Which Countries Count?: *Lawrence v. Texas* and the Selection of Foreign Persuasive Authority', *Virginia Journal of International Law* 45:2 (2005) 357–449.

Goodwin-Gill, G. S. and Lambert, H. (eds.), *The Limits of Transnational Law: Refugee Law, Policy Harmonization and Judicial Dialogue in the European Union* (Cambridge: Cambridge University Press, 2010).

Groppi, T., 'A User-Friendly Court. The Influence of Supreme Court of Canada Decisions Since 1982 on Court Decisions in Other Liberal Democracies', *Supreme Court Law Review* 36 (2007) 337–364.

Hallo de Wolf, A. and Wallace, D., 'The Overseas Exchange of Human Rights Jurisprudence: The US Supreme Court in the European Court of Human Rights', *International Criminal Justice Review* 19:3 (2009) 1–21.

Hamann, A. and Ruiz Fabri, H., 'Transnational Networks and Constitutionalism', *International Journal of Constitutional Law* 6:3–4 (2008) 481–508.

Harding, S. 'Comparative Reasoning and Judicial Review', *Yale Journal of International Law* 28 (2003) 409–464.

Harris, D., *et al.* (eds.), *Law of the European Convention on Human Rights*, 3rd ed. (Oxford: Oxford University Press, 2014).

Hart, N., 'Complementary Protection and Transjudicial Dialogue: Global Best Practice or Race to the Bottom?', *International Journal of Refugee Law* 28:2 (2016) 171–209.

Helfer, L., 'Consensus, Coherence and the European Convention on Human Rights', *Cornell International Law Journal* 26:1 (1993) 133–165.

'Redesigning the European Court of Human Rights: Embeddedness as a Deep Structural Principle of the European Human Rights Regime', *European Journal of International Law* 19:1 (2008) 125–159.

Helfer, L., and Slaughter, A.-M., 'Toward a Theory of Effective Supranational Adjudication', *Yale Law Journal*, 107:2 (1997) 273–391.

Henkin, L., 'A New Birth of Constitutionalism: Genetic Influences and Genetic Defects', *Cardozo Law Review* 14:3–4 (1993) 533–547.

Heringa, A., 'The Consensus Principle – The Role of "Common Law" in the ECHR Case Law', *Maastricht Journal of European and Comparative Law* 3:2 (1996) 106–145.

Hill, K., 'Comparative Law, Law Reform and Legal Theory', *Oxford Journal of Legal Studies* 9:1 (1989) 101–115.

Hirji, Z. (ed.), *Diversity and Plurality in Islam: Historical and Contemporary Discourses amongst Muslims* (New York: IB Tauris, 2010).

Hirschl, R., 'The Question of Case Selection in Comparative Constitutional Law', *American Journal of Comparative Law* 53:1 (2005) 125–156.

Jackson, V., 'Constitutional Comparisons: Convergence, Resistance, Engagement', *Harvard Law Review* 119:1 (2005) 109–128.

Constitutional Engagement in a Transnational Era (Oxford: Oxford University Press, 2010).

Jacobs, F. G., 'Judicial Dialogue and the Cross-Fertilization of Legal Systems: The European Court of Justice', *Texas International Law Journal* 38:3 (2003) 547–557.

Jaremba, U. and Mak, E., 'Interviewing Judges in the Transnational Context', *Law and Method* 5 (2014) 1–15.

Keller, H. and Stone-Sweet, A. (eds.), *A Europe of Rights: The Impact of the ECHR on National Legal Systems* (Oxford: Oxford University Press, 2008).

Kennedy, D., 'One, Two, Three, Many Legal Orders: Legal Pluralism and the Cosmopolitan Dream', *New York University Review of Law & Social Change* 31:3 (2007) 641–660.

Killander, M. (ed.), *International Law and Human Rights Litigation in Africa* (Cape Town: Pretoria University Law Press, 2010).

King, M. and Thornhill, C. (eds.), *Luhmann on Law and Politics: Critical Appraisals and Applications* (Oxford: Hart Publishing, 2006).

Kirby, M., 'Commentaries: Transnational Judicial Dialogue, Internationalisation of Law and Australian Judges', *Melbourne Journal of International Law* 9:1 (2008) 171–189.

'Domestic Courts and International Human Rights Law: The Ongoing Judicial Conversation', *Utrecht Law Review* 6:1 (2010) 168–181.

Koch, C., 'Judicial Dialogue for Legal Multiculturalism', *Michigan Journal of International Law* 25:4 (2003–2004) 879–903.

Koh, H., 'International Law as Part of Our Law', *American Journal of International Law* 98:1 (2004) 43–57.

Koskenniemi, M., 'The Fate of Public International Law: Between Technique and Politics', *Modern Law Review* 70:1 (2007) 1–30.

Krotoszynski, R., '"I'd Like the World to Sing (in Perfect Harmony)": International Judicial Dialogue and the Muses – Reflections in the Perils and the Promise of International Judicial Dialogue', *Michigan Law Review* 104:6 (2006) 1321–1359.

Kurczewski, J. and Sullivan, B. 'The Bill of Rights and the Emerging Democracies', *Law and Contemporary Problems* 65:2 (2002) 251–294.

L'Heurreux-Dube, C., 'The Importance of Dialogue: Globalization and the International Impact of the Rehnquist Court', *Tulsa Law Journal* 34:15 (1998) 15–40.

La Forest, G. V., 'The Expanding Role of the Supreme Court of Canada in International Law Issues', *Canadian Yearbook of International Law* 34 (1996) 89–102.

Lambert, H., 'Transnational Judicial Dialogue, Harmonization and the Common European Asylum System', *International and Comparative Law Quarterly* 58:3 (2009) 519–543.

Larson, J., 'Importing Constitutional Norms from a "Wider Civilisation": *Lawrence*, the Rehnquist Court's Use of Foreign and International Law in Domestic Constitutional Interpretation', *Ohio State Law Journal* 65:5 (2004) 1283–1329.

Lavranos, N., 'The *Solange*-Method as a Tool for Regulating Competing Jurisdictions Among International Courts and Tribunals', *Loyola of Los Angeles International and Comparative Law Review* 30:3 (2008) 275–334.

Law, D. S. and Chang, W.-C., 'The Limits of Global Judicial Dialogue', *Washington Law Review* 86:3 (2011) 523–578.

Law, D. S. and Versteeg, M., 'The Declining Influence of the United States Constitution', *New York University Law Review* 87:3 (2012) 762–858.

Lazega, E. 'Mapping Judicial Dialogue Across National Borders: An Explanatory Network Study of Learning from Lobbying among European Intellectual Property Judges', *Utrecht Law Review* 8:2 (2012) 115–128.

Levit, J. K., 'Bottom-Up International Lawmaking: Reflections on the New Haven School of International Law', *Yale Journal of International Law* 32:2 (2007) 393–420.

Likosky, M. (ed.), *Transnational Legal Processes: Globalisation and Power Disparities* (London: Butterworths, 2002).

Lyke, S. B., 'Brown Abroad: An Empirical Analysis of Foreign Judicial Citation and the Metaphor of Cosmopolitan Conversation', *Vanderbilt Journal of Transnational Law* 45:1 (2012) 83–144.

MacGregor, E. F. and Gil, R. S., 'Foreign Precedents in Mexican Constitutional Adjudication', *Mexican Law Review* 4:2 (2012) 293–307.

MacIntyre, J. M., 'The Use of American Cases in Canadian Courts', *University of British Columbia Law Review* 2:3 (1964–1966) 478–490.

Mahoney, P., Matscher, F. and Petzold, H. (eds.), *Protecting Human Rights: The European Perspective. Studies in Memory of Rolv Ryssdal* (Köln: Carl Heymanns Verlag KG, 2000).

Mak, E., 'Why do Dutch and UK Judges Cite Foreign Law?', *Cambridge Law Journal* 70:2 (2011) 420–450.

Judicial Decision-Making in a Globalised World: A Comparative Analysis of the Changing Practices of Western Highest Courts (Oxford: Hart Publishing, 2013).

Manfredi, C.P., 'The Use of United States Decisions by the Supreme Court of Canada under the Charter of Rights and Freedoms', *Canadian Journal of Political Science* 23:3 (1990) 499–518.

Markesinis, B. and Fedtke, J., *Engaging with Foreign Law* (Oxford: Oxford University Press, 2009).

Judicial Recourse to Foreign Law (Abingdon: Routledge, 2006).

Marochkin, S. Y., 'International Law in the Courts of the Russian Federation: Practice of Application', *Chinese Journal of International Law* 6:2 (2007) 329–344.

Martinek, M., 'Comparative Jurisprudence – What Good Does It Do – History, Tasks, Methods, Achievements and Perspectives of an Indispensable Discipline of Legal Research and Education', *Journal of South African Law* 1 (2013) 39–57.

Martinez, J. S., 'Towards an International Judicial System', *Stanford Law Review* 56:2 (2003) 429–529.

Martinico, G. and Pollicino, O., *The Interaction between Europe's Legal Systems. Judicial Dialogue and the Creation of Supranational Laws* (Cheltenham: Edward Elgar, 2012).

McCormick, P., 'Waiting for Globalization: An Empirical Study of the McLachlin Court's Foreign Judicial Citations', *Ottawa Law Review* 41:2 (2010) 209–244.

McCrudden, C., 'Common Law of Human Rights?: Transnational Judicial Conversations on Constitutional Rights', *Oxford Journal of Legal Studies* 20:4 (2000) 499–532.

Merry, S. E., 'From Law and Colonialism to Law and Globalization: A Review Essay on Martin Chanok, Law, Custom, and Social Order: The Colonial Experience in Malawi and Zambia Zambia', *Law and Social Inquiry* 28:2 (2003) 269–290.

Michaels, R., 'Global Legal Pluralism', *Annual Review of Law and Social Science* 5 (2009) 1–35.

Muller, S. and Richards, S. (eds.), *Highest Courts and Globalisation* (The Hague: Asser Press, 2010).

Müllerson, R., Fitzmaurice, M. and Andenæs, M. (eds.), *Constitutional Reforms and International Law in Central and Eastern Europe* (The Hague: Brill, 1997).

Murphy, C., 'Human Rights Law and the Challenges of Explicit Judicial Dialogue', Jean Monnet Working Paper, *NYU School of Law* 12:10 (2012) 1–32.

Murray, J. L., 'Judicial Cosmopolitanism', *Judicial Studies Institute Journal* 8:2 (2008) 1–17.

Neuman, G., 'Import, Export, and Regional Consent in the Inter-American Court of Human Rights', *European Journal of International Law* 19:1 (2008) 101–123.

'The Uses of International Law in Constitutional Interpretation', *American Journal of International Law* 98:1 (2004) 82–91.

Neves, M., *Transconstitucionalismo* (São Paulo: Martins Fontes, 2009).

Nollkaemper, A., 'The Role of Domestic Courts in the Case Law of the International Court of Justice?', *Chinese Journal of International Law* 5:2 (2006) 301–322.

National Courts and the International Rule of Law (Oxford: Oxford University Press, 2011).

Örücü, E. (ed.), *Judicial Comparativism in Human Rights Cases* (London: British Institute for International and Comparative Law, 2003).

Osiatynski, W., 'Paradoxes of Constitutional Borrowing', *International Journal of Constitutional Law* 1:2 (2003) 244–268.

Palombella G. and Walker N. (eds.), *Relocating the Rule of Law* (Portland: Hart Publishing, 2009).

Peters, A., 'Supremacy Lost: International Law Meets Domestic Constitutional Law', *Vienna Online Journal on International Constitutional Law* 3:3 (2009) 170–198.

Petrov, R. and Kalinichenko, P., 'The Europeanization of Third Country Judiciaries through the Application of the EU Aquis: The Cases of Russia and Ukraine', *International and Comparative Law Quarterly* 60:2 (2011) 325–353.

Posner, E. A. and Sunstein, C. R., 'The Law of Other States', *Stanford Law Review* 59:1 (2006) 131–179.

Prost, M., 'All Shouting the Same Slogans: International Law's Unity and the Politics of Fragmentation', *Finnish Yearbook of International Law* 17 (2006) 1–29.

Ramsey, M., 'International Materials and Domestic Rights: Reflections on Atkins and Lawrence', *American Journal of International Law* 98:1 (2004) 69–82.

Roach, K., 'Constitutional, Remedial and International Dialogues about Rights: The Canadian Experience', *Texas Journal of International Law* 40:3 (2004–2005) 537–577.

Roberts, A., 'Comparative International Law? The Role of National Courts in Creating and Enforcing International Law', *International and Comparative Law Quarterly* 60:1 (2011) 57–93.

Romano, C., 'Deciphering the Grammar of the International Jurisprudential Dialogue', *New York University Journal of International Law and Politics* 41:4 (2008) 755–787.

Rosenkrantz, C. F., 'Against Borrowings and Other Non-Authoritative Uses of Foreign Law', *International Journal of Constitutional Law* 1:2 (2003) 269–295.

Rozakis, C., 'The European Judge as Comparatist', *Tulane Law Review* 80:1 (2005–2006) 257–279.

Sadurski, W., 'Partnering with Strasbourg: Constitutionalisation of the European Court of Human Rights, the Accession of Central and East European States to the Council of Europe, and the Idea of Pilot Judgments', *Human Rights Law Review* 9:3 (2009) 397–453.

Schultz, T., 'Carving up the Internet: Jurisdiction, Legal Orders, and the Private/Public International Law Interface', *European Journal of International Law* 19:4 (2008) 799–839.

Senden, H., *Interpretation of Fundamental Rights in a Multilevel Legal System: An Analysis of the European Court of Human Rights and the Court of Justice of the European Union* (Cambridge: Intersentia, 2011).

Shany, Y., 'National Courts as International Actors: Jurisdictional Implications', *Rivista di Diritto Pubblico Italiano, Comunitario e Comparato* 15:1 (2009) 1–31.

Shelton, D. (ed.), *International Law and Domestic Legal Orders, Incorporation, Transformation and Persuasion* (Oxford: Oxford University Press, 2011).

Slaughter, A.-M., 'A Global Community of Courts', *Harvard International Law Journal* 44:1 (2003) 191–291.

A New World Order (Princeton: Princeton University Press, 2004).

'A Typology of Transjudicial Communication', *University of Richmond Law Review* 29:1 (1994–1995) 99–139.

'Judicial Globalization', *Virginia Journal of International Law* 40:4 (2000) 1103–1124.

'The Real New World Order', *Foreign Affairs* 76:5 (1997) 183–197.

Slaughter, A.-M., Stone Sweet, A. and Weiler, J. (eds.), *The European Court and National Courts: Doctrine and Jurisprudence. Legal Change in Its Social Context* (Oxford: Hart Publishing, 1998).

Sloss, D. (ed.), *The Role of Domestic Courts in Treaty Enforcement: A Comparative Study* (Cambridge: Cambridge University Press, 2009).

Smith, A., 'Making Itself at Home: Understanding Foreign Law in Domestic Jurisprudence: The Indian Case', *Berkeley Journal of International Law* 24:1 (2006) 218–273.

Smith, J. and Wiest, D., 'The Uneven Geography of Global Civil Society: National and Global Influences on Transnational Association', *Social Forces* 84:2 (2005) 621–652.

Smithey, S. I., 'A Tool, Not A Master. The Use of Foreign Case Law in Canada and South Africa', *Comparative Political Studies* 34:10 (2001) 1188–1211.

Staes, D., 'The Use of Documents Other than the European Convention on Human Rights and Its Protocols before the European Court of Human Rights. Reflections From and Upon a Users' Perspective', *Human Rights and International Legal Discourse* 2 (2014) 186–214.

Stephan, P. B., 'Courts on Courts: Contracting for Engagement and Indifference in International Judicial Encounters', *Virginia Law Review* 100:1 (2014) 17–111.

Strauss, A., 'Beyond National Law: The Neglected Role of International Law of Personal Jurisdiction in Domestic Courts', *Harvard International Law Journal* 36:2 (1995) 373–425.

Teubner, G. (ed.), *Global Law without a State* (Brookfield: Dartmouth Pub Co, 1996).

Treves, T., et al. (eds.), *Civil Society, International Courts and Compliance Bodies* (The Hague: T.M.C. Asser Press, 2005).

Tripathi, P. 'Foreign Precedents and Constitutional Law', *Columbia Law Review* 57:3 (1957) 319–347.

Trochev, A., 'All Appeals Lead to Strasbourg? Unpacking the Impact of the European Court of Human Rights on Russia' *Demokratizatsiya: The Journal of Post-Soviet Democratization* 17:2 (2009) 145–178.

Tushnet, M. 'The Possibilities of Comparative Constitutional Law', *Yale Law Journal* 108:6 (1999) 1225–1309.

Twining, W., 'Diffusion of Law: A Global Perspective', (2004) *Journal of Legal Pluralism and Unofficial Law* 36:49 (2004) 1–45.

Voeten, E., 'Borrowing and Non-borrowing among International Courts', *The Journal of Legal Studies* 39:2 (2010) 547–576.

von Bogdandy, A., 'Pluralism, Direct Effect, and the Ultimate Say: On the Relationship between International and Domestic Constitutional Law', *International Journal of Constitutional Law* 6:3–4 (2008) 397–413.

Voßkuhle, A., 'Multilevel Cooperation of the European Constitutional Courts: Der Europäische Verfassungsgerichtsverbund', *European Constitutional Review* 6:2 (2010) 175–198.

Waaldijk, K., 'Others May Follow: The Introduction of Marriage, Quasi-Marriage and Semi-Marriage for Same-Sex Couples in Europe', *New England Law Review* 38:3 (2003–2004) 569–589.

Waldron, J., 'Foreign Law and the Modern Ius Gentium', *Harvard Law Review* 119:1 (2005) 125–147.

Walker, N., 'Beyond Boundary Disputes and Basic Grids: Mapping the Global Disorder of Normative Orders', *International Journal of Constitutional Law* 6:3–4 (2008) 373–396.

Waters, M. A., 'Creeping Monism: The Judicial Trend Toward Interpretive Incorporation of Human Rights Treaties', *Columbia Law Review* 107:3 (2007) 628–706.

'Mediating Norms and Identity: The Role of Transnational Judicial Dialogue in Creating and Enforcing International Law', *Georgetown Law Journal* 93:2 (2005) 487–574.

Waters, M. A., 'Normativity in the "New" Schools: Assessing the Legitimacy of International Legal Norms Created by Domestic Courts', *Yale Journal of International Law* 32:2 (2007) 455–484.

Weisbrud, M., 'Using International Law to Interpret National Constitutions – Conceptual Problems: Reflections on Justice Kirby's Advocacy of International Law in Domestic Constitutional Interpretation', *American University International Law Review* 21:3 (2006) 365–379.

Wells, M., 'International Norms in Constitutional Law', *Georgia Journal of International and Comparative Law* 32:2 (2004) 429–436.

Wildhaber, L., 'The European Convention on Human Rights and International Law', *The International and Comparative Law Quarterly* 56:2 (2007) 217–231.

Wildhaber, L., Hjartarson, A. and Donnelly, S., 'No Consensus on Consensus? The Practice of the European Court of Human Rights', *Human Rights Law Journal* 33:7–12 (2013) 248–263.

Young, M. (ed.), *Regime Interaction in International Law: Facing Fragmentation* (Oxford: Oxford University Press, 2010).

INDEX